Sven Hassel (handwritten signature)

(1982)

THE LIFE AND TIMES
OF
MARTIN LUTHER

THE LIFE AND TIMES

OF

MARTIN LUTHER

by

J. H. Merle D'Aubigné

Selections from D'Aubigné's famed
History of the Reformation of the Sixteenth Century

Translated from the French by H. White
and revised by the author

MOODY PRESS

CHICAGO

Moody Press Edition 1978

Second Printing, 1980

FROM THE AUTHOR'S PREFACE

CHRISTIANITY is neither an abstract doctrine nor an external organization. It is a life from God communicated to mankind, or rather to the Church. This new life is contained essentially in the person of Jesus Christ, and it is given to all those who are united to Him, whether Episcopalians, Presbyterians, Baptists, or others. For this union is effected neither by the baptism of adults, nor by the episcopacy, nor by general assemblies; but solely by faith in certain divine facts that Christ has accomplished, His humble incarnation, His atoning death, and His glorious resurrection. From this intimate union of Christians with Christ there necessarily results an intimate union of Christians with all those who receive the life of Christ; for the life that is in one is the life that is in all; and all together, Episcopalians, Presbyterians, Congregationalists, Baptists, and others, form not a simple plurality, but also, and chief of all, a living and organic unity.

The history of the Reformation is the history of one of the greatest outpourings of the life that cometh from God. May this work contribute to unite always more and more all those who are partakers of that divine life.

J. H. Merle D'Aubigné

Eaux Vives, near Geneva, February, 1846

CONTENTS

CHAPTER   PAGE

1. Early Life and Training 11
2. Entrance into a Convent 19
3. Study of Scripture in the Original Languages 26
4. Conversion, Ordination; Professorship at Wittenberg . . 35
5. Journey to Rome 49
6. Now Doctor of Divinity 58
7. Justification by Faith 65
8. Theses—Beginning the Reformation 73
9. The Court Sermon 78
10. Theses Against Pelagianism 83
11. Nets to Catch Silver 90
12. Certificates of Salvation? 99
13. Ninety-five Theses Posted 109
14. Theses Published and Circulated 120
15. "All Taught of God" 128
16. Tetzel's Reply 135
17. Obelisks and Asterisks 143
18. Luther at Heidelberg 153
19. Letter to Leo X 162
20. Philip Melancthon 178
21. Departure for Augsburg 186
22. Cajetan and Serra Longa 191
23. Luther's Release from His Order 200
24. A New Adversary 207
25. Luther's Protest to De Vio 211
26. An Evening of Communion 216
27. Wittenberg Again, Safe and Sound 225
28. Roman Thunders 231
29. Seeds of Truth over Every Land 237
30. Eck Recommences the Combat 250
31. Eck and Carlstadt on Free Will 261
32. The Church's Foundation—Peter or Christ? 271

CHAPTER   PAGE

33. Luther on Galatians and the Lord's Supper 283
34. Charles V Elected Emperor 291
35. Erasmus Defends Luther 295
36. Ecclesiastical or Spiritual State? 303
37. Zwingli of Helvetia; Luther's Condemnation . . . 313
38. Melancthon Weds Catherine Krapps 321
39. The Gospel Across the Alps 326
40. The Little Book, *Christian Liberty* 330
41. Bull at Wittenberg—Zwingli's Intervention . . . 338
42. Books to Ashes 343
43. Luther Flings Bull to the Flames 349
44. Coronation of Charles V 358
45. Luther Overwhelmed with Acclamation 367
46. The Diet of Worms 374
47. Aleander's Activity and Accusations 382
48. Luther Reflects on the Magnificat 393
49. The Safe-Conduct to Worms 399
50. Luther's Courage 405
51. Luther at Erfurt 409
52. Luther Appears before the Diet of Worms 415
53. "But the Cause Is Thine!" 427
54. Charles Keeps His Word 435
55. Luther's Departure from Worms 442
56. The Edict of Worms 450
57. Luther's Captivity in the Wartburg 459
58. His Labors While a Captive 463
59. Luther Abandons Monachism 469
60. The Idol of Halle 474
61. The Translation of the Bible 480
62. Emancipation of the Monks—the Fall of the Mass . . 486
63. The New Prophets 496
64. Luther Returns to Wittenberg 505
65. "I Put Forward God's Word" 512
66. Melancthon's Theology 521
67. Henry VIII Attacks 529
68. Progress of the Reformation 540
69. Luther's Marriage 547

Chapter 1

EARLY LIFE AND TRAINING

IN MORA, a village near the Thuringian forests, dwelt an ancient and numerous family of the name of Luther. It was customary with the Thuringian peasants, that the eldest son always inherited the dwelling and the paternal fields, while the other children departed elsewhere in quest of a livelihood. One of these, John Luther, married Margaret Lindemann, the daughter of an inhabitant of Neustadt, in the see of Wurzburg. The married couple quitted the plains of Eisenach, and went to settle in the little town of Eisleben in Saxony, to earn their bread by the sweat of their brows.

John Luther was an upright man, diligent in business, frank, and carrying the firmness of his character even to obstinacy. With a more cultivated mind than that of most men of his class, he read much. Books were then rare; but John omitted no opportunity of procuring them. They formed his relaxation in the intervals of repose, snatched from his severe and constant labors. Margaret possessed all the virtues that can adorn a good and pious woman. Her modesty, her fear of God and her prayerful spirit were particularly remarked. She was looked upon by the matrons of the neighborhood as a model whom they should strive to imitate.

It is not known precisely how long they had been living at Eisleben, when, on the tenth of November, one hour before midnight, Margaret gave birth to a son. Melancthon often questioned his friend's mother as to the period of his birth. "I well remember the day and the hour," replied she, "but I am not certain about the year." But Luther's brother James, an honest and upright man, has recorded that in the opinion of the whole family the future reformer was born on St. Martin's eve, November 10, 1483, and Luther himself wrote on a Hebrew Psalter which is still in existence: "I was born in the year 1483." The first thought of his pious parents was to dedicate to God by the holy rite of baptism the child that He had given them. On the morrow, which happened to be Tuesday, the father with gratitude and joy carried his son to St. Peter's Church, and there he received the seal of his consecration to the Lord. They called him Martin in commemoration of the day.

The child was not six months old when his parents quitted Eisleben to repair to Mansfeldt, which is only five leagues distant. The mines of that neighborhood were then very celebrated. John Luther, who was a hard-working man, feeling that perhaps he would be called upon to bring up a numerous family, hoped to gain a better livelihood for himself and his children in that town. It was here that the understanding and strength of young Luther received their first development; here his activity began to display itself, and here his character was declared in his words and in his actions. The plains of Mansfeldt and the banks of the Wipper were the theater of his first sports with the children of the neighborhood.

The first period of their abode at Mansfeldt was difficult to the worthy John and his wife. At first they lived in great poverty. "My parents," said the reformer, "were very poor. My father was a poor wood-cutter, and my mother has often carried wood upon her back, that she might procure the means of bringing up her children. They endured the severest labor for our sakes." The example of the parents whom he revered and the habits they inspired in him early accustomed Luther to labor and frugality. How many times, doubtless, he accompanied his mother to the wood, there to gather up his little fagot!

There are promises of blessing on the labor of the righteous, and John Luther experienced their realization. Having attained somewhat easier circumstances, he established two smelting furnaces at Mansfeldt. Beside these furnaces little Martin grew in strength, and with the produce of this labor his father afterwards provided for his studies. "It was from a miner's family," says the good Mathesius, "that the spiritual founder of Christendom was to go forth: an image of what God would do in purifying the sons of Levi through him, and refining them like gold in His furnaces." Respected by all for his integrity, for his spotless life, and good sense, John Luther was made councilor of Mansfeldt, capital of the earldom of that name. Excessive misery might have crushed the child's spirit: the competence of his paternal home expanded his heart and elevated his character.

John took advantage of his new position to court the society which he preferred. He had a great esteem for learned men, and often invited to his table the clergy and schoolmasters of the place. His house offered a picture of those social meetings of his fellow-citizens, which did honor to Germany at the commencement of the sixteenth century. It was a mirror in which were reflected the numerous images that followed one another on the agitated scene of the times. The child profited by them. No doubt the sight of these men, to whom so much respect was shown in his father's house, excited more than once in little Martin's heart the ambitious desire of becoming himself one day a schoolmaster or a learned man.

As soon as he was old enough to receive instruction, his parents endeavored to impart to him the knowledge of God, to train him up in His fear, and to mold him to Christian virtues. They exerted all their care in this earliest domestic education. The father would often kneel at the child's bedside, and fervently pray aloud, begging the Lord that his son might remember His name and one day contribute to the propagation of the truth. The parent's prayer was listened to most graciously. And yet his tender solicitude was not confined to this.

His father, anxious to see him acquire the elements of that learning for which he himself had so much esteem, invoked God's blessing upon him, and sent him to school. Martin was still very young. His father, or Nicholas Emler, a young man of Mansfeldt, often carried him to the house of George Emilius, and afterwards returned to fetch him home. Emler in after years married one of Luther's sisters.

His parents' piety, their activity and austere virtue, gave the boy a happy impulse, and formed in him an attentive and serious disposition. The system of education which then prevailed made use of chastisement and fear as the principal incentives to study. Margaret, although sometimes approving the too great severity of her husband, frequently opened her maternal arms to her son to console him in his tears. Yet even she herself overstepped the limits of that wise precept: "He that loveth his son, chasteneth him betimes." Martin's impetuous character gave frequent occasion for punishment and reprimand. "My parents," said Luther in after life, "treated me harshly, so that I became very timid. My mother one day chastised me so severely about a nut, that the blood came. They seriously thought that they were doing right; but they could not distinguish character, which, however, is very necessary in order to know when, or where, or how chastisement should be inflicted. It is necessary to punish; but the apple should be placed beside the rod."

At school the poor child met with treatment no less severe. His master flogged him fifteen times successively in one morning. "We must," said Luther, when relating this circumstance—"we must whip children, but we must at the same time love them." With such an education Luther learned early to despise the charms of a merely sensual life. "What is to become great, should begin small," justly observes one of his oldest biographers; "and if children are brought up too delicately and with too much kindness from their youth, they are injured for life."

Martin learned something at school. He was taught the heads of his Catechism, the Ten Commandments, the Apostles' Creed, the Lord's Prayer, some hymns, some forms of prayer, and a Latin grammar written in the fourth century by Donatus, who was St. Jerome's master, and which, improved in the eleventh century by one Remigius, a French monk, was long held in great repute in every school. He further studied the calendar of Cisio Janus, a very singular work, composed in the tenth or eleventh century: in fine, he learned all that could be taught in the Latin school of Mansfeldt.

But the child's thoughts do not appear to have been directed to God at that time. The only religious sentiment that could then be discovered in him was fear. Every time he heard Jesus Christ spoken of, he turned pale with fright; for the Saviour had only been represented to him as an offended Judge. This servile fear—so alien to true religion—may perhaps have prepared him for the glad tidings of the gospel, and for that joy which he afterwards felt, when he learned to know Him who is meek and lowly in heart.

John Luther wished to make his son a scholar. The day that was everywhere beginning to dawn had penetrated even into the house of the Mansfeldt miner, and there it awakened ambitious thoughts. The persevering application of his son and the boy's remarkable disposition made John conceive the liveliest expectations. Accordingly, in 1497, when Martin had attained the age of fourteen years, his father resolved to part with him, and send him to the Franciscan school at Magdeburg. His mother was obliged to consent, and Martin prepared to quit the paternal roof.

Magdeburg was like a new world to Martin. In the midst of numerous privations, for he scarcely had enough to live upon, he inquired—he listened. Andrew Proles, provincial of the Augustine order, was at that time warmly advocating the necessity of reforming religion and the Church. It was not he, however, who deposited in the young man's heart the first germ of the ideas that he afterwards developed.

This was a rude apprenticeship for Luther. Thrown upon the world at the age of fourteen, without friends or protectors, he trembled in the presence of his masters, and in the hours of recreation he painfully begged his bread in company with children poorer than himself. "I used to beg with my companions for a little food," said he, "that we might have the means of providing for our wants. One day, at the time the Church celebrates the festival of Christ's nativity, we were wandering together through the neighboring villages, going from house to house, and singing in four parts the usual carols on the infant Jesus, born at Bethlehem. We stopped before a peasant's house that stood by itself at the extremity of the village. The farmer, hearing us sing our Christmas hymns, came out with some food which he intended to give us. He called out in a high voice and with a harsh tone, 'Boys, where are you?' Frightened at these words, we ran off as fast as our legs would carry us. We had no reason to be alarmed, for the farmer offered us assistance with great kindness; but our hearts, no doubt, were rendered fearful by the threats and tyranny with which the teachers were then accustomed to rule over their pupils, so that a sudden panic had seized us. At last, however, as the farmer continued calling after us, we stopped, forgot our fears, ran back to him, and received from his hands the food intended for us." "It is thus," adds Luther, "that we are accustomed to tremble and flee, when our conscience is guilty and alarmed. We are afraid even of those who are our friends, and who would willingly do us every good."

A year had scarcely passed away, when John and Margaret, hearing what difficulty their son found in supporting himself at Magdeburg, sent him to Eisenach, where there was a celebrated school, and in which town they had many relatives. They had other children, and although their means had increased, they could not maintain their son in a place where he was unknown. The furnaces and the industry of John Luther did little more than provide for the support of his family. He hoped that when Martin arrived at Eisenach he would more easily find the means of subsistence, but he was not more fortunate in this town. His relations took no care of him, or perhaps, being very poor themselves, they could not give him any assistance.

When the young scholar was pinched by hunger, he was compelled, as at Magdeburg, to join with his schoolfellows in singing from door to door to obtain a morsel of bread. Sometimes the voices of the youths formed a harmonious concert. Often, instead of food, the poor and modest Martin received nothing but harsh words. Then, overwhelmed with sorrow, he shed many tears in secret, and thought with anxiety of the future.

One day, he had already been repulsed from three houses and was preparing to return fasting to his lodgings, when, having reached the square of St. George, he stopped motionless, plunged in melancholy reflections, before the house of a worthy citizen. Must he for want of bread renounce his studies, and return to labor with his father in the mines of Mansfeldt? Suddenly a door opened—a woman appeared on the threshold. It was Ursula, the wife of Conrad Cotta, and a daughter of the burgomaster of Ilefeld. The Eisenach chronicles style her "the pious Shunamite," in remembrance of the woman who constrained the prophet Elisha to stay and eat bread with her. The Christian Shunamite had already more than once noticed the youthful Martin in the assemblies of the faithful; she had been affected by the sweetness of his voice and by his devotion. She had heard the harsh words, and seeing him stand thus sadly before her door, she came to his aid, beckoned him to enter, and gave him food to appease his hunger.

Conrad approved of his wife's benevolence: he even found so much pleasure in the boy's society that a few days after he took him to live entirely with him. Henceforward his studies were secured; he was not obliged to return to the mines of Mansfeldt there to bury the talents that God had entrusted to him. At a time when he knew not what would become of him, God opened the heart and the house of a Christian family. This event begat in him that confidence in God which the severest trials could not afterwards shake.

Luther lived in Cotta's house a very different kind of life from that which he had hitherto known. His existence glided away calmly, free from want aand care; his mind became more serene, his character more cheerful, and his heart more open. All his faculties awoke at the mild rays of charity, and he began to exult with life, joy, and happiness. His prayers were more fervent, his thirst for knowledge greater, and his progress in study more rapid.

To literature and science he added the charms of the fine arts, for they also were advancing in Germany. The men whom God destines to act upon their contemporaries are themselves at first influenced and carried away by all the tendencies of the age in which they live. Luther learned to play on the flute and on the lute. With this latter instrument he used often to accompany his fine alto voice, and thus cheered his heart in the hours of sadness. He took delight in showing by his melody his lively gratitude towards his foster mother, who was passionately fond of music. He himself loved it even to old age, and composed the words and tunes of some of the finest hymns that Germany possesses. Many have even passed into our language.

These were happy times for young Luther; he could never think of them without emotion. One of Conrad's sons who came many years after to study at Wittenberg, when the poor scholar of Eisenach had become the first doctor of the age, was received with joy at his table and under his roof. He wished to make some returns to the son for the kindness he had received from his parents. It was in remembrance of this Christian woman who had fed him when all the world repulsed him, that he gave utterance to this beautiful thought: "There is nothing sweeter on earth than the heart of a woman in which piety dwells."

Luther was never ashamed of these days in which, oppressed by hunger, he begged in sadness the money necessary for his studies and his livelihood. Far from that, he used to reflect with gratitude on the extreme poverty of his youth. He looked upon it as one of the means that God had employed to make him what he afterwards became, and he accordingly thanked Him for it. The poor children who were obliged to follow the same kind of life touched his heart. "Do not despise," said he, "the boys who go singing through the streets, begging a little bread for the love of God (*panem propter Deum*): I also have done the same. It is true that somewhat later my father supported me with much love and kindness at the University of Erfurt, maintaining me by the sweat of his brow; yet I have been a poor beggar. And now, by means of my pen, I have risen so high that I would not change lots with the Grand Turk himself. Should all the riches of the earth be heaped one upon another, I would not take them in exchange for what I possess. And yet I should not be where I am if I had not gone to school—if I had not learned to write." Thus did this great man see in these his first humble beginnings the origin of all his glory. He never forgot to recall that the voice whose accents thrilled the empire and the world once used to beg for a morsel of bread in the streets of a small town. The Christian finds a pleasure in such recollections, because they remind him that it is in God alone he should glory.

The strength of his understanding, the liveliness of his imagination, the excellence of his memory, soon carried him beyond all his schoolfellows. He made rapid progress, especially in Latin, in eloquence, and in poetry. He wrote speeches and composed verses. As he was cheerful, obliging, and had what is called "a good heart," he was beloved by his masters and by his schoolfellows.

Among the professors he attached himself particularly to John Trebonius, a learned and eloquent man who had all that regard for youth which is so well calculated to encourage them. Martin had noticed that whenever Trebonius entered the schoolroom, he raised his cap to salute the pupils—a great condescension in those pedantic times! This had delighted the young man for it revealed to him his own value as an individual. The respect of the master had elevated the scholar in his own estimation. The colleagues of Trebonius, who did not adopt the same custom, one day expressed their astonishment at his extreme condescension. He replied, "There are among these boys men of whom God will one day make burgomasters, chancellors, doctors, and magistrates. Although you do not yet see them with the badges of their dignity, it is right that you should treat them with respect." Doubtless the young scholar listened with pleasure to these words, and perhaps imagined himself already with the doctor's cap.

Chapter 2

ENTRANCE INTO A CONVENT

L<small>UTHER</small> had now reached his eighteenth year. He had tasted the sweets of literature; he burned with a desire for knowledge. He sighed for a university education, and wished to repair to one of those fountains of learning where he could slake his thirst for erudition. His father required him to study the law. Full of hope in the talents of his son, he wished that he should cultivate them and make them generally known. He already pictured him discharging the most honorable functions among his fellow-citizens, gaining the favor of princes, and shining on the theater of the world. It was determined that the young man should go to Erfurt.

Luther arrived at this university in 1501. Jodocus, surnamed the Doctor of Eisenach, was teaching there the scholastic philosophy with success. Melancthon regretted that at that time nothing was taught at Erfurt but a system of dialectics bristling with difficulties. His thought was that if Luther had met with other professors, if they had taught him the milder and calmer discipline of true philosophy, the violence of his nature might have been moderated. The new disciple applied himself to study the philosophy of the Middle Ages in the works of Occam, Duns Scotus, Bonaventure, and Thomas Aquinas. In later times all this scholastic divinity was his aversion. He trembled with indignation whenever Aristotle's name was pronounced in his presence. He went so far as to say that if Aristotle had not been a man, he should not have hesitated to take him for the devil. But a mind so eager for learning as his required other ailments; he began to study the masterpieces of antiquity, the writings of Cicero, Virgil, and other classic authors. He was not content, like the majority of students, with learning their productions by heart; he endeavored to fathom their thoughts, to imbibe the spirit which animated them, to appropriate their wisdom to himself, to comprehend the object of their writings, and to enrich his mind with their pregnant sentences and brilliant images. He often addressed questions to his professors, and soon outstripped his fellow-students. Blessed with a retentive memory and a strong imagination, all that he read or heard remained constantly present to his mind; it was as if he had seen it himself. "Thus shone Luther in his early years. The whole university," says Melancthon, "admired his genius."

But even at this period the young man of eighteen did not study merely to cultivate his intellect; he had those serious thoughts, that heart directed heavenwards, which God gives to those of whom He resolves to make His most zealous ministers. Luther was aware of his entire dependence upon God,—simple and powerful conviction, which is at once the cause of deep humility and of great actions! He fervently invoked the divine blessing upon his labors. Every morning he began the day with prayers; he then went to church, and afterwards applied himself to his studies, losing not a moment in the whole course of the day. "To pray well," he was in the habit of saying, "is the better half of study."

The young student passed in the university library all the time he could snatch from his academic pursuits. Books were as yet rare, and it was a great privilege for him to profit by the treasures brought together in this vast collection. One day—he had then been two years at Erfurt and was twenty years old—he opened many books in the library one after another, to learn their writers' names. One volume that he came to attracted his attention. He had never until this hour seen its like. He read the title—it was a Bible, a rare book, unknown in those times. His interest was greatly excited and he was filled with astonishment at finding other matters than those fragments of the Gospels and epistles that the Church had selected to be read to the people during public worship every Sunday throughout the year. Until that day he had imagined that they composed the whole Word of God. Now he saw many pages, many chapters, many books of which he had had no idea! His heart beat fast as he held the divinely inspired Volume in his hand. With eagerness and with indescribable emotion he turned over these leaves from God.

The first page on which he fixed his attention told the story of Hannah and of the young Samuel. He read eagerly and his soul could hardly contain the joy it felt. The child Samuel whom his parents lend to the Lord as long as he lived; the song of Hannah, in which she declares that Jehovah "raiseth up the poor out of the dust, and lifteth the beggar from the dunghill, to set them among princes"; Samuel's service in the temple in the presence of the Lord; those sacrificers—the sons of Heli—wicked men who live in debauchery, and "make the Lord's people to transgress";—all this history, all this revelation that he had discovered, excited feelings till then unknown. He returned home with a full heart. "Oh! that God would give me such a book for myself," he thought. Luther was as yet ignorant both of Greek and Hebrew. It is scarcely probable that he had studied these languages during the first two or three years of his residence at the university. The Bible that had filled him with such transports was in Latin. He soon returned to the library to pore over his treasure, then came repeatedly, in his astonishment and joy, to read it further. The first glimmerings of a new truth were beginning to dawn upon his mind.

Thus God led him to the discovery of that Book of which he was to give the admirable translation which Germany has used for three centuries. That may have been the first time that the precious volume had been taken down from its place in the library of Erfurt. That Book, deposited on the unknown shelves of a gloomy hall, was about to become the Book of Life to a whole nation. In that Bible the Reformation lay hidden.

It was in the same year that Luther took his first academic degree —that of bachelor. The excessive labor he had expended in order to pass his examination brought on a dangerous illness. Death seemed imminent, and serious reflections occupied his mind. His case excited general interest. "It is a pity," his friends thought, "to see so many expectations blighted so early." Among the many friends who came to visit him was a venerable priest who had noticed Luther's work at Mansfeldt in his academic career. The young man could not conceal the thoughts that occupied his mind. "Soon," said he, "I shall be called away from this world." But the old man kindly replied, "My dear bachelor, take courage; you will not die of this illness. Our God will yet make of you a man who, in turn, shall console many. For

God layeth His cross upon those whom He loveth, and they who bear it patiently acquire much wisdom." These words impressed Luther. When he was so near death he had heard the voice of a priest reminding him that God, as Samuel's mother said, raiseth up the miserable. The old man had poured sweet consolation into his heart and had revived his spirits; never would he forget it. "This was the first prediction that the worthy doctor heard," says Mathesius, Luther's friend, who records the incident, "and he often used to call it to mind." We may easily comprehend in what sense Mathesius calls the priest's words a prediction.

When Luther recovered, there was a great change in him. The Bible, his illness, the words of the aged priest—all seem to have made a new appeal, but as yet he had not made the great decision. Another circumstance awakened serious thoughts within him. At the festival of Easter, probably in the year 1503, Luther was on his way to pass a short time with his family. According to the custom of the age, he was wearing a sword; as he struck it with his foot, the blade fell out, cutting one of the principal arteries. His companion having dashed off for assistance, Luther found himself alone. Unable to check the flow of blood, he lay down on his back and put his finger on the wound. In spite of this, the blood continued to flow, and Luther, feeling the approach of death, cried out, "O Mary, help me!" At last a surgeon arrived from Erfurt and bound up the cut. The wound opened in the night, and Luther fainted, again calling loudly upon the Virgin. "At that time," said he in after years, "I should have died relying upon Mary." Soon after that he invoked a more powerful Saviour.

He continued his studies. In 1505 he was admitted master of arts and doctor of philosophy. The University of Erfurt was then the most celebrated in all Germany. The other schools were inferior in comparison with it. The ceremony was conducted, as usual, with great pomp. A procession by torchlight came to pay honor to Luther. The festival was magnificent. It was a general rejoicing. Luther, encouraged perhaps by these honors, felt disposed to apply himself entirely to the law, in conformity with his father's wishes.

But the will of God was different. While Luther was occupied with various studies, and beginning to teach the physics and ethics of Aristotle, with other branches of philosophy, his heart never ceased to cry to him that religion was the one thing needful, and that above all things he should secure his salvation. He knew the displeasure that God manifests against sin; he called to mind the penalties that God's Word denounces against the sinner; and he asked himself, with apprehension whether he was sure of possessing the divine favor. His conscience answered, No! His character was prompt and decided; he resolved to do all that might ensure him a firm hope of immortality. Two events occurred, one after the other, to disturb his soul, and to hasten his resolution.

Among his closest friends at the university was one named Alexis. One morning a report was spread in Erfurt that Alexis had been assassinated. Luther hastened to ascertain the truth of this rumor. This sudden loss of his friend agitated him, and his mind was filled with keenest terror as he asked himself, "What would become of me, if I were thus called away without warning?"

It was in the summer of 1505 that Luther, whom the ordinary university vacations left at liberty, resolved to go to Mansfeldt, to revisit the dear scenes of his childhood and to embrace his parents. Perhaps also he wished to open his heart to his father, to sound him on the plan that he was forming in his mind, and to obtain his permission to engage in another profession. He foresaw all the difficulties. The idle life of the majority of priests was displeasing to the active miner of Mansfeldt. Besides, the ecclesiastics were but little esteemed in the world. For the most part their revenues were scanty, and the father, who had made great sacrifices to maintain his son at the university, and who now saw him teaching publicly in a celebrated school, although only in his twentieth year, was not likely to renounce the proud hopes he had cherished.

We are ignorant of what transpired during Luther's stay at Mansfeldt. Perhaps the decided wish of his father made him fear to open his heart to him. He again left his father's house to take his seat on the benches of the academy. He was already within a short distance of Erfurt, when he was overtaken by a violent storm, such as often occurs in those mountains. The lightning flashed—the bolt fell at his feet. Luther threw himself upon his knees, thinking that his hour, perhaps, had come. Death, the judgment, and eternity, with all their terrors, summoned him and he heard a voice that he could no longer resist. "Encompassed with the anguish and terror of death," as he expressed it, he made a vow that if the Lord should deliver him from this danger, he would abandon the world, and devote himself entirely to God.

After rising from the ground, having still present to him that death which must one day overtake him, he examined himself seriously, and asked what he ought to do. The thoughts that had agitated him now returned with greater force. He had endeavored, it is true, to fulfill all his duties, but what was the state of his soul? Could he appear before the tribunal of a terrible God with an impure heart? He must become holy. He had now as great a thirst for holiness as he had had formerly for knowledge. But where could he find it, or how could he attain it? The university provided him with the means of satisfying his first desires. Who should calm that anguish and quench the fire that now consumed him? To what school of holiness should he direct his steps? He resolved to enter a cloister; the monastic life would save him. Oftentimes had he heard of its power to transform the heart, to sanctify the sinner, and to make man perfect! He would enter a monastic order, and there become holy; thus would he secure eternal life.

Such was the event that changed the calling, the whole destiny of Luther. In this we perceive the finger of God. It was His powerful hand that on the highway cast down the young master of arts, the candidate for the bar, the future lawyer, to give an entirely new direction to his life. Rubianus, one of Luther's friends at the University of Erfurt, wrote thus to him many years later: "Divine Providence looked at what you were one day to become, when on your return from your parents, the fire from heaven threw you to the ground, like another Paul, near the city of Erfurt, and withdrawing you from our society, drove you into the Augustine order." Analagous circumstances have marked the conversion of the two greatest instruments that divine Providence has used in the two greatest revolutions that have been effected upon the earth: the apostle Paul and Luther.

Luther re-entered Erfurt, but his resolution was unalterable. It was not without a pang that he prepared to break the ties so dear to him. Telling his intention to no one, he invited his university friends to a cheerful but frugal supper. Music once more enlivened their social meeting—Luther's farewell to the world. Henceforth, instead of these amiable companions of his pleasures and his studies, he would have monks; instead of this gay and witty conversation—the silence of the cloister; and for these merry songs—the solemn strains of the quiet chapel. God was calling him, and he must sacrifice everything. Now, for the last time, he shared in the joys of his youth! The repast excited his friends; Luther himself was the soul of the party. But at the very moment that they were giving way to their gaiety, Luther could no longer hide his serious thoughts and he revealed his intention to his astonished friends. They endeavored to shake it, but in vain. That very night Luther, perhaps fearful of their pleadings, quit his lodgings, leaving behind him his clothes and books, taking only *Virgil* and *Plautus*; he had no Bible as yet. *Virgil* and *Plautus*—an epic poem and comedies—striking picture of Luther's mind! In effect a whole epic had taken place within him—a beautiful, sublime poem; but as he had a disposition inclined to gaiety, wit, and humor, he combined more than one feature with the serious and stately groundwork of his life.

Provided with these two books, he repaired alone, in the darkness of night, to the convent of the hermits of St. Augustine. He asked admittance; the gate opened and closed again. Behold him, separated forever from his parents, from the companions of his studies, and from the world! It was August 17, 1505: Luther was then twenty-one years old.

Chapter 3

STUDY OF SCRIPTURE IN THE ORIGINAL LANGUAGES

WITH GOD AT LAST! Luther's soul was in safety; he was now about to find that holiness which he so much desired. The monks were astonished at the sight of the youthful doctor. They extolled his courage and his contempt of the world. He did not, however, forget his friends. He wrote to them, bidding farewell to them and to the world, and on the next day he sent these letters, with the clothes he had worn till then, and returned to the university his ring of master of arts, that nothing might remind him of the world he had renounced.

His friends at Erfurt were struck with astonishment. Must so eminent a genius go and hide himself in that monastic state,—a partial death? Filled with the liveliest sorrow, they hastily repaired to the convent in the hope of inducing Luther to retrace so afflicting a step: but all was useless. For two whole days they surrounded the convent and almost besieged it, in the hope of seeing Luther come forth. But the gates remained closely shut and barred. A month elapsed without anyone's being able to see or speak to the new monk.

Luther had also hastened to communicate to his parents the great change that had taken place in his life. His father was amazed and trembled for his son, as Luther tells us in the dedication of his work on monastic vows, addressed to his father. His weakness, his youth, the violence of his passions, all led John Luther to fear that when the first moment of enthusiasm was over, the habits of the cloister would make the young man fall either into despair or into some great sin.

He knew that this kind of life had already been the destruction of many. Besides, the councilor-miner of Mansfeldt had formed very different plans for his son. He had hoped that he would contract a rich and honorable marriage. Now all his ambitious projects had been overthrown in one night by this imprudent step.

John wrote a very angry letter to his son, in which he spoke to him in a contemptuous tone, as Luther informs us. He had addressed him always in a friendly manner after he had taken his master-of-arts degree. He withdrew all his favor, and declared him disinherited from his paternal affection. In vain did John Luther's friends, and doubtless his wife, endeavor to soften him; in vain did they say: "If you would offer a sacrifice to God, let it be what you hold best and dearest,—even your son, your Isaac." The inexorable councilor of Mansfeldt would listen to no one.

Not long after, however (Luther tells us in a sermon preached at Wittenberg, January 20, 1544), the plague appeared. It deprived John Luther of two of his sons. About that time someone came and told the bereaved father that the monk of Erfurt was dead also! . . . His friends seized the opportunity of reconciling the father to the young novice. "If it should be a false alarm," they said to him, "at least sanctify your affliction by cordially consenting to your son's becoming a monk!" "Well! so be it!" replied John Luther, with a heart bruised, yet still half rebellious, "and God grant he may prosper!" Some time after this, when Luther, who had been reconciled to his father, related to him the event that had induced him to enter a monastic order: "God grant," replied the worthy miner, "that you may not have taken for a sign from heaven what was merely a delusion of the devil."

There was not then in Luther that which was afterwards to make him the reformer. Of this his entrance into the convent is a strong proof. It was a proceeding in conformity with the tendencies of the age from which he was soon to contribute his endeavors to liberate the Church. He who was destined to become the great teacher of the world was as yet its slavish imitator. A new stone had been added to the edifice of ritual by the very man who was erelong to destroy it. Luther looked to himself for salvation, to human works and observances. He knew not that salvation comes wholly from God. He sought after his own glory and righteousness and was unmindful of the righteousness and glory of the Lord. But what he was ignorant of as yet, he learned soon after. In the cloister of Erfurt was brought about the mighty transformation which substituted in his heart God and His wisdom for the world and its traditions. It prepared him for the mighty revolution of which he was to be the most illustrious instrument.

When Martin Luther entered the convent, he changed his name, and assumed that of Augustine. The monks had received him with joy. It was no slight gratification to see one of the most esteemed doctors of the age abandon the university for a house belonging to their order. Nevertheless they treated him harshly, and imposed on him the meanest occupations. They wished to humble the doctor of philosophy and to teach him that his learning did not raise him above his brethren. By this means they thought to prevent him from devoting himself so much to his studies, from which the convent could reap no advantage. The former master of arts had to perform the offices of porter, to open and shut the gates, to wind up the clock, to sweep the church, and to clean out the cells. Then, when the poor monk, who was doorkeeper, sexton, and menial servant of the cloister, had finished his work: *Cum sacco per civitatem!* "Away with your wallet through the town!" cried the friars, and laden with his bread-bag, he wandered through all the streets of Erfurt, begging from house to house, obliged perhaps to present himself at the doors of those who had once been his friends or his inferiors.

On his return, he had either to shut himself up in a low and narrow cell, whence he could see nothing but a small garden a few feet square, or recommence his humble tasks. Naturally disposed to devote himself entirely to whatever he undertook, he had become a monk with all his soul. Besides, how could he have a thought of sparing his body, or have had any regard for what might please the flesh? It was not thus that he could acquire the humility, the sanctity which he had come to seek within the cloister.

The poor monk, oppressed with toil, hastened to employ in study all the moments that he could spare from these mean occupations. He voluntarily withdrew from the society of the brethren to give himself up to his beloved pursuits; but they soon found it out. Surrounding him with murmurs, they tore him from his books, exclaiming, "Come, come! It is not by studying, but by begging bread, corn, eggs, fish, meat, and money that a monk renders himself useful to the cloister." Luther submitted; he laid aside his books, and took up his bag again. Far from repenting at having taken upon himself such a yoke, he was willing to go through with his task. It was then that the inflexible perseverance with which he always carried out the resolutions he had once formed, began to be developed in his mind.

The resistance he made to these assaults gave a stronger temper to his will. God tried him in small things, that he might learn to remain unshaken in great ones. Besides, to be able to deliver his age from the superstitions under which it groaned, it was necessary for him first to feel their weight.

This severe apprenticeship did not, however, last so long as Luther may have feared. The prior of the convent, at the intercession of the university to which Luther belonged, freed him from the humiliating duties that had been laid upon him. The youthful monk then returned to his studies with new zeal. The works of the fathers of the Church, especially of St. Augustine, attracted his attention. The exposition of the Psalms by this illustrious doctor, and his book *On the Letter and the Spirit*, were his favorite study. Nothing struck him more than the sentiments of this father on the corruption of man's will and on divine grace. He felt by his own experience the reality of that corruption and the necessity for that grace. The words of St. Augustine corresponded with the sentiments of his own heart. If he could have belonged to any other school than that of Jesus Christ, it undoubtedly would have been to that of the doctor of Hippo. He knew almost by rote the works of Peter d'Ailly and of Gabriel Biel. He was much taken with a saying of the former, that, if the Church had not decided to the contrary, it would have been preferable to concede that the bread and wine were really taken in the Lord's Supper, and not mere accidents.

He also carefully studied the theologians Occam and Gerson, who both expressed themselves so freely on the authority of the popes. To this course of reading he added other exercises. He was heard in the public discussions unraveling the most complicated trains of reasoning, and extricating himself from a labyrinth whence none but he could have found an outlet. His hearers were filled with astonishment.

But he had not entered the cloister to acquire the reputation of a

great genius; it was to seek food for his piety. He therefore regarded
these labors as mere digressions. He loved above all things to draw
wisdom from the pure source of the Word of God. He found in the
convent a Bible fastened by a chain, and to this chained Bible he
was continually returning. He had but little understanding of the
Word, yet it was his most pleasing study. It sometimes happened that
he passed a whole day meditating upon a single passage. At other
times he learned fragments of the Prophets by heart. He especially
desired to acquire from the writings of the prophets and of the
apostles a perfect knowledge of God's will, to grow up in greater fear
of His name, and to nourish his faith by the sure testimony of the
Word.

It would appear that about this time he began to study the Scriptures in their original languages, and to lay the foundation of the
most perfect and most useful of his labors—the translation of the
Bible. He made use of Reuchlin's Hebrew Lexicon, which had just
appeared. John Lange, one of the friars of the convent, a man
skilled in Greek and Hebrew, and one with whom he always remained closely connected, probably was his first instructor. He also
made much use of the learned commentaries of Nicholas Lyra, who
died in 1340. It was from this circumstance that Pflug, afterwards
bishop of Naumburg, said: *Si Lyra non lyrasset, Lutherus non saltas-
set*.[1]

The young monk studied with such industry and zeal that frequently he did not repeat the daily prayers for three or four weeks
together. But he soon grew alarmed at the thought that he had trans-
gressed the rules of his order. He then shut himself up to repair his
negligence. He began to repeat conscientiously all the prayers he had
omitted, without a thought of either eating or drinking. Once, for
seven weeks together, he scarcely closed his eyes in sleep.

Burning with desire to attain that holiness in quest of which he
had entered the cloister, Luther gave way to all the rigor of an
ascetic life. He endeavored to crucify the flesh by fastings, mortifications, and watchings. Shut up in his cell, as in a prison, he struggled unceasingly against the deceitful thoughts and the evil inclina-
tions of his heart. A little bread and a small herring were often his
only food. Besides, he was naturally of very abstemious habits. Thus

[1] If Lyra had not touched his lyre, Luther had never danced.

he was frequently seen by his friends, long after he had ceased to think of purchasing heaven by his abstinence, to content himself with the poorest food, and remain even four days in succession without eating or drinking. This we have on the testimony of Melancthon, a witness, in every respect, worthy of credit. We may judge from this circumstance of the small value to be attached to the stories that ignorance and prejudice have circulated as to Luther's intemperance. At this period in his life, nothing was too great a sacrifice that might enable him to become a saint—to acquire heaven. Never did the Romish church possess a more pious monk. Never did cloister witness more severe or indefatigable exertions to purchase eternal happiness. When Luther became a reformer, and declared that heaven was not to be obtained by means such as these, he knew whereof he spoke. "I was indeed a pious monk," wrote he to Duke George of Saxony, "and followed the rules of my order more strictly than I can express. If ever a monk could obtain heaven by his monkish works, I should certainly have been entitled to it. Of this all the friars who have known me can testify. If it had continued much longer, I should have carried my mortifications even to death, by means of my watchings, prayers, reading, and other labors."

Luther did not find in the tranquillity of the cloister and in monkish perfection that peace of mind which he had looked for there. He wished to have the assurance of his salvation; this was the great desire of his soul. Without it, there was no repose for him. But the fears that had agitated him in the world pursued him to his cell. Nay, they were increased. The faintest cry of his heart re-echoed loud beneath the silent arches of the cloister. God had led him there that he might learn to know himself and to despair of his own strength and virtue. His conscience, enlightened by the divine Word, told him what it was to be holy, but he was filled with terror at finding, neither in his heart nor in his life, that image of holiness which he had thoughtfully considered with admiration in the Word of God. A sad discovery, and one that is made by every sincere man! No righteousness within, no righteousness without! all was omission, sin, impurity! The more ardent the character of Luther, the stronger was that secret and constant resistance which man's nature opposes to good; and it plunged him into despair.

The monks and divines of the day encouraged him to satisfy the divine righteousness by meritorious works. "But what works," thought he, "can come from a heart like mine? How can I stand before the holiness of my Judge with works polluted in their very source?" "I saw that I was a great sinner in the eyes of God," he wrote later, "and I did not think it possible for me to propitiate Him by my own merits."

He was agitated and yet dejected, avoiding the trifling and often stupid conversation of other monks. The latter, unable to comprehend the storms that tossed his soul, looked upon him with surprise, and reproached him for his silence and his gloomy air. One day, Cochloeus tells us, as they were saying mass in the chapel, Luther had carried thither all his anxiety, and was in the choir in the midst of the brethren, sad and heart-stricken. Already the priest had prostrated himself, the incense had been burnt before the altar, the Gloria sung, and they were reading the Gospel, when Luther, poor monk, unable any longer to repress his anguish, cried out in a mournful tone, as he fell on his knees, "It is not I—it is not I." All were thunderstruck and the ceremony was interrupted for a moment. Perhaps Luther thought he heard some reproach of which he knew himself innocent; perhaps he declared his unworthiness of being one of those to whom Christ's death had brought the gift of eternal life. Cochloeus says that they were reading the story of the dumb man from whom Christ expelled a devil. It is possible that this cry of Luther, if the account be true, had reference to this circumstance, and that, although speechless like the dumb man, he protested by such an exclamation that his silence came from other causes than demoniacal possession. Indeed, Cochloeus says that the monks sometimes attributed the sufferings of their brother to a secret intercourse with the devil, and this writer himself entertained that opinion.

A tender conscience inclined Luther to regard the slightest fault as a great sin. He had hardly discovered it before he endeavored to expiate it by the severest mortifications, which only served to point out to him the uselessness of all human remedies. "I tortured myself almost to death," said he, "in order to procure peace with God for my troubled heart and agitated conscience, but surrounded with thick darkness, I found peace nowhere."

The practices of monastic holiness, which lulled so many consciences to sleep, and to which Luther himself had had recourse in his distress, soon appeared to him the unavailing remedies of a deceptive religion. "While I was yet a monk, I no sooner felt assailed by any temptation than I cried out—I am lost! Immediately I had recourse to a thousand methods to stifle the cries of my conscience. I went every day to confession, but that was of no use to me. Then, bowed down by sorrow, I tortured myself by the multitude of my thoughts.—Look, exclaimed I, thou art still envious, impatient, passionate! . . . It profiteth thee nothing, O wretched man, to have entered this sacred order."

And yet Luther, imbued with the prejudices of his time, had from early youth considered the observances, whose worthlessness he had just discovered, as a certain remedy for diseased souls. What could he think of the strange discovery he had just made in the solitude of the cloister? It is possible, then, to dwell within the sanctuary, and yet bear in one's bosom a man of sin! He had received another garment, but not another heart. His expectations were disappointed; where could he stop? Were all these rules and observances mere human inventions? Such a supposition appeared to him, at one time a temptation of the devil, and at another an irresistible truth. By turns contending with the holy voice that spoke to his heart, and with the venerable institutions that time had sanctioned, Luther passed his life in a continual struggle. The young monk crept like a shadow through the long galleries of the cloister that re-echoed with his sorrowful moanings. His body wasted away; his strength began to fail him; sometimes he remained like one dead.

On one occasion, overwhelmed with sorrow, he shut himself up in his cell, and for several days and nights allowed no one to approach him. One of his friends, Lucas Edemberger, feeling anxious about the unhappy monk, and having a presentiment of the condition in which he was, took with him some boys who were in the habit of singing in the choirs, and knocked at the door of the cell. No one opened—no one answered. The good Edemberger, still more alarmed, broke open the door. Luther lay insensible upon the floor, giving no signs of life. His friend strove in vain to recall him to his senses; but he remained motionless. Then the choristers began to sing a sweet hymn. Their clear voices acted like a charm on this one, to whom music was ever one of his greatest pleasures; gradually he recovered his strength, his consciousness, and life. If music could restore his serenity for a few moments, he required another and a stronger remedy to heal him thoroughly: he needed that mild and subtle sound of the gospel, which is the voice of God Himself. He knew it well, therefore his troubles and his terrors led him to study with fresh zeal the writings of the prophets and of the apostles.

Chapter 4

CONVERSION, ORDINATION; PROFESSOR-SHIP AT WITTENBERG

LUTHER was not the first monk who had undergone such trials. The gloomy walls of the cloisters often concealed the most abominable vices; often, however, they hid Christian virtues that expanded there in silence, and which, had they been exposed to the eyes of the world, would have excited universal admiration. The possessors of these virtues, living only with themselves and with God, attracted no attention, and were often unknown to the modest convent in which they were enclosed: their lives were known only to God. Sometimes these humble solitaries fell into that mystic theology,—sad "disease" of the noblest minds!—which in earlier ages had been the delight of the first monks on the banks of the Nile, and which unprofitably consumes the souls of those who become its victims.

Yet if one of these men was called to some high station, he displayed virtues in it whose salutary influence was long and widely felt. The candle thus was set on a candlestick; it illumined the whole house, and many were awakened by this light. Thus from generation to generation were these pious souls propagated; they were seen shining like isolated torches at the very times when the cloisters were often receptacles of darkness.

One such torch in the German convents was a young man named John Staupitz. He was descended from a noble Misnian family, and from his tenderest youth had had a taste for knowledge and a love of virtue. Feeling the need of retirement to devote himself to letters, he soon discovered that philosophy and the study of nature could not do much towards eternal salvation. He therefore began to study theology, but especially endeavored to unite practice with knowledge. "For," says one of his biographers, "it is in vain that we assume the name of divine (clergyman, versed in divinity), if we do not confirm that noble title by our lives." The study of the Bible and of the Augustine theology, the knowledge of himself, the battles that he, like Luther, had had to fight against the deceits and lusts of his heart, led him to the Redeemer. He found peace for his soul in faith in Christ. The doctrine of election by grace had taken strong hold of his mind. The integrity of his life, the extent of his knowledge, the eloquence of his speech, not less than a striking exterior and dignified manners, recommended him to his contemporaries. Frederick the Wise, elector of Saxony, made him his friend, employed him in various embassies, and founded the University of Wittenberg under his direction. This disciple of St. Paul and St. Augustine was the first dean of the theological faculty of that school from which the light was one day to issue to illumine the schools and churches of so many nations. Present at the Lateran council, as proxy of the Archbishop of Saltzburg, he became provincial of his order in Thuringia and Saxony, and afterwards vicar-general of the Augustines for all Germany.

John Staupitz was grieved at the corruption of morals and the errors of doctrine that were devastating the Church. His own writings on the love of God, on Christian faith, and on conformity with the death of Christ, as well as the testimony of Luther, confirm this. But he considered the former evil of more importance than the latter. Besides the mildness and indecision of his character, his desire not to go beyond the sphere of action he thought assigned to him made him more fit to be the restorer of a convent than the reformer of the Church. He would have wished to raise none but distinguished men to important offices, but not finding them, he submitted to employ others. "We must plow," said he, "with such horses as we can find; and with oxen, if there are no horses."

We have noted the anguish and the internal struggles to which Luther was a prey in the convent of Erfurt. It was at this time that a visitation of the vicar-general was announced, for Staupitz came to make his usual inspection. This friend of Frederick, the founder of the University of Wittenberg, and chief of the Augustines, exhibited much kindness to monks under his authority. One of these brothers attracted his attention. He was a young man of middle height, whom study, fasting, and prolonged vigils had so wasted away that all his bones might be counted. His eyes, that were in later life compared to a falcon's, were sunken; his manner was dejected; his countenance betrayed an agitated mind, the prey of a thousand struggles, but yet strong and resolute. His whole appearance was grave, melancholy, and solemn: Staupitz, whose discernment had been exercised by long experience, easily discovered what was passing in his mind, and marked the youthful monk above all who surrounded him. He felt drawn to him, and had a presentiment of his great destiny. He had had to struggle, like Luther, and therefore he could understand him. Above all, he could point out to him the road to peace, which he himself had found. What he learned of the circumstances that had brought the young Augustine into the convent still more increased his sympathy. He requested the prior to treat him with greater mildness, and took advantage of the opportunities afforded by his station to win the confidence of the youthful brother. Approaching him with affection, he endeavored by every means to dispel his timidity, which was increased by the respect and fear that a man of such exalted rank as Staupitz must necessarily inspire.

Luther's heart, which harsh treatment had closed till then, opened at last and expanded. "As in water face answereth to face, so the heart of man to man." Luther's heart found an echo in that of Staupitz. The vicar-general understood him. The monk felt a confidence towards him that he had as yet experienced for none. He revealed to him the cause of his dejection, described the horrible thoughts that perplexed him. Then began in the cloister of Erfurt those conversations so full of wisdom and of instruction. Up to this time no one had understood Luther. One day, when at the table in the refectory, the young monk, dejected and silent, scarcely touched his food. Staupitz, who looked earnestly at him, said at last, "Why are you so sad, brother Martin?" "Ah!" replied Luther, with a deep sigh, "I do not know what will become of me!" "These temptations," resumed Staupitz, "are more necessary to you than eating and drinking." These two men did not stop there; and erelong in the silence of the cloister there took place conversation which powerfully contributed to lead forth the future reformer from his state of darkness.

"It is in vain," said Luther despondingly to Staupitz, "that I make promises to God: sin is ever the strongest."

"O my friend!" replied the vicar-general, as he looked back on his own experience, "more than a thousand times have I sworn to our holy God to live piously, and I have never kept my vows. Now I swear no longer, for I know that I cannot keep my solemn promises. If God will not be merciful towards me for the love of Christ, and grant me a happy departure, when I must quit this world, I shall never, with the aid of all my vows and all my good works, stand before Him. I must perish."

The young monk was terrified at the thought of divine justice. He laid open all his fears to the vicar-general. He was alarmed at the unspeakable holiness of God and His sovereign majesty. "Who may abide the day of his coming? and who shall stand when he appeareth?" (Mal. 3:2).

Staupitz resumed: he knew where he had found peace, and he resolved to point it out to the young man. "Why," said he, "do you torment yourself with all these speculations and these high thoughts? . . . Look at the wounds of Jesus Christ, to the blood that He has shed for you; it is there that the grace of God will appear to you. Instead of torturing yourself on account of your sins, throw yourself into the Redeemer's arms. Trust in Him—in the righteousness of His life—in the atonement of His death. Do not shrink back; God is not angry with you; it is you who are angry with God. Listen to the Son of God. He became man to give you the assurance of divine favor. He says to you, 'You are My sheep; you hear My voice; no man shall pluck you out of My hand.'"

But Luther did not find in himself the repentance which he thought necessary for salvation, and he made the reply which is the usual answer of distressed and timid minds: "How can I dare believe in the favor of God, so long as there is no real conversion in me? I must be changed before He will accept me."

His venerable guide showed him that there can be no real conversion so long as man fears God as a severe Judge. "What will you say then," asked Luther, "to so many consciences to which a thousand insupportable tasks are prescribed in order that they may gain heaven?"

Then he heard this reply of the vicar-general, but he could not believe that it came from man; it seemed to him like a voice from heaven. "There is no real repentance except that which begins with the love of God and of righteousness. What others imagine to be the end and accomplishment of repentance is, on the contrary, only its beginning. In order that you may be filled with the love of what is good, you must first be filled with love for God. If you desire to be converted, do not be curious about all these mortifications and all these tortures. Love Him who first loved you!"

Luther listened—he listened again. These consolations filled him with joy till then unknown, and imparted to him new light. "It is Jesus Christ," thought he in his heart: "Yes, it is Jesus Christ Himself who so wonderfully consoles me by these sweet and healing words."

These words, indeed, penetrated to the bottom of the young monk's heart, like the sharp arrow of a strong man. In order to repent, we must love God. Guided by this new light, he began to compare the Scriptures. He looked out all the passages that treat of repentance and conversion. Luther himself tells us that these words, till then so dreaded, "are become to me an agreeable pastime and the sweetest of recreations. All the passages of Scripture that used to alarm me seem now to run to me from every part,—to smile and sport around me."

"Hitherto," he exclaims, "although I carefully dissembled the state of my soul before God, and endeavored to express towards Him a love which was a mere constraint and a fiction, there was no expression in Scripture so bitter to me as that of repentance. But now there is none so sweet or more acceptable. Oh! how delightful are all God's precepts when we read them not only in books, but also in our Saviour's precious wounds!"

Luther had been consoled by Staupitz' words, but he nevertheless fell sometimes into despondency. Sin was again felt in his timid conscience, and then all his previous despair banished the joy of salvation. "O my sin! my sin! my sin!" cried the young monk one day in the presence of the vicar-general, with a tone of profound anguish. "Well! would you only be a sinner in appearance," replied the latter, "and have also a Saviour only in appearance? Then," added Staupitz with authority, "know that Jesus Christ is the Saviour even of those who are great, real sinners, and deserving of utter condemnation."

It was not alone the sin he discovered in his heart that agitated Luther; the troubles of his conscience were augmented by those of reason. If the holy precepts of the Bible alarmed him, some of the doctrines of that divine Book still more increased his tortures. The truth, which is the great medium by which God confers peace on man, must necessarily begin by taking away from him the false security that destroys him. The doctrine of election particularly disturbed this young man. It launched him into a boundless field of inquiry. Must he believe that it was man who first chose God for his portion, or that God first elected man? The Bible, history, daily experience, the works of Augustine,—all had shown him that we must always and in every case ascend to that First Cause, to that sovereign will by which everything exists, and on which everything depends. But his ardent spirit would have desired to go still further; he would have wished to penetrate into the secret councils of God, to unveil His mysteries, to see the invisible, and to comprehend the incomprehensible. Staupitz checked him. He told him not to presume to fathom the hidden God, but to confine himself to what He has manifested to us in Jesus Christ. "In Him," the Lord has said, "you will find what I am, and what I require. Nowhere else, neither in heaven nor in earth, will you discover it."

The vicar-general did still more. He showed Luther the fatherly designs of Providence in permitting these temptations and these various struggles that his soul was to undergo. He made him view them in a light well calculated to revive his courage. By such trials God prepares for Himself the souls that He destines for some important work. We must prove the vessel before we launch it into the wide sea. If there is an education necessary for every man, there is a particular one for those who are destined to act upon their generation. This is what Staupitz represented to the monk of Erfurt. "It is not in vain," he assured Luther, "that God exercises you in so many conflicts: you will see that He will employ you, as His servant, for great purposes."

Luther listened with astonishment and humility. He was inspired with courage, and he discovered strength in himself which he had not even suspected. The wisdom and prudence of an enlightened friend gradually revealed the strong man to himself. Staupitz went further; he gave him many valuable directions for his studies, exhorting him, henceforward, to derive all his theology from the Bible, and to put away the systems of the schools. "Let the study of the Scriptures," said he, "be your favorite occupation." Never was good advice better followed out. What particularly delighted Luther was the present Staupitz made him of a Bible, but it was not that red leather-bound Latin one, the property of the convent, which it had been his desire to possess and to carry about with him. He had wanted that one because he was so familiar with its pages, and knew where to find each passage. Nevertheless, at last he was master of the Treasure of God. Henceforward he studied the Scriptures, and especially the epistles of St. Paul, with ever increasing zeal. To these he added the works of St. Augustine alone. All that he read was imprinted deeply in his mind. His struggles had prepared his heart to understand the Word. The soil had been plowed deep; the incorruptible Seed sank into it with power. When Staupitz quitted Erfurt, a new dawn had risen upon Luther!

But the work was not yet finished. The vicar-general had prepared the way: God reserved its accomplishment for an humbler instrument. The conscience of the young Augustine had not yet found repose. His body gave way at last under the conflict and the tension of his soul. He was attacked by illness that brought him to the brink of the grave. This was in the second year of his abode in the convent. All his distresses and all his fears were aroused at the approach of death. His own impurity and the holiness of God again disturbed his mind. One day, as he lay overwhelmed with despair, an aged monk entered his cell, and addressed a few words of comfort to him. Luther opened his heart to him, and made known the fears by which he was tormented. The venerable man was incapable of following up that soul in all its doubts, as Staupitz had done, but he knew his Credo, and had found in it much consolation to his heart. He therefore applied the same remedy to his young brother.

Leading him back to that Apostles' creed which Luther had learned in early childhood at the school of Mansfeldt, the aged monk repeated this article with kind good nature: "I believe in the forgiveness of sins." These simple words, which the pious brother pronounced with sincerity in this decisive moment, diffused great consolation in Luther's heart. "I believe," he repeated to himself erelong on his bed of sickness, "I believe in the forgiveness of sins!"—"Ah!"

said the monk, "you must believe not only in the forgiveness of David's and of Peter's sins, for this even the devils believe. It is God's command that we believe our own sins are forgiven us." How delightful did this commandment seem to poor Luther! "Hear what St. Bernard says in his discourse on the Annunciation," added the aged brother: "The testimony of the Holy Ghost in thy heart is this: Thy sins are forgiven thee." From this moment light sprang up in the heart of the young monk of Erfurt. The word of grace had been pronounced; he had believed in it. He disclaimed all merit of salvation, and resigned himself confidingly to the grace of God in Jesus Christ. He did not at first perceive the consequences of the principle he had admitted; he was still sincere in his attachment to the Church, and yet he had no further need of her, for he had received salvation immediately from God Himself; henceforth Roman Catholicism was no more for him. He advanced,—he sought in the writings of the apostles and prophets for all that could strengthen the hope which filled his heart. Each day he invoked support from on high, and each day also the light increased in his soul.

Luther's mental health restored that of his body. He soon rose from his bed of sickness, for he had received a new life in a two-fold sense. The festival of Christmas, following soon, gave him an opportunity of tasting abundantly all the consolations of faith. He took part in these holy solemnities with sweet emotion; and when in the ceremonial of the day he had to chant these words, O beata culpa quoe talem meruisti Redemptorem, his whole being responded Amen, and thrilled with joy.

Luther had been two years in the cloister, and was to be ordained priest. He had received much, and saw with delight the prospect afforded by the sacerdotal office of freely distributing what he had freely received. He wished to take advantage of the ceremony that was about to take place to become thoroughly reconciled with his father. He invited him to be present, and even requested him to fix the day. John Luther, who was not yet entirely pacified with regard to his son, nevertheless accepted the invitation, and named Sunday, May 2, 1507.

Among the number of Luther's friends was the vicar of Eisenach, John Braun, who had been a faithful counselor to him during his residence in that city. Luther wrote to him on April 22. This is the oldest letter of the reformer, and it bears the following address: "To John Braun, holy and venerable priest of Christ and of Mary." It is only in Luther's two earliest letters that the name of Mary is found.

"God, who is glorious and holy in all His works," says the candidate for the priesthood, "having most graciously condescended to raise me up—me, a wretched and in all respects unworthy sinner, and to call me by His sole and most free mercy to His sublime ministry; I ought, in order to testify my gratitude for such divine and magnificent goodness (as far at least as mere dust and ashes can do it) to fulfill with my whole heart the duties of the office intrusted to me."

At last the day arrived. The miner of Mansfeldt did not fail to be present at his son's ordination. He gave him indeed no unequivocal mark of his affection and of his generosity by presenting him on the occasion with twenty florins.

The ceremony took place. Hieronymus, bishop of Brandenburg, officiated. At the moment of conferring on Luther the power of celebrating mass, he placed the chalice in his hands, and uttered these solemn words, *Accipe potestatem sacrificandi pro vivis et mortuis:* "Receive the power of sacrificing for the quick and the dead."

Luther at that time listened calmly to these words, which conferred on him the power of doing the work belonging to the Son of God; but he shuddered at them in after years. "If the earth did not then open and swallow us both up," said he, "it was owing to the great patience and long-suffering of the Lord."

The father afterwards dined at the convent with his son, the young priest's friends, and the monks. The conversation turned to Martin's entrance into the monastery. The brothers loudly extolled it as a most meritorious work, upon which the inflexible John, turning to his son, asked: "Have you not read in Scripture, that you should obey your father and mother?" These words struck Luther; they presented in quite a new aspect the action that had brought him into the convent, and they long re-echoed in his heart.

Shortly after his ordination, Luther, by the advice of Staupitz, made little excursions on foot into the neighboring parishes and convents, either to divert his mind and give his body the necessary exercise, or to accustom him to preaching.

The festival of Corpus Christi was to be celebrated with great pomp at Eisleben. The vicar-general would be present, and Luther repaired there also. He still had need of Staupitz, and sought every opportunity of meeting this enlightened guide who directed his soul into the path of life. The procession was numerous and brilliant. Staupitz himself bore the consecrated host, Luther following in his sacerdotal robes. The thought that it was Jesus Christ Himself whom the vicar-general carried, the idea that the Saviour was there in person before him, suddenly struck Luther's imagination, and filled him with such terror that he could scarcely proceed. The perspiration dropped from his face; he staggered, and thought he should die of anguish and fright. At length the procession was over; the host that had awakened all the fears of the monk was solemnly deposited in the sanctuary; and Luther, finding himself alone with Staupitz, fell into his arms and confessed his dread. Then the good vicar-general, who had long known that gentle Saviour who does not break the bruised reed, said to him mildly: "It was not Jesus Christ, my brother; He does not alarm; He gives consolation only."

Luther was not destined to remain hidden in an obscure convent. The time had come for his removal to a wider stage. Staupitz, with whom he always remained in close communication, saw clearly that the young monk's disposition was too active to be confined within so narrow a circle. He spoke of him to the Elector Frederick of Saxony, and this enlightened prince invited Luther, probably about the end of the year 1508, to become professor at the University of Wittenberg. On this field he was to fight many hard battles. Luther felt that his true vocation was there. He was asked to go to his new post with all speed and in the hurry of moving he had not time to write to the one whom he styled his master and well-beloved father —John Braun, curate of Eisenach. A few months later he wrote, "My departure was so hasty that those with whom I was living were almost ignorant of it. I am farther away, I confess: but the better part of me remains with you." Luther had spent three years in the cloister at Erfurt.

In the year 1502, Frederick the Elector had founded a new University at Wittenberg. He declared in the charter confirming the privileges of this high school that he and his people would look to it as to an oracle. At that time he had little thought how remarkably this language would be verified. Two men of the opposition that had been formed against the scholastic system—Pollich of Mellerstadt, doctor of medicine, law, and philosophy, and Staupitz—had had great influence in the establishment of this academy. The university declared that it selected St. Augustine for its patron—a choice that was very significant. This new institution, which possessed great liberty and which was considered as a court of final appeal in all cases of difficulty, was admirably fitted to become the cradle of the Reformation, and it powerfully contributed to the development of Luther and of his work.

On his arrival at Wittenberg, he repaired to the Augustine convent, where a cell was allotted to him; for though a professor, he did not cease to be a monk. He had been called to teach physics and dialectics. When he was assigned to this duty, regard had probably been paid to the philosophical studies he had pursued at Erfurt and to the degree of master of arts which he had taken. Thus Luther, who hungered and thirsted after the Word of God, was compelled to devote himself almost exclusively to the study of the Aristotelian scholastic philosophy. He had need of that Bread of Life which God gives to the world, and yet he was forced to occupy himself with human subtleties. What a restraint, and what sighs it called forth!

"By God's grace, I am well," he wrote to Braun, "except that I have to study philosophy with all my might. From the first moment of my arrival at Wittenberg, I was earnestly desirous of exchanging it for that of theology; but," he added, lest it should be supposed he meant the theology of the day, "it is of a theology which seeks the kernel in the nut, the wheat in the husk, the marrow in the bones, that I am speaking. Be that as it may, God is God," he continued with that confidence which was the soul of his life; "man is almost always mistaken in his judgments; but this is our God. He will lead us with goodness for ever and ever." The studies that Luther was then obliged to pursue were of great service to him, in enabling him subsequently to combat the errors of the schoolmen.

But he could not stop there. The desire of his heart was about to be accomplished. That same power, which some years before had driven Luther from the legal profession into a monastic life, was now impelling him from philosophy towards the Bible. He zealously applied himself to the acquisition of the ancient languages, particularly of Greek and Hebrew, in order to draw knowledge and learning from the very springs whence they gushed forth. He was all his life indefatigable in labor. A few months after his arrival at the university, he solicited the degree of bachelor of divinity. He obtained it at the end of March 1509, with the particular summons to devote himself to biblical theology,—*ad Biblia.*

Every day, at one in the afternoon, Luther was called to lecture on the Bible; it was a precious hour both for the professor and his pupils, and it led them deeper and deeper into the divine meaning of those revelations so long lost to the people and to the schools!

He began his course by explaining the Psalms, and thence passed to the Epistle to the Romans. It was more particularly while meditating on this portion of Scripture that the light of truth penetrated his heart. In the retirement of his quiet cell, he used to consecrate whole hours to the study of the divine Word, this epistle of the apostle Paul lying open before him. On one occasion, having reached the seventeenth verse of the first chapter, he read this passage from the prophet Habakkuk, "The just shall live by faith." This precept struck him. There is then for the just a life different from that of other men: and this life is the gift of faith. This promise, which he received into his heart as if God Himself had placed it there, unveiled to him the mystery of the Christian life and increased this life in him. Years after, in the midst of his numerous occupations, he imagined he still heard these words: "The just shall live by faith."

Luther's prepared lectures had little similarity with what had been heard till then. It was not an eloquent rhetorician or a pedantic schoolman that spoke; but a Christian who had felt the power of revealed truths, one who drew them forth from the Bible, poured them out from the treasures of his heart, and presented them all full of life to his astonished hearers. It was not the teaching of a man, but of God.

This entirely new method of expounding the truth made a great disturbance; the news of it spread far and wide, and attracted to the newly established university a crowd of youthful foreign students. Even many professors attended Luther's lectures, and among others Mellerstadt, frequently styled "the light of the world," first rector of the university, who already at his previous post at Leipzig had earnestly combated the ridiculous instructions of scholasticism, had denied the "the light created on the first day was Theology," and had maintained that the study of literature should be the foundation of that science. "This monk," said he, "will put all the doctors to shame; he will bring in a new doctrine, and reform the the whole church; for he builds upon the Word of Christ, and no one in the world can either resist or overthrow that Word, even should he attack it with all the arms of philosophy, of the Sophists, Scotists, Albertists, Thomists, and with all the Tartaretus." *

Staupitz, who was the instrument of God to develop the gifts and treasures hidden in Luther, requested him to preach in the church of the Augustines. The young professor shrank from this proposal. He desired to confine himself to his academic duties; he trembled at the thought of increasing them by those of the ministry. In vain did Staupitz solicit him: "No! no!" he replied, "it is no slight thing to speak before men in the place of God." What affecting humility in this great reformer of the Church! Staupitz persisted; but the ingenious Luther, says one of his biographers, found fifteen arguments, pretexts, and evasions to defend himself against this invitation. At length, the chief of the Augustines persevering in his attack, Luther said: "Ah, doctor, by doing this you deprive me of life. I shall not be able to hold out three months."—"Well! so be it in God's name," replied the vicar-general, "for our Lord God has also need on high of devoted and skillful men." Luther was forced to yield.

In the middle of the square at Wittenberg stood an ancient wooden chapel, thirty feet long and twenty feet wide, whose walls propped up on all sides were falling into ruin. An old pulpit made of planks received the preacher. It was in this wretched place that the preaching of the Reformation began. It was God's will that that which was to restore His glory should have the humblest of beginnings. The foundations of the new Augustine Church had just been laid, and meanwhile this miserable place of worship was used. "This building," adds Myconius, one of Luther's contemporaries, who records these circumstances, "may well be compared to the stable in which Christ was born. It was in this wretched enclosure that God willed, so to speak, that His well-beloved Son should be born a second time.

* Favorite works with the scholastic divines in the Middle Ages.

Among those thousands of cathedrals and parish churches with which the world is filled, there was not one at that time which God chose for the glorious preaching of eternal life."

Luther preached: everything about the new minister was striking. His expressive countenance, his noble air, his clear and sonorous voice, captivated all his hearers. Before his time, the majority of preachers had sought rather what might amuse their congregation than what would convert them. The great seriousness that pervaded all Luther's sermons, and the joy with which the knowledge of the gospel had filled his heart, imparted to his eloquence an authority, a warmth, and an unction that his predecessors had not possessed. "Endowed with a ready and lively genius," says one of his opponents, "with a good memory, and employing his mother-tongue with wonderful facility, Luther was inferior to none of his contemporaries in eloquence. Speaking from the pulpit as if he were agitated by some violent emotion, suiting the action to his words, he affected his hearers' minds in a surprising manner, and carried them like a torrent wherever he pleased. So much strength, grace, and eloquence are rarely found in these children of the North." "He had," says Bossuet, "a lively and impetuous eloquence that charmed and led away the people."

Soon the little chapel could not hold the hearers who crowded to it. The council of Wittenberg then nominated Luther their chaplain, and invited him to preach in the city church. The impression he there produced was greater still. The energy of his genius, the eloquence of his style, and the excellency of the doctrines that he proclaimed, equally astonished his hearers. His reputation extended far and wide, and Frederick the Wise himself came once to Wittenberg to hear him.

This was the beginning of a new life for Luther. The slow tempo of the cloister had been succeeded by great activity. Freedom, labor, the earnest and constant action to which he could now devote himself at Wittenberg, succeeded in re-establishing harmony and peace within him. Now he was in his place, and the work of God was soon to display its majestic progress.

Chapter 5

JOURNEY TO ROME

LUTHER was teaching both in the academic hall and in the church, when he was interrupted in his labors. In 1510, or according to others in 1511 or 1512, he was sent to Rome. Seven convents of his order were at variance on certain points with the vicar-general. The acuteness of Luther's mind, his powerful language, and his talents for discussion, were the cause of his selection as agent for these seven monasteries before the pope. This divine dispensation was necessary for Luther. It was requisite that he should know Rome. He had always imagined Rome to be the abode of sanctity.

Setting out from Wittenberg, he traveled south across the Alps; but he had scarcely descended into the plains of the rich and voluptuous Italy, before he found subjects of astonishment and scandal. The poor monk from Germany was entertained in a wealthy convent of the Benedictines on the banks of the Po, in Lombardy. The revenues of this monastery amounted to thirty-six thousand ducats; twelve thousand were devoted to the table, twelve thousand were set apart for the buildings, and the remainder for the wants of the monks. The splendor of the apartments, the richness of dress, and the delicacy of food, confounded Luther. Marble, silk, luxury in all its forms—what a sight for the humble brother of the poor convent of Wittenberg! He was astonished and silent; but when Friday came, what was his surprise at seeing the table spread with an abundance of meat. Upon this he resolved to speak. "The Church and the pope," said he, "forbid such things." The Benedictines were irritated. This was a reprimand from an unpolished German. But Luther persisted, and perhaps may have threatened to make these irregularities known, therefore some thought the simplest course would be to get rid of their importunate guest. The porter of the convent forewarned him of the danger he incurred by a longer stay. He accordingly quitted this monastery, and reached Bologna, where he fell dangerously ill. Some have attributed this to the effects of poison; but it is more reasonable to suppose that the change of diet affected the frugal monk whose usual food was bread and herrings. The sickness was not unto death, but to the glory of God. He again relapsed into the sorrow and dejection so natural to him. To die thus, far from Germany, in a foreign land—what a sad fate! The distress of mind that he had felt at Erfurt returned with renewed force. The sense of his sinfulness troubled him; the prospect of God's judgment filled him once more with dread. But at the very moment that these terrors had reached their highest pitch, the words of St. Paul, "The just shall live by faith," recurred forcibly to his memory and enlightened his soul like a ray from heaven. Restored and comforted, he soon regained his health and resumed his journey towards Rome, expecting to find there a very different manner of life from that of the Lombard convents. He was impatient to efface, by the sight of Roman holiness, the melancholy impressions left on his mind by his sojourn on the banks of the Po.

After a toilsome journey under a burning Italian sun, at the beginning of summer, he drew near the seven-hilled city. His heart was moved within him: his eyes sought after the Queen of the world and of the Church. As soon as he discovered the Eternal City in the distance—the city of St. Peter and St. Paul, the metropolis of Catholicism—he fell on his knees, exclaiming, "Holy Rome, I salute thee!"

Now in Rome, Luther, the Wittenberg professor stood in the midst of the eloquent ruins of the consular and imperial city—of the Rome of so many martyrs and confessors of Jesus Christ. Here had lived that Plautus and that Virgil whose works he had carried with him into the cloister, and all the great men over whose history his heart had so often beat with emotion. He beheld their statues,—the ruins of the monuments that bore witness to their glory. All that glory—all that power had fled; his feet trampled on dust! At each step he called to mind the sad presentiments of Scipio shedding his tears as he looked upon ruins—the burning palaces and tottering walls of Carthage, and exclaimed, "Thus will it one day be with Rome!" "And in truth," said Luther, "the Rome of the Scipios and

Caesars has become a corpse. There are such heaps of rubbish that the foundations of the houses are now where once stood the roofs. It is there," added he, as he threw a melancholy glance over these ruins, "it is there that once the riches and the treasures of the world were gathered together." All these fragments, against which his feet stumbled at every step, proclaimed to Luther that what is strongest in the eyes of man may be easily destroyed by the breath of the Lord.

But with these profane ashes were mingled other and holier ones: he recalled them to mind. The burial place of the martyrs was not far from that of the generals and conquerors of Rome. Christian Rome with its sufferings had more power over the heart of the Saxon monk than pagan Rome with all its glory. Here was the place where that letter arrived in which Paul wrote, "The just shall live by faith." He was not far from Appii Forum and the Three Taverns. Here was the house of Narcissus—there the palace of Caesar, where the Lord delivered the apostle from the jaws of the lion. Oh, how these recollections strengthened the heart of the monk of Wittenberg!

But Rome at this time presented the warlike Julius II filling the papal chair, and not Leo X as some distinguished German historians have said, doubtless through inattention. Luther often related a trait in the character of this pope. When the news reached him that his army had been defeated by the French before Ravenna, he was repeating his daily prayers: he flung away the book, exclaiming with a terrible oath: "And Thou too art become a Frenchman . . . Is it thus Thou dost protect Thy Church? . . ." Then turning in the direction of the country to whose arms he thought to have recourse, he added: "Saint Switzer, pray for us!" Ignorance, levity, and dissolute manners, a profane spirit, a contempt for all that was sacred, a scandalous traffic in divine things—such was the spectacle afforded by this unhappy city.

Because it was the period of the feast of St. John, Luther heard the Romans repeating a proverb current among them: "Happy the mother whose son performs mass on St. John's eve!"—"Oh, how I should rejoice to render my mother happy!" said Luther to himself. Margaret's pious son endeavored to repeat a mass on that day; but he could not, the throng was too great.

Fervent and meek, he visited all the churches and chapels; he believed in all that was told him; he devoutly performed all the holy practices that were required, happy in being able to execute so many good works from which his fellow-countrymen were debarred. "Oh! how I regret," said the pious German to himself, "that my father and mother are still alive! What pleasure I should have in delivering them from the fire of purgatory by my masses, my prayers, and by so many other admirable works!" He had found the light; but the darkness was not entirely expelled from his understanding. His heart was converted; his mind was not yet enlightened: he had faith and love, but without knowledge. It was no trifling matter to emerge from that thick night which had persisted for so many centuries.

Several times Luther repeated mass at Rome. He officiated with all the unction and dignity that such an action appeared to him to require. What affliction seized his heart after he witnessed the sad mechanism of the Roman priests, as they celebrated the sacrament of the altar! They laughed at his simplicity. The priests at an adjoining altar, to one at which he ministered, had already repeated seven masses before he had finished one. "Quick, quick!" repeated one of them, "send our Lady back her Son"; making impious allusion to the transubstantiation of the bread into the body and blood of Jesus Christ. At another time Luther had only just reached the Gospel, when the priest beside him had terminated the mass. "Passa, passa!" cried the latter to him, "make haste! have done with it at once."

His astonishment was still greater when he later found in the dignitaries what he had already observed in the inferior clergy. He had hoped and expected better things of them.

It was the fashion at the papal court to attack Christianity. You could not pass for a well-bred man, unless you entertained some erroneous or heretical opinion on the doctrines of the Church. They had endeavored to convince Erasmus, by means of certain extracts from Pliny, that there was no difference between the souls of men and of beasts. Some of the pope's youthful courtiers maintained that the orthodox faith was the result of the crafty devices of a few saints.

Luther's coming from the German Augustines procured him invitations to numerous meetings of distinguished ecclesiastics. One day he was at table with several prelates, who displayed openly their buffoonery and impious conversation. They did not scruple to utter a thousand mockeries, thinking, no doubt, that he was of the same mind. Among other things, they related, laughing and priding themselves upon it, how, when they were repeating mass at the altar, instead of the sacramental words that were to transform the bread and wine into the flesh and blood of our Saviour, they pronounced over the elements this derisive expression: *Panis es, et panis manebis; vinum es, et vinum manebis.*[1] Then, they explained that they elevated the host, and all the people bowed down and worshiped it. Luther could hardly believe his ears. His disposition, one of animation and even gaiety in the society of friends, was serious whenever sacred matters were concerned. The mockeries of Rome were a stumbling block to him. "I was," said he, "a thoughtful and pious young monk. Such language grieved me bitterly. If 'tis thus they speak at Rome, freely and publicly at the dinner table, what would it be if their actions corresponded to their words, and if all—pope, cardinals, and courtiers—thus repeat the mass! And how they must have deceived me, who have heard them read devoutly so great a number!"

Luther had thought to find the edifice of the Church encompassed with splendor and strength, but its doors were broken down, and the walls damaged by fire. He witnessed the desolation of the sanctuary, and drew back with horror. All his dreams had been of holiness,—he had discovered profanation.

The disorders without the churches were not less shocking. "The police of Rome is very strict and severe," said he. "The judge or captain patrols the city every night on horseback with three hundred followers; he arrests every one that is found in the streets: if they meet an armed man, he is hung, or thrown into the Tiber. And yet the city is filled with disorder and murder; whilst in those places where the Word of God is preached uprightly and in purity, peace and order prevail, without calling for the severity of the law." . . . "No one can imagine what sins and infamous actions are committed in Rome," he said at another time; "they must be seen and heard to be believed. Thus, they are in the habit of saying, 'If there is a hell, Rome is built over it': it is an abyss whence issues every kind of sin."

Thus Rome made a deep impression upon Luther's mind; it was increased erelong. "The nearer we approach Rome, the greater number of bad Christians we meet with," he said, many years afterward.

[1] Bread thou art, and bread thou shalt remain; wine thou art, and wine thou shalt remain.

"There is a vulgar proverb, that he who goes to Rome the first time, looks out for a knave; the second time, he finds him; and the third, he brings him away with him. But people are now become so clever, that they make these three journeys in one." Machiavelli, one of the most profound geniuses of Italy, but also one of unenviable notoriety, who was living at Florence when Luther passed through that city on his way to Rome, has made the same remark: "The strongest symptom," said Machiavelli, "of the approaching ruin of Christianity [by which he meant Roman Catholicism] is, that the nearer people approach the capital of Christendom, the less Christian spirit is found in them. The scandalous examples and the crimes of the court of Rome are the cause why Italy has lost every principle of piety and all religious feeling. We Italians," this great historian continues, "are indebted to the Church and the priests for having become impious and immoral." Luther, somewhat later, was aware of the great importance of this journey. "If they would give me one hundred thousand florins," said he, "I would not have missed seeing Rome!"

This visit was very advantageous to him in regard to learning. Like Reuchlin, Luther took advantage of his Italian residence to penetrate deeper into the meaning of the Holy Scriptures. He took lessons in Hebrew from a celebrated rabbi, named Elias Levita. While in Rome he partly acquired that knowledge of the divine Word, under the attacks of which Rome was destined to fall.

This journey was important to Luther in another respect. Not only was the veil withdrawn, and the sardonic sneer, the mocking incredulity which lay concealed behind superstitions revealed, but the living faith that God had implanted in him was powerfully strengthened.

He at first gave himself up to all the observances which the Church enjoined for the expiation of sin. One day wishing to obtain an indulgence promised by the pope to all who should ascend on their knees what is called Pilate's Staircase, the Saxon monk was humbly creeping up those steps, which he was told had been miraculously transported from Jerusalem to Rome. While he was performing this meritorious act, he thought he heard a voice of thunder crying from the bottom of his heart, as at Wittenberg and Bologna, "The just shall live by faith." These words twice before struck him like the voice of an angel from God. They now resounded unceasingly and powerfully within him. He rose in amazement from the steps up which he was dragging his body: he shuddered at himself; he was ashamed of seeing to what a depth superstition had plunged him, therefore he fled far from the scene of his folly.

This powerful text had a mysterious influence on the life of Luther. It was a creative sentence both for the reformer and for the Reforma - tion. It was in these words God then said, "Let there be light! and there was light."

Frequently a truth must be presented many times to our minds in order that it may produce the due effect. Luther had profoundly studied the Epistle to the Romans, yet the doctrine of justification by faith taught in it had never appeared so clear. Now he comprehended that righteousness which alone can stand before God; now he received for himself from the hand of Christ that obedience which God of His free gift imputes to the sinner, as soon as he raises his eyes with humility to the crucified Son of Man. This was the decisive epoch of Luther's inner life. The faith which had saved him from the terrors of death became the very soul of his theology. It was his stronghold in every danger; the principle which gave energy to his preaching and strength to his charity; the foundation of his peace, the encouragement to his labors, his comfort in life and in death.

This great doctrine of a salvation proceeding from God and not from man was not only the power of God to save Luther's soul; it became in a still greater degree the power of God to reform the Church: an effectual weapon which had been wielded by the apostles,—a weapon too long neglected, but taken at last, in all its primitive brightness, from the arsenal of the omnipotent God. When Luther rose from his knees on Pilate's Staircase, in agitation and amazement at those words which Paul had addressed fifteen centuries before to the inhabitants of that same metropolis,—Truth, till then a melancholy captive, and fettered in the Church, rose also to fall no more.

Here it is well to listen to what Luther says: "Although I was a holy and blameless monk, my conscience was nevertheless full of trouble and anguish. I could not endure those words—'the righteousness of God.' I had no love for that holy and just God who punishes sinners. I was filled with secret anger against Him: I hated Him, because, not content with frightening by the law and the miseries of life us wretched sinners, already ruined by original sin, He still further increased our tortures by the gospel . . . But when, by the Spirit of God, I understood the words,—when I learned how the justification of the sinner proceeds from the free mercy of our Lord through faith . . . then I felt born again like a new man; I entered through the open door into the very paradise of God. Henceforward, also, I saw the beloved and Holy Scriptures with other eyes. I perused the Bible,—I brought together a great number of passages that taught me the nature of God's work. And as previously I had detested with all my heart these words, 'the righteousness of God,' I began from that hour to value and to love them, as the sweetest and most consoling words in the Bible. In very truth, this language of St. Paul was to me the true gate of Paradise."

When, on solemn occasions, Luther was called to confess this doctrine, he always recovered his enthusiasm and rough energy. "I see," observed he at an important moment, "that the devil is continually attacking this fundamental article by means of his doctors, and that in this respect he can never cease or take any repose. Well then, I, Doctor Martin Luther, unworthy herald of the gospel of our Lord Jesus Christ, confess this article, that faith alone without works justifies before God; and I declare that it shall stand and remain forever in despite of the emperor of the Romans, the emperor of the Turks the emperor of the Tartars, the emperor of the Persians,—in spite of the pope and all the cardinals, with the bishops, priests, monks, and nuns,—in spite of kings, princes, and nobles,—and in spite of all the world and of the devils themselves; and that if they endeavor to fight against this truth, they will draw the fires of hell upon their heads. This is the true and holy gospel, and the declaration of me, Doctor Luther, according to the teaching of the Holy Ghost . . . There is no one who has died for our sins, if not Jesus Christ the Son of God. I say it once again, should all the world and all the devils tear each other to pieces and burst with rage, that it is not the less true. And if it is He alone that taketh away our sins, it cannot be ourselves and our own works. But good works follow redemption, as the fruit grows on the tree. That is our doctrine—that is what is taught by the Holy Ghost and by all the communion of saints. We hold fast to it in the name of God. Amen!"

Thus Luther found what had been overlooked, at least to a certain degree, by doctors and reformers, even by the most illustrious of them. In Rome God gave him this clear view of the fundamental doctrine of Christianity. He had gone to Rome, city of the pontiffs, for the solution of certain difficulties concerning a monastic order: he brought away from it in his heart the salvation of the Church.

Chapter 6

NOW DOCTOR OF DIVINITY

LUTHER quitted Rome, and returned to Wittenberg: his heart was full of sorrow and indignation. Turning his eyes with disgust from the pontifical city, he directed them with hope to the Holy Scriptures—to that new life which the Word of God seemed then to promise to the world. This Word increased in his heart by all that the Church lost. He separated from the one to cling to the other. The whole of the Reformation was in that one movement. It set God in the place of the priest.

Staupitz and the elector did not lose sight of the monk whom they had called to the University of Wittenberg. The vicar-general, it seems, had a presentiment of the work that was to be done in the world, and that, finding it too difficult for himself, he wished to urge Luther toward it. There is nothing more remarkable,—nothing, perhaps, more mysterious than this person, who is seen everywhere urging forward Luther in the path where God calls him, and then going to end his days sadly in a cloister. The preaching of the young professor had made a deep impression on the prince; he had admired the strength of his understanding, the forcibleness of his eloquence, and the excellency of the matters that he expounded. The elector and his friend, desirous of advancing a man of such great promise, resolved that he should take the high degree of doctor of divinity. Staupitz went to the convent, and took Luther into the garden, where, alone with him under a tree that Luther in after years delighted to point out to his disciples, the venerable father said to him: "My friend, you must now become Doctor of the Holy Scriptures." Luther shrank at the very thought: this eminent honor startled him. "Seek a more worthy person," replied he. "As for me, I cannot consent to it." The vicar-general persisted: "Our Lord God has much to do in the Church: He has need at this time of young and vigorous doctors." These words, adds Melancthon, were perhaps said playfully, yet the event corresponded with them; for generally many omens precede all great revolutions. It is not necessary to suppose that Melancthon here speaks of miraculous prophecies. The most incredulous age—that which preceded the present one—saw an exemplification of this remark. How many presages, without there being anything miraculous in them, announced the revolution in which it closed!

"But I am weak and sickly," replied Luther. "I have not long to live. Look out for some strong man."—"The Lord has work in heaven as well as on earth," replied the vicar-general; "dead or alive, He has need of you in His council."

"It is the Holy Ghost alone that can make a doctor of divinity," then urged the monk still more alarmed. "Do what your convent requires," said Staupitz, "and what I, your vicar-general, command; for you have promised to obey us."—"But my poverty," resumed the brother; "I have no means of defraying the expenses incidental to such a promotion."—"Do not be uneasy about that," replied his friend; "the prince has done you the favor to take all the charges upon himself." Pressed on every side, Luther thought it his duty to give way.

It was about the end of the summer of 1512 that Luther set out for Leipzig to receive from the elector's treasurers the money necessary for his promotion. But according to court custom, the money did not arrive. The brother growing impatient wished to depart, but monastic obedience detained him. At length, on October 4, he received fifty florins from Pfeffinger and John Doltzig. In the receipt which he gave them, he employs no other title than that of monk. "I, Martin," wrote he, "brother of the order of Hermits." Luther hastened to return to Wittenberg.

Andrew Bodenstein of the city of Carlstadt was at that time dean of the theological faculty, and it is by the name of Carlstadt that this doctor is generally known. He was also called A. B. C. Melancthon first gave him this designation on account of the three initials of his name. Bodenstein acquired in his native country the first elements of learning. He was of a serious and gloomy character, perhaps inclined to jealousy, and of a restless temper, but full of desire for knowledge, and of great capacity. He frequented several universities to augment his stores of learning, and studied theology at Rome. On his return from Italy, he settled at Wittenberg, and became doctor of divinity. "At this time," he said afterwards, "I had not yet read the Holy Scriptures." This remark gives us a very correct idea of what theology then was. Carlstadt, besides his functions of professor, was canon and archdeacon. Such was the man who in after years was destined to create a schism in the Reformation. At this time he saw in Luther only an inferior; but the Augustine erelong became an object of jealousy to him. "I will not be less great than Luther," said he one day. Very far from anticipating at that period the great destinies of the young professor, Carlstadt conferred on his future rival the highest dignity of the university.

On October 18, 1512, Luther was received licentiate in divinity, and took the following oath: "I swear to defend the evangelical truth with all my might." On the day following, Bodenstein solemnly conferred on him, in the presence of a numerous assembly, the insignia of doctor of divinity. He was made a biblical doctor, and not a doctor of sentences, and was thus called to devote himself to the study of the Bible, and not to that of human traditions. He then pledged himself by an oath, as he himself relates, to his well-beloved and Holy Scriptures. He promised to preach them faithfully, to teach them with purity, to study them all his life, and to defend them, both in disputation and in writing, against all false teachers, so far as God should give him ability.

This solemn oath was Luther's call to the Reformation. By imposing on his conscience the holy obligation of searching freely and boldly proclaiming the Christian truth, this oath raised the new doctor above the narrow limits to which his monastic vow would perhaps have confined him. Called by the university, by his sovereign, in the name of the imperial majesty and of the see of Rome itself, and bound before God by the most solemn oath, he became from that hour the most intrepid herald of the Word of Life. On that memorable day Luther was armed champion of the Bible.

We may accordingly look upon this oath, sworn to the Holy Scriptures, as one of the causes of the revival of the Church. The sole and infallible authority of the Word of God was the primary and fundamental principle of the Reformation. Every reform in detail that was afterwards carried out in the doctrine, morals, or government of the Church, and in its worship, was but a consequence of this first principle. In these days we can scarcely imagine the sensation produced by this elementary and simple but long-neglected truth. A few men of enlarged views foresaw its immense consequences. Erelong the courageous voices of all the reformers proclaimed this mighty principle: "The Christians receive no other doctrines than those founded on the express words of Jesus Christ, of the apostles, and of the prophets. No man, no assembly of doctors, has a right to prescribe new ones."

Luther's position was changed. The summons that he had received became to the reformer as one of those extraordinary calls which the Lord addressed to the prophets under the Old Covenant, and to the apostles under the New. The solemn engagement that he made produced so deep an impression upon his soul that the recollection of this oath was sufficient, in after years, to console him in the midst of the greatest dangers and of the fiercest conflicts. And when he saw all Europe agitated and shaken by the Word that he had proclaimed; when the accusations of Rome, the reproaches of many pious men, the doubts and fears of his own too sensible heart, seemed likely to make him hesitate, fear, and fall into despair,—he called to mind the oath that he had taken, and remained steadfast, calm, and full of joy. "I have gone forward in the Lord's name," said he in a critical moment, "and I have placed myself in His hands. His will be done! Who prayed Him to make me a doctor? . . . If it was He who created me such, let Him support me; or else if He repent of what He has done, let Him deprive me of my office. . . . This tribulation, therefore, alarms me not. I seek one thing only, which is to preserve the favor of God in all that He has called me to do with Him." At another time he said: "He who undertakes anything without a divine call, seeks his own glory. But I, Doctor Martin Luther, was forced to become a doctor. Popery desired to stop me in the performance of my duty: but you see what has happened to it, and worse still will befall it. They cannot defend themselves against me. I am determined, in God's name, to tread upon the lions, to trample dragons and serpents under foot. This will begin during my life, and will be accomplished after my death."

From the period of his oath, Luther no longer sought the truth for himself alone: he sought it also for the Church. Still full of the recollections of Rome, he saw confusedly before him a path in which he had promised to walk with all the energy of his soul. The spiritual life that had hitherto been manifested only within him, now extended itself without. This was the third epoch of his development. His entrance into the cloister had turned his thoughts toward God; the knowledge of the remission of sins and of the righteousness of faith had emancipated his soul; his doctor's oath gave him that baptism of fire by which he became a reformer of the Church.

His ideas were soon directed in a general manner towards the Reformation. In an address that he had written, as it would seem, to be delivered by the provost of Lietzkau at the Lateran council, he declared that the corruption of the world originated in the teaching of so many fables and traditions, instead of preaching the pure Word of God. The Word of Life, in his view, alone had the power of effecting the spiritual regeneration of man. Thus then already he made the salvation of the world depend upon the re-establishment of sound doctrine, and not upon a mere reformation of manners. Yet Luther was not entirely consistent with himself; he still entertained contradictory opinions: but a spirit of power beamed from all his writings. He courageously broke the bonds with which the systems of the schools had fettered the thoughts of men; he everywhere passed beyond the limits within which previous ages had so closely confined him, and opened up new paths. God was with him.

The first adversaries that he attacked were those famous schoolmen, whom he had himself so much studied, and who then reigned supreme in all the academies. He accused them of Pelagianism, and forcibly inveighing against Aristotle, the father of the schools, and against Thomas Aquinas, he undertook to hurl them both from the throne whence they governed, the one philosophy, and the other theology.

"Aristotle, Porphyry, the sententiary divines [the schoolmen]," he wrote to Lange, "are useless studies in our days. I desire nothing more earnestly than to unveil to the world that comedian who has deceived the Church by assuming a Greek mask, and to show his deformity to all." In every public discussion he was heard repeating: "The writings of the apostles and prophets are surer and more sublime than all the sophisms and all the divinity of the schools." Such language was new, but men gradually became used to it. About a year after he was able to write with exultation: "God is at work. Our theology and St. Augustine advance admirably and prevail in our university. Aristotle is declining: he is tottering towards his eternal ruin that is near at hand. The lectures on the Sentences produce nothing but weariness. No one can hope for hearers, unless he professes the biblical theology." Happy the university of which such testimony can be given!

At the same time that Luther was attacking Aristotle, he took the side of Erasmus and Reuchlin against their enemies. He entered into communication with these great men and with other scholars, such as Pirckheimer, Mutianus, and Hütten, who belonged more or less to the same party. He also, about this period, formed another friendship that was of great importance through the whole course of his life.

There was at that time at the elector's court a person remarkable for his wisdom and his candor: this was George Spalatin. He was born at Spalatus or Spalt in the bishopric of Eichstadt, and had been originally curate of the village of Hohenkirch, near the Thuringian forests. He was afterwards chosen by Frederick the Wise to be his secretary, chaplain, and tutor to his nephew, John Frederick, who was one day to wear the electoral crown. Spalatin was a simple-hearted man in the midst of the court: he appeared timid in the presence of great events; circumspect and prudent, like his master, before the ardent Luther, with whom he corresponded daily. Like Staupitz, he was better suited for peaceful times. Such men are necessary: they are like those delicate substances in which jewels and crystal are wrapped to secure them from the injuries of transport. They seem useless; and yet without them all these precious objects would be broken and lost. Spalatin was not a man to effect great undertakings; but he faithfully and noiselessly performed the task imposed upon him. He was at first one of the principal aids of his master in collecting those relics of saints, of which Frederick was so long a great admirer. But he, as well as the prince, turned by degrees towards the truth. The faith, which then reappeared in the Church, did not lay such violent hold upon him as upon Luther: it guided him by slower methods. He became Luther's friend at court; the minister through whom passed all matters between the reformer and the princes; the mediator between the Church and the State. The elector honored Spalatin with great intimacy: they always traveled together in the same carriage. Nevertheless the atmosphere of the court oppressed the good chaplain: he was affected by profound melancholy; he could have desired to quit all these honors, and become once more a simple pastor in the forests of Thuringia. But Luther consoled him, and exhorted him to remain firm at his post. Spalatin acquired general esteem: princes and learned men showed him the most sincere regard. Erasmus used to say, "I inscribe Spalatin's name not only among those of my principal friends, but still further among those of my most honored protectors; and that, not upon paper, but on my heart."

Reuchlin's quarrel with the monks was then making a great noise in Germany. The most pious men were often undecided what part they should take; for the monks were eager to destroy the Hebrew books in which blasphemies against Christ were to be found. The elector commissioned his chaplain to consult the doctor of Wittenberg on this matter, as his reputation was already great. Here is Luther's answer: it is the first letter he addressed to the court-preacher:—

"What shall I say? These monks pretend to cast out Beelzebub, but it is not by the finger of God. I cease not from groaning and lamenting over it. We Christians are beginning to be wise outwardly, and mad inwardly. There are in every part of our Jerusalem blasphemies, a hundred times worse than those of the Jews, and all there are filled with spiritual idols. It is our duty with holy zeal to carry out and destroy these internal enemies. But we neglect that which is most urgent; and the devil himself persuades us to abandon what belongs to us, at the same time that he prevents us from correcting what belongs to others."

Chapter 7

JUSTIFICATION BY FAITH

LUTHER did not lose himself in this quarrel. A living faith in Christ filled his heart and his life. "Within my heart," said he, "reigns alone (and it ought thus to reign alone) faith in my Lord Jesus Christ, who is the beginning, middle, and end of all the thoughts that occupy my mind by day and night."

All his hearers listened with admiration as he spoke, whether from the professor's chair or from the pulpit, of that faith in Jesus Christ. His teaching diffused great light. Men were astonished that they had not earlier acknowledged truths that appeared so evident in his mouth. "The desire of self-justification," said he, "is the cause of all the distresses of the heart. But he who receives Jesus Christ as a Saviour, enjoys peace; and not only peace, but purity of heart. All sanctification of the heart is a fruit of faith. For faith is a divine work in us, which changes us and gives us a new birth, emanating from God Himself. It kills the old Adam in us; and, by the Holy Ghost which is communicated to us, it gives us a new heart and makes us new men. It is not by empty speculations," he again exclaimed, "but by this practical method that we can obtain a saving knowledge of Jesus Christ."

It was at this time that Luther preached those discourses on the Ten Commandments that have come down to us under the title of *Popular Declamations*. They contain errors no doubt; Luther became enlightened only by degrees. "The path of the just is as the shining light, that shineth more and more unto the perfect day." But what truth, simplicity, and eloquence are found in these discourses! How well can we understand the effect that the new preacher must have produced upon his audience and upon his age! We will quote but one passage taken from the beginning.

Luther ascended the pulpit of Wittenberg, and read these words: "Thou shalt have no other gods before me" (Exod. 20:3). Then turning to the people who crowded the sanctuary, he said, "All the sons of Adam are idolaters, and have sinned against this first commandment."

Doubtless this strange assertion startled his hearers. He proceeded to justify it, and continued: "There are two kinds of idolatry—one external, the other internal.

"The external, in which man bows down to wood and stone, to beasts and to the heavenly host.

"The internal, in which man, fearful of punishment, or seeking his own pleasure, does not worship the creature, but loves him in his heart, and trusts in him. . . ."

"What kind of religion is this? You do not bend the knee before riches and honors, but you offer them your heart, the noblest portion of yourselves . . . Alas! you worship God in body, but the creature in spirit.

"This idolatry prevails in every man until he is healed by the free gift of the faith that is in Christ Jesus.

"And how shall this cure be accomplished?

"Listen. Faith in Christ takes away from you all trust in your own wisdom, righteousness, and strength; it teaches you that if Christ had not died for you, and had not thus saved you, neither you nor any other creature would have been able to do it. Then you learn to despise all those things that are unavailing to you.

"Nothing now remains to you but Jesus Christ—Christ alone,— Christ all-sufficient for your soul. Hoping for nothing from any creature, you have only Christ, from whom you hope for everything, and whom you love above every thing.

"Now Christ is the one, sole, and true God. When you have Him for your God, you have no other gods."

It is in this manner Luther shows how the soul is brought back to God, by the gospel, according to the words of Jesus Christ: "I am the way; . . . no man cometh unto the Father but by me." The man who speaks thus to his age aims at something more than the correction of a few abuses; he is earnest above all things to establish true religion. His work is not merely negative; it is primarily positive.

Luther afterwards turned his discourse against the superstitions which then filled Christendom—the signs and mysterious characters, the observance of certain days and months, familiar spirits, phantoms, the influence of the stars, witchcraft, metamorphoses, *incubi and succubi,* the patronage of saints, and so on; one after another he attacked these idols, and with vigorous arm overthrew all these false gods.

It was particularly in his lecture-room, before an enlightened and youthful audience, hungering for the truth, that he displayed all the treasures of God's Word. "He explained Scripture in such a manner," says his illustrious friend Melanchthon, "that, in the judgment of all pious and well-informed men, it was as if a new morn had risen upon the doctrine after a long night of darkness. He showed the difference that existed between the law and the gospel. He refuted the then prevalent error of the churches and of the schools, that men by their works merit the remission of sins, and become righteous before God by an outward discipline. He thus led men's hearts back to the Son of God. Like John the Baptist, he pointed to the Lamb of God that has taken away the sins of the world; he explained how sin is freely pardoned on account of the Son of God, and that man receives this blessing through faith. He made no change in the ceremonies. On the contrary, the established discipline had not in his order a more faithful observer and defender. But he endeavored more and more to make all understand that these grand and essential doctrines of conversion, of the remission of sins, of faith, and of the true consolation that is to be found in the cross. Pious minds were struck and penetrated by the sweetness of this doctrine; the learned received it with joy. One might have said that Christ, the apostles, and the prophets, were now issuing from the obscurity of some impure dungeon."

The firmness with which Luther relied on the Holy Scriptures imparted great authority to his teaching. But other circumstances added still more to his strength. In him every action of his life corresponded with his words. It was known that these discourses did not proceed merely from his lips: they had their source in his heart, and were practiced in all his works. And when, somewhat later, the Reformation burst forth, many influential men, who saw with regret these divisions in the Church, won over beforehand by the holiness of the reformer's life and by the beauty of his genius, not only did not oppose him, but, further still, embraced that doctrine to which he gave testimony by his works. The more men loved Christian virtues, the more they inclined to the reformer. All honest divines were in his favor. This is what was said by those who knew him, and particularly by the wisest man of his age, Melanchthon, and by Erasmus, the illustrious opponent of Luther. Envy and prejudice have dared to speak of his disorderly life. Wittenberg was changed by this preaching of faith, and that city became the focus of a light that was soon to illumine all Germany, and to shine on all the Church.

It was in 1516 that Luther published the work of an anonymous mystic theologian (probably Ebland, priest at Frankfurt), entitled *Theologia Germanica*, in which the author shows how man may attain perfection by the three methods of purification, illumination, and communion. Luther never gave himself up to the mystic theology, but he received from it a salutary impression. It confirmed him in his disgust for the dry teaching of the schoolmen, in his contempt for the works and observances so much trumpeted by the Church, and in the conviction that he felt of man's spiritual helplessness and of the necessity of grace, and in his attachment to the Bible. "I prefer," he wrote to Staupitz, "the mystics and the Bible to all the schoolmen"; thus placing the former teachers in the next rank to the sacred writers. Perhaps, also, the *Theologia Germanica* aided him in forming a sounder idea on the sacraments, and above all on the mass. The author maintains that the eucharist gives Christ to man, and does not offer up Christ to God. Luther accompanied this publication by a preface, in which he declared that, next to the Bible and St. Augustine, he had never met with a book in which he had learned more of God, Christ, man, and of all things. Already many doctors began to speak ill of the Wittenberg professors, and accused them of innovation. "One would say," continues Luther, "that there had never lived men before us who taught as we teach. Yes, in truth, there have been many. But the anger of God, which our sins have deserved, has prevented us from seeing and hearing them. For a long time the universities have banished the Word of God into a corner. Let them read this book, and then let them say whether our theology is new, for this is not a new book."

But if Luther derived from the mystic divinity whatever good it contained, he did not take the bad also. The great error of mysticism is to overlook the free gift of salvation. We are about to notice a remarkable example of the purity of his faith.

Luther had an affectionate and tender heart, and desired to see those whom he loved in possession of that light which had guided him into the paths of peace. He took advantage of every opportunity that occurred, as professor, preacher, or monk, as well as of his extensive correspondence, to communicate his treasure to others. One of his former brethren in the convent of Erfurt, the monk George Spenlein, was then residing in the convent of Memmingen, perhaps after having spent a short time at Wittenberg. Spenlein had commissioned the doctor to sell various articles that he had left with him—a tunic of Brussels cloth, a work by an Eisenach doctor, and a hood. Luther carefully discharged this commission. He received, he says in a letter to Spenlein, dated April 7, 1516, one florin for the tunic, half a florin for the book, and a florin for the hood, and remitted the amount to the father-vicar, to whom Spenlein owed three florins. But Luther quickly passed from this account of a monk's wardrobe to a more important subject.

"I should be very glad to know," wrote he to friar George, "what is the state of your soul. Is it not tired of its own righteousness? Does it not breathe freely at last, and does it not confide in the righteousness of Christ? In our days, pride seduces many, and especially those who labor with all their might to become righteous. Not understanding the righteousness of God that is given to us freely in Christ Jesus, they wish to stand before Him on their own merits. But that cannot be. When you were living with me, you were in that error, and so was I. I am yet struggling unceasingly against it, and I have not yet entirely triumphed over it.

"Oh, my dear brother, learn to know Christ and Him crucified. Learn to sing unto Him a new song, to despair of yourself, and to say to Him: Thou, Lord Jesus Christ, art my righteousness, and I am Thy sin. Thou hast taken what was mine, and hast given me what was Thine. What Thou wast not, Thou didst become, in order that I might become what I was not!—Beware, my dear George, of pretending to such purity as no longer to confess yourself a sinner: for Christ dwells only with sinners. He came down from heaven, where He was living among the righteous, in order to live also among sinners. Meditate carefully upon this love of Christ, and you will taste all its unspeakable consolation. If our labors and afflictions could give peace to the conscience, why should Christ have died? You will not find peace, save in Him, by despairing of yourself and of your works, and in learning with what love He opens His arms to you, taking all your sins upon Himself, and giving thee all His righteousness."

Thus the powerful doctrine which had already saved the world in the apostolic age, and which was destined to save it a second time in the days of the Reformation, was clearly and forcibly explained by Luther. Passing over the many ages of ignorance and superstition that had intervened, in this he gave his hand to St. Paul.

Spenlein was not the only man whom he sought to instruct in this fundamental doctrine. The little truth that he found in this respect in the writings of Erasmus made him uneasy. It was of great importance to enlighten a man whose authority was so great, and whose genius was so admirable. But how was he to do it? His court-friend, the Elector's chaplain, was much respected by Erasmus: it was to him that Luther applied. "What displeases me in Erasmus, who is a man of such extensive learning, is, my dear Spalatin," wrote Luther, "that by the righteousness of works and of the law, of which the apostle speaks, he understands the fulfilling of the ceremonial law. The righteousness of the law consists not only in ceremonies, but in all the works of the Decalogue. Even if these works should be accomplished without faith in Christ, they may, it is true, produce a Fabricius, a Regulus, and other men perfectly upright in the eyes of the world; but they then deserve as little to be styled righteousness, as the fruit of the medlar to be called a fig. For we do not become righteous, as Aristotle maintains, by performing righteous works; but when we are become righteous, then we perform such works. The man must first be changed, and afterwards the works. Abel was first accepted by God, and then his sacrifice." Luther continues: "Fulfill, I beseech you, the duty of a friend and of a Christian by communicating these matters to Erasmus." This letter is dated: "In haste, from the corner of our convent, October 19, 1516." It places in its true light the relation between Luther and Erasmus. It shows the sincere interest he felt in what he thought would be really beneficial to this illustrious writer. Undoubtedly, the opposition shown by Erasmus to the truth compelled Luther somewhat later to combat him openly;

but he did not do so until he had sought to enlighten his antagonist.

Then was declared the principle that what constitutes the real goodness of an action is not its outward appearance, but the spirit in which it is performed. This was aiming a deadly blow at all those superstitious observances which for ages had oppressed the Church, and prevented Christian virtues from growing up and flourishing within it.

"I am reading Erasmus," said Luther on another occasion. "But he daily loses his credit with me. I like to see him rebuke with so much firmness and learning the groveling ignorance of the priests and monks; but I fear that he does not render great service to the doctrine of Jesus Christ. What is of man is dearer to him than what is of God. We are living in dangerous times. A man is not a good and judicious Christian because he understands Greek and Hebrew. Jerome who knew five languages, is inferior to Augustine who understood but one; although Erasmus thinks the contrary. I very carefully conceal my opinions concerning Erasmus, through fear of giving advantage to his adversaries. Perhaps the Lord will give him understanding in His time."

The helplessness of man—the omnipotence of God, were the two truths that Luther desired to re-establish. That is but a sad religion and a wretched philosophy by which man is directed to his own natural strength. Ages have tried in vain this so much boasted strength; and while man has, by his own natural powers, arrived at great excellence in all that concerns his earthly existence, he has never been able to scatter the darkness that conceals from his soul the knowledge of the true God, or to change a single inclination of his heart. The highest degree of wisdom attained by ambitious minds, or by souls thirsting with the desire of perfection, has been to despair of themselves. It is therefore a generous, a comforting, and a supremely true doctrine which unveils our own impotency in order to proclaim a power from God by which we can do all things. That truly is a great reformation which vindicates on earth the glory of heaven, and which pleads before man the rights of the Almighty God.

No one knew better than Luther the intimate and indissoluble bond that unites the gratuitous salvation of God with the free works of man. No one showed more plainly than he that it is only by receiving all from Christ that man can impart much to his brethren. He always represented these two actions—that of God and that of man—in the same picture. And thus it is that, after explaining to the friar Spenlein what is meant by saving righteousness, he added, "If thou firmly believest those things, as is thy duty (for cursed is he who does not believe them), receive thy brethren who are still ignorant and in error, as Jesus Christ has received thee. Bear with them patiently. Make their sins thine own; and if thou hast any good thing, impart it to them. 'Receive ye one another,' says the apostle, 'as Christ also received us, to the glory of God' (Rom. 15:7). It is a deplorable righteousness that cannot bear with others because it finds them wicked, and which thinks only of seeking the solitude of the desert, instead of doing them good by long-suffering, prayer, and example. If thou art the lily and the rose of Christ, know that thy dwelling-place is among thorns. Only take care lest by thy impatience, by thy rash judgments, and thy secret pride, thou dost not thyself become a thorn. Christ reigns in the midst of His enemies. If He had desired to live only among the good, and to die for those only who loved Him, for whom, I pray, would He have died, and among whom would He have lived?"

It is affecting to see how Luther practiced these charitable precepts. An Augustine monk of Erfurt, George Leiffer, was exposed to many trials. Luther became informed of this, and within a week after writing the preceding letter to Spenlein, he came to him with words of comfort. "I learn that you are agitated by many tempests, and that your soul is tossed to and fro by the waves . . . The cross of Christ is divided among all the world, and each man has his share. You should not, therefore, reject that which has fallen to you. Receive it rather as a holy relic, not in a vessel of silver or of gold, but in what is far better—in a heart of gold,—in a heart full of meekness. If the wood of the cross has been so sanctified by the body and blood of Christ that we consider it as the most venerable relic, how much more should the wrongs, persecutions, sufferings, and hatred of men, be holy relics unto us, since they have not only been touched by Christ's flesh, but have been embraced, kissed, and blessed by His infinite charity."

Chapter 8

THESES—BEGINNING THE
REFORMATION

LUTHER'S TEACHING produced its natural fruits. Many of his disciples already felt themselves impelled to profess publicly the truths which their master's lessons had revealed to them. Among his hearers was a young scholar, Bernard of Feldkirchen, professor of Aristotle's physics in the university, and who five years later was the first of the evangelical ecclesiastics who entered into the bonds of matrimony.

It was Luther's wish that Feldkirchen should mantain, under his presidence, certain theses or propositions in which his principles were laid down. The doctrines professed by Luther thus gained additional publicity. The disputation took place in 1516, and was Luther's first attack upon the dominion of the Sophists and upon the papacy, as he himself characterizes it. Weak as it was, it caused him some uneasiness. "I allow these propositions to be printed," said he many years after, when publishing them in his works, "principally that the greatness of my cause, and the success with which God has crowned it, may not make me vain. For they fully manifest my humiliation, that is to say, the infirmity and ignorance, the fear and trembling with which I began this conflict. I was alone: I had thrown myself imprudently into this business. Unable to retract, I conceded many important points to the pope, and I even adored him."

Some of the propositions were as follows:

"The old Adam is the vanity of vanities; he is the universal vanity; and he renders all other creatures vain, however good they may be.

"The old Adam is called the flesh, not only because he is led by the lusts of the flesh, but further, because should he be chaste, prudent, and righteous, he is not born again of God by the Holy Ghost.

"A man who has no part in the grace of God cannot keep the commandments of God, or prepare himself, either wholly or in part, to receive grace, but he rests of necessity under the power of sin.

"The will of man without grace is not free, but is enslaved, and that too with its own consent.

"Jesus Christ, our strength and our righteousness, He who trieth the heart and reins, is the only discerner and judge of our merits.

"Since all is possible, by Christ, to the believer, it is superstitious to seek for other help, either in man's will or in the saints."

This disputation made a great disturbance, and it has been considered as the beginning of the Reformation.

The hour drew nigh in which the Reformation was to burst forth. God hastened to prepare the instrument that He had determined to employ. The elector, having built a new church at Wittenberg, to which he gave the name of All Saints, sent Staupitz into the Low Countries to collect relics for the ornament of the new edifice. The vicar-general commissioned Luther to replace him during his absence, and in particular to make a visitation of the forty monasteries of Misnia and Thuringia.

Luther repaired first to Grimma, and thence to Dresden. Everywhere he endeavored to establish the truths that he had discovered, and to enlighten the members of his order: "Do not bind yourselves to Aristotle, or to any other teacher of a deceitful philosophy," said he to the monks, "but read the Word of God with diligence. Do not look for salvation in your own strength or in your good works, but in the merits of Christ and in God's grace."

An Augustine monk of Dresden had fled from his convent, and was at Mentz, where the prior of the Augustines had received him. Luther wrote to the latter, begging him to send back the stray sheep, and added these words so full of charity and truth: "I know that offenses must needs come. It is no marvel that man falls; but it is so that he rises again and stands upright. Peter fell that he might know he was but a man. Even in our days the cedars of Lebanon are seen to fall. The very angels—a thing that exceeds all imagination!—have fallen in heaven, and Adam in paradise. Why then should we be surprised if a reed is shaken by the whirlwind, or if a smoking taper is extinguished?"

From Dresden Luther proceeded to Erfurt, and reappeared to discharge the functions of vicar-general in that very convent where, eleven years before, he had wound up the clock, opened the gates, and swept out the church. He nominated to the priorship of the convent his friend the Bachelor John Lange, a learned and pious but severe man; he exhorted him to affability and patience. "Put on," wrote he to him shortly after, "put on a spirit of meekness towards the prior of Nuremberg: this is but proper, seeing that he has assumed a spirit of bitterness and harshness. Bitterness is not expelled by bitterness, that is to say, the devil by the devil; but sweetness dispels bitterness, that is to say, the finger of God casts out the evil spirit." We must, perhaps, regret that Luther did not on various occasions remember this excellent advice.

At Neustadt on the Orla there was nothing but disunion. Dissensions and quarrels reigned in the convent, and all the monks were at war with their prior. They assailed Luther with their complaints. The prior Michael Dressel, or Tornator, as Luther calls him, translating his name into Latin, on his side laid all his troubles before the doctor. "Peace, peace!" said he. "You seek peace," replied Luther, "but it is the peace of the world, and not the peace of Christ that you seek. Do you not know that our God has set His peace in the midst of war? He whom no one disturbs has not peace. But he who, troubled by all men and by the things of this life, bears all with tranquillity and joy—he possesses the true peace. You say with Israel: Peace, peace! and there is no peace. Say rather with Christ: The cross, the cross! and there will be no cross. For the cross ceases to be a cross as soon as we can say with love: O blessed cross, there is no wood like thine!" On his return to Wittenberg, Luther, desiring to put an end to these dissensions, permitted the monks to elect another prior.

Luther returned to Wittenberg after an absence of six weeks. He was grieved by all that he had seen; but the journey gave him a better knowledge of the Church and of the world, increased his confidence in his intercourse with society, and afforded him many opportunities of founding schools, of pressing this fundamental truth that "holy Scripture alone shows us the way to heaven," and of exhorting the brethren to live together in holiness, chastity, and peace. There is no doubt that much good seed was sown in the different Augustine convents during this journey of the reformer. The monastic orders, which had long been the support of Rome, did perhaps more for the Reformation than against it. This is true in particular of the Augustines. Almost all the pious men of liberal and elevated mind, who were living in the cloisters, turned towards the gospel. A new and generous blood erelong circulated through these orders, which were, so to speak, the arteries of the German church. As yet nothing was known in the world of the new ideas of the Wittenberg Augustine, while they were already the chief topic of conversation in the chapters and monasteries. Many a cloister thus became a nursery of reformers. As soon as the great struggle took place, pious and able men issued from obscurity and abandoned the seclusion of a monastic life for the active career of ministers of God's Word. At the period of this inspection of 1516 Luther awakened many drowsy souls by his words. Hence this year has been named "the morning star of the gospel-day."

Luther resumed his usual occupation. He was at this period overwhelmed with labor: it was not enough that he was professor, preacher, and confessor; he was burdened still further by many temporal occupations having reference to his order and his convent. "I have need almost continually," writes he, "of two secretaries; for I do nothing else all the day long but write letters. I am preacher to the convent; I read the prayers at table; I am pastor and parish minister; director of studies; the prior's vicar—that is to say, prior eleven times over!—inspector of the fish-ponds at Litzkau; counsel to the inns of Herzberg at Torgau; lecturer on Saint Paul, and commentator on the Psalms . . . I have rarely time to repeat the daily prayers and to sing a hymn; without speaking of my struggles with flesh and blood, with the devil and the world . . . Learn from this what an idle man I am!"

About this time the plague broke out in Wittenberg. A great number of the students and teachers quitted the city. Luther remained. "I am not certain," wrote he to his friend at Erfurt, "if the plague will let me finish the Epistle to the Galatians. Its attacks are sudden and violent: it is making great ravages among the young in particular. You advise me to fly. Whither shall I fly? I hope that the world will no come to an end, if Brother Martin dies. If the pestilence spreads, I shall disperse the brothers in every direction; but as for me, my place is here; duty does not permit me to desert my post, until He who has called me shall summon me away. Not that I have no fear of death (for I am not Paul, I am only his commentator); but I hope that the Lord will deliver me from fear." Such was the resolution of the Wittenberg doctor. Shall he whom the pestilence could not force to retire a single step, shrink before Rome? Shall he yield through fear of the scaffold?

Chapter 9

THE COURT SERMON

LUTHER displayed the same courage before the mighty of this world that he had shown amidst the most formidable evils. The elector was much pleased with the vicar-general, who had made a rich harvest of relics in the Low Countries. Luther gives an account of them to Spalatin; and this affair of the relics, occurring at the very moment when the Reformation is about to begin, is a singular circumstance. Most certainly, the reformers had little idea to what point they were tending. A bishopric appeared to the elector the only recompense worthy the services of the vicar-general. Luther, to whom Spalatin wrote on the subject, strongly disapproved of such an idea. "There are many things which please your prince," replied he, "and which, nevertheless, are displeasing to God. I do not deny that he is skillful in the matters of this world; but in what concerns God and the salvation of souls, I account him, as well as his councilor Pfeffinger, sevenfold blind. I do not say this behind their backs, like a slanderer; do not conceal it from them, for I am ready myself, and on all occasions, to tell them both to their faces. Why would you," continues he, "surround this man [Staupitz] with all the whirlwinds and tempests of episcopal cares?"

The elector was not offended with Luther's frankness. "The prince," wrote Spalatin, "often speaks of you, and in honorable terms." Frederick sent the monk some very fine cloth for a gown. "It would be too fine," said Luther, "if it were not a prince's gift. I am not worthy that any man should think of me, much less a prince, and so great a prince as he. Those are my best friends who think the worst of me. Thank our prince for his kindness to me; but I cannot allow myself to be praised either by you or by any man; for all praise of man is vain, and only that which comes from God is true."

The excellent chaplain was unwilling to confine himself to his court functions. He wished to make himself useful to the people; but like many individuals in any age, he desired to do it without offense and without irritation, by conciliating the general favor. "Point out," he wrote to Luther, "some work that I may translate into our mother tongue; one that shall give general satisfaction, and at the same time be useful." "Agreeable and useful!" replied Luther; "such a question is beyond my ability. The better things are the less they please. What is more salutary than Jesus Christ? And yet He is to the majority a savor of death. You will tell me that you wish to be useful only to those who love what is good. In that case, make them hear the voice of Jesus Christ: you will be useful and agreeable, depend upon it, to a very small number only; for the sheep are rare in this region of wolves."

Luther, however, recommended to his friend the sermons of the Dominican Tauler. "I have never read," said he, "either in Latin or in our own language, a theology sounder, or more in conformity with the gospel. Taste, then, and see how sweet the Lord is, but not till after you have first tasted and felt how bitter is everything that we are ourselves."

It was in the course of the year 1517 that Luther entered into communication with Duke George of Saxony. The house of Saxony had at that time two chiefs. Two princes, Ernest and Albert, carried off in their youth from the castle of Altenburg by Kunz of Kaufungen, had, by the treaty of Leipzig, become the founders of the two houses which still bear their names. The Elector Frederick, son of Ernest, was at the period we are describing, the head of the Ernestine branch; and his cousin Duke George, of the Albertine. Dresden and Leipzig were both situated in the states of this duke, whose residence was in the former of these cities. His mother, Sidonia, was daughter of George Podiebrad, king of Bohemia. The long struggle that Bohemia had maintained with Rome, since the time of John Huss, had not been without influence on the prince of Saxony. He had often manifested a desire for a Reformation. "He has imbibed it with his mother's milk," said the priests; "he is by birth an enemy of the clergy." He annoyed the bishops, abbots, canons, and monks in many ways; and his cousin, the Elector Frederick, was compelled more than once to interfere in their behalf. It seemed that Duke George would be one of the warmest partisans of a Reformation. The devout Frederick, on the other hand, who had in former years worn the spurs of Godfrey in the Holy Sepulcher, and girding himself with the long and heavy sword of the conqueror of Jerusalem, had made oath to fight for the Church, like that ancient and valiant knight, appeared destined to be the most ardent champion of Rome. But in all that concerns the gospel, the anticipations of human wisdom are frequently disappointed. The reverse of what we might have supposed took place. The duke would have been delighted to humiliate the Church and the clergy, to humble the bishops, whose princely retinue far surpassed his own; but it was another thing to receive into his heart the evangelical doctrine that would humble it, to acknowledge himself a guilty sinner, incapable of being saved, except by grace alone. He would willingly have reformed others, but he cared not to reform himself. He would perhaps have set his hand to the task of compelling the Bishop of Mentz to be contented with a single bishopric, and to keep no more than fourteen horses in his stables, as he said more than once; but when he saw another than himself step forward as a reformer,—when he beheld a simple monk undertake this work, and the Reformation gaining numerous partisans among the people, the haughty grandson of the Hussite king became the most violent adversary of the reform to which he had before shown himself favorable.

In the month of July 1517, Duke George requested Staupitz to send him an eloquent and learned preacher. Luther was recommended to him as a man of extensive learning and irreproachable conduct. The prince invited him to preach at Dresden in the castle-chapel, on the feast of St. James the Elder.

The day arrived. The duke and his court repaired to the chapel to hear the Wittenberg preacher. Luther joyfully seized this opportunity of testifying to the truth before such an assemblage. He selected his text from the Gospel of the day: "Then came to him the mother of Zebedee's children with her sons" (Matt. 20:20–23). He preached on the unreasonable desires and prayers of men; and then spoke emphatically on the assurance of salvation. He established it on this foundation, that those who receive the Word of God with faith are the true disciples of Jesus Christ, elected to eternal life. He next treated of gratuitous election, and showed that this 'doctrine, if presented in union with the work of Christ, has great power to dispel the terrors of conscience; so that men, instead of flying far from the righteous God, at the sight of their own unworthiness, are gently led to seek their refuge in Him. In conclusion, he related an allegory of three virgins from which he deduced edifying instructions.

The Word of truth made a deep impression on his hearers. Two of them in particular seemed to pay very great attention to the sermon of the Wittenberg monk. The first was a lady of respectable appearance, who was seated on the court benches, and on whose features a profound emotion might be traced. It was Madame de la Sale, first lady to the duchess. The other was a licentiate in canon law, Jerome Emser, councilor and secretary to the duke. Emser possessed great talents and extensive information. A courtier and skillful politician, he would have desired to be on good terms with the two contending parties—to pass at Rome for a defender of the papacy, and at the same time shine in Germany among the learned men of the age. But under this pliant mind was concealed a violent character. It was in the palace-chapel at Dresden that Luther and Emser first met; they were afterwards to break more than one lance together.

The dinner hour arrived for the inhabitants of the palace, and in a short time the ducal family and the persons attached to the court were assembled at table. The conversation naturally fell on the preacher of the morning. "How were you pleased with the sermon?" said the duke to Madame de la Sale. "If I could hear but one more like it," replied she, "I should die in peace." "And I," replied George angrily, "would rather give a large sum not to have heard it; for such discourses are only calculated to make people sin with assurance."

The master having thus made known his opinion, the courtiers gave way uncontrolled to their dissatisfaction. Each one had his censure ready. Some maintained that in his allegory of the three Virgins, Luther had in view three ladies of the court; on which there arose interminable babbling. They rallied the three ladies from the monk of Wittenberg had thus, they said, publicly pointed out. He is an ignorant fellow, said some; he is a proud monk, said others. Each one made his comment on the sermon, and put what he pleased into the preacher's mouth. The truth had fallen into the midst of a court that was little prepared to receive it. Every one mangled it after his own fashion. But while the Word of God was thus an occasion of stumbling to many, it was for the first lady a stone of uprising. Falling sick a month after, she confidently embraced the grace of the Saviour, and died with joy.

As for the duke, it was not perhaps in vain that he heard this testimony to the truth. Whatever may have been his opposition to the Reformation during his life, we know that at his death he declared that he had no hope save in the merits of Jesus Christ.

It was natural that Emser should do the honors to Luther in his master's name. He invited him to supper. Luther refused; but Emser persisted, and prevailed on him to come. Luther thought he should only meet a few friends; but he soon perceived that a trap had been laid for him. A master of arts from Leipzig and several Dominicans were with the prince's secretary. The master of arts, having no mean opinion of himself, and full of hatred towards Luther, addressed him in a friendly and honeyed manner; but he soon got into a passion, and began to shout with all his might. The combat began. The dispute turned, says Luther, on the trumpery of Aristotle and St. Thomas. At last Luther defied the master of arts to define with all the learning of the Thomists what is the fulfilling of God's commandments. The embarrassed disputant put a good face on the matter. "Pay me my fee," said he holding out his hand, "da pastum." One would have said that he wished to give a regular lesson, taking his fellow-guests for his pupils. "At this foolish reply," added the reformer, "we all burst into laughter, and then we parted."

During this conversation a Dominican was listening at the door. He longed to enter and spit in Luther's face: but he checked himself, and boasted of it afterwards. Emser, charmed at seeing his guests disputing, and appearing himself to preserve a due moderation, was earnest in excuses to Luther for the manner in which the evening had passed.

Chapter 10

THESES AGAINST PELAGIANISM

LUTHER returned zealously to work. He was preparing six or seven young theologians who were shortly to undergo an examination for a license to teach. What rejoiced him most of all was that their promotion would tend to the discredit of Aristotle. "I should desire to multiply the number of his enemies as soon as possible," said he. With this intent he published certain theses which merit our attention.

Luther had already treated the great subject of free will in the Feldkirchen theses; now he went deeper into the question. There had been, from the very commencement of Christianity, a struggle more or less keen between the two doctrines of man's liberty and his enslavement. Some schoolmen had taught, like Pelagius and other doctors, that man possessed of himself the liberty or the power of loving God and of performing good works. Luther denied this liberty; not to deprive man of it, but in order that man might obtain it. The struggle in this great question is not therefore, as is generally said, between liberty and slavery: it is between a liberty proceeding from man, and one that comes from God. Those who style themselves the partisans of liberty say to man: "Thou hast the power of performing good works; thou hast no need of greater liberty." The others, who are called the partisans of servitude, say on the contrary: "True liberty is what thou needest, and God offers it thee in His gospel." On the one side, they speak of liberty to perpetuate slavery; on the other, they speak of slavery to give liberty. Such was the contest in the times of St. Paul, of St. Augustine, and of Luther. Those who say, "Change nothing," are the champions of slavery: the others who say, "Let your fetters fall off," are the champions of liberty.

But we should deceive ourselves were we to sum up all the Reformation in that particular question. It is one of the numerous doctrines maintained by the Wittenberg doctor, and that is all. It would be indulging in a strange delusion to pretend that the Reformation was a fatalism,—an opposition to liberty. It was a noble emancipation of the human mind. Snapping the numerous bonds with which the hierarchy had bound men's minds,—restoring the ideas of liberty, of right, of free examination, it set free its own age, ourselves, and the remotest posterity. But let it not be said that the Reformation delivered man from every human despotism, but made him a slave by proclaiming the sovereignty of grace. It desired, no doubt, to lead back the human will, to confound it with and render it entirely subject to the divine will; but what kind of philosophy is that which does not know that an entire conformity with the will of God is the only, supreme, and perfect liberty; and that man will be really free only when sovereign righteousness and eternal truth alone have dominion over him?

The following are some of the ninety-nine propositions that Luther put forth in the Church against the Pelagian rationalism of the scholastic theology:—

"It is true that man who has become a corrupt tree, can will or do nought but evil.

"It is false that the will, left to itself, can do good as well as evil; for it is not free, but in bondage.

"It is not in the power of man's will to choose or reject whatever is offered to it.

"Man cannot of his own nature will God to be God. He would prefer to be God himself, and that God were not God.

"The excellent, infallible, and sole preparation for grace, is the eternal election and predestination of God.

"It is false to say that if man does all that he can, he removes the obstacles to grace.

"In a word, nature possesses neither a pure reason nor a good will.

"On the side of man there is nothing that goes before grace, unless it be impotency and even rebellion.

"There is no moral virtue without pride or without sorrow, that is to say, without sin.

"From beginning to end, we are not masters of our actions, but their slaves.

"We do not become righteous by doing what is righteous; but having become righteous, we do what is righteous.

"He who says that a divine, who is not a logician, is a heretic and an empiric, maintains an empirical and heretical proposition.

"There is no form of reasoning (of syllogism) that holds with the things of God.

"If the form of the syllogism could be applied to divine things, we should have *knowledge* and not *belief* of the article of the Holy Trinity.

"In a word, Aristotle is to divinity, as darkness to light.

"Man is a greater enemy to the grace of God than he is to the law itself.

"He who is without God's grace sins continually, even should he neither rob, murder, nor commit adultery.

"He sins, in that he does not fulfill the law spiritually.

"Not to kill, not to commit adultery, externally only and with regard to the actions, is the righteousness of hypocrites.

"The law of God and the will of man are two adversaries, that without the grace of God can never be reconciled.

"What the law commands, the will never wishes, unless through fear or love it puts on the appearance of willing.

"The law is the taskmaster of the will, who is not overcome but by the Child that is born unto us (Isa. 9:6).

"The law makes sin abound, for it exasperates and repels the will.

"But the grace of God makes righteousness abound through Jesus Christ, who causes us to love the law.

"Every work of the law appears good outwardly, but inwardly it is sin.

"The will, when it turns toward the law without the grace of God, does so in its own interest alone.

"Cursed are all those who perform the works of the law.

"Blessed are all those who perform the works of God's grace.

"The law which is good, and in which we have life, is the love of God shed abroad in our hearts by the Holy Ghost (Rom. 5:5).

"Grace is not given in order that the work may be done more frequently and more easily, but because without grace there can be no work of love.

"To love God is to hate oneself and to know nothing out of God."

Thus Luther ascribes to God all the good that man can do. There is no question of repairing, of patching up, if we may use the expression, man's will: an entirely new one must be given him. God only has been able to say this, because God alone can accomplish it. This is one of the greatest and most important truths that the human mind can conceive.

But while Luther proclaimed the powerlessness of man, he did not fall into the other extreme. He says in the eighth thesis: "It does not hence follow that the will is naturally depraved; that is to say, that its nature is that of evil itself, as the Manichees have taught." Originally man's nature was essentially good: it has turned away from the good, which is God, and inclined toward evil. Yet its holy and glorious origin still remains; and it is capable, by the power of God, of recovering this origin. It is the business of Christianity to restore it to him. It is true that the gospel displays man in a state of humiliation and impotency, but between two glories and two grandeurs: a past glory from which he has been precipitated, and a future glory to which he is called. There lies the truth: man is aware of it, and if he reflects ever so little, he easily discovers that all which is told him of his present purity, power, and glory is but a fiction with which to lull and soothe his pride.

Luther in his theses protested not only against the pretended goodness of man's will, but still more against the pretended light of his understanding in respect to divine things. In truth, Scholasticism had exalted his reason as well as his will. This theology, as some of its doctors have represented it, was at bottom nothing but a kind of rationalism. This is indicated by the propositions we have cited. One might fancy them directed against the rationalism of our days. In the theses that were the signal of the Reformation, Luther censured the Church and the popular superstitions which had added indulgences, purgatory, and so many other abuses to the gospel. In those we have just quoted, he assailed the schools and rationalism, which had taken away from that very gospel the doctrine of the sovereignty of God, of His revelation, and of His grace. The Reformation attacked rationalism before it turned against superstition. It proclaimed the rights of God before it cut off the excrescences of man. It was positive before it became negative. This has not been sufficiently observed; and yet if we do not notice it, we cannot justly appreciate that religious revolution and its true nature.

However this may be, the truths that Luther had just enunciated with so much energy were very novel. It would have been an easy matter to support these propositions at Wittenberg; for there his influence predominated. But it might have been said that he had chosen a field where he knew that no combatant would dare appear. By offering battle in another university, he would give them greater publicity; and it was by publicity that the Reformation was effected. He turned his eyes to Erfurt, whose theologians had shown themselves so irritated against him.

He therefore transmitted these propositions to John Lange, prior of Erfurt, and wrote to him: "My suspense as to your decision upon these paradoxes is great, extreme, too great perhaps, and full of anxiety. I strongly suspect that your theologians will consider as paradoxical, and even as kakodoxical (unsound doctrine) what is in my opinion very orthodox. Pray inform me, as soon as possible, of your sentiments upon them. Have the goodness to declare to the faculty of theology, and to all, that I am prepared to visit you, and to maintain these propositions publicly, either in the university, or in the monastery." It does not appear that Luther's challenge was accepted. The monks of Erfurt were contented to let him know that these propositions had greatly displeased them.

But he desired to send them also into another quarter of Germany. For this purpose he turned his eyes on an individual who plays a great part in the history of the Reformation, and whom we must learn to know.

A distinguished professor, by name John Meyer, was then teaching at the University of Ingolstadt in Bavaria. He was born at Eck, a village in Swabia, and was commonly styled Doctor Eck. He was a friend of Luther, who esteemed his talents and his information. He was full of intelligence, had read much, and possessed an excellent memory. He united learning with eloquence. His gestures and his voice expressed the vivacity of his genius. Eck, as regards talent, was in the south of Germany what Luther was in the north. They were the two most remarkable theologians of that epoch, although having very different tendencies. Ingolstadt was almost the rival of Witten-berg. The reputation of these two doctors attracted from every quar-ter, to the universities where they taught, a crowd of students eager to listen to their teaching. Their personal qualities, not less than their learning, endeared them to their disciples. The character of Dr. Eck has been attacked; but one trait of his life will show that, at this period at least, his heart was not closed against generous impulses.

Among the students whom his reputation had attracted to Ingol-stadt, was a young man named Urban Regius, born on the shores of an Alpine lake. He had studied first at the University of Friburg in Brisgau. On his arrival at Ingolstadt, Urban followed the philosoph-ical courses, and gained the professor's favor. Compelled to provide for his own wants, he was obliged to undertake the charge of some young noblemen. He had not only to watch over their conduct and their studies, but even to provide with his own money the books and clothing of which they stood in need. These youths dressed with elegance, and were fond of good living. Regius, in his embarrassed condition, entreated the parents to withdraw their sons.—"Take courage," was their reply. His debts increased; his creditors became pressing: he knew not what to do. The emperor was at that time col-lecting an army against the Turks. Recruiting parties arrived at Ingolstadt, and in his despair Urban enlisted. Dressed in his military uniform, he appeared in the ranks at their final review previous to leaving the town. At that moment Dr. Eck came into the square with several of his colleagues. To his great surprise he recognized his pupil among the recruits. "Urban Regius!" said he, fixing on him a piercing glance. "Here!" replied the young soldier. "Pray, what is the cause of this change?" The young man told his story. "I will take the matter upon myself," replied Eck, who then took away his halberd and bought him off. The parents, threatened by the doctor with their prince's displeasure, sent the money necessary to pay their children's expenses. Urban Regius was saved, and became somewhat later one of the bulwarks of the Reformation.

It was through Dr. Eck that Luther thought of making his proposi-tions on Pelagianism and scholastic rationalism known in the south of the empire. He did not, however, send them direct to the Ingolstadt professor, but forwarded them to a common friend, the excellent Christopher Scheurl, secretary to the city of Nurenberg. "I forward you," said he, "my propositions, which are altogether paradoxical, and even kakistodoxical, as it would appear to many. Communicate them to our dear Eck, that most learned and ingenious man, in order that I may see and hear what he thinks of them." It was thus Luther spoke at that time of Dr. Eck: such was the friendship that united them. It was not Luther that broke it off.

But it was not on this field that the battle was to be fought. These propositions turned on doctrines of perhaps greater importance than those which two months later set the Church in flames; and yet, in despite of Luther's challenges, they passed unnoticed. At most, they were read within the walls of the schools, and created no sensation beyond them. It was because they were only university propositions, or theological doctrines; while the theses which followed had reference to an evil that had grown up among the people, and which was then breaking bounds on every side throughout Germany. So long as Luther was content to revive forgotten doctrines, men were silent; but when he pointed out abuses that injured all the world, everybody listened.

And yet in neither case did Luther propose more than to excite one of those theological discussions so frequent in the universities. This was the circle to which his thoughts were restricted. He had no idea of becoming a reformer. He was humble, and his humility bordered on distrust and anxiety. "Considering my ignorance," said he, "I deserve only to be hidden in some corner, without being known to anyone under the sun." But a mighty hand drew him from this corner in which he would have desired to remain unknown to the world. A circumstance, independent of Luther's will, threw him into the field of battle, and the war began.

Chapter 11

NETS TO CATCH SILVER

A GREAT AGITATION prevailed at that time among the German people. The Church had opened a vast market upon earth. From the crowds of purchasers, and the shouts and jokes of the sellers, it might have been called a fair, but a fair conducted by monks. The merchandise that they were extolling, and which they offered at a reduced price, was, said they, the salvation of souls!

These dealers traversed the country in a handsome carriage, accompanied by three horsemen, living in great state and spending freely. One might have thought it some archbishop on a progress through his diocese with his retinue and officers, and not a common chapman (tradesman) or a begging monk. When the procession approached a town, a deputy waited on the magistrate, and said, "The Grace of God and of the Holy Father is at your gates." Instantly everything was in motion in the place. The clergy, the priests and the nuns, the council, the schoolmasters and their pupils, the trades with their banners, men and women, young and old, went out to meet these merchants, bearing lighted tapers in their hands, and advancing to the sound of music and of all the bells, "so that they could not have received God Himself with greater honor," says a historian. The salutations being exchanged, the procession moved towards the church. The pontiff's bull of grace was carried in front on a velvet cushion, or on cloth of gold. The chief of the indulgence-merchants came next, holding a large red wooden cross in his hand. All the procession thus moved along amidst singing, prayers, and the smoke of incense. The sound of the organ and loud music welcomed the merchant-monk and his attendants into the temple. The cross that he had carried was placed in front of the altar: on it were suspended the arms of the pope, and so long as it remained there, the clergy of the place, the penitentiaries, and the under-commissaries with white wands, came daily after vespers, or before the salutation, to render it homage. This great affair excited a lively sensation in the quiet cities of Germany.

One person in particular attracted the attention of the spectators at these sales. It was he who carried the red cross, and who played the chief part. He was robed in the Dominican dress, and moved with an air of arrogance. His voice was sonorous and seemed in its full strength, although he had already attained his sixty-third year. This man, the son of a Leipzig goldsmith named Diez, was known as John Diezel, or Tetzel. He had studied in his native city, had taken the degree of bachelor in 1487, and two years after had entered the Dominican order. Numerous honors had been heaped upon his head. Bachelor of divinity, prior of the Dominicans, apostle commissary, inquisitor, he had from the year 1502 uninterruptedly filled the office of dealer in indulgences. The skill that he had acquired as subordinate had soon procured him the nomination as chief commissary. He received eighty florins a month; all his expenses were paid; a carriage and three horses were at his disposal; but his subsidiary profits, as may be easily imagined, far exceeded his stipend. In 1507 he gained at Friburg two thousand florins in two days. If he had the office of a mountebank, he possessed the manners also. Convicted at Inspruck of adultery and infamous conduct, his vices had nearly caused his death. The Emperor Maximilian had ordered him to be put into a sack and thrown into the river. The Elector Frederick of Saxony interfered and obtained his pardon. But the lesson that he had received had not taught him modesty. He led two of his children about with him. Miltitz, the pope's legate, mentions this fact in one of his letters. It would have been difficult to find in all the convents of Germany a man better qualified than Tetzel for the business with which he was charged. With the theology of a monk and the zeal and spirit of an inquisitor, he united the greatest effrontery; and the circumstance that most especially facilitated his task was his skill in inventing those extravagant stories by which the people's minds are captivated. To him all means were good that filled his chest. Raising his voice and displaying the eloquence of a mountebank, he offered his indulgences to all comers, and knew better than any tradesman how to extol his wares.

When the cross had been erected and the arms of the pope suspended from it, Tetzel went into the pulpit, and with a tone of assurance began to extol the value of indulgences, in the presence of a crowd whom the ceremony had attracted to the holy place. The people listened and stared as they heard of the admirable virtues that he announced. A Jesuit historian, speaking of the Dominican monks whom Tetzel had taken with him, says: "Some of these preachers failed not, as usual, to go beyond the matter they were treating of, and so far to exaggerate the worth of indulgences that they gave the people cause to believe that they were assured of their salvation, and of the deliverance of souls from purgatory, so soon as they had given their money." If such were the disciples, we may easily imagine what the master must have been. Let us listen to one of the harangues he delivered after the elevation of the cross.

"Indulgences are the most precious and the most noble of God's gifts.

"This cross (pointing to the red cross) has as much efficacy as the very cross of Jesus Christ.

"Come and I will give you letters, all properly sealed, by which even the sins that you intend to commit may be pardoned.

"I would not change my privileges for those of St. Peter in heaven; for I have saved more souls by my indulgences than the apostle by his sermons.

"There is no sin so great that an indulgence cannot remit; and even if any one (which is doubtless impossible) had offered violence to the blessed Virgin Mary, mother of God, let him pay—only let him pay well, and all will be forgiven him.

"Reflect then, that for every mortal sin you must, after confession and contrition, do penance for seven years, either in this life or in purgatory: now, how many mortal sins are there not committed in a day, how many in a week, how many in a month, how many in a year, how many in a whole life! . . . Alas! these sins are almost infinite, and they entail an infinite penalty in the fires of purgatory. And now, by means of these letters of indulgence, you can once in your life, in every case except four, which are reserved for the apostolic see, and afterwards in the article of death, obtain a plenary remission of all your penalties and all your sins!"

Tetzel even entered into financial calculations. "Do you not know," said he, "that if any one desires to visit Rome, or any country where travelers incur danger, he sends his money to the bank, and for every hundred florins that he wishes to have, he gives five or six or ten more, that by means of the letters of this bank he may be safely repaid his money at Rome or elsewhere . . . And you, for a quarter of a florin, will not receive these letters of indulgence, by means of which you may introduce into paradise, not a vile metal, but a divine and immortal soul, without its running any risk."

Tetzel then passed to another subject.

"But more than this," said he; "indulgences avail not only for the living, but for the dead.

"For that, repentance is not even necessary.

"Priest! noble! merchant! wife! youth! maiden! do you not hear your parents and your other friends who are dead, and who cry from the bottom of the abyss: 'We are suffering horrible torments! a trifling alms would deliver us; you can give it, and you will not!'"

All shuddered at these words uttered by the thundering voice of the imposter-monk.

"At the very instant," continued Tetzel, "that the money rattles at the bottom of the chest, the soul escapes from purgatory, and flies liberated to heaven.

"O stupid and brutish people, who do not understand the grace so richly offered! Now heaven is everywhere opened! . . . Do you refuse to enter now? When, then, will you enter? . . . Now you can ransom so many souls! . . . Stiffnecked and thoughtless man! with twelve groats you can deliver your father from purgatory, and you are ungrateful enough not to save him! I shall be justified in the day of judgment; but you—you will be punished so much the more severely for having neglected so great salvation. I declare to you, though you should have but a single coat, you ought to strip it off and sell it, in order to obtain this grace . . . The Lord our God no longer reigns. He has resigned all power to the pope."

Then seeking to make use of other arms besides, he added: "Do you know why our most Holy Lord distributes so rich a grace? It is

to restore the ruined Church of St. Peter and St. Paul, so that it may
not have its equal in the world. This Church contains the bodies of
the holy apostles Peter and Paul, and those of a multitude of martyrs.
These saintly bodies, through the present state of the building, are
now, alas! . . . beaten upon, inundated, polluted, dishonored, reduced to rottenness, by the rain and the hail . . . Alas! shall these
sacred ashes remain longer in the mire and in degradation?"

This description failed not to produce an impression on many, who
burned with a desire to come to the aid of poor Leo X, who had not
the means of sheltering the bodies of St. Peter and St. Paul from the
weather.

The orator next turned against the cavilers and traitors who opposed his work: "I declare them excommunicated!" exclaimed he.

Then addressing the docile souls and making an impious application of Scripture, he exclaimed: "Blessed are the eyes which see the
things that ye see: for I tell you, that many prophets and kings have
desired to see those things which ye see, and have not seen them; and
to hear those things which ye hear, and have not heard them!" And
in conclusion, pointing to the strong box in which the money was received, he generally finished his pathetic discourse by three appeals
to his auditory: "Bring—bring—bring!" "He used to shout these
words with such a horrible bellowing," wrote Luther, "that one
would have said it was a mad bull rushing on the people and goring
them with his horns." When his speech was ended, he left the pulpit, ran towards the money-box, and in sight of all the people flung
into it a piece of money, taking care that it should rattle loudly.

Such were the discourses that Germany listened to with astonishment in the days when God was preparing Luther.

The speech being concluded, the indulgence was considered as
"having established its throne in the place with due solemnity." Confessionals decorated with the pope's arms were ranged about: the
under-commissaries and the confessors whom they selected were
considered the representatives of the apostolic penitentiaries of Rome
at the time of a great jubilee; and on each of their confessionals were
posted in large characters, their names, surnames, and titles.

Then thronged the crowd around the confessors. Each came with
a piece of money in his hand. Men, women, and children, the poor,
and even those who lived on alms—all found money. The peniten-

tiaries, after having explained anew to each individual privately the greatness of the indulgence, addressed this question to the penitents: "How much money can you conscientiously spare to obtain a remission?" The demand, said the Instructions of the Archbishop of Mentz to the Commissaries, should be made at this moment, in order that the penitents might be better disposed to contribute.

Four precious graces were promised to those who should aid in building the basilic of St. Peter. "The first grace that we announce to you," said the commissaries, in accordance with the letter of their instructions, "is the full pardon of every sin." Next followed three other graces: first, the right of choosing a confessor, who, whenever the hour of death appeared at hand, should give absolution from all sin, and even from the greatest crimes reserved for the apostolic see; secondly, a participation in all the blessings, works, and merits of the Catholic Church, prayers, fasts, alms, and pilgrimages; thirdly, redemption of the souls that are in purgatory.

To obtain the first of these graces, it was requisite to have contrition of heart and confession of mouth, or at least an intention of confessing. But as for the three others, they might be obtained without contrition, without confession, simply by paying. Christopher Columbus, extolling the value of gold, had said ere this with great seriousness: "Whoever possesses it can introduce souls into paradise." Such was the doctrine taught by the Archbishop of Mentz and by the papel commissaries.

"As for those," said they, "who wish to deliver souls from purgatory and procure the pardon of all their offenses, let them put money into the chest; contrition of heart or confession of mouth is not necessary. Let them only hasten to bring their money; for thus will they perform a work most useful to the souls of the dead, and to the building of the Church of St. Peter." Greater blessings could not be offered at a lower rate.

The confession over, and that was soon done, the faithful hastened to the vendor. One alone was charged with the sale. His stall was near the cross. He cast inquiring looks on those who approached him. He examined their manner, their gait, their dress, and he required a sum proportionate to the appearance of the individual who presented himself. Kings, queens, princes, archbishops, bishops, were according to the scale, to pay twenty-five ducats for an ordinary indulgence. Abbots, counts, and barons, ten. The other nobles, the rectors, and all those who possessed an income of five hundred florins, paid six. Those who had two hundred florins a year paid one; and others, only a half. Moreover, if this tariff could not be carried out to the letter, full powers were given the apostolical commissary; and all was to be arranged according to the data of "sound reason," and the generosity of the donor. For particular sins, Tetzel had a particular tax. For polygamy it was six ducats; for sacrilege and perjury, nine ducats; for murder, eight ducats; for witchcraft, two ducats. Samson, who exercised the same trade in Switzerland as Tetzel in Germany, had a somewhat different scale. For infanticide he required four *livres tournois* (or sterling each worth about 20 cents then); and for parricide or fratricide, one ducat (worth $2.25).

The apostolical commissaries sometimes met with difficulties in their trade. It frequently happened, both in towns and villages, that the men were opposed to this traffic, and forbade their wives to give anything to these merchants. What could their pious spouses do? "Have you not your dowry, or other property, at your own disposal?" asked the vendors. "In that case you can dispose of it for so holy a work, against the will of your husbands."

The hand that had given the indulgence could not receive the money; this was forbidden under the severest penalties: there were good reasons to fear lest that hand should prove unfaithful. The penitent was himself to drop the price of his pardon into the chest. They showed an angry countenance against all who daringly kept their purses closed.

If among the crowd of those who thronged the confessionals there should be found a man whose crime had been public, though it was one that the civil laws could not reach, he was to begin by doing public penance. They first led him into a chapel or the vestry; there they stripped off his garments, took off his shoes, and left him nothing but a shirt. They crossed his arms over his bosom: placed a taper in one hand, and a rod in the other. The penitent then walked at the head of a procession to the red cross. Here he remained kneeling until the chants and the offertory were over. After this the commissary struck up the psalm, Miserere Mei! The confessors immediately drew near the penitent, and conducted him through the station towards the commissary, who, taking the rod and striking him thrice gently on the back, said to him: "God have pity on thee and pardon thy sin!" He then began to sing the Kyrie eleison (Lord have mercy upon us): the penitent was led to the front of the cross, where the confessor gave him the apostolical absolution, and declared him reinstated in the communion of the faithful. Sad mummery, concluded by the words of Holy Scripture, that, in such a moment, were mere profanity!

We give one of these letters of absolution. It is worth while learning the contents of these diplomas which led to the Reformation of the Church.

"May our Lord Jesus Christ have pity on thee, N. N., and absolve thee by the merits of His most holy passion! And I, in virtue of the apostolical power that has been confided to me, absolve thee from all ecclesiastical censures, judgments, and penalties which thou mayst have incurred; moreover, from all excesses, sins, and crimes that thou mayst have committed, however great and enormous they may be, and from whatsoever cause, were they even reserved for our most holy father the pope and for the apostolic see. I blot out all the stains of inability and all marks of infamy that thou mayst have drawn upon thyself on this occasion. I remit the penalties that thou mayst have drawn upon thyself on this occasion. I restore thee anew to participation in the sacraments of the Church. I incorporate thee afresh in the communion of saints, and re-establish thee in the purity and innocence which thou hadst at thy baptism. So that in the hour of death, the gate by which sinners enter the place of torments and punishment shall be closed against thee, and, on the contrary, the gate leading to the paradise of joy shall be open. And if thou shouldst not die for long years, this grace will remain unalterable until thy last hour shall arrive.

"In the name of the Father, Son, and Holy Ghost. Amen.

"Friar John Tetzel, commissary, has signed this with his own hand."

With what skill are presumptuous and lying words here foisted in between holy and Christian expressions!

All the believers were required to confess in the place where the red cross was set up. None were excepted but the sick and aged, and pregnant women. If, however, there chanced to be in the neighborhood some noble in his castle, some great personage in his palace, there was also an exemption for him, as he would not like to be mixed up with this crowd, and his money was well worth the pains of fetching it from his mansion.

Was there any convent whose chiefs, opposed to Tetzel's commerce, forbade their monks to visit the places where the Indulgence had set up its throne, they found means of remedying the evil by sending them confessors, who were empowered to absolve them contrary to the rules of their order and the will of their superiors. There was no vein in the gold mine that they did not find the means of working.

Then came what was the end and aim of the whole business: the reckoning of the money. For greater security, the chest had three keys; one was in Tetzel's keeping; the second in that of a treasurer delegated by the house of Fugger of Augsburg, to whom this vast enterprise had been consigned; the third was confided to the civil authority. When the time was come, the money-boxes were opened before a public notary, and the contents were duly counted and registered. Must not Christ arise and drive out these profane money-changers from the sanctuary?

When the mission was over, the dealers relaxed from their toils. The instructions of the commissary-general forbade them, it is true, to frequent taverns and places of bad repute; but they cared little for this prohibition. Sin could have but few terrors for those who made so easy a traffic in it. "The collectors led a disorderly life," says a Romanist historian; "they squandered in taverns, gambling-houses, and places of ill-fame, all that the people had saved from their necessities."

Chapter 12

CERTIFICATES OF SALVATION?

L ET US TURN to the scenes which this sale of the pardon of sins at that time gave rise to in Germany. There are characteristics which, of themselves alone, depict the times. We prefer using the language of the men whose history we are narrating.

At Magdeburg, Tetzel refused to absolve a rich lady, unless (as he declared to her) she would pay one hundred florins in advance. She requested the advice of her usual confessor, who was a Franciscan: "God grants the remission of sins gratuitously," replied the monk, "He does not sell it." He begged her, however, not to communicate to Tetzel the counsel she had received from him. But this merchant having notwithstanding heard a report of this opinion so contrary to his interests, exclaimed: "Such a counselor deserves to be banished or to be burnt."

Tetzel rarely found men enlightened enough, and still more rarely men who were bold enough to resist him. In general he easily managed the superstitious crowd. He had set up the red cross of the indulgences at Zwickau, and the worthy parishioners had hastened to drop into his strong-box the money that would deliver them. He was about to leave with a well-stored purse, when, on the eve of his departure, the chaplains and their acolytes asked him for a farewell supper. The request was just. But how contrive it? The money was already counted and sealed up. On the morrow he caused the great bell to be tolled. The crowd rushed into the church; each one imagined something extraordinary had happened, seeing that the business was over. "I had resolved," said he, "to depart this morning; but last night I was awakened by groans. I listened attentively . . . they

99

came from the cemetery . . . Alas! it was some poor soul calling upon me and earnestly entreating me to deliver it from the torments by which it is consumed! I shall stay, therefore, one day longer, in order to move the compassion of all Christian hearts in favor of this unhappy soul. I myself will be the first to give, and he that does not follow my example will merit condemnation." What heart would not have replied to this appeal? Who knows, besides, what soul it is thus crying from the cemetery? The offerings were abundant, and Tetzel entertained the chaplains and their acolytes with a joyous repast, the expense of which was defrayed by the offerings given in behalf of the soul of Zwickau.

The indulgence-merchants had visited Hagenau in 1517. The wife of a shoemaker, taking advantage of the authorization given in the commissary-general's instructions, had procured a letter of indulgence, contrary to her husband's will, and had paid a gold florin. She died shortly after. As the husband had not caused a mass to be said for the repose of her soul, the priest charged him with contempt of religion, and the magistrate of Hagenau summoned him to appear in court. The shoemaker put his wife's indulgence in his pocket, and went to answer the accusation.—"Is your wife dead?" asked the magistrate.—"Yes," replied he.—"What have you done for her?"—"I have buried her body, and commended her soul to God."—"But have you had a mass said for the repose of her soul?"—"I have not: it was of no use: she entered heaven at the moment of her death."—"How do you know that?"—"Here is the proof." As he said these words, he drew the indulgence from his pocket, and the magistrate, in presence of the priest, read in so many words, that, at the moment of her death, the woman who had received it would not go into purgatory, but would at once enter into heaven. "If the reverend gentleman maintains that a mass is still necessary," added the widower, "my wife has been deceived by our most holy father the pope; if she has not been, it is the priest who deceives me." There was no reply to this, and the shoemaker was acquitted. Thus did the plain sense of the people condemn these pious frauds.

One day as Tetzel was preaching at Leipzig, and mingling with his sermon some of these stories, two students quitted the church in indignation, exclaiming: "It is impossible for us to listen any longer to this monk's jokes and puerilities." One of them, we are informed, was the youthful Camerarius, who afterwards became Melancthon's intimate friend and biographer.

But of all the young men of the age, the one on whom Tetzel made the deepest impression was doubtless Myconius, afterwards celebrated as a reformer and historian of the Reformation. He had received a Christian education. "My son," his father, a pious Franconian, would often say to him, "pray frequently; for all things are given to us gratuitously from God alone. The blood of Christ," added he, "is the only ransom for the sins of the whole world. O my son, though three men only should be saved by Christ's blood, believe, and believe with assurance, that thou art one of those three men. It is an insult to the Saviour's blood to doubt that He can save." And then, cautioning his son against the traffic that was now beginning to be established in Germany: "Roman indulgences," said he again, "are nets to catch silver, and which serve to deceive the simpleminded. Remission of sins and eternal life are not to be purchased with money."

At the age of thirteen Frederick was sent to the school at Annaberg to finish his studies. Tetzel arrived in this city shortly after, and remained there two years. The people flocked in crowds to hear his sermons. "There is no other means of obtaining eternal life," cried Tetzel in a voice of thunder, "than the satisfaction of works. But this satisfaction is impossible for man. He can therefore only purchase it from the Roman pontiff."

When Tetzel was about to quit Annaberg, his sermons became more earnest. "Soon," cried he in threatening accents, "I shall take down the cross, shut the gates of heaven, and extinguish the brightness of the sun of grace that beams before your eyes." And then assuming a tender tone of exhortation: "Now is the accepted time; behold, now is the day of salvation." Again raising his voice, the priestly Stentor, who was addressing the inhabitants of a country whose wealth consisted in its mines, shouted out: "Bring your money, citizens of Annaberg! contribute bounteously in favor of indulgences, and your mines and your mountains shall be filled with pure silver!" Finally, at Whitsuntide, he declared that he would distribute his letters to the poor gratuitously, and for the love of God.

The youthful Myconius was one of Tetzel's hearers. He felt an ardent desire to take advantage of this offer. "I am a poor sinner," said he to the commissaries in Latin, "and I have need of a gratuitous pardon."—"Those alone," replied the merchants, "can have part in Christ's merits who lend a helping hand to the Church, that is to say, who give money."—"What is the meaning, then," asked Myconius, "of those promises of a free gift posted on the gates and walls of the churches?"—"Give at least a groat," said Tetzel's people, after having vainly interceded with their master in favor of the young man. "I cannot."—"Only six deniers."—"I am not worth so many." The Dominicans feared that he came on purpose to entrap them. "Listen," said they, "we will make you a present of the six deniers." The young man replied indignantly: "I will have no bought indulgences. If I desired to buy them, I should only have to sell one of my schoolbooks. I desire a gratuitous pardon, and for the love of God alone. You will render an account to God for having allowed a soul to be lost for six deniers."—"Who sent you to entrap us?" exclaimed the vendors. —"Nothing but the desire of receiving God's pardon could have made me appear before such great gentlemen," replied the young man, as he withdrew.

"I was very sad at being thus sent away unpitied. But I felt, however, a Comforter within me, who said that there was a God in heaven who pardons repentant souls without money and without price, for the love of His Son Jesus Christ. As I took leave of these folks, the Holy Spirit touched my heart. I burst into tears, and prayed to the Lord with anguish: 'O God!' cried I, 'since these men have refused to remit my sins, because I had no money to pay them, do Thou, Lord, have pity on me, and pardon them of Thy pure grace.' I repaired to my chamber; I prayed to my crucifix which was lying on my desk; I put it on a chair, and fell down before it. I cannot describe to you what I experienced. I begged God to be a Father to me, and to do with me whatever He pleased. I felt my nature changed, converted, transformed. What had delighted me before, now became an object of disgust. To live with God and to please Him was my earnest, my only desire."

Thus did Tetzel himself prepare the Reformation. By flagrant abuses, he cleared the way for a purer doctrine; and the indignation he aroused in a generous youth was one day to burst forth with power. We may form some idea of this by the following anecdote.

A Saxon nobleman, who had heard Tetzel at Leipzig, was much

displeased by his falsehoods. Approaching the monk, he asked him if he had the power of pardoning sins that men have an intention of committing. "Most assuredly," replied Tetzel, "I have received full powers from his holiness for that purpose."—"Well, then," answered the knight, "I am desirous of taking a slight revenge on one of my enemies, without endangering his life. I will give you ten crowns if you will give me a letter of indulgence that shall fully justify me." Tetzel made some objections; they came, however, to an arrangement by the aid of thirty crowns. The monk quitted Leipzig shortly after. The nobleman and his attendants lay in wait for him in a wood between Jüterbock and Treblin; they fell upon him, gave him a slight beating, and took away the well-stored indulgence-chest the inquisitor was carrying with him. Tetzel made a violent outcry, and carried his complaint before the courts. But the nobleman showed the letter which Tetzel had signed himself, and which exempted him beforehand from every penalty. Duke George, whom this action had at first exceedingly exasperated, no sooner read the document than he ordered the accused to be acquitted.

This traffic everywhere occupied men's thoughts, and was everywhere talked of. It was the topic of conversation in castles, in academies, and in the burghers' houses, as well as in taverns, inns, and all places of public resort. Opinions were divided; some believed, others felt indignant. As for the sensible part of the nation, they rejected with disgust the system of indulgences. This doctrine was so opposed to the Holy Scriptures and to morality, that every man who had any knowledge of the Bible, or any natural light, internally condemned it, and only waited for a signal to oppose it. On the other hand, the scoffers found ample food for raillery. The people, whom the dissolute lives of the priests had irritated for many years, and whom the fear of punishment still kept within certain bounds, gave vent to all their hatred. Complaints and sarcasms might everywhere be heard on the love of money that devoured the clergy.

They did not stop there. They attacked the power of the keys and the authority of the sovereign pontiff. "Why," said they, "does not the pope deliver at once all the souls from purgatory by a holy charity and on account of their great wretchedness, since he delivers so many for love of perishable money and of the cathedral of St. Peter? Why are they always celebrating festivals and anniversaries for the dead?

Why does not the pope restore or permit the resumption of the benefices and prebends founded in favor of the dead, since it is now useless and even reprehensible to pray for those whom the indulgences
have delivered forever? What means this new holiness of God and
of the pope, that for love of money they grant to an impious man, and
an enemy of God, to deliver from purgatory, a pious soul, the beloved of the Lord, rather than deliver it themselves gratuitously
through love, and because of its great misery?"

Stories were told of the gross and immortal conduct of the traf-
fickers in indulgences. To pay their bills to the carriers who transported them and their merchandise, the inn-keepers with whom they
lodged, or whoever had done them any service, they gave a letter of
indulgence for four souls, for five, or for any number according to
circumstances. Thus these certificates of salvation circulated in the
inns and markets like bank notes or other paper money. "Pay! pay!"
said the people, "that is the head, belly, tail, and all the contents of
their sermons."

A miner of Schneeberg met a seller of indulgences. "Must we
credit,", asked he, "what you have so often told us of the power of
indulgences and of the papal authority, and believe that we can, by
throwing a penny into the chest, ransom a soul from purgatory?"
The merchant affirmed it was so. "Ah!" resumed the miner, "what a
merciless man, then, the pope must be, since for want of a wretched
penny he leaves a poor soul crying in the flames so long! If he has
no ready money, let him store up some hundred thousand crowns,
and deliver all these souls at once. We poor people would very readily
repay him both interest and capital."

The Germans were wearied with this scandalous traffic that was
carried on in the midst of them. They could not longer endure the
impositions of these master-cheats of Rome, as Luther called them.
No bishop, no theologian, however, dared oppose their quackery and
their frauds. All minds were in suspense. Men asked one another
if God would not raise up some mighty man for the work that was to
be done; but nowhere did he appear.

Luther, as far as we know, heard of Tetzel for the first time at
Grimma in 1516, just as he was commencing his visitation of the
churches. It was reported to Staupitz, who was still with Luther, that
there was a seller of indulgences at Wurzen named Tetzel, who was

making a great noise. Some of his extravagant expressions were quoted, and Luther exclaimed with indignation: "If God permit, I will make a hole in his drum."

Tetzel was returning from Berlin, where he had met with the most friendly reception from the Elector Joachim, the farmer-general's brother, when he took his station at Jüterbock. Staupitz, taking advantage of the confidence the Elector Frederick placed in him, had often called his attention to the abuses of the indulgences and the scandalous lives of the vendors. The princes of Saxony, indignant at this disgraceful traffic, had forbidden the merchant to enter their provinces. He was therefore compelled to remain in the territories of his patron the Archbishop of Magdeburg; but he approached Saxony as near as he could. Jüterbock was only four miles from Wittenberg. "This great purse-thresher," said Luther, "began to thresh bravely throughout the country, so that the money began to leap and fall tinkling into the box." The people flocked from Wittenberg to the indulgence-market of Jüterbock.

At this period Luther still respected the Church and the pope. "I was at that time," said he, "a monk, and a most furious papist, so intoxicated, nay, so drowned in the Roman doctrines, that I would have willingly aided, if I could, in killing anyone who should have had the audacity to refuse the slightest obedience to the pope. I was a very Saul, as there are many still." But at the same time his heart was ready to catch fire for anything that he recognized as truth and against everything he believed to be error. "I was a young doctor fresh from the forge, ardent and rejoicing in the Word of the Lord."

Luther was one day seated in the confessional at Wittenberg. Many of the townspeople came successively, and confessed themselves guilty of great excesses. Adultery, licentiousness, usury, ill-gotten gains—such were the crimes acknowledged to the minister of the Word by those souls of which he was one day to give an account. He reprimanded, corrected, instructed. But what is his astonishment when these individuals replied that they would not abandon their sins? . . . Greatly shocked, the pious monk declared that since they would not promise to change their lives, he could not absolve them. The unhappy creatures then appealed to their letters of indulgence; they showed them, and maintained their virtue. But Luther replied that he had nothing to do with these papers, and added: "Except ye repent, ye shall all likewise perish." They cried out and protested; but the doctor was immovable. They must cease to do evil and learn to do well, or else there was no absolution. "Have a care," added he, "how you listen to the clamors of these indulgence-merchants: you have better things to do than buy these licenses which they sell at so vile a price."

The inhabitants of Wittenberg, in great alarm, hastily returned to Tetzel: they told him that an Augustine monk had treated his letters with contempt. At this intelligence, the Dominican bellowed his anger. He stormed from the pulpit, employing insults and curses; and to strike the people with greater terror, he had a fire lighted several times in the market-place, declaring that he had received an order from the pope to burn all heretics who presumed to oppose his most holy indulgences.

Such was the fact that was not the cause but the first occasion of the Reformation. A pastor, seeing the sheep of his fold in a course in which they must perish, sought to withdraw them from it. As yet he had no thought of reforming the Church and the world. He had seen Rome and her corruptions; but still he did not rise up against her. He had a presentiment of some of the abuses under which Christendom groaned; but he did not think of correcting them. He did not desire to become a reformer. He had no more plan for the reformation of the Church than he had had for the reformation of himself. God willed a reform, and elected Luther to be its instrument. The same remedy which had been so efficacious in healing his own wounds, the hand of God would apply by him to the sores of Christendom. He remained tranquil in the sphere that was assigned to him. He walked simply wherever his Master called him. He fulfilled at Wittenberg the duties of professor, preacher, and pastor. He was seated in the temple where the members of his church came and opened their hearts to him. It was there—on that field—that the evil attacked him, and error sought him out. They would prevent him from executing his office. His conscience, bound to the Word of God, revolted. Was it not God who called him? To resist was a duty, therefore a right. He must speak. Thus, says Mathesius, were the events ordained by that God who desired to restore Christendom by means of the forgemaster's son, and to pass through His furnaces the impure doctrine of the Church in order to purify it.

It is not requisite, after this statement, to refute a lying imputation, invented by some of Luther's enemies after his death. It has been said that the jealousy peculiar to religious orders—vexation at seeing a disgraceful and reprobated traffic confided to the Dominicans rather than to the Augustines, who had hitherto possessed it—led the Wittenberg professor to attack Tetzel and his doctrines. The well-established fact, that this speculation had been first offered to the Franciscans who would have nothing to do with it, is sufficient to refute this fable repeated by writers who have copied one another. Cardinal Pallavicini himself affirmed that the Augustines had never held this commission. Besides, we have witnessed the travail of Luther's soul. His conduct needed no other interpretation. It was necessary for him to confess aloud the doctrine to which he owed his happiness. In Christianity, when a man has found a treasure for himself, he desires to impart it to others. In our days we should give up these puerile and unworthy explanations of the great revolution of the sixteenth century. It requires a more powerful lever to raise the world. The Reformation was not in Luther only; his age must have given it birth.

Luther, who was impelled equally by obedience to the Word of God and charity towards men, ascended the pulpit. He forearmed his hearers, but with gentleness, as he says himself. His prince had obtained from the pope special indulgences for the castle-chapel at Wittenberg. Some of the blows that he was aiming at the inquisitor's indulgences might fall on those of the elector. It mattered not! he hazarded disgrace. If he sought to please men, he would not be Christ's servant.

"No one can prove by Scripture that the righteousness of God requires a penalty or satisfaction from the sinner," said the faithful minister of the Word to the people of Wittenberg. "The only duty it imposes is a true repentance, a sincere conversion, a resolution to bear the cross of Christ, and to perform good works. It is a great error to pretend of oneself to make satisfaction for our sins to God's righteousness; God pardons them gratuitously by His inestimable grace.

"The Christian Church, it is true, requires something of the sinner, and which consequently can be remitted. But that is all. . . . Yet farther, these indulgences of the Church are tolerated only because of the idle and imperfect Christians who will not zealously perform good works; for they move no one to sanctification, but leave each man in his imperfection."

Next attacking the pretenses under which indulgences were published, he continued: "They would do much better to contribute for love of God to the building of St. Peter's, than to buy indulgences with this intention. . . . But, say you, shall we then never purchase any? . . . I have already told you, and I repeat it, my advice is that no one should buy them. Leave them for drowsy Christians: but you should walk apart and for yourselves! We must turn the faithful aside from indulgences, and exhort them to the works which they neglect."

Finally, glancing at his adversaries, Luther concluded in these words: "And should any cry out that I am a heretic (for the truth I preach is very prejudicial to their strong box), I care but little for their clamors. They are gloomy and sick brains, men who have never tasted the Bible, never read the Christian doctrine, never comprehended their own doctors, and who lie rotting in the rags and tatters of their own vain opinions . . . May God grant both them and us a sound understanding! Amen." After these words the doctor quitted the pulpit, leaving his hearers in great emotion at such daring language.

This sermon was printed, and made a profound impression on all who read it. Tetzel replied to it, and Luther answered again; but these discussions did not take place till the year 1518.

Chapter 13

NINETY-FIVE THESES POSTED

L UTHER'S WORDS produced little change. Tetzel continued his traffic and his impious discourses without disturbing himself. Would Luther resign himself to these crying abuses, and would he keep silence? As pastor, he had earnestly exhorted those who had recourse to his services; as preacher, he had uttered a warning voice from the pulpit. It still remained for him to speak as a theologian; he had yet to address not merely a few souls in the confessional, not merely the assembly of the faithful at Wittenberg, but all those who were, like himself, teachers of the Word of God. His resolution was made.

It was not the Church he thought of attacking; it was not the pope he was bringing to the bar; on the contrary, it was his respect for the pope that would not allow him to be silent longer on the monstrous claims by which the pontiff was discredited. He must take the pope's part against those impudent men who dared to mingle his venerable name with their scandalous traffic. Far from thinking of a revolution which should overthrow the primacy of Rome, Luther believed he had the pope and Catholicism for his allies against these bare-faced monks.

The festival of All-Saints was a very important day for Wittenberg, and, above all, for the church the elector had built there and which he had filled with relics. On that day the priests used to bring out these relics, ornamented with gold, silver, and precious stones, and exhibit them before the people, who were astonished and dazzled at such magnificence. Whoever visited the church on that festival, and made confession, obtained a rich indulgence. Accordingly, on this great anniversary, pilgrims came to Wittenberg in crowds.

On October 31, 1517, at noon on the day preceding the festival, Luther walked boldly toward the church to which a superstitious crowd of pilgrims was going, and posted upon the door ninety-five theses against the doctrine of indulgences. Neither the elector, nor Staupitz, nor Spalatin, nor any of his most intimate friends, had been notified of his intention.

Luther therein declared, in a kind of preface, that he had written these theses with the express desire of setting the truth in the full light of day. He declared himself ready to defend them on the morrow, in the university, against all opponents. Great was the attention they excited: they were read and passed from mouth to mouth. Erelong the pilgrims, the university, and the whole city, were in commotion.

We give some of these propositions, written with the pen of the monk, and posted on the door of the church of Wittenberg:

"1. When our Lord and Master Jesus Christ says *repent,* He means that the whole life of believers upon earth should be a constant and perpetual repentance.

"2. This word cannot be understood of the sacrament of penance (i.e., confession and satisfaction), as administered by the priest.

"3. Still the Lord does not mean to speak in this place solely of internal repentance; internal repentance is null, if it produce not externally every kind of mortification of the flesh.

"4. Repentance and sorrow—i.e., true penance—endure as long as a man is displeased with himself—that is, until he passes from this life into eternity.

"5. The pope is unable and desires not to remit any other penalty than that which he has imposed of his own good pleasure, or conformably to the canons—i.e., the papal ordinances.

"6. The pope cannot remit any condemnation, but only declare and confirm the remission of God, except in the cases that appertain to himself. If he does otherwise, the condemnation remains entirely the same.

"8. The laws of ecclesiastical penance ought to be imposed solely on the living, and have no regard to the dead.

"21. The commissaries of indulgences are in error when they say that by the papal indulgence a man is delivered from every punishment and is saved.

"25. The same power that the pope has over purgatory throughout the Church, each bishop possesses individually in his own diocese, and each priest in his own parish.

"27. They preach mere human follies who maintain that as soon as the money rattles in the strong box, the soul flies out of purgatory.

"28. This is certain that as soon as the money tinkles, avarice and love of gain arrive, increase, and multiply. But the support and prayers of the Church depend solely on God's will and good pleasure.

"32. Those who fancy themselves sure of salvation by indulgences will go to perdition along with those who teach them so.

"35. They are teachers of antichristian doctrines who pretend that to deliver a soul from purgatory, or to buy an indulgence, there is no need of either sorrow or repentance.

"36. Every Christian who truly repents of his sins, enjoys an entire remission both of the penalty and of the guilt, without any need of indulgences.

"37. Every true Christian, whether dead or alive, participates in all the blessings of Christ or of the Church, by God's gift, and without a letter of indulgence.

"38. Still we should not contemn the papal dispensation and pardon; for this pardon is a declaration of the pardon of God.

"40. True repentance and sorrow seek and love the punishment; but the mildness of indulgence absolves from the punishment, and begets hatred against it.

"42. We should teach Christians that the pope has no thought or desire of comparing in any respect the act of buying indulgences with any work of mercy.

"43. We should teach Christians that he who gives to the poor, or lends to the needy, does better than he who purchases an indulgence.

"44. For the work of charity increaseth charity, and renders a man more pious; whereas the indulgence does not make him better, but only renders him more self-confident, and more secure from punishment.

"45. We should teach Christians that whoever sees his neighbor in want, and yet buys an indulgence, does not buy the pope's indulgence, but incurs God's anger.

"46. We should teach Christians that if they have no superfluity, they are bound to keep for their own households the means of procuring necessaries, and ought not to squander their money in indulgences.

"47. We should teach Christians that the purchase of an indulgence is a matter of free choice and not of commandment.

"48. We should teach Christians that the pope, having more need of prayers offered up in faith than of money, desires prayer more than money when he dispenses indulgences.

"49. We should teach Christians that the pope's indulgence is good, if we put no confidence in it; but that nothing is more hurtful, if it diminishes our piety.

"50. We should teach Christians that if the pope knew of the extortions of the preachers of indulgences, he would rather the mother-church of St. Peter were burned and reduced to ashes, than see it built up with the skin, the flesh, and the bones of his flock.

"51. We should teach Christians that the pope (as it is his duty) would distribute his own money to the poor whom the indulgence-sellers are now stripping of their last farthing, even were he compelled to sell the mother-church of St. Peter.

"52. To hope to be saved by indulgences is a lying and an empty hope; although even the commissary of indulgences, nay farther, the pope himself, should pledge their souls to guarantee it.

"53. They are the enemies of the pope and of Jesus Christ, who, by reason of the preaching of indulgences, forbid the preaching of the Word of God.

"55. The pope can have no other thought than this: If the indulgence, which is a lesser matter, be celebrated with ringing of a bell, with pomp and ceremony, much more should we honor and celebrate the gospel, which is a greater thing, with a hundred bells, and with a hundred pomps and ceremonies.

"62. The true and precious treasure of the Church is the holy gospel of the glory and grace of God.

"65. The treasures of the gospel are nets in which in former times the rich and those in easy circumstances were caught.

"66. But the treasures of the indulgence are nets with which they now catch the riches of the people.

"67. It is the duty of bishops and pastors to receive the commissaries of the apostolical indulgences with every mark of respect.

"68. But it is still more their duty to ascertain with their eyes and ears that the said commissaries do not preach the dreams of their own imagination, instead of the orders of the pope.

"71. Cursed be he who speaks against the indulgence of the pope.

"72. But blessed be he who speaks against the foolish and impudent language of the preachers of indulgences.

"76. The indulgence of the pope cannot take away the smallest daily sin, as far as regards the guilt or the offense.

"79. It is blasphemy to say that the cross adorned with the arms of the pope is as effectual as the cross of Christ.

"80. The bishops, pastors, and theologians who permit such things to be told the people, will have to render an account of them.

"81. This shameless preaching, these impudent commendations of indulgences, make it difficult for the learned to defend the dignity and honor of the pope against the calumnies of the preachers, and the subtle and crafty questions of the common people.

"86. Why, say they, does not the pope, who is richer than the richest Croesus, build the mother-church of St. Peter with his own money, rather than with that of poor Christians?

"92. Would that we were quit of all these preachers who say to the Church: Peace! peace! and there is no peace.

"94. We should exhort Christians to diligence in following Christ, their Head, through crosses, death, and hell.

"95. For it is far better to enter into the kingdom of heaven through much tribulation than to acquire a carnal security by the consolations of a false peace."

Such was the commencement of the work. The germs of the Reformation were contained in these propositions of Luther's. The abuses of indulgences were attacked therein, and this is their most striking feature; but beneath these attacks there was a principle which, although attracting the attention of the multitude in a less degree, was one day to overthrow the edifice of popery. The evangelical doctrine of a free and gratuitous remission of sins was there for the first time publicly professed. The work must now increase in strength. It was evident, indeed, that whoever had this faith in the remission of sins, announced by the Wittenberg doctor; that whoever had this repentance, this conversion, and this sanctification, the necessity of which he so earnestly inculcated, would no longer care for human ordinances, would escape from the toils and swaddling-bands of Rome, and would acquire the liberty of the children of God. All errors would fall down before this truth. By it, light had begun to enter Luther's mind; by it, also, the light would be diffused over the Church. A clear knowledge of this truth is what preceding reformers had lacked; and hence the unfruitfulness of their exertions. Luther himself acknowledged afterwards that in proclaiming justification by faith, he had laid the axe to the root of the tree. "It is doctrine we attack in the adherents of the papacy," said he. "Huss and Wycliffe only attacked their lives. Everything depends on the Word, which the pope has taken from us and falsified. I have vanquished the pope, because my doctrine is of God, and his is of the devil."

In our days, too, we have forgotten this main doctrine of justification by faith, although in a sense opposed to that of our fathers. "In the time of Luther," observes one of our contemporaries, "the remission of sins cost money at least; but in our days, each man supplies himself gratis." There is a great similarity between these two errors. There is perhaps more forgetfulness of God in ours, than in that of the sixteenth century. The principle of justification by the grace of God, which brought the Church out of so much darkness at the period of the Reformation, can alone renew our generation, put an end to its doubts and waverings, destroy the selfishness that preys upon it, establish righteousness and morality among the nations, and, in short, reunite the world to God from whom it has been separated.

But if Luther's theses were strong by the strength of the truth they proclaimed, they were not the less so by the faith of their champion. He had boldly drawn the sword of the Word: he had done so in reliance on the power of truth. He had felt that by leaning on God's promises, he could afford to risk something, to use the language of the world. "Let him who desires to begin a good work," said he when speaking of this daring attack, "undertake it with confidence in the goodness of his cause, and not, which God forbid! expecting the support and consolation of the world. Moreover, let him have no fear of man, or of the whole world; for these words will never lie: 'It is good to trust in the Lord, and assuredly he that trusteth in the Lord shall not be confounded.' But let him that will not or who cannot risk something with confidence in God, take heed how he undertakes anything." Luther, after having posted his theses on the gate of All-Saints' Church, retired, no doubt, to his tranquil cell, full of the peace and joy that spring from an action done in the Lord's name, and for the sake of eternal truth.

Whatever be the boldness that prevailed in these propositions, they still bespeak the monk who refused to admit a single doubt on the authority of the See of Rome. But, while attacking the doctrine of indulgences, Luther had unwittingly touched on certain errors, whose discovery could not be agreeable to the pope, seeing that sooner or later they would call his supremacy in question. Luther was not so far-sighted; but he was sensible of the extreme boldness of the step he had just taken, and consequently thought it his duty to soften down their audacity, as far as he could in conformity with the truth. He therefore set forth these theses as doubtful propositions on which he solicited the information of the learned; and appended to them, conformably with the established usage, a solemn declaration that he did not mean to affirm or say anything contrary to the Holy Scriptures, the Fathers of the Church, and the rights and decretals (decrees) of the Roman See.

Frequently, in after years, as he contemplated the immense and unexpected consequences of this courageous attack, Luther was astonished at himself, and could not understand how he had ventured to make it. An invisible and mightier hand than his held the clue, and led the herald of truth along a path that was still hidden from him, and, from the difficulties of which he would perhaps have shrunk, if he had foreseen them, and if he had advanced alone and of his own accord. "I entered into this controversy," said he, "without any definite plan, without knowledge or inclination; I was taken quite unawares, and I call God, the searcher of hearts, to witness."

Luther had become acquainted with the source of the abuses. Someone brought him a little book, adorned with the arms of the Archbishop of Mentz and Magdeburg, which contained the regulations to be followed in the sale of indulgences. It was this young prelate, then, this graceful prince, who had prescribed, or at least sanctioned, all this. In him Luther saw only a superior whom he should fear and respect. Not wishing to beat the air at hazard, but rather to address those who are charged with the government of the Church, Luther sent him a letter, abounding at once in frankness and humility. It was on the very day he posted up the theses that the doctor wrote to Albert:—

"Pardon me, most reverend Father in Christ and most illustrious prince, if I, who am but the dregs of men, have the presumption to write to your Sublime Highness. The Lord Jesus Christ is my witness that, feeling how small and despicable I am, I have long put off doing it. . . . May your Highness condescend to cast a single glance on a grain of dust, and of your episcopal mildness graciously receive my petition.

"Certain individuals are hawking the papal indulgences up and down the country, in your Grace's name. I am unwilling so much to blame the clamors of these preachers (for I have not heard them), as the false ideas of the simple and ignorant people, who, in purchasing indulgences, fancy themselves assured of salvation. . . .

"The souls intrusted to your care, most excellent Father, are taught, not unto life, but unto death. The severe and just account that will be required of you increases from day to day. . . . I could no longer be silent. No! Man is not saved by the work or the office of his bishop. . . . Even the righteous are saved with difficulty . . . and narrow is the way which leadeth unto life. Wherefore, then, do these preachers of indulgences by their empty fables inspire the people with a carnal security?

"Indulgences alone, to hear them, ought to be proclaimed and extolled. . . . What! is it not the principal, the sole duty of the bishops to instruct the people in the gospel, and in the charity of Christ Jesus? Christ Himself has nowhere ordained the preaching of indulgences; but He has forcibly commanded the preaching of the gospel. How dreadful, then, and how dangerous, for a bishop to allow the gospel to be silent, and that the noise of indulgences alone should re-echo incessantly in the ears of his flock! . . .

"Most worthy Father in God, in the instructions to the commissaries, which have been published in your Grace's name (no doubt without your knowledge), it is said, that the indulgences are the most precious treasure—that by them man is reconciled to God, and that repentance is not necessary to those who purchase them.

"What can I, what ought I to do, most worthy Bishop, most serene Prince? I beg your Highness, in the name of our Lord Jesus Christ, to cast a look of paternal vigilance on this affair, to suppress the book entirely, and to order the preachers to deliver other sermons before the people. If you do not so, fear lest you should one day hear some voice uplifted in refutation of these preachers, to the great dishonor of your most serene Highness."

Luther, at the same time, forwarded his theses to the archbishop, and added a postscript inviting him to read them, in order to convince himself on how slight a foundation the doctrine of indulgences was based.

Thus, Luther's whole desire was for the sentinels of the Church to awaken and resolve to put an end to the evils that were laying it waste. Nothing could be more noble and more respectful than this letter from a monk to one of the greatest princes of the Church and the Empire. Never did man act more in accordance with this precept of Christ: "Render to Caesar the things that are Caesar's, and to God the things that are God's." This is not the course of those fiery revolutionists who "despise dominion and speak evil of dignities." It is the cry of a Christian conscience—of a priest who gives honor to all, but who fears God above everything. All his prayers, all his entreaties, were unavailing. The youthful Albert, engrossed by pleasures and ambitious designs, made no reply to so solemn an appeal. The Bishop of Brandenburg, Luther's ordinary, a learned and pious man, to whom he sent his theses, replied that he was attacking the power of the Church; that he would bring upon himself much trouble and vexation; that the thing was above his strength; and he earnestly advised him to keep quiet. The princes of the Church stopped their ears against the voice of God, which was manifested with such energy and tenderness through the mouth of Luther. They would not understand the signs of the times; they were struck with that blindness which has caused the ruin of so many powers and dignities. "They both thought," said Luther afterwards, "that the pope would be too strong for a poor mendicant friar like me."

But Luther could judge better than the bishops of the disastrous effects of indulgences on the manners and lives of the people, for he was in direct communication with them. He saw continually and near at hand what the bishops knew only through unfaithful reports. Although the bishops failed him, God did not. The Head of the Church, who sitteth in the heavens, and to whom all power is given upon earth, had Himself prepared the soil and deposited the seed in the hands of His minister; he gave wings to the seeds of truth, and he scattered it in an instant throughout the length and breadth of His Church.

No one appeared next day at the university to attack Luther's propositions. The Tetzel traffic was too much decried, and too shameful, for anyone but himself or his followers to dare take up the glove. But these theses were destined to be heard elsewhere than under the arched roof of an academic hall. Scarcely had they been nailed to the church door of Wittenberg than the feeble sounds of the hammer were followed throughout all Germany by a mighty blow that reached even the foundations of haughty Rome, threatening with sudden ruin the walls, the gates, the pillars of popery, stunning and terrifying her champions, and at the same time awakening thousands from the sleep of error.

These theses spread with the rapidity of lightning. A month had not elapsed before they were at Rome. "In a fortnight," says a contemporary historian, "they were in every part of Germany, and in four weeks they had traversed nearly the whole of Christendom, as if the very angels had been their messengers, and had placed them before the eyes of all men. No one can believe the noise they made." Somewhat later they were translated into Dutch and Spanish, and a traveler sold them in Jerusalem. "Everyone," said Luther, "complained of the indulgences: and as all the bishops and doctors had kept silence, and nobody was willing to bell the cat, poor Luther became a famous doctor, because (as they said) there came one at last who ventured to do it. But I did not like this glory, and the tune was nearly too high for my voice."

Many of the pilgrims, who had thronged to Wittenberg from every quarter for the feast of All-Saints, carried back with them, instead of indulgences, the famous theses of the Augustine monk. By this means they contributed to their circulation. Everyone read them, meditated and commented on them. Men conversed about them in all the convents and in all the universities. The pious monks, who had entered the cloisters to save their souls—all upright and honorable men, were delighted at this simple and striking confession of the truth, and heartily desired that Luther would continue the work he had begun. At length one man had found courage to undertake the perilous struggle. This was a reparation accorded to Christendom:

the public conscience was satisfied. Piety saw in these theses a blow aimed at every superstition; the new theology hailed in it the defeat of the scholastic dogmas; princes and magistrates considered them as a barrier raised against the invasions of the ecclesiastical power; and the nation rejoiced at seeing so positive a veto opposed by this monk to the cupidity of the Roman chancery.

"When Luther attacked this fable," remarked to Duke George of Saxony, a man very worthy of belief, and one of the principal rivals of the reformer, namely Erasmus, "the whole world applauded, and there was a general assent." "I observe," said he at another time to Cardinal Campeggio, "that the greater their evangelical piety and the purer their morals, the less are men opposed to Luther. His life is praised even by those who cannot endure his faith. The world was weary of a doctrine so full of puerile fables and human ordinances, and thirsted for that living, pure, and hidden water which springs from the veins of the evangelists and apostles. Luther's genius was fitted to accomplish these things, and his zeal would naturally catch fire at so glorious an enterprise."

Chapter 14

THESES PUBLISHED AND CIRCULATED

WE MUST FOLLOW these propositions into whatever place they penetrated—into the studies of the learned, the cells of the monks, and the halls of princes, to form an idea of the various but prodigious effects they produced in Germany.

Reuchlin received them. He was wearied of the rude combat he had to fight against the monks. The strength displayed by the new combatant in his theses reanimated the dispirited champion of literature, and restored joy to his desponding heart. "Thanks be to God!" exclaimed he after reading them, "at last they have found a man who will give them so much to do that they will be compelled to let my old age end in peace."

The cautious Erasmus was in the Low Countries when these propositions reached him. He internally rejoiced at witnessing his secret wishes for the rectifying of abuses expressed with so much courage: he approved of the author, exhorting him only to greater moderation and prudence. Nevertheless, when someone reproached Luther's violence in his presence: "God," said he, "has given men a physician who cuts deep into the flesh, because the malady would otherwise be incurable."

Doctor Flek, prior of the monastery of Steinlausitz, had long discontinued reading the Mass, but without telling anyone the real cause. One day he found Luther's theses posted up in the refectory: he went up to them, began to read, and had only perused a few, when, unable to contain his joy, he exclaimed: "Ah! ah! he whom we have so long expected is come at last, and he will show you monks a trick or two!" Then looking into the future, says Mathesius, and playing on the meaning of the name Wittenberg: "All the world," said he, "will go and seek wisdom on that mountain and will find it." He wrote to the doctor to continue the glorious struggle with boldness. Luther styles him a man full of joy and consolation.

The ancient and renowned episcopal see of Wurzburg was filled at that time by Lorenzo de Bibra, a pious, wise, and worthy man, according to the testimony of his contemporaries. When a gentleman came and informed him that he intended placing his daughter in a convent: "Rather give her a husband," said he. And then he added: "If you require money for her dowry, I will lend it you." The emperor and all the princes held him in the highest esteem. He mourned over the disorders of the Church, and above all, over those of the convents. The theses reached his palace also; he read them with great joy, and publicly declared that he approved of Luther. Somewhat later, he wrote to the Elector Frederick: "Do not let the pious Doctor Martin go, for they do him wrong." The elector was delighted at this testimony, and communicated it to the reformer with his own hand.

The Emperor Maximilian, predecessor of Charles the Fifth, read and admired the theses of the monk of Wittenberg; he perceived his ability, and foresaw that this obscure Augustine might one day become a powerful ally for Germany in her struggle against Rome. He accordingly said to the Elector of Saxony through his envoy: "Take great care of the monk Luther, for the time may come when we shall have need of him." And shortly after, being in diet with Pfeffinger, the elector's privy counselor, he said to him: "Well! what is your Augustine doing? In truth his propositions are not contemptible. He will play the monks a pretty game."

At Rome, even in the Vatican, these theses were not so badly received as might have been imagined. Leo X judged rather as a patron of letters than as pope. The amusement they gave him made him forget the severe truths they contained; and as Sylvester Prierio, the master of the sacred palace, who had the charge of examining the books, requested him to treat Luther as a heretic, he replied: "Brother Martin Luther is a very fine genius, and all that is said against him is mere monkish jealousy."

There were few men on whom Luther's theses produced a deeper impression than the scholar of Annaberg, whom Tetzel had so mercilessly repulsed. Myconius had entered a convent. On the very night of his arrival he dreamed he saw immense fields of wheat all glistening with ripe ears. "Cut," said the voice of his guide; and when he alleged his want of skill, his conductor showed him a reaper working with inconceivable activity. "Follow him, and do as he does," said the guide. Myconius, as eager after holiness as Luther had been, devoted himself while in the monastery to all the vigils, fasts, mortifications, and practices invented by men. But at last he despaired of ever attaining his object by his own exertions.

He neglected his studies, and employed himself in manual labors only. At one time he would bind books; at another, work at the turner's lathe, or any laborious occupation. This outward activity was unable to quiet his troubled conscience. God had spoken to him, and he could no longer fall back into his previous lethargy. This state of anguish endured several years. It has been sometimes imagined that the paths of the reformers were smooth, and that when they had renounced the observances of the Church, nothing but pleasure and comfort awaited them. It is not considered that they arrived at the truth through internal struggles a thousand times more painful than the observances to which salvish minds easily submitted.

At length the year 1517 arrived; Luther's theses were published; they were circulated through Christendom, and penetrated also into the monastery where the scholar of Annaberg was concealed. He hid himself in a corner of the cloister with another monk, John Voigt, that he might read them at his ease. Here were the selfsame truths he had heard from his father; his eyes were opened; he felt a voice within him responding to that which was then reechoing through Germany, and great consolation filled his heart. "I see plainly," said he, "that Martin Luther is the reaper I saw in my dream, and who taught me to gather the ears." He began immediately to profess the doctrine that Luther had proclaimed. The monks grew alarmed as they heard him; they argued with him, and declared against Luther and against his convent. "This convent," replied Myconius, "is like our Lord's sepulcher: they wish to prevent Christ's resurrection, but they will fail." At last his superiors, finding they could not convince him, prohibited him for a year and a half from all intercourse with the world, permitting him neither to write nor receive letters, and threatening him with imprisonment for life.

But the hour of his deliverance was at hand. Being afterwards nominated pastor of Zwickau, he was the first who declared against the papacy in the churches of Thuringia. "Then," said he, "was I enabled to labor with my venerable father Luther in the gospel-harvest." Jonas describes him as a man capable of doing everything he undertook.

No doubt there were others besides to whose souls Luther's propositions were a signal of life. They kindled a new flame in many cells, cottages, and palaces. Whereas those who had entered the convents in quest of good cheer, an idle life, or respect and honors, says Mathesius, began to load the name of Luther with reproaches, the monks who lived in prayer, fasting, and mortification returned thanks to God as soon as they heard the cry of that eagle, whom Huss had announced a century before. Even the common people, who did not clearly understand the theological question but who knew only that this man assailed the empire of the lazy and mendicant monks, welcomed him with bursts of acclamation. An immense sensation was produced in Germany by these daring propositions. Some of the reformer's contemporaries, however, foresaw the serious consequences to which they might lead and the numerous obstacles they would encounter. They expressed their fears aloud, and rejoiced with trembling.

"I am much afraid," wrote Bernard Adelmann, to his friend Pirck-heimer, "that the worthy man must give way at last before the avarice and power of the partisans of indulgences. His representations have produced so little effect that the Bishop of Augsburg, our primate and metropolitan, has just ordered, in the pope's name, fresh indulgences for St. Peter's at Rome. Let him haste to secure the aid of princes; let him beware of tempting God; for he must be void of common sense if he overlooks the imminent peril he incurs." Adelmann was delighted on hearing it rumored that Henry VIII had invited Luther to England. "In that country," thought the canon, "he will be able to teach the truth in peace." Many thus imagined that the doctrine of the gospel required the support of the civil power. They knew not that it advances without this power, and is often trammeled and enfeebled by it.

Albert Kranz, the famous historian, was at Hamburg on his death-bed, when Luther's theses were brought to him: "Thou art right, brother Martin," said he, "but thou wilt not succeed. . . . Poor monk! Go to thy cell and cry: Lord! have mercy upon me!"

An aged priest of Hexter in Westphalia, having received and read the theses in his parsonage, shook his head and said in Low German: "Dear Brother Martin! if you succeed in overthrowing this purgatory and all these paper-dealers, you will be a fine fellow indeed!" Erbenius, who lived a century later, wrote the following doggerel under these words:

> "What would the worthy parson say,
> If he were living at this day?"

Not only did a great number of Luther's friends entertain fears as to this proceeding, but many even expressed their disapprobation.

The Bishop of Brandenburg, grieved at seeing so violent a quarrel break out in his diocese, would have desired to stifle it. He resolved to effect this by mildness. "In your theses on indulgences," said he to Luther, through the Abbot of Lenin, "I see nothing opposed to the Catholic truth; I myself condemn these indiscreet proclamations; but for the love of peace and for regard to your bishop, discontinue writing upon this subject." Luther was confounded at being addressed with such humility by so great a dignitary. Led away by the first impulse of his heart, he replied with emotion: "I consent: I would rather obey than perform miracles if that were possible."

The elector beheld with regret the commencement of a combat that was justifiable no doubt, but the results of which could not be foreseen. No prince was more desirous of maintaining the public peace than Frederick. Yet, what an immense conflagration might not be kindled by this spark! What violent discord, what rending of nations, might not this monkish quarrel produce! The elector gave Luther frequent intimations of the uneasiness he felt.

Even in his own order and in his own convent at Wittenberg, Luther met with disapprobation. The prior and sub-prior were terrified at the outcry made by Tetzel and his companions. They repaired trembling and alarmed to Brother Martin's cell, and said: "Pray do not bring disgrace upon our order! The other orders, and especially the Dominicans, are already overjoyed to think that they will not be alone in their shame." Luther was moved at these words; but he soon recovered, and replied: "Dear fathers! if this work be not of God, it will come to naught; but if it be, let it go forward." The prior and sub-prior made no answer. "The work is still going forward," added Luther, after recounting this anecdote, "and, God willing, it will go on better and better unto the end. Amen."

Luther had many other attacks to endure. At Erfurt, he was blamed for the violent and haughty manner in which he condemned the opinions of others: this is the reproach usually made against those men who possess that strength of conviction which proceeds from the Word of God. He was also accused of precipitation and levity.

"They require moderation in me," answered Luther, "and they trample it under foot in the judgment they pass on me! . . . We can always see the mote in our brother's eye, and we overlook the beam in our own. . . . Truth will not gain more by my rashness. I desire to know [continues he, addressing Lange] what errors you and your theologians have found in my theses? Who does not know that a man rarely puts forth any new idea without having some appearance of pride, and without being accused of exciting quarrels? If humility herself should undertake something new, her opponents would accuse her of pride! Why were Christ and all the martyrs put to death? Because they seemed to be proud contemners of the wisdom of the time, and because they advanced novelties, without having first humbly taken counsel of the oracles of the ancient opinions.

"Do not let the wise of our days expect from me humility, or rather hypocrisy, enough to ask their advice, before publishing what duty compels me to say. Whatever I do will be done, not by the prudence of men, but by the counsel of God. If the work be of God, who shall stop it? If it be not, who can forward it? Not my will, nor theirs, nor ours; but thy will, O Holy Father, which art in heaven."—What courage, what noble enthusiasm, what confidence in God, and above all, what truth in these words, and what truth for all ages!

The reproaches and accusations which were showered upon Luther from every quarter could not fail, however, to produce some impression on his mind. He had been deceived in his hopes. He had expected to see the heads of the Church and the most distinguished scholars in the nation publicly unite with him; but the case was far otherwise. A word of approbation which escaped in the first moment of astonishment was all the best-disposed accorded him; on the contrary, many whom he had hitherto respected the most, were loudest in their censure. He felt himself alone in the Church, alone against Rome, alone at the foot of that ancient and formidable building whose foundations penetrated to the center of the earth, whose walls soared to the clouds, and against which he had aimed so daring a blow. He was troubled and dispirited. Doubts, which he fancied he had overcome, returned to his mind with fresh force. He trembled at the thought that he had the whole authority of the Church against him: to withdraw from that authority, to be deaf to that voice which people had obeyed for centuries, to set himself in opposition to that Church which he had been accustomed from his infancy to venerate as the mother of the faithful . . . he, an insignificant monk . . . was an effort too great for human power! No step cost him dearer than this. And it was this, accordingly, which decided the Reformation.

No one can paint better than himself the combat in his own soul: "I began this business," said he, "with great fear and trembling. Who was I then, I, a poor, wretched, contemptible friar, more like a corpse than a man; who was I to oppose the majesty of the pope, before whom not only the kings of the earth and the whole world trembled, but even, if I may so speak, heaven and hell were constrained to obey the signal of his eyes? . . . No one can know what my heart suffered during these first two years, and into what despondency, I may say into what despair, I was sunk. Those haughty spirits who have since attacked the pope with such great hardihood can form no idea of it, although with all their skill they would have been unable to do him the least harm, if Jesus Christ had not already inflicted through me, His weak and unworthy instrument, a wound that shall never be healed. . . . But while they were content to look on and leave me alone in the danger, I was not so cheerful, so tranquil, nor so confident; for at that time I was ignorant of many things which now, thank God, I know. There were, it is true, many pious Christians who were pleased with my propositions, and valued them highly; but I could not acknowledge them and consider them as the instruments of the Holy Ghost; I looked only to the pope, to the cardinals, bishops, theologians, lawyers, monks, and priests. . . . It was from them I expected to witness the influence of the Spirit. However, after gaining the victory over all their arguments by Scripture, I at last surmounted through Christ's grace, but with great anguish, toil, and pain, the only argument that still checked me, namely, that I should 'Listen to the Church'; for, from the bottom of my heart, I reverenced the pope's Church as the true Church; and I did so with far more sincerity and veneration than all those scandalous and infamous corrupters who, to oppose me, now extol it so mightily. If I had despised the pope, as those men really despise him in their hearts who praise him so much with their lips, I should have trembled lest the earth should have instantly opened and swallowed me up alive like Korah and his company."

How honorable are these combats to Luther! What sincerity, what uprightness of mind they display! And by these painful assaults which he had to sustain from within and from without, he is rendered more worthy of our esteem than he would have been by an intrepidity unaccompanied by any such struggles. This travail of his soul clearly demonstrates the truth and divinity of his work. We see that the cause and the principle were both in heaven. Who will dare assert, after all the features we have pointed out, that the Reformation was a political affair? No; it was not the effect of man's policy, but of God's power. If Luther had been urged forward solely by human passions, he would have sunk under his fears; his errors, his scruples, would have smothered the fire kindled in his soul; and he would have shed upon the Church a mere passing ray, as many zealous pious men have done whose names have been handed down to us. But now God's time was come; the work could not be stopped; the emancipation of the Church must be accomplished.

Luther was appointed at least to prepare the way for that complete enfranchisement and those extensive developments which are promised to the reign of Jesus Christ. He experienced, accordingly, the truth of that glorious promise: "Even the youths shall faint and be weary and the young men shall utterly fall: but they that wait upon the Lord shall renew their strength; they shall mount up with wings as eagles." That divine power which filled the heart of the Wittenberg doctor, and which had impelled him to the combat, soon restored to him all his early resolution.

Chapter 15

"ALL TAUGHT OF GOD"

THE REPROACHES, the timidity, and the silence of his friends had discouraged Luther; the attacks of his enemies produced a contrary effect: this is a case of frequent occurrence. The adversaries of the truth, who hope by their violence to do their own work, are doing that of God Himself. Tetzel took up the gauntlet, but with a feeble hand. Luther's sermon, which had been for the people what the theses had been for the learned, was the object of his first reply. He refuted this discourse point by point, after his own fashion; he then announced that he was preparing to meet his adversary more fully in certain theses which he would maintain at the University of Frankfurt-on-the-Oder. "Then," said he, replying to the conclusion of Luther's sermon, "each man will be able to judge who is the heresiarch, heretic, schismatic; who is mistaken, rash, and slanderous. Then it will be clear to the eyes of all who it is that has a dull brain, that has never felt the Bible, never read the Christian doctrines, never understood his own doctors. . . . In support of the propositions I advance, I am ready to suffer all things—prisons, scourging, drowning, and the stake."

One thing struck us, as we read Tetzel's reply—the difference between the German employed by him and Luther. One might say they were several ages apart. A foreigner, in particular, sometimes finds it difficult to understand Tetzel, while Luther's language is almost entirely that of our own days. A comparison of their writings is sufficient to show that Luther is the creator of the German language. That is, no doubt, one of his least merits, but still it is one.

Luther replied without naming Tetzel; Tetzel had not named him.

But there was no one in Germany who could not write at the head of their publications the names they thought proper to conceal. Tetzel, in order to set a higher value upon his indulgences, endeavored to confound the repentance required by God with the penance imposed by the Church. Luther sought to clear up this point.

"To save words," said he, in his picturesque language, "I have thrown to the winds (which, besides, have more leisure than I) his other remarks, which are mere artificial flowers and dry leaves, and will content myself with examining the foundations of his edifice of burs.

"The penance imposed by the holy Father cannot be that required by Christ; for what the holy Father imposes he can dispense with; and if these two penances were one and the same thing, it would follow that the pope takes away what Christ imposes, and destroys the commandment of God. . . . Well! if he likes it, let him abuse me [continues Luther, after quoting other erroneous interpretations by Tetzel], let him call me heretic, schismatic, slanderer, and whatever he pleases: I shall not be his enemy for that, and I shall pray for him as for a friend. . . . But I cannot suffer him to treat the Holy Scriptures, our consolation (Rom. 15:4), as a sow treats a sack of oats."

We must accustom ourselves to find Luther sometimes making use of coarse expressions, and such as are too familiar for our age: it was the fashion of the times; and there will generally be found under these words, which would now shock the conventional usages of language, a strength and propriety which redeem their vulgarity. He thus continues:

"He who purchases indulgences, repeat our adversaries, does better than he who gives alms to a poor man who is not reduced to the last extremity. Now, should we hear the news that the Turks are profaning our churches and our crosses, we could hear it without shuddering; for we have in the midst of us the worst of Turks, who profane and annihilate the only real sanctuary, the Word of God, that sanctifieth all things. Let him who desires to follow this precept, beware of feeding the hungry, or of clothing the naked, before they die, and consequently have no more need of assistance."

It is important to compare Luther's zeal for good works with what he says on justification by faith. The man that has any experience and any knowledge of Christianity, does not require this new proof of a truth, the evidence of which he has himself felt: namely, the more we are attached to justification by faith, the more we see the necessity of works, and the more we become attached to their practice; while any laxity with regard to the doctrine of faith necessarily brings with it laxity of morals. Luther, and Saint Paul before him and Howard after him, are proofs of the first assertion; every man without faith, and there are many such in the world, is a proof of the second.

When Luther comes to Tetzel's invectives, he answers them in this manner: "When I hear these invectives, I fancy it is an ass braying at me. I am delighted with them, and I should be very sorry were such people to call me a good Christian." We must represent Luther as he was, with all his weaknesses. A turn for jesting, and even for coarse jesting, was one of them. The Reformer was a great man, a man of God, no doubt; but he was still a man and not an angel, and he was not even a perfect man. Who has the right to require perfection in him?

"Finally," added he, challenging his adversary to battle, "although it is not usual to burn heretics for such matters, here am I at Wittenberg, I, Doctor Martin Luther! Is there any inquisitor who is determined to chew iron and to blow up rocks? I beg to inform him that he has a safe-conduct to come hither, open gates, bed and board secured to him, and all by the gracious cares of our worthy prince, Duke Frederick, elector of Saxony, who will never protect heresy."

We see that Luther was not wanting in courage. He relied upon the Word of God; and it is a rock that never fails us in the storm. But God in His faithfulness afforded him other assistance. The burst of joy by which the multitude welcomed Luther's theses, had been soon followed by a gloomy silence. The learned had timidly retreated before the calumnies and abuse of indulgences, seeing them attacked at last, had not failed, by a contradiction that is by no means rare, to discover that the attack was unseasonable. The greater portion of the reformer's friends were alarmed. Many had fled away. But when the first terror was over, a contrary movement took place in their minds. The monk of Wittenberg, who for some time had been almost alone in the midst of the Church, soon gathered around him again a numerous body of friends and admirers.

There was one who, although timid, yet remained faithful during this crisis, and whose friendship was his consolation and support. This was Spalatin. Their correspondence was not interrupted. "I thank you," said Luther, speaking of a particular mark of friendship that he had received, "but what am I not indebted to you?" It was on November 11, 1517, eleven days after the publication of the theses, and consequently at the very time when the fermentation of men's minds was greatest, that Luther delighted thus to pour out his gratitude into his friend's heart. It is interesting to witness in this very letter to Spalatin, this strong man, who had just performed the bravest action, declaring whence all this strength was derived. "We can do nothing of ourselves: we can do everything by God's grace. All ignorance is invincible for us: no ignorance is invincible for the grace of God. The more we endeavor, of ourselves, to attain wisdom, the nearer we approach to folly. It is untrue that this invincible ignorance excuses the sinner; otherwise there would be no sin in the world."

Luther had not sent his propositions either to the prince or to any of his court. It would appear that the chaplain expressed some astonishment to his friend in consequence. "I was unwilling," replied Luther, "that my theses should reach our most illustrious prince, or any of his court, before they had been received by those who think themselves especially designated in them, for fear they should believe I had published them by the prince's order, or to conciliate his favor, and from opposition to the Bishop of Mentz. I understand there are many persons who dream such things. But now I can safely swear that my theses were published without the knowledge of Duke Frederick."

If Spalatin consoled his friend and supported him by his influence, Luther, on his part, endeavored to answer the questions put to him by the unassuming chaplain. Among others, the latter asked one that has been often proposed in our days: "What is the best method of studying Scripture?"

"As yet, most excellent Spalatin," Luther replied, "you have only asked me things that were in my power. But to direct you in the study of the Holy Scriptures is beyond my ability. If, however, you absolutely wish to know my method, I will not conceal it from you.

"It is very certain, that we cannot attain to the understanding of

Scripture either by study or by the intellect. Your first duty is to begin by prayer. Entreat the Lord to grant you, of His great mercy, the true understanding of His Word. There is no other interpreter of the Word of God than the Author of this Word, as He Himself has said: 'They shall be all taught of God.' Hope for nothing from your own labors, from your own understanding: trust solely in God, and in the influence of His Spirit. Believe this on the word of a man who has had experience." We here see how Luther arrived at the possession of the truth which he preached. It was not, as some pretend, by trusting to a presumptuous reason; it was not, as others maintain, by giving way to malignant passions. The purest, the sublimest, the holiest source—God Himself, consulted in humility, confidence, and prayer—was that at which he drank. But in our days he has found few imitators, and hence it is there are not many who understand him. To every serious mind these words of Luther's are of themselves a justification of the Reformation.

Luther found further consolation in the friendship of respectable laymen. Christopher Scheurl, the excellent secretary of the imperial city of Nuremberg, gave him the most affecting marks of his regard. We know how dear are the expressions of sympathy to a man's heart when he sees himself attacked on every side. The secretary of Nuremberg did still more: he desired to increase the number of Luther's friends, and with this intent requested him to dedicate one of his works to Jerome Ebner, a celebrated Nuremberg lawyer. "You entertain a high opinion of my studies," modestly answered the reformer; "but I have a very mean one of them. Nevertheless, I have desired to conform with your wishes. I have sought . . . but among all my stores, that I have never found so paltry before, nothing presented itself that did not appear utterly unworthy of being dedicated to so great a man by so mean a person as myself." Affecting humility! It is Luther who speaks, and it is to Doctor Ebner, whose name is unknown to us, that he compares himself. Posterity has not ratified this decision.

Luther, who had done nothing to circulate his theses, had not sent them to Scheurl any more than to the Elector and his court. The secretary of Nuremberg expressed his astonishment at this. "My design," answered Luther, "was not to give my theses such publicity. I only desired to confer on their contents with some of those who remain with us or near us. If they had been condemned, I would have destroyed them. If they had been approved of, I purposed publishing them. But they have now been printed over and over again, and circulated so far beyond all my hopes, that I repent of my offspring; not because I fear the truth should be made known to the people, 'twas this alone I sought; but that is not the way to instruct them. They contain questions that are still doubtful to me, and if I had thought my theses would have created such a sensation, there are some things I should have omitted, and others I should have asserted with greater confidence." In after years Luther thought differently. Far from fearing he had said too much, he declared that he ought to have said much more. But the apprehensions he manifested to Scheurl do honor to his sincerity. They show that he had no premeditated plan, no party spirit, no self-conceit, and that he sought for truth alone. When he had discovered it fully, he changed his tone. "You will find in my earlier writings," said he many years after, "that I very humbly conceded many things to the pope, and even important things, that now I regard and detest as abominable and blasphemous."

Scheurl was not the only respectable layman who, at this time, gave testimony of his friendship with Luther. The celebrated painter, Albert Durer, sent him a present, perhaps one of his pictures, and the doctor warmly expressed his gratitude for the kindness.

Thus Luther practically experienced the truth of these words of divine wisdom: "A friend loveth at all times; and a brother is born for adversity." But he remembered them also for others, and pleaded the cause of the whole nation. The elector had just imposed one tax, and there was talk of another, probably by the advice of his counselor Pfeffinger, against whom Luther often vented his biting sarcasms. The doctor boldly placed himself in the breach: "Let not your highness despise the prayer of a poor beggar," said he. "I beseech you, in God's name, not to impose a new tax. My heart was bruised as well as the hearts of many of those who are most devoted to you, when they saw how far the last had injured your good fame, and the popularity your highness enjoyed. It is true that the Lord has given you an exalted understanding, so that you see into these matters farther than I or your subjects can. But perhaps it is God's will that a mean understanding should instruct a greater, in order that no one should trust to himself, but solely in the Lord our God, whom I pray to preserve your health of body for our good, and your soul for eternal blessedness. Amen." Thus it is that the gospel, which calls upon us to honor kings, makes us also plead the cause of the people. To a nation it proclaims its duties, and reminds the prince of his subjects' rights. The voice of a Christian like Luther, resounding in the cabinet of a sovereign, might often supply the place of a whole assembly of legislators.

In this same letter, in which Luther addresses a severe lesson to the elector, he does not fear to make a request, or rather to remind him of a promise to give him a new coat. This freedom of Luther, at a time when he might fear he had displeased Frederick, does equal honor to the prince and to the reformer. "But if it is Pfeffinger who has charge of it," added he, "let him give it me in reality, not in protestations of friendship. He knows how to spin fine speeches, but they never produce good cloth." Luther imagined that by the faithful counsel he had given his prince, he had well earned his court-dress. But, however that may be, he had not received it two years after, and he asked for it again. This seems to indicate that Frederick was not so much influenced by Luther as has been supposed.

Chapter 16

TETZEL'S REPLY

Men's minds had thus recovered a little from their first alarm. Luther himself felt inclined to declare that his theses had not the scope attributed to them. New events might turn aside the general attention, and this blow aimed at the Romish doctrine be lost in air like so many others. But the partisans of Rome prevented the affair from ending thus. They fanned the flame instead of quenching it.

Tetzel and the Dominicans replied with insolence to the attack that had been made on them. Burning with the desire of crushing the impudent monk who had dared to trouble their commerce, and of conciliating the favor of the Roman pontiff, they uttered a cry of rage; they maintained that to attack the indulgence ordained by the pope was to attack the pope himself, and they summoned to their aid all the monks and divines of their school. Tetzel indeed felt that an adversary like Luther was too much for him alone. Greatly disconcerted at the doctor's attack, and exasperated to the highest degree, he quitted the vicinity of Wittenberg, and repaired to Frankfurt-on-the-Oder, where he arrived in the month of November, 1517. The university of this city, like that of Wittenberg, was of recent date; but it had been founded by the opposite party. Conrad Wimpina, an eloquent man, the ancient rival of Pollich of Mellerstadt, and one of the most distinguished theologians of the age, was a professor there. Wimpina cast an envious glance on the doctor and University of Wittenberg. Their reputation galled him. Tetzel requested him to answer Luther's theses, and Wimpina wrote two lists of antitheses, the object of the first being to defend the doctrine of indulgences, and the second, the authority of the pope.

On January 20, 1518, took place that disputation prepared so long beforehand, announced with so much pomp, and on which Tetzel founded such great hopes. On every side he had sounded a call for recruits. Monks had been sent from all the cloisters in the neighborhood, and they met to the number of about three hundred. Tetzel read his theses. They even contained this declaration, "that whoever says that the soul does not escape out of purgatory so soon as the money tinkles in the chest, is in error."

But above all, he put forward propositions according to which the pope seemed actually seated as God in the temple of God, according to the apostle's expression (II Thess. 2:4). It was convenient for this shameless trafficker to take shelter, with all his disorders and scandals, under the mantle of the pope.

He declared himself ready to maintain the following propositions before the numerous assembly by which he was surrounded:

3. "We should teach Christians that the pope, by the greatness of his power, is above the whole universal Church, and superior to the councils, and that we should implicitly obey his decrees.

4. "We should teach Christians that the pope alone has the right of deciding in all matters of Christian faith; that he alone and no one besides him has power to interpret the meaning of Scripture according to his own views, and to approve or condemn all the words or writings of other men.

5. "We should teach Christians that the judgment of the pope cannot err, in matters concerning the Christian faith, or which are necessary to the salvation of the human race.

6. "We should teach Christians that, in matters of faith, we should rely and repose more on the pope's sentiments, as made known by his decisions, than on the opinions of all the learned, which are derived merely from Scripture.

8. "We should teach Christians that those who injure the honor or dignity of the pope, are guilty of high treason, and deserve to be accursed.

17. "We should teach Christians that there are many things which the Church regards as indisputable articles of universal truth, although they are not to be found in the canon of the Bible or in the writings of the ancient doctors.

44. "We should teach Christians to regard as obstinate heretics all

who declare by their words, acts, or writings, that they will not retract their heretical propositions, even should excommunication after
excommunication fall upon them like hail or rain.

48. "We should teach Christians that those who protect the errors
of heretics, and who, by their authority, prevent them from being
brought before the judge who has a right to hear them, are excommunicated; that if in the space of a year they do not change their
conduct, they will be declared infamous, and cruelly punished with
divers chastisements, according to the law, and for a warning to other
men.

50. "We should teach Christians that those who scribble so many
books and waste so much paper, who dispute and preach publicly
and wickedly about oral confession, the satisfaction of works, the
rich and great indulgences of the Bishop of Rome, and his power;
that the persons who take part with those who preach or write such
things, who are pleased with their writings, and circulate them
among the people and over the world; that those who speak in private of these things, in a contemptuous and shameless manner,
should expect to incur the penalties before mentioned, and to precipitate themselves, and others with them, into eternal condemnation
at the judgment day, and into merited disgrace even in this world.
For 'if so much as a beast touch the mountain, it shall be stoned.'"

We see that Tetzel did not attack Luther only. He probably had
the Elector of Saxony in view in his 48th thesis. These propositions,
besides, savor strongly of the Dominican. To threaten every contra-
dictor with cruel punishments was the argument of an inquisitor, to
which there were no means of replying. The three hundred monks
whom Tetzel had collected stared and listened with admiration to
what he had said. The theologians of the university were too fearful
of being ranked with the abettors of heresy, or else were too strongly
attached to Wimpina's principles to attack openly the astonishing
theses that had just been read.

All this affair, about which there had been so much noise, seemed
then destined to be a mere sham fight; but among the crowd of
students present at the disputation was a youth about twenty years
of age, named John Knipstrow. He had read Luther's theses, and had
found them conformable to the doctrines of Scripture. Indignant at
beholding the truth publicly trodden under foot, without anyone ap-

pearing in its defense, this young man raised his voice, to the great astonishment of all the assembly, and attacked the presumptuous Tetzel. The poor Dominican, who had not reckoned on any opposition, was quite confused. After a few exertions, he deserted the field of battle, and gave way to Wimpina. The latter resisted more vigorously; but Knipstrow pressed him so closely, that to finish a struggle so unbecoming in his eyes, the president (Wimpina himself) declared the disputation over, and immediately proceeded to confer the degree of doctor upon Tetzel in recompense of this glorious combat. In order to get rid of the young orator, Wimpina had him sent to the convent of Pyritz in Pomerania, with an order that he should be strictly watched. But this dawning light was removed from the banks of the Oder, only to diffuse not long after a greater brilliancy throughout Pomerania. When God thinks fit, He employs even learners to confound the teachers.

Tetzel, wishing to retrieve the check he had experienced, had recourse to the *ultima ratio* of Rome and of the inquisitors—to fire. He caused a pulpit and a scaffold to be erected in one of the public walks in the environs of Frankfurt. Thither he repaired in solemn procession, with his insignia of inquisitor of the faith. He gave vent to all his violence from the pulpit. He hurled thunderbolts and exclaimed with his stentorian voice that the heretic Luther deserved to suffer death at the stake. Next, placing the doctor's propositions and sermon on the scaffold, he burnt them. He knew better how to do this than to maintain his theses. At this time he met with no gainsayers: his victory was complete. The impudent Dominican re-entered Frankfurt in triumph. When powerful parties are vanquished, they have recourse to certain demonstrations, which we may well accord to them as some consolation for their disgrace.

These second theses of Tetzel's form an important epoch in the Reformation. They changed the ground of dispute: they transported it from the indulgence-markets to the halls of the Vatican, and diverted it from Tetzel to the pope. In the place of that despicable broker whom Luther had so firmly grasped, they substituted the sacred person of the head of the Church. Luther was filled with astonishment. It is probable that he would erelong have taken this step himself; but his enemies spared him the trouble. It was henceforward no question of a discredited traffic, but of Rome itself; and the blow by which a daring hand had tried to demolish Tetzel's shop shook the very foundations of the pontifical throne.

Tetzel's theses served as a rallying cry to the troops of Rome. An uproar against Luther broke out among the monks, infuriated at the appearance of a more formidable adversary than either Reuchlin or Erasmus. Luther's name resounded everywhere from the pulpits of the Dominicans, who addressed themselves to the passions of the people. They called the bold doctor a madman, a seducer, and a demoniac. His doctrine was cried down as the most horrible heresy. "Only wait a fortnight, or a month at most," said they, "and this notorious heretic will be burned." If it had depended solely on the Dominicans, the fate of Jerome and of Huss would soon have been that of the Saxon doctor also; but God was watching over him. His life was destined to accomplish what the ashes of the Bohemian reformer had begun; for each does the work of God, one by his death, the other by his life. Many began to exclaim that the whole University of Wittenberg was deeply tainted with heresy, and pronounced it infamous. "Let us drive out that villain and all his partisans," continued they. In many places these cries succeeded in exciting the passions of the multitude. The public attention was directed against those who shared Luther's opinions; and wherever the monks were the strongest, the friends of the gospel experienced the effects of their hatred. It was thus, with regard to the Reformation, that our Saviour's prophecy began to be accomplished: "Men will revile you, and persecute you, and say all manner of evil against you falsely, for my sake." In every age this is the recompense bestowed by the world on the decided friends of the gospel.

When Luther was informed of Tetzel's theses, and of the general attack of which they were the signal, his courage immediately took fire. He felt the necessity of opposing such adversaries face to face; and his intrepid soul had no difficulty in coming to such a decision. But at the same time their weakness revealed to him his own strength, and inspired him with the consciousness of what he really was.

He did not, however, give way to those sentiments of pride so natural to man's heart. "I have more difficulty to refrain from despising my adversaries," wrote he about this time to Spalatin, "and from sinning in this way against Jesus Christ, than I should have in conquering them. They are so ignorant of human and divine things that it is disgraceful to have to fight against them. And yet it is this very ignorance which gives them their inconceivable arrogance and their brazen face." But the strongest encouragement to his heart, in the midst of this general hostility, was the intimate conviction that his cause was that of truth. "Do not be surprised," wrote he to Spalatin at the beginning of 1518, "that I am so grossly insulted. I listen to their abuse with joy. If they did not curse me, we could not be so firmly assured that the cause I have undertaken is that of God Himself. Christ has been set up for a sign to be spoken against. . . . I know [said he on another occasion] that from the very beginning of the world, the Word of God has been of such a nature, that whoever desired to publish it to the world has been compelled, like the apostles, to abandon all things, and to expect death. If it were not so it would not be the Word of Jesus Christ." This peace in the midst of agitation is a thing unknown to the heroes of the world. We see men who are at the head of a government, or of a political party, sink under their toils and vexations. The Christian generally acquires new vigor in his struggle. It is because he possesses a mysterious source of repose and of courage unknown to him whose eyes are closed against the gospel.

One thing, however, sometimes agitated Luther: the thought of the dissensions his courageous opposition might produce. He knew that a single word might set the world on fire. At times his imagination beheld prince arrayed against prince, and perhaps people against people. His patriotic heart was saddened; his Christian charity alarmed. He would have desired peace; and yet he must speak, for such was the Lord's will. "I tremble," said he, "I shudder at the idea that I may be an occasion of discord between such mighty princes."

He still kept silence with regard to Tetzel's propositions concerning the pope. Had he been carried away by passion, he would, no doubt, have instantly fallen upon that astonishing doctrine, under the shelter of which his adversary sought to protect himself. But he did not; and in his delay, his reserve and silence, there is something grave and solemn, which sufficiently reveals the spirit that animated him. He waited, but not from weakness: for the blow was all the stronger.

Tetzel, after his auto-da-fe (pronouncement of judgment) at Frankfurt, had hastened to send his theses into Saxony. They would serve as an antidote (he thought) against Luther's. A man from

Halle, commissioned by the inquisitor to circulate his theses, arrived at Wittenberg. The students of the university, still indignant that Tetzel should have burned their master's propositions, had scarcely heard of his arrival before they sought him out, surrounded him, mobbed and frightened him. "How can you dare bring such things here?" said they. Some of them bought part of the copies he had with him, others seized the remainder. They thus became masters of his whole stock, amounting to eight hundred copies; and then, unknown to the elector, the senate, the rector, Luther, and all the professors, they posted the following words on the university boards: "Whoever desires to be present at the burning and funeral of Tetzel's theses, must come to the market place at two o'clock."

Crowds assembled at the appointed hour, and the Dominican's propositions were consigned to the flames in the midst of noisy acclamations. One copy escaped the conflagration, which Luther sent afterwards to his friend Lange of Erfurt. These generous but imprudent youths followed the precept of the ancients, "Eye for eye, and tooth for tooth," and not that of Jesus Christ. But when doctors and professors set the example at Frankfurt, can we be astonished that it was followed by young students at Wittenberg? The news of this academical execution soon spread through all Germany, and made a great disturbance. Luther was deeply pained at it.

"I am surprised," wrote he to his old master, Jodocus, at Erfurt, "you should have believed I allowed Tetzel's theses to be burned! Do you think I have so taken leave of my senses? But what could I do? When I am concerned, everybody believes whatever is told of me. Can I stop the mouths of the whole world? Well! let them say, hear, and believe whatever they like concerning me. I shall work so long as God gives me strength, and with His help I shall fear nothing. . . . What will come of it [said he to Lange] I know not, except that the peril in which I am involved becomes greater on this very account." This act shows how the hearts of the young already glowed for the cause which Luther defended. This was a sign of great importance; for a movement which has taken place among the youth is soon of necessity propagated throughout the whole nation.

The theses of Tetzel and of Wimpina, although little esteemed, produced a certain effect. They aggravated the dispute; they widened the rent in the mantle of the Church; they brought questions of the highest interest into the controversy. The chiefs of the Church began, accordingly, to take a nearer view of the matter and to declare strongly against the Reformer. "Truly, I do not know on whom Luther relies," said the Bishop of Brandenburg, "since he thus ventures to attack the power of the bishops." Perceiving that this new conjuncture called for new measures, the bishop came himself to Wittenberg. But he found Luther animated with that interior joy which springs from a good conscience, and determined to give battle. The bishop saw that the Augustine monk obeyed a power superior to his own, and he returned in anger to Brandenburg. One day during the winter of 1518, as he was seated before the fire, he said, turning to those who surrounded him: "I will not lay my head down in peace, until I have thrown Martin into the fire, like this brand"; and he flung the billet into the flames. The revolution of the sixteenth century was not destined to be accomplished by the heads of the Church, any more than that of the first century had been by the Sanhedrim and by the synagogue. The chiefs of the clergy in the sixteenth century were opposed to Luther, to the Reformation, and to its ministers, as they had been to Jesus Christ, to the gospel, to His apostles, and, as too frequently happens, in every age, to the truth.—"The bishops," said Luther, speaking of the visit the prelate of Brandenburg had paid him, "begin to perceive that they ought to have done what I am doing, and they are ashamed of it. They call me proud and arrogant—I will not deny that I am so; but they are not the people to know either what God is, or what we are."

Chapter 17

OBELISKS AND ASTERISKS

A MORE FORMIDABLE resistance than that made by Tetzel was already opposed to Luther. Rome had answered. A reply had gone forth from the walls of the sacred palace. It was not Leo X who had condescended to speak of theology: " 'Tis a mere monkish squabble," he said one day; "the best way is not to meddle with it." And at another time he observed, "It is a drunken German that has written these theses: when the perfumes have passed off, he will talk very differently." A Roman Dominican, Sylvester Mazzolini of Prierio or Prierias, master of the sacred palace, filled the office of censor, and it was in this capacity that he first became acquainted with the theses of the Saxon monk.

A Romish censor and Luther's theses, what a contrast! Freedom of speech, freedom of inquiry, freedom of belief, come into collision in the city of Rome with that power which claims to hold in its hands the monopoly of intelligence, and to open and shut at pleasure the mouth of Christendom. The struggle of Christian liberty which engenders children of God, with pontifical despotism which produces slaves of Rome, is typified, as it were, in the first days of the Reformation, in the encounter of Luther and Prierio.

The Roman censor, prior-general of the Dominicans, empowered to decide on what Christendom should profess or conceal, and on what it ought to know or be ignorant of, hastened to reply. He published a writing, which he dedicated to Leo X. In it he spoke contemptuously of the German monk, and declared with Romish assurance "that he should like to know whether this Martin had an iron nose or a brazen head, which cannot be broken!" And then, under the form of a dialogue, he attacked Luther's theses, employing by turns ridicule, insult, and menaces.

This combat between the Augustine of Wittenberg and the Dominican of Rome was waged on the very question that is the principle of the Reformation, namely: "What is the sole infallible authority for Christians?" Here is the system of the Church, as set forth by its most independent organs:

The letter of the written Word is dead without the spirit of interpretation, which alone reveals its hidden meaning. Now, this spirit is not given to every Christian, but to the Church—that is, to the priests. It is great presumption to say that He who promised the Church to be with her always, even to the end of the world, could have abandoned her to the power of error. It will be said, perhaps, that the doctrine and constitution of the Church are no longer such as we find them in the sacred oracles. Undoubtedly: but this change is only in appearance; it extends only to the form and not to the substance. We may go further: this change is progressive. The vivifying power of the divine Spirit has given a reality to what in Scripture was merely an idea; it has filled up the outline of the Word; it has put a finishing touch to its rude sketches; it has completed the work of which the Bible only gave the first rough draft. We must therefore understand the sense of the Holy Scriptures as settled by the Church, under the guidance of the Holy Spirit. From this point the Catholic doctors diverge. General councils, said some (and Gerson was one of them), are the representatives of the Church. The pope, said others, is the depositary of the spirit of interpretation, and no one has a right to understand the Scriptures otherwise than as decreed by the Roman pontiff. This was the opinion of Prierio.

Such was the doctrine opposed by the master of the sacred palace to the infant Reformation. He put forward propositions, on the power of the Church and of the pope, at which the most shameless flatterers of the Church of Rome would have blushed. Here is one of the principles he advanced at the head of his writing: "Whoever relies not on the teaching of the Roman Church, and of the Roman pontiff, as the infallible rule of faith, from which the Holy Scriptures themselves derive their strength and their authority, is a heretic."

Then, in a dialogue in which Luther and Mazzolini are the speakers, the latter seeks to refute the doctor's propositions. The opinions of the Saxon monk were altogether strange to a Roman censor; and accordingly, Mazzolini shows that he understood neither the emotions of his heart, nor the springs of his conduct. He measured the doctor of the truth by the petty standard of the servants of Rome. "My dear Luther," said he, "if you were to receive from our lord the pope a good bishopric and a plenary indulgence for repairing your Church, you would sing in a softer strain, and you would extol the indulgences you are now disparaging!" The Italian, so proud of his elegant manners, occasionally assumes the most scurrilous tone: "If it is the nature of dogs to bite," said he to Luther, "I fear you had a dog for your father." The Dominican at last wonders at his own condescension in speaking to the rebellious monk; and ends by showing his adversary the cruel teeth of an inquisitor. "The Roman Church," says he, "the apex of whose spiritual and temporal power is in the pope, may constrain by the secular arm those who, having once received the faith, afterward go astray. It is not bound to employ reason to combat and vanquish rebels."

These words, traced by the pen of a dignitary of the Roman court, were very significant. Still, they did not frighten Luther. He believed, or feigned to believe, that this dialogue was not written by Mazzolini, but by Ulric Hütten, or by another of the contributors to the *Letters of some Obscure Men;* who, said he, in his satirical humor, and in order to excite Luther against Prierio, had compiled this mass of absurdities. He had no desire to behold the See of Rome excited against him. However, after having kept silence for some time, his doubts (if he had any) were dispelled: he set to work, and his answer was ready in two days.

The Bible had moulded the reformer and begun the Reformation. Luther needed not the testimony of the Church in order to believe. His faith had come from the Bible itself; from within and not from without. He was so intimately convinced that the evangelical doctrine was immovably founded on the Word of God that in his eyes all external authority was useless. This experiment made by Luther opened a new futurity to the Church. The living source that had welled forth for the monk of Wittenberg was to become a river to slake the thirst of nations.

In order that we may comprehend the Word, the Spirit of God must give understanding, said the Church; and it was right so far.

But its error had been in considering the Holy Spirit as a monopoly accorded to a certain class, and supposing that it could be confined exclusively within assemblies or colleges, in a city or in a conclave. "The wind bloweth where it listeth," said the Son of God, speaking of God's Spirit; in another place "they shall be all taught of God." The corruption of the Church, the ambition of the pontiffs, the passions of the councils, the quarrels of the clergy, the pomp of the prelates, had banished far from the sacerdotal abodes that Holy Ghost, that Spirit of humility and peace. It had deserted the assemblies of the proud, the palaces of the mighty ones of the Church, and had taken up its dwelling with simple Christians and humble priests. It had fled from a domineering hierarchy, that had often trampled under foot and shed the blood of the poor; from a proud and ignorant clergy, whose chiefs were better skilled in using the sword than the Bible; and dwelt at one time with despised sects, and at another with men of intelligence and learning. The holy cloud, that had departed from the sumptuous basilics and proud cathedrals, had descended into the obscure abodes of the humble, or into the quiet studies, those tranquil witnesses of a conscientious inquiry. The Church, degraded by its love of power and of riches, dishonored in the eyes of the people by the venal use it made of the doctrine of life; the Church, which sold salvation to replenish the treasuries drained by its haughtiness and debauchery,—had forfeited all respect, and sensible men no longer attached any value to her testimony. Despising so debased an authority, they joyfully turned towards the divine Word, and to its infallible authority, as toward the only refuge remaining to them in such a general disorder.

The age, therefore, was prepared. The bold movement by which Luther changed the resting place of the sublimest hopes of the human heart, and with a hand of power transported them from the walls of the Vatican to the rock of the Word of God, was saluted with enthusiasm. This is the work that the reformer had in view in his reply to Prierio.

He passed over the principles which the Dominican had set forth in the beginning of his work: "But," said he, "following your example, I will also lay down certain fundamental principles.

"The first is this expression of St. Paul: 'Though we, or an angel

from heaven, preach any other gospel unto you than that which we
have preached unto you, let him be accursed.'

"The second is this passage from St. Augustine to St. Jerome: 'I
have learned to render to the canonical books alone the honor of
believing most firmly that none of them has erred; as for the others,
I do not believe in what they teach, simply because it is they who
teach them.'"

Here we see Luther laying down with a firm hand the essential
principles of the Reformation: the Word of God, the whole Word of
God, nothing but the Word of God. "If you clearly understand these
points," continues he, "you will also understand that your Dialogue
is wholly overturned by them; for you have only brought forward the
expressions and the opinions of St. Thomas." Then, attacking his
adversary's axioms, he frankly declares that he believes popes and
councils can err. He complains of the flatteries of the Roman courtiers, who ascribe both temporal and spiritual power to the pope. He
declares that the Church exists virtually in Christ alone, and repre-
sentatively in the councils. And then coming to Prierio's insinuation:
"No doubt you judge of me after yourself," said he, "but if I aspired
to an episcopal station, of a surety I should not use the language that
is so grating to your ears. Do you imagine I am ignorant how bishoprics and the priesthood are obtained at Rome? Do not the very
children sing in the streets those well-known words:—

> "'Of all foul spots the world around,
> The foulest spot in Rome is found.'"

Such songs as these had been current at Rome before the election
of one of the latter popes. Nevertheless, Luther speaks of Leo with
respect: "I know," said he, "that we may compare him to Daniel in
Babylon; his innocence has often endangered his life." He concludes
by a few words in reply to Prierio's threats: "Finally, you say that the
pope is at once pontiff and emperor, and that he is mighty to compel
obedience by the secular arm. Do you thirst for blood? . . . I protest that you will not frighten me either by your rodomontades (brag-
gings) or by the threatening noise of your words. If I am put to death,
Christ lives, Christ my Lord, and the Lord of all, blessed for evermore. Amen."

Thus, with a firm hand, Luther erected against the infidel altar of the papacy the altar of the only infallible and Holy Word of God, before which he desired every knee to bow, and on which he declared himself ready to offer up his life.

Prierio published an answer, and then a third book, *On the Irrefragable Truth of the Church and of the Roman Pontiff*, in which, relying upon the ecclesiastical law, he asserted that although the pope should make the whole world go with him to hell, he could neither be condemned nor deposed. The pope was at last obliged to impose silence on Prierio.

A new adversary erelong entered the lists; he also was a Dominican. James Hochstraten, inquisitor at Cologne, whom we have already seen opposing Reuchlin and the friends of letters, shuddered at Luther's boldness. It was necessary for monkish darkness and fanaticism to come in contact with him who was destined to give them a mortal blow. Monachism had sprung up as the primitive truth began to disappear. Since then, monks and errors grew up side by side. The man had now appeared who was to accelerate their ruin; but these robust champions could not abandon the field of battle without a struggle. It lasted all the reformer's life; but in Hochstraten this combat is singularly personified: Hochstraten and Luther; the free and courageous Christian with the impetuous slave of monkish superstitions! Hochstraten lost his temper, grew furious, and called loudly for the heretic's death. . . . It is by the stake he wished to secure the triumph of Rome. "It is high treason against the Church," exclaimed he, "to allow so horrible a heretic to live one hour longer. Let the scaffold be instantly erected for him!" This murderous advice was, alas! but too effectually carried out in many countries; the voices of numerous martyrs, as in the primitive times of the Church, gave testimony to the truth, even in the midst of flames. But in vain were the sword and the stake invoked against Luther. The Angel of the Lord kept watch continually around him and preserved him.

Luther answered Hochstraten in few words, but with great energy: "Go," said he in conclusion, "go, thou raving murderer, who criest for the blood of thy brethren; it is my earnest desire that thou forbearest to call me Christian and faithful, and that thou continuest, on the contrary, to decry me as a heretic. Understandest thou these things, blood-thirsty man! enemy of the truth! and if thy mad rage should hurry thee to undertake anything against me, take care to act with circumspection, and to choose thy time well. God knows what is my purpose, if He grant me life. . . . My hope and my expectation, God willing, will not deceive me." Hochstraten was silent.

A more painful attack awaited the reformer. Doctor Eck, the celebrated professor of Ingolstadt, the deliverer of Urban Regius, and Luther's friend, had received the famous theses. Eck was not a man to defend the abuse of indulgences; but he was a doctor of the schools and not of the Bible; well-versed in the scholastic writings, but not in the Word of God. If Prierio had represented Rome, if Hochstraten had represented the monks, Eck represented the schoolmen. The schools, which for five centuries past had domineered over Christendom, far from giving way at the first blow of the reformer, rose up haughtily to crush the man who dared pour out upon them the floods of his contempt. Eck and Luther, the School and the Word, had more than one struggle; but it was now that the combat began.

Eck could not but find errors in many of Luther's positions. Nothing leads us to doubt the sincerity of his convictions. He as enthusiastically maintained the scholastic opinions, as Luther did the declarations of the Word of God. We may even suppose that he felt no little pain when he found himself obliged to oppose his old friend; it would seem, however, from the manner of his attack, that passion and jealousy had some share in his motives.

He gave the name of *Obelisks* to his remarks against Luther's theses. Desirous at first of saving appearances, he did not publish his work, but was satisfied with communicating it confidentially to his ordinary, the Bishop of Eichstadt. But the *Obelisks* were soon extensively circulated, either through the indiscretion of the bishop or by the doctor himself. A copy fell into the hands of Link, a friend of Luther and preacher at Nuremberg. The latter hastened to send it to the reformer. Eck was a far more formidable adversary than Tetzel, Prierio, or Hochstraten: the more his work surpassed theirs in learning and in subtlety, the more dangerous it was. He assumed a tone of compassion towards his "feeble adversary," being well aware that pity inflicts more harm than anger. He insinuated that Luther's propositions circulated the Bohemian poison, that they savored of Bohemia, and by these malicious allusions, he drew upon Luther the unpopularity and hatred attached in Germany to the name of Huss and to the schismatics of his country.

The malice that pervaded this treatise exasperated Luther; but the thought that this blow came from an old friend grieved him still more. Is it then at the cost of his friend's affections that he must uphold the truth? Luther poured out the deep sorrow of his heart in a letter to Egranus, pastor at Zwickau. "In the *Obelisks* I am styled a venomous man, a Bohemian, a heretic, a seditious, insolent, rash person. . . . I pass by the milder insults, such as drowsy-headed, stupid, ignorant, contemner of the sovereign pontiff, etc. This book is brimful of the blackest outrages. Yet he who penned them is a distinguished man, with a spirit full of learning, and a learning full of spirit; and, what causes me the deepest vexation, he is a man who was united to me by a great and recently contracted friendship: it is John Eck, doctor of divinity, chancellor of Ingolstadt, a man celebrated and illustrious by his writings. If I did not know Satan's thoughts, I should be astonished at the fury which has led this man to break off so sweet and so new a friendship, and that, too, without warning me, without writing to me, without saying a single word."

But if Luther's heart was wounded, his courage was not cast down. On the contrary, he rose up invigorated for the contest. "Rejoice, my brother," said he to Egranus, whom a violent enemy had likewise attacked, "rejoice, and do not let these flying leaves affright thee. The more my adversaries give way to their fury, the farther I advance. I leave the things that are behind me, in order that they may bay at them, and I pursue what lies before me, that they may bay at them in their turn."

Eck was aware how disgraceful his conduct had been, and endeavored to vindicate himself in a letter to Carlstadt. In it he styled Luther "their common friend," and cast all the blame on the Bishop of Eichstadt, at whose solicitation he pretended to have written his work. He said that it had not been his intention to publish the *Obelisks*; that he would have felt more regard for the bonds of friendship that united him to Luther; and demanded in conclusion, that Luther, instead of disputing publicly with him, should turn his weapons against the Frankfurt divines. The professor of Ingolstadt, who had not feared to strike the first blow, began to be alarmed when he reflected on the strength of that adversary whom he had so imprudently attacked. Willingly would he have eluded the struggle; but it was too late.

All these fine phrases did not persuade Luther, who was yet inclined to remain silent. "I will swallow patiently," said he, "this sop, worthy of Cerberus." But his friends differed from him: they solicited, they even constrained him to answer. He therefore replied to the *Obelisks* by his *Asterisks,* opposing (as he said, playing on the words) to the rust and livid hue of the Ingolstadt doctor's *Obelisks,* the light and dazzling brightness of the stars of heaven. In this work he treated his adversary with less severity than he had shown his previous antagonists; but his indignation pierced through his words.

He showed that in these chaotic *Obelisks* there was nothing from the Holy Scriptures, nothing from the Fathers of the Church, nothing from the ecclesiastical canons; that they were filled with scholastic glosses, opinions, mere opinions and empty dreams; in a word, the very things that Luther had attacked. The *Asterisks* are full of life and animation. The author is indignant at the errors of his friend's book; but he pities the man. He professes anew the fundamental principle which he laid down in his answer to Prierio: "The supreme pontiff is a man, and may be led into error; but God is truth, and cannot err." Farther on, employing the *argumentum ad hominem* (argument founded on the principles of an opponent himself) against the scholastic doctor, he says to him, "It would be great impudence assuredly for anyone to teach in the philosophy of Aristotle, what he cannot prove by the authority of that ancient author.—You grant it. —It is, *a fortiori* (all the more) the most impudent of all impudence to affirm in the Church and among Christians what Christ Himself has not taught. Now, where is it found in the Bible that the treasure of Christ's merits is in the hands of the pope?"

He adds further: "As for the malicious reproach of Bohemian heresy, I bear this calumny with patience through love of Christ. I live in a celebrated university, in a well-famed city, in a respectable bishopric, in a powerful duchy, where all are orthodox, and where, undoubtedly, so wicked a heretic would not be tolerated."

Luther did not publish the *Asterisks;* he communicated them solely to his friends. They were not given to the public till long after.

This rupture between the two doctors of Ingolstadt and Wittenberg made a great sensation in Germany. They had many friends in common. Scheurl especially, who appears to have been the man by whom the two doctors had been connected, was alarmed. He was one of those who desired to see a thorough reform in the German church by means of its most distinguished organs. But if, at the very outset, the most eminent theologians of the day should fall to blows; if, while Luther came forward with novelties, Eck became the representative of antiquity, what disruption might not be feared! Would not numerous partisans rally round each of these two chiefs, and would not two hostile camps be formed in the bosom of the empire?

Scheurl endeavored therefore to reconcile Eck and Luther. The latter declared his willingness to forget everything; that he loved the genius, that he admired the learning of Doctor Eck, and that what his old friend had done had caused him more pain than anger. "I am ready," said he to Scheurl, "for peace and for war: but I prefer peace. Apply yourself to the task; grieve with us that the devil has thrown among us this beginning of discord, and afterwards rejoice that Christ in His mercy has crushed it." About the same time he wrote Eck a letter full of affection: but Eck made no reply; he did not even send him any message. It was no longer a season for reconciliation. The contest daily grew warmer. Eck's pride and implacable spirit soon broke entirely the last ties of that friendship.

Chapter 18

LUTHER AT HEIDELBERG

MEANWHILE it had become necessary for the fire that had been lighted at Wittenberg to be kindled in other places. Luther, not content with announcing the gospel truth in the place of his residence, both to the students of the academy and to the people, was desirous of scattering elsewhere the seed of sound doctrine. In the spring of 1518, a general chapter of the Augustine order was to be held at Heidelberg. Luther was summoned to it as one of the most distinguished men of the order. His friends did all they could to dissuade him from undertaking this journey. In truth, the monks had endeavored to render Luther's name odious in all the places through which he would have to pass. To insults they added menaces. It would require but little to excite a popular tumult on his journey of which he might be the victim. "Or else," said his friends, "they will effect by fraud and stratagem, what they dare not do by violence." But Luther never suffered himself to be hindered in the accomplishment of a duty by the fear of danger, however imminent. He therefore closed his ears to the timid observations of his friends: he pointed to Him in whom he trusted, and under whose guardianship he was ready to undertake so formidable a journey. Immediately after the festival of Easter, he set out calmly on foot, April 13, 1518.

He took with him a guide named Urban, who carried his little baggage, and who was to accompany him as far as Wurtzburg. What thoughts must have crowded into the heart of this servant of the Lord during his journey! At Weissenfels, the pastor, whom he did not know, immediately recognized him as the Wittenberg doctor, and gave him a hearty welcome. At Erfurt, two other brothers of the

Augustine order joined them. At Judenbach, they fell in with the elector's personal councilor, Degenhard Pfeffinger, who entertained them at the inn where they had found him. "I had the pleasure," wrote Luther to Spalatin, "of making this rich lord a few groats poorer; you know how I like on every opportunity to levy contributions on the rich for the benefit of the poor, especially if the rich are my friends." He reached Coburg, overwhelmed with fatigue. "All goes well, by God's grace," wrote he, "except that I acknowledge having sinned in undertaking this journey on foot. But for that sin I have no need, I think, of the remission of indulgences; for my contrition is perfect, and the satisfaction plenary. I am overcome with fatigue, and all the conveyances are full. Is not this enough, and more than enough, of penance, contrition, and satisfaction?"

The reformer of Germany, unable to find room in the public conveyances, and no one being willing to give up his place, was compelled, notwithstanding his weariness, to leave Coburg the next morning humbly on foot. He reached Wurtzburg the second Sunday after Easter, toward evening. Here he sent back his guide.

In this city resided the Bishop of Bibra, who had received his theses with so much approbation. Luther was the bearer of a letter to him from the Elector of Saxony. The bishop, delighted at the opportunity of becoming personally acquainted with this bold champion of the truth, immediately invited him to the episcopal palace. He went and met him at the door, conversed affectionately with him, and offered to provide him with a guide to Heidelberg. But at Wurtzburg Luther had met his two friends, the vicar-general Staupitz, and Lange, the prior of Erfurt, who had offered him a place in their carriage. He therefore thanked Bibra for his kindness; and on the morrow the three friends quitted Wurtzburg. They thus traveled together for three days, conversing with one another. On April 21 they arrived at Heidelberg. Luther went and lodged at the Augustine convent.

The Elector of Saxony had given him a letter for the Count Palatine Wolfgang, duke of Bavaria. Luther repaired to his magnificent castle, the situation of which excites the admiration of strangers. The monk from the plains of Saxony had a heart to admire the situation of Heidelberg, where the two beautiful valleys of the Rhine and the Neckar unite. He delivered his letter to James Simler, steward of the household. The latter on reading it observed: "In truth you have here a valuable letter of credit." The count-palatine received Luther with much kindness, and frequently invited him to his table, together with Lange and Staupitz. So friendly a reception was a source of great comfort to Luther. "We were very happy, and amused one another with agreeable and pleasant conversation," said he; "eating and drinking, examining all the beauties of the palatine palace, admiring the ornaments, arms, cuirasses (armor); everything remarkable contained in this celebrated and truly regal castle."

But Luther had another task to perform. Having arrived at a university which exercised great influence over the west and south of Germany, he was there to strike a blow that should shake the churches of these countries. He began, therefore, to write some theses which he purposed maintaining in a public disputation. Such discussions were not unusual; but Luther felt that this one, to be useful, should lay forcible hold upon men's minds. His disposition, besides, naturally led him to present truth under a paradoxical form. The professors of the university would not permit the discussion to take place in their large theater; and Luther was obliged to take a hall in the Augustine convent. April 26 was the day appointed for the disputation.

Heidelberg, at a later period, received the evangelical doctrine: those who were present at the conference in the convent might have foreseen that it would one day bear fruit.

Luther's reputation attracted a large audience; professors, students, courtiers, citizens, came in crowds. The following are some of the doctor's *Paradoxes*; for so he designated his theses. Perhaps even in our days they would still bear this name; it would, however, be easy to translate them into obvious propositions:

"1. The law of God is a salutary doctrine of life. Nevertheless, it cannot aid man in attaining to righteousness; on the contrary, it impedes him.

"3. Man's works, however fair and good they may be, are, however, to all appearance, nothing but deadly sins.

"4. God's works, however unsightly and bad they may appear, have however an everlasting merit.

"7. The works of the righteous themselves would be mortal sins, unless, being filled with a holy reverence for the Lord, they feared that their works might in truth be mortal sins.

"9. To say that works done out of Christ are truly dead, but not deadly, is a dangerous forgetfulness of the fear of God.

"13. Since the fall of man, free will is but an idle word; and if man does all he can, he still sins mortally.

"16. A man who imagines to arrive at grace by doing all that he is able to do, adds sin to sin, and is doubly guilty.

"18. It is certain that man must altogether despair of himself, in order to be made capable of receiving Christ's grace.

"21. A theologian of the world calls evil good, and good evil; but a theologian of the cross teaches aright on the matter.

"22. The wisdom which endeavors to learn the invisible perfections of God in His works, puffs up, hardens, and blinds a man.

"23. The law calls forth God's anger, kills, curses, accuses, judges, and condemns whatsoever is not in Christ.

"24. Yet this wisdom is not evil; and the law is not to be rejected; but the man who studies not the knowledge of God under the cross, turns to evil whatever is good.

"25. That man is not justified who performs many works; but he who, without works, has much faith in Christ.

"26. The law says, Do this! and what it commands is never done. Grace says, Believe in Him! and immediately all things are done.

"28. The love of God finds nothing in man, but creates in him what He loves. The love of man proceeds from his Well-Beloved."

Five doctors of divinity attacked these theses. They had read them with all the astonishment that novelty excites. Such theology appeared very extravagant; and yet they discussed these points, according to Luther's own testimony, with a courtesy that inspired him with much esteem for them, but at the same time with earnestness and discernment. Luther, on his side, displayed wonderful mildness in his replies, unrivaled patience in listening to the objections of his adversaries, and all the quickness of St. Paul in solving the difficulties opposed to him. His replies were short, but full of the Word of God, and excited the admiration of his hearers. "He is in all respects like Erasmus," said many; "but surpasses him in one thing: he openly professes what Erasmus is content merely to insinuate."

The disputation was drawing to an end. Luther's adversaries had retired with honor from the field; the youngest of them, Doctor

George Niger, alone continued the struggle with the powerful champion. Alarmed at the daring propositions of the monk, and not knowing what further arguments to have recourse to, he exclaimed, with an accent of fear: "If our peasants heard such things, they would stone you to death!" At these words the whole auditory burst into a loud laugh.

Never had an assembly listened with so much attention to a theological discussion. The first words of the reformer had aroused their minds. Questions which shortly before would have been treated with indifference, were now full of interest. On the countenances of many of the hearers a looker-on might have seen reflected the new ideas which the bold assertions of the Saxon doctor had awakened in their minds.

Three young men in particular were deeply moved. One of them, Martin Bucer by name, was a Dominican, twenty-seven years of age, who, notwithstanding the prejudices of his order, appeared unwilling to lose one of the doctor's words. He was born in a small town of Alsace, and had entered a convent at sixteen. He soon displayed such capacity that the most enlightened monks entertained the highest expectations of him: "He will one day be the ornament of our order," said they. His superiors had sent him to Heidelberg to study philosophy, Greek, and Hebrew. At that period Erasmus published several of his works, which Bucer read with avidity.

Soon appeared the earliest writings of Luther. The Alsatian student hastened to compare the reformer's doctrines with the Holy Scriptures. Some misgivings as to the truth of the popish religion arose in his mind. It was thus that the light was diffused in those days. The elector-palatine took particular notice of the young man. His strong and sonorous voice, his graceful manners and eloquent language, the freedom with which he attacked the vices of the day, made him a distinguished preacher. He was appointed chaplain to the court, and was fulfilling his functions when Luther's journey to Heidelberg was announced. What joy for Bucer! No one repaired with greater eagerness to the hall of the Augustine convent. He took with him paper, pens, and ink, intending to take down what the doctor said. But while his hand was swiftly tracing Luther's words, the finger of God, in more indelible characters, wrote on his heart the great truths he heard. The first gleams of the doctrine of grace were diffused through his soul during this memorable hour. The Dominican was gained over to Christ.

Not far from Bucer stood John Brentz or Brentius, then nineteen years of age. He was the son of a magistrate in a city of Swabia, and at thirteen had been entered as student at Heidelberg. None manifested greater application. He rose at midnight and began to study. This habit became so confirmed, that during his whole life he could not sleep after that hour. In later years he consecrated these tranquil moments to meditation on the Scriptures. Brentz was one of the first to perceive the new light then dawning on Germany. He welcomed it with a heart abounding in love. He eagerly perused Luther's words. But what was his delight when he heard the writer himself at Heidelberg! One of the doctor's propositions more especially startled the youthful scholar; it was this: "That man is not justified before God who performs many works; but he who, without works, has much faith in Jesus Christ."

A pious woman of Heilbronn on the Neckar, wife of a senator of that town, named Snepf, had imitated Hannah's example, and consecrated her firstborn son to the Lord, with a fervent desire to see him devote himself to the study of theology. This young man, who was born in 1495, made rapid progress in learning; but either from taste, or from ambition, or in compliance with his father's wishes, he applied to the study of jurisprudence. The mother was grieved to behold her child, Ehrhard, pursuing another career than that to which she had consecrated him. She admonished him, entreated him, prayed him continually to remember the vow she had made on the day of his birth. Overcome at last by his mother's perseverance, Ehrhard Snepf gave way. Erelong he felt such a taste for his new studies, that nothing in the world could have diverted him from them.

He was very intimate with Bucer and Brentz, and they were friends until death; "for," says one of their biographers, "friendships based on the love of letters and of virtue never fail." He was present with his two friends at the Heidelberg discussion. The *Paradoxes* and courage of the Wittenberg doctor gave him a new impulse. Rejecting the vain opinion of human merits, he embraced the doctrine of the free justification of the sinner.

The next day Bucer went to Luther. "I had a familiar and private conversation with him," said Bucer; "a most exquisite repast, not of dainties, but of truths that were set before me. To whatever objection I made, the doctor had a reply, and explained everything with the greatest clearness. Oh! would to God that I had time to write more!" Luther himself was touched with Bucer's sentiments. "He is the only brother of his order," wrote he to Spalatin, "who is sincere; he is a young man of great promise. He received me with simplicity, and conversed with me very earnestly. He is worthy of our confidence and love."

Brentz, Snepf, and many others, excited by the new truths that began to dawn upon their minds, also visited Luther; they talked and conferred with him; they begged for explanations on what they did not understand. The reformer replied, strengthening his arguments by the Word of God. Each sentence imparted fresh light to their minds. A new world was opening before them.

After Luther's departure, these noble-minded men began to teach at Heidelberg. They felt it their duty to continue what the man of God had begun, and not allow the flame to expire which he had lighted up. The scholars will speak, when the teachers are silent. Brentz, although still so young, explained the Gospel of St. Matthew, at first in his own room, and afterwards, when the chamber became too small, in the theater of philosophy. The theologians, envious at the crowd of hearers this young man drew around him, became irritated. Brentz then took orders, and transferred his lectures to the college of the Canons of the Holy Ghost. Thus the fire already kindled in Saxony now glowed in Heidelberg. The centers of light increased in number. This period has been called the seedtime of the Palatinate.

But it was not the Palatinate alone that reaped the fruits of the Heidelberg disputation. These courageous friends of the truth soon became shining lights in the Church. They all attained to exalted stations, and took part in many of the debates which the Reformation occasioned. Strasburg, and England a little later, were indebted to Bucer for a purer knowledge of the truth. Snepf first declared it at Marburg, then at Stuttgart, Tubingen, and Jena. Brentz, after having taught at Heidelberg, continued his labors for a long period at Tubingen, and at Halle in Swabia. We shall meet with these three men again in the course of our history.

This disputation carried forward Luther himself. He increased daily in the knowledge of the truth. "I belong to those," said he, "who improve by writing and by teaching others, and not to those who from nothing become on a sudden great and learned doctors."

He was overjoyed at seeing with what avidity the students of the schools received the dawning truth, and this consoled him when he found the old doctors so deep-rooted in their opinions. "I have the glorious hope," said he, "that as Christ, when rejected by the Jews, turned to the Gentiles, we shall now also behold the new theology, that has been rejected by these graybeards with their empty and fantastical notions, welcomed by the rising generation."

The chapter being ended, Luther thought of returning to Wittenberg. The count-palatine gave him a letter for the elector, dated May first, in which he said "that Luther had shown so much skill in the disputation, as greatly to contribute to the renown of the University of Wittenberg." He was not allowed to return on foot. The Nuremberg Augustines conducted him as far as Wurtzburg, from whence he proceeded to Erfurt with the friars from that city. As soon as he arrived he repaired to the house of his old teacher, Jodocus. The aged professor, much grieved and scandalized at the path his disciple had taken, was in the habit of placing before all Luther's propositions a theta, the letter employed by the Greeks to denote condemnation. He had written to the young doctor in terms of reproach, and the latter desired to reply in person to these letters. Not having been admitted, he wrote to Jodocus: "All the university, with the exception of one licentiate, think as I do. More than this; the prince, the bishop, many other prelates, and all our most enlightened citizens, declare with one voice, that up to the present time they had neither known nor understood Jesus Christ and His gospel. I am ready to receive your corrections; and although they should be severe, they will appear to me very gentle. Open your heart, therefore, without fear; unburden your anger. I will not and I cannot be vexed with you. God and my conscience are my witnesses!"

The old doctor was moved by these expressions of his former pupil. He was willing to try if there were no means of removing the damnatory theta. They conversed on the matter, but the result was unfavorable. "I made him understand at least," said Luther, "that all their sentences were like that beast which is said to devour itself. But talking to a deaf man is labor in vain. These doctors obstinately cling to their petty distinctions, although they confess there is nothing to confirm them but the light of natural reason, as they call it—a dark chaos truly to us who preach no other light than Jesus Christ, the true and only light."

Luther quitted Erfurt in the carriage belonging to the convent, which took him to Eisleben. From thence the Augustines of the place, proud of a doctor who had shed such glory on their order and on their city, his native place, conveyed him to Wittenberg with their own horses and at their own expense. Every one desired to bestow some mark of affection and esteem on this extraordinary man, whose fame was constantly increasing.

He arrived on the Saturday after Ascension Day. The journey had done him good, and his friends thought him improved in appearance and stronger than before his departure. They were delighted at all he had to tell them. Luther rested some time after the fatigues of his journey and his dispute at Heidelberg; but this rest was only a preparation for severer toils.

Chapter 19

LETTER TO LEO X

TRUTH at last had raised her head in the midst of Christendom. Victorious over the inferior ministers of the papacy, she was now to enter upon a struggle with its chief in person.

It was after his return from Heidelberg that he took this bold step. His early theses on the indulgences had been misunderstood. He determined to explain their meaning with greater clearness. From the clamors that a blind hatred extorted from his enemies, he had learned how important it was to win over the most enlightened part of the nation to the truth. He resolved to appeal to its judgment by setting forth the bases on which his new convictions were founded. It was requisite at once to challenge the decision of Rome: he did not hesitate to send his explanations thither. While he presented them with one hand to the enlightened and impartial readers of his nation, with the other he laid them before the throne of the sovereign pontiff.

These explanations of his theses, which he styled *Resolutions*, were written in a very moderate tone. Luther endeavored to soften down the passages that had occasioned the greatest irritation, and thus gave proof of genuine humility. But at the same time he showed himself to be unshaken in his convictions, and courageously defended all the propositions which truth obliged him to maintain. He repeated once more, that every truly penitent Christian possesses remission of sins without papal indulgences; that the pope, like the meanest priest, can do no more than simply declare what God has already pardoned; that the treasury of the merits of the saints, administered by the pope, was a pure chimera, and that the Holy Scriptures were the sole rule of faith. But let us hear his own statement on some of these points.

He begins by establishing the nature of real repentance. "The Greek word," said he, "signifies, put on a new spirit, a new mind, take a new nature, so that ceasing to be earthly, you may become heavenly. . . . Christ is a teacher of the spirit and not of the letter, and His words are spirit and life. He teaches, therefore, a repentance in spirit and in truth, and not those outward penances that can be performed by the proudest sinners without humiliation. He wills a repentance that can be effected in every situation of life,—under the kingly purple, under the priest's cassock, under the prince's hat,—in the midst of those pomps of Babylon where a Daniel lived, as well as under the monk's frock and the beggar's rags."

Further on we meet with this bold language: "I care not for what pleases or displeases the pope. He is a man like other men. There have been many popes who loved not only errors and vices, but still more extraordinary things. I listen to the pope as pope, that is to say, when he speaks in the canons, according to the canons, or when he decrees some article in conjunction with a council, but not when he speaks after his own ideas. Were I to do otherwise, ought I not to say with those who know not Christ, that the horrible massacres of Christians by which Julius II was stained, were the good deeds of a gentle shepherd towards Christ's flock?"

"I cannot help wondering," continues Luther, "at the simplicity of those who have asserted that the two swords of the gospel represent one the spiritual, the other the secular power. Yes! the pope wields a sword of iron; it is thus he exhibits himself to Christendom, not as a tender father, but as a formidable tyrant. Alas! an angry God has given us the sword we longed for, and taken away that which we despised. In no part of the world have there been more terrible wars than among Christians. . . . Why did not that acute mind which discovered this fine commentary, interpret in the same subtle manner the history of the two keys intrusted to St. Peter, and lay it down as a doctrine of the Church, that one key serves to open the treasures of heaven, the other the treasures of the earth?"

"It is impossible," says Luther in another place, "for a man to be a Christian without having Christ; and if he has Christ, he possesses at the same time all that belongs to Christ. What gives peace to our consciences is this—by faith our sins are no longer ours, but Christ's, on whom God has laid them all; and, on the other hand, all Christ's righteousness belongs to us, to whom God has given it. Christ lays His hand on us, and we are healed. He casts His mantle over us, and we are sheltered; for He is the glorious Saviour blessed for evermore."

With such views of the riches of salvation by Jesus Christ, there was no longer any need of indulgences.

While Luther attacks the papacy, he speaks honorably of Leo X. "The times in which we live are so evil," said he, "that even the most exalted individuals have no power to help the Church. We have at present a very good pope in Leo X. His sincerity, his learning, inspire us with joy. But what can be done by this one man, amiable and gracious as he is? He was worthy of being pope in better days. In our age we deserve none but such men as Julius II and Alexander VI."

He then comes to the point: "I will say what I mean, boldly and briefly: the Church needs a reformation. And this cannot be the work either of a single man, as the pope, or of many men, as the cardinals and councils; but it must be that of the whole world, or rather it is a work that belongs to God alone. As for the time in which such a reformation should begin, He alone knows who has created all time. . . . The dike is broken, and it is no longer in our power to restrain the impetuous and overwhelming billows."

This is a sample of the declarations and ideas which Luther addressed to his enlightened fellow countrymen. The festival of Whitsuntide was approaching; and at the same period in which the apostles gave to the risen Saviour the first testimony of their faith, Luther, the new apostle, published this spirit-stirring book, in which he ardently called for a resurrection of the Church. On Saturday, May 22, 1518, the eve of Pentecost, he sent the work to his ordinary the bishop of Brandenburg with the following letter:—

"Most worthy Father in God! It is now some time since a new and unheard-of doctrine touching the apostolic indulgences began to make a noise in this country; the learned and the ignorant were troubled by it; and many persons, some known, some personally unknown to me, begged me to declare by sermon or by writing what I thought of the novelty, I will not say the impudence, of this doctrine. At first I was silent and kept in the background. But at last things came to such a pass, that the pope's holiness was compromised.

"What could I do? I thought it my duty neither to approve nor condemn these doctrines, but to originate a discussion on this important subject, until the Holy Church should decide.

"As no one accepted the challenge I had given to the whole world, and since my theses have been considered, not as matters for discussion, but as positive assertions, I find myself compelled to publish an explanation of them. Condescend therefore to receive these trifles, which I present to you, most merciful bishop. And that all the world may see that I do not act presumptuously, I entreat your reverence to take pen and ink, and blot out, or even throw into the fire and burn, anything that may offend you. I know that Jesus Christ needs neither my labors nor my services, and that He will know how to proclaim His glad tidings to the Church without my aid. Not that the bulls and the threats of my enemies alarm me; quite the contrary. If they were not so impudent, so shameless, no one should hear of me; I would hide myself in a corner, and there study alone for my own good. If this affair is not God's, it certainly shall no longer be mine or any other man's, but a thing of nought. Let the honor and the glory be His to whom alone they belong!"

Luther was still filled with respect for the head of the Church. He supposed Leo to be a just man and a sincere lover of the truth. He resolved, therefore, to write to him. A week after, on Trinity Sunday, May 30, 1518, he penned a letter, of which we give a few specimens.

"To the most blessed Father Leo X sovereign bishop, Martin Luther, and Augustine friar, wishes eternal salvation.

"I am informed, most holy Father, that wicked reports are in circulation about me, and that my name is in bad odor with your holiness. I am called a heretic, apostate, traitor, and a thousand other insulting names. What I see fills me with surprise, what I learn fills me with alarm. But the only foundation of my tranquillity remains,—a pure and peaceful conscience. Deign to listen to me, most holy Father,—to me who am but a child and unlearned."

After relating the origin of the whole matter, Luther thus continues: "In all the taverns nothing was heard but complaints against the avarice of the priests, and attacks against the power of the keys and of the sovereign bishop. Of this the whole of Germany is a witness. When I was informed of these things, my zeal was aroused for the glory of Christ, as it appeared to me; or, if another explanation be sought, my young and warm blood was inflamed.

"I forewarned several princes of the Church; but some laughed at me, and others turned a deaf ear. The terror of your name seemed to restrain everyone. I then published my disputation.

"And behold, most holy Father, the conflagration that is reported to have set the whole world on fire.

"Now what shall I do? I cannot retract, and I see that this publication draws down upon me an inconceivable hatred from every side. I have no wish to appear before the world; for I have no learning, no genius, and am far too little for such great matters; above all, in this illustrious age, in which Cicero himself, were he living, would be compelled to hide himself in some dark corner.

"But in order to quiet my adversaries, and to reply to the solicitations of many friends, I here publish my thoughts. I publish them, holy Father, that I may be in greater safety under the shadow of your wings. All those who desire it will thus understand with what simplicity of heart I have called upon the ecclesiastical authority to instruct me, and what respect I have shown to the power of the keys. If I had not behaved with propriety, it would have been impossible for the most serene lord Frederick, duke and elector of Saxony, who shines among the friends of the apostolic and Christian faith, to have ever endured in his University of Wittenberg a man so dangerous as I am asserted to be.

"For this reason, most holy Father, I fall at the feet of your holiness, and submit myself to you, with all that I have and with all that I am. Destroy my cause, or espouse it: declare me right or wrong; take away my life or restore it, as you please. I shall acknowledge your voice as the voice of Jesus Christ, who presides and speaks through you. If I have merited death, I shall not refuse to die; the earth is the Lord's, and all that is therein. May He be praised through all eternity! Amen. May He uphold you forever! Amen.

"Written the day of the Holy Trinity, in the year 1518.

"Martin Luther, Augustine Friar."

What humility and truth in Luther's fear, or rather in the avowal he makes that his warm young blood was perhaps too hastily inflamed! In this we behold the sincerity of a man who, presuming not on himself, dreads the influence of his passions in the very acts most in conformity with the Word of God. This language is widely different from that of a proud fanatic. Luther had an earnest desire to gain

over Leo to the cause of truth, to prevent all schism, and to cause the
Reformation, the necessity of which he proclaimed, to proceed from
the head of the Church. Assuredly he should not be accused of destroying that unity in the Western Church which so many persons
of all parties have since regretted. He sacrificed everything to maintain it—everything except the truth. It was not he, it was his adversaries, who, by refusing to acknowledge the fullness and sufficiency
of the salvation wrought by Jesus Christ, rent our Saviour's vesture,
even at the foot of the cross.

After writing this letter, and on the very same day, Luther wrote
to his friend Staupitz, vicar-general of his order. It was by his instrumentality that he desired the Solutions and letter should reach
Leo.

"I beg of you," says he, "to accept with kindness these trifles that
I send you, and to forward them to the excellent Pope Leo X. Not
that I desire by this to draw you into the peril in which I am involved; I am determined to encounter the danger alone. Jesus Christ
will see if what I have said proceeds from Him or from me—Jesus
Christ, without whose will the pope's tongue cannot move, and the
hearts of kings cannot decide.

"As to those who threaten me, I reply in the words of Reuchlin:
'He who is poor has nothing to fear, since he has nothing to lose.' I
have neither property nor money, and I do not desire any. If formerly
I possessed any honor, any reputation, let Him who has begun to deprive me of them complete His task. All that is left to me is a
wretched body, weakened by many trials. Should they kill me by
stratagem or by force, to God be the glory! They will thus, perhaps,
shorten my life by an hour or two. It is enough for me that I have a
precious Redeemer, a powerful High Priest, Jesus Christ my Lord.
As long as I live will I praise Him. If another will not unite with me
in these praises, what is that to me?"

In these words we read Luther's inmost heart.

While he was thus looking with confidence towards Rome, Rome
already entertained thoughts of vengeance against him. As early as
the third of April, Cardinal Raphael of Rovera had written to the
Elector Frederick, in the pope's name, intimating that his orthodoxy
was suspected, and cautioning him against protecting Luther. "Cardinal Raphael," said the latter, "would have had great pleasure in

seeing me burned by Frederick." Thus was Rome beginning to sharpen her weapons against Luther. It was through his protector's mind that she resolved to aim the first blow. If she succeeded in destroying that shelter under which the monk of Wittenberg was reposing, he would become an easy prey to her.

The German princes were very tenacious of their reputation for orthodoxy. The slightest suspicion of heresy filled them with alarm. The court of Rome had skillfully taken advantage of this disposition. Frederick, moreover, had always been attached to the religion of his forefathers, and hence Raphael's letter made a deep impression on his mind. But it was a rule with the elector never to act precipitately. He knew that truth was not always on the side of the strongest. The disputes between the empire and Rome had taught him to mistrust the interested views of that court. He had found out that to be a Christian prince, it was not necessary to be the pope's slave.

"He was not one of those profane persons," said Melancthon, "who order all changes to be arrested at their very commencement. Frederick submitted himself to God. He carefully perused the writings that appeared, and did not allow that to be destroyed which he believed to be true." It was not from want of power; for, besides being sovereign in his own states, he enjoyed in the empire a respect very little inferior to that which was paid to the emperor himself.

It is probable that Luther gained some information of this letter of Cardinal Raphael's transmitted to the elector on the seventh of July. Perhaps it was the prospect of excommunication which the Roman missive seemed to forbode that induced him to enter the pulpit of Wittenberg on the fifteenth of the same month, and to deliver a sermon on that subject, which made a deep impression. He drew a distinction between external and internal excommunication; the former excluding only from the services of the Church, the latter from communion with God. "No one," said he, "can reconcile the fallen sinner with God, except the Eternal One. No one can separate man from God, except man himself by his own sins. Blessed is he who dies under an unjust excommunication! While he suffers a grievous punishment at the hands of men for righteousness' sake, he receives from the hand of God the crown of everlasting happiness."

Some of the hearers loudly commended this bold language; others were still more exasperated by it.

But Luther no longer stood alone. Although his faith required no other support than that of God, a phalanx which defended him against his enemies had grown up around him. The German people had heard the voice of the reformer. From his sermons and writings issued those flashes of light which aroused and illumined his contemporaries. The energy of his faith poured forth in torrents of fire on their frozen hearts. The life that God had placed in this extraordinary mind communicated itself to the dead body of the Church. Christendom, motionless for so many centuries, became animated with religious enthusiasm. The people's attachment to the Romish superstitions diminished day by day; there were always fewer hands that offered money to purchase forgiveness; and at the same time Luther's reputation continued to increase. The people turned towards him, and saluted him with love and respect, as the intrepid defender of truth and liberty.

Undoubtedly, all men did not see the depth of the doctrines he proclaimed. For the greater number it was sufficient to know that he stood up against the pope, and that the dominion of the priests and monks was shaken by the might of his word. In their eyes, Luther's attack was like those beacon fires kindled on the mountains, which announce to a whole nation that the time to burst their chains has arrived. The reformer was not aware of what he had done, until the people hailed him as their leader. But for a great number also, Luther's coming was something more than this. The Word of God, which he so skillfully wielded, pierced their hearts like a two-edged sword. In many bosoms was kindled an earnest desire of obtaining the assurance of pardon and eternal life. Since the primitive ages, the Church had never witnessed such hungering and thirsting after righteousness. If the eloquence of Peter the Hermit and of St. Bernard had inspired the people of the Middle Ages to assume a perishable cross, the eloquence of Luther prevailed on those of his day to take up the real cross—the truth which saves. The scaffolding which then encumbered the Church had stifled everything; the form had destroyed the life. The powerful language given to this man diffused a quickening breath over the soil of Christendom.

At the first outburst, Luther's writings had carried away believers and unbelievers alike: the unbelievers, because the positive doctrines that were afterwards to be settled had not been as yet fully developed;

the believers, because their germs were found in that living faith which his writings proclaimed with so much power. Accordingly, the influence of these writings was immense; they filled Germany and the world. Everywhere prevailed a secret conviction that men were about to witness, not the establishment of a sect, but a new birth of the Church and society. Those who were then born of the breath of the Holy Ghost rallied around him who was its organ. Christendom was divided into two parties: the one contended with the Spirit against the form, and the other with the form against the Spirit. On the side of the form were, it is true, all the appearances of strength and grandeur; on the side of the Spirit were helplessness and insignificance. But form, void of Spirit, is but a feeble body, which the first breath of wind may throw down. Its apparent power serves but to excite hostility and to precipitate its destruction. Thus, the simple Word of truth had raised a powerful army for Luther.

This army was very necessary, for the nobles began to be alarmed, and the empire and the Church were already uniting their power to get rid of this troublesome monk. If a strong and courageous prince had then filled the imperial throne, he might have taken advantage of this religious agitation, and the reliance upon the Word of God and upon the nation. But Maximilian was too old, and he had determined besides on making every sacrifice in order to attain the great object of his life, the aggrandizement of his house, and consequently the elevation of his grandson. The emperor was at that time holding an imperial diet at Augsburg. Six electors had gone thither in person at his summons. All the Germanic states were there represented. The kings of France, Hungary, and Poland had sent their ambassadors. These princes and envoys displayed great magnificence. The Turkish war was one of the causes for which the diet had been assembled. The legate of Leo X earnestly urged the meeting on this point. The states, learning wisdom from the bad use that had formerly been made of their contributions, and wisely counseled by the Elector Frederick, were satisfied with declaring they would reflect on the matter, and at the same time produced fresh complaints against Rome. A Latin discourse, published during the diet, boldly pointed out the real danger to the German princes. "You desire to put the Turk to flight," said the author. "This is well; but I am very much afraid that you are mistaken in the person. You should look for him in Italy, and not in Asia."

Another affair of no less importance was to occupy the diet. Maximilian desired to have his grandson Charles, already king of Spain and Naples, proclaimed king of the Romans, and his successor in the imperial dignity. The pope knew his own interests too well to desire to see the imperial throne filled by a prince whose power in Italy might be dangerous to himself. The emperor imagined he had already won over most of the electors and of the states; but he met with a vigorous resistance from Frederick. All solicitations proved unavailing; in vain did the ministers and the best friends of the elector unite their entreaties to those of the emperor; he was immovable, and showed on this occasion (as it has been remarked) that he had firmness of mind not to swerve from a resolution which he had once acknowledged to be just. The emperor's design failed.

Henceforward this prince sought to gain the good will of the pope, in order to render him favorable to his plans; and to give a more striking proof of his attachment, he wrote to him as follows, on the fifth of August: "Most holy Father, we have learned that a friar of the Augustine order, named Martin Luther, has presumed to maintain certain propositions on the traffic of indulgences; a matter that displeases us the more because this friar has found many protectors, among whom are persons of exalted station. If your holiness and the very reverend fathers of the Church (i.e., the cardinals) do not soon exert your authority to put an end to these scandals, these pernicious teachers will not only seduce the simple people, but they will involve great princes in their destruction. We will take care that whatever your holiness may decree in this matter for the glory of God Almighty shall be enforced throughout the whole empire."

This letter must have been written immediately after some warm discussion between Maximilian and Frederick. On the same day, the elector wrote to Raphael of Rovera. He had learned, no doubt, that the emperor was writing to the Roman pontiff, and to parry the blow, he put himself in communication with Rome.

"I shall never have any other desire," says he, "than to show my submission to the universal Church.

"Accordingly, I have never defended either the writings or the sermons of Doctor Martin Luther. I learn, besides, that he has always offered to appear, under a safe-conduct, before impartial, learned, and Christian judges, in order to defend his doctrine, and to submit, in case he should be convicted of error by the Scriptures themselves."

Leo X, who up to this time had let the business follow its natural course, aroused by the clamors of the theologians and monks, nominated an ecclesiastical commission at Rome empowered to try Luther. Sylvester Prierio, the reformer's great enemy, was at once accuser and judge. The case was soon prepared, and the court summoned Luther to appear before it in person within sixty days.

Luther was tranquilly awaiting at Wittenberg the good effects that he imagined his submissive letter to the pope would produce, when on the seventh of August, two days only after the letters of Maximilian and of Frederick were sent off, he received the summons of the Roman tribunal. "At the very moment I was expecting a blessing," said he, "I saw the thunderbolt fall upon me. I was the lamb that troubled the water the wolf was drinking. Tetzel escaped, and I was to permit myself to be devoured."

This summons caused general alarm in Wittenberg; for whatever course Luther might take he could not escape danger. If he went to Rome, he would there become the victim of his enemies. If he refused to appear, he would be condemned for contumacy, as was usual, without the power of escaping; for it was known that the legate had received orders to do everything he could to exasperate the emperor and the German princes against the doctor. His friends were filled with consternation. Shall the preacher of truth risk his life in that great city drunk with the blood of the saints and of the martyrs of Jesus? Shall a head be raised in the midst of enslaved Christendom, only to fall? Shall this man also be struck down—this man whom God appears to have formed to withstand a power that hitherto nothing had been able to resist? Luther himself saw that no one could save him but the elector; yet he would rather die than compromise his prince. At last his friends agreed on an expedient that would not endanger Frederick. Let him refuse Luther a safe-conduct, and then the reformer would have a legitimate excuse for not appearing at Rome.

On the eighth of August, Luther wrote to Spalatin begging him to employ his influence with the elector to have his cause heard in

Germany. "See what snares they are laying for me," wrote he also to Staupitz, "and how I am surrounded with thorns. But Christ lives and reigns, the same yesterday, today, and forever. My conscience assures me that I have been teaching the truth, although it appears still more odious because I teach it. The Church is the womb of Rebecca. The children must struggle together, even to the risk of the mother's life. As for the rest, pray the Lord that I feel not too much joy in this trial. May God not lay this sin to their charge."

Luther's friends did not confine themselves to consultations and complaints. Spalatin wrote, on the part of the elector, to Renner the emperor's secretary: "Doctor Martin Luther willingly consents to be judged by all the universities of Germany, except Leipzig, Erfurt, and Frankfurt-on-the-Oder, which have shown themselves partial. It is impossible for him to appear at Rome in person."

The University of Wittenberg wrote a letter of intercession to the pope: "The weakness of his frame," they said, speaking of Luther, "and the dangers of the journey, render it difficult and even impossible for him to obey the order of your holiness. His distress and his prayers incline us to sympathize with him. We therefore entreat you, most holy Father, as obedient children, to look upon him as a man who has never been tainted with doctrines opposed to the tenets of the Roman Church."

The university, in its solicitude, wrote the same day to Charles of Miltitz, a Saxon gentleman and the pope's chamberlain, in high estimation with Leo X. In this letter they gave Luther a more decided testimony than they had ventured to insert in the first. "The reverend father Martin Luther, an Augustine," it ran, "is the noblest and most distinguished member of our university. For many years we have seen and known his talents, his learning, his profound acquaintance with the arts and literature, his irreproachable morals, and his truly Christian behavior."

This active charity shown by all who surrounded Luther is his noblest eulogy.

While men were anxiously looking for the result of this affair, it was terminated more easily than might have been expected. The legate De Vio, mortified at his ill success in the commission he had received to excite a general war against the Turks, wished to exalt and give luster to his embassy in Germany by some other brilliant act. He thought that if he could extinguish heresy he should return to Rome with honor. He therefore entreated the pope to intrust this business to him. Leo, for his part, was highly pleased with Frederick for his strong opposition to the election of the youthful Charles. He felt that he might yet stand in need of his support. Without further reference to the summons, he commissioned the legate, by a brief dated August 23, to investigate the affair in Germany. The pope lost nothing by this course of proceeding. Even if Luther could not be prevailed on to retract, the noise and scandal of his presence at Rome would be avoided.

"We charge you," said Leo, "to summon personally before you, to prosecute and constrain without any delay, and as soon as you shall have received this paper from us, the said Luther, who has already been declared a heretic by our dear brother Jerome, bishop of Ascoli."

The pope then proceeded to utter the severest threats against Luther:

"Invoke for this purpose the arm and the aid of our very dear son in Christ, Maximilian, and of the other princes of Germany, and of all the communities, universities, and potentates, ecclesiastic or secular. And, if you get possession of his person, keep him in safe custody, that he may be brought before us."

We see that this indulgent concession from the pope was only a surer way of inveigling Luther to Rome. Next followed milder measures:

"If he return to his duty, and beg forgiveness for so great a misdeed, of his own accord and without solicitation, we give you power to receive him into the unity of our holy mother the Church."

The pope soon returned to his maledictions:

"If he persist in his obstinacy, and you cannot secure his person, we authorize you to outlaw him in every part of Germany; to banish, curse, and excommunicate all prelates, religious orders, universities, communities, counts, dukes, and potentates (the Emperor Maximilian always excepted), who shall not aid in seizing the aforesaid Martin Luther and his adherents, and send them to you under good and safe guard.—And if, which God forbid, the said princes, communities, universities, and potentates, or any belonging to them, shall in any manner offer an asylum to the said Martin and his adherents, give him privately or publicly, by themselves or by others, succor and counsel, we lay under interdict all these princes, communities, universities, and potentates, with their cities, towns, countries, and villages, as well as the cities, towns, countries, and villages in which the said Martin may take refuge, so long as he shall remain there, and three days after he shall have quitted them."

This audacious see, which claims to be the earthly representative of Him who said: "God sent not his Son into the world to condemn the world, but that the world through him might be saved," continued its anathemas; and after pronouncing the penalties against ecclesiastics, went on to say:

"As for the laymen, if they do not immediately obey your orders without delay or opposition, we declare them infamous (the most worthy emperor always excepted), incapable of performing any lawful act, deprived of Christian burial, and stripped of all the fiefs (landed estates) they may hold either from the apostolic see, or from any lord whatsoever."

Such was the fate destined for Luther. The monarch of Rome invoked everything for his destruction. Nothing was spared, not even the quiet of the grave. His ruin appears certain. How could he escape from this vast conspiracy? But Rome was deceived; the movement, begun by the Spirit of God, could not be checked by the decrees of her chancery.

The pope had not even preserved the appearances of a just and impartial examination. Luther had been declared a heretic, not only before he had been heard, but even before the expiration of the time allowed for his appearance. The passions, and never do they show themselves more violently than in religious discussions, overleap all forms of justice. It is not only in the Roman Church, but in the Protestant churches that have turned aside from the gospel, and wherever the truth is not found, that we meet with such strange proceedings in this respect. Everything is lawful against the gospel. We frequently see men who in every other case would scruple to commit the least injustice, not fearing to trample under foot all rule and law, whenever Christianity, or the testimony that is paid to it, is concerned.

When Luther became acquainted with this brief, he thus expressed his indignation:

"This is the most remarkable part of the affair: the brief was issued on the twenty-third of August—I was summoned on the seventh —so that between the brief and the summons sixteen days elapsed. Now, make the calculation, and you will find that my Lord Jerome, bishop of Ascoli, proceeded against me, pronounced judgment, condemned me, and declared me a heretic, before the summons reached me, or at the most within sixteen days after it had been forwarded to me. Now, where are the sixty days accorded me in the summons? They began on the seventh of August, and they should end on the seventh of October. . . . Is this the style and fashion of the Roman court, which on the same day summons, exhorts, accuses, judges, condemns, and declares a man guilty who is so far from Rome, and who knows nothing of all these things? What reply can they make to this? No doubt they forgot to clear their brains with hellebore (an herb) before having recourse to such trickery."

But while Rome secretly deposited her thunders in the hands of her legate, she sought by sweet and flattering words to detach from Luther's cause the prince whose power she dreaded most. On the same day (August 23, 1518), the pope wrote to the Elector of Saxony. He had recourse to the wiles of that ancient policy which we have already noticed, and endeavored to flatter the prince's vanity.

"Dear son," wrote the pontiff, "when we think of your noble and worthy family; of you who are its ornament and head; when we call to mind how you and your ancestors have always desired to uphold the Christian faith, and the honor and dignity of the holy see, we cannot believe that a man who abandons the faith can rely upon your highness's favor, and daringly give the rein to his wickedness. Yet it is reported to us from every quarter that a certain friar, Martin Luther, hermit of the order of St. Augustine, has forgotten, like a child of the evil one and despiser of God, his habit and his order, which consist in humility and obedience, and that he boasts of fearing neither the authority nor the punishment of any man, being assured of your favor and protection.

"But as we know that he is deceived, we have thought fit to write to your highness, and to exhort you in the Lord to watch over the honor of your name, as a Christian prince, the ornament, glory, and sweet savor of your noble family; to defend yourself from these calumnies; and to guard yourself not only from so serious a crime as that imputed to you, but still further even from the suspicion that the rash presumption of this friar tends to bring upon you."

Leo X at the same time informed the elector that he had commissioned the cardinal of St. Sixtus to investigate the matter, and requested him to deliver Luther into the legate's hands, "for fear," added he, still returning to his first argument, "the pious people of our own or of future times should one day lament and say: 'The most pernicious heresy with which the Church of God has been afflicted sprung up under the favor and support of that high and worthy family.'"

Thus had Rome taken her measures. With one hand she scattered the intoxicating incense of flattery; in the other she held concealed her terrors and revenge.

All the powers of the earth, emperor, pope, princes, and legates, began to rise up against this humble friar of Erfurt, whose internal struggles we have already witnessed. "The kings of the earth set themselves, and the rulers take counsel against the Lord, and against His anointed."

Chapter 20

PHILIP MELANCTHON

BEFORE this letter and the brief had reached Germany, and while Luther was still afraid of being compelled to appear at Rome, a fortunate event brought consolation to his heart. He needed a friend into whose bosom he could pour out his sorrows, and whose faithful affection would comfort him in his hours of dejection. God gave him such a friend in Melancthon.

George Schwartzerd was a skillful master-armorer of Bretten, a small town in the Palatinate. On the fourteenth of February 1497, his wife bore him a son, who was named Philip, and who became famous in after years under the name of Melancthon. George, who was highly esteemed by the palatine princes, and by those of Bavaria and Saxony, was a man of perfect integrity. Frequently he would refuse from purchasers the price they offered him; and if he found they were poor, would compel them to take back their money. It was his habit to leave his bed at midnight, and offer a fervent prayer upon his knees. If the morning came without his having performed this pious duty, he was dissatisfied with himself all the rest of the day. His wife Barbara was the daughter of a respectable magistrate named John Reuter. She possessed a tender disposition, rather inclined to superstition, but in other respects discreet and prudent. To her we are indebted for these well-known German rhymes:

> "Alms-giving impoverisheth not.
> Church-going hindereth not.
> To grease the car delayeth not.
> Ill-gotten wealth profiteth not.
> God's Book deceiveth not."

And the following rhymes also:

> "Those who love to squander
> More than their fields render,
> Will surely come to ruin,
> Or a rope be their undoing."

Philip was not eleven years old when his father died. Two days before he expired, George called his son to his bedside, and exhorted him to have the fear of God constantly before his eyes. "I foresee," said the dying armorer, "that terrible tempests are about to shake the world. I have witnessed great things, but greater still are preparing. May God direct and guide thee!" After Philip had received his father's blessing, he was sent to Spier that he might not be present at his parent's death. He departed weeping bitterly.

The lad's grandfather, the worthy bailiff Reuter, who himself had a son, performed a father's duty to Philip, and took him and his brother George into his own house. Shortly after this he engaged John Hungarus to teach the three boys. The tutor was an excellent man, and in after years proclaimed the gospel with great energy, even to an advanced age. He overlooked nothing in the young man. He punished him for every fault, but with discretion: "It is thus," said Melancthon in 1554, "that he made a scholar of me. He loved me as a son, I loved him as a father; and we shall meet, I hope, in heaven."

Philip was remarkable for the excellence of his understanding and his facility in learning and explaining what he had learned. He could not remain idle and was always looking for someone to discuss with him the things he had heard. It frequently happened that well-educated foreigners passed through Bretten and visited Reuter. Immediately the bailiff's grandson would go up to them, enter into conversation, and press them so hard in the discussion that the hearers were filled with admiration. With strength of genius he united great gentleness, and thus won the favor of all. He stammered; but like the illustrious Grecian orator, he so diligently set about correcting this defect, that in after life no traces of it could be perceived.

On the death of his grandfather, the youthful Philip with his brother and his young uncle John, was sent to the school at Pforzheim. These lads resided with one of their relations, sister to the fa-

mous Reuchlin. Eager in the pursuit of knowledge, Philip, under the
tuition of George Simmler, made rapid progress in learning, and particularly in Greek, of which he was passionately fond. Reuchlin frequently came to Pforzheim. At his sister's house he became acquainted with her young boarders, and was soon struck with Philip's
replies. He presented him with a Greek grammar and a Bible. These
two books were to be the study of his whole life.

When Reuchlin returned from his second journey to Italy, his
young relative, then twelve years old, celebrated the day of his arrival
by representing before him, with the aid of some friends, a Latin
comedy which he had himself composed. Reuchlin, charmed with
the young man's talents, tenderly embraced him, called him his dear
son, and placed sportively upon his head the red hat he had received
when he had been made doctor. It was at this time that Reuchlin
changed the name of Schwartzerd into that of Melancthon; both
words, the one in German and the other in Greek, signifying black
earth. Most of the learned men of that age thus translated their
names into Greek or Latin.

Melancthon, at twelve years of age, went to the University of
Heidelberg, and here he began to slake his ardent thirst for knowledge. He took his bachelor's degree at fourteen. In 1512, Reuchlin invited him to Tubingen, where many learned men were assembled.
He attended by turns the lectures of the theologians, doctors, and
lawyers. There was no branch of knowledge that he deemed unworthy his study. Praise was not his object, but the possession and the
fruits of learning.

The Holy Scriptures especially engaged his attention. Those who
frequented the church of Tubingen had remarked that he frequently held a book in his hands, which he was occupied in reading
between the services. This unknown volume appeared larger than
the prayer books, and a report was circulated that Philip used to read
profane authors during those intervals. But the suspected book
proved to be a copy of the Holy Scriptures, printed shortly before at
Basle by John Frobenius. All his life he continued this study with
the most unceasing application. He always carried this precious
volume with him, even to the public assemblies to which he was invited. Rejecting the empty systems of the schoolmen, he adhered to
the plain word of the Gospel. "I entertain the most distinguished and

splendid expectations of Melancthon," wrote Erasmus to Œcolampadius about this time; "God grant that this young man may long survive us. He will entirely eclipse Erasmus." Nevertheless, Melancthon shared in the errors of his age. "I shudder," he observed at an advanced period of his life, "when I think of the honor I paid to images, while I was yet a papist."

In 1514, he was made doctor of philosophy, and then began to teach. He was seventeen years old. The grace and charm that he imparted to his lessons formed the most striking contrast to the tasteless method which the doctors, and above all the monks, had pursued till then. He took an active part in the struggle in which Reuchlin was engaged with the learning-haters of the day. Agreeable in conversation, mild and elegant in his manners, beloved by all who knew him, he soon acquired great authority and solid reputation in the learned world.

It was at this time that the elector formed the design of inviting some distinguished scholar to the University of Wittenberg as professor of the ancient languages. He applied to Reuchlin, who recommended Melancthon. Frederick foresaw the celebrity that this young man would confer on an institution so dear to him, and Reuchlin, charmed at beholding so noble a career opening before his young friend, wrote to him these words of the Almighty to Abraham: " 'Get thee out of thy country, and from thy kindred, and from thy father's house, and I will make thy name great, and thou shalt be a blessing.' Yea," continued the old man, "I hope that it will be so with thee, my dear Philip, my handiwork and my consolation." In this invitation Melancthon acknowledged a call from God. At his departure the university was filled with sorrow; yet it contained individuals who were jealous and envious of him. He left his native place, exclaiming: "The Lord's will be done!" He was then twenty-one years of age.

Melancthon traveled on horseback, in company with several Saxon merchants, as a traveler joins a caravan in the deserts; for, says Reuchlin, he was unacquainted both with the roads and the country. He presented his respects to the elector, whom he found at Augsburg. At Nuremberg he saw the excellent Pirckheimer, whom he had known before; at Leipzig he formed an acquaintance with the learned Hellenist Mosellanus. The university of this last city gave a banquet in his honor. The repast was academical. The dishes succeeded one another in great variety, and at each new dish one of the professors rose and addressed Melancthon in a Latin speech he had prepared beforehand. The latter immediately replied extemporaneously. At last, wearied with so much eloquence, he said: "Most illustrious men, permit me to reply to your harangues once for all; for, being unprepared, I cannot put such varieties into my answers as you have done in your addresses." After this, the dishes were brought in without the accompaniment of a speech.

Reuchlin's youthful relative arrived in Wittenberg on the twenty-fifth of August 1518, two days after Leo X had signed the brief addressed to Cajetan, and the letter to the elector.

The Wittenberg professors did not receive Melancthon so favorably as those of Leipzig had done. The first impression he made on them did not correspond with their expectations. They saw a young man, who appeared younger than he really was, of small stature, and with a feeble and timid air. Was this the illustrious doctor whom Erasmus and Reuchlin, the greatest men of the day, extolled so highly? Neither Luther, with whom he first became acquainted, nor his colleague, entertained any great hopes of him when they saw his youth, his shyness, and his diffident manners.

On the twenty-ninth of August, four days after his arrival, he delivered his inaugural discourse. All the university was assembled. This lad, as Luther calls him, spoke in such elegant latinity (idiom), and showed so much learning, an understanding so cultivated, and a judgment so sound, that all his hearers were struck with admiration.

When the speech was finished, all crowded round him with congratulations; but no one felt more joy than Luther. He hastened to impart to his friends the sentiments that filled his heart. "Melancthon," wrote he to Spalatin on August 31, "delivered four days after his arrival so learned and so beautiful a discourse that everyone listened with astonishment and admiration. We soon recovered from the prejudices excited by his stature and appearance; we now praise and admire his eloquence; we return our thanks to you and to the prince for the service you have done us. I ask for no other Greek master. But I fear that his delicate frame will be unable to support our mode of living, and that we shall be unable to keep him long on account of the smallness of his salary. I hear that the Leipzig people are already boasting of their power to take him from us. O my dear Spalatin, beware of despising his age and his personal appearance. He is a man worthy of every honor."

Melancthon began immediately to lecture on Homer and the Epistle of St. Paul to Titus. He was full of ardor. "I will make every effort," wrote he to Spalatin, "to conciliate the favor of all those in Wittenberg who love learning and virtue." Four days after his inauguration, Luther wrote again to Spalatin: "I most particularly recommend to you the very learned and very amiable Grecian, Philip. His lecture room is always full. All the theologians in particular go to hear him. He is making every class, upper, lower, and middle, begin to read Greek."

Melancthon was able to respond to Luther's affection. He soon found in him a kindness of disposition, a strength of mind, a courage, a discretion, that he had never found till then in any man. He venerated, he loved him. "If there is anyone," said he, "whom I dearly love, and whom I embrace with my whole heart, it is Martin Luther."

Thus did Luther and Melancthon meet; they were friends until death. We cannot too much admire the goodness and wisdom of God in bringing together two men so different and yet so necessary to one another. Luther possessed warmth, vigor, and strength; Melancthon clearness, discretion, and mildness. Luther gave energy to Melancthon, Melancthon moderated Luther. They were like substances in a state of positive and negative electricity, which mutually act upon each other. If Luther had been without Melancthon, perhaps the torrent would have overflowed its banks; Melancthon, when Luther was taken from him by death, hesitated and gave way, even where he should not have yielded. Luther did much by power; Melancthon perhaps did no less by following a gentler and more tranquil method. Both were upright, openhearted, generous; both ardently loved the Word of eternal life, and obeyed it with a fidelity and devotion that governed their whole lives.

Melancthon's arrival at Wittenberg effected a revolution not only in that university, but in the whole of Germany and in all the learned world. The attention he had bestowed on the Greek and Latin classics and on philosophy had given a regularity, clearness, and precision to his ideas, which shed a new light and an indescribable beauty on every subject that he took in hand. The mild spirit of the gospel fertilized and animated his meditations, and in his lectures the driest pursuits were clothed with a surpassing grace that captivated all hearers. The barrenness that scholasticism had cast over education was at an end. A new manner of teaching and of studying began with Melancthon. "Thanks to him," says an illustrious German historian, "Wittenberg became the school of the nation."

It was indeed highly important that a man who knew Greek thoroughly should teach in that university, where the new developments of theology called upon masters and pupils to study in their original language the earliest documents of the Christian faith. From this time Luther zealously applied to the task. The meaning of a Greek word, of which he had been ignorant until then, suddenly cleared up his theological ideas. What consolation and what joy did he not feel, when he saw, for instance, that the Greek word which, according to the Latin Church, signifies a penance, a satisfaction required by the Church, a human expiation, really meant in Greek a transformation or conversion of heart! A thick mist was suddenly rolled away from his eyes. The two significations given to this word suffice of themselves to characterize the two Churches.

The impulse Melancthon gave to Luther in the translation of the Bible is one of the most remarkable circumstances of the friendship between these two great men. As early as 1517, Luther had made some attempts at translations. He had procured as many Greek and Latin books as were within his reach. And now, with the aid of his dear Philip, he applied to his task with fresh energy. Luther compelled Melancthon to share in his researches; consulted him on the difficult passages: and the work, which was destined to be one of the great labors of the reformer, advanced more safely and more speedily.

Melancthon, on his side, became acquainted with the new theology. The beautiful and profound doctrine of justification by faith filled him with astonishment and joy; but he received with independence the system taught by Luther, and molded it to the peculiar form of his mind; for, although he was only twenty-one years old, he was one of those geniuses who attain early to a full possession of all their powers, and who think for themselves from the very first.

The zeal of the teachers was soon communicated to the disciples. It was decided to reform the method of instruction. With the elector's consent, certain courses that possessed a merely scholastic importance were suppressed; at the same time the study of the classics received a fresh impulse. The school of Wittenberg was transformed, and the contrast with other universities became daily more striking. All this, however, took place within the limits of the Church, and none suspected they were on the eve of a great contest with the pope.

Chapter 21

DEPARTURE FOR AUGSBURG

No doubt Melancthon's arrival at a moment so critical brought a pleasing change to the current of Luther's thoughts; no doubt, in the sweet outpourings of a dawning friendship, and in the midst of the biblical labors to which he devoted himself with fresh zeal, he sometimes forgot Rome, Prierio, Leo, and the ecclesiastical court before which he was to appear. Yet these were but fugitive moments, and his thoughts always returned to that formidable tribunal before which his implacable enemies had summoned him. With what terror would not such thoughts have filled a soul whose object had been anything else than the truth! But Luther did not tremble; confident in the faithfulness and power of God, he remained firm, and was ready to expose himself alone to the anger of enemies more terrible than those who had kindled John Huss's pile.

A few days after Melancthon's arrival, and before the resolution of the pope transferring Luther's citation from Rome to Augsburg could be known, Luther wrote thus to Spalatin: "I do not require that our sovereign should do the least thing in defense of my theses; I am willing to be given up and thrown into the hands of my adversaries. Let him permit all the storm to burst upon me. What I have undertaken to defend, I hope to be able to maintain, with the help of Christ. As for violence, we must needs yield to that, but without abandoning the truth."

Luther's courage was infectious: the mildest and most timid men, as they beheld the danger that threatened this witness to the truth, found language full of energy and indignation. The prudent, the pacific Staupitz wrote to Spalatin on the seventh of September: "Do not cease to exhort the prince, your master and mine, not to allow himself to be frightened by the roaring of the lions. Let him defend the truth, without anxiety either about Luther, Staupitz, or the order. Let there be one place at least where men may speak freely and without fear. I know that the plague of Babylon, I was nearly saying of Rome, is let loose against whoever attacks the abuses of those who sell Jesus Christ. I have myself seen a preacher thrown from the pulpit for teaching the truth; I saw him, although it was a festival, bound and dragged to prison. Others have witnessed still more cruel sights. For this reason, dearest Spalatin, prevail upon his highness to continue in his present sentiments."

At last the order to appear before the cardinal-legate at Augsburg arrived. It was now with one of the princes of the Roman Church that Luther had to deal. All his friends entreated him not to set out. They feared that even during the journey snares might be laid for his life. Some busied themselves in finding an asylum for him. Staupitz himself, the timid Staupitz, was moved at the thought of the dangers to which brother Martin would be exposed—that brother whom he had dragged from the seclusion of the cloister, and whom he had launched on that agitated sea in which his life was now endangered. Alas! would it not have been better for the poor brother to have remained forever unknown! It was too late. At least he would do everything in his power to save him. Accordingly he wrote from his convent at Salzburg, on the fifteenth of September, soliciting Luther to flee and seek an asylum with him. "It appears to me," said he, "that the whole world is enraged and combined against the truth. The crucified Jesus was hated in like manner. I do not see that you have anything else to expect but persecution. Erelong no one will be able without the pope's permission to search the Scriptures, and therein look for Jesus Christ, which Jesus Christ however commands. You have but few friends: I would to God that fear of your adversaries did not prevent those few from declaring themselves in your favor! The wisest course is for you to abandon Wittenberg for a season and come to me. Then we shall live and die together. This is also the prince's opinion," adds Staupitz.

From different quarters Luther received the most alarming intelligence. Count Albert of Mansfeldt bid him beware of undertaking the journey, for several powerful lords had sworn to seize his person, and strangle or drown him. But nothing could frighten him. He had no intention of profiting by the vicar-general's offer. He would not go and conceal himself in the obscurity of a convent at Salzburg; he would remain faithfully on that stormy scene where the hand of God had placed him. It was by persevering in despite of his adversaries, by proclaiming the truth aloud in the midst of the world, that the reign of this truth advanced. Why then should he flee? He was not one of those who draw back to perish, but of those who keep the faith to the saving of their souls. This expression of the Master whom he desired to serve, and whom he loved more than life, re-echoed incessantly in his heart: "Whosoever shall confess me before men, him will I also confess before my Father who is in heaven." At all times do we find in Luther and in the Reformation this intrepid courage, this exalted morality, this infinite charity, which the first advent of Christianity had already made known to the world. "I am like Jeremiah," says Luther at the time of which we are speaking, "a man of strife and contention; but the more their threats increase, the more my joy is multiplied. My wife and my children are well provided for; my fields, my houses, and my goods are in order. They have already destroyed my honor and my reputation. One single thing remains; it is my wretched body; let them take it; they will thus shorten my life by a few hours. But as for my soul, they cannot take that. He who desires to proclaim the Word of Christ to the world must expect death at every moment."

The elector was then at Augsburg. Shortly before quitting the diet in that city, he had paid the legate a visit. The cardinal, highly flattered with this condescension from so illustrious a prince, promised Frederick, that if the monk appeared before him, he would listen to him in a paternal manner, and dismiss him kindly. Spalatin, by the prince's order, wrote to his friend, that the pope had appointed a commission to hear him in Germany; that the elector would not permit him to be dragged to Rome; and that he must prepare for his journey to Augsburg. Luther resolved to obey. The notice he had received from the Count of Mansfeldt induced him to ask a safe-conduct from Frederick. The latter replied that it was unnecessary, and sent him only letters of recommendation to some of the most distinguished councilors of Augsburg. He also provided him with money for the journey; and the poor defenseless reformer set out on foot to place himself in the hands of his enemies.

What must have been his feelings as he quitted Wittenberg and took the road to Augsburg, where the pope's legate awaited him! The object of this journey was not like that to Heidelberg, a friendly meeting; he was about to appear before the Roman delegate without a safe-conduct; perhaps he was going to death. But his faith was not one of mere outward show; with him it was a reality. Hence it gave him peace, and he could advance without fear, in the name of the Lord of hosts, to bear his testimony to the gospel.

He arrived at Weimar on September 28, and lodged in the Cordeliers' monastery. One of the monks could not take his eyes off him; it was Myconius. He then saw Luther for the first time; he wished to approach him, to say that he was indebted to him for peace of mind, and that his whole desire was to labor with him. But Myconius was too strictly watched by his superiors: he was not allowed to speak to Luther.

The Elector of Saxony was then holding his court at Weimar, and it is on this account probably that the Cordeliers gave the doctor a welcome. The day following his arrival was the festival of St. Michael. Luther said mass, and was invited to preach in the palace chapel. This was a mark of favor his prince loved to confer on him. He preached extempore, in presence of the court, selecting his text (Matt. 18:1-11) from the Gospel of the day. He spoke forcibly against hypocrites, and those who boast of their own righteousness. But he said not a word about angels, although such was the custom on St. Michael's day.

The courage of the Wittenberg doctor, who was going quietly and on foot to answer a summons which had terminated in death to so many of his predecessors, astonished all who saw him. Interest, admiration, and sympathy prevailed by turns in their hearts. John Kestner, purveyor to the Cordeliers, struck with apprehension at the thought of the dangers which awaited his guest, said to him: "Brother, in Augsburg you will meet with Italians who are learned men and subtle antagonists and who will give you enough to do. I fear you will not be able to defend your cause against them. They will cast you into the fire, and their flames will consume you." Luther solemnly replied: "Dear friend, pray to our Lord God who is in heaven, and put up a paternoster for me and for His dear Son Jesus, whose cause is mine, that He may be favorable to Him. If He maintain His cause, mine is maintained; but if He will not maintain it, of a truth it is not I who can maintain it, and it is He who will bear the dishonor."

Luther continued his journey on foot, and arrived at Nuremberg. As he was about to present himself before a prince of the Church, he wished to appear in a becoming dress. His own was old, and all the worse for the journey. He therefore borrowed a frock from his faithful friend Wenceslas Link, preacher at Nuremberg.

Luther doubtless did not confine his visits to Link; he saw in like manner his other Nuremberg friends, Scheurl the townclerk, the illustrious painter Albert Durer (to whose memory that city erected a statue), and others besides. He derived strength from the conversation of these excellent ones of the earth, while many monks and laymen felt alarmed at his journey, and endeavored to shake his resolution, beseeching him to retrace his steps. The letters he wrote from this city show the spirit which then animated him: "I have met," said he, "with pusillanimous men who wish to persuade me not to go to Augsburg; but I am resolved to proceed. The Lord's will be done! Even at Augsburg, even in the midst of His enemies, Christ reigns. Let Christ live; let Luther die, and every sinner, according as it is written! May the God of my salvation be exalted! Farewell! persevere, stand fast, for it is necessary to be rejected either by God or by man: but God is true, and man is a liar."

Link and an Augustine monk named Leonard could not make up their minds to permit Luther to go alone to face the dangers that threatened him. They knew his disposition, and were aware that, abounding as he did in determination and courage, he would probably be wanting in prudence. They therefore accompanied him. When they were about five leagues from Augsburg, Luther, whom the fatigues of the journey and the various agitations of his mind had probably exhausted, was seized with violent pains in the stomach. He thought he should die. His two friends in great alarm hired a wagon in which they placed the doctor. On the evening of the seventh of October they reached Augsburg, and alighted at the Augustine convent. Luther was very tired; but he soon recovered. No doubt his faith and the vivacity of his mind speedily recruited his weakened body.

Chapter 22

CAJETAN AND SERRA LONGA

IMMEDIATELY on his arrival, and before seeing any one, Luther, desirous of showing the legate all due respect, begged Link to go and announce his presence. Link did so, and respectfully informed the cardinal, on the part of the Wittenberg doctor, that the latter was ready to appear before him whenever he should give the order. The legate was delighted at this news. At last he had this impetuous heretic within his reach, and promised himself that the reformer should not quit the walls of Augsburg as he had entered them. At the same time that Link waited upon the legate, the monk Leonard went to inform Staupitz of Luther's arrival. The vicar-general had written to the doctor that he would certainly come and see him as soon as he knew that he had reached Augsburg. Luther was unwilling to lose a minute in informing him of his presence.

The diet was over. The emperor and the electors had already separated. The emperor, it is true, had not yet quitted the place, but was hunting in the neighborhood. The ambassador of Rome remained alone in Augsburg. If Luther had gone thither during the diet, he would have met with powerful supporters; but everything now seemed destined to bend beneath the weight of the papal authority.

The name of the judge before whom Luther was to appear was not calculated to encourage him. Thomas de Vio, surnamed Cajetan, from the town of Gaeta in the kingdom of Naples, where he was born in 1469, had given great promise from his youth. At sixteen, he had entered the Dominican order, contrary to the express will of his parents. He had afterwards become general of his order, and cardinal of the Roman Church. But what was worse for Luther, this learned doctor was one of the most zealous defenders of that scholastic theology which the reformer had always treated so unmercifully. His mother, we are informed, had dreamed during her pregnancy that St. Thomas in person would instruct the child to which she was about to give birth, and would introduce him into heaven. Accordingly De Vio, when he became a Dominican, had changed his name from James to Thomas. He had zealously defended the prerogatives of the papacy, and the doctrines of Thomas Aquinas, whom he looked upon as the pearl of theologians. Fond of pageantry and show, he construed almost seriously the Roman maxim, that legates are above kings, and surrounded himself with a brilliant train. On the first of August, he had performed a solemn mass in the cathedral of Augsburg, and, in presence of all the princes of the empire, had placed the cardinal's hat on the head of the Archbishop of Mentz, who knelt before him, and had delivered to the emperor himself the hat and sword which the pope had consecrated.

Such was the man before whom the Wittenberg monk was about to appear, dressed in a frock that did not belong to him. Further, the legate's learning, the austerity of his disposition, and the purity of his morals, ensured him an influence and authority in Germany that other Roman courtiers would not easily have obtained. It was no doubt to this reputation for sanctity that he owed this mission. Rome perceived that it would admirably forward her designs. Thus even the good qualities of Cajetan rendered him still more formidable. Besides, the affair intrusted to him was by no means complicated. Luther was already declared a heretic. If he would not retract, the legate must send him to prison; and if he escaped, whoever should give him an asylum was to be excommunicated. This was what the dignitary of the Church before whom Luther was summoned had to perform on behalf of Rome.

Luther had recovered his strength during the night. On Saturday morning (October 8), being already reinvigorated after his journey, he began to consider his strange position. He was resigned, and awaited the manifestation of God's will by the course of events. He had not long to wait. A person, unknown to him, sent to say (as if entirely devoted to him) that he was about to pay him a visit, and that Luther should avoid appearing before the legate until after this interview. The message proceeded from an Italian courtier named Urban of Serra Longa, who had often visited Germany as envoy from the Margrave of Montferrat. He had known the Elector of Saxony, to whom he had been accredited, and after the margrave's death, he had attached himself to the Cardinal de Vio.

The art and address of this individual presented the most striking contrast with the noble frankness and generous integrity of Luther. The Italian soon arrived at the Augustine monastery. The cardinal had sent him to sound the reformer, and prepare him for the recantation expected from him. Serra Longa imagined that his sojourn in Germany had given him a great advantage over the other courtiers in the legate's train; he hoped to make short work with this German monk. He arrived attended by two domestics, and professed to have come of his own accord, from friendship towards a favorite of the Elector of Saxony, and from attachment to the holy Church. After having most cordially saluted Luther, the diplomatist added in an affectionate manner:

"I am come to offer you good advice. Be wise, and become reconciled with the Church. Submit to the cardinal without reserve. Retract your offensive language. Remember the Abbot Joachim of Florence: he had published, as you know, many heretical things, and yet he was declared no heretic, because he retracted his errors."

Upon this Luther spoke of justifying what he had done.

Serra Longa.—"Beware of that! . . . Would you enter the lists against the legate of his holiness?"

Luther.—"If they convince me of having taught anything contrary to the Roman Church, I shall be my own judge, and immediately retract. The essential point will be to know whether the legate relies on the authority of St. Thomas more than the faith will sanction. If he does so, I will not yield."

Serra Longa.—"Oh, oh! You intend to break a lance then!"

The Italian then began to use language which Luther styles horrible. He argued that one might maintain false propositions, provided they brought in money and filled the treasury; that all discussion in the universities against the pope's authority must be avoided; that, on the contrary, it should be asserted that the pope could, by a single nod, change or suppress articles of faith; and so he ran on, in a similar strain. But the wily Italian soon perceived that he was forgetting himself; and returning to his mild language, he endeavored to persuade Luther to submit to the legate in all things, and to retract his doctrine, his oaths, and his theses.

The doctor, who was at first disposed to credit the fair professions of the orator Urban (as he calls him in his narrative), was now convinced that they were of little worth, and that he was much more on the legate's side than on his. He consequently became less communicative and was content to say that he was disposed to show all humility, to give proofs of his obedience, and render satisfaction in those things in which he might have erred. At these words Serra Longa exclaimed joyfully: "I shall hasten to the legate; you will follow me presently. Everything will go well, and all will soon be settled."

He went away. The Saxon monk, who had more discernment than the Roman courtier, thought to himself: "This crafty Sinon * has been badly taught and trained by his Greeks." Luther was in suspense between hope and fear; yet hope prevailed. The visit and the strange professions of Serra Longa, whom he afterwards called a bungling mediator, revived his courage.

The councilors and other inhabitants of Augsburg, to whom the elector had recommended Luther, were all eager to see the monk whose name already resounded throughout Germany. Peutinger, the imperial councilor, one of the most eminent patricians of the city, who frequently invited Luther to his table; the councilor Langemantel; Doctor Auerbach of Leipzig; the two brothers Adelmann, both canons, and many more, repaired to the Augustine convent. They cordially saluted this extraordinary man who had undertaken so long a journey to place himself in the hands of the Roman agents. "Have you a safe conduct?" asked they. "No," replied the intrepid monk. "What boldness!" they all exclaimed. "It was a polite expression," says Luther, to designate my rashness and folly." All unanimously entreated him not to visit the legate before obtaining a safe-conduct from the emperor himself. It is probable the public had already heard something of the pope's brief, of which the legate was the bearer.

* The Greek who, by a false tale, induced the Trojans to drag the wooden horse into Troy. Vergil's Aeneid

"But," replied Luther, "I set out for Augsburg without a safe-conduct, and have arrived safely."

"The elector has recommended you to us; you ought therefore to obey us, and do all that we tell you," answered Langemantel affectionately but firmly.

Doctor Auerbach coincided with these views, and added: "We know that at the bottom of his heart the cardinal is exceedingly irritated against you. One cannot trust these Italians."

The canon Adelmann urged the same thing: "You have been sent without protection, and they have forgotten to provide you with that which you needed most."

His friends undertook to obtain the requisite safe-conduct from the emperor. They then told Luther how many persons, even in elevated rank, had a leaning in his favor. "The minister of France himself, who left Augsburg a few days ago, has spoken of you in the most honorable manner." This remark struck Luther, and he remembered it afterwards. Thus several of the most respectable citizens in one of the first cities of the Empire were already gained over to the Reformation.

The conversation had reached this point when Serra Longa returned. "Come," said he to Luther, "the cardinal is waiting for you. I will myself conduct you to him. But you must first learn how to appear in his pressence: when you enter the room in which he is, you will prostrate yourself with your face to the ground; when he tells you to rise, you will kneel before him; and you will wait his further orders before you stand up. Remember you are about to appear before a prince of the Church. As for the rest, fear nothing: all will speedily be settled without difficulty."

Luther, who had promised to follow this Italian as soon as he was invited, found himself in a dilemma. However, he did not hesitate to inform him of the advice of his Augsburg friends, and spoke of a safe-conduct.

"Beware of asking for anything of the kind," immediately replied Serra Longa; "you do not require one. The legate is kindly disposed towards you, and ready to end this business in a friendly manner. If you ask for a safe-conduct, you will ruin everything."

"My gracious lord, the Elector of Saxony," replied Luther, "recommended me to several honorable men in this city. They advise me to undertake nothing without a safe-conduct: I ought to follow their advice. For if I did not, and anything should happen, they will write to the elector, my master, that I would not listen to them."

Luther persisted in his determination, and Serra Longa was compelled to return to his chief, and announce the shoal on which his mission had struck, at the very moment he flattered himself with success.

Thus terminated the conferences of that day with the orator of Montferrat.

Another invitation was sent to Luther, but with a very different view. John Frosch, prior of the Carmelites, was an old friend. Two years before, as licentiate in theology, he had defended some theses, under the presidence of Luther. He came to see him, and begged him earnestly to come and stay with him. He claimed the honor of entertaining the doctor of Germany as his guest. Already men did not fear to pay him homage even in the face of Rome; already the weak had become the stronger. Luther accepted the invitation, and left the convent of the Augustines for that of the Carmelites.

The day did not close without serious reflections. Serra Longa's eagerness and the fears of the councilors alike pointed out the difficulties of Luther's position. Nevertheless, he had God in heaven for his protector; guarded by Him he could sleep without fear.

The next day was Sunday, on which he obtained a little more repose. Yet he had to endure fatigues of another kind. All the talk of the city was about Doctor Luther, and everybody desired to see, as he wrote to Melancthon, "this new Erostratus, who had caused so vast a conflagration." They crowded round him in his walks, and the good doctor smiled, no doubt, at this singular excitement.

But he had to undergo importunities of another kind. If the people were desirous of seeing him, they had a still greater wish to hear him. He was requested on all sides to preach. Luther had no greater joy than to proclaim the gospel. It would have delighted him to preach Jesus Christ in this large city, and in the solemn circumstances in which he was placed. But he evinced on this occasion, as on many others, a just sentiment of propriety, and great respect for his superiors. He refused to preach, for fear the legate should think he did it to annoy and to brave him. This moderation and this discretion were assuredly as good as a sermon.

The cardinal's people, however, did not permit him to remain quiet. They renewed their persuasions. "The cardinal," said they, "gives you assurances of his grace and favor: what are you afraid of?" They employed a thousand reasons to persuade him to wait upon De Vio. "He is a very merciful father," said one of these envoys. But another approached and whispered in his ear: "Do not believe what they tell you. He never keeps his word." Luther persisted in his resolution.

On Monday morning (October 10), Serra Longa again returned to the charge. The courtier had made it a point of honor to succeed in his negotiation. He had scarcely arrived when he said in Latin: "Why do you not wait upon the cardinal? He is expecting you most indulgently: the whole matter lies in six letters: *Revoca*, retract. Come! you have nothing to fear."

Luther thought to himself that these six letters were very important ones; but without entering into any discussion on the merits of the things to be retracted, he replied: "I will appear as soon as I have a safe-conduct."

Serra Longa lost his temper on hearing these words. He insisted— he made fresh representations; but Luther was immovable. Becoming still more angry, he exclaimed: "You imagine, no doubt, that the elector will take up arms in your defense, and for your sake run the risk of losing the territories he received from his forefathers?"

Luther—"God forbid!"

Serra Longa—"When all forsake you, where will you take refuge?"

Luther, looking to heaven with an eye of faith, "Under heaven."

Serra Longa was silent for a moment, struck with the sublimity of this unexpected answer. He then resumed the conversation:

"What would you do if you held the legate, pope, and cardinals in your hands, as they have you now in theirs?"

Luther—"I would show them all possible honor and respect. But with me the Word of God is before everything."

Serra Longa, smiling, and snapping his fingers in the manner of the Italians: "Eh, eh! all honor! . . . I do not believe a word of it."

He then went out, sprang into his saddle, and disappeared.

Serra Longa did not return to Luther; but he long remembered the resistance he had met with from the reformer, and that which his master was soon after to experience in person. We shall find him at a later period loudly calling for Luther's blood.

Serra Longa had not long quitted the doctor when the safe-conduct arrived. Luther's friends had obtained it from the imperial councilors. It is probable that the latter had consulted the emperor on the subject, as he was not far from Augsburg. It would even appear from what the cardinal said afterwards, that from unwillingness to displease him, his consent also had been asked. Perhaps this was the reason why Serra Longa was set to work upon Luther; for open opposition to the security of a safe-conduct would have disclosed intentions that it was desirable to keep secret. It was a safer plan to induce Luther himself to desist from the demand. But they soon found out that the Saxon monk was not a man to give way.

Luther was now to appear. In demanding a safe-conduct, he did not lean upon an arm of flesh; for he was fully aware that an imperial safe-conduct had not preserved John Huss from the stake. He only wished to do his duty by submitting to the advice of his master's friends. The Lord would decide his fate. If God should require his life, he would be ready joyfully to resign it. At this solemn moment, he felt the need of communing once again with his friends, above all with Melancthon, who was so dear to his heart, and he took advantage of a few moments of leisure to write to him.

"Show yourself a man," said he, "as you do at all times. Teach our beloved youths what is upright and acceptable to God. As for me, I am going to be sacrificed for you and for them, if such is the Lord's will. I would rather die, and even (which would be my greater misfortune) be forever deprived of your sweet society, than retract what I felt it my duty to teach, and thus ruin perhaps by my own fault the excellent studies to which we are now devoting ourselves.

"Italy, like Egypt in times of old, is plunged in darkness so thick that it may be felt. No one in that country knows anything of Christ, or of what belongs to Him; and yet they are our lords and our masters in faith and in morals. Thus the wrath of God is fulfilled among us, as the prophet saith: 'I will give children to be their princes, and babes shall rule over them.' Do your duty to God, my dear Philip, and avert His anger by pure and fervent prayer."

The legate, being informed that Luther would appear before him on the morrow, assembled the Italians and Germans in whom he had the greatest confidence, in order to concert with them the method he should pursue with the Saxon monk. Their opinions were divided. We must compel him to retract, said one; We must seize him and put him in prison, said another; It would be better to put him out of the way, thought a third; We should try to win him over by gentleness and mildness, was the opinion of a fourth. The cardinal seemed to have resolved on beginning with the last method.

Chapter 23

LUTHER'S RELEASE FROM HIS ORDER

THE DAY fixed for the interview arrived at last. The legate knowing that Luther had declared himself willing to retract everything that could be proved contrary to the truth, was full of hope; he doubted not that it would be easy for a man of his rank and learning to reclaim this monk to obedience to the Church.

Luther repaired to the legate's residence, accompanied by the prior of the Carmelites, his host and his friend; by two friars of the same convent; by Doctor Link and an Augustine, probably the one that had come from Nuremberg with him. He had scarcely entered the legate's palace when all the Italians who formed the train of this prince of the Church crowded round him; everyone desired to see the famous doctor, and they thronged him so much that he could with difficulty proceed. Luther found the apostolic nuncio and Serra Longa in the hall where the cardinal was waiting for him. His reception was cold, but civil, and conformable with Roman etiquette. Luther, in accordance with the advice he had received from Serra Longa, prostrated himself before the cardinal; when the latter told him to rise, he remained on his knees; and at a fresh order from the legate, he stood up. Many of the most distinguished Italians in the legate's court found their way into the hall in order to be present during the interview; they particularly desired to see the German monk humble himself before the pope's representative.

The legate remained silent. He hated Luther as an adversary of the theological supremacy of St. Thomas, and as the chief of a new, active, and hostile party in a rising university, whose first steps had disquieted the Thomists. He was pleased at seeing Luther fall down before him, and thought, as a contemporary observed, that he was about to recant. The doctor on his part humbly waited for the prince to address him; but as he did not speak, Luther understood this silence as an invitation to begin, and he did so in these words:

"Most worthy Father, in obedience to the summons of his papal holiness, and in compliance with the orders of my gracious lord the Elector of Saxony, I appear before you as a submissive and dutiful son of the holy Christian Church, and acknowledge that I have published the propositions and theses ascribed to me. I am ready to listen most obediently to my accusation, and if I have erred, to submit to instruction in the truth."

The cardinal, who had determined to assume the appearance of a tender and compassionate father towards an erring child, then adopted the most friendly tone; he praised and expressed his delight at Luther's humility, and said to him: "My dear son, you have disturbed all Germany by your dispute on indulgences. I understand that you are a very learned doctor in the Holy Scriptures, and that you have many followers. For this reason, if you desire to be a member of the Church, and to find a gracious father in the pope, listen to me."

After this prelude, the legate did not hesitate to declare at once what he expected of him, so confident was he of Luther's submission. "Here are three articles," said he, "which by the command of our holy Father, Pope Leo X, I have to set before you. First, You must bethink yourself, own your faults, and retract your errors, propositions, and sermons; secondly, You must promise to abstain in the future from propagating your opinions; and, thirdly, Bind yourself to behave with greater moderation, and avoid everything that may grieve or disturb the Church."

Luther—"Most holy Father, I beg you will show me the pope's brief, by virtue of which you have received full powers to treat of this matter."

Serra Longa and the other Italians opened their eyes with astonishment at this demand, and although the German monk had already appeared to them a very strange kind of man, they could not conceal their amazement at such a daring request. Christians, accustomed to ideas of justice, desire that justice should be observed towards others and towards themselves; but those who act habitually in an arbitrary manner, are surprised when they are called upon to proceed according to the usual rules, formalities, and laws.

De Vio—"This request, my dear son, cannot be granted. You must confess your errors, keep a strict watch upon your words for the future, and not return like a dog to his vomit, so that we may sleep without anxiety or disturbance; then, in accordance with the order and authorization of our most holy Father the Pope, I will arrange the whole business."

Luther—"Condescend, then, to inform me in what I have erred."

At this new request, the Italian courtiers, who had expected to see the poor German fall down on his knees and beg pardon, were still more astonished than before. None of them would have deigned to reply to so impertinent a question. But De Vio, who thought it ungenerous to crush this petty monk with the weight of his authority, and who, besides, trusted to gain an easy victory by his learning, consented to tell Luther of what he was accused, and even to enter into discussion with him. We must do justice to the general of the Dominicans. We must acknowledge that he showed more equity, a greater sense of propriety, and less passion, than have been often shown in similar matters since. He replied in a condescending tone:

"Most dear son! here are two propositions that you have advanced, and which you must retract before all: First, The treasure of indulgences does not consist of the sufferings and merits of our Lord Jesus Christ; second, The man who receives the holy sacrament must have faith in the grace that is presented to him."

Each of these propositions, in truth, struck a mortal blow at the Romish commerce. If the pope had not the power of dispensing at his pleasure the merits of the Saviour; if, in receiving the drafts which the brokers of the Church negotiated, men did not receive a portion of this infinite righteousness, this paper-money would lose its value, and would be as worthless as a heap of rags. It was the same with the sacraments. Indulgences were more or less an extraordinary branch of Roman commerce; the sacraments were a staple commodity. The revenue they produced was of no small amount. To assert that faith was necessary before they could confer a real benefit on the soul of a Christian, took away all their charms in the eyes of the people; for it is not the pope who gives faith: it is beyond his province; it proceeds from God alone. To declare its necessity was therefore depriving Rome both of the speculation and the profit. By attacking these two doctrines, Luther had imitated Jesus Christ, who at the very beginning of His ministry had overthrown the tables of the money-changers, and driven the dealers out of the temple. "Make not my Father's house a house of merchandise," He had said.

"In confuting your errors," said Cajetan, "I will not appeal to the authority of St. Thomas and other doctors of the schools; I will rely entirely on Holy Scripture, and talk with you in all friendliness."

But De Vio had scarcely begun to bring forward his proofs before he departed from the rule he had declared that he would follow. He combated Luther's first proposition by an Extravagance of Pope Clement, and the second by all sorts of opinions from the schoolmen. The discussion turned first on this papal constitution in favor of indulgences. Luther, indignant at hearing what authority the legate ascribed to a decree of Rome, exclaimed:—

"I cannot receive such constitutions as sufficient proofs on matters so important. For they pervert the Holy Scriptures, and never quote them to the purpose."

De Vio—"The pope has power and authority over all things."

Luther (quickly)—"Except Scripture!"

De Vio (sneering)—"Except Scripture! . . . Do you not know that the pope is above councils; he has recently condemned and punished the Council of Basle."

Luther—"The university of Paris has appealed from this sentence."

De Vio—"These Paris gentlemen will receive their deserts."

The dispute between the cardinal and Luther then turned upon the second point, namely, the faith that Luther declared necessary for the efficacy of the sacraments. Luther, according to his custom, quoted various passages of Scripture in favor of the opinion he maintained; but the legate treated them with ridicule. "It is of faith in general that you are speaking," said he. "No," replied Luther. One of the Italians, the legate's master of the ceremonies, irritated at Luther's resistance and replies, was burning with the desire to speak. He continually endeavored to put in a word, but the legate imposed silence on him. At last he was compelled to reprimand him so sharply, that the master of the ceremonies quitted the hall in confusion.

"As for indulgences," said Luther to the legate, "if it can be shown that I am mistaken, I am very ready to receive instruction. We may pass over that and yet be good Christians. But as to the article of faith, if I made the slightest concession, I should renounce Jesus Christ. I cannot—I will not yield on this point, and with God's grace I will never yield."

De Vio (growing angry)—"Whether you will, or whether you will not, you must retract that article this very day, or, upon that article alone, I shall reject and condemn your whole doctrine."

Luther—"I have no will but the Lord's. Let Him do with me as seemeth good to Him. But if I had four hundred heads, I would rather lose them all than retract the testimony which I have borne to the holy Christian faith."

De Vio—"I did not come here to dispute with you. Retract, or prepare to suffer the penalty you have deserved."

Luther saw clearly that it was impossible to put an end to the subject by a conference. His opponent sat before him as if he were himself pope, and pretended that he would receive humbly and submissively all that was said to him; and yet he listened to Luther's replies, even when they were founded on Holy Scripture, with shrugging of shoulders, and every mark of irony and contempt. He thought the wiser plan would be to answer the cardinal in writing. This means, thought he, gives at least one consolation to the oppressed. Others will be able to judge of the matter, and the unjust adversary, who by his clamors remains master of the field of battle, may be frightened at the consequences.

Luther having shown a disposition to retire, the legate said, "Do you wish me to give you a safe-conduct to go to Rome?"

Nothing would have pleased Cajetan better than the acceptance of this offer. He would thus have been freed from a task of which he now began to perceive the difficulties; and Luther, with his heresy, would have fallen into hands that would soon have arranged everything. But the reformer, who saw the dangers that surrounded him, even in Augsburg, took care not to accept an offer that would have delivered him up, bound hand and foot, to the vengeance of his enemies. He therefore rejected it, as often as De Vio proposed it; and he did so very frequently. The legate dissembled his vexation at Luther's refusal; he took refuge in his dignity, and dismissed the monk with a compassionate smile, under which he endeavored to conceal his disappointment, and at the same time with the politeness of a man who hopes for better success another time.

Luther had scarcely reached the court of the palace before that babbling Italian, the master of the ceremonies, whom his lord's reprimands had compelled to quit the hall of conference, overjoyed at being able to speak without being observed by Cajetan, and burning with desire to confound the abominable heretic with his luminous reasonings, ran after him, and began, as he walked along, to deal out his sophisms. But Luther, disgusted with this foolish individual, replied to him by one of those sarcasms which he had so much at command, and the poor master slunk away abashed, and returned in confusion to the cardinal's palace.

Luther did not carry away a very exalted opinion of his adversary. He had heard from him, as he wrote afterwards to Spalatin, propositions quite opposed to sound theology, and which in the mouth of another would have been considered arch-heresies. And yet De Vio was reckoned the most learned of the Dominicans. Next after him was Prierio. "We may conclude from this," says Luther, "what they must be who are in the tenth or the hundredth rank."

On the other hand, the noble and decided bearing of the Wittenberg doctor had greatly surprised the cardinal and his courtiers. Instead of a poor monk asking pardon as a favor, they had found a man of independence, a firm Christian, an enlightened doctor, who required that unjust accusations should be supported by proofs, and who victoriously defended his own doctrine. Every one in Cajetan's palace cried out against the pride, obstinacy, and effrontery of the heretic. Luther and De Vio had learned to know each other, and both prepared for their second interview.

A very agreeable surprise awaited Luther on his return to the Carmelite convent. The vicar-general of the Augustine order, his friend and father, Staupitz, had arrived at Augsburg. Unable to prevent Luther's journey to that city, Staupitz gave his friend a new and touching proof of his attachment by going thither himself in the hope of being useful to him. This excellent man foresaw that the conference with the legate might have the most serious consequences. He was equally agitated by his fears and by his friendship for Luther. After so painful an interview, it was a great comfort to the doctor to embrace so dear a friend. He told him how impossible it had been to obtain an answer of any value, and how the cardinal had insisted solely upon a recantation, without having essayed to convince him. "You must positively," said Staupitz, "reply to the legate in writing."

After what he had learned of the first interview, Staupitz entertained but little hopes from another. He therefore resolved upon an act which he now thought necessary; he determined to release Luther from the obligations of his order. By this means Staupitz thought to attain two objects: if, as everything seemed to forebode, Luther should fail in this undertaking, he would thus prevent the disgrace of his condemnation from being reflected on the whole order: and if the cardinal should order him to force Luther to be silent or to retract, he would have an excuse for not doing so. The ceremony was performed with the usual formalities. Luther saw clearly what he must now expect. His soul was deeply moved at the breaking of those bonds which he had taken upon him in the enthusiasm of youth. The order he had chosen rejected him; his natural protectors forsook him. He became a stranger among his brethren. But although his heart was filled with sadness at the thought, all his joy returned when he directed his eyes to the promises of a faithful God, who has said: "I will never leave thee nor forsake thee."

The emperor's councilors informed the legate, through the Bishop of Trent, that Luther was provided with an imperial safe-conduct, and at the same time enjoined him to take no proceedings against the doctor. De Vio lost his temper, and abruptly answered in truly Romish language: "It is well; but I will execute the pope's orders." We know what they were.

Chapter 24

A NEW ADVERSARY

THE NEXT DAY both parties prepared for a second interview, which it seemed would be decisive. Luther's friends, who were resolved to accompany him to the legate's palace, went to the Carmelite convent. Peutinger and the Dean of Trent, both imperial councilors, and Staupitz, arrived successively. Shortly after, the doctor had the pleasure of seeing them joined by the knight Philip of Feilitzsch and Doctor Ruhel, councilors of the elector, who had received their master's order to be present at the conferences, and to protect Luther's liberty. They had reached Augsburg the previous evening. They were to keep close to him, says Mathesius, as the knight of Chlum stood by John Huss at Constance. The doctor moreover took a notary, and, accompanied by all his friends, he repaired to the legate's palace.

At this moment Staupitz approached him: he fully comprehended Luther's position; he knew that unless his eyes were fixed on the Lord, who is the Deliverer of His people, he must fall. "My dear brother," said he, seriously, "bear constantly in mind that you have begun these things in the name of the Lord Jesus Christ." Thus did God environ his humble servant with consolation and encouragement.

When Luther arrived at the cardinal's, he found a new adversary: this was the prior of the Dominicans of Augsburg, who sat beside his chief. Luther, conformably with the resolution he had taken, had written his answer. The customary salutations being finished, he read the following declaration with a loud voice:—

"I declare that I honor the holy Roman Church, and that I shall continue to honor her. I have sought after truth in my public disputations, and everything that I have said I still consider as right, true, and Christian. Yet I am but a man, and may be deceived. I am therefore willing to receive instruction and correction in those things wherein I may have erred. I declare myself ready to reply orally or in writing to all the objections and charges that the lord legate may bring against me. I declare myself ready to submit my theses to the four universities of Basle, Freiburg in Brisgau, Louvain, and Paris, and to retract, whatever they shall declare erroneous. In a word, I am ready to do all that can be required of a Christian. But I solemnly protest against the method that has been pursued in this affair, and against the strange pretension of compelling me to retract without having refuted me."

Undoubtedly nothing could be more reasonable than these propositions of Luther's, and they must have greatly embarrassed a judge who had been tutored beforehand as to the judgment he should pronounce. The legate, who had not expected this protest, endeavored to hide his confusion by affecting to smile at it, and by assuming an appearance of mildness. "This protest," said he to Luther, with a smile, "is necessary; I have no desire to dispute with you either privately or publicly; but I propose arranging this matter with the kindness of a parent." The sum of the cardinal's policy consisted in laying aside the stricter forms of justice, which protect the accused, and treating the whole affair as one of mere administration between a superior and an inferior: a convenient method, that opens a wider field for arbitrary proceedings.

Continuing with the most affectionate air, De Vio said: "My dear friend, abandon, I beseech you, so useless an undertaking; bethink yourself, acknowledge the truth, and I am prepared to reconcile you with the Church and the sovereign bishop . . . Retract, my friend, retract; such is the pope's wish. Whether you will or whether you will not, is of little consequence. It would be a hard matter for you to kick against the pricks."

Luther, who saw himself treated as if he were already a rebellious child and an outcast from the Church, exclaimed: "I cannot retract! but I offer to reply, and that too in writing. We had debating enough yesterday."

De Vio was irritated at this expression, which reminded him that he had not acted with sufficient prudence; but he recovered himself, and said with a smile: "Debated! my dear son, I have not debated with you: besides, I have no wish to debate; but, to please the most serene Elector Frederick, I am ready to listen to you, and to exhort you in a friendly and paternal manner."

Luther could not understand why the legate was so much scandalized at the term he had employed; for (thought he) if I had not wished to speak with politeness, I ought to have said, not debated, but disputed and wrangled, for that is what we really did yesterday.

De Vio, who felt that in the presence of the respectable witnesses who attended this conference, he must at least appear anxious to convince Luther, reverted to the two propositions, which he had pointed out as fundamental errors, being firmly resolved to permit the reformer to speak as little as possible. Using his Italian volubility, he overwhelmed the doctor with objections, without waiting for any reply. At one time he jeered, at another scolded; he declaimed with passionate warmth; mingled together the most heterogeneous matters; quoted St. Thomas and Aristotle; clamored, stormed against all who thought differently from himself. More than ten times Luther tried to speak; but the legate immediately interrupted him and overwhelmed him with threats. Retract! retract! this was all that was required. He raved, he domineered, he alone was permitted to speak. Staupitz took upon himself to check the legate. "Pray, allow brother Luther time to reply to you," said he. But De Vio began again; he quoted the Extravagances and the opinions of St. Thomas; he had resolved to have all the talk to himself during this interview. If he could not convince, and if he dared not strike, he would do his best to stun by his violence.

Luther and Staupitz saw very clearly that they must renounce all hope, not only of enlightening De Vio by discussion, but still more of making any useful confession of faith. Luther therefore reverted to the request he had made at the beginning of the sitting, and which the cardinal had then eluded. Since he was not permitted to speak, he begged that he might at least be permitted to transmit a written reply to the legate. Staupitz seconded this petition; several of the spectators joined their entreaties to his, and Cajetan, notwithstanding his repugnance to every thing that was written, for he remembered that such writings are lasting, at length consented. The meeting broke up. The hopes that had been entertained of seeing the matter arranged at this interview were deferred; they must wait and see the issue of the next conference.

The permission which the general of the Dominicans had given Luther to take time for his reply, and to write his answer, to the two distinct accusations touching indulgences and faith, was no more than strict justice required, and yet we must give De Vio credit for this mark of moderation and impartiality.

Luther quitted the cardinal, delighted that his request had been granted. On his way to Cajetan, and on his return, he was the object of public attention. All enlightened men were as much interested in his affair as if they were to be tried themselves. It was felt that the cause of the gospel, of justice, and of liberty, was then pleading at Augsburg. The lower classes alone held with Cajetan, and they no doubt gave the Reformer some significant proofs of their sentiments, for he took notice of them.

It became more evident every day that the legate would hear no other words from Luther than these: "I retract," and Luther was resolved not to pronounce them. What would be the issue of so unequal a struggle? How could it be imagined that all the power of Rome matched against a single man should fail to crush him? Luther saw this; he felt the weight of that terrible hand under which he had voluntarily placed himself; he lost all hope of returning to Wittenberg, of seeing his dear Philip again, of mingling once more with those generous youths in whose hearts he so delighted to scatter the seeds of life. He beheld the sentence of excommunication suspended over his head, and doubted not that it would soon fall upon him. These prospects afflicted his soul, but he was not cast down. His trust in God was not shaken. God could break the instrument He had been pleased to make use of until this hour; but He would uphold the truth. Happen what may, Luther felt he must defend it to the last. He therefore began to prepare the protest that he intended to present to the legate. He devoted part of October 13 to this task.

Chapter 25

LUTHER'S PROTEST TO DE VIO

O N FRIDAY (October 14) Luther returned to the cardinal, accompanied by the elector's councilors. The Italians crowded around him as usual, and were present at the conference in great numbers. Luther advanced and presented his protest to the cardinal. His courtiers regarded this paper with astonishment—a paper so presumptuous in their eyes. This is what the Wittenberg doctor declared to their master:

"You attack me on two points. First, you oppose to me the constitution of Pope Clement VI, in which it is said that the treasure of indulgences is the merit of the Lord Jesus Christ and of the saints—which I deny in my theses.

"Panormitanus declares in his first book that in whatever concerns the holy faith, not only a general council, but still further, each believer, is above the pope, if he can bring forward the declarations of Scripture and allege better reasons than the pope. The voice of our Lord Jesus Christ is far above the voice of all men, whatever be the names they bear.

"My greatest cause of grief and of serious reflection is, that this constitution contains doctrines entirely at variance with the truth. It declares that the merits of the saints are a treasure, while the whole of Scripture bears witness that God rewards us far more richly than we deserve. The prophet exclaims: 'Enter not into judgment with thy servant, O Lord, for in thy sight shall no man living be justified!' 'Woe be to men, however honorable and however praiseworthy their lives may have been,' says Augustine, 'if a judgment from which mercy was excluded should be pronounced upon them!'

"Thus the saints are not saved by their merits, but solely by God's mercy, as I have declared. I maintain this, and in it I stand fast. The words of Holy Scripture, which declare that the saints have not merit enough, must be set above the words of men, which affirm that they have an excess. For the pope is not above the Word of God, but below it."

Luther did not stop here: he showed that if indulgences cannot be the merits of the saints, they cannot any the more be the merits of Christ. He proved that indulgences are barren and fruitless, since their only effect is to exempt men from performing good works, such as prayer and almsgiving. "No," exclaimed he, "the merits of Jesus Christ are not a treasure of indulgence exempting man from good works, but a treasure of grace which quickeneth. The merits of Christ are applied to the believer without indulgences, without the keys, by the Holy Ghost alone, and not by the pope. If anyone has an opinion better founded than mine," he added, terminating what referred to this first point, "let him make it known to me, and then will I retract."

"I affirm," said he, coming to the second article, "that no man can be justified before God if he has not faith; so that it is necessary for a man to believe with a perfect assurance that he has obtained grace. To doubt of this grace is to reject it. The faith of the righteous is his righteousness and his life."

Luther proved his proposition by a multitude of declarations from Scripture.

"Condescend, therefore, to intercede for me with our most holy father the pope," he added, "in order that he may not treat me with such harshness. My soul is seeking for the light of truth. I am not so proud or so vainglorious as to be ashamed of retracting if I have taught false doctrines. My greatest joy will be to witness the triumph of what is according to God's Word. Only let not men force me to do anything that is against the voice of my conscience."

The legate took the declaration from Luther's hands. After glancing over it, he said coldly: "You have indulged in useless verbiage: you have penned many idle words; you have replied in a foolish manner to the two articles, and have blackened your paper with a great number of passages from Scripture that have no connection with the subject." Then, with an air of contempt, De Vio flung

Luther's protest aside, as if it were of no value, and recommencing in the tone which had been so successful in the previous interview, he began to exclaim with all his might that Luther ought to retract. The latter was immovable. "Brother! brother!" cried De Vio in Italian, "on the last occasion you were very tractable, but now you are very obstinate." The cardinal then began a long speech, extracted from the writings of St. Thomas; he again extolled the constitution of Clement VI; and persisted in maintaining that by virtue of this constitution it is the very merits of Jesus Christ that are dispensed to the believer by means of indulgences. He thought he had reduced Luther to silence; the later sometimes interrupted him; but De Vio raved and stormed without intermission, and claimed, as on the previous day, the sole right of speaking.

This method had partially succeeded the first time; but Luther was not a man to submit to it on a second occasion. His indignation burst out at last; it was his turn to astonish the spectators, who believed him already conquered by the prelate's volubility. He raised his sonorous voice, seized upon the cardinal's favorite objection, and made him pay dearly for his rashness in venturing to enter into discussion with him. "Retract, retract!" repeated De Vio, pointing to the papal constitution. "Well, if it can be proved by this constitution," said Luther, "that the treasure of indulgences is the very merits of Jesus Christ, I consent to retract, according to your Eminence's good will and pleasure."

The Italians, who had expected nothing of the kind, opened their eyes in astonishment at these words, and could not contain their joy at seeing their adversary caught in the net. As for the cardinal, he was beside himself; he laughed aloud, but with a laugh in which anger and indignation were mingled; he sprang forward, seized the book which contained this famous constitution; looked for it, found it, and, exulting in the victory he thought certain, read the passage aloud with panting eagerness. The Italians were elated; the elector's councilors were uneasy and embarrassed; Luther was waiting for his adversary. At last, when the cardinal came to these words: "The Lord Jesus Christ has acquired this treasure by His sufferings," Luther stopped him: "Most worthy father," said he, "pray, meditate and weigh these words carefully: 'He has acquired.' Christ has acquired a treasure by His merits; the merits, therefore, are not the treasure; for, to speak philosophically, the cause and effect are very different matters. The merits of Jesus Christ have acquired for the pope the power of giving certain indulgences to the people; but it is not the very merits of our Lord that the hand of the pontiff distributes. Thus, then, my conclusion is the true one, and this constitution, which you invoke with so much noise testifies with me to the truth I proclaim."

De Vio still held the book in his hands, his eyes resting on the fatal passage; he could make no reply. He was caught in the very snare he had laid, and Luther held him there with a strong hand, to the inexpressible astonishment of the Italian courtiers around him. The legate would have eluded the difficulty, but had not the means: he had long abandoned the testimony of Scripture and of the Fathers; he had taken refuge in this Extravagance of Clement VI, and lo! he was caught. Yet he was too cunning to betray his confusion. Desirous of concealing his disgrace, the prince of the Church suddenly quitted this subject, and violently attacked other articles. Luther, who perceived this skillful maneuver, did not permit him to escape; he tightened and closed on every side the net in which he had taken the cardinal, and rendered all escape impossible. "Most reverend Father," said he, with an ironical, yet very respectful tone, "your eminence cannot, however, imagine that we Germans are ignorant of grammar: to be a treasure, and to acquire a treasure, are two very different things."

"Retract!" said De Vio; "retract! or if you do not, I shall send you to Rome to appear before judges commissioned to take cognizance of your affair. I shall excommunicate you with all your partisans, with all who are or who may be favorable to you, and reject them from the Church. All power has been given me in this respect by the holy apostolic see. Think you that your protectors will stop me? Do you imagine that the pope cares anything for Germany? The pope's little finger is stronger than all the German princes put together."

"Deign," replied Luther, "to forward to Pope Leo X, with my humble prayers, the answer which I have transmitted you in writing."

At these words, the legate, highly pleased at finding a moment's release, again assumed an air of dignity, and said to Luther with pride and anger:

"Retract, or return no more."

These words struck Luther. This time he would reply in another way than by speeches: he bowed and left the hall, followed by the elector's councilors. The cardinal and the Italians, remaining alone, looked at one another in confusion at such a result.

Thus the Dominican system, covered with the brilliancy of the Roman purple, had haughtily dismissed its humble adversary. But Luther was conscious that there was a power—the Christian doctrine, the truth—that no secular or spiritual authority could ever subdue. Of the two combatants, he who withdraw remained master of the field of battle.

This is the first step by which the Church separated from the papacy.

Luther and De Vio did not meet again; but the reformer had made a deep impression on the legate, which impression was never effaced. What Luther had said about faith, what De Vio read in the subsequent writings of the Wittenberg doctor, greatly modified the cardinal's opinions. The theologians of Rome beheld with surprise and discontent the sentiments he advanced on justification in his commentary on the Epistle to the Romans. The Reformation did not recede, did not retract; but its judge, he who had not ceased from crying, "Retract! Retract!" changed his views, and indirectly retracted his errors. Thus was crowned the unshaken fidelity of the Reformer.

Luther returned to the monastery where he had been entertained. He had stood fast; he had given testimony to the truth; he had done his duty. God would perform the rest! His heart overflowed with peace and joy.

Chapter 26

AN EVENING OF COMMUNION

Y ET THE RUMORS that reached him were not very encouraging: it was reported in the city, that if he did not retract, he was to be seized and thrown into a dungeon. The vicar-general of his order, Staupitz himself, it was affirmed, had given his consent. Luther could not believe what was said of his friend. No! Staupitz would not deceive him! As for the cardinal's designs, to judge from his words, there could be no doubt about them. Yet he would not flee from the danger; his life, like the truth itself, was in powerful hands, and, despite the threatening peril, he was resolved not to quit Augsburg.

The legate soon repented of his violence; he felt that he had gone beyond his part, and endeavored to retrace his steps. Staupitz had scarcely finished his dinner (on the morning of the interview, and the dinner-hour was noon), before he received a message from the cardinal, inviting him to his palace. Staupitz went thither attended by Wenceslas Link. The vicar-general found the legate alone with Serra Longa. De Vio immediately approached Staupitz, and addressed him in the mildest language. "Endeavor," said he, "to prevail upon your monk, and induce him to retract. Really, in other respects, I am well pleased with him, and he has no better friend than myself."

Staupitz—"I have already done so, and I will again advise him to submit to the Church in all humility."

De Vio—"You will have to reply to the arguments he derives from the Holy Scriptures."

Staupitz—"I must confess, my lord, that is a task beyond my abilities: for Doctor Martin Luther is superior to me both in genius and knowledge of the Holy Scriptures."

The cardinal smiled, no doubt, at the vicar-general's frankness. Besides, he knew himself how difficult it would be to convince Luther. He continued, addressing both Staupitz and Link:

"Are you aware, that, as partisans of an heretical doctrine, you are yourselves liable to the penalties of the Church?"

Staupitz—"Condescend to resume the conference with Luther, and order a public discussion on the controverted points."

De Vio, alarmed at the very thought—"I will no longer dispute with that beast, for it has deep eyes and wonderful speculations in its head."

Staupitz at length prevailed on the cardinal to transmit to Luther in writing what he was required to retract.

The vicar-general returned to Luther. Staggered by the representations of the cardinal, he endeavored to persuade him to come to an arrangement. "Refute, then," said Luther, "the declarations of Scripture that I have advanced."

"It is beyond my ability," said Staupitz.

"Well then!" replied Luther, "It is against my conscience to retract, so long as these passages of Scripture are not explained differently. What! The cardinal professes, as you inform me, that he is desirous of arranging this affair without any disgrace or detriment to me! Ah! these are Roman expressions, which signify in good German that it will be my eternal shame and ruin. What else can he expect who, through fear of men and against the voice of his conscience, denies the truth?"

Staupitz did not persist; he only informed Luther that the cardinal had consented to transmit to him in writing the points which he would be required to retract. He then no doubt informed him also of his intention of quitting Augsburg, where he had no longer anything to do. Luther communicated to him a plan he had formed for comforting and strengthening their souls. Staupitz promised to return, and they separated for a short time.

Alone in his cell, Luther turned his thoughts towards the friends dearest to his heart. His ideas wandered to Weimar and to Wittenberg. He desired to inform the elector of what was passing; and, fearful of being indiscreet by addressing the prince himself, he wrote to Spalatin, and begged the chaplain to inform his master of the state of affairs. He detailed the whole transaction, even to the promise given by the legate to send him the controverted points in writing, and finished by saying: "This is the posture of affairs; but I have neither hope nor confidence in the legate. I will not retract a syllable. I will publish the reply I gave him, in order that, if he should proceed to violence, he may be covered with shame in all Christendom."

The doctor then profited by the few moments that still remained to write to his Wittenberg friends.

"Peace and happiness," wrote he to Doctor Carlstadt. "Accept these few words as if they were a long letter, for time and events are pressing. At a better opportunity I will write to you and others more fully. Three days my business has been in hand, and matters are now at such a point that I have no longer any hope of returning to you, and I have nothing to look for but excommunication. The legate positively will not allow me to dispute either publicly or privately. He desires not to be a judge," says he, "but a father to me; and yet he will not allow me to dispute either publicly or privately. He desires not to be a judge," says he, "but a father to me; and yet he will hear no other words from me than these: 'I retract, and acknowledge my error.' And these I will not utter.

"The dangers of my cause are so much the greater that its judges are not only implacable enemies, but, still further, men incapable of understanding it. Yet the Lord God lives and reigns: to His protection I commit myself, and I doubt not that, in answer to the prayers of a few pious souls, He will send me deliverance; I imagine I feel them praying for me.

"Either I shall return to you without having suffered any harm; or else, struck with excommunication, I shall have to seek a refuge elsewhere.

"However that may be, conduct yourself valiantly, stand fast, and glorify Christ boldly and joyfully. . . .

"The cardinal always styles me his dear son. I know how much I must believe of that. I am nevertheless persuaded that I should be the most acceptable and dearest man to him in the world, if I would pronounce the single word *Revoco,* I retract. But I will not become a heretic by renouncing the faith by which I became a Christian. I would rather be exiled, accursed, and burned to death.

"Farewell, my dear doctor; show this letter to our theologians, to Amsdorff, to Philip, to Otten, and the rest, in order that you may pray for me and also for yourselves; for it is your cause that I am pleading here. It is that of faith in the Lord Jesus Christ, and in the grace of God."

Sweet thought, which ever fills with consolation and with peace all those who have borne witness to Jesus Christ, to His divinity, to His grace, when the world pours upon them from every side its judgments, its exclusions, and its disgrace: "Our cause is that of faith in the Lord!" And what sweetness also in the conviction expressed by the reformer: "I feel that they are praying for me!" The Reformation was the work of piety and prayer. The struggle between Luther and De Vio was that of a religious element which reappeared full of life with the expiring relics of the wordy dialectics of the middle ages.

Thus did Luther converse with his absent friends. Staupitz soon returned; Doctor Ruhel and the Knight of Feilitzsch, both envoys from the elector, also called upon Luther after taking leave of the cardinal. Some other friends of the gospel joined them. Luther, seeing thus assembled these generous men, who were on the point of separating, and from whom he was perhaps to part forever, proposed that they should celebrate the Lord's Supper together. They agreed, and this little band of faithful men communicated in the body and blood of Jesus Christ. What feelings swelled the hearts of the reformer's friends at the moment when, celebrating the Eucharist with him, they thought it was perhaps the last time they would be permitted to do so! What joy, what love animated Luther's heart, as he beheld himself so graciously accepted by his Master at the very moment that men rejected him! How solemn must have been that communion! How holy that evening!

The next day, Luther waited for the articles the legate was to send him; but not receiving any message, he begged his friend Wenceslas Link to go to the cardinal. De Vio received Link in the most affable manner, and assured him that he had no desire but to act like a friend. He said, "I no longer regard Luther as a heretic. I will not excommunicate him this time, unless I receive further orders from Rome. I have sent his reply to the pope by an express." And then, to show his friendly intentions, he added: "If Doctor Luther would only retract what concerns indulgences, the matter would soon be finished; for, as to what concerns faith in the sacraments, it is an article that each one may understand and interpret in his own fashion."

Spalatin, who records these words, adds this shrewd but just remark: "It follows clearly that Rome looks to money rather than to the holy faith and the salvation of souls."

Link returned to Luther: he found Staupitz with him, and gave them an account of his visit. When he came to the unexpected concession of the legate: "It would have been well," said Staupitz, "if Doctor Wenceslas had had a notary and witnesses with him to take down these words in writing; for, if such a proposal were made known, it would be very prejudicial to the Romans."

However, in proportion to the mildness of the prelate's language, the less confidence did these worthy Germans place in him. Many of the good men to whom Luther had been recommended held counsel together: "The legate," said they, "is preparing some mischief by this courier of whom he speaks, and it is very much to be feared that you will all be seized and thrown into prison."

Staupitz and Wenceslas therefore resolved to quit the city; they embraced Luther, who persisted in remaining at Augsburg, and departed hastily for Nuremberg, by two different roads, not without much anxiety respecting the fate of the courageous witness they were leaving behind them.

Sunday passed off quietly enough. But Luther in vain waited for the legate's message: the latter sent none. At last he determined to write. Staupitz and Link, before setting out, had begged him to treat the cardinal with all possible respect. Luther had not yet made trial of Rome and of her envoys: this was his first experiment. If deference did not succeed he would take a warning. Not a day passed in which he did not condemn himself, and groan over his facility in giving utterance to expressions stronger than the occasion required: why should he not confess to the cardinal what he confessed daily to God? Besides, Luther's heart was easily moved, and he suspected no evil. He took up his pen, and with a sentiment of the most respectful goodwill, wrote to the cardinal as follows:—

"Most worthy Father in God, once more I approach you, not in person, but by letter, entreating your paternal goodness to listen to me graciously. The reverend Dr. Staupitz, my very dear father in Christ, has called upon me to humble myself, to renounce my own sentiments, and to submit my opinions to the judgment of pious and impartial men. He has also praised your fatherly kindness, and has thoroughly convinced me of your favorable disposition towards me. This news has filled me with joy.

"Now, therefore, most worthy Father, I confess, as I have already done before, that I have not shown (as has been reported) sufficient modesty, meekness, or respect for the name of the sovereign pontiff; and, although I have been greatly provoked, I see that it would have been better for me to have conducted my cause with greater humility, mildness, and reverence, and not to have answered a fool according to his folly, lest I should be like unto him.

"This grieves me very much, and I ask forgiveness. I will publicly confess it to the people from the pulpit, as indeed I have often done before. I will endeavor, by God's grace, to speak differently. Nay more: I am ready to promise, freely and of my own accord, not to utter another word on the subject of indulgences, if this business is arranged. But also, let those who made me begin, be compelled on their part to be more moderate henceforth in their sermons, or to be silent.

"As for the truth of my doctrine, the authority of St. Thomas and other doctors cannot satisfy me. I must hear (if I am worthy to do so) the voice of the Bride, which is the Church. For it is certain that she hears the voice of the Bridegroom, which is Christ.

"In all humility and submission, I therefore entreat your paternal love to refer all this business, so unsettled up to this day, to our most holy lord Leo X, in order that the Church may decide, pronounce, and ordain, and that I may retract with a good conscience, or believe with sincerity."

As we read this letter, another reflection occurs to us. We see that Luther was not acting on a preconceived plan, but solely by virtue of convictions impressed successively on his mind and on his heart. Far from having any settled system, any well-arranged opposition, he frequently and unsuspectingly contradicted himself. Old convictions still reigned in his mind, although opposite convictions had already entered it. And yet, it is in these marks of sincerity and truth that men have sought for arguments against the Reformation; it is because it followed the necessary laws of progression which are imposed upon all things in the human mind, that some have written the history of its variations; it is in these very features, that show its sincerity and which consequently make it honorable, that one of the most eminent Christian geniuses has found his strongest objections! Inconceivable perversity of the human mind!

Luther received no answer to his letter. Cajetan and his courtiers, after being so violently agitated, had suddenly become motionless. What could be the reason? Might it not be the calm that precedes the storm? Some persons were of Pallavicini's opinion: "The cardinal was waiting," he observed, "until this proud monk, like an inflated bellows, should gradually lose the wind that filled him, and become thoroughly humble." Others, imagining they understood the ways of Rome better, felt sure that the legate intended to arrest Luther, but that, not daring to proceed to such extremities on his own account, because of the imperial safe-conduct, he was waiting a reply from Rome to his message. Others could not believe that the cardinal would delay so long. "The Emperor Maximilian," said they (and this may really be the truth), "will have no more scruple to deliver Luther over to the judgment of the Church, notwithstanding the safe-conduct, than Sigismond had to surrender Huss to the Council of Constance. The legate is perhaps even now negotiating with the emperor. Maximilian's authorization may arrive any minute. The more he was opposed to the pope before, the more will he seem to flatter him now, until the imperial crown encircles his grandchild's head. There is not a moment to be lost." "Draw up an appeal to the pope," said the noble-minded men who surrounded Luther, "and quit Augsburg without delay."

Luther, whose presence in this city had been useless during the last four days, and who had sufficiently proved, by his remaining after the departure of the Saxon councilors sent by the elector to watch over his safety, that he feared nothing, and that he was ready to answer any charge, yielded at length to his friends' solicitations. But first he resolved to inform De Vio of his intention: he wrote to him on Tuesday, the eve of his departure. This second letter is in a firmer tone than the other. It would appear that Luther, seeing all his advances were unavailing, began to lift up his head in the consciousness of his integrity and of the injustice of his enemies.

"Most worthy Father in God," wrote he to De Vio, "your paternal kindness has witnessed,—I repeat it, witnessed and sufficiently acknowledged my obedience. I have undertaken a long journey, through great dangers, in great weakness of body, and despite my extreme poverty; at the command of our most holy lord, Leo X, I have appeared in person before your eminence; lastly, I have thrown my-self at the feet of his holiness, and I now wait his good pleasure, ready to submit to his judgment, whether he should condemn or acquit me. I therefore feel that I have omitted nothing which it becomes an obedient child of the Church to do.

"I think, consequently, that I ought not uselessly to prolong my sojourn in this town; besides, it would be impossible, my resources are failing me; and your paternal goodness has loudly forbidden me to appear before you again, unless I will retract.

"I therefore depart in the name of the Lord, desiring, if possible, to find some spot where I may dwell in peace. Many persons, of greater importance than myself, have requested me to appeal from your paternal kindness, and even from our most holy lord, Leo X, ill informed, to the pope when better informed. Although I know that such an appeal will be far more acceptable to our most serene high-ness the elector than a retraction, nevertheless, if I had consulted my own feelings only, I should not have done so. . . . I have committed no fault; I ought therefore to fear nothing."

Luther having written this letter, which was not given to the legate until after his departure, prepared to quit Augsburg. God had pre-served him till this hour, and he praised the Lord for it with all his heart; but he must not tempt God. He embraced his friends Peu-tinger, Langemantel, the Adelmanns, Auerbach, and the prior of the Carmelites, who had shown him such Christian hospitality. On Wednesday, before daybreak, he was up and ready to set out. His friends had recommended him to take every precaution for fear that he should be prevented, if his intentions were known. He followed their advice as far as possible. A pony that Staupitz had left for him was brought to the door of the convent. Once more he bade his brethren adieu; he then mounted and set off, without a bridle for his horse, without boots or spurs, and unarmed. The magistrate of the city had sent him as a guide one of the horse-police who was well acquainted with the roads. This servant conducted him in the dark through the silent streets of Augsburg. They directed their course to a small gate in the wall of the city. One of the councilors, Lange-mantel, had given orders that it should be opened. He was still in the power of the legate. The hand of Rome might grasp him yet. No doubt, if the Italians knew their prey was escaping them, they would utter a cry of rage. Who could say that the intrepid adversary of

Rome would not yet be seized and thrown into a dungeon? . . . At length Luther and his guide arrived at the little gate; they passed through. They were out of Augsburg. Soon they put their horses to a gallop, and rode speedily away.

Luther, on his departure, had left his appeal to the pope in the hands of the prior of Pomesaw. His friends had recommended that it should not be transmitted to the legate. The prior was commissioned to have it posted upon the cathedral gates two or three days after the doctor's departure, in the presence of a notary and witnesses. This was done.

In this paper, Luther declared that he appealed from the most holy Father the Pope, ill informed, to the most holy lord and Father in Christ, Leo X of that name, by the grace of God, better informed. This appeal had been drawn up in the customary form and style, by aid of the imperial notary, Gall of Herbrachtingen, in presence of two Augustine monks, Bartholomew Utzmair, and Wenzel Steinbies. It was dated October 16.

When the cardinal was informed of Luther's departure, he was thunderstruck, and even frightened and alarmed, as he assured the elector in his letter. Indeed there was good cause to be annoyed. This departure, which so abruptly terminated the negotiations, disconcerted the hopes with which he had so long flattered his pride. He had been ambitious of the honor of healing the wounds of the Church, of restoring the tottering influence of the pope in Germany; and the heretic had escaped not only unpunished, but even without being humbled. The conference had served only to exhibit in a stronger light, on the one hand, Luther's simplicity, integrity, and firmness; and on the other, the imperious and unreasonable proceedings of the pope and his ambassador. Since Rome had gained nothing, she had lost; her authority, not having been strengthened, had received a fresh check. What would they say in the Vatican? What messages would be received from Rome? The difficulties of his position would be forgotten; the unlucky issue of this affair would be attributed to his want of skill. Serra Longa and the Italians were furious at seeing themselves with all their dexterity outwitted by a German monk. De Vio could hardly conceal his irritation. Such an insult called for vengeance, and we shall soon witness him breathing out his wrath in a letter to the elector.

Chapter 27

WITTENBERG AGAIN, SAFE AND SOUND

LUTHER and his guide continued their flight far from the walls of Augsburg. He spurred his horse, and galloped as fast as the poor animal's strength would permit. He called to mind the real or supposed flight of John Huss, the manner in which he was caught, and the assertion of his adversaries, who pretended that Huss having by his flight annulled the emperor's safe-conduct, they had the right of condemning him to the flames. These anxious thoughts, however, did not long occupy Luther's mind. Having escaped from a city in which he had passed ten days under the hand of Rome, he was free; now that he inhaled the fresh breezes of the country, traversed the villages and rural districts, and beheld himself wonderfully delivered by the arm of the Lord, his whole being returned thanks to the Almighty. He could now say: "Our soul is escaped as a bird out of the snare of the fowlers: the snare is broken, and we are escaped. Our help is in the name of the Lord, who made heaven and earth." Thus Luther's heart overflowed with joy. But his thoughts were turned on De Vio also: "The cardinal would have liked to have me in his hands to send me to Rome. He is vexed, no doubt, at my escape. He imagined I was in his power at Augsburg; he thought he had me; but he was holding an eel by the tail. Is it not disgraceful that these people set so high a value upon me? They would give a heap of crowns to have me in their clutches, while our Lord Jesus Christ was sold for thirty pieces of silver."

The first day he traveled fourteen leagues. When he reached the inn where he was to pass the night, he was so fatigued (his horse was a very hard trotter, a historian tells us) that, when he dismounted, he could not stand upright, and lay down upon a bundle of straw. He nevertheless obtained some repose. On the morrow he continued his journey. At Nuremberg he met with Staupitz, who was visiting the convents of his order. It was in this city that he first saw the brief sent by the pope to Cajetan about him. He was indignant at it, and it is very probable that if he had seen this brief before leaving Wittenberg, he would never have gone to the cardinal. "It is impossible to believe," said he, "that any thing so monstrous could have proceeded from any sovereign pontiff."

All along the road Luther was an object of general interest. He had not yet yielded in any one point. Such a victory, gained by a mendicant monk over the representative of Rome, filled every heart with admiration. Germany seemed avenged of the contempt of Italy. The eternal Word had received more honor than the word of the pope. This vast power, which for so many centuries tyrannized the world, had received a formidable check. Luther's journey was like a triumph. Men rejoiced at the obstinacy of Rome, in the hope that it would lead to her destruction. If she had not insisted on preserving her shameful gains; if she had been wise enough not to despise the Germans; if she had reformed crying abuses: perhaps, according to human views, all would have returned to that death-like state from which Luther had awakened. But the papacy would not yield; and the doctor would see himself compelled to bring to light many other errors, and to go forward in the knowledge and manifestation of the truth.

On the twenty-sixth of October Luther reached Graefenthal, on the verge of the Thuringian forests. Here he met with Count Albert of Mansfeldt, the same person who had so strongly dissuaded him from going to Augsburg. The count, laughing heartily at his singular equipage, compelled him to stop and be his guest. Luther soon resumed his journey.

He hastened forward, desiring to be at Wittenberg on the thirty-first of October, under the impression that the elector would be there for the festival of All-Saints, and that he should see him. The brief which he had read at Nuremberg had disclosed to him all the perils of his situation. In fact, being already condemned at Rome, he could not hope either to stay at Wittenberg, to obtain an asylum in a convent, or to find peace and security in any other place. The elector's protection might perhaps be able to defend him; but he was far from being sure of it. He could no longer expect anything from the two friends whom he had possessed hitherto at the court of the prince. Staupitz had lost the favor he had so long enjoyed, and was quitting Saxony. Spalatin was beloved by Frederick, but had not much influence over him. The elector himself was not sufficiently acquainted with the doctrine of the gospel to encounter manifest danger for its sake. Luther thought, however, that he could not do better than return to Wittenberg, and there await what the eternal and merciful God would do with him. If, as many expected, he were left unmolested, he resolved to devote himself entirely to study and to the education of youth.

Luther re-entered Wittenberg on October 30. All his expedition had been to no purpose. Neither the elector nor Spalatin had come to the feast. His friends were overjoyed at seeing him again among them. He hastened to inform Spalatin of his arrival. "I returned to Wittenberg today safe and sound, by the grace of God," said he, "but how long I shall stay here I do not know. . . . I am filled with joy and peace, and can hardly conceive that the trial which I endure can appear so great to so many distinguished personages."

De Vio had not waited long after Luther's departure to pour forth all his indignation to the elector. His letter breathes vengeance. He gives Frederick an account of the conference with an air of assurance. "Since brother Martin," says he in conclusion, "cannot be induced by paternal measures to acknowledge his error, and remain faithful to the Catholic Church, I beg your highness will send him to Rome, or expel him from your states. Be assured that this difficult, mischievous, and envenomed business cannot be protracted much longer; for so soon as I have informed our most holy lord of all this artifice and wickedness, it will be brought to an end." In a postscript, written with his own hand, the cardinal entreats the elector not to tarnish his honor and that of his illustrious ancestors for the sake of a miserable little friar.

Never perhaps did Luther's soul feel a nobler indignation than when he read the copy of this letter forwarded to him by the elector. The thought of the sufferings he was destined to undergo, the value of the truth for which he was contending, contempt inspired by the conduct of the Roman legate,—all agitated his heart together. His reply, written in the midst of this agitation, was full of that courage, sublimity, and faith which he always displayed in the most trying circumstances of his life. He gave, in his turn, an account of the Augsburg conference; and after describing the cardinal's behavior, he continued:

"I should like to answer the legate in the place of the elector:

" 'Prove that you speak of what you understand,' I would say to him; let the whole matter be committed to writing: then I will send brother Martin to Rome, or else I will myself seize him and put him to death. I will take care of my conscience and of my honor, and will permit no stain to tarnish my glory. But so long as your positive knowledge shuns the light, and is made known by its clamors only, I can put no faith in darkness.

"It is thus I would reply, most excellent prince.

"Let the reverend legate, or the pope himself, specify my errors in writing; let them give their reasons; let them instruct me, for I am a man who desires instruction, who begs and longs for it, so that even a Turk would not refuse to grant it. If I do not retract and condemn myself when they have proved that the passages which I have cited ought to be understood in a different sense from mine, then, most excellent elector, let your highness be the first to prosecute and expel me; let the university reject me, and overwhelm me with its anger.
. . . Nay more, and I call heaven and earth to witness, may the Lord Jesus Christ cast me out and condemn me! . . . The words that I utter are not dictated by vain presumption, but by an unshaken conviction. I am willing that the Lord God withdraw His grace from me, and that every one of God's creatures refuse me His countenance, if, when a better doctrine has been shown me, I do not embrace it.

"If they despise me on account of my low estate, me a poor little mendicant friar, and if they refuse to instruct me in the way of truth, then let your highness entreat the legate to inform you in writing wherein I have erred; and if they refuse even your highness this favor, let them write their views either to his imperial majesty, or to some archbishop of Germany. What can I or what ought I to say more?

"Let your highness listen to the voice of your conscience and of your honor, and not send me to Rome. No man can require you to do so, for it is impossible I can be safe in Rome. The pope himself is not safe there. It would be commanding you to betray Christian blood. They have paper, pens, and ink: they have also notaries without number. It is easy for them to write wherein and wherefore I have erred. It will cost them less to instruct me when absent by writing, than to put me to death by stratagem when among them.

"I resign myself to banishment. My adversaries are laying their snares on every side, so that I can nowhere live in security. In order that no evil may happen to you on my account, I leave your territories in God's name. I will go wherever the eternal and merciful God will have me. Let Him do with me according to his pleasure!

"Thus then, most serene Elector, I reverently bid you farewell. I commend you to the everlasting God, and give you eternal thanks for all your kindness toward me. Whatever be the people among whom I shall dwell in future, I shall ever remember you, and pray continually and gratefully for the happiness of yourself and of your family. . . . I am still, thanks be to God, full of joy: and praise Him because Christ, the Son of God, thinks me worthy to suffer in such a cause. May He ever protect your illustrious highness! Amen."

This letter, so abounding in truth, made a deep impression on the elector. "He was shaken by a very eloquent letter," says Maimbourg. Never could he have thought of surrendering an innocent man to the hands of Rome; perhaps he would have desired Luther to conceal himself for a time, but he resolved not to appear to yield in any manner to the legate's menaces. He wrote to his councilor Pfeffinger, who was at the emperor's court, telling him to inform this prince of the real state of affairs, and to beg him to write to Rome, so that the business might be concluded, or at least that it might be settled in Germany by impartial judges.

A few days after, the elector replied to the legate: "Since Doctor Martin has appeared before you at Augsburg, you should be satisfied. We did not expect that you would endeavor to make him retract, without having convinced him of his errors. None of the learned men in our principality have informed me that Martin's doctrine is impious, anti-Christian, or heretical." The prince refused, moreover, to send Luther to Rome, or to expel him from his states.

This letter, which was communicated to Luther, filled him with joy. "Gracious God!" wrote he to Spalatin, "with what delight I have read it again and again! I know what confidence may be put in these words, at once so forcible and moderate. I fear that the Romans will not understand their full bearing; but they will at least understand that what they think already finished is as yet hardly begun. Pray, return my thanks to the prince. It is strange that he (De Vio) who, a short time ago, was a mendicant monk like myself, does not fear to address the mightiest princes disrespectfully, to call them to account, to threaten, to command them, and to treat them with such inconceivable haughtiness. Let him learn that the temporal power is of God, and that its glory may not be trampled under foot."

What had doubtless encouraged the elector to reply to the legate in a tone the latter had not expected, was a letter addressed to him by the University of Wittenberg. It had good reason to declare in the doctor's favor, for it flourished daily more and more, and was eclipsing all the other schools. A crowd of students flocked thither from all parts of Germany to hear this extraordinary man, whose teaching appeared to open a new era to religion and learning. These youths who came from every province, halted as soon as they discovered the steeples of Wittenberg in the distance; they raised their hands to heaven, and praised God for having caused the light of truth to shine forth from this city, as from Zion in times of old, and whence it spread even to the most distant countries. A life and activity till then unknown animated the university. "Our students here are as busy as ants," wrote Luther.

Chapter 28

ROMAN THUNDERS

LUTHER, imagining he might soon be expelled from Germany, was engaged in publishing a report of the Augsburg conference. He desired that it should remain as a testimony of the struggle between him and Rome. He saw the storm ready to burst, but did not fear it. He waited from day to day for the anathemas that were to be sent from Italy; and he put everything in order, that he might be prepared when they arrived. "Having tucked up my robe and girt my loins," said he, "I am ready to depart, like Abraham, without knowing whither I go; or rather well knowing, since God is everywhere." He intended leaving a farewell letter behind him. "Be bold enough," wrote he to Spalatin, "to read the letter of an accursed and excommunicated man."

His friends felt great anxiety and fear on his account. They entreated him to deliver himself as a prisoner into the elector's hands, in order that this prince might keep him somewhere in security.

His enemies could not understand whence he derived this confidence. One day as the conversation turned upon him at the court of the Bishop of Brandenburg, and it was asked on what support he could rely: "On Erasmus," said some; "on Capito, and other learned men who are in his confidence."—"No, no," replied the bishop, "the pope would care very little about those folks. It is in the University of Wittenburg and the Duke of Saxony that he trusts." Thus both parties were ignorant of the Stronghold in which the reformer had taken refuge.

Thoughts of departure passed through Luther's mind. They did not originate in fear of danger, but in foresight of the continually increasing obstacles that a free confession of the truth would meet with in Germany. "If I remain here," said he, "the liberty of speaking and writing many things will be torn from me. If I depart, I shall freely pour forth the thoughts of my heart, and devote my life to Christ."

France was the country where Luther hoped to have the power of announcing the truth without opposition. The liberty enjoyed by the doctors and University of Paris appeared to him worthy of envy. Besides, he agreed with them on many points. What would have happened had he been removed from Wittenberg to France? Would the Reformation have been established there, as in Germany? Would the power of Rome have been dethroned there? And would France, which was destined to see the hierarchical principles of Rome and the destructive principles of an irreligious philosophy long contend within her bosom, have become a great center of evangelical light? It is useless to indulge in vain conjectures on this subject; but perhaps Luther at Paris might have changed in some degree the destinies of Europe and France.

Luther's soul was deeply moved. He used to preach frequently in the city church, in the room of Simon Heyens Pontanus, pastor of Wittenberg, who was almost always sick. He thought it his duty, at all events, to take leave of that congregation to whom he had so frequently announced salvation. He said in the pulpit one day: "I am a very unstable and uncertain preacher. How often already have I not left you without bidding you farewell? . . . If this case should happen again, and that I cannot return, accept my farewell now." Then, after adding a few words, he concluded by saying with moderation and gentleness: "Finally, I warn you not to be alarmed should the papal censures be discharged upon me. Do not blame the pope, or bear any ill-will, either to him or to any other man; but trust all to God."

The moment seemed to have come at last. The prince informed Luther that he desired him to leave Wittenberg. The wishes of the elector were too sacred for him not to hasten to comply with them. He therefore made preparations for his departure, without well knowing whither he should direct his steps. He desired however to see his friends once more around him, and with this intent prepared a farewell repast. Seated at the same table with them, he enjoyed

their sweet conversation, their tender and anxious friendship. A letter
was brought to him. . . . It came from the court. He opened it and
read; his heart sank; it contained a fresh order for his departure. The
prince inquired why he delayed so long. His soul was overwhelmed
with sadness. Yet he resumed his courage, and raising his head, said
firmly and joyfully, as he turned his eyes on those about him:
"Father and mother abandon me, but the Lord takes me up." Leave
he must. His friends were deeply moved.—What would become of
him? If Luther's protector rejected him, who would receive him? And
the gospel, the truth, and this admirable work . . . all would doubtless perish with its illustrious witness. The Reformation seemed to
hang upon a thread, and at the moment Luther quit the walls of
Wittenberg would this thread break? Luther and his friends said
little. Struck with the blow that had fallen upon their brother, tears
rolled down their cheeks. But shortly after, a new messenger arrived.
Luther opened the letter, not doubting that it contained a fresh
order. But, O powerful hand of the Lord! for a time he was saved.
Everything was changed. "Since the pope's new envoy hopes that all
may be arranged by a conference, remain for the present." How important was this hour! And what would have happened if Luther,
ever anxious to obey his sovereign's will, had left Wittenberg immediately on receiving the first letter? Never were Luther and the cause
of the Reformation lower than at that moment. It appeared that their
fate was decided: an instant sufficed to change it. Having reached
the lowest degree of his career, the Wittenberg doctor rose rapidly,
and his influence from this time continued increasing. The Almighty
commands (in the language of the prophet), and his servants go
down to the depths, and mount up again to heaven.

By Frederick's order, Spalatin summoned Luther to Lichtenberg,
to have an interview with him. They conversed a long time on the
situation of affairs. "If the censures arrive from Rome," said Luther,
"certainly I shall not stay at Wittenberg."—"Beware," said Spalatin,
"of being too precipitate in going to France!" He left them, telling
him to wait for further orders. "Only commend my soul to Christ,"
said Luther to his friends. "I see that my adversaries are still more
determined in their designs to ruin me; but meanwhile Christ
strengthens me in my resolution to concede nothing."

Luther now published his *Report of the Conference at Augsburg.*

Spalatin had written to him, on the part of the elector, not to do so; but the letter came too late. As soon as the publication had taken place, the prince gave his sanction: "Great God!" said Luther in his preface, "what a new, what an amazing crime to seek for light and truth! . . . and above all in the Church, that is to say, in the kingdom of truth."—"I send you my Report," wrote he to Link: "it is keener no doubt than the legate expects; but my pen is ready to produce much greater things. I do not know myself whence these thoughts arise. In my opinion, the work is not yet begun, so far are the great ones at Rome mistaken in looking for the end. I will send you what I have written, in order that you may judge whether I have guessed rightly that the Antichrist of whom St. Paul speaks now reigns in the court of Rome. I think I shall be able to show that he is worse nowadays than the Turks themselves."

Sinister reports reached Luther from every side. One of his friends wrote to him that the new envoy from Rome had received an order to lay hold of him and deliver him up to the pope. Another related that while traveling he had met with a courtier, and that the conversation turning on the matters that were now occupying all Germany, the latter declared that he had undertaken to deliver Luther into the hands of the sovereign pontiff. "But the more their fury and their violence increase," wrote the reformer, "the less I tremble."

At Rome they were much displeased with Cajetan. The vexation felt at the ill-success of this business was at first vented on him. The Roman courtiers thought they had reason to reproach him for having been deficient in that prudence and address which, if we must believe them, were the chief qualities in a legate, and for not having relaxed, on so important an occasion, the strictness of his scholastic theology. It is all his fault, said they. His clumsy pedantry spoiled all. Why did he exasperate Luther by insults and threats, instead of alluring him by the promise of a rich bishopric, or even of a cardinal's hat? These mercenaries judged the reformer by themselves. Still the failure must be retrieved. On the one hand, Rome must declare herself; on the other, she must conciliate the elector, who might be very serviceable to her in the choice they would soon have to make of an emperor.

As it was impossible for Roman ecclesiastics to suspect whence Luther derived his courage and his strength, they imagined that the elector was implicated more deeply in the affair than he really was. The pope therefore resolved to pursue another course. He caused a bull to be published in Germany by his legate, in which he confirmed the doctrine of indulgences, precisely in the points attacked, but in which he made no mention either of Luther or of the elector. As the reformer had always declared that he would submit to the decision of the Roman Church, the pope imagined that he would now either keep his word, or exhibit himself openly as a disturber of the peace of the Church, and a contemner of the holy apostolic see. In either case, the pope could not but gain; no advantage however is derived by obstinately opposing the truth. In vain had the pope threatened with excommunication whoever should teach otherwise than he ordained; the light is not stopped by such orders. It would have been wiser to moderate by certain restrictions the pretensions of the sellers of indulgences. This decree from Rome was therefore a new fault. By legalizing crying abuses, it irritated all wise men, and rendered Luther's reconciliation impossible. "It was thought," says a Roman Catholic historian, a great enemy to the Reformation, "that this bull had been issued solely for the benefit of the pope and the begging friars, who began to find that no one would purchase their indulgences."

Cardinal De Vio published the decree at Lintz, in Austria, on the thirteenth of December, 1518; but Luther had already placed himself beyond its reach. On November 28, he had appealed, in the chapel of Corpus Christi, at Wittenberg, from the pope to a general council of the Church. He foresaw the storm that was about to burst upon him; he knew that God alone could disperse it; but he did what it was his duty to do. He must, no doubt, quit Wittenberg, if only on the elector's account, as soon as the Roman anathemas arrived: he would not, however, leave Saxony and Germany without a striking protest. He therefore drew one up, and that it might be ready for circulation as soon as the Roman thunders reached him, as he expressed it, he had it printed under the express condition that the bookseller should deposit all the copies with him. But this man, covetous of gain, sold almost every one, while Luther was calmly waiting to receive them. The doctor was vexed, but the thing was done. This bold protest was soon circulated everywhere. In it Luther declared anew that he had no intention of saying anything against the holy Church or the authority of the apostolic see, and of the pope when well-advised. "But," continues he, "seeing that the pope, who is God's vicar upon earth, may, like any other man, err, sin, and lie, and that an appeal to a general council is the only means of safety against that injustice which it is impossible to resist, I am obliged to have recourse to this step."

Here we see the Reformation launched on a new career. It was no longer made dependent on the pope and on his resolutions, but on a general council. Luther addressed the whole Church, and the voice that proceeded from the chapel of Corpus Christi must be heard throughout all the Lord's fold. The reformer was not wanting in courage; of this he had just given a new proof. Will God be far from him? This we shall learn from the different periods of the Reformation.

Chapter 29

SEEDS OF TRUTH OVER EVERY LAND

DANGERS HAD GATHERED round Luther and the Reformation. The appeal of the Wittenberg doctor to a general council was a new assault upon the papal power. A bull of Pius II had pronounced the greater excommunication against the emperors who should dare be guilty of such an act of revolt. Frederick of Saxony, as yet weak in the evangelical doctrine, was ready to banish Luther from his states. A new message from Leo X would therefore have driven the reformer among strangers, who might have feared to compromise themselves by receiving a monk under the anathema of Rome. And if any of the nobles had drawn the sword in his defense, these simple knights, despised by the mighty princes of Germany, would have been crushed in their perilous enterprise.

But at the very moment that the courtiers of Leo X were urging him to measures of severity, and when another blow would have placed his adversary in his hands, this pope suddenly changed his policy. He entered upon a course of conciliation and apparent mildness. We may reasonably presume that he was deceived as to the elector's sentiments, and thought them more favorable to Luther than they really were; we may admit that the public voice and the spirit of the age—powers then quite new—appeared to surround Luther with an impregnable rampart; we may suppose, as one of his historians has done, that he followed the impulses of his judgment and of his heart, which inclined to mildness and moderation; but this new mode of action, adopted by Rome at such a moment, was so strange that it was impossible not to recognize in it a higher and a mightier hand.

A Saxon noble, the pope's chamberlain and canon of Mentz (Treves) and Meissen, was then at the Roman court. He had contrived to make himself important. He boasted of being distantly related to the Saxon princes, so that the Roman courtiers sometimes gave him the title of Duke of Saxony. In Italy, he made a foolish display of his German nobility; in Germany, he was an awkward imitator of the elegance and manners of the Italians. He was fond of wine, and his residence at the court of Rome had increased this vice. The Roman courtiers, however, entertained great expectations of him. His German origin, his insinuating manners, his skill in business,—all led them to hope that Charles of Miltitz (for such was his name) would by his prudence succeed in arresting the mighty revolution that threatened.

It was important to conceal the real object of the mission of the Roman chamberlain. This was effected without difficulty. Four years previously, the pious elector had petitioned the pope for the Golden Rose. This rose, the most beautiful of flowers, represented the body of Jesus Christ; it was consecrated yearly by the sovereign pontiff, and sent to one of the chief princes in Europe. It was resolved to give it this year to the elector. Miltitz departed with a commission to examine the state of affairs, and to gain over Spalatin and Pfeffinger, the elector's councilors. He carried private letters for them. In this manner, by seeking to conciliate those who surrounded the prince, Rome hoped erelong to have her formidable adversary in her power.

The new legate, who arrived in Germany in December 1518, was engaged during his journey in sounding the public opinion. To his great surprise he found, that wherever he went, the majority of the inhabitants were partisans of the Reformation. They spoke of Luther with enthusiasm. For one person favorable to the pope, there were three favorable to the reformer. Luther has transmitted to us one of the incidents of his mission. "What do you think of the papal chair?" the legate would frequently ask the landladies and maid-servants at the inns. On one occasion one of these poor women artlessly replied: "What can we know of the papal chair, whether it is of wood or of stone?"

The mere rumors of the new legate's arrival filled the elector's court, the University and town of Wittenberg, and the whole of Saxony, with suspicion and distrust. "Thanks be to God, Luther is still alive," wrote Melancthon in affright. It was affirmed that the Roman legate had received orders to get Luther into his power either by violence or stratagem. Every one recommended the doctor to be on his guard against the treachery of Miltitz. "He is coming," said they, "to seize you and give you up to the pope. Trustworthy persons have seen the briefs he is bringing with him."—"I await God's will," replied Luther.

Miltitz indeed came bearing letters for the elector, for his councilors, and for the bishops and the burgomaster of Wittenberg. He brought with him seventy apostolical briefs. If the flattery and the favors of Rome attained their end—if Frederick delivered Luther into his hands, these seventy briefs were, in some measure, to serve as passports. He would produce and post up one in each of the cities through which he would have to pass, and by this means he hoped to succeed in dragging his prisoner to Rome without opposition.

The pope appeared to have taken every precaution. Already in the electoral court they did not know what course to adopt. They would have resisted violence; but how could they oppose the head of Christendom, who spoke with so much mildness, and with so great an appearance of reason? Would it not be desirable, they said, for Luther to conceal himself, until the storm had passed over? An unexpected event extricated Luther, the elector, and the Reformation, from this difficult position. The aspect of the world suddenly changed.

On January 12, 1519, Maximilian, emperor of Germany, expired. Frederick of Saxony, in conformity with the Germanic constitution, became administrator of the empire. Henceforth the elector no longer feared the projects of nuncios. New interests began to agitate the court of Rome, which forced it to be cautious in its negotiations with Frederick, and arrested the blow that Miltitz and De Vio undoubtedly were meditating.

The pope earnestly desired to prevent Charles of Austria, already king of Naples, from filling the imperial throne. He thought that a neighboring king was more to be feared than a German monk. Desirous of securing the elector, who might be of great use to him in this affair, he resolved to let the monk rest, that he might the better oppose the king; but both advanced in despite of him. Thus changed Leo X.

Another circumstance also contributed to turn aside the storm that threatened the Reformation. Political troubles broke out immediately after Maximilian's death. In the south of the empire, the Swabian confederation desired to punish Ulric of Württemberg, who had been unfaithful to it; in the north, the Bishop of Hildesheim threw himself with an armed force upon the bishopric of Minden and on the territories of the Duke of Brunswick. In the midst of all this agitation, how could the great ones of the age attach any importance to a dispute about the remission of sins? But God especially advanced the cause of the Reformation by the wisdom of the elector, now become vicar of the empire, and by the protection he granted to the new teachers. "The tempest suspended its rage," says Luther, "the papal excommunication began to fall into contempt. Under the shadow of the elector's viceroyalty, the gospel circulated far and wide, and popery suffered great damage in consequence."

Besides, during an interim the severest prohibitions naturally lost their force. All became easier and more free. The ray of liberty that shone upon these beginnings of the Reformation powerfully developed the yet tender plant; and already it might have been seen how favorable political liberty would be to the progress of evangelical Christianity.

Miltitz, who had reached Saxony before the death of Maximilian, had hastened to visit his old friend Spalatin; but he had no sooner begun his complaints against Luther, than Spalatin broke out against Tetzel. He made the nuncio acquainted with the falsehoods and blasphemies of the indulgence-merchant, and declared that all Germany ascribed to the Dominican the divisions by which the Church was rent.

Miltitz was astonished. Instead of being the accuser, he found himself the accused. All his anger was immediately directed against Tetzel. He summoned him to appear at Altenburg and justify his conduct.

The Dominican, as cowardly as he was boastful, fearing the people whom his impositions had exasperated, had discontinued passing from town to town, and had hidden himself in the college of St. Paul at Leipzig. He turned pale on receiving Miltitz's letter. Even Rome abandons him; she threatens and condemns him; she wishes to draw him from the only asylum in which he thinks himself secure, and to expose him to the anger of his enemies. Tetzel refused to obey the nuncio's summons. "Certainly," wrote he to Miltitz on December 31, 1518, "I should not care about the fatigue of the journey, if I could leave Leipzig without danger to my life; but the Augustine Martin Luther has so excited and aroused the men of power against me that I am nowhere safe. A great number of Luther's partisans have sworn my death; I cannot, therefore, come to you." What a striking contrast is here between these two men, the one residing in the college of St. Paul at Leipzig, the other in the Augustine cloister at Wittenberg! The servant of God displayed an intrepid courage in the presence of danger; the servant of men, a contemptible cowardice.

Miltitz had been ordered to employ persuasive measures in the first instance; and it was only when these failed that he was to produce his seventy briefs, and at the same time make use of all the favors of Rome to induce the elector to restrain Luther. He therefore intimated his desire to have an interview with the reformer. Their common friend, Spalatin, offered his house for that purpose, and Luther quitted Wittenberg on the second or third of January to visit Altenburg.

In this interview Miltitz exhausted all the cunning of a diplomatist and of a Roman courtier. Luther had scarcely arrived when the nuncio approached him with great demonstrations of friendship. "Oh!" thought Luther, "how his violence is changed into gentleness! This new Saul came to Germany, armed with more than seventy apostolical briefs, to drag me alive and in chains to that murderous Rome; but the Lord has thrown him to the ground by the way."

"My dear Martin," said the pope's chamberlain, in a fawning tone, "I thought you were an old theologian who, seated quietly at his fireside, was laboring under some theological crotchet; but I see you are still a young man and in the prime of life. Do you know," continued he, assuming a graver tone, "that you have drawn away everybody from the pope and attached them to yourself?" Miltitz was not ignorant that the best way of seducing mankind is to flatter their pride; but he did not know the man he had to deal with. "If I had an army of twenty-five thousand men," added he, "I do not think I should be able to carry you to Rome." Rome with all her power was sensible of her weakness compared with this poor monk; and the monk felt strong compared with Rome. "God stays the waves of the sea upon the shore," said Luther, "and He stays them—with sand!"

The nuncio, believing he had now prepared his adversary's mind, continued in these terms: "Bind up the wound that you yourself have inflicted on the Church, and that you alone can heal. Beware," said he, dropping a few tears, "beware of raising a tempest that would cause the destruction of Christendom." He then gradually proceeded to hint that a retractation alone could repair the mischief; but he immediately softened down whatever was objectionable in this word, by giving Luther to understand that he felt the highest esteem for him, and by storming against Tetzel. The snare was laid by a skillful hand: how could it fail to catch the prey? "If, at the outset, the Archbishop of Mentz had spoken to me in this manner," said the reformer afterwards, "this business would not have created so much disturbance."

Luther then replied, and set forth with calmness, but with dignity and force, the just complaints of the Church; he did not conceal his great indignation against the Archbishop of Mentz, and complained in a noble manner of the unworthy treatment he had received from Rome, notwithstanding the purity of his intentions. Miltitz, who had not expected to hear such decided language, was able however to suppress his anger.

"I offer," resumed Luther, "to be silent for the future on this matter, and to let it die away of itself, provided my opponents are silent on their part; but if they continue attacking me, a serious struggle will soon arise out of a trifling quarrel. My weapons are quite prepared. . . . I will do still more [he added a moment after]; I will write to his holiness, acknowledging I have been a little too violent, and I will declare to him that it is as a faithful son of the Church that I opposed discourses which drew upon them the mockeries and insults of the people. I even consent to publish a writing desiring all those who read my works not to see in them any attacks upon the Roman Church, and to continue under its authority. Yes! I am willing to do and to bear everything; but as for a retractation, never expect one from me."

Miltitz saw by Luther's firm tone that the wisest course would be to appear satisfied with what the reformer so readily promised. He merely proposed they should choose an archbishop to arbitrate on some points that were still to be discussed. "Be it so," said Luther;

"but I am very much afraid that the pope will not accept any judge; in that case I will not abide by the pope's decision, and then the struggle will begin again. The pope will give the text, and I shall make my own comments upon it."

Thus ended the first interview between Luther and Miltitz. They had a second meeting in which the truce or rather the peace was signed. Luther immediately informed the elector of what had taken place. "Most serene prince and most gracious lord," wrote he, "I hasten most humbly to acquaint your electoral highness that Charles of Miltitz and myself are at last agreed, and have terminated this matter by deciding upon the following articles:—

"1. Both parties are forbidden to preach, write, or do anything further in the discussion that has been raised.

"2. Miltitz will immediately inform the holy Father of the state of affairs. His holiness will empower an enlightened bishop to investigate the matter, and to point out the erroneous articles I should retract. If they prove me to be in error I shall willingly recant, and will do nothing derogatory to the honor or authority of the holy Roman Church."

When the agreement had been thus effected, Miltitz appeared overjoyed. "These hundred years past," exclaimed he, "no question has occasioned more anxiety to the cardinals and Roman courtiers than this. They would rather have given ten thousand ducats than consent to its being prolonged."

The pope's chamberlain spared no marks of attention to the monk of Wittenberg. At one time he manifested his joy, at another he shed tears. This show of sensibility moved the reformer but little; still he avoided showing what he thought of it. "I pretended not to understand the meaning of these crocodile's tears," said he.

Miltitz gave Luther an invitation to supper, which the latter accepted. His host laid aside all the severity connected with his mission, and Luther indulged in all the cheerfulness of his disposition. The repast was joyous, and when the moment of departure was come, the legate opened his arms to the heretical doctor, and kissed him. "A Judas kiss," thought Luther; "I pretended not to understand these Italian artifices," wrote he to Staupitz.

Was that kiss destined to reconcile Rome and the dawning Reformation? Miltitz hoped so, and was delighted at the thought; for he

had a nearer view than the Roman courtiers of the terrible consequences the papacy might suffer from the Reformation. If Luther
and his adversaries are silenced, thought he, the dispute will be
ended; and Rome, by calling up favorable circumstances, will regain
all her former influence. It appeared, then, that the termination of the
contest was at hand. Rome had opened her arms, and the reformer
seemed to have cast himself into them. But this work was not of man,
but of God. The error of Rome lay in regarding as a mere monkish
quarrel what was in reality an awakening of the Church. The kisses
of a papal chamberlain could not check the renewal of Christendom.

Miltitz being of opinion that he would by this means reclaim the
erring Lutherans, behaved most graciously to all of them, accepted
their invitations, and sat down with the heretics; but soon becoming
inebriated (it is a pope who relates this), the pontifical nuncio was
no longer master of his tongue. The Saxons led him to speak of the
pope and the court of Rome, and Miltitz, confirming the old proverb,
in vino veritas (when wine is in, the wit comes out.—Old English
proverb), gave an account in the openness of his heart of all the
practices and disorders of the papacy. His companions smiled, urging
and pressing him to continue; everything was exposed; they took
notes of what he said; and these scandals were afterwards made matter of public reproach against the Romans, at the Diet of Worms, in
the presence of all Germany. Pope Paul III complained, alleging they
had put things in his envoy's mouth that were utterly destitute of
foundation, and in consequence ordered his nuncios, whenever they
were invited out, to make a pretense of accepting the invitations, to
behave graciously, and to be guarded in their conversation.

Miltitz, faithful to the arrangement he had just concluded, went
from Altenburg to Leipzig, where Tetzel was residing. There was
no necessity to silence him, for sooner than speak he would have concealed himself if possible in the center of the earth. But the nuncio
resolved to vent all his anger on him. As soon as he reached Leipzig,
he summoned the wretched Tetzel before him, overwhelmed him
with the pope's displeasure. This was not enough. An agent from the
house of Fugger, who was then in the city, was confronted with
him. Miltitz laid before the Dominican the accounts of this establishment, the papers he had himself signed, and proved that he had
squandered or stolen considerable sums of money. The unhappy

man, whom in the day of his triumph nothing could alarm, bent under the weight of these just accusations: he fell into despair, his health suffered, he knew not where to hide his shame. Luther was informed of the wretched condition of his old adversary, and he alone was affected by it. "I am sorry for Tetzel," wrote he to Spalatin. He did not confine himself to words: it was not the man but his actions that Luther hated. At the very moment that Rome was venting her wrath on the Dominican, Luther sent him a letter full of consolation. But all was unavailing. Tetzel, a prey to remorse, terrified by the reproaches of his best friends, and dreading the pope's anger, died very miserably not long after. It was believed that grief accelerated his death.

Luther, in accordance with the promise he had given Miltitz, wrote the following letter to the pope on the third of March:

"Blessed Father! May your holiness condescend to incline your paternal ear, which is that of Christ Himself, towards your poor sheep, and listen kindly to his bleating. What shall I do, most holy Father? I cannot bear the lightnings of your anger, and I know not how to escape them. I am called upon to retract. I would most readily do so, could that lead to the desired result. But the persecutions of my adversaries have circulated my writings far and wide, and they are too deeply graven on the hearts of men, to be by any possibility erased. A recantation would only still more dishonor the Church of Rome, and draw from the lips of all a cry of accusation against her. Most holy Father! I declare in the presence of God and of all His creatures, that I have neved desired, and that I shall never desire, to weaken, either by force or stratagem, the power of the Roman Church or of your holiness. I confess that nothing in heaven or in earth should be preferred above that Church, except Jesus Christ alone—the Lord of all."

These words might appear strange and even reprehensible in Luther's mouth, did we not remember that he reached the light not suddenly, but by a slow and progressive course. They are a very important evidence that the Reformation was not simply an opposition to the papacy, it was not a war waged against certain forms; nor was it the result of a merely negative tendency. Opposition to the pope was in the second line of the battle: a new life, a positive doctrine was the generating principle. "Jesus Christ, the Lord of all, and who must be preferred above all," even above Rome itself, as Luther writes at the end of his letter, was the essential cause of the Revolution of the sixteenth century.

It is probable that shortly before this time the pope would not have passed over unnoticed a letter in which the monk of Wittenberg plainly refused to retract. But Maximilian was dead: men's minds were occupied with the choice of his successor, and in the midst of the intrigues which then agitated the pontifical city, Luther's letter was disregarded.

The reformer made a better use of his time than his powerful adversary. While Leo X was occupied with his interests as a temporal prince, and was making every exertion to exclude a formidable neighbor from the throne, Luther grew each day in knowledge and in faith. He studied the papal decrees, and the discoveries he made therein greatly modified his ideas. "I am reading the decrees of the pontiffs," wrote he to Spalatin, "and (I whisper this in your ear) I do not know whether the pope is Antichrist himself, or his apostle, so greatly is Christ misrepresented and crucified in them."

Yet he still felt esteem for the ancient Church of Rome, and had no thought of separating from it. "That the Roman Church," said he in the explanation which he had promised Miltitz to publish, "is honored by God above all others is what we cannot doubt. Saint Peter, Saint Paul, forty-six popes, many hundreds of thousands of martyrs, have shed their blood in its bosom. Although everything is now in a very wretched state there, this is not a sufficient reason for separating from it. On the contrary, the worse things are going on within it, the more should cling to it; for it is not by separation that we shall make it better. We must not desert God on account of the devil; or abandon the children of God who are still in the Roman communion, because of the multitude of the ungodly. There is no sin, there is no evil that should destroy charity or break the bond of union. For charity can do all things, and to unity nothing is difficult."

It was not Luther who separated from Rome: it was Rome that separated from Luther, and thus rejected the ancient faith of the Catholic Church, of which he was then the representative. It was not Luther who deprived Rome of her power, and made her bishop descend from a throne which he had usurped: the doctrines he proclaimed, the word of the apostles which God manifested anew in the Universal Church with great power and admirable purity could alone prevail against that dominion which had for centuries enslaved the Church.

These declarations, which were published by Luther at the end of February, did not entirely satisfy Miltitz and De Vio. These two had retired within the ancient walls of Treves. There, assisted by the prince-archbishop, they hoped to accomplish together the object in which each of them had failed separately. The two nuncios felt clearly that nothing more was to be expected from Frederick, now invested with supreme power in the empire. They saw that Luther persisted in his refusal to retract. The only means of success were to deprive the heretical monk of the elector's protection and to entice him into their hands. Once at Treves, in the states of an ecclesiastical prince, the reformer would be very skillful if he escaped without having fully satisfied the demands of the sovereign pontiff. They immediately applied themselves to the task. "Luther," said Miltitz to the Elector-archbishop of Treves, "has accepted your Grace as arbitrator. Summon him before you." The Elector of Treves accordingly wrote on the third of May to the Elector of Saxony, requesting him to send Luther to him. De Vio, and afterwards Miltitz himself, wrote also to Frederick, informing him that the Golden Rose had arrived at Augsburg. This (thought they) is the moment for striking a decisive blow.

But circumstances had changed: neither Frederick nor Luther permitted himself to be shaken. The elector comprehended his new position. He no longer feared the pope, much less his agents. The reformer, seeing Miltitz and De Vio united, foresaw the fate that awaited him if he complied with their invitation. "Everywhere," said he, "and in every manner they seek after my life." Besides, he had appealed to the pope, and the pope, busied in intrigues with crowned heads, had not replied. Luther wrote to Miltitz: "How can I set out without an order from Rome, in the midst of the troubles by which the Empire is agitated? How can I encounter so many dangers, and incur such heavy expense, seeing that I am the poorest of men?"

The Elector of Treves, a prudent and moderate man, and a friend of Frederick's, was desirous of keeping on good terms with the latter. Besides, he had no desire to interfere in this matter unless he was positively called upon. He therefore arranged with the Elector of Saxony to put off the inquiry until the next diet, which did not take place until two years after, when it assembled at Worms.

While a providential hand thus warded off, one by one, the dangers by which Luther was threatened, he himself was boldly advancing towards a goal which he did not suspect. His reputation increased; the cause of truth grew in strength; the number of students at Wittenberg was augmented, and among them were the most distinguished young men of Germany. "Our town," wrote Luther, "can hardly receive all those who are flocking to it"; and on another occasion: "The number of students increases considerably, like an overflowing river."

But it was no longer in Germany alone that the reformer's voice was heard. It had passed the frontiers of the empire, and had begun to shake, among the different nations of Europe, the foundations of the Romish power. Frobenius, a celebrated printer at Basle, had published a collection of Luther's works. It was rapidly circulated. At Basle, the bishop himself commended Luther. The cardinal of Sion, after reading his works, exclaimed with a slight tone of irony, playing upon his name: "O Luther! thou art a real Luther!"

Erasmus was at Louvain when Luther's writings reached the Low Countries. The prior of the Augustines of Antwerp, who had studied at Wittenberg, and who, according to the testimony of Erasmus, was a follower of true primitive Christianity, read them with eagerness, as did other Belgians. But those who consulted their own interests only, remarked the sage of Rotterdam, and who fed the people with old wives' tales, broke out into gloomy fanaticism. "I cannot describe to you," wrote Erasmus to Luther, "the emotion, the truly tragic sensation which your writings have occasioned."

Frobenius sent six hundred copies of these works into France and Spain. They were sold publicly in Paris. The doctors of the Sorbonne, as it would appear, read them with approbation. "It is high time," said some of them, "that those who devote themselves to biblical studies should speak out freely." In England these books were received with still greater eagerness. Some Spanish merchants translated them into their mother-tongue, and forwarded them from Antwerp to their own country. "Certainly these merchants must have been of Moorish descent," says Pallavicini.

Calvi, a learned bookseller of Pavia, carried a great number of copies to Italy, and circulated them in all the transalpine cities. It was not the love of gain that inspired this man of letters, but a desire of contributing to the revival of piety. The energy with which Luther maintained the cause of Christ filled him with joy. "All the learned men of Italy," wrote he, "will unite with me, and we will send you verses composed by our most distinguished writers."

Frobenius, in transmitting a copy of his publication to Luther, related all these joyful tidings, and added: "I have sold every copy, except ten; and I have never made so good a speculation." Other letters informed Luther of the joy caused by his works. "I am delighted," said he, "that the truth is so pleasing, although she speaks with so little learning and in so barbarous a tone."

Such was the commencement of the awakening in the various countries of Europe. If we except Switzerland, and even France, where the gospel had already been preached, the arrival of the Wittenberg doctor's writings everywhere forms the first page in the history of the Reformation. A printer of Basle scattered the first germs of truth. At the very moment when the Roman pontiff thought to stifle the work in Germany, it began in France, the Low Countries, Italy, Spain, England, and Switzerland.

Chapter 30

ECK RECOMMENCES THE COMBAT

WHILE THE COMBAT was beginning beyond the confines of the empire, it appeared dying away within. The most impetuous of the Roman champions, the Franciscans of Juterbock, who had imprudently attacked Luther, had hastily become silent after the reformer's vigorous reply. The papal partisans were mute: Tetzel was no longer in a condition to fight. Luther was entreated by his friends not to continue the discussion, and he had promised compliance. The theses were passing into oblivion. This treacherous peace rendered the eloquence of the reformer powerless. The Reformation appeared checked. "But," said Luther somewhat later, when speaking of this epoch, "men imagine vain things; for the Lord awoke to judge the people. God does not guide me," he said in another place; "He pushes me forward, He carries me away. I am not master of myself. I desire to live in repose; but I am thrown into the midst of tumults and revolutions."

Eck the scholastic, Luther's old friend, and author of the *Obelisks*, was the man who recommenced the combat. He was sincerely attached to the papacy, but seems to have had no true religious sentiments, and to have been one of that class of men, so numerous in every age, who look upon science, and even theology and religion, as the means of acquiring worldly reputation. Vainglory lies hidden under the priests's cassock no less than under the warrior's coat of mail. Eck had studied the art of disputation according to the rules of the schoolmen and had become a master in this sort of controversy. While the knights of the middle ages and the warriors in the time of the Reformation sought for glory in the tournament, the schoolmen struggled for it in disputations—a spectacle of frequent occurrence in the universities. Eck, who entertained no mean idea of himself, and who was proud of his talents, of the popularity of his cause, and of the victories he had gained in eight universities of Hungary, Lombardy, and Germany, ardently desired to have an opportunity of trying his strength and skill against the reformer. He had spared no exertion to acquire the reputation of being one of the most learned men of the age. He was constantly endeavoring to excite some new discussion, to make a sensation, and aimed at procuring, by means of his exploits, all the enjoyments of life. A journey that he had made to Italy had been, according to his own account, one long series of triumphs. The most learned scholars had been forced to subscribe to his theses.

This experienced gladiator fixed his eyes on a new field of battle, in which he thought the victory already secure. The little monk who had suddenly grown into a giant—that Luther, whom hitherto no one had been able to vanquish, galled his pride and excited his jealousy. Perhaps in seeking his own glory, Eck might ruin Rome. But his scholastic vanity was not to be checked by such a consideration. *Theologians, as well as princes, have more than once sacrificed the general interest to their personal glory.* We shall see what circumstances afforded the Ingolstadt doctor the means of entering the lists with his importunate rival.

The zealous but too ardent Carlstadt was still on friendly terms with Luther. These two theologians were closely united by their attachment to the doctrine of grace, and by their admiration for Saint Augustine. Carlstadt was inclined to enthusiasm, and possessed little discretion: he was not a man to be restrained by the skill and policy of a Miltitz. He had published some theses in reply to Dr. Eck's *Obelisks*, in which he defended Luther and their common faith. Eck had answered him; but Carlstadt did not let him have the last word. The discussion grew warm. Eck, desirous of profiting by so favorable an opportunity, had thrown down the gauntlet, and the impetuous Carlstadt had taken it up. God made use of the passions of these two men to accomplish His purposes. Luther had not interfered in their disputes, and yet he was destined to be the hero of the fight. There are men who by the force of circumstances are always brought upon the stage. It was agreed that the discussion should take place at Leipzig. Such was the origin of that Leipzig disputation which became so famous.

Eck cared little for disputing with and even conquering Carlstadt: Luther was his great aim. He therefore made every exertion to allure him to the field of battle, and with this view published thirteen theses, which he pointed expressly against the chief doctrines already set forth by the reformer. The thirteenth was thus drawn up: "We deny that the Roman Church was not raised above the other churches before the time of Pope Sylvester; and we acknowledge in every age, as the successor of St. Peter and the vicar of Jesus Christ, him who has filled the chair and held the faith of St. Peter." Sylvester lived in the time of Constantine the Great; by this thesis, Eck denied, therefore, that the primacy enjoyed by Rome had been conferred on it by that emperor.

Luther, who had reluctantly consented to remain silent, was deeply moved as he read these propositions. He saw that they were aimed at him, and felt that he could not honorably avoid the contest. "This man," said he, "calls Carlstadt his antagonist, and at the same time attacks me. But God reigns. He knows what He will bring out of this tragedy. It is neither Doctor Eck nor myself that will be at stake: God's purpose will be accomplished. Thanks to Eck, this affair, which hitherto has been mere play, will become serious, and inflict a deadly blow on the tyranny of Rome and of the Roman pontiff."

Rome herself had broken the truce. She did more; in renewing the signal of battle, she began the contest on a point that Luther had not yet attacked. It was the papal supremacy to which Doctor Eck drew the attention of his adversaries. In this he followed the dangerous example that Tetzel had already set. Rome invited the blows of the gladiator; and, if she left some of her members quivering on the arena, it was because she had drawn upon herself his formidable arm.

The pontifical supremacy once overthrown, the whole edifice would crumble into ruin. The greatest danger was impending over the papacy, and yet neither Miltitz nor Cajetan took any steps to prevent this new struggle. Did they imagine that the Reformation would be vanquished, or were they struck with that blindness which often hurries along the mighty to their destruction?

Luther, who had set a rare example of moderation by remaining silent so long, fearlessly replied to the challenge of his antagonist. He immediately published some new theses in opposition to those of Doctor Eck. The last was conceived in these words: "It is by contemptible decretals of Roman pontiffs, composed within the last four centuries, that they would prove the primacy of the Church of Rome; but this primacy is opposed by all the credible history of eleven centuries—by the declarations of Holy Scripture—and by the resolutions of the Council of Nice, the holiest of all councils."

"God knows," wrote he at the same time to the elector, "that I was firmly resolved to keep silence, and that I was glad to see this struggle terminated at last. I have so strictly adhered to the treaty concluded with the papal commissary that I have not replied to Sylvester Prierio, notwithstanding the insults of my adversaries, and the advice of my friends. But now Doctor Eck attacks me, and not only me, but the University of Wittenberg also. I cannot suffer the truth to be thus covered with opprobrium."

At the same time Luther wrote to Carlstadt: "Most excellent Andrew, I would not have you enter upon this dispute, since they are aiming at me. I shall joyfully lay aside my serious occupations to take my part in the sports of these flatterers of the Roman pontiff."— Then addressing his adversary, he cries disdainfully from Wittenberg to Ingolstadt: "Now, my dear Eck, be brave, and gird thy sword upon thy thigh, thou mighty man! If I could not please thee as mediator, perhaps I shall please thee better as antagonist. Not that I imagine I can vanquish thee; but because, after all the triumphs thou hast gained in Hungary, Lombardy, and Bavaria (if at least we are to believe thee), I shall give thee opportunity of gaining the title of conqueror of Saxony and Misnia, so that thou shalt forever be hailed with the glorious title of August."

All Luther's friends did not share in his courage; for no one had hitherto been able to resist the sophisms of Doctor Eck. But their greatest cause of alarm was the subject of the discussion: the pope's primacy. The courtiers of the elector were alarmed. Spalatin, the prince's confidant and Luther's intimate friend, was filled with anxiety. Frederick was uneasy: even the sword of the knight of the holy sepulcher, with which he had been invested at Jerusalem, would be of little avail in this war. The reformer alone did not blench. The Lord (thought he) will deliver him into my hands. The faith by which he was animated gave him the means of encouraging his friends: "I entreat you, my dear Spalatin," said he, "do not give way to fear. You well know that if Christ had not been on my side, all that I have hitherto done must have been my ruin. Quite recently has not the Duke of Pomerania's chancellor received news from Italy that I had turned Rome topsy-turvy, and that they knew not how to quiet the agitation? So that it was resolved to attack me, not according to the rules of justice, but by Roman artifices (such was the expression used), meaning, I suppose, poison, ambush, or assassination.

"I restrain myself, and from love to the elector and the university suppress many things that I would publish against Babylon, if I were elsewhere. O my poor Spalatin, it is impossible to speak with truth of the Scriptures and of the Church without arousing the beast. Never expect to see me free from danger unless I abandon the teaching of sound divinity. If this matter be of God, it will not come to an end before all my friends have forsaken me, as Christ was forsaken by His disciples. Truth will stand alone, and will triumph by its own right hand, not by mine, nor yours, nor any other man's. If I perish, the world will not perish with me. But, wretch that I am, I fear I am unworthy to die in such a cause."—"Rome," he wrote again about the same time, "Rome is eagerly longing to kill me, and I am wasting my time in braving her. I have been assured that an effigy of Martin Luther was publicly burned in the Campo di Fiore at Rome, after being loaded with execrations. I await their furious rage. The whole world," he continued, "is moved, and totters in body and mind; what will happen, God only knows. For my part, I foresee wars and disasters. The Lord have mercy on us!"

Luther wrote letter upon letter to Duke George, begging this prince, in whose states Leipzig was situated, to give him permission to go and take part in the disputation; but he received no answer. The grandson of the Bohemian king, alarmed by Luther's proposition on the papal authority, and fearing the recurrence of those wars in Saxony of which Bohemia had so long been the theater, would not consent to the doctor's request. The latter therefore resolved to publish an explanation of the thirteenth thesis. But this writing, far from persuading the duke, made him only the more resolved; he positively refused the sanction required by the reformer to take a share in the disputation, allowing him only to be present as a spectator. This annoyed Luther very much: yet he had but one desire—to obey God. He resolved to go—to look on—and to wait his opportunity.

At the same time the prince forwarded to his utmost ability the disputation between Eck and Carlstadt. George was attached to the old doctrine; but he was upright, sincere, a friend to free inquiry, and did not think that every opinion should be judged heretical simply because it was offensive to the court of Rome. More than this, the elector used his influence with his cousin; and George, gaining confidence from Frederick's language, ordered that the disputation should take place.

Adolphus, bishop of Merseburg, in whose diocese Leipzig was situated, saw more clearly than Miltitz and Cajetan the danger of leaving such important questions to the chances of single combat. Rome dared not expose to such hazard the hard-earned fruits of many centuries. All the Leipzig theologians felt no less alarm, and entreated their bishop to prevent the discussion. Upon this, Adolphus made the most energetic representations to Duke George, who very sensibly replied: "I am surprised that a bishop should have so great a dread of the ancient and praiseworthy custom of our fathers—the investigation of doubtful questions in matters of faith. If your theologians refuse to defend their doctrines, it would be better to employ the money spent on them in maintaining old women and children, who at least could spin while they were singing."

This letter had but little effect on the bishop and his theologians. *There is a secret consciousness in error that makes it shrink from examination, even when talking most of free inquiry.* After having imprudently advanced, it retreated with cowardice. Truth gave no challenge, but it stood firm; error challenged to the combat, and ran away. Besides, the prosperity of Wittenberg was an object of jealousy to the University of Leipzig. The monks and priests of the latter city begged and entreated their flocks from the pulpit to flee from the new heretics. They vilified Luther; they depicted him and his friends in the blackest colors in order to excite the ignorant classes against the doctors of the Reformation. Tetzel, who was still living, awoke to cry out from the depth of his retreat: "It is the devil who urges them to this contest."

All the Leipzig professors did not, however, entertain the same opinions: some belonged to the class of indifferents, always ready to laugh at the faults of both parties. Among this body was the Greek professor, Peter Mosellanus. He cared very little about either John Eck, Carlstadt, or Martin Luther; but he flattered himself that he would derive much amusement from their disputation. "John Eck, the most illustrious of goose-quill gladiators and of braggadocios," wrote he to his friend Erasmus, "John Eck, who like the Aristophanic Socrates despises even the gods themselves, will have a bout with Andrew Carlstadt. The match will end in loud cries. Ten such men as Democritus would find matter for laughter in it."

The timid Erasmus, on the contrary, was alarmed at the very idea of a combat, and his prudence would have prevented the discussion. "If you would take Erasmus's word," wrote he to Melancthon, "you would labor rather in cultivating literature than in disputing with its enemies. I think that we should make greater progress by this means. Above all, let us never forget that we ought to conquer not only by our eloquence, but also by mildness and moderation." Neither the alarm of the priests nor the discretion of the pacificators could any longer prevent the combat. Each man got his arms ready.

While the electors were meeting at Frankfurt to choose an Emperor (June, 1519), the theologians assembled at Leipzig for an act, unnoticed by the world at large, but whose importance was destined to be quite as great for posterity.

Eck came first to the rendezvous. On the twenty-first of June he entered Leipzig with Poliander, a young man whom he had brought from Ingolstadt to write an account of the disputation. Every mark of respect was paid to the scholastic doctor. Robed in his sacerdotal garments, and at the head of a numerous procession, he paraded the streets of the city on the festival of Corpus Christi. All were eager to see him: the inhabitants were on his side, he tells us himself; "yet," adds he, "a report was current in the town that I should be beaten in this combat."

On the day succeeding the festival (Friday, June 24), which was the Feast of Saint John, the Wittenbergers arrived. Carlstadt, who was to contend with Dr. Eck, sat alone in his carriage, and preceded all the rest. Duke Barnim of Pomerania, who was then studying at Wittenberg and who had been named honorary rector of the uni-

versity, came next in an open carriage: at each side were seated the
two great divines—the fathers of the Reformation—Luther and
Melancthon. The latter would not quit his friend. "Martin, the
soldier of the Lord," he had said to Spalatin, "has stirred up this
fetid pool. My spirit is vexed when I think of the disgraceful conduct
of the papal theologians. Be firm, and abide with us!" Luther himself
had wished that his Achates, as he called him, should accompany
him.

John Lange, vicar of the Augustines, many doctors of law, several
masters of arts, two licentiates in theology, and other ecclesiastics,
among whom was Nicholas Amsdorff, closed the procession. Amsdorff, sprung from a noble family, valuing little the brilliant career
to which his illustrious birth might have called him, had dedicated
himself to theology. The theses on indulgences had brought him to
a knowledge of the truth. He had immediately made a bold confession of faith. Possessing a strong mind and an ardent character, Amsdorff frequently excited Luther, who was naturally vehement
enough, to acts that were perhaps imprudent. Born in exalted rank,
he had no fear of the great, and he sometimes spoke to them with a
freedom bordering on rudeness. "The gospel of Jesus Christ," said
he one day before an assembly of nobles, "belongs to the poor and
afflicted—not to you, princes, lords, and courtiers, who live continually in luxury and pleasures."

But these persons alone did not form the procession from Wittenberg. A great number of students followed their teachers: Eck affirms
that they numbered two hundred. Armed with pikes and halberds,
they surrounded the carriages of the doctors, ready to defend them,
and proud of their cause.

Such was the order in which the cortege of the reformers arrived
in Leipzig. They had already entered by the Grimma gate and advanced as far as St. Paul's cemetery, when one of the wheels of
Carlstadt's carriage gave way. The archdeacon, whose vanity was delighted at so solemn an entry, rolled into the mud. He was not hurt,
but was compelled to proceed to his lodgings on foot. Luther's carriage, which followed next, rapidly outstripped him, and bore the
reformer in safety to his quarters. The inhabitants of Leipzig, who
had assembled to witness the entry of the Wittenberg champions,

looked upon this accident as an evil omen to Carlstadt: and erelong the whole city was of opinion that he would be vanquished in the combat, but that Luther would come off victorious.

Adolphus of Merseburg was not idle. As soon as he heard of the approach of Luther and Carlstadt, and even before they had alighted from their carriages, he ordered placards to be posted upon the doors of all the churches, forbidding the opening of the disputation under pain of excommunication. Duke George, astonished at this audacity, commanded the town council to tear down the placards, and committed to prison the bold agent who had ventured to execute the bishop's order. George had repaired to Leipzig, attended by all his court, among whom was that Jerome Emser at whose house in Dresden Luther had passed a remarkable evening. George made the customary presents to the respective combatants. "The duke," observed Eck with vanity, "gave me a fine deer; but he only gave a fawn to Carlstadt."

Immediately on hearing of Luther's arrival, Eck went to visit the Wittenberg doctor. "What is this!" asked he; "I am told that you refuse to dispute with me!"

Luther.—"How can I, since the duke has forbidden me?"

Eck.—"If I cannot dispute with you, I care little about meeting Carlstadt. It was on your account I came here." Then after a moment's silence he added: "If I can procure you the duke's permission, will you enter the lists with me?"

Luther, joyfully.—"Procure it for me, and we will fight."

Eck immediately waited on the duke, and endeavored to remove his fears. He represented to him that he was certain of victory, and that the papal authority, far from suffering in the dispute, would come forth covered with glory. The ringleader must be attacked: if Luther remained standing, all would stand with him; if he fell, everything would fall with him. George granted the required permission.

The duke had caused a large hall to be prepared in his palace of the Pleissenburg. Two pulpits had been erected opposite each other; and tables were placed for the notaries commissioned to take down the discussion, and benches had been arranged for the spectators. The pulpits and benches were covered with handsome hangings. Over the pulpit of the Wittenberg doctor was suspended the portrait of Saint Martin, whose name he bore; over that of Doctor Eck, a representation of Saint George the champion. "We shall see," said the presumptous Eck, as he looked at this emblem, "whether I shall not ride over my enemies." Everything announced the importance that was attached to this contest.

On the twenty-fifth of June, both parties met at the palace to hear the regulations that were to be observed during the disputation. Eck, who had more confidence in his declamations and gestures than in his arguments, exclaimed, "We will dispute freely and extemporaneously; and the notaries shall not take down our words in writing."

Carlstadt.—"It has been agreed that the disputation should be reported, published, and submitted to the judgment of all men."

Eck.—"To take down everything that is said is dispiriting to the combatants, and prolongs the battle. There is an end to that animation which such a discussion requires. Do not check the flow of eloquence."

The friends of Doctor Eck supported his proposition, but Carlstadt persisted in his objections. The champion of Rome was obliged to give way.

Eck.—"Be it so; it shall be taken down. But do not let the notes be published before they have been submitted to the examination of chosen judges."

Luther.—"Does then the truth of Doctor Eck and his followers dread the light?"

Eck.—"We must have judges."

Luther.—"What judges?"

Eck.—"When the disputation is finished, we will arrange about selecting them."

The object of the partisans of Rome was evident. If the Wittenberg divines accepted judges, they were lost: for their adversaries were sure beforehand of them. If they refused these judges, they would be covered with shame, for their opponents would circulate the report that they were afraid to submit their opinions to impartial arbitrators.

The judges whom the reformers demanded were, not any particular individual whose opinion had been previously formed, but all Christendom. They appealed to this universal suffrage. Besides, it was a slight matter to them if they were condemned, if, while pleading their cause before the whole world, they brought a few souls to the knowledge of the truth. "Luther," says a Romanist historian, "required all men for his judges; that is, such a tribunal that no urn could have been vast enough to contain the votes."

They separated. "See what artifices they employ," said Luther and his friends one to another. "They desire no doubt to have the pope or the universities for judges."

In fact, on the next morning the Romanist divines sent one of their number to Luther, who was commissioned to propose that their judge should be—the pope! . . . "The pope!" said Luther; "how can I possibly agree to this?"

"Beware," exclaimed all his friends, "of acceding to conditions so unjust." Eck and his party held another council. They gave up the pope, and proposed certain universities. "Do not deprive us of the liberty which you had previously granted," answered Luther. "We cannot give way on this point," they replied. "Well then!" exclaimed Luther, "I will take no part in the discussion!"

Again the parties separated, and this matter was a general topic of conversation throughout the city. "Luther," everywhere exclaimed the Romanists, "Luther will not dispute! . . . He will not acknowledge any judge!" His words were commented on and misrepresented, and his adversaries endeavored to place them in the most unfavorable light. "What! does he really decline the discussion?" said the reformer's best friends. They went to him and expressed their alarm. "You refuse to take any part in the discussion!" cried they. "Your refusal will bring everlasting disgrace on your university and on your cause." This was attacking Luther on his weakest side. "Well, then!" replied he, his heart overflowing with indignation, "I accept the conditions imposed upon me; but I reserve the right of appeal, and except against the court of Rome."

Chapter 31

ECK AND CARLSTADT ON FREE WILL

THE TWENTY-SEVENTH OF JUNE was the day appointed for the opening of the discussion. Early in the morning the two parties assembled in the college of the university, and thence went in procession to the Church of Saint Thomas, where a solemn mass was performed by order and at the expense of the duke. After the service they proceeded to the ducal palace. At their head were Duke George and the Duke of Pomerania; after them came counts, abbots, knights, and other persons of distinction, and last of all the doctors of the two parties. A guard composed of seventy-six citizens, armed with halberds, accompanied the train, with banners flying, and to the sound of martial music. It halted at the castle gates.

The procession having reached the palace, each took his station in the hall appointed for the discussion. Duke George, the hereditary Prince John, Prince George of Anhalt, then twelve years old, and the Duke of Pomerania, occupied the seats assigned them.

Mosellanus ascended the pulpit to remind the theologians, by the duke's order, in what manner they were to dispute. "If you fall to quarrelling," said the speaker, "what difference will there be between a theologian in discussion and a shameless duelist? What is your object in gaining the victory, if it be not to recover a brother from the error of his ways? . . . It appears to me that each of you should desire less to conquer than to be conquered!"

When this address was terminated, sacred music resounded through the halls of the Pleissenburg; all the assembly knelt down, and the ancient hymn of invocation to the Holy Ghost, *Veni Sancte Spiritus* (Come, Holy Spirit) was sung. This was a solemn moment in the annals of the Reformation. Thrice the invocation was repeated, and while this solemn strain was heard, the defenders of the old doctrine and the champions of the new: the churchmen of the Middle Ages and those who sought to restore the Church of the Apostles, here assembled and confounded with one another, humbly bent their heads to the earth. The ancient tie of one and the same communion still bound together all those different minds; the same prayer still proceeded from all those lips, as if pronounced by one heart.

These were the last moments of outward—of dead unity: a new unity of spirit and of life was about to begin. The Holy Ghost was invoked upon the Church, and was preparing to answer and to renovate Christendom.

The signing and the prayers being ended, they all rose up. The discussion was about to open; but as it was past the hour of noon, it was deferred until two o'clock.

The duke invited to his table the principal persons who were to be present at the discussion. After the repast, they returned to the castle. The great hall was filled with spectators. Disputations of this kind were the public meetings of that age. It was here that the representatives of their day agitated the questions that occupied all minds. The speakers were soon at their posts. That the reader may form a better idea of their appearance, we will give their portraits as drawn by one of the most impartial witnesses of the contest.

"Martin Luther is of middle stature, and so thin, in consequence of his studies, that his bones may almost be counted. He is in the prime of life, and has a clear and sonorous voice. His knowledge and understanding of the Holy Scriptures is unparalleled; he has the Word of God at his fingers' ends. Besides this, he possesses great store of arguments and ideas. One might perhaps desire a little more judgment in arranging his subjects. In conversation he is pleasing and affable; there is nothing harsh or austere about him; he can accommodate himself to everyone; his manner of speaking is agreeable and unembarrassed. He displays firmness, and has always a cheerful air, whatever may be his adversaries' threats; so that it is difficult to believe that he could undertake such great things without the divine protection. He is blamed, however, for being more caustic, when reproving others, than becomes a theologian, particularly when putting forward novelties in religion.

"Carlstadt is of shorter stature; his complexion is dark and sunburnt, his voice unpleasing, his memory less trustworthy than Luther's, and he is more inclined to anger. He possesses, however, though in a smaller degree, the qualities that distinguish his friend.

"Eck is tall, broad-shouldered, and has a strong and thorough German voice. He has good lungs, so that he would be heard well in a theater, and would even make an excellent towncrier. His accent is rather vulgar than elegant. He has not that gracefulness so much extolled by Fabius and Cicero. His mouth, his eyes, and his whole countenance give you the idea of a soldier or a butcher rather than of a divine. He has an excellent memory, and if he had only as much understanding, he would be really a perfect man. But he is slow of comprehension, and is wanting in judgment, without which all other qualities are useless. Hence, in disputing, he heaps together, without selection or discernment, a mass of passages from the Bible, quotations from the Fathers, and proofs of all kinds. He has, besides, an impudence almost beyond conception. If he is embarrassed, he breaks off from the subject he is treating of, and plunges into another; he sometimes even takes up his adversary's opinion, clothing it in other words, and with extraordinary skill attributes to his opponent the absurdity he had been himself defending."

Such, according to Mosellanus, were the men at that time attracting the attention of the crowd which thronged the great hall of the Pleissenburg.

The dispute began between Eck and Carlstadt.

Eck's eyes were fixed for a moment on certain objects that lay on the desk of his adversary's pulpit, and which seemed to disturb him; they were the Bible and the Holy Fathers. "I decline the discussion," exclaimed he suddenly, "if you are permitted to bring your books with you." Surprising that a divine should have recourse to books in order to dispute! Eck's astonishment was still more marvellous. "It is the figleaf which this Adam makes use of to hide his shame," said Luther. "Did not Augustine consult his books when arguing with the Manicheans?" What did that matter? Eck's partisans raised a great clamor. The other side did the same. "The man has no memory," said Eck. At last it was arranged, according to the wish of the Chancellor of Ingolstadt, that each should rely upon his memory and his tongue only. "Thus, then," said many, "the object of this disputation will not be to discover the truth, but what praise is to be conferred on the tongue and the memory of the disputants."

As we are unable to give the details of this discussion, which lasted seventeen days, we shall, as an historian expresses it, imitate the painters who, when they have to represent a battle, set the most memorable actions in the foreground and leave the others in the distance.

The subject of discussion between Eck and Carlstadt was important. "Man's will, before his conversion," said Carlstadt, "can perform no good work: every good work comes entirely and exclusively from God, who gives man first the will to do, and then the power of accomplishing." This truth proclaimed by Scripture, says: "It is God which worketh in you both to will and to do of his good pleasure"; and by Saint Augustine, who, in his dispute with the Pelagians, had enunciated it in nearly the same terms. Every work in which the love of God and obedience toward Him do not exist is deprived in the eyes of the Almighty of all that can render it good, even should it originate in the best of human motives. Now there is in man a natural opposition to God—an opposition that the unaided strength of man cannot surmount. He has neither the will nor the power to overcome it. This must therefore be effected by the divine will.

This is the whole question of free will—so simple, and yet so decried by the world. Such had been the doctrine of the Church. But the schoolmen had so explained it that it was not recognizable. Undoubtedly (said they) the natural will of man can do nothing really pleasing to God; but it can do much toward rendering men meet to receive the grace of God, and more worthy to obtain it. They called these preparations a merit of congruity: "because it is congruous," said Thomas Aquinas, "that God should treat with particular favor him who makes a good use of his own will." And, as regards the conversion to be effected in man, undoubtedly it must be accomplished by the grace of God, which (according to the schoolmen) should bring it about, but not to the exclusion of his natural powers. These powers (said they) were not destroyed by sin: sin only opposes an obstacle to their development; but so soon as this obstacle is removed (and it was this, in their opinion, that the grace of God had to effect) the action of these powers begins again. The bird, to use one of their favorite comparisons, that has been tied for some time, has in this state neither lost its ability nor forgotten the art of flying; but some hand must loose the bonds, in order that he may again make use of his wings. This is the case with man, said they.

Such was the question agitated between Eck and Carlstadt. At first Eck had appeared to oppose all Carlstadt's propositions on this subject; but finding his position untenable, he said: "I grant that the will has not the power of doing a good work, and that it receives this power from God."—"Do you acknowledge then," asked Carlstadt, overjoyed at obtaining so important a concession, "that every good work comes entirely from God?"—"The whole good work really proceeds from God, but not wholly," cunningly replied the scholastic doctor.—"Truly, this is a discovery not unworthy of the science of divinity," exclaimed Melancthon.—"An entire apple," continued Eck, "is produced by the sun, but not entirely and without the co-operation of the plant." Most certainly it has never yet been maintained that an apple is produced solely by the sun.

Well then, said the opponents, plunging deeper into this important and delicate question of philosophy and religion, let us inquire how God acts upon man, and how man conducts himself under this action. "I acknowledge," said Eck, "that the first impulse in man's conversion proceeds from God, and that the will of man in this instance is entirely passive." Thus far the two parties were agreed. "I acknowledge," said Carlstadt, "that after this first impulse which proceeds from God, something must come on the part of man,—something that St. Paul denominates will, and which the fathers entitle consent." Here again they were both agreed: but from this point they diverged.

"This consent of man," said Eck, "comes partly from our natural will, and partly from God's grace." "No," said Carlstadt; "God must entirely create this will in man." Upon this Eck manifested anger and astonishment at hearing words so fitted to make man sensible of his nothingness. "Your doctrine," exclaimed he, "converts a man into a stone, a log, incapable of any reaction!" "What!" replied the reformers, "the faculty of receiving this strength which God produces in him, this faculty which (according to us) man possesses, does not sufficiently distinguish him from a log or a stone?"—"But," said their antagonist, "by denying that man has any natural ability, you contradict all experience." "We do not deny," replied they, "that man possesses a certain ability, and that he has the power of reflection, meditation, and choice. We consider this power and ability as mere instruments that can produce no good work, until the hand of God has set them in motion. They are like a saw in the hands of a sawyer."

The great doctrine of free will was here discussed; and it was easy to demonstrate that the doctrine of the reformers did not deprive man of his liberty as a moral agent and make him a mere passive machine. The liberty of a moral agent consists in his power of acting conformably to his choice. Every action performed without external constraint, and in consequence of the determination of the soul itself, is a free action. The soul is determined by motives; but we continually observe the same motives acting differently on different minds. Many men do not act in conformity with the motives of which, however, they acknowledge the full force. This inefficacy of motives proceeds from the obstacles opposed to them by the corruption of the understanding and of the heart. But God, by giving man a new heart and a new spirit, removes these obstacles; and by removing them, far from depriving him of his liberty, He takes away, on the contrary, everything that would prevent him from acting freely, from listening to the voice of his conscience, and, in the words of the gospel, "makes him free indeed" (John 8:36).

A trivial circumstance interrupted the discussion. We learn from Eck that Carlstadt had prepared a number of arguments; and, like many public speakers, he was reading what he had written. Eck saw in this the tactics of a mere learner, and objected to it. Carlstadt, embarrassed, and fearing that he should break down if he were deprived of his papers, persisted. "Ah!" exclaimed the schoolman, proud of the advantage he thought he had obtained, "his memory is not so good as mine." The point was referred to the arbitrators, who permitted the reading of extracts from the Fathers, but decided that in other respects the disputants should speak extempore.

This first part of the disputation was often interrupted by the noise of the spectators. They were in commotion, and frequently raised their voices. Any proposition that offended the ears of the majority immediately excited their clamors, and then the galleries were often called to order. The disputants themselves were sometimes carried away by the heat of discussion.

Near Luther sat Melancthon, who attracted almost as much attention as his neighbor. He was of small stature, and appeared little more than eighteen years old. Luther, who was a head taller, seemed connected with him in the closest friendship; they came in, went out, and took their walks together. "To look at Melancthon," wrote a Swiss theologian who studied at Wittenberg, "you would say he was a mere boy; but in understanding, learning, and talent, he is a giant, and I cannot comprehend how such heights of wisdom and genius can be found in so small a body." Between the sittings, Melancthon conversed with Carlstadt and Luther. He aided them in preparing for the combat, and suggested the arguments with which his extensive learning furnished him. During the discussion he remained quietly seated among the spectators, and carefully listened to the words of the theologians. From time to time, however, he came to the assistance of Carlstadt; and when the latter was near giving way under the powerful declamation of the Chancellor of Ingolstadt, the young professor whispered a word, or slipped him a piece of paper, on which the answer was written. Eck having perceived this on one occasion, and feeling indignant that this grammarian, as he called him, should dare interfere in the discussion, turned towards him and said haughtily: "Hold your tongue, Philip; mind your studies, and do not disturb me." Perhaps Eck at that time foresaw how formidable an opponent he would afterwards find in this young man. Luther was offended at the gross insult directed against his friend. "Philip's judgment," said he, "has greater weight with me than that of a thousand Doctor Ecks."

The calm Melancthon easily detected the weak points of the discussion. "We cannot help feeling surprised," said he, with that wisdom and beauty which we find in all his words, "when we think of the violence with which these subjects were treated. How could anyone expect to derive any profit from it? The Spirit of God loves retirement and silence: it is then that He penetrates deep into our hearts. The Bride of Christ does not dwell in the streets and market places, but leads her Spouse into the house of her mother."

Each party claimed the victory. Eck strained every nerve to appear the conqueror. As the points of divergence almost touched each other, he frequently exclaimed that he had convinced his opponent; or else, like another Proteus (said Luther), he suddenly turned round, put forth Carlstadt's opinions in other words, and asked him, with a tone of triumph, if he did not find himself compelled to yield. And the unskillful auditors, who could not detect the maneuver of the sophist, applauded and exulted with him. In many respects they were not equally matched. Carlstadt was slow, and on some occasions did not reply to his adversary's objections until the next day. Eck, on the contrary, was a master in his science, and found whatever he required at the very instant. He entered the hall with a disdainful air; ascended the rostrum with a firm step; and there he tossed himself about, paced to and fro, spoke at the full pitch of his sonorous voice, had a reply ready for every argument, and bewildered his hearers by his memory and skill. And yet, without perceiving it, Eck conceded during the discussion much more than he had intended. His partisans laughed aloud at each of his devices; "but (said Luther) I seriously believe that their laughter was mere pretense, and that in their hearts they were annoyed at seeing their chief, who had commenced the battle with so many bravados, abandon his standard, desert his army, and become a shameless runaway."

Three or four days after the opening of the conference, the disputation was interrupted by the festival of Peter and Paul the apostles.

On this occasion the Duke of Pomerania requested Luther to preach before him in his chapel. Luther cheerfully consented. But the place was soon crowded, and as the number of hearers kept increasing, the assembly was transferred to the great hall of the castle, in which the discussion was held. Luther preached on the grace of God and the power of Saint Peter. What Luther ordinarily maintained before an audience composed of men of learning, he then set before the people. Christianity causes the light of truth to shine upon the humblest as well as the most elevated minds; it is this which distinguishes it from every other religion and from every system of philosophy. The theologians of Leipzig, who had heard Luther preach, hastened to report to Eck the scandalous words with which their ears had been shocked. "You must reply," exclaimed they; "you must publicly refute these subtle errors." Eck desired nothing better. All the churches were open to him, and four times in succession he went into the pulpit to cry down Luther and his sermon. Luther's friends were indignant at this. They demanded that the Wittenberg divine should be heard in his turn. But it was all in vain. The pulpits were open to the adversaries of the evangelical doctrine; they were closed against those who proclaimed it. "I was silent," said Luther, "and was forced to suffer myself to be attacked, insulted, and calumniated, without even the power of excusing or defending myself."

It was not only the ecclesiastics who manifested their opposition to the evangelical doctors: the citizens of Leipzig were, in this respect, of the same opinion as the clergy. A blind fanaticism had rendered them the dupes of the falsehood and hatred that the priests were attempting to propagate. The principal inhabitants did not visit either Luther or Carlstadt. If they met them in the street, they did not salute them, and endeavored to prejudice the duke against them. But on the contrary they paid frequent visits to the Doctor of Ingolstadt, and ate and drank with him. The latter feasted with them, entertaining them with a description of the costly banquets to which he had been invited in Germany and Italy, sneering at Luther who had imprudently rushed upon his invincible sword, slowly quaffing the beer of Saxony the better to compare it with that of Bavaria, and casting amorous glances (he boasts of it himself) on the frail fair ones of Leipzig. His manners, which were rather free, did not give a favorable idea of his morals. They were satisfied with offering Luther the wine usually presented to the disputants. Those who were favorably disposed towards him, concealed their feelings from the public; many, like Nicodemus of old, visited him stealthily and by night. Two men alone honorably distinguished themselves by publicly declaring their friendship for him. They were Doctor Auerback, whom we have already seen at Augsburg, and Doctor Pistor the younger.

The greatest agitation prevailed in the city. The two parties were like two hostile camps, and they sometimes came to blows. Frequent quarrels took place in the taverns between the students of Leipzig and those of Wittenberg. It was generally reported, even in the meetings of the clergy, that Luther carried a devil about with him shut up in a little box. "I don't know whether the devil is in the box or merely under his frock," said Eck insidiously; "but he is certainly in one or the other."

Several doctors of the two parties had lodgings during the disputation in the house of the printer Herbipolis. They became so outrageous that their host was compelled to station a police officer, armed with a halberd, at the head of the table, with orders to prevent the guests from coming to blows. One day Baumgartner, an indulgence-merchant, quarreled with a gentleman, a friend of Luther's and gave way to such a violent fit of anger that he expired. "I was one of those who carried him to his grave," said Froschel, who relates the circumstance. In this manner did the general ferment in men's minds display itself. Then the speeches in the pulpits found an echo in the drawing-room and in the streets.

Duke George, although strongly biased in Eck's favor, did not display so much passion as his subjects. He invited Eck, Luther and Carlstadt to meet each other at his table. He even begged Luther to come and see him in private; but it was not long before he displayed all the prejudices with which he had been inspired against the reformer. "By your work on the Lord's Prayer," said the duke with displeasure, "you have misled the consciences of many. There are some people who complain that they have not been able to repeat a single Pater Noster for four days together."

Chapter 32

THE CHURCH'S FOUNDATION—
PETER OR CHRIST?

O N THE FOURTH OF JULY the discussion between Eck and Luther commenced. Everything seemed to promise that it would be more violent, more decisive, and more interesting than that which had just concluded, and which had gradually thinned the hall. The two combatants entered the arena resolved not to lay down their arms until victory declared in favor of one or the other. The general expectation was aroused, for the papal primacy was to be the subject of discussion. Christianity has two great adversaries: hierarchism and rationalism. Rationalism, in its application to the doctrine of man's ability, had been attacked by the reformers in the previous part of the Leipzig disputation. Hierarchism, considered in what is at once its summit and its base—the doctrine of papal authority—was to be contested in the second.

On the one side appeared Eck, the champion of the established religion, vaunting of the discussions he had maintained, as a general boasts of his campaigns. On the other side advanced Luther, who seemed destined to reap persecution and ignominy from this struggle, but who still presented himself with a good conscience, a firm resolution to sacrifice everything in the cause of truth, and an assurance grounded in faith in God and in the deliverance He grants to all who trust in Him. New convictions had sunk deep into his soul; they were not as yet arranged into a system; but in the heat of the combat they flashed forth like lightning. Serious and daring, he showed a resolution that made light of every obstacle. On his features might be seen the traces of the storms his soul had encountered, and the courage with which he was prepared to meet fresh tempests. These combatants, both sons of peasants and the representatives of the two tendencies that still divide Christendom, were about to enter upon a contest on which depended, in great measure, the future prospects of the State and of the Church. At seven in the morning the two disputants were in their pulpits, surrounded by a numerous and attentive assembly.

Luther stood up, and with a necessary precaution, he said modestly:

"In the name of the Lord, Amen! I declare that the respect I bear to the sovereign pontiff would have prevented my entering upon this discussion, if the excellent Dr. Eck had not dragged me into it."

Eck—"In Thy name, gentle Jesus! before descending into the lists, I protest before you, most noble lords, that all that I may say is in submission to the judgment of the first of all sees, and of him who is its possessor."

After a brief silence, Eck continued:

"There is in the Church of God a primacy that cometh from Christ Himself. The Church militant was formed in the image of the Church triumphant. Now the latter is a monarchy in which the hierarchy ascends step by step up to God, its sole Chief. For this reason Christ has established a similar order upon earth. What a monster the Church would be if it were without a head!"

Luther, turning towards the assembly—"When Dr. Eck declares that the universal Church must have a head, he says well. If there is any one among us who maintains the contrary, let him stand up! As for me, it is no concern of mine."

Eck—"If the Church militant has never been without a head, I should like to know who it can be, if not the Roman pontiff?"

Luther—"The Head of the Church militant is Christ Himself, and not a man. I believe this on the testimony of God's Word. He must reign, says Scripture, till He hath put all enemies under His feet. Let us not listen to those who banish Christ to the Church triumphant in heaven. His kingdom is a kingdom of faith. We cannot see our Head, and yet we have one."

Eck, who did not consider himself beaten, had recourse to other arguments, and resumed:

"It is from Rome, according to Saint Cyprian, that sacerdotal unity has proceeded."

Luther—"For the Western Church, I grant it. But is not this same Roman Church the offspring of that of Jerusalem? It is the latter, properly speaking, that is the nursing mother of all the churches."

Eck—"Saint Jerome declares that if an extraordinary power, superior to all others, were not given to the pope, there would be in the churches as many sects as there were pontiffs."

Luther—"Given: that is to say, if all the rest of believers consent to it, this power might be conceded to the chief pontiff by human right. And I will not deny that if all the believers in the world agree in recognizing as first and supreme pontiff either the Bishop of Rome, or of Paris, or of Magdeburg, we should acknowledge him as such from the respect due to this general agreement of the Church; but that has never been seen yet, and never will be seen. Even in our own day, does not the Greek Church refuse its assent to Rome?"

Luther was at that time prepared to acknowledge the pope as chief magistrate of the Church, freely elected by it; but he denied that he was pope of divine right. It was not till much later that he denied that submission was in any way due to him: and this step he was led to take by the Leipzig disputation. But Eck had ventured on ground better known to Luther than to himself. The latter could not, indeed, maintain his thesis that the papacy had existed during the preceding four centuries only. Eck quoted authorities of an earlier date, to which Luther could not reply. Criticism had not yet attacked the False Decretals. But the nearer the discussion approached the primitive ages of the Church, the greater was Luther's strength. Eck appealed to the Fathers; Luther replied to him from the Fathers, and all the bystanders were struck with his superiority over his rival.

"That the opinions I set forth are those of Saint Jerome," said he, "I prove by the Epistle of St. Jerome himself to Evagrius: 'Every bishop,' says he, 'whether at Rome, Eugubium, Constantinople, Rhegium, Tanis, or Alexandria, is partaker of the same merit and of the same priesthood. The power of riches, the humiliation of poverty, are the only things that make a difference in the rank of the bishops.' "

From the writings of the Fathers, Luther passed to the decisions of the councils, which consider the Bishop of Rome as only the first among his peers.

"We read," said he, "in the decree of the Council of Africa, 'The bishop of the first see shall neither be called prince of the pontiffs, nor sovereign pontiff, nor by any other name of that kind; but only bishop of the first see.' If the monarchy of the Bishop of Rome was of divine right," continued Luther, "would not this be an heretical injunction?"

Eck replied by one of those subtle distinctions that were so familiar to him:

"The bishop of Rome, if you will have it so, is not universal bishop, but bishop of the universal Church."

Luther—"I shall make no reply to this: let our hearers form their own opinion of it."—"Certainly," added he directly, "this is an explanation very worthy of a theologian, and calculated to satisfy a disputant who thirsts for glory. It is not for nothing, it seems, that I have remained at great expense at Leipzig, since I have learned that the pope is not, in truth, the universal bishop, but the bishop of the universal Church!"

Eck—"Well then, I will come to the point. The worthy doctor calls upon me to prove that the primacy of the Church of Rome is of divine right. I will prove it by this expression of Christ: "Thou art Peter, and on this rock will I build my church." Saint Augustine, in one of his epistles, has thus explained the meaning of this passage: 'Thou art Peter, and on this rock (that is to say, on Peter) I will build my church.' It is true that in another place the same father has explained that by this rock we should understand Christ Himself, but he has not retracted his former exposition."

Luther—"If the reverend doctor desires to attack me, let him first reconcile these contradictions in Saint Augustine. For it is most certain that Augustine has said many times that the rock was Christ, and perhaps not more than once that it was Peter himself. But even should Saint Augustine and all the Fathers say that the apostle is the rock of which Christ speaks, I would resist them, single-handed, in reliance upon the Holy Scriptures, that is, on divine right; for it is written: 'Other foundation can no man lay than that is laid, which is Jesus Christ.' Peter himself terms Christ the chief cornerstone, and a living stone on which we are built up a spiritual house."

Eck—"I am surprised at the humility and modesty with which the reverend doctor undertakes to oppose, alone, so many illustrious Fathers, and pretends to know more than the sovereign pontiffs, the councils, the doctors, and the universities! . . . It would be surprising, no doubt, if God had hidden the truth from so many saints and martyrs—until the advent of the reverend father!"

Luther—"The Fathers are not against me. Saint Augustine and Saint Ambrose, both most excellent doctors, teach as I teach. *Super isto articulo fidei, fundata est Ecclesia* (The Church is founded on that article of faith), says Saint Ambrose, when explaining what is meant by the rock on which the Church is built. Let my opponent then set a curb upon his tongue. To express himself as he does will only serve to excite contention, and not be to discuss like a true doctor."

Eck had no idea that his opponent's learning was so extensive, and that he would be able to extricate himself from the toils that were drawn around him. "The reverend doctor," said he, "has come well armed into the lists. I beg your lordships to excuse me if I do not exhibit such accuracy of research. I came here to discuss, and not to make a book."

Eck was surprised but not beaten. As he had no more arguments to adduce, he had recourse to a wretched and spiteful trick, which, though it did not vanquish his antagonist, would at least embarrass him greatly. If the accusation of being Bohemian, a heretic, a Hussite, could be fixed upon Luther, he would be vanquished; for the Bohemians were objects of abhorrence in the Church. The scene of combat was not far from the frontiers of Bohemia; Saxony, after the sentence pronounced on John Huss by the Council of Constance, had been exposed to all the horrors of a long and ruinous war; it was its boast to have resisted the Hussites at that time; the University of Leipzig had been founded in opposition to the tendencies of John Huss; and this discussion was going on in the presence of princes, nobles, and citizens, whose fathers had fallen in that celebrated contest. To insinuate that Luther and Huss were of one mind would be to inflict a most terrible blow on the former.

It was to this stratagem that the Ingolstadt doctor now had recourse: "From the earliest times, all good Christians have acknowledged that the Church of Rome derives its primacy direct from Christ

Himself, and not from human right. I must confess, however, that the Bohemians, while they obstinately defended their errors, attacked this doctrine. I beg the worthy father's pardon, if I am an enemy of the Bohemians, because they are enemies of the Church, and if the present discussion has called these heretics to my recollection; for, in my humble opinion, the doctor's conclusions are in every way favorable to these errors. It is even asserted that the Hussites are loudly boasting of it."

Eck had calculated well: his partisans received this perfidious insinuation with the greatest favor. There was a movement of joy among the audience. "These insults," said the reformer afterwards, "tickled them much more agreeably than the discussion itself."

Luther—"I do not like and I never shall like a schism. Since on their own authority the Bohemians have separated from our unity, they have done wrong, even if the divine right had pronounced in favor of their doctrines; for the supreme, divine right is charity and oneness of mind."

It was during the morning sitting of the fifth of July that Luther had made use of this language. The meeting broke up shortly after, as it was the hour of dinner. Luther felt ill at ease. Had he not gone too far in thus condemning the Christians of Bohemia? Did they not hold the doctrines that Luther was now maintaining? He saw all the difficulties of his position. Should he rise up against a council that condemned John Huss, or should he deny that sublime idea of a universal Christian Church which had taken full possession of his mind? The unshaken Luther did not hesitate. He would do his duty, whatever might be the consequences. Accordingly when the assembly met again at two in the afternoon, he was the first to speak. He said with firmness:

"Among the articles of faith held by John Huss and the Bohemians, there are some that are most Christian. This is a positive certainty. Here, for instance, is one: 'That there is but one universal Church'; and here is another: 'It is not necessary for salvation to believe the Roman Church superior to all others.' It is of little consequence to me whether these things were said by Wycliffe or by Huss . . . they are truth."

Luther's declaration produced a great sensation among his hearers. Huss—Wycliffe—those odious names, pronounced with approbation by a monk in the midst of a Catholic assembly! An almost general murmur ran round the hall. Duke George himself felt alarmed. He fancied he saw that banner of civil war upraised in Saxony which had for so many years desolated the states of his maternal ancestors. Unable to suppress his emotion, he placed his hands on his hips, shook his head, and exclaimed aloud, so that all the assembly heard him, "He is carried away by rage!" The whole meeting was agitated: they rose up, each man speaking to his neighbor. Those who had given way to drowsiness awoke. Luther's friends were in great perplexity, while his enemies exulted. Many who had thus far listened to him with pleasure began to entertain doubts of his orthodoxy. The impression produced on Duke George's mind by these words was never effaced; from this moment he looked upon the reformer with an evil eye, and became his enemy.

Luther did not suffer himself to be intimidated by these murmurs. One of his principal arguments was that the Greeks had never recognized the pope, and yet they had never been declared heretics; that the Greek Church had existed, still existed, and would exist, without the pope, and that it as much belonged to Christ as the Church of Rome did. Eck, on the contrary, impudently maintained that the Christian and the Roman Church were one and the same; that the Greeks and Orientals, in abandoning the pope, had also abandoned the Christian faith, and were indisputably heretics. "What!" exclaimed Luther, "are not Gregory of Nazianzum, Basil the Great, Epiphanius, Chrysostom, and an immense number besides of Greek bishops—are they not saved? and yet they did not believe that the Church of Rome was above the other Churches! . . . It is not in the power of the Roman pontiffs to make new articles of faith. The Christian believer acknowledges no other authority than Holy Scripture. This alone is the right divine. I beg the worthy doctor to concede that the Roman pontiffs were men, and that he will not make them gods."

Eck then resorted to one of those jests which give a specious air of triumph to him who employs them.

"The reverend father is a very poor cook," said he; "he has made a terrible hodgepodge of Greek saints and heretics; so that the odor of sanctity in the one prevents us from smelling the poison of the others."

Luther, interrupting Eck with warmth—"The worthy doctor is becoming abusive. In my opinion, there is no communion between Christ and Belial."

Luther made a great advance. In 1516 and 1517, he had only attacked the sermons of the indulgence-hawkers and the scholastic doctrines, but had respected the papal degrees. Somewhat later he rejected those degrees, and appealed to a council.

These theological disputes, to which the men of the world would be unwilling to consecrate a few brief moments, had been followed and listened to for twenty successive days with great attention; laymen, knights, and princes had manifested a constant interest. But, on the contrary, some of the Leipzig theologians, friends of Doctor Eck, slept soundly, as an eye witness informed the historian. It was necessary to wake them up at the close of the disputation, for fear they would lose their dinners.

Luther quitted Leipzig first; Carlstadt followed him; but Eck remained several days after their departure.

No decision had been reached on the discussion. Everyone commented on it according to his own feelings. "At Leipzig," said Luther, "there was great loss of time, but no seeking after truth. We have been examining the doctrines of our adversaries these two years past, so that we have counted all their bones. Eck, on the contrary, has hardly grazed the surface; but he has made more noise in one hour than we have in two long years."

The Leipzig disputation was not destined, however, to pass away in smoke. Every work performed with devotion bears fruit. Luther's words sunk with irresistible power into the minds of his hearers. Many of those who daily thronged the hall of the castle were subdued by the truth. It was especially in the midst of its most determined adversaries that its victories were gained. Doctor Eck's secretary, familiar friend, and disciple, Poliander, was won to the Reformation; and in the year 1522, he publicly preached the gospel at Leipzig. John Cellarius, professor of Hebrew, a man violently opposed to the reformed doctrines, was touched by the words of the eloquent doctor, and began to search the Scriptures more deeply. Erelong he gave up his station, and went to Wittenberg to study at Luther's feet. Some time after he was pastor at Frankfurt and at Dresden.

Among those who had taken their seats on the benches reserved for the court and who surrounded Duke George, was George of Anhalt, a young prince, twelve years old, descended from a family celebrated for their combats against the Saracens. He was then studying at Leipzig under a private tutor. An eager desire for learning and an ardent thirst for truth already distinguished this illustrious youth. He was frequently heard repeating these words of Solomon: "Lying lips become not a prince." The discussion at Leipzig awakened serious reflections in this boy, and excited a decided partiality for Luther. Some time after, he was offered a bishopric. His brothers and all his relations entreated him to accept it, wishing to push him to the highest dignities in the Church.

But he was determined in his refusal. On the death of his pious mother, who was secretly well disposed towards Luther, he became possessed of all the reformer's writings. He offered up constant and fervent prayers to God beseeching Him to turn his heart to the truth, and often, in the solitude of his closet, he exclaimed with tears: "Deal with Thy servant according to Thy mercy, and teach me Thy statutes." His prayers were heard. Convinced and carried away, he fearlessly ranged himself on the side of the gospel. In vain did his guardians, and particularly Duke George, besiege him with entreaties and remonstrances. He was inflexible, and George exclaimed, half convinced by the reasoning of his ward: "I cannot answer him; but I will still remain in my own Church, for it is a hard matter to break in an old dog." We shall meet again with this amiable prince, one of the noblest characters of the Reformation, who preached in person to his subjects the words of everlasting life, and to whom has been applied the saying of Dion on the Emperor Marcus Antoninus: "He was consistent during the whole of his life; he was a good man, one in whom there was no guile."

But it was the students in particular who received Luther's words with enthusiasm. They felt the difference between the spirit and energy of the Wittenberg doctor and the sophistical distinctions, the empty speculations of the Chancellor of Ingolstadt. They saw that Luther relied upon the Word of God, and that Eck's opinions were grounded on human tradition. The effect was instantaneous. The lecture rooms of the University of Leipzig were speedily deserted after the disputation. One circumstance, indeed, contributed to this result: the plague seemed on the point of breaking out in that city. But there were other universities (Erfurt, Ingolstadt, etc.) to which the students might have gone. The power of truth drew them to Wittenberg, where the number of students was soon doubled.

Among those who removed from the one university to the other was observed a youth of sixteen years, of melancholy disposition, speaking seldom, and who, in the midst of the conversations and sports of his fellow students, often appeared absorbed in his own reflections. His parents had at first thought him of weak intellect; but they soon found him so quick in learning and so constantly occupied with his studies that they formed the greatest expectations of him. His uprightness and candor, his modesty and piety, won him the affection of all, and Mosellanus pointed him out as a model to the whole university. His name was Gaspard Cruciger, a native of Leipzig. The new student of Wittenberg was afterwards the friend of Melancthon, and Luther's assistant in the translation of the Bible.

The Leipzig disputation bore still greater fruits. Here it was that the theologian of the Reformation received his call. Melancthon sat modest and silent listening to the discussion, in which he took very little part. Till that time literature had been his sole occupation. The conference gave him a new impulse, and launched the eloquent professor into the career of theology. From that hour his extensive learning bowed before the Word of God. He received the evangelical truths with the simplicity of a child; explained the doctrine of salvation with a grace and perspicuity that charmed all his hearers; and trod boldly in that path so new to him, for, said he, "Christ will never abandon His followers." The two friends walked together, contending for liberty and truth,—the one with the energy of St. Paul, the other with the meekness of St. John. Luther admirably expressed the difference of their callings. "I was born," said he, "to contend on the field of battle with factions and with wicked spirits. This is why my works abound with war and tempests. It is my task to uproot the stock and the stem, to clear away the briars and underwood, to fill up the pools and the marshes. I am the rough woodman who has to prepare the way and smooth the road. But Philip advances quietly and softly; he tills and plants the ground; sows and waters it joyfully, according to the gifts that God has given him with so liberal a hand."

If Melancthon, the tranquil sower, was called to the work by the disputation of Leipzig, Luther, the hardy woodman, felt his arm strengthened by it, and his courage reinvigorated. The greatest effect of this discussion was that wrought in Luther himself. "The scales of scholastic theology," said he, "fell then entirely from before my eyes, under the triumphant presidence of Doctor Eck." The veil which the School and the Church had conjointly drawn before the sanctuary was rent for the reformer from top to bottom. Driven to new inquiries, he arrived at unexpected discoveries. With as much indignation as astonishment, he saw the evil in all its magnitude. Searching into the annals of the Church, he discovered that the supremacy of Rome had no other origin than ambition on the one hand, and ignorant credulity on the other.

The narrow point of view under which he had hitherto looked upon the Church was succeeded by a deeper and more extended range. He recognized in the Christians of Greece and of the East true members of the Catholic Church; and instead of a visible chief, seated on the banks of the Tiber, he adored, as sole Chief of the people of God, an invisible and eternal Redeemer, who according to His promise, is daily in the midst of every nation upon earth, with all who believe in His name. The Latin Church was no longer in Luther's estimation the universal Church; he saw the narrow barriers of Rome fall down, and exulted in discovering beyond them the glorious dominions of Christ. From that time he comprehended how a man might be a member of Christ's Church, without belonging to the pope's. But, above all, the writings of John Huss produced a deep impression upon him. He there found, to his great surprise, the doctrine of St. Paul and of St. Augustine—that doctrine at which he himself had arrived after so many struggles. "I believed and I taught all the doctrines of John Huss without being aware of it: and so did Staupitz. In short, although unconscious of it, we are all Hussites. Paul and Augustine were so themselves. I am confounded, and know not what to think. Oh! how terribly have men deserved the judgments of God, seeing that the gospel truth, which has been unveiled and published this century past, has been condemned, burned, and stifled. . . . Woe, woe to the world!"

Luther separated from the papacy, and then felt toward it a decided aversion and holy indignation. All the witnesses that in every age had risen up against Rome came in turns before him and testified against her, each revealing some abuse or error. "Oh! what thick darkness!" exclaimed he.

He was not allowed to be silent on this sad discovery. The insolence of his adversaries, their pretended triumph and the efforts they made to extinguish the light, decided his soul. He advanced along the path in which God conducted him, without anxiety as to the goal to which it would lead him. Luther pointed to this moment as that of his emancipation from the papal yoke. "Learn from me," said he, "how difficult a thing it is to throw off errors confirmed by the example of all the world, and which, through long habit, have become a second nature to us. I had then been seven years reading and publicly explaining the Holy Scriptures with great zeal, so that I knew them almost by heart. I had also all the firstfruits of knowledge and faith in our Lord Jesus Christ. I knew that we are justified and saved not by our works, but by faith in Christ; and I even maintained openly that the pope is not the head of the Christian Church by divine right. And yet I could not see the consequences that flowed from this. What is not of God must needs be of the devil." Luther adds further on: "I no longer permit myself to be indignant against those who are still attached to the pope, since I, who had for so many years studied the Holy Scriptures so attentively, still clung with so much obstinacy to popery."

Such were the real results of the Leipzig disputation—results of more importance than the disputation itself. It was like those first successes which discipline an army and excite its courage.

Chapter 33

LUTHER ON GALATIANS
AND THE LORD'S SUPPER

E CK GAVE WAY to all the intoxication of what he wished to represent as a victory. He inveighed against Luther; heaped charge upon charge against him; wrote to Frederick; and desired, like a skillful general, to take advantage of the confusion that always follows a battle to obtain important concessions from that prince. While waiting for the measures that were to be taken against his adversary's person, he called down fire upon his writings, even on those he had not read. He begged the elector to summon a provincial council: "Let us exterminate these vermin," said the coarse doctor, "before they multiply beyond all bounds."

It was not against Luther alone that he vented his anger. His imprudence called Melancthon into the lists. The latter, connected by tender ties of friendship with the excellent Œcolampadius, wrote him an account of the disputation, speaking of Dr. Eck in terms of commendation. Nevertheless, the pride of the Chancellor of Ingolstadt was wounded. He immediately took up the pen against "that grammarian of Wittenberg, who was not ignorant, indeed, of Latin and Greek, but who had dared publish a letter in which he had insulted him—Dr. Eck."

Melancthon replied, and this was his first theological writing. It is characterized by all that exquisite urbanity which distinguished this excellent man. Laying down the fundamental principles of hermeneutics, he showed that we ought not to interpret Scripture by the Fathers, but the Fathers by Scripture. "How often has not Jerome been mistaken!" said he; "how frequently Augustine! how frequently Ambrose! how often their opinions are different! and how often they retract their errors! There is but one Scripture, inspired by the Holy Ghost, and pure and true in all things.

"Luther does not follow certain ambiguous explanations of the ancients, say they; and why should he? When he explains the passage of Saint Matthew: 'Thou art Peter, and upon this rock I will build my church,' he says the same thing as Origen, who alone is a host; as Augustine in his homily; and as Ambrose in his sixth book upon Saint Luke; I will mention no others. What then, will you say the Fathers contradict one another? And is there any thing astonishing in that? I believe in the Fathers because I believe in Scripture. The meaning of Scripture is one and simple, like heavenly truth itself. It is obtained by comparing Scripture with Scripture: it is deduced from the thread and connection of the discourse. There is a philosophy that is enjoined us as regards Holy Scripture: and that is, to bring all human opinions and maxims to it, as to a touchstone by which to try them."

It had been a long time since such powerful truths had been set forth so arrestingly. The Word of God was restored to its place, and the Fathers to theirs. The simple method by which we may arrive at the real meaning of Scripture was firmly laid down. The Word floated above all the difficulties and all the explanations of the School. Melancthon furnished the means of replying to all those who, like Dr. Eck, should perplex this subject, even to the most distant ages. The feeble grammarian had risen up, and the broad, sturdy shoulders of the scholastic gladiator had bent under the movement of his arm.

The weaker Eck was, the louder he clamored. By his boastings and his accusations he hoped to secure the victory that he had lost in his discussions. The monks and all the partisans of Rome re-echoed his clamors. From every part of Germany, reproaches were poured upon Luther; but he remained unaffected by them. "The more I find my name covered with opprobrium, the more do I glory in it," said he at the conclusion of the explanations he published on the Leipzig propositions. "The truth, that is to say Christ, must needs increase, and I must decrease. The voice of the Bride and the Bridegroom causes me a joy that far surpasses the terrors inspired by these clamors. Men are not the authors of my sufferings, and I entertain no hatred toward them. It is Satan, the prince of wickedness, who desires to terrify me. But He who is within us is mightier than he that is in the world. The judgment of our contemporaries is bad; that of posterity will be better."

If the Leipzig disputation augmented Luther's enemies in Germany, it also increased the number of his friends in foreign countries. "What Huss was in Bohemia in other days, you now are in Saxony, dear Martin," wrote the Bohemian brethren to him; "for this reason, pray and be strong in the Lord!"

About this time the war broke out between Luther and Emser, then professor at Leipzig. The latter wrote to Dr. Zack, a zealous Roman Catholic of Prague, a letter in which his design appeared to be to deprive the Hussites of their notion that Luther belonged to their party. Luther could not doubt that by seeming to justify him, the learned Leipziger was endeavoring to fix upon him the suspicion of adhering to the Bohemian heresy, and he accordingly resolved to tear aside the veil under which his former host of Dresden desired to conceal his hostility. With this intent he published a letter, addressed "To Emser the Goat" (his adversary's crest was a goat), and concluded by these words, so clearly depicting his character: "My maxim is,—to love all men, but to fear none."

While new friends and enemies thus sprang up around Luther, his old friends seemed to be deserting him. Staupitz, who had brought the reformer from the obscurity of his cloister at Erfurt, began to evince some coolness toward him. Luther had soared too high for Staupitz, who could not follow him. "You abandon me," wrote Luther to him. "All day long I have been very sad on your account, as a weaned child cries after its mother. I dreamed of you last night; you were leaving me, while I groaned and shed bitter tears. But you stretched out your hand, bade me be calm, and promised to return to me again."

The pacificator Miltitz was desirous of making a fresh attempt to calm the agitation of men's minds. But what hold could he have over men still agitated by the emotions that struggle had excited? His endeavors proved unavailing. He was the bearer of the famous Golden Rose presented to the elector, but the latter did not condescend to receive it in person. Frederick knew the artifices of Rome, and all hope of deceiving him was relinquished.

Luther, far from retreating, advanced daily. It was at this time that he aimed one of his most violent blows against error in his Commentary on the Epistle to the Galatians. The second Commentary is undoubtedly superior to the first; but in the first he expounded with great power the doctrine of justification by faith. Each expression of the new apostle was full of life, and God made use of him to introduce a knowledge of Himself into the hearts of the people. "Christ gave Himself for our sins," said Luther to his contemporaries. "It was not silver or gold that He gave for us; it was not a man; it was not all the angels; it was Himself that He gave, apart from whom there is nothing great. And He gave this inestimable treasure—for our sins. Where now are those who vaunt of the power of our will? Where are all the lessons of moral philosophy? Where are the power and the strength of the law? Since our sins were so great that nothing could take them away except a ransom so immeasurable, shall we still claim to obtain righteousness by the strength of our own will, by the power of the law, or by the teaching of men? What shall we do with all these artifices, with all these delusions? Alas! we shall cover our iniquities with a false righteousness, and we shall make hypocrites of ourselves, whom nothing in the world can save."

But while Luther was thus laying down the doctrine that there is no salvation for men out of Christ, he also showed that this salvation transforms man, and makes him abound in good works. "He who has truly heard the Word of Christ, and who keeps it, is immediately clothed with the spirit of charity. If you love the man who has made you a present of twenty florins (coin first struck in 1252), or done you any important service, or in any other manner testified his affection, how much more ought you to love Him who has given you not gold or silver, but Himself, who has even received so many wounds for your sake, who for you has sweated drops of blood, and who died for you; in a word, who, by paying for all your sins, has swallowed up death, and obtained for you in heaven a Father full of love! . . . If you love Him not, you have not heard with your heart the things that He has done; you have not believed them, for faith worketh by love."

"This Epistle is my epistle," said Luther, speaking of the Epistle to the Galatians: "I am wedded to it."

His adversaries compelled him to advance more quickly than he would have done without them. At this period Eck incited the Franciscans of Juterbock to attack him again. Luther, in reply, not content with repeating what he had already taught, attacked errors that he had newly discovered. "I should like to know," said he, "in what part of Scripture the power of canonizing the saints has been given to the popes; and also what necessity, what utility there is in canonizing them. . . . For that matter," added he sarcastically, "let them canonize as much as they like!"

Luther's new attacks remained unanswered. The blindness of his enemies was as favorable to him as his own courage. They passionately defended secondary matters, and when Luther laid his hand on the foundations of the Roman doctrine, they saw them shaken without uttering a word. They busied themselves in defending the outworks. Their intrepid adversary was advancing into the body of the place, and there boldly planting the standard of truth. Accordingly, they were afterwards astonished when they beheld the fortress they were defending undermined and on fire, and crumbling into ruins in the midst of the flames, while they were flattering themselves that it was impregnable, and were still braving those who led the assault. Thus are all great catastrophes effected.

The Sacrament of the Lord's Supper was now beginning to occupy Luther's thoughts. He looked in vain for this holy supper in the Mass. One day, shortly after his return from Leipzig, he went into the pulpit. Let us listen to his words, for they are the first he uttered on a subject that has since rent the Church of the Reformation into two parties. He said: "In the holy sacrament of the altar there are three things we must observe: the sign, which should be outward, visible, and in a bodily shape; the thing signified, which is inward, spiritual, and in the mind of man; and faith, which makes use of both." If definitions had been carried no farther, unity would have been maintained.

Luther continued: "It would be a good thing if the Church, by a general council, should order both kinds to be given to the believer; not however that one kind is not sufficient, for faith alone would suffice." This bold language pleased his hearers. A few of them were however alarmed and irritated. "It is false and scandalous," said they.

The preacher continued: "There is no closer, deeper, or more indivisible union than that which takes place between the food and the body which the food nourishes. Christ is so united to us in the sacrament that He acts as if he were ourselves. Our sins assail Him; His righteousness defends us."

But Luther was not satisfied with setting forth the truth; he attacked one of the most fundamental errors of Rome. That Church maintains that the Sacrament operates of itself, independently of the disposition of the communicant. Nothing can be more convenient than that opinion. Hence the ardor with which the sacrament is sought. Luther attacked this doctrine, and opposed it by the contrary doctrine, by virtue of which faith and the concurrence of the heart are necessary.

This energetic protest was of a nature to overthrow the ancient superstitions; and yet it is most astonishing that no one paid any attention to it. Rome passed by that which should have called up a shriek of distress, and fell impetuously on the unimportant remark Luther had made at the beginning of his discourse, touching the communion in both kinds. This sermon having been published in December, a cry of heresy was raised in every quarter. "It is nothing more nor less than the doctrine of Prague," was the observation at the court of Dresden, where the sermon arrived during the festival of Christmas; "the work, besides, is in German, in order that the common people may understand it." The prince's devotion was disturbed, and on the third day of the festival he wrote to his cousin Frederick: "Since the publication of this sermon, the number of those who receive the Eucharist in both kinds has increased in Bohemia by six thousand. Your Luther, from being a professor at Wittenberg, is about to become bishop of Prague and arch-heretic!"

"He was born in Bohemia!" said some, "of Bohemian parents; he was brought up in Prague, and taught from Wycliffe's books!"

Luther thought it his duty to contradict these rumors in a writing wherein he seriously gives an account of his family. "I was born at Eisleben," said he, "and christened in St. Peter's Church. Dresden is the nearest place to Bohemia that I have ever visited."

Duke George's letter did not estrange the elector from Luther. A few days after, this prince invited the doctor to a splendid banquet which he gave the Spanish ambassador, and there Luther valiantly contended against Charles's minister. The elector had begged him, through his chaplain, to defend his cause with moderation. "Too much folly is displeasing to men," replied Luther to Spalatin; "but too much discretion is displeasing to God. The gospel cannot be defended without tumult and without scandal. The Word of God is a sword,—a war,—a ruin,—a stumbling-block,—a destruction,—a poison; and, as Amos says, it meets us like a bear in the road or a lioness in the forest. I seek nothing, I ask nothing. There is One greater than I, who seeketh and asketh. If He should fall, I lose nothing; if He stand, I am profited nothing."

Everything announced that Luther would need faith and courage now more than ever. Eck was forming plans of revenge. Instead of the laurels that he had reckoned on gaining, the Leipzig gladiator had become the laughingstock of all the sensible men of his nation. Several biting satires were published against him. One was the *Epistle of Ignorant Canons,* written by Œcolampadius, and which cut Eck to the quick. Another was a *Complaint against Eck,* probably from the pen of the excellent Pirckheimer of Nuremberg, overflowing with a sarcasm and dignity of which Pascal's *Provincial Letters* can alone give us any idea.

Luther manifested his displeasure at several of these writings. "It is better to attack openly," said he, "than to bite from behind a hedge."

What a disappointment for the Chancellor of Ingolstadt! His fellow countrymen abandoned him. He prepared to cross the Alps to seek foreign support. Wherever he went, he vented his threats against Luther, Melancthon, Carlstadt, and the elector himself. "From his lofty language," said the Wittenberg doctor, "one might take him to be God Almighty." Inflamed with anger and the desire of revenge, Eck published, in February, 1520, a work on the primacy of St. Peter. In this treatise, which was utterly destitute of all sound criticism, he maintained that this apostle was the first of the popes, and had dwelt twenty-five years in Rome. After this Eck set out for Italy, to receive the reward of his pretended triumphs, and to forge in Rome, under the shadow of the papal capitol, more powerful thunderbolts than the frail weapons of the schoolmen that had shivered in his hands.

Luther foresaw all the perils that his opponent's journey might draw upon him; but he feared not. Spalatin, in alarm, begged him to propose peace. "No," replied Luther, "so long as he continues his

clamors, I cannot withdraw my hands from the contest. I trust everything to God. I consign my bark to the winds and to the waves. The
battle is the Lord's. Why should you imagine that Christ will advance His cause by peace? Did He not fight with His own blood, and
all the martyrs after Him?"

Such, at the opening of the year 1520, was the position of the combatants of Leipzig. The one was rousing all the papacy to crush his
rival: the other waited for war with the same calmness that men look
for peace. The new year was destined to see the storm burst forth.

Chapter 34

CHARLES V ELECTED EMPEROR

A NEW ACTOR was about to appear on the stage. God designed to bring the Wittenberg monk face to face with the most powerful monarch that had appeared in Christendom since the days of Charlemagne. He selected a prince whose scepter extended over a considerable part of the old world, and even over the new, so that (according to a celebrated saying) the sun never went down on his vast dominions; and to him He opposed that lowly Reformation, begun in the secluded cell of a convent at Erfurt by the anguish and the sighs of a poor monk. The history of this monarch and of his reign was destined, it would seem, to teach the world an important lesson. It was to show the nothingness of all the strength of man when it presumes to measure itself with the weakness of God. If a prince, a friend to Luther, had been called to the imperial throne, the success of the Reformation might have been ascribed to his protection. If even an emperor opposed to the new doctrines, but yet a weak ruler, had worn the diadem, the triumph of this work might have been accounted for by the weakness of the monarch. But it was the haughty conqueror at Pavia who was destined to vail his pride before the power of God's Word; and the whole world beheld the man, who found it an easy task to drag Francis I a prisoner to Madrid, obliged to lower his sword before the son of a poor miner.

The emperor Maximilian was dead, and the electors had met at Frankfurt to choose a successor. This was an important event for all Europe under the existing circumstances. All Christendom was occupied with this election. Maximilian had not been a great prince; but his memory was dear to the people. They were delighted to call to recollection his presence of mind and his good nature. Luther used often to converse with his friends about him, and one day related the following anecdote of this monarch.

A mendicant was once following him and begging alms, calling him brother; "for [said he] we are both descended from the same father, Adam. I am poor [continued he], but you are rich, and you ought therefore to help me." The emperor turned round at these words, and said to him: "There is a penny for you; go to all your other brothers, and, if each one gives you as much, you will be richer than I am."

It was not a good-natured Maximilian that was destined to wear the imperial crown. The times were changing; men of overweening ambition were about to dispute the throne of the emperors of the West; a strong hand was to grasp the reins of the empire, and long and bloody wars were on the point of succeeding a profound peace.

Three kings claimed the crown of the Caesars from the assembly at Frankfurt. A youthful prince, grandson of the last emperor, born in the first year of the century, and consequently nineteen years old, appeared first. His name was Charles, and he was born at Ghent. His paternal grandmother, Mary, daughter of Charles the Bold, had bequeathed to him Flanders and the rich domains of Burgundy. His mother, Joanna, daughter of Ferdinand of Aragon and Isabella of Castile, and wife of Philip the Emperor Maximilian's son, had transmitted to him the united crowns of the two Spains, Naples, and Sicily, to which Christopher Columbus had added a new world. His grandfather's death now put him in possession of the hereditary states of Austria.

This young prince, endowed with great intelligence, and amiable whenever it pleased him to be so, joined to a taste for military exercises, in which the famous dukes of Burgundy had long distinguished themselves, and to the subtlety and penetration of the Italians, an extensive knowledge of public affairs which he had acquired under the direction of Chièvres; for, from the age of fifteen years, he had attended all the deliberations of his councils. Qualities so various were covered and concealed, as it were, by his Spanish taciturnity and reserve; there was an air of melancholy in his long visage. "He was pious and silent," said Luther; "I will wager that he does not talk so much in a year as I do in a day." If Charles had grown up under free and Christian influences, he would perhaps have been one of the most meritorious princes recorded in history; but politics absorbed his whole life, and blighted his naturally amiable character.

The youthful Charles, not content with the scepters he already grasped in his hand, aspired to the imperial dignity. "It is a beam of sunshine that casts a splendor upon the house on which it falls," said many; "but stretch forth the hand to seize it, and you find nothing." Charles, on the contrary, looked upon it as the summit of all earthly grandeur, and a means of obtaining a magical influence over the minds of nations.

Francis I, king of France, was the second candidate. The young officers of the court of this chivalrous sovereign were ever repeating that he ought, like Charlemagne, to be emperor of all the West, and, reviving the exploits of the knights of old, to attack the Crescent that threatened the empire, crush the infidels, and recover the Holy Sepulcher.

"You should convince the dukes of Austria that the imperial crown is not hereditary," said the ambassadors of Francis to the electors. "Besides, in the present state of affairs, Germany requires, not a youth of nineteen, but a prince who with a tried judgment combines talents already proved. Francis will unite the arms of France and Lombardy with those of Germany to make war on the Mussulmans. As sovereign of the duchy of Milan, he is already a member of the empire." The French ambassadors strengthened their arguments by four hundred thousand crowns which they expended in buying votes, and in banquets which the guest generally quitted in a state of inebriation.

Lastly, Henry VIII of England, jealous of the influence the choice of the electors would give Francis or Charles, also entered the lists; but he soon left these two powerful rivals to dispute the crown between them.

The electors were not very favorably disposed towards either. "Our people," thought they, "will consider the King of France as a foreign master, and this master may wrest even from us that independence of which the great lords of his own kingdom have recently been deprived." As for Charles, it was an old maxim with the electors never to select a prince who already played an important part in the empire. The pope participated in these fears. He was opposed to the King of Naples, his neighbor, and to the King of France whose enterprising spirit alarmed him. "Choose rather one of yourselves," was the advice he sent to the electors. The Elector of Treves proposed to nominate

Frederick of Saxony; and the imperial crown was laid at the feet of this friend to Luther.

Such a choice would have gained the approbation of the whole of Germany. Frederick's wisdom and love for the people were well known. During the revolt of Erfurt, he had been advised to take the city by storm. He refused, that he might avoid bloodshed. "But it will not cost five men," was the reply. "A single man would be too many," answered the prince. It appeared that the election of the protector of the Reformation would secure the triumph of that work. Ought not Frederick to have seen a call from God in this wish of the electors? Who could have been better suited to preside over the destinies of the empire than this wise prince? Who could have been stronger against the Turks than a truly Christian emperor? The refusal of the Elector of Saxony, so extolled by historians, may have been a fault on the part of this prince. Perhaps to him must be partly ascribed the contests that devastated Germany in after days. But it is a difficult matter to decide whether Frederick deserves to be blamed for want of faith, or honored for his humility. He thought that the very safety of the empire required him to refuse the crown. "We need an emperor more powerful than myself to preserve Germany," said this modest and disinterested prince. "The Turk is at our gates. The King of Spain, whose hereditary possessions of Austria border on the threatened frontier, is its natural defender."

The Roman legate, seeing that Charles would be elected, declared that the pope withdrew his objections; and on the twenty-eighth of June the grandson of Maximilian was nominated emperor. "God," said Frederick not long after, "hath given him to us in His favor and in His anger." The Spanish envoys offered thirty thousand gold florins to the Elector of Saxony as a testimonial of their master's gratitude; but this prince refused them, and forbade his ministers to accept of any present. At the same time, he secured the liberties of Germany by a capitulation to which Charles's envoys swore in his name. The circumstances under which the latter assumed the imperial crown seemed, moreover, to give a stronger pledge than the oaths in favor of German liberty and of the work of the Reformation. This youthful prince was jealous of the laurels that his rival Francis I had gathered at Marignan. Charles quitted Spain in May, 1520, and was crowned at Aix-la-Chapelle on the twenty-second of October.

Chapter 35

ERASMUS DEFENDS LUTHER

Luther had foreseen that the cause of the Reformation would soon be carried before the new emperor. He wrote to Charles, while this prince was yet at Madrid: "If the cause that I defend," said he, "is worthy of appearing before the throne of the Majesty of heaven, it ought not to be unworthy of engaging the attention of a prince of this world. O Charles! first of the kings of the earth! I throw myself a suppliant at the feet of your most serene majesty. Deign to receive under the shadow of your wings, not me, but the cause of that eternal truth, for the defense of which God has intrusted you with the sword." The young monarch laid aside this singular letter from a German monk and made no reply to it.

While Luther was vainly turning towards Madrid, the storm seemed to increase around him. Fanaticism was kindling in Germany. Hochstraten, indefatigable in his attempts at persecution, had extracted certain theses from Luther's writings. At his demand, the universities of Cologne and Louvain had condemned these works. That of Erfurt, still exasperated at Luther's preference for Wittenberg, was about to follow their example. But having been informed of it, the doctor wrote to Lange so spirited a letter that the Erfurt divines were dismayed and kept silent. The condemnation pronounced at Cologne and Louvain sufficed, however, to inflame men's minds. Nay, more: the priests of Meissen, who had espoused Emser's quarrel, said publicly (Melancthon is our authority) that he who should kill Luther would be without sin. "Now is the time," said Luther, "when men will think they do Christ a service by putting us to death." These homicidal words were destined to produce their fruit in due season.

One day, says a biographer, as Luther was in front of the Augustine cloister, a stranger, who held a pistol concealed under his cloak, accosted him in these words: "Why do you go thus alone?"—"I am in God's hands," replied Luther. "He is my strength and my shield. What can man do unto me?" Upon this the stranger turned pale (adds the historian), and fled away trembling. Serra Longa, the ambassador at the Augsburg conference, wrote to the elector about this time: "Let not Luther find an asylum in the states of your highness; let him be rejected of all, and stoned in the face of heaven; that will be more pleasing to me than if I received ten thousand crowns from you."

But it was particularly in the direction of Rome that the storm was gathering. Valentine Teutleben, a Thuringian nobleman, vicar to the archbishop of Mentz, and a zealous partisan of the papacy, was the Elector of Saxony's representative at the papal court. Teutleben, ashamed of the protection accorded by his master to a heretical monk, was impatient at seeing his mission paralyzed by this imprudent conduct. He imagined that, by alarming the elector, he would induce him to abandon the rebellious divine. "They will not listen to me here," wrote he to his master, "because of the protection you show to Luther."

But the Romans were deceived if they thought to frighten the prudent Frederick. This prince was aware that the will of God and the movements of nations were more irresistible than the decrees of the papal chancery. He ordered his envoy to intimate to the pope that, far from defending Luther, he had always left him to defend himself; besides, he had already called upon him to quit Saxony and the university; that the doctor had declared his willingness to obey, and that he would not then be in the electoral states, if the legate himself, Charles of Miltitz, had not entreated the prince to keep him near at hand, for fear that, by going to other countries, Luther would act with greater liberty than even in Saxony. Frederick went farther than this: he desired to enlighten Rome. "Germany," continues he in his letter, "now possesses a great number of learned men, well taught in every language and science; the laity themselves begin to have understanding, and to love the Holy Scriptures; if, therefore, the reasonable conditions of Dr. Luther are rejected, there is great cause to fear that peace will never be re-established. Luther's doctrine has struck deep root into many hearts. If, instead of refuting it by the testimony of the Bible, you strive to destroy him by the thunderbolts of the ecclesiastical authority, great scandals will arise, and ruinous and terrible revolts will be excited."

The elector, having the greatest confidence in Luther, communicated Teutleben's letter to him, with another that he had received from Cardinal Saint George. The reformer was agitated as he read them. He immediately perceived the dangers by which he was surrounded. His soul was for a time quite overwhelmed. But it was in such moments that the whole strength of his faith shone forth. Often weak and ready to fall into dejection, he rose again, and appeared greater in the midst of the tempest. He longed to be delivered from such trials; but he saw at what price peace was offered to him, and he indignantly rejected it. "Hold my peace!" exclaimed he, "I am disposed to do so, if they will permit me: that is, if they will make others keep silence. If any one desires my places, let him take them; if any one desires to destroy my writings, let him burn them. I am ready to keep quiet, provided they do not require that the truth of the gospel should be silent also. I do not ask for a cardinal's hat; I ask not for gold, or for anything that Rome values. There is nothing in the world they cannot obtain from me, provided they will not shut up the way of salvation against Christians. Their threats do not alarm me, their promises cannot seduce me."

Animated with such sentiments, Luther soon recovered his militant disposition, and preferred the Christian warfare to the calm of solitude. One night was sufficient to bring back his desire of overthrowing Rome. "I have taken my part," wrote he on the morrow; "I despise the fury of Rome, and contemn her favors. No more reconciliation, no more communication with her forever. Let her condemn me, let her burn my writings! In my turn, I will condemn and publicly burn the pontifical law,—that nest of every heresy. The moderation I have hitherto shown has been unavailing; I now renounce it!"

His friends were far from being thus tranquil. Great was the consternation at Wittenberg. "We are in a state of extraordinary expectation," said Melancthon; "I would rather die than be separated from Luther. If God does not help us, we shall all perish."—"Our dear Luther is still alive," wrote he a month later, in his anxiety; "may it please God to grant him a long life! for the Roman accusers are making every exertion to put him to death. Let us pray that this sole avenger of sacred theology may long survive."

These prayers were heard. The warning the elector had given Rome through his envoy was not without foundation. Luther's words had found an echo everywhere—in cottages and convents, in the homes of the citizens and in the castles of the nobles, in the universities and in the palaces of kings. "If my life," he had said to Duke John of Saxony, "has been instrumental to the conversion of a single man, I shall willingly consent to see all my books perish." It was not one man, it was a great multitude, that had found the light in the writings of the humble doctor. Everywhere, accordingly, were men to be found ready to protect him. The sword intended to slay him was forging in the Vatican; but heroes were springing up in Germany to shield him with their bodies. At the moment when the bishops were chafing with rage, when princes kept silence, when the people were in expectation, and when the first murmurs of the thunder were beginning to be heard from the Seven Hills, God aroused the German nobles to make a rampart for His servant.

Sylvester of Schaumburg, one of the most powerful knights of Franconia, sent his son to Wittenberg at this time with a letter for the reformer. "Your life is in danger," wrote he. "If the support of the electors, princes, or magistrates fail you, I entreat you to beware of going to Bohemia, where in former times learned men have had much to undergo; rather come to me. God willing, I shall soon have collected more than a hundred gentlemen, and with their help I shall be able to protect you from every danger."

Francis of Sickingen, the hero of his age, of whose intrepid courage we have already been witnesses, loved the reformer because he found him worthy of being loved, and also because he was hated by the monks. "My services, my goods, and my body, all that I possess," wrote he to Luther, "are at your disposal. You desire to maintain the Christian truth: I am ready to aid you in the work." Harmurth of Cronberg spoke in the same language. Lastly, Ulric of Hütten, the poet and valiant knight of the sixteenth century, never ceased speaking in Luther's favor. But what a contrast between these two men! Hütten wrote to the reformer: "It is with swords and with bows, with javelins and bombs, that we must crush the fury of the devil." Luther on receiving these letters exclaimed: "I will not have recourse to arms and bloodshed in defense of the gospel. By the Word the earth has been subdued; by the Word the Church has been saved; and by the Word also it shall be re-established."—"I do not despise his offer," said he at another time on receiving Schaumburg's letter, which we have mentioned above, "but I will rely upon none but Jesus Christ." It was not thus the Roman pontiffs spoke when they waded in the blood of the Waldenses and Albigenses. Hütten felt the difference between his cause and Luther's, and he accordingly wrote to him with noble-mindedness: "As for me, I am busied with the affairs of men; but you soar far higher, and are occupied solely with those of God." He then set out to win, if possible, Charles and Ferdinand to the side of truth.

Luther at this time met with a still more illustrious protector. Erasmus, whom the Romanists so often quote against the Reformation, raised his voice and undertook the reformer's defense, after his own fashion, however, that is to say, without any show of defending him. On the first of November, 1519, this patriarch of learning wrote to Albert, elector of Mentz and primate of all Germany, a letter in which, after describing in vivid colors the corruption of the Church, he said: "This is what stirred up Luther, and made him oppose the intolerable imprudence of certain doctors. For what other motive can we ascribe to a man who seeks not honors and who cares not for money? Luther has dared doubt the virtue of indulgences; but others before him had most unblushingly affirmed it. He feared not to speak, certainly with little moderation, against the power of the Roman pontiff; but others before him had extolled it without reserve. He had dared contemn the decrees of St. Thomas, but the Dominicans had set them almost above the gospel. He has dared give utterance to his scruples about confession, but the monks continually made use of this ordinance as a net in which to catch and enslave the consciences of men. Pious souls were grieved at hearing that in the universities there was little mention of the evangelical doctrine; that in the assemblies of Christians very little was heard of Christ; that nothing was there talked of, except the power of the pontiff, and the opinions of the Romish doctors; and that the whole sermon was a mere matter of lucre, flattery, ambition, and imposture. It is to such a state of affairs that we should ascribe Luther's violent language." Such was Erasmus's opinion on the state of the Church and on the reformer. This letter, which was published by Ulric Hütten, then residing at the court of Mentz, made a profound impression.

At the same time, men more obscure than Erasmus and than all the knights, but who were destined to be more powerful auxiliaries, rallied round Luther in every direction. Doctor Botzhemus Abstemius, canon of Constance, wrote to him thus: "Now that you have become the friend of the universe, or at least of the better part of the world, that is to say, of good and true Christians, you must also become mine, whether you will or not! I am so delighted with your writings that nothing gives me greater pleasure than to be living at a time when not only profane but also sacred literature is resuming its pristine splendor." And at nearly the same period Gaspard Hedio, preacher at Basle, wrote to the reformer: "Most dear sir, I see that your doctrine is of God, and that it cannot be destroyed; that it becomes daily more efficacious; and that every hour it is winning souls to Christ by turning them away from sin and attracting them to real piety. Do not halt therefore, O liberator, but exert all your power to restore the yoke of Christ, so light and easy to bear. Be yourself the general, and we will follow after you, like soldiers whom nothing can tear from you."

Thus at one time Luther's enemies oppressed him, at another his friends sprang up to defend him. "My bark," said he, "floats to and fro, the sport of the winds; hope and fear prevail by turns; but what matters it!" And yet these testimonies of sympathy were not without influence upon the mind. "The Lord reigns," said he, "I see Him there, as if I could touch Him." Luther felt that he was not alone; his words had borne fruit, and this thought filled him with fresh courage. The fear of compromising the elector no longer checked him, when he found other defenders ready to brave the anger of Rome. He became more free, and if possible more determined. This is an important epoch in the development of Luther's character. "Rome ought to understand," wrote he at this period to the elector's chaplain, "that, even should she succeed by her threats in expelling me from Wittenberg, she would only injure her cause. It is not in Bohemia, but in the very heart of Germany that those are to be found who are ready to defend me against the thunders of the papacy. If I have not done my enemies all the harm I am preparing for them, they must ascribe it neither to my moderation nor to their tyranny, but to the elector's name and to the interests of the University of Wittenberg, which I feared to compromise: now that I have such fears no longer, they will see me fall with fresh vigor upon Rome and upon her courtiers."

And yet it was not on the great that Luther fixed his hopes. He had been often solicited to dedicate a book to Duke John, the elector's brother. He had not done so. "I am afraid," said he, "that the suggestion comes from himself. Holy Scripture should subserve the glory of God's name alone." Luther now recovered from his fears, and dedicated his sermon on *Good Works* to Duke John. This is one of the writings in which the reformer lays down with the greatest force the doctrine of justification by faith,—that powerful truth, whose strength he sets far above the sword of Hütten, the army of Sickengen, and the protection of dukes and electors.

"The first, the noblest, the sublimest of all works," says he, "is faith in Jesus Christ. It is from this work that all other works must proceed: they are but the vassals of faith, and receive their efficacy from it alone.

"If a man feels in his heart the assurance that what he has done is acceptable to God, the work is good, if it were merely the lifting up of a straw; but if he have not this assurance, his work is not good, even should he raise the dead. To trust firmly in God, and to feel an assurance that we are accepted by Him, is what a Christian, strong in grace, alone is capable of doing.

"A Christian who possesses faith in God does everything with liberty and joy; while the man who is not at one with God is full of care and kept in bondage; he asks himself with anguish how many works he should perform; he runs to and fro; he questions this man and that; he nowhere finds peace, and does everything with sorrow and fear.

"Consequently, I have always extolled faith. But in the world it is otherwise. There, the essential thing is to have many works—works high and great, and of every dimension, without caring whether they are quickened by faith. Thus, men build their peace, not on God's good pleasure, but on their own merits, that is to say, on sand (Matt. 7:26, 27).

"To preach faith [it has been said] is to prevent good works; but if a man should possess the strength of all men united, or even of all creatures, this sole obligation of living in faith would be a task too great for him ever to accomplish. If I say to a sick man: 'Be well, and thou shalt have the use of thy limbs,' will anyone say that I forbid him to use his limbs? Must not health precede labor? It is the same when we preach faith: it should go before works, in order that the works themselves should exist.

"Where then, you will say, can we find this faith, and how can we receive it? This is in truth what it is most important to know. Faith comes solely from Jesus, who was promised and given freely.

"O man! figure Jesus Christ to yourself, and contemplate how God in Him has shown thee His mercy, without any merit on thy part going before. Draw from this image of His grace the faith and assurance that all thy sins are forgiven thee. Works cannot produce it. It flows from the blood, and wounds, and death of Christ; thence it wells forth into our hearts. Christ is the Rock whence flow milk and honey" (Deut. 32).

As we cannot notice all Luther's writings, we have quoted a few short passages from this discourse on *Good Works,* in consequence of the opinion the reformer himself entertained of it. "In my own judgment," said he, "it is the best I ever published." And he added immediately this deep reflection: "But I know that when I please myself with what I write, the infection of that bad leaven hinders it from pleasing others." Melancthon, in forwarding this discourse to a friend, accompanied it with these words: "There is no one among all the Greek and Latin writers who has come nearer than Luther to the spirit of St. Paul."

Chapter 36

ECCLESIASTICAL OR SPIRITUAL STATE?

B UT THERE WAS another evil in the Church besides the substitution of a system of meritorious works for the grand idea of grace and amnesty. A haughty power had arisen in the midst of the shepherds of Christ's flock. Luther prepared to attack this usurped authority. Already a vague and distant rumor announced the success of Dr. Eck's intrigues at Rome. This rumor aroused the militant spirit of the reformer, who, in the midst of all his troubles, had studied in his retirement the rise, progress, and usurpations of the papacy. His discoveries had filled him with surprise. He no longer hesitated to make them known, and to strike the blow which, like Moses' rod in ancient times, was to awaken a people who had long slumbered in captivity. Even before Rome had time to publish her formidable bull, it was he who hurled his declaration of war against her. "The time to be silent is past," exclaimed he; "the time to speak is come! At last, we must unveil the mysteries of Antichrist." On the twenty-third of June, 1520, he published his famous *Appeal to his Imperial Majesty and to the Christian Nobility of the German Nation, on the Reformation of Christianity*. This work was the signal of the attack that was to decide both the rupture and the victory.

"It is not through presumption," said he at the opening of this address, "that I, a man of the people, venture to speak to your lordships. The misery and oppression that at this hour weigh down all the states of Christendom, and particularly Germany, extort from me a cry of distress. I must call for help; I must see if God will not give His Spirit to some man in our own country, and thus stretch forth His hand to save our wretched nation. God has placed over us a young and generous prince, and has thus filled our hearts with great expectations. But on our part we must do everything that lies in our power.

"Now the first requisite is, not to trust in our own strength, or in our lofty wisdom. If we begin a good work with confidence in ourselves, God overthrows and destroys it. Frederick I, Frederick II, and many other emperors besides, before whom the world trembled, have been trodden under foot by the popes, because they trusted more in their own strength than in God. Therefore they could not but fall. It is against the powers of hell that we have to contend in this struggle. Hoping nothing from the strength of arms, humbly trusting in the Lord, looking more to the distress of Christendom than to the crimes of the wicked—this is how we must set to work. Otherwise the work will have a prosperous look at the beginning; but suddenly, in the midst of the contest, confusion will enter in, evil minds will cause incalculable disasters, and the whole world will be deluged with blood. The greater our power, the greater also is our danger, if we do not walk in the fear of the Lord."

After this prelude, Luther continues thus:

"The Romans have raised around themselves three walls to protect them against every kind of reformation. Have they been attacked by the temporal power?—they have asserted that it had no authority over them, and that the spiritual power was superior to it. Have they been rebuked by Holy Scripture?—they have replied that no one is able to interpret it except the pope. Have they been threatened with a council?—no one but the sovereign pontiff has authority to convoke one.

"They have thus despoiled us of the three rods destined to correct them, and have given themselves up to every wickedness. But now may God be our helper, and give us one of those trumpets that overthrew the walls of Jericho. With our breath let us throw down those barriers of paper and straw which the Romans have built around them, and upraise the rods which punish the wicked, by exposing the wiles of the devil."

Luther now began the attack. He shook to its foundation that papal monarchy which for ages had combined the people of the West in one body under the scepter of the Roman bishop. That there is no sacerdotal caste in Christianity is the truth which he powerfully set forth at the beginning—a truth hidden from the eyes of the Church from the earliest ages.

"It has been said," writes Luther, "that the pope, the bishops, the priests, and all those who people the convents, form the spiritual or ecclesiastical state; and that the princes, the nobility, the citizens, and peasants, form the secular or lay estate. This is a fine story. Let no person, however, be startled at it. All Christians belong to the spiritual state, and there is no other difference between them than that arising from the functions which they discharge. We have all one baptism, one faith; and this it is which constitutes the spiritual man. The unction, the tonsure, ordination, consecration by the bishop or the pope, may make a hypocrite, but never a spiritual man. We are all consecrated priests by baptism, as Saint Peter says: 'Ye are priests and kings,' although it does not belong to all to exercise such offices, for no one can take what is common to all without the consent of the community. But if we possess not this divine consecration, the pope's anointing can never make a priest. If ten brothers, sons of a king, having equal claims to the inheritance, select one of them to administer it for them, they would all be kings, and yet only one of them would be the administrator of their common power. So it is with the Church. If a few pious laymen were banished to a desert place, and if, not having among them a priest consecrated by a bishop, they should agree to choose one of their own number, married or not, this man would be as truly a priest as if all the bishops in the world had consecrated him. Thus Augustine, Ambrose, and Cyprian, were elected.

"Hence it follows that laymen and priests, princes and bishops, or, as they say, the clergy and laity, have nothing but their functions to distinguish them. They have all the same estate, but have not all the same work to perform.

"If this be true, why should not the magistrate chastise the clergy? The secular power was established by God to punish the wicked and to protect the good. And it must be allowed to act throughout all Christendom, whomsoever it may touch, be he pope, bishop, priest, monk, or nun. St. Paul says to all Christians: 'Let every one (and consequently the pope also) be subject unto the higher powers, for they bear not the sword in vain.'"

Luther, having in like manner overthrown the two other walls, passed in review all the corruptions of Rome. He set forth, in an eminently popular style of eloquence, the evils that had been pointed out for centuries past. Never had a nobler protest been heard. The assembly before which Luther spoke was the Church; the power whose corruptions he attacked was that papacy which for ages had oppressed all nations with its weight; and the reformation he so loudly called for was destined to exercise its powerful influence over all Christendom,—in all the world, so long as the human race shall endure.

He began with the pope. "It is a horrible thing," said he, "to behold the man who styles himself Christ's vicegerent displaying a magnificence that no emperor can equal. Is this being like the poor Jesus, or the humble Peter? He is (say they) the lord of the world! But Christ, whose vicar he boasts of being, has said, 'My kingdom is not of this world.' Can the dominions of a vicar extend beyond those of his Superior?"

Luther now proceeded to describe the effects of the papal rule. "Do you know what is the use of cardinals? I will tell you. Italy and Germany have many convents, religious foundations, and richly endowed benefices. How can this wealth be drawn to Rome? Cardinals have been created; these cloisters and prelacies have been given to them; and now. . . . Italy is almost deserted, the convents are in ruins, the bishoprics devoured, the cities decayed, the inhabitants corrupted, religious worship is expiring, and preaching abolished! . . . And why is this? Because all the wealth of the churches must go to Rome. The Turk himself would never have so ruined Italy!" Luther next turned to his fellow countrymen:

"And now they have come into Germany; they begin tenderly; but let us be on our guard, or Germany will erelong be like Italy! We have already a few cardinals. Before the Germans comprehend our design (think they) they will no longer have either bishopric, convent, or benefice, penny or farthing left. Antichrist must possess the treasures of the earth. Thirty or forty cardinals will be created in one day. Bamberg will be given to one, the bishopric of Wurtzburg to another; rich cures will be attached to them, until the cities and churches are desolate. And then the pope will say: 'I am Christ's vicar, and the shepherd of His flocks. Let the Germans be submissive!' "

Luther's indignation was kindled:

"What! shall we Germans endure such robberies and such extortions from the pope? If the kingdom of France has been able to defend itself, why should we permit ourselves to be thus ridiculed and laughed at? Oh! if they only despoiled us of our goods! But they lay waste the churches, fleece the sheep of Christ, abolish religious worship, and annihilate the Word of God."

Luther here exposed "the practices of Rome" to obtain the money and the revenues of Germany. Annats, palliums, commendams, administrations, reversions, incorporations, reserves, etc.—he passed them all in review; and then he said: "Let us endeavor to check such desolation and wretchedness. If we desire to march against the Turks, let us march against those who are the worst Turks of all. If we hang thieves, and decapitate highway robbers, let us not permit Romish avarice to escape, which is the greatest of thieves and robbers, and that too in the name of St. Peter and of Jesus Christ! Who can suffer this? Who can be silent? All that the pope possesses, has he not gained by plunder? For he has neither bought it, nor inherited it from St. Peter, nor gained it by the sweat of his brow! Whence then has he all this?"

Luther proposed remedies for these evils, and called energetically upon the nobility of Germany to put an end to these Romish depredations. He then came to the reformation of the pope himself: "Is it not ridiculous," says he, "that the pope pretends to be the lawful heir to the empire? Who gave it him? Was it Jesus Christ, when He said: 'The kings of the Gentiles exercise lordship over them . . . but ye shall not be so' (Luke 22: 25, 26)? How is it possible to govern an empire, and at the same time preach, pray, study, and take care of the poor? Jesus Christ forbade His ministers to carry with them either gold or two coats, because they would be unable to discharge the duties of their ministry if they were not free from all other care; and yet the pope would govern the empire and still remain pope."

Luther continued: "Let the pope renounce every claim on the kingdom of Naples and Sicily. He has no more right to it than I have. It is unjustly and in opposition to all the commandments of Christ that he possesses Bologna, Imola, Ravenna, the Romagna, the March of Ancona, etc. 'No man that warreth, [says Saint Paul] entangleth himself with the affairs of this life' (II Tim. 2:4). Yet the pope, who pretends to be the leader of the Church militant, entangles himself with the affairs of this life more than any emperor or king. We must relieve him from all this toil. Let the emperor put the Bible and a prayerbook into the pope's hands, in order that he may leave the cares of government to kings, and confine himself to preaching and praying."

Luther would no more suffer the pope's spiritual power in Germany than his temporal power in Italy. "First of all," said he, "we must expel from every German state those papal legates, with their pretended benefits which they sell us at their weight in gold, and which are downright impositions. They take our money, and for what? to legalize their ill-gotten gains, to absolve from all oaths, to teach us to be wanting in fidelity, to instruct us how to sin, and to lead us direct to hell."

The Christian tribune pursued his course, he summoned before him all the corruptions that form the papal train, and purposed sweeping from the floor of the Church the rubbish by which it was encumbered. He began with the monks:

"And now then I come to that sluggish troop which promises much but does little. Do not be angry, my dear sirs, my intentions are good: what I have to say is a truth at once sweet and bitter: namely, no more cloisters must be built for mendicant friars. We have, indeed, too many already, and would to God that they were all pulled down. Strolling through a country like beggars never has done and never can do good."

The marriage of the clergy now has its turn, and this is the first time Luther speaks of it:

"To what a sad state have the clergy fallen, and how many priests do we not find burdened with women, and children, and remorse, and yet no one comes to their aid! It is all very well for the pope and the bishops to let things go on as before, and for that to continue lost which is lost; but I am determined to save my conscience, and to open my mouth freely: after that, let the pope, the bishops, and any one who pleases, take offence at it! . . . I assert, then, that according to the appointment of Christ and His apostles, each city should have a pastor or bishop, and that this pastor may have a wife, as Saint

Paul writes to Timothy: 'A bishop must be the husband of one wife' (I Tim. 3:2), and as is still practised in the Greek Church. But the devil has persuaded the pope, as the same apostle says to Timothy (I Tim. 4:1–3), to forbid the clergy to marry. Hence have proceeded miseries so numerous that we cannot mention all. What is to be done? How can we save so many pastors, in whom we have no fault to find, except that they live with a woman, to whom they would with all their heart be legitimately married? Ah! let them quiet their consciences! let them take this woman as their lawful wife, and let them live virtuously with her, not troubling themselves whether the pope is pleased or not. The salvation of your soul is of greater consequence to you than tyrannical and arbitrary laws, that do not emanate from the Lord."

It is in this way that the Reformation aimed at restoring purity of morals in the Church. The reformer continues:

"Let all festivals be abolished, and let none but Sunday be observed; or if people desire to keep the great Christian festivals, let them be celebrated only in the morning, and let the rest of the day be like any other working day. For as on those days men do nothing but drink, gamble, indulge in every sin, or remain idle, they offend God on the festivals more than at other times."

He next attacked the commemorations, which he styled mere taverns; and after them the fasts and religious fraternities. He not only desired to put an end to abuses, he wished also to put away schism. "It is high time," said he, "that we busied ourselves seriously with the cause of the Bohemians—that we put a stop to envy and hatred, and that we united with them." After proposing some excellent means of reconciliation, he added: "We must convince heretics by Scripture, as did the ancient Fathers, and not subdue them by fire. In this latter system, the executioners would be the most learned doctors in the world. . . . Oh! would to God that on both sides we stretched forth our hands in brotherly humility, instead of being inflexible in the sentiment of our strength and of our right! Charity is more necessary than the papacy of Rome. I have now done all that is in my power. If the pope and his adherents oppose this, the responsibility will fall on them. The pope should be ready to renounce his papacy, all his possessions, and all his honors, if he could by that means save a single soul. But he would rather see all the world perish than bate even a hairsbreadth of the power he has usurped! . . . I am clear of these things."

Luther next proceeded to the universities and schools:

"I am much afraid that the universities will prove to be the great gates of hell, unless they diligently labor in explaining the Holy Scriptures, and engraving them in the hearts of youth. I advise no one to place his child where the Scriptures do not reign paramount. Every institution in which men are not unceasingly occupied with the Word of God must become corrupt." Weighty words, upon which governments, learned men, and parents in every age should seriously meditate!

Toward the end of this appeal he returned to the empire and to the emperor:

"The pope, unable to manage at his will the ancient masters of the Roman empire, conceived a plan of taking away their title and their empire, and bestowing them on us Germans. Thus it happened that we became the vassals of the pope. For the pope took possession of Rome, and compelled the emperor by an oath never to reside there; whence it is that the emperor is emperor of Rome, without Rome. We possess the name: the pope has the country and the cities. We have the title and arms of the empire; the pope has its treasures, power, privileges, and liberties. The pope eats the fruit, and we play with the husk. It is thus that the pride and tyranny of the Romans have always abused our simplicity.

"But now may God, who has given us such an empire, be our helper! Let us act in conformity with our name, title, and arms; let us preserve our liberty; and let the Romans learn to appreciate what God has given us by their hands! They boast of having given us an empire. Well, then, let us take what belongs to us! Let the pope resign to us Rome and every portion of the empire that he still holds! Let him put an end to his taxes and extortions! Let him restore our liberty, our power, our property, our honor, our souls, and our bodies! Let the empire be all that an empire ought to be, and let the sword of princes no longer be constrained to bow before the hypocritical pretensions of a pope!"

In these words there are not only energy and enthusiasm, but also a lofty strain of reasoning. Did any orator ever speak thus to the nobility of the empire, and to the emperor himself? Far from being surprised that so many German states separated from Rome, ought we not rather to feel astonished that all Germany did not march to the banks of the Tiber to resume that imperial power whose attributes the popes had so imprudently placed on the brow of its sovereign?

Luther concluded this courageous appeal in these words:

"I can very well imagine that I have pitched my song too high, proposed many things that will seem impossible, and attacked many errors rather too violently. But what can I do? Let the world be offended with me, rather than God! . . . They can but take away my life. I have often proposed peace to my adversaries. But God, by their instrumentality, has compelled me continually to cry louder and louder against them. I have still another song in reserve against Rome. If their ears itch, I will sing it them, and loudly too. Dost thou clearly understand, O Rome, what I mean?" . . .

This was probably an allusion to a work on the papacy that Luther had some intention of publishing, but which was withheld. About this time the Rector Burkhardt wrote to Spengler: "There is also a little treatise *De execranda Venere Romanorum*; but it is kept in reserve." The title promised something very offensive; and we should rejoice that Luther had the moderation not to publish this writing.

"If my cause is just," continued he, "it will be condemned by all the world, and justified only by Christ in heaven. Let them come on, then, pope, bishops, priests, monks, and doctors! let them put forth all their zeal! let them give the rein to all their fury! These are, in truth, the men who ought to persecute the truth, as every age has witnessed."

Whence did this monk acquire so clear an understanding of public affairs, which even the states of the empire often found so difficult to elucidate? Whence did this German derive the courage which made him raise his head in the midst of a nation so long enslaved, and aim such violent blows at the papacy? What was the mysterious power that animated him? Might we not be led to say that he had heard these words addressed by God to a man of the olden time: "Behold,

I have made thy face strong against their faces. . . . As an adamant harder than flint have I made thy forehead: fear them not, neither be dismayed at their looks" (Ezek. 3:8, 9).

This exhortation, which was addressed to the German nobility, soon reached all those for whom it had been written. It circulated through Germany with inconceivable rapidity. Luther's friends trembled; Staupitz and those who desired to employ mild measures found the blow too severe. "In our days," replied Luther, "every thing that is handled gently falls into oblivion, and no one cares about it." At the same time he gave striking evidence of single-mindedness and humility. He did not yet know himself. "I cannot tell what to say of myself," wrote he. "Perhaps I am Philip's [Melancthon's] forerunner. I am preparing the way for him, like Elias, in spirit and in power. It is he who will one day trouble Israel and the house of Ahab."

But there was no need to wait for another than him who had already appeared. The *Appeal to the German Nobility* was published on June 26, 1520; in a short time four thousand copies were sold, a number unprecedented in those days. The astonishment was universal. This writing produced a powerful sensation among the people. The vigor, life, perspicuity, and generous boldness that breathed throughout, made it a truly popular work. The people felt at last that he who spoke to them loved them also. The confused views of a great number of wise men were cleared up. The Romish usurpations became evident to every mind. Even the elector's court, so circumspect and timid, did not disapprove of the reformer: it waited patiently. But the nobility and the people did not wait. The nation was reanimated. Luther's voice had shaken it; it was won over, and rallied round the standard that he had uplifted. Nothing could have been more advantageous to the reformer than this publication. In the palaces and castles, in the homes of the citizens and the cottages of the peasants, all were now prepared, and defended as it were with a breastplate, against the sentence of condemnation that was about to fall upon this prophet of the people. All Germany was on fire. Let the bull arrive! not by such means will the conflagration be extinguished.

Chapter 37

ZWINGLI OF HELVETIA; LUTHER'S CONDEMNATION

EVERY PREPARATION was made at Rome for condemning the defender of the liberty of the Church. That Church had long been living in a state of haughty security. For several years the monks had been accusing Leo X of caring only for luxury and pleasure, of occupying himself solely with the chase, the theater, and music, while the Church was tottering to its fall. At length, aroused by the clamors of Dr. Eck, who had come from Leipzig to invoke the power of the Vatican, pope, cardinals, monks, and all Rome, awoke and thought of saving the papacy.

Rome indeed was compelled to have recourse to the severest measures. The gauntlet had been thrown down; the combat must be to the death. Luther did not attack the abuses of the Roman pontificate, but the pontificate itself. At his command he would have had the pope descend humbly from his throne, and become a simple pastor or bishop on the banks of the Tiber. All the dignitaries of the Roman hierarchy were to renounce their wealth and their worldly glory, and become elders and deacons of the churches of Italy. All that splendor and power, which for ages had dazzled the West, was to vanish and give place to the humble simplicity of the primitive Christian worship. God might have brought this about; He will do so in His own time; but it could not be expected from man. And even should any pope have been so disinterested or bold as to be willing to overthrow the ancient and costly edifice of the Roman Church, thousands of priests and bishops would have stretched out their hands to prevent its fall. The pope had received his power on the express condition of maintaining what was confided to him.

Rome thought herself divinely appointed to the government of the Church. We cannot therefore be astonished that she prepared to strike the most terrible blows. And yet she hesitated at first. Many cardinals and the pope himself were opposed to violent measures. The skillful Leo saw clearly that a decision, the execution of which depended on the very doubtful compliance of the civil power, might seriously compromise the authority of the Church. He was aware, besides, that the violent measures hitherto employed had only served to aggravate the mischief. Is it not possible to gain over this Saxon monk? asked the Roman politicians of one another. Will all the power of the Church, will all the craft of Italy fail?—They must negotiate still.

Eck accordingly met with powerful obstacles. He neglected nothing that might prevent such impious concessions. In every quarter of Rome he vented his rage and called for revenge. The fanatical portion of the monks soon leagued with him. Strengthened by their alliance, he assailed the pope and cardinals with fresh courage. In his opinion, every attempt at conciliation would be useless. These (said he) are idle dreams with which you soothe yourselves at a distance from the danger. He knew the peril, for he had contended with the audacious monk. He saw that there should be no delay in cutting off this gangrened limb, for fear the disease should infect the whole body. The impetuous disputant of Leipzig parried objection after objection, and with difficulty persuaded the pope. He desired to save Rome in spite of herself. He made every exertion, passing many hours together in deliberation in the pontiff's cabinet. He excited the court and the cloisters, the people and the Church. "Eck is stirring up the bottomless pit against me," said Luther; "he is setting fire to the forests of Lebanon."

But at the very moment when Dr. Eck was most sure of victory, there existed even in Rome a respectable party to a certain extent favorable to Luther. On this point we have the testimony of a Roman citizen, one of whose letters, written in January, 1521, has fortunately been preserved. "You should know," says he, "that in Rome there is scarcely an individual, at least among men of sound judgment, who is not aware that in many respects Luther speaks the truth." These respectable persons resisted the demands of Dr. Eck. "We should take more time for reflection," said they; "Luther should be opposed by moderation and by reason, and not by anathemas." Leo X was again staggered. But immediately all that was bad in Rome burst out into violent fury. Eck mustered his recruits, and from all quarters, but especially from among the Dominicans, auxiliaries rallied around him, overflowing with anger and apprehension lest their victim should escape. "It is unbecoming the dignity of the Roman pontiff," said they, "to give a reason to every little wretch that presumes to raise his head; on the contrary, these obstinate people should be crushed by force, lest others, after them, should imitate their audacity. It was in this way that the punishment of John Huss, and of his disciple Jerome, terrified many; and if the same thing had been done to Reuchlin, Luther would never have dared what he has done."

At the same time the theologians of Cologne, Louvain, and other universities, and even princes of Germany, either by letter or through their envoys, daily urged the pope in private by the most pressing entreaties. But the most earnest solicitations proceeded from a banker who, by his wealth, possessed great influence at Rome, and who was familiarly styled "the king of crowns." This banker was Fugger, the treasurer of the indulgences. Inflamed with anger against Luther, and very uneasy about his profits and his wares, the Augsburg merchant strained every nerve to exasperate the pope: "Employ force against Luther," said he, "and I will promise you the alliance and support of several princes." It would even appear that it was he who had sent Eck to Rome.

This gave the decisive blow. The "king of crowns" was victor in the pontifical city. It was not the sword of the Gaul, but well-stored purses that were on this occasion thrown into the balance. Eck prevailed at last. The politicians were defeated by the fanatics in the papal councils. Leo gave way, and Luther's condemnation was resolved upon. Eck breathed again. His pride was flattered by the thought that it was he who had decided the destruction of his heretical rival, and thus saved the Church. "It was fortunate," said he, "that I came to Rome at this time, for they were but little acquainted with Luther's errors. It will one day be known how much I have done in this cause."

Few were more active in supporting Doctor Eck than Sylvester

Mazzolini de Prierio, master of the sacred palace. He had just published a work in which he maintained that not only did the infallible decision of all controverted points belong to the pope alone, but that the papal dominion was the fifth monarchy prophesied by Daniel, and the only true monarchy; that the pope was the first of all ecclesiastical princes, the father of all secular rulers, the chief of the world, and, essentially, the world itself. In another writing, he affirmed that the pope is as much superior to the emperor as gold is more precious than lead; that the pope may elect and depose both emperors and electors; establish and annul positive rights, and that the emperor, though backed by all the laws and nations of Christendom, cannot decide the least thing against the pope's will.

Such was the voice that issued from the palace of the sovereign pontiff; such was the monstrous fiction which, combined with the scholastic doctrines, pretended to extinguish the dawning truth. If this fable had not been unmasked as it has been, and even by learned men in the Romish communion, there would have been neither true religion nor true history. The papacy is not only a lie in the face of the Bible; it is so even in the face of the annals of all nations. Thus the Reformation, by breaking its charm, emancipated not only the Church, but also kings and people. It has been said that the Reformation was a political work; in this sense it is true; but this is only a secondary sense.

Thus did God send forth a spirit of infatuation on the Roman doctors. The separation between truth and error had now become necessary; and error was the instrument of its accomplishment. If they had come to an agreement, it could only have been at the expense of truth; but to take away the smallest part of itself, is to prepare the way for its complete annihilation. It is like the insect which is said to die if one of its antennae be removed. Truth requires entirety in all its members in order to display that energy by which it is enabled to gain wide and salutary victories, and to propagate itself through future ages. To mingle a little error with truth is like throwing a grain of poison into a well-filled dish; this one grain is sufficient to change the nature of the food, and will cause death, slowly perhaps, but surely. Those who defend Christ's doctrine against the attacks of its adversaries, as jealously keep watch upon its remotest outworks as upon the body of the place; for no sooner has the enemy gained a footing in the least of these positions, than his victory is not far distant.

The Roman pontiff resolved, at the period we have now reached, to rend the Church. Wherever the Word of God is, there is life. Luther, however great his courage, would probably have kept silence if Rome had been silent herself, and had affected to make a few apparent concessions. But God had not abandoned the Reformation to the weak heart of man. Luther was in the hands of One more far-sighted than himself. Divine Providence made use of the pope to break every link between the past and the future, and to turn the reformer into a new path, unknown and undistinguishable to his eyes, the approaches of which he never could have found unaided. The pontifical bull was the letter of divorcement that Rome gave to the pure Church of Jesus Christ in the person of him who was then its humble but faithful representative; and the Church accepted it, from that hour to depend solely on her Head who is in heaven.

While, at Rome, Luther's condemnation was urged forward with so much violence that a humble priest, living in one of the simple towns of Helvetia, and who had never held any communication with the reformer, was deeply affected at the thought of the blow impending over him; and, while the friends of the Wittenberg doctor trembled and remained silent, this child of the Swiss mountains resolved to employ every means in his power to arrest the formidable bull. His name was Ulrich Zwingli. William des Faucons, secretary to the pope's legate in Switzerland, and who, in the legate's absence, was intrusted with the affairs of Rome, was his friend. "So long as I live," had said the nuncio *ad interim* to him a few days before, "you may count on my doing all that can be expected from a true friend." The Helvetian priest, trusting to this assurance, went to the nuncio's office (such at least is the conclusion we draw from one of his letters). He had no fear on his own part of the dangers to which the evangelical faith exposed him; he knew that a disciple of Christ should always be ready to lay down his life. "All that I ask of Christ for myself," said he to a friend to whose bosom he confided his anxiety about Luther, "is that I may endure with the heart of a man the evils that await me. I am a vessel of clay in His hands; let Him dash me in pieces or strengthen me, as seemeth good to Him." But the Swiss evangelist feared for the Christian Church, if so formidable a blow should strike the reformer. He endeavored to persuade the representative of Rome to enlighten the pope, and to employ all the means in his power to prevent Luther's excommunication. "The dignity of the holy see itself is interested in this," said Zwingli, "for if matters should come to such a point, Germany, overflowing with enthusiasm for the gospel and for the doctor who preaches it, will despise the pope and his anathemas." This intervention proved of no effect: it would appear also that, even at the time it was made, the blow had been already struck. Such was the first occasion in which the paths of the Saxon doctor and of the Swiss priest met. We shall again find the latter in the course of this history, and see him growing up and increasing to a lofty stature in the Church of the Lord.

Luther's condemnation being once resolved upon, new difficulties were raised in the consistory. The theologians were of opinion that the fulmination should be issued immediately; the lawyers, on the contrary, that it should be preceded by a summons. "Was not Adam first summoned?" said they to their theological colleagues; "so too was Cain: 'Where is thy brother Abel?' demanded the Almighty." To these singular arguments drawn from the Holy Scriptures the canonists added motives derived from the natural law: "The evidence of a crime," said they, "cannot deprive a criminal of his right of defense." It was pleasing to find these principles of justice in this Roman assembly. But these scruples were not to the taste of the divines in the assembly, who, instigated by passion, thought only of going immediately to work.

One man in particular then came forward whose opinions must of necessity have had great influence: this was De Vio, cardinal Cajetan, still laboring under extreme vexation at his defeat in Augsburg, and the little honor or profit he had derived from his German mission. De Vio, who had returned to Rome in ill health, was carried to the assembly on his couch. He would not miss this paltry triumph, which afforded him some little consolation. Although defeated at Augsburg, he desired to take part at Rome in condemning this indomitable monk, before whom he had witnessed the failure of all his learning, skill, and authority. Luther was not there to reply: De Vio thought himself invincible. "I have seen enough to know," said he, "that if the Germans are not kept under by fire and sword, they will entirely throw off the yoke of the Roman Church." Such a declaration from Cajetan could not fail to have great weight. The cardinal was avenged of his defeat and of the contempt of Germany. A final conference, which Eck attended, was held in the pope's presence at his villa of Malliano. On the fifteenth of June the Sacred College decided on the condemnation, and sanctioned the famous bull.

"Arise, O Lord," said the Roman pontiff, speaking at this solemn moment as God's vicegerent and head of the Church, "arise, judge Thy cause, and call to mind the opprobrium which madmen continually heap on Thee! Arise, O Peter; remember thy Holy Roman Church, mother of all churches, and queen of the faith! Arise, O Paul, for behold a new Porphyry attacks thy doctrines and the holy popes, our predecessors. Lastly, arise, ye assembly of saints, the holy Church of God, and intercede with the Almighty!"

The pope then proceeds to quote from Luther's works forty-one pernicious, scandalous, and poisonous propositions, in which the latter set forth the holy doctrines of the gospel. The following propositions are included in the list:

"To deny that sin remains in the child after baptism, is to trample under foot both Saint Paul and our Lord Jesus Christ."

"A new life is the best and sublimest penance."

"To burn heretics is contrary to the will of the Holy Ghost," and so on.

"So soon as this bull shall be published," continued the pope, "the bishops shall make diligent search after the writings of Martin Luther that contain these errors, and burn them publicly and solemnly in the presence of the clergy and laity. As for Martin himself, what have we not done? Imitating the long-suffering of God Almighty, we are still ready to receive him again into the bosom of the Church, and we grant him sixty days in which to forward us his recantation in a paper, sealed by two prelates; or else, which would be far more agreeable to us, for him to come to Rome in person, in order that no one may entertain any doubts of his obedience. Meanwhile, and from this very moment, he must give up preaching, teaching, and writing, and commit his works to the flames. And if he does not retract in the space of sixty days, we by these presents condemn both him and his adherents as open and obstinate heretics." The pope then pronounced a number of excommunications, maledictions, and interdicts, against Luther and his partisans, with orders to seize their persons and send them to Rome. We may easily conceive what would become of these noble-minded confessors of the gospel in the papal dungeons.

Thus the tempest gathered over Luther's head. It might have been imagined, after the affair of Reuchlin, that the court of Rome would no longer make common cause with the Dominicans and the Inquisition. But now the latter had the ascendancy, and the ancient alliance was solemnly renewed. The bull was published; and for centuries Rome had not pronounced a sentence of condemnation that her arm had not followed up with death. This murderous message was about to leave the Seven Hills, and reach the Saxon monk in his cell. The moment was aptly chosen. It might be supposed that the new emperor, who had so many reasons for courting the pope's friendship, would be eager to deserve it by sacrificing to him an obscure monk. Already Leo X, the cardinals, nay all Rome, exulted in their victory, and fancied they saw their enemy at their feet.

Chapter 38

MELANCTHON WEDS
CATHERINE KRAPPS

WHILE THE INHABITANTS of the eternal city were thus agitated, more tranquil scenes were passing at Wittenberg. Melancthon was there diffusing a mild but brilliant light. From fifteen hundred to two thousand auditors, assembling from Germany, England, the Low Countries, France, Italy, Hungary, and Greece, were often gathered round him. He was twenty-four years of age, and had not entered the ecclesiastical state. There were none in Wittenberg who were not delighted to receive the visits of this young professor, at once so learned and so amiable. Foreign universities, Ingolstadt in particular, desired to attract him within their walls. His Wittenberg friends were eager to retain him among them by the ties of marriage. Although Luther wished that his dear friend Philip might find a consort, he openly declared that he would not be his adviser in this matter. Others took this task upon themselves.

The young doctor frequented, in particular, the house of the burgomaster Krapp, who belonged to an ancient family. Krapp had a daughter named Catherine, a woman of mild character and great sensibility. Melancthon's friends urged him to demand her in marriage; but the young scholar was absorbed in his books, and would hear no mention of anything besides. His Greek authors and his Testament were his delight. The arguments of his friends he met with other arguments. At length they extorted his consent. All the preliminary steps were arranged, and Catherine was given him to wife. He received her very coldly, and said with a sigh: "It is God's will! I must renounce my studies and my pleasures to comply with the wishes of my friends." He appreciated, however, Catherine's good qualities. "The young woman," said he, "has just such a character and education as I should have asked of God. Certainly she deserves a better husband." Matters were settled in the month of August; the betrothal took place on the twenty-fifth of September, and at the end of November the wedding was celebrated. Old John Luther with his wife and daughters visited Wittenberg on this occasion. Many learned men and people of note were present at the nuptials.

The young bride felt as much affection as the young professor gave evidence of coldness. Always anxious about her husband, Catherine grew alarmed at the least prospect of any danger that threatened her dear partner. Whenever Melancthon proposed taking any step of such a nature as to compromise himself, she overwhelmed him with entreaties to renounce it. "I was compelled," wrote Melancthon on one such occasion, "to give way to her weakness . . . such is our lot." How many infidelities in the Church may have had a similar origin! Perhaps we should ascribe to Catherine's influence the timidity and fears with which her husband has so often been reproached.

Catherine was an affectionate mother as well as loving wife. She was liberal in her alms to the poor. "O God! do not abandon me in my old age, when my hair begins to turn gray!" such was the daily prayer of this pious and timid woman. Melancthon was soon conquered by his wife's affection. When he had once tasted the joys of domestic life, he felt all their sweetness: he was formed for such pleasures. Nowhere did he feel himself happier than with Catherine and his children. A French traveler one day finding "the master of Germany" rocking his child's cradle with one hand, and holding a book in the other, started back with surprise. But Melancthon, without being disconcerted, explained to him with so much warmth the value of children in the eyes of God, that the stranger quitted the house wiser (to use his own words) than he had entered it.

Melancthon's marriage gave a domestic circle to the Reformation. There was from this time one house in Wittenberg always open to those who were inspired by the new life. The concourse of strangers was immense. They came to Melancthon on a thousand different matters; and the established regulations of his household enjoined him to refuse nothing to anyone. The young professor was extremely disinterested whenever good was to be done. When all his money was spent, he would secretly carry his plate to some merchant, caring little about depriving himself of it, since it gave him wherewithal to comfort the distressed. "Accordingly it would have been impossible for him to provide for the wants of himself and family," says his friend Camerarius, "if a divine and secret blessing had not from time to time furnished him the means." His good nature was extreme. He possessed several ancient gold and silver medals, remarkable for their inscriptions and figures. He showed them one day to a stranger who called upon him. "Take any one you like," said Melancthon.—"I should like them all," replied the stranger. "I confess," said Philip, "that this unreasonable request displeased me a little at first; I nevertheless gave them to him."

There was in Melancthon's writings a perfume of antiquity, which did not however prevent the sweet savor of Christ from exhaling from every part, and which communicated to them an inexpressible charm. There is not one of his letters addressed to his friends in which we are not reminded in the most natural manner of the wisdom of Homer, Plato, Cicero, and Pliny, Christ ever remaining his Master and his God. Spalatin had asked him the meaning of this expression of Jesus Christ, "Without me ye can do nothing" (John 15:5). Melancthon referred him to Luther. *"Cur agam gestum, spectante Roscio?* [1] to use Cicero's words," said he. He then continued: "This passage signifies that we must be absorbed in Christ, so that we ourselves no longer act, but Christ lives in us. As the divine nature was incorporated with the human in the person of Christ, so man must be incorporated with Jesus Christ by faith."

The illustrious scholar generally retired to rest shortly after supper. At two or three o'clock in the morning he was again at his studies. It was during these early hours that his best works were written. His manuscripts usually lay on the table exposed to the view of every visitor, so that he was robbed of several. When he had invited any of his friends to his house, he used to beg one of them to read, before sitting down to table, some small composition in prose or verse. He always took some young men with him during his journeys,

[1] How can I declaim in the presence of Roscius?

conversing with them in a manner at once amusing and instructive. If the conversation languished, each of them had to recite in turn passages extracted from the ancient poets. He made frequent use of irony, tempering it, however, with great mildness. "He scratches and bites," said he of himself, "and yet he does no harm."

Learning was his passion. The great object of his life was to diffuse literature and knowledge. Let us not forget that in his estimation the Holy Scriptures ranked far above the writings of pagan authors. "I apply myself solely to one thing," said he, "the defense of letters. By our example we must excite youth to the admiration of learning, and induce them to love it for its own sake, and not for the advantage that may be derived from it. The destruction of learning brings with it the ruin of everything that is good: religion, morals, divine and human things. The better a man is, the greater his ardor in the preservation of learning; for he knows that of all plagues ignorance is the most pernicious."

Some time after his marriage, Melancthon, in company with Camerarius and other friends, made a journey to Bretten in the Palatinate, to visit his beloved mother. As soon as he caught sight of his birthplace, he got off his horse, fell on his knees, and returned thanks to God for having permitted him to see it once more. Margaret almost fainted with joy as she embraced her son. She wished him to stay at Bretten, and begged him earnestly to adhere to the faith of his fathers. Melancthon excused himself in this respect, but with great delicacy, lest he should wound his mother's feelings. He had much difficulty in leaving her again; and whenever a traveler brought him news from his natal city, he was as delighted as if he had once more returned (to use his own words) to the joys of his childhood. Such was the private life of one of the greatest instruments of the religious Revolution of the sixteenth century.

A disturbance, however, occurred to trouble these domestic scenes and the studious activity of Wittenberg. The students came to blows with the citizens. The rector displayed great weakness. We may imagine what was Melancthon's sorrow at beholding the excesses committed by these disciples of learning. Luther was indignant: he was far from desiring to gain popularity by an unbecoming conciliation. The opprobrium these disorders reflected on the university pierced him to the heart. He went into the pulpit, and preached forcibly against these seditions, calling upon both parties to submit to the magistrates. His sermon occasioned great irritation: "Satan," said he in one of his letters, "being unable to attack us from without, desires to injure us from within. I am not afraid of him; but I fear lest God's anger should light upon us, because we have not becomingly received His Word. These last three years I have been thrice exposed to great danger; at Augsburg in 1518, at Leipzig in 1519, and now in 1520 at Wittenberg. It is neither by wisdom nor by arms that the renovation of the Church will be accomplished, but by humble prayers, by a faith full of courage, that puts Christ on our side. My dear friend, unite thy prayers with mine, for fear the wicked spirit should make use of this small spark to kindle a great conflagration."

Chapter 39

THE GOSPEL ACROSS THE ALPS

BUT MORE TERRIBLE COMBATS than these awaited Luther. Rome was brandishing the sword with which she was about to strike the gospel. The rumor of the condemnation that was destined to fall upon him, far from dispiriting the reformer, augmented his courage. He manifested no anxiety to parry the blows of this haughty power. It was by inflicting more terrible blows himself that he would neutralize those of his adversaries. While the transalpine assemblies were thundering out anathemas against him, he bore the sword of the Word into the midst of the Italian people. Letters from Venice spoke of the favor with which Luther's sentiments were received there. He burned with desire to send the gospel across the Alps. Evangelists were wanted to carry it thither. "I wish," said he, "that we had living books, that is, preachers, and that we could multiply and protect them everywhere, in order that they might convey to the people a knowledge of holy things. The prince could not undertake a more glorious task. If the people of Italy should receive the truth, our cause would then be impregnable."

It does not appear that Luther's project was realized. In later years, it is true, evangelical men, even Calvin himself, sojourned for a short period in Italy; but for the present Luther's designs were not carried out. He had addressed one of the mighty princes of the world: if he had appealed to men of humble rank, but full of zeal for the kingdom of God, the result might have been different. At that period, the idea generally prevailed, that everything should be done by governments; and the association of simple individuals—that power which is now effecting such great things in Christendom—was almost unknown.

If Luther did not succeed in his projects for propagating the truth in distant countries, he was only the more zealous in announcing it himself. It was at this time that he preached, at Wittenberg, his sermon on the Mass. In this discourse he inveighed against the numerous sects of the Romish Church, and reproached it, with reason, for its want of unity. "The multiplicity of spiritual laws," says he, "has filled the world with sects and divisions. Priests, monks, and laymen have come to hate each other more than the Christians hate the Turks. What do I say? Priests against priests, and monks against monks, are deadly enemies. Each one is attached to his own sect, and despises all others. The unity and charity of Christ are at an end." He next attacked the doctrine that the mass is a sacrifice, and has some virtue in itself. "What are most precious in every sacrament, and consequently in the eucharist," says he, "are the promises and the Word of God. Without faith in this Word and these promises, the sacrament is dead: it is a body without a soul, a vessel without wine, a purse without money, a type without fulfillment, a letter without spirit, a casket without jewels, a scabbard without a sword."

Luther's voice was not, however, confined to Wittenberg; and if he did not find missionaries to bear his instructions to distant lands, God had provided a missionary of a new kind. The printing-press was the successor of the Evangelists. This was the breeching-battery employed against the Roman fortress. Luther had prepared a mine, the explosion of which shook the edifice of Rome to its lowest foundations. This was the publication of his famous book on the *Babylonish Captivity of the Church*, which appeared on October 6, 1520. Never did man in so critical a position display greater courage.

In this work he first set forth with haughty irony all the advantages for which he was indebted to his enemies:

"Whether I will it or not, I become wiser every day, urged on as I am by so many illustrious masters. Two years ago, I attacked indulgences, but with so much indecision and fear that I am now ashamed of it. There is no cause for astonishment in this, for I was alone when I set this stone rolling." He thanked Prierio, Eck, Emser, and his other adversaries: "I denied that the papacy was of divine origin, but I granted that it was of human right. Now, after reading all the subtleties on which these gentry have set up their idol, I know that the papacy is none other than the kingdom of Babylon, and the violence of Nimrod the mighty hunter. I therefore beseech all my friends and all the booksellers to burn the books that I have written on this subject, and to substitute this one proposition in their place: The papacy is a vigorous chase led by the Roman bishop, to catch and destroy souls."

Luther next proceeded to attack the prevailing errors on the sacraments, monastic vows, etc. He reduced the seven sacraments of the Church to three; namely, baptism, penance, and the Lord's Supper. After explaining the true nature of this Supper, he passed on to baptism; and it is here in particular that he laid down the excellence of faith, and vigorously attacked Rome. "God," said he, "has preserved this sacrament alone free from human traditions. God has said: 'He that believeth and is baptized shall be saved.' This promise of God should be preferred before all the glory of works, all vows, all satisfactions, all indulgences, and all inventions of man. Now, upon this promise, if we receive it with faith, depends our whole salvation. If we believe, our hearts are strengthened by the divine promise; and though the believer should be forsaken of all, this promise in which he believes will never forsake him. With it, he will resist the adversary who lies in wait for his soul, and be prepared to meet remorseless death, and stand before the judgment seat of God. It will be his consolation in all his trials to say: God's promises never deceive; of their truth I received a pledge at my baptism; if God is for me, who shall be against me? Oh, how rich is the Christian that has been baptized! Nothing can destroy him except he refuse to believe.

"Perhaps to what I have said on the necessity of faith, they will object to me the baptism of little children. But as the Word of God is mighty to change even the heart of a wicked man, who is however neither less deaf nor ignorant than a little child; in like manner also the prayers of the Church, to which all things are possible, change the little child, by the faith that it pleases God to pour into his heart, and thus purifies and renews it."

After having thus explained the doctrine of baptism, Luther wielded it as a weapon of offense against the papacy. In fact, if the Christian finds all his salvation in the renewal of his baptism by faith, what need has he of the Romish ordinances?

"For this reason, I declare," says Luther, "that neither the pope, nor the bishop, nor any man whatsoever, has authority to impose the least thing on a Christian, unless it be with his own consent. All that is done without it is an act of tyranny. We are free as regards all men. The vow that we made at our baptism is sufficient of itself, and is more than we can ever fulfill. All other vows may therefore be abolished. Let every man who enters the priesthood or any religious order clearly understand that the works of a monk or of a priest differ in no respect before God from those of a peasant who tills his fields, or of a woman who manages her house. God estimates all things by the standard of faith. And it often happens that the simple labor of a serving man or maiden is more acceptable to God than the fasts and works of a monk, because the latter are void of faith. . . . Christians are God's true people, led captive to Babylon, where everything has been taken from them which baptism hath given."

Such were the weapons by which that religious revolution whose history we are retracing was effected. First, the necessity of faith was re-established, and then the reformers employed it as a weapon to dash to atoms every superstition. It is with this power of God, which removes mountains, that they attacked so many errors.

Luther terminated this famous writing on the *Captivity of Babylon* with these words:

"I hear that new papal excommunications are about to be fabricated against me. If it be true, this present book must be considered as part of my future recantation. The remainder will soon follow, to prove my obedience; and the complete work will form, with Christ's aid, such a whole as Rome has never heard or seen the like."

Chapter 40

THE LITTLE BOOK, CHRISTIAN LIBERTY

AFTER SUCH A PUBLICATION, all hope of reconciliation between Luther and the pope must of necessity have vanished. The incompatibility of the reformer's faith with the doctrines of the Church must have struck the least discerning; but precisely at that very time fresh negotiations had been opened. Five weeks before the publication of the *Captivity of Babylon*, at the end of August, 1520, the general chapter of the Augustine monks was held at Eisleben. The venerable Staupitz there resigned the general vicarship of the order, and it was conferred on Wenceslas Link, the same who had accompanied Luther to Augsburg. The indefatigable Miltitz suddenly arrived in the midst of the proceedings. He was ardently desirous of reconciling Luther with the pope. His vanity, his avarice, and above all, his jealousy and hatred, were deeply interested in this result. Eck and his boastings annoyed him; he knew that the Ingolstadt doctor had been decrying him at Rome, and he would have made every sacrifice to baffle, by a peace that should be promptly concluded, the schemes of this importunate rival. The interests of religion were mere secondary matters in his eyes. One day, as he relates, he was dining with the Bishop of Leissen. The guests had already made pretty copious libations, when a new work of Luther's was laid before them. It was opened and read; the bishop grew angry; the official swore; but Miltitz burst into a hearty laugh. He dealt with the Reformation as a man of the world; Eck as a theologian.

Aroused by the arrival of Dr. Eck, Miltitz addressed the chapter of the Augustines in a speech, delivered with a strong Italian accent, thinking thus to impose on his simple fellow-countrymen. "The whole Augustine order," said he, "is compromised in this affair. Show me the means of restraining Luther." "We have nothing to do with the doctor," replied the fathers, "and cannot give you advice." They relied no doubt on the release from the obligations to his order which Staupitz had given Luther at Augsburg. Miltitz persisted: "Let a deputation from this venerable chapter wait upon Luther, and entreat him to write to the pope, assuring him that he has never plotted against his person. That will be sufficient to put an end to the matter." The chapter complied with the nuncio's demand, and commissioned, no doubt at his own request, the former vicar-general and his successor (Staupitz and Link) to speak to Luther. This deputation immediately set out for Wittenberg, bearing a letter from Miltitz to the doctor, filled with expressions of the greatest respect. "There is no time to lose," said he; "the thunderstorm, already gathering over the reformer's head, will soon burst forth; and then all will be over."

Neither Luther nor the deputies who shared in his sentiments expected any success from a letter to the pope. But that was an additional reason for not refusing to write one. Such a letter could only be a mere matter of form, which would set the justice of Luther's cause in a still stronger light. "This Italianized Saxon [Miltitz]," thought Luther, "is no doubt looking to his own private interest in making the request. Well, then, let it be so! I will write, in conformity with the truth, that I have never entertained any designs against the pope's person. I must be on my guard against attacking the see of Rome itself too violently. Yet I will sprinkle it with its own salt."

But not long after, the doctor was informed of the arrival of the bull in Germany; on the third of October, he told Spalatin that he would not write to the pope, and on the sixth of the same month, he published his book on the *Captivity of Babylon*. Miltitz was not even yet discouraged. The desire of humbling Eck made him believe in impossibilities. On the second of October, he had written to the elector full of hope: "All will go on well; but, for the love of God, do not delay any longer to pay me the pension that you and your brother have given me these several years past. I require money to gain new friends at Rome. Write to the pope, pay homage to the young cardinals, the relations of his holiness, in gold and silver pieces from the electoral mint, and add to them a few for me also, for I have been robbed of those that you gave me."

Even after Luther had been informed of the bull, the intriguing Miltitz was not discouraged. He requested to have a conference with Luther at Lichtemberg. The elector ordered the latter to go there; but his friends, and above all, the affectionate Melancthon, opposed it. "What!" thought they; "accept a conference with the nuncio in so distant a place, at the very moment when the bull is to appear which commands Luther to be seized and carried to Rome! Is it not clear that, as Dr. Eck is unable to approach the reformer on account of the open manner in which he has shown his hatred, the crafty chamberlain has taken upon himself to catch Luther in his toils?"

These fears had no power to stop the Wittenberg doctor. The prince had commanded, and he would obey. "I am setting out for Lichtemberg," he wrote to the chaplain on the eleventh of October; "pray for me." His friends would not abandon him. Towards evening of the same day, he entered Lichtemberg on horseback, accompanied by thirty cavaliers, among whom was Melancthon. The papal nuncio arrived about the same time with a train of four persons. Was not this moderate escort a mere trick to inspire confidence in Luther and his friends?

Miltitz was very pressing in his solicitations, assuring Luther that the blame would be thrown on Eck and his foolish vaunting, and that all would be concluded to the satisfaction of both parties. "Well then!" replied Luther, "I offer to keep silence henceforward, provided my adversaries are silent likewise. For the sake of peace, I will do everything in my power."

Miltitz was filled with joy. He accompanied Luther as far as Wittenberg. The reformer and the nuncio entered side by side into that city which Doctor Eck was already approaching, presenting with a threatening hand the formidable bull that was intended to crush the Reformation. "We shall bring this business to a happy conclusion," wrote Miltitz to the elector immediately; "thank the pope for the rose, and at the same time send forty or fifty florins to the Cardinal Quatuor Sanctorum."

Luther had now to fulfill his promise of writing to the pope. Before bidding Rome farewell forever, he was desirous of proclaiming to her once more some important and salutary truths. Many readers, from ignorance of the sentiments that animated the writer, will consider his letter as a caustic writing, a bitter and insolent satire.

All the evils that afflicted Christendom he sincerely ascribed to Rome; on this ground, his language cannot be regarded as insolent, but as containing the most solemn warnings. The greater his affection for Leo, and the greater his love for the Church of Christ, the more he desires to lay bare the extent of its wound. The energy of his expressions is a scale by which to measure the energy of his affections. The moment had come for striking a decisive blow. We may almost imagine we see a prophet going round the city for the last time, reproaching it with its abominations, revealing the judgments of the Almighty, and calling out "Yet a few days more!"

The following is Luther's letter:

"To the most holy Father in God, Leo X, Pope at Rome, be all health in Christ Jesus our Lord. Amen.

"From the midst of the violent battle which for three years I have been fighting against dissolute men, I cannot hinder myself from sometimes looking towards you, O Leo, most holy Father in God! And although the madness of your impious flatterers has constrained me to appeal from your judgment to a future council, my heart has never been alienated from your holiness, and I have never ceased praying constantly and with deep groaning for your prosperity and for that of your pontificate.

"It is true that I have attacked certain anti-Christian doctrines, and have inflicted a deep wound upon my adversaries, because of their impiety. I do not repent of this, for I have the example of Christ before me. What is the use of salt, if it hath lost its pungency, or of the edge of the sword, if it cuts not? Cursed be the man who does the Lord's work coldly! Most excellent Leo, far from ever having entertained an evil thought with reference to you, I wish you the most precious blessings for eternity. I have done but one thing—upheld the Word of truth. I am ready to submit to you in everything; but as for this Word, I will not—I cannot abandon it. He who thinks differently from me thinks erroneously.

"It is true that I have attacked the court of Rome; but neither you nor any man on earth can deny that it is more corrupt than Sodom and Gomorrah; and that the impiety prevailing there is past all hope of cure. Yes! I have been filled with horror at seeing that under your name the poor people of Christ have been made a sport of. This I opposed, and I will oppose it again; not that I imagine I shall be able, despite the opposition of flatterers, to prosper in anything connected with this Babylon, which is confusion itself; but I owe it to my brethren, in order that some may escape, if possible, from these terrible scourges.

"You are aware that Rome for many years past has inundated the world with all that could destroy both body and soul. The Church of Rome, once the foremost in sanctity, is become the most licentious den of robbers, the most shameless of all brothels, the kingdom of sin, of death, and of hell, which Antichrist himself, if he were to appear, could not increase in wickedness. All this is clearer than the sun at noonday.

"And yet, O Leo! you sit like a lamb in the midst of wolves, like Daniel in the lions' den! What can, you do alone against such monsters? Perhaps there are three or four cardinals who combine learning with virtue. But what are they against so great a number! You would all die of poison, before being able to make trial of any remedy. The fate of the court of Rome is decreed; God's wrath is upon it, and will consume it. It hates good advice, dreads reform, will not mitigate the fury of its impiety, and thus deserves that men should speak of this city as of its mother: We would have healed Babylon, but she is not healed; forsake her. It was for you and your cardinals to have applied the remedy; but the sick man mocks the physician, and the horse will not obey the rein.

"Full of affection for you, most excellent Leo, I have always regretted that you, who are worthy of better times, should have been raised to the pontificate in such days as these. Rome merits you not, nor those who resemble you; she deserves to have Satan himself for her king. So true it is that he reigns more than you in that Babylon. Would to God that, laying aside that glory which your enemies so loudly extol, you would exchange it for some small living, or would support yourself on your paternal inheritance; for none but Iscariots deserve such honor. . . . O my dear Leo, of what use are you in this Roman court, except that the basest men employ your name and power to ruin fortunes, destroy souls, multiply crimes, oppress the faith, the truth, and the whole Church of God? O Leo! Leo! you are the most unhappy of men, and you sit on the most dangerous of thrones! I tell you the truth because I mean you well.

"Is it not true that under the spreading firmament of heaven there is nothing more corrupt or more detestable than the Romish court? It infinitely exceeds the Turks in vices and corruption. Once it was the gate of heaven, now it is the mouth of hell; a mouth which the wrath of God keeps open so wide, that on witnessing the unhappy people rushing into it, I cannot but utter a warning cry, as in a tempest, that some at least may be saved from the terrible gulf.

"Behold, O Leo, my Father! why I have inveighed against this death-dealing see. Far from rising up against your person, I thought I was laboring for your safety, by valiantly attacking that prison, or rather that hell, in which you are shut up. To inflict all possible mischief on the court of Rome is performing your duty. To cover it with shame, is to do Christ honor; in a word, to be a Christian, is not to be a Roman.

"Yet finding that by succoring the see of Rome I lose both my labor and my pains, I transmitted to it this writing of divorcement, and said: Farewell, Rome! 'He that is unjust, let him be unjust still; and he which is filthy, let him be filthy still!' And I devoted myself to the tranquil and solitary study of the Holy Scripture. Then Satan opened his eyes, and awoke his servant John Eck, a great adversary of Jesus Christ, in order to challenge me again to the lists. He was desirous of establishing not the primacy of Saint Peter, but his own, and for that purpose to lead the conquered Luther in his triumphal train. His be the blame of all the disgrace with which the see of Rome is covered."

Luther relates his communications with De Vio, Miltitz, and Eck; and then continues:

"Now then, I come to you, most holy Father, and, prostrate at your feet, I beseech you to curb, if that be possible, these enemies of peace. But I cannot retract my doctrine. I cannot permit any rules of interpretation to be imposed on the Scriptures. The Word of God, which is the fountain whence all true liberty flows, must not be bound.

"O Leo! my Father! listen not to those flattering sirens who would persuade you that you are not a mere man, but a demigod, and can command and require whatever you please. You are the servant of servants, and the place where you are seated is the most dangerous and miserable of all. Believe those who depreciate you, and not those who extol you. I am perhaps too bold in presuming to teach so exalted a majesty, which ought to instruct all men. But I see the dangers that surround you at Rome; I see you driven to and fro, like the waves of the sea in a storm. Charity urges me, and it is my duty to utter a cry of warning and of safety.

"That I may not appear empty-handed before your holiness, I present you a small book which I have dedicated to you, and which will inform you of the subjects on which I should be engaged, if your parasites permitted me. It is a little matter, if its size be considered; but a great one, if we regard its contents; for the sum of the Christian life is therein contained. I am poor, and have nothing else to offer you; besides, have you need of any other than spiritual gifts? I commend myself to your holiness, whom may the Lord Jesus preserve forever! Amen!"

The little book which Luther presented to the pope was his discourse on *Christian Liberty,* in which the reformer demonstrates incontrovertibly, how, without infringing the liberty given by faith, a Christian may submit to all external ordinances in a spirit of liberty and charity. Two truths serve as a foundation to the whole argument: "The Christian is free and master in all things. The Christian is in bondage and a servant in all and to all. He is free and a master by faith; he is a servant and a slave by love."

He first explained the power of faith to make a Christian free: "Faith unites the soul to Christ, as a wife to her husband," said Luther to the pope. "All that Christ has, becomes the property of the believing soul; all that the soul has, becomes the property of Christ. Christ possesses every blessing and eternal salvation: they are henceforward the property of the soul. The soul possesses every vice and sin; they become henceforth the property of Christ. It is then the blessed exchange commences: Christ, who is God and man, Christ who has never sinned, and whose holiness is immaculate, Christ the Almighty and Everlasting, appropriating by His nuptial ring, that is, by faith, all the sins of the believer's soul, these sins are swallowed up and lost in Him; for there is no sin that can stand before His infinite righteousness. Thus, by means of faith, the soul is delivered from every sin, and clothed with the eternal righteousness of her Husband, Jesus Christ. Blessed union! the rich, noble, and holy Spouse, Jesus Christ, unites in marriage with that poor, guilty, and despised wife, delivers her from every ill, and adorns her with the most costly blessings. . . . Christ, a priest and king, shares this honor and glory with every Christian. The Christian is a king, and consequently possesses all things; he is a priest, and consequently possesses God. And it is faith, and not works, that brings him to such honor. The Christian is free of all things, above all things, faith giving him abundantly of every thing."

In the second part of his discourse, Luther gave another view of the truth. "Although the Christian is thus made free, he voluntarily becomes a slave, to act toward his brethren as God has acted towards him through Jesus Christ. I desire [said he] to serve freely, joyfully, and gratuitously, a Father who has thus lavished upon me all the abundance of His blessings: I wish to become all things for my neighbor, as Christ has become all things for me."

"From faith," continued Luther, "proceeds the love of God; from love proceeds a life full of liberty, charity, and joy. Oh! how noble and elevated is the Christian life! But, alas! no one knows it, no one preaches it. By faith the Christian ascends to God: by love, he descends even to man, and yet he abides ever with God. This is true liberty—a liberty which surpasses all others as much as the heavens are above the earth."

Such is the work with which Luther accompanied his letter to Leo.

Chapter 41

BULL AT WITTENBERG— ZWINGLI'S INTERVENTION

WHILE the reformer was thus addressing the Roman pontiff for the last time, the bull which anathematized him was already in the hands of the chiefs of the German Church, and at the threshold of Luther's dwelling place. It would appear that no doubts were entertained at Rome of the success of the step just taken against the Reformation. The pope had commissioned two high functionaries of his court, Caraccioli and Aleander, to bear it to the Archbishop of Mentz, desiring him to see it put in execution. But Eck himself appeared in Saxony as the herald and agent of the great pontifical work.

The choice had long been doubtful. "Eck," wrote an inhabitant of Rome about this time, "was peculiarly adapted for this mission by his impudence, his dissimulation, his lies, his flattery, and other vices, that are held in high esteem at Rome: but his fondness for drinking (a failing towards which the Italians entertain a great aversion), was rather against his election." The influence, however, of his patron Fugger, "the king of crowns," prevailed in the end. This bad habit was even metamorphosed into a virtue in the case of Dr. Eck. "He is just the man we want," said many of the Romans; "for these drunken Germans, what can be better than a drunken legate? Their temerity can only be checked by an equal degree of temerity." Further, it was whispered about that no man of sincerity and good sense would undertake such a mission; and that even could such a man be found, the magnitude of the danger would soon make him abandon the place. The idea of nominating Aleander as Dr. Eck's colleague

338

seemed most excellent. "A worthy pair of ambassadors," said some; "both are admirably suited for this work, and perfectly matched in effrontery, impudence, and debauchery."

The doctor of Ingolstadt had felt more than any other man the force of Luther's attack; he had seen the danger, and stretched forth his hand to steady the tottering edifice of Rome. He was, in his own opinion, the Atlas destined to bear on his sturdy shoulders the ancient Roman world now threatening to fall to ruins. Proud of the success of his journey to Rome,—proud of the commission he had received from the sovereign pontiff,—proud of appearing in Germany with the new title of prothonotary and pontifical nuncio,—proud of the bull he held in his hands, and which contained the condemnation of his indomitable rival, his present mission was a more magnificent triumph than all the victories he had gained in Hungary, Bavaria, Lombardy, and Saxony, and from which he had previously derived so much renown.

But this pride was soon to be brought low. The pope, by confiding the publication of the bull to Eck, had committed a fault destined to destroy its effect. So great a distinction, accorded to a man not filling an elevated station in the Church, offended all sensible men. The bishops, accustomed to receive the bulls direct from the Roman pontiff, were displeased that this should be published in their dioceses by a nuncio created for the occasion. The nation, that had laughed at the pretended conqueror at Leipzig at the moment of his flight to Italy, was astonished and indignant at seeing him recross the Alps, bearing the insignia of a papal nuncio, and furnished with power to crush her chosen men. Luther considered this judgment brought by his implacable opponent as an act of personal revenge; this condemnation was in his idea (says Pallavicini) the treacherous dagger of a mortal enemy, and not the lawful axe of a Roman lictor. This paper was no longer regarded as the bull of the supreme pontiff, but as the bull of Doctor Eck. Thus the edge was blunted and weakened beforehand by the very man who had prepared it.

The Chancellor of Ingolstadt had made all haste to Saxony. 'Twas there he had fought; 'twas there he wished to publish his victory. He succeeded in posting up the bull at Meissen, Merseburg, and Brandenburg, toward the end of September. But in the first of these cities it was stuck up in a place where no one could read it, and the bishops of the three sees did not press its publication. Even his great protector, Duke George, forbade the council of Leipzig to make it generally known before receiving an order from the Bishop of Merseburg; and this order did not come till the following year. "These difficulties are merely for form's sake," thought John Eck at first; for everything in other respects seemed to smile upon him. Duke George himself sent him a gilt cup filled with ducats. Even Miltitz, who had hastened to Leipzig at the news of his rival's presence, invited him to dinner. The two legates were boon companions, and Miltitz thought he could more effectually sound his rival over the bottle. "When he had drunk pretty freely, he began," says the pope's chamberlain, "to boast at a fine rate; he displayed his bull, and related how he intended bringing that scoundrel Martin to reason."

But erelong the Ingolstadt doctor observed that the wind was changing. A great alteration had taken place in Leipzig during the past year. On St. Michael's day, some students posted up placards in ten different places, in which the new nuncio was sharply attacked. In alarm he fled to the cloister of St. Paul, in which Tetzel had already taken refuge, refused to see anyone, and prevailed upon the rector to bring these youthful adversaries to account. But poor Eck gained little by this. The students wrote a ballad upon him, which they sung in the streets: Eck heard it from his retreat. Upon this he lost all his courage; the formidable champion trembled in every limb. Each day he received threatening letters. One hundred and fifty students arrived from Wittenberg, boldly exclaiming against the papal envoy. The wretched apostolical nuncio could hold out no longer. "I have no wish to see him killed," said Luther, "but I am desirous that his schemes should fail." Eck quitted his asylum by night, escaped secretly from Leipzig, and went and hid himself at Coburg. Miltitz, who relates this, boasted of it more than the reformer. This triumph was not of long duration; all the conciliatory plans of the chamberlain failed, and he came to a melancholy end. Miltitz, being intoxicated, fell into the Rhine at Mentz, and was drowned.

Gradually, however, Eck's courage revived. He repaired to Erfurt, whose theologians had given the Wittenberg doctor several proofs of their jealousy. He insisted that the bull should be published in this city; but the students seized the copies, tore them in pieces, and flung the fragments into the river, saying: "Since it is a bull [a bubble], let it float!" "Now," said Luther, when he was informed of this, "the pope's paper is a real bull [bubble]."

Eck did not dare appear at Wittenberg; he sent the bull to the rector, threatening to destroy the university if he did not conform to it. At the same time he wrote to Duke John, Frederick's brother and coregent: "Do not misconstrue my proceedings," said he; "for I am fighting on behalf of the faith, which costs me much care, toil, and money."

The Bishop of Brandenburg could not, even had he so wished, act in Wittenberg in his quality of ordinary; for the university was protected by its privileges. Luther and Carlstadt, both condemned by the bull, were invited to be present at the deliberations that took place on its contents. The rector declared that, as the bull was not accompanied by a letter from the pope, he would not publish it. The university already enjoyed in the surrounding countries a greater authority than the pontiff himself. Its declaration served as a model for the elector's government. Thus the spirit that was in Luther triumphed over the bull of Rome.

While this affair was thus violently agitating the public mind in Germany, a solemn voice was heard in another country of Europe. One man, foreseeing the immense schism that the papal bull would cause in the Church, stood forward to utter a serious warning and to defend the reformer. It was the same Swiss priest whom we have mentioned before, Ulrich Zwingli, who, without any relations of friendship with Luther, published a writing full of wisdom and dignity,—the first of his numerous works. A brotherly affection seemed to attract him towards the reformer of Wittenberg. "The piety of the pontiff," said he, "calls upon him to sacrifice gladly all that he holds dearest, for the glory of Christ his king and the public peace of the Church. Nothing is more injurious to his dignity than his defending it by bribery or by terror. Before even Luther's writings had been read, he was cried down among the people as a heretic, a schismatic, and as Antichrist himself. No one had given him warning, no one had refuted him; he begged for a discussion, and they were content to condemn him. The bull that is now published against him displeased even those who honor the pope's grandeur; for throughout it betrays signs of the impotent hatred of a few monks, and not those becoming the mildness of a pontiff, the vicar of a Saviour full of compassion. All men acknowledge that the true doctrine of the gospel of Jesus Christ has greatly degenerated, and that we need a striking public revival of laws and morality. Look to all men of learning and virtue; the greater their sincerity, the stronger is their attachment to the evangelical truth, and the less are they scandalized at Luther's writings. There is no one but confesses that these books have made him a better man, although perhaps they may contain passages that he does not approve of. Let men of pure doctrine and acknowledged probity be chosen; let those princes above all suspicion, the Emperor Charles, the King of England, and the King of Hungary, themselves appoint the arbitrators; let these men read Luther's writings, hear him personally, and let their decision be ratified! May the teaching and truth of Christ prevail!

This proposition emanating from the country of the Swiss led to no results. The great divorce must be accomplished; Christendom must be rent in twain; and even in its wounds will the remedy for all its ills be found.

Chapter 42

BOOKS TO ASHES

IN TRUTH, what signified all this resistance of students, rectors, and priests? If the mighty hand of Charles united with the pope's, would they not crush those scholars and grammarians? Who would withstand the power of the pontiff of Christendom, and of the Emperor of the West? The bolt was discharged; Luther was cut off from the Church; the gospel seemed lost. At this solemn moment, the reformer did not conceal from himself the perils that surrounded him. He cast his looks to heaven. He prepared to receive, as from the hand of the Lord, the blow that seemed destined to destroy him. His soul reposed at the foot of the throne of God. "What will happen?" said he. "I know not, and I care not to know, feeling sure that He who sitteth in heaven hath foreseen from all eternity the beginning, continuation, and end of all this affair. Wherever the blow may reach me, I fear not. The leaf of a tree does not fall to the ground without the will of our Father. How much less we ourselves. . . . It is a little matter to die for the Word, since this Word, which was made flesh for us, died itself at first. We shall arise with it, if we die with it, and passing where it has gone before, we shall arrive where it has arrived, and abide with it through all eternity."

Sometimes, however, Luther could not restrain the contempt inspired by the maneuvers of his enemies; we then find in him that mixture of sublimity and irony which characterized him. "I know nothing of Eck," said he, "except that he has arrived with a long beard, a long bull, and a long purse; but I laugh at his bull."

On the third of October he was informed of the papal brief. "It is come at last, this Roman bull," said he. "I despise and attack it as

impious, false, and in every respect worthy of Eck. It is Christ Himself who is condemned therein. No reasons are given in it: I am cited
to Rome, not to be heard, but that I may eat my words. I shall treat
it as a forgery although I believe it true. Oh, that Charles V would
act like a man! And that for the love of Christ he would attack these
wicked spirits! I rejoice in having to bear such ills for the best of
causes."

It was not in Saxony alone that the thunders of Rome had caused
alarm. A tranquil family of Swabia, one that had remained neutral,
found its peace suddenly disturbed. Bilibald Pirckheimer of Nuremberg, one of the most distinguished men of his day, early bereft of his
beloved wife Crescentia, was attached by the closest ties of affection
to his two young sisters, Charity, abbess of Saint Clare, and Clara,
a nun in the same convent. These two pious young women served
God in this seclusion, and divided their time between study, the care
of the poor, and meditation on eternal life. Bilibald, a statesman,
found some relaxation from his public cares in the correspondence he
kept with them. They were learned, read Latin, and studied the
Fathers; but there was nothing they loved so much as the Holy Scriptures. They had never had any other instructor than their brother.
Charity's letters bear the impress of a delicate and loving mind. Full
of the tenderest affection for Bilibald, she feared the least danger on
his account. Pirckheimer, to encourage this timid creature, composed
a dialogue between Charitas and Veritas (Charity and Truth), in
which Veritas strives to give confidence to Charitas. Nothing could
have been more touching, or better adapted to console a tender and
anxious heart.

What must have been Charity's alarm when she heard it rumored
that Bilibald's name was posted up under the pope's bull on the
gates of the cathedral beside that of Luther! In fact, Eck, impelled by
blind fury, had associated with Luther six of the most distinguished
men in Germany: Carlstadt, Feldkirchen, Egranus, who cared little
about it, Adelmann, Pirckheimer, and his friend Spengler, whom the
public functions with which they were invested rendered particularly
sensible to this indignity. Great was the agitation in the convent of
St. Claire. How could they endure Bilibald's shame? Nothing is so
painful to relatives as trials of this nature. The danger was truly
urgent. In vain did the city of Nuremberg, the Bishop of Bamberg,

and even the Dukes of Bavaria, intercede in favor of Spengler and Pirckheimer: these noble minded men were compelled to humble themselves before Dr. Eck, who made them feel all the importance of a Roman prothonotary, and compelled them to write a letter to the pope, in which they declared that they did not adhere to the doctrines of Luther, except so far as they were conformable with the Christian faith. At the same time Adelmann, with whom Eck had once disputed, as he rose from table, after a discussion on the great question then filling every mind, was forced to appear before the bishop of Augsburg, and clear himself upon oath from all participation in the Lutheran heresy. Yet vengeance and anger proved bad counselors to Eck. The names of Bilibald and of his friends brought discredit on the bull. The character of these eminent men, and their numerous connections, served to increase the general irritation.

Luther at first pretended to doubt the authenticity of the bull. "I hear," said he in the first of his writings on the subject, "that Eck has brought a new bull from Rome, which resembles him so much that it might be called *Doctor Eck*—so full is it of falsehood and error. He would have us believe that it is the pope's doing, while it is only a forgery." After having set forth the reasons for his doubts, Luther concluded by saying: "I must see with my own eyes the lead, the seal, the strings, the clause, the signature of the bull, in fact the whole of it, before I value all these clamors even at a straw!"

But no one doubted, not even Luther himself, that it really emanated from the pope. Germany waited to see what the reformer would do. Would he stand firm? All eyes were fixed on Wittenberg. Luther did not keep his contemporaries long in suspense. He replied with a terrible discharge of artillery, publishing on the fourth of November, 1520, his treatise, *Against the bull of Antichrist*.

"What errors, what deceptions," said he, "have crept among the poor people under the mantle of the Church and of the pretended infallibility of the pope! How many souls have thus been lost! how much blood spilled! how many murders committed! how many kingdoms devastated! . . .

"I can pretty clearly distinguish," said he ironically, a little further on, "between skill and malice, and I set no high value on a malice so unskillful. To burn books is so easy a matter that even children can do it; much more, then, the holy Father and his doctors. It would be well for them to show greater ability than that which is required to burn books. . . . Besides, let them destroy my works! I desire nothing better; for all my wish has been to lead souls to the Bible, so that they might afterwards neglect my writings. Great God! if we had a knowledge of Scripture, what need would there be of any books of mine? . . . I am free, by the grace of God, and bulls neither console nor alarm me. My strength and my consolation are in a place where neither men nor devils can reach them."

Luther's tenth proposition, condemned by the pope, was thus drawn up: "No man's sins are forgiven, unless he believes they are forgiven when the priest absolves him." By condemning this, the pope denied that faith was necessary in the sacrament. "They pretend," exclaimed Luther, "that we must not believe our sins are forgiven when we receive ablution from the priest. And what then ought we to do? . . . Listen, Christians, to this news from Rome. Condemnation is pronounced against that article of faith which we profess when we say: 'I believe in the Holy Ghost, the Holy Catholic Church, the forgiveness of sins.' If I were certain that the pope had really issued this bull at Rome, (and he had no doubt about it), and that it was not invented by Eck, that prince of liars, I should like to proclaim to all Christians that they ought to consider the pope as the real Antichrist spoken of in Scripture. And if he would not discontinue publicly to proscribe the faith of the Church, then . . . let even the temporal sword resist *him*, rather than the Turk! . . . For the Turk permits us to believe, but the pope forbids it."

While Luther was speaking thus forcibly, his dangers were increasing. His enemies' plan was to expel him from Wittenberg. If Luther and Wittenberg can be separated, Luther and Wittenberg will be ruined. One blow would thus free Rome both from the heretical doctor and the heretical university. Duke George, the Bishop of Merseburg, and the Leipzig theologians secretly applied themselves to the task. When Luther heard of it, he said: "I place the whole matter in God's hands." These intrigues were not entirely ineffectual: Adrian, Hebrew professor at Wittenberg, suddenly turned against the doctor. Great strength of faith was required to bear up against the blow inflicted by the court of Rome. There are some characters that will go along with the truth only to a certain point. Such was

Adrian. Alarmed by this condemnation, he quitted Wittenberg, and repaired to Dr. Eck at Leipzig.

The bull was beginning to be carried into execution. The voice of the pontiff of Christendom was not powerless. For ages, fire and sword had taught submission to his decrees. The burning piles were erected at his voice. Everything seemed to announce that a terrible catastrophe would shortly put an end to the daring revolt of this Augustine monk. In October, 1520, Luther's books were taken away from all the booksellers' shops in Ingolstadt, and put under seal. The Elector-archbishop of Mentz, moderate as he was, felt obliged to banish Ulrich of Hütten from his court, and to imprison his printer. The papal nuncios had besieged the youthful emperor: Charles declared that he would protect the old religion; and in some of his hereditary possessions scaffolds were erected, on which the writings of the heretic were to be reduced to ashes. Princes of the Church and councilors of state were present at these autos-da-fé.

Eck behaved with insolence, in every quarter threatening the great and the learned, and "filling everything with his smoke," as Erasmus says. "The pope," said Eck, "who has overthrown so many counts and dukes, will know how to bring these wretched grammarians to their senses. We must tell the Emperor Charles himself: 'You are but a cobbler.'" And his colleague Aleander, frowning like a schoolmaster who threatens his pupils with the rod, said to Erasmus: "We shall know how to get at this Duke Frederick, and teach him reason." Aleander was quite elated with his success. To hear the haughty nuncio talk, one would have thought that the fire which consumed Luther's books at Mentz was "the beginning of the end." These flames (said they one to another at Rome) will spread terror far and wide. It was so with many timid and superstitious minds; but even in the hereditary states of Charles, the only places in which they dared carry out the bull, the people, and sometimes the nobles, often replied to these pontifical demonstrations by ridicule or by expressions of indignation.

"Luther," said the doctors of Louvain, when they appeared before Margaret, governor of the Netherlands, "Luther is overturning the Christian faith." "Who is Luther?" asked the princess. "An ignorant monk." "Well, then," replied she, "do you who are so wise and so numerous write against him. The world will rather believe many wise men than an isolated and unlearned man." The Louvain doctors preferred an easier method. They erected a vast pile at their own expense. A great multitude thronged the place of execution. Students and citizens might be seen hastily traversing the crowd, bearing large volumes under their arms, which they threw into the flames. Their zeal edified both monks and doctors; but the trick was afterwards discovered—it was the *Sermones Discipuli, Tartaretus,* and other scholastic and papistical works, they had been throwing into the fire, instead of Luther's writings!

The Count of Nassau, viceroy of Holland, replied to the Dominicans who solicited permission to burn the doctor's books: "Go and preach the gospel with as much purity as Luther does, and you will have to complain of nobody." As the conversation turned upon the reformer at a banquet when the leading princes of the empire were present, the Lord of Ravenstein said aloud: "In the space of four centuries, a single Christian has ventured to raise his head, and him the pope wishes to put to death!"

Luther, sensible of the strength of his cause, remained tranquil in the midst of the tumult the bull had created. "If you did not press me so earnestly," said he to Spalatin, "I should keep silence, well knowing that the work must be accomplished by the counsel and power of God." The timid man was for speaking out, the strong desired to remain silent. Luther discerned a power that escaped the eyes of his friend. "Be of good cheer," continued the reformer. "It is Christ who has begun these things, and it is He that will accomplish them, whether I be banished or put to death. Jesus Christ is here present, and He who is within us is greater than he who is in the world."

Chapter 43

LUTHER FLINGS BULL TO THE FLAMES

Duty obliged Luther to speak, that the truth might be manifested to the world. Rome had struck the blow: he would show how he had received it. The pope had put him under the ban of the Church; he would put the pope under the ban of Christendom. Hitherto the pontiff's commands had been all-powerful; he would oppose sentence to sentence, and the world should know which had the greater strength. "I desire," said he, "to set my conscience at rest, by disclosing to all men the danger that threatens them"; and at the same time he prepared to make a fresh appeal to a general council. An appeal from the pope to a council was a crime. It is therefore by a new attack on the pontifical power that Luther presumes to justify those by which it had been preceded.

On the seventeenth of November, a notary and five witnesses, among whom was Cruciger, met at ten o'clock in the morning in one of the halls of the Augustine convent where Luther resided. There, the public officer (Sarctor of Eisleben) immediately proceeded to draw up the minute of his protest, the reformer in presence of these witnesses said with a solemn tone of voice:

"Considering that a general council of the Christian Church is above the pope, especially in matters of faith;

"Considering that the power of the pope is not above but inferior to Scripture; and that he has no right to slaughter the sheep of Christ's flock, and throw them into the jaws of the wolf;

"I, Martin Luther, an Augustine friar, doctor of the Holy Scriptures at Wittenberg, appeal by these presents, in behalf of myself and of those who are or who shall be with me, from the most holy pope Leo to a future general and Christian council.

"I appeal from the said pope, first, as an unjust, rash, and tyrannical judge, who condemns me without a hearing, and without giving
any reasons for his judgment; secondly, as a heretic and an apostate,
misled, hardened, and condemned by the Holy Scriptures, who commands me to deny that Christian faith is necessary in the use of the
sacraments; thirdly, as an enemy, an antichrist, an adversary, an
oppressor of Holy Scripture, who dares set his own words in opposition to the Word of God; fourthly, as a despiser, a calumniator, a
blasphemer of the holy Christian Church and of a free council, who
maintains that a council is nothing of itself.

"For this reason, with all humility, I entreat the most serene, most
illustrious, excellent, generous, noble, powerful, wise, and prudent
lords, namely, Charles emperor of Rome, the electors, princes, counts,
barons, knights, gentlemen, councilors, cities and communities of the
whole German nation, to adhere to my protest, and to resist with me
the antichristian conduct of the pope, for the glory of God, the
defense of the Church and of the Christian doctrine, and for the
maintenance of the free councils of Christendom; and Christ, our
Lord, will reward them bountifully by His everlasting grace. But if
there be any who scorn my prayer, and continue to obey that impious
man the pope, rather than God, I reject by these presents all responsibility, having faithfully warned their consciences, and I abandon
them, as well as the pope and his adherents, to the supreme judgment
of God."

Such was Luther's bill of divorce; such was his reply to the
pontiff's bull. A great seriousness pervaded the whole of this declaration. The charges he brought against the pope were of the gravest
description, and it was not heedlessly that he made them. This protest was circulated through Germany, and was sent to most of the
courts of Christendom.

Luther had, however, a still more daring step in reserve, although
that which he had just taken appeared the extreme of audacity. He
would in no respect be behindhand with Rome. The monk of Wittenberg would do all that the sovereign pontiff dared do. He gave
judgment for judgment; he raised pile for pile. The son of the
Medici and the son of the miner of Mansfeldt had gone down into
the lists; and in that desperate struggle, which shook the world, one
did not strike a blow which the other did not return. On the tenth

of December, a placard was posted on the walls of the University of Wittenberg, inviting the professors and students to be present at nine o'clock in the morning, at the Eastern gate, near the Holy Cross. A great number of doctors and students assembled, and Luther, walking at their head, conducted the procession to the appointed place. How many burning piles had Rome erected during the course of ages! Luther resolved to make a better application of the great Roman principle. It was only a few old papers that were about to be destroyed; and fire, thought he, is intended for that purpose. A scaffold had been prepared. One of the oldest masters of arts set fire to it. As the flames rose high into the air, the formidable Augustine, wearing his frock, approached the pile, carrying the Canon Law, the Decretals, the Clementines, the papal Extravagants, some writings by Eck and Emser, and the pope's bull. The Decretals having been first consumed, Luther held up the bull, and said: "Since thou hast vexed the Holy One of the Lord, may everlasting fire vex and consume thee!" He then flung it into the flames. Never had war been declared with greater energy and resolution. After this Luther calmly returned to the city, and the crowd of doctors, professors, and students, testifying their approval by loud cheers, re-entered Wittenberg with him. "The Decretals," said Luther, "resemble a body whose face is meek as a young maiden's, whose limbs are full of violence like those of a lion, and whose tail is filled with wiles like a serpent. Among all the laws of the popes, there is not one word that teaches us who is Jesus Christ." "My enemies," said he on another occasion, "have been able, by burning my books, to injure the cause of truth in the minds of the common people, and destroy their souls; for this reason, I consumed their books in return. A serious struggle has just begun. Hitherto I have been only playing with the pope. I began this work in God's name; it will be ended without me and by His might. If they dare burn my books, in which more of the gospel is to be found (I speak without boasting) than in all the books of the pope, I can with much greater reason burn theirs, in which no good can be discovered."

If Luther had commenced the Reformation in this manner, such a step would undoubtedly have entailed the most deplorable results. Fanaticism might have been aroused by it, and the Church thrown into a course of violence and disorder. But the reformer had prefaced his work by seriously explaining the lessons of Scripture. The foundations had been wisely laid. Now, a powerful blow, such as he had just given, might not only be without inconvenience, but even accelerate the moment in which Christendom would throw off its bonds.

Luther thus solemnly declared that he separated from the pope and his church. This might appear necessary to him after his letter to Leo X. He accepted the excommunication that Rome had pronounced. He showed the Christian world that there was now war unto death between him and the pope. He burned his ships upon the beach, and in so doing imposed on himself the necessity of advancing and of combating.

Luther had re-entered Wittenberg. On the morrow, the lecture room was more crowded than usual. All minds were in a state of excitement; a solemn feeling pervaded the assembly; they waited expecting an address from the doctor. He lectured on the Psalms—a course that he had commenced in the month of March in the preceding year. Having finished his explanations, he remained silent a few minutes, and then continued energetically: "Be on your guard against the laws and statutes of the pope. I have burned his Decretals, but this is merely child's play. It is time, and more than time, that the pope were burned; that is [explaining himself immediately], the see of Rome, with all its doctrines and abominations." Then assuming a more solemn tone, he added: "If you do not contend with your whole heart against the impious government of the pope, you cannot be saved. Whoever takes delight in the religion and worship of popery, will be eternally lost in the world to come."

"If you reject it," continued he, "you must expect to incur every kind of danger, and even to lose your lives. But it is far better to be exposed to such perils in this world than to keep silence! So long as I live, I will denounce to my brethren the sore and the plague of Babylon, for fear that many who are with us should fall back like the rest into the bottomless pit."

We can scarcely imagine the effect produced on the assembly by this discourse, the energy of which surprises us. "Not one among us," adds the candid student who has handed it down, "unless he be a senseless log of wood, doubts that this is truth pure and undefiled. It is evident to all believers that Dr. Luther is an angel of the living God, called to feed Christ's wandering sheep with the Word of God."

This discourse and the act by which it was crowned mark an important epoch in the Reformation. The dispute at Leipzig had inwardly detached Luther from the pope. But the moment in which he burned the bull was that in which he declared in the most formal manner his entire separation from the Bishop of Rome and his church, and his attachment to the universal Church, such as it had been founded by the apostles of Jesus Christ. At the Eastern gate of the city he lit up a fire that has been burning for three centuries.

"The pope," said he, "has three crowns; and for this reason: the first is against God, for he condemns religion; the second against the emperor, for he condemns the secular power; the third is against society, for he condemns marriage." When he was reproached with inveighing too severely against popery: "Alas!" replied he, "would that I could speak against it with a voice of thunder, and that each of my words were a thunderbolt!"

The firmness spread to Luther's friends and fellow countrymen. A whole nation rallied around him. The University of Wittenberg in particular grew daily more attached to this hero, to whom it was indebted for its importance and glory. Carlstadt then raised his voice against that "furious lion of Florence," which tore all human and divine laws, and trampled under foot the principles of eternal truth. Melancthon, also, about this time addressed the states of the empire in a writing characterized by the elegance and wisdom peculiar to this amiable man. It was in reply to a work attributed to Emser, but published under the name of Rhadinus, a Roman divine. Never had Luther himself spoken with greater energy; and yet there was a grace in Melancthon's language that won its way to every heart.

After showing by various passages of Scripture that the pope is not superior to the other bishops, "What is it," says he to the states of the empire, "that prevents our depriving the pope of the rights that we have given him? It matters little to Luther whether our riches, that is to say, the treasures of Europe, are sent to Rome; but the great cause of his grief and ours is, that the laws of the pontiffs and the reign of the pope not only endanger the souls of men but entirely ruin them. Each one may judge for himself whether it is becoming or not to contribute his money for the maintenance of Roman luxury; but to judge of religion and its sacred mysteries is not within the scope of the commonalty. It is on this ground, then, that Luther appeals to your faith and zeal, and that all pious men unite with him,—some aloud, others with sighs and groans. Call to remembrance that you are Christians, ye princes of a Christian people, and wrest these sad relics of Christendom from the tyranny of Antichrist. They are deceivers who pretend that you have no authority over priests. That same spirit which animated Jehu against the priests of Baal, urges you, by this precedent, to abolish the Roman superstition, which is much more horrible than the idolatry of Baal." Thus spoke the gentle Melancthon to the princes of Germany.

A few cries of alarm were heard among the friends of the Reformation. Timid minds inclined to extreme measures of conciliation, and Staupitz, in particular, expressed the deepest anxiety. "All this matter has been hitherto mere play," wrote Luther to him. "You have said yourself, that if God does not do these things, it is impossible they can be done. The tumult becomes more and more tumultuous, and I do not think it will ever be appeased, except at the last day." Thus did Luther encourage these affrighted minds.

"The papacy," continued he, "is no longer what it was yesterday and the day before. Let it excommunicate and burn my writings! . . . Let it slay me! . . . It shall not check that which is advancing. Some great portent is at our doors. I burned the bull, at first with great trembling, but now I experience more joy from it than from any action I have ever done in my life."

We involuntarily stop, and are delighted at reading in Luther's great soul the mighty future that was preparing. "O my father," said he to Staupitz in conclusion, "pray for the Word of God and for me. I am carried away and tossed about by these waves."

Thus war was declared on both sides. The combatants threw away their scabbards. The Word of God reasserted its rights, and deposed him who had taken the place of God Himself. Society was shaken. In every age selfish men are not wanting who would let human society sleep on in error and corruption; but wise men, although they may be timid, think differently. "We are well aware," said the gentle and moderate Melancthon, "that statesmen have a dread of innovation; and it must be acknowledged that, in this sad confusion which is denominated human life, controversies, and even those which proceed from the justest causes, are always tainted with some evil. It is requisite, however, that in the Church, the Word and commandments of God should be preferred to every mortal thing. God threatens with His eternal anger those who endeavor to suppress the truth. For this reason it was a duty, a Christian duty, incumbent on Luther, and from which he could not draw back, especially as he was a doctor of the Church of God, to reprove the pernicious errors which unprincipled men were disseminating with inconceivable effrontery. If controversy engenders many evils, as I see to my great sorrow," adds the wise Philip, "it is the fault of those who at first propagated error, and of those who, filled with diabolical hatred, are now seeking to uphold it."

But all men did not think thus. Luther was overwhelmed with reproaches: the storm burst upon him from every quarter of heaven. "He is quite alone," said some; "he is a teacher of novelties," said others.

"Who knows," replied Luther, sensible of the call that was addressed to him from on high, "if God has not chosen and called me, and if they ought not to fear that, by despising me, they despise God Himself? Moses was alone at the departure from Egypt; Elijah was alone in the reign of King Ahab; Isaiah alone in Jerusalem; Ezekiel alone in Babylon. . . . God never selected as a prophet either the high-priest or any other great personage; but ordinarily he chose low and despised men, once even the shepherd Amos. In every age, the saints have had to reprove the great, kings, princes, priests, and wise men, at the peril of their lives. . . . And was it not the same under the New Testament? Ambrose was alone in his time; after him, Jerome was alone; later still, Augustine was alone. . . . I do not say that I am a prophet; but I say that they ought to fear, precisely because I am alone and they are many. I am sure of this, that the Word of God is with me, and that it is not with them.

"It is said also," continued he, "that I put forward novelties, and that it is impossible to believe that all the other doctors were so long in error.

"No! I do not preach novelties. But I say that all Christian doctrines have been lost sight of by those who should have preserved them; namely, the learned and the bishops. Still I doubt not that the truth remained in a few hearts, even were it with infants in the cradle. Poor peasants and simple children now understand Jesus Christ better than the pope, the bishops, and the doctors.

"I am accused of rejecting the holy doctors of the Church. I do not reject them; but, since all these doctors endeavor to prove their writings by Holy Scripture, Scripture must be clearer and surer than they are. Who would think of proving an obscure passage by one that was obscurer still? Thus, then, necessity obliges me to have recourse to the Bible, as all the doctors have done, and to call upon it to pronounce upon their writings; for the Bible alone is lord and master.

"But (say they) men of power persecute him. Is it not clear, according to Scripture, that the persecutors are generally wrong, and the persecuted right; that the majority has ever been on the side of falsehood, and the minority on that of truth? Truth has in every age caused an outcry."

Luther next examines the propositions condemned in the bull as heretical, and demonstrates their truth by proofs drawn from the Holy Scriptures. With what vigor especially does he not maintain the doctrine of grace!

"What! before and without grace, nature can hate sin, avoid it, and repent of it; while even after grace is come, this nature loves sin, seeks it, longs for it, and never ceases contending against grace, and being angry with it; a state which all the saints mourn over continually! . . . It is as if men said that a strong tree, which I cannot bend by the exertion of all my strength, would bend of itself, as soon as I left it, or that a torrent which no dikes or barriers can check, would cease running as soon as it was left alone. . . . No! it is not by reflecting on sin and its consequences that we arrive at repentance; but it is by contemplating Jesus Christ, His wounds, and His infinite love. The knowledge of sin must proceed from repentance, and not repentance from the knowledge of sin. Knowledge is the fruit, repentance is the tree. In my country, the fruit grows on the tree; but it would appear that in the states of the holy Father the tree grows on the fruit."

The courageous doctor, although he protested, still retracted some of his propositions. Our astonishment will cease when we see the manner in which he did it. After quoting the four propositions on indulgences, condemned by the bull, he simply added:

"In submission to the holy and learned bull, I retract all that I have ever taught concerning indulgences. If my books have been justly burned, it is certainly because I made concessions to the pope on the doctrine of indulgences; for this reason I condemn them to the flames."

He retracts also with respect to John Huss: "I now say that not a few articles, but all the articles of John Huss are wholly Christian. By condemning John Huss, the pope has condemned the gospel. I have done five times more than he, and yet I much fear I have not done enough. Huss only said that a wicked pope is not a member of Christendom; but if Peter himself were now sitting at Rome, I should deny that he was pope by divine appointment.

Chapter 44

CORONATION OF CHARLES V

THE MIGHTY WORDS of the reformer sank deep into men's hearts, and contributed to their emancipation. The sparks that flew from every one of them were communicated to the whole nation. But still a greater question remained to be solved. Would the prince in whose states Luther was residing, favor or oppose the execution of the bull? The reply appeared doubtful. The elector, as well as all the princes of the empire, was at Aix-la-Chapelle. Here the crown of Charlemagne was placed on the head of the youngest but most powerful monarch of Christendom. An unusual pomp and magnificence were displayed in this ceremony. Charles V, Frederick, princes, ministers, and ambassadors, repaired immediately to Cologne. Aix-la-Chapelle, where the plague was raging, seemed to pour its whole population into this ancient city on the banks of the Rhine.

Among the crowd of strangers who thronged this city were the two papal nuncios, Marino Caraccioli and Jerome Aleander. Caraccioli, who had already been ambassador at the court of Maximilian, was commissioned to congratulate the new emperor, and to treat with him on political matters. But Rome had discovered that, to succeed in extinguishing the Reformation, it was necessary to send into Germany a nuncio specially accredited for this work, and of a character, skill, and activity fitted for its accomplishment. Aleander had been selected. This man, afterwards invested with the purple of the cardinals, would appear to have been descended from a family of respectable antiquity, and not from Jewish parents, as it has been said. The guilty Borgia invited him to Rome to be the secretary of his son —of that Caesar before whose murderous sword all Rome trembled.

"Like master, like man," says an historian, who thus compares Alean-der to Alexander VI. This judgment is in our opinion too severe.

After Borgia's death, Aleander applied to his studies with fresh ardor. His knowledge of Greek, Hebrew, Chaldee, and Arabic, gained him the reputation of being the most learned man of his age. He devoted himself with his whole heart to everything he under-took. The zeal with which he studied languages was by no means inferior to that which he exerted afterwards in persecuting the Reformation. Leo X attached him to his own service. Some historians speak of his epicurean manners; Romanists, of the integrity of his life. It would appear that he was fond of luxury, parade, and amuse-ment. "Aleander is living at Venice like a groveling epicurean, and in high dignity," wrote his old friend Erasmus concerning him. All are agreed in confessing that he was violent, prompt in his actions, full of ardor, indefatigable, imperious, and devoted to the pope. Eck was the fiery and intrepid champion of the schools: Aleander, the haughty ambassador of the proud court of the pontiffs. He seemed born to be a nuncio.

Rome had made every preparation to destroy the monk of Witten-berg. The duty of attending the coronation of the emperor, as the pope's representative, was a mere secondary mission in Aleander's eyes, yet calculated to facilitate his task by the respect it secured for him. But he was specially charged to prevail upon Charles tp crush the rising Reformation.

As soon as Aleander arrived at Cologne, he and Caraccioli set every wheel in motion to have Luther's heretical works burned throughout the empire, but particularly under the eyes of the Ger-man princes assembled in that city. Charles V had already given his consent with regard to his hereditary states. The agitation of men's minds was excessive. "Such measures," said they to Charles's min-isters and the nuncios themselves, "far from healing the wound, will only increase it. Do you imagine that Luther's doctrines are found only in those books that you are throwing into the fire? They are written, where you cannot reach them, in the hearts of the nation. . . . If you desire to employ force, it must be that of countless swords unsheathed to massacre a whole nation. A few logs of wood piled up to burn a few sheets of paper will effect nothing; and such arms are unbecoming the dignity of an emperor and of a pontiff."

The nuncio defended his burning piles: "These flames," said he, "are a sentence of condemnation written in colossal characters, equally intelligible to those who are near and those who are afar off,—to the learned and ignorant,—and even to those who cannot read."

But it was not in reality papers and books that the nuncio wanted: it was Luther himself. "These flames," resumed he, "are not sufficient to purify the infected air of Germany. If they terrify the simple, they do not punish the wicked. We require an imperial edict against Luther's person."

Aleander did not find the emperor so compliant when the reformer's life was in question, as when his books only were concerned.

"As I have but recently ascended the throne," said he to Aleander, "I cannot without the advice of my councilors and the consent of the princes strike such a blow as this against a numerous faction surrounded by so many powerful defenders. Let us first learn what our father, the Elector of Saxony, thinks of this matter; we shall afterwards see what reply we can make to the pope." The nuncios, therefore, proceeded to make trial of their artifices and eloquence on the elector.

The first Sunday in November, Frederick having attended mass in the Greyfriars' convent, Caraccioli and Aleander begged an audience. He received them in the presence of the Bishop of Trent and several of his councilors. Caraccioli first presented the papal brief. Of a milder disposition than Aleander, he thought it his duty to win over the prince by his flatteries, and began by eulogizing him and his ancestors. "It is to you," said he, "that we look for the salvation of the Roman Church and of the Roman Empire."

But the impetuous Aleander, wishing to come to the point, hastily stepped forward and interrupted his colleague, who modestly gave way: "It is to me and Eck," said he, "that this business of Martin's has been intrusted. Look at the imminent dangers into which this man is plunging the Christian republic. If we do not make haste to apply some remedy, the empire is ruined. Why were the Greeks destroyed, but because they abandoned the pope? You cannot remain united to Luther without separating from Jesus Christ. I require two things of you, in the name of his holiness: first, that you will burn Luther's writings; secondly, that you will inflict on him the punishment he deserves, or at least that you will deliver him up to the pope.

The emperor and all the princes of the empire have declared their willingness to accede to our request; you alone hesitate still."

Frederick replied, through the medium of the Bishop of Trent: "This matter is too serious to be settled now. We will let you know our determination."

The situation in which Frederick was placed was a difficult one. What part ought he to take? On the one side were the emperor, the princes of the empire, and the supreme pontiff of Christendom, whose authority the elector had as yet no idea of throwing off; on the other, a monk, a feeble monk; for it was he only that they demanded. Charles's reign had just commenced. Ought Frederick, the oldest and wisest of all the princes of Germany, to sow disunion in the empire? Besides, how could he renounce that ancient piety which led him even to the sepulcher of Christ?

Other voices were then heard. A young prince, who afterwards wore the electoral crown, and whose reign was signalized by the greatest misfortunes, John Frederick, son of Duke John, the elector's nephew, and Spalatin's pupil, a youth seventeen years of age, had received in his heart a sincere love for the truth, and was firmly attached to Luther. When he saw the reformer struck by the Roman anathemas, he embraced his cause with the warmth of a young Christian and of a youthful prince. He wrote to the doctor and to his uncle, nobly entreating the latter to protect Luther against his enemies. On the other hand, Spalatin, frequently it is true very dejected, Pontanus, and the other councilors who were with the elector at Cologne, represented to the prince that he ought not to abandon the reformer.

In the midst of this general agitation, one man alone remained tranquil: it was Luther. While it was sought to preserve him by the influence of the great, the monk in his cloister at Wittenberg thought that it was rather for him to save the great ones of this world. "If the gospel," wrote he to Spalatin, "was of a nature to be propagated or maintained by the powers of this world, God would not have intrusted it to fishermen. It belongs not to the princes and pontiffs of this age to defend the Word of God. They have enough to do to shelter themselves from the judgments of the Lord and of His Anointed. If I speak, it is in order that they may attain a knowledge of the divine Word, and that by it they may be saved."

Luther's expectation was not to be deceived. That faith, which a convent at Wittenberg concealed, exerted its power in the palaces of Cologne. Frederick's heart, shaken perhaps for a moment, grew stronger by degrees. He was indignant that the pope, in defiance of his earnest entreaties to examine into the matter in Germany, had decided upon it at Rome at the request of a personal enemy of the reformer, and that in his absence this opponent should have dared publish in Saxony a bull that threatened the existence of the university and the peace of his subjects. Besides, the elector was convinced that Luther was wronged. He shuddered at the thought of delivering an innocent man into the hands of his cruel enemies. Justice was the principle on which he acted, and not the wishes of the pope. He came to the determination of not giving way to Rome. On the fourth of November, Frederick's councilors (in the presence of the Bishop of Trent), replied that he had seen with much pain the advantage that Dr. Eck had taken of his absence to involve in the condemnation several persons who were not named in the bull; that since his departure from Saxony, it was possible that an immense number of learned and ignorant men, of the clergy and laity, might have united and adhered to the cause and appeal of Luther; that neither his imperial majesty nor any other person had shown that Luther's writings had been refuted, and that they deserved only to be thrown into the fire; and finally he requested that Doctor Luther should be furnished with a safe-conduct, so that he might appear before a tribunal of learned, pious, and impartial judges.

After this declaration, Aleander, Caraccioli, and their followers, retired to deliberate. This was the first time that the elector had publicly made known his intentions with regard to the reformer. The nuncios had expected quite a different course from him. Now (they had thought) that the elector, by maintaining his character for impartiality, would draw dangers upon himself the whole extent of which he could not foresee, he would not hesitate to sacrifice the monk. Thus Rome had reasoned. But her machinations were doomed to fail before a force that did not enter into her calculations —the love of justice and of truth.

Being re-admitted into the presence of the elector's councilors, the imperious Aleander said: "I should like to know what the elector would think, if one of his subjects should choose the king of France, or any other foreign prince, for judge." Seeing that nothing could shake the Saxon councilors, he said: "We will execute the bull; we will hunt out and burn Luther's writings. As for his person," added he, affecting a contemptuous indifference, "the pope is not desirous of staining his hands with the blood of the wretched man."

The news of the reply the elector had made to the nuncios having reached Wittenberg, Luther's friends were filled with joy. Melancthon and Amsdorff, especially, indulged in the most flattering anticipations. "The German nobility," said Melancthon, "will direct their course by the example of this prince, whom they follow in all things, as their Nestor. If Homer styled his hero the bulwark of the Greeks, why should we not call Frederick the bulwark of the Germans?"

The oracle of courts, the torch of the schools, the light of the world, Erasmus, was then at Cologne. Many princes had invited him, to be guided by his advice. At the epoch of the Reformation, Erasmus was the leader of the moderates; he imagined himself to be so, but without just cause; for when truth and error meet face to face, justice lies not between them. He was the chief of that philosophical and academical party which, for ages, had attempted to correct Rome, but had never succeeded; he was the representative of human wisdom, but that wisdom was too weak to batter down the high places of popery. It needed that wisdom from God, which men often call foolishness, but at whose voice mountains crumble into dust. Erasmus would neither throw himself into the arms of Luther, nor sit at the pope's feet. He hesitated, and often wavered between these two powers, attracted at one time towards Luther, then suddenly repelled in the direction of the pope. "The last spark of Christian piety seems nearly extinguished," said he in his letter to Albert; "and 'tis this which has moved Luther's heart. He cares neither for money nor honors." But this letter, which the imprudent Ulrich of Hütten had published, caused Erasmus so much annoyance, that he determined to be more cautious in the future. Besides, he was accused of being Luther's accomplice, and the latter offended him by his imprudent language. "Almost all good men are for Luther," said he; "but I see that we are tending towards a revolt. . . . I would not have my name joined with his. That would injure me without serving him." "So be it," replied Luther; "since that annoys you, I promise never to make mention either of you or of your friends." Such was the man to whom both the partisans and enemies of the Reformation applied.

The elector, knowing that the opinion of a man so much respected as Erasmus would have great influence, invited the illustrious Dutchman to visit him. Erasmus obeyed the order. This was on the fifth of December. Luther's friends could not see this step without secret uneasiness. The elector was standing before the fire, with Spalatin at his side, when Erasmus was introduced. "What is your opinion of Luther?" immediately demanded Frederick. The prudent Erasmus, surprised at so direct a question, sought at first to elude replying. He screwed up his mouth, bit his lips, and said not a word. Upon this the elector, raising his eyebrows, as was his custom when he spoke to people from whom he desired to have a precise answer (says Spalatin), fixed his piercing glance on Erasmus. The latter, not knowing how to escape from his confusion, said at last, in a half jocular tone: "Luther has committed two great faults: he has attacked the crown of the pope and the bellies of the monks." The elector smiled, but gave his visitor to understand that he was in earnest. Erasmus then laying aside his reserve, said: "The cause of all this dispute is the hatred of the monks toward learning, and the fear they have of seeing their tyranny destroyed. What weapons are they using against Luther?—clamor, cabals, hatred, and libels. The more virtuous a man is, and the greater his attachment to the gospel, the less is he opposed to Luther. The severity of the bull has aroused the indignation of all good men, and no one can recognize in it the gentleness of a vicar of Christ. Two only, out of all the universities, have condemned Luther; and they have only condemned him, not proved him in the wrong. Do not be deceived; the danger is greater than some men imagine. Arduous and difficult things are pressing on. To begin Charles's reign by so odious an act as Luther's imprisonment, would be a mournful omen. The world is thirsting for evangelical truth; let us beware of setting up a blamable opposition. Let this affair be inquired into by serious men—men of sound judgment; this will be the course most consistent with the dignity of the pope himself!"

Thus spoke Erasmus to the elector. Such frankness may perhaps astonish the reader; but Erasmus knew whom he was addressing.

Spalatin was delighted. He went out with Erasmus, and accompanied him as far as the house of the Count of Nuenar, provost of Cologne, where Erasmus was residing. The latter, in an impulse of frankness, on retiring to his study, took a pen, sat down, wrote a summary of what he had said to the elector, and forwarded the paper to Spalatin; but erelong the fear of Aleander came over the timid Erasmus; the courage that the presence of the elector and his chaplain had communicated to him had evaporated; and he begged Spalatin to return the too daring paper, for fear it should fall into the hands of the terrible nuncio. But it was too late.

The elector, feeling re-assured by the opinion of Erasmus, spoke to the emperor in a more decided tone. Erasmus himself endeavored, in nocturnal conferences, like those of Nicodemus of old, to persuade Charles's councilors that the whole business should be referred to impartial judges. Perhaps he hoped to be named arbitrator in a cause which threatened to divide the Christian world. His vanity would have been flattered by such an office. But at the same time, and not to lose his credit at Rome, he wrote the most submissive letters to Leo, who replied with a kindness that seriously mortified Aleander. From love to the pope, the nuncio would willingly have reprimanded the pope; for Erasmus communicated these letters from the pontiff, and they added still more to his credit. The nuncio complained of it to Rome. "Pretend not to notice this man's wickedness," was the reply; "prudence enjoins this: we must leave a door open to repentance."

Charles at the same time adopted a "see-saw" system, which consisted in flattering the pope and the elector, and appearing to incline by turns towards each, according to the necessities of the moment. One of his ministers, whom he had sent to Rome on Spanish business, arrived at the very moment that Doctor Eck was clamorously urging on Luther's condemnation. The wily ambassador immediately saw what advantage his master might derive from the Saxon monk. "Your Majesty," he wrote on the twelfth of May, 1520, to the emperor, who was still in Spain, "ought to go into Germany, and show some favor to a certain Martin Luther, who is at the Saxon court, and who by the sermons he preaches gives much anxiety to the court of Rome." Such from the commencement was the view Charles took of the Reformation. It was of no importance for him to know on which side truth or error might be found, or to discern what the great interests of the German nation required. His only question was what policy demanded, and what should be done to induce the pope to support the emperor. And this was well known at Rome. Charles's ministers intimated to Aleander the course their master intended following. "The emperor," said they, "will behave toward the pope as he behaves toward the emperor; for he has no desire to increase the power of his rivals, and particularly of the King of France." At these words the imperious nuncio gave way to his indignation. "What!" replied he, "supposing the pope should abandon the emperor, must the latter renounce his religion? If Charles wishes to avenge himself thus . . . let him tremble! this baseness will turn against himself." But the nuncio's threats did not shake the imperial diplomatists.

Chapter 45

LUTHER OVERWHELMED
WITH ACCLAMATION

IF THE legates of Rome failed with the mighty ones of this world, the inferior agents of the papacy succeeded in spreading trouble among the lower ranks. The army of Rome had heard the commands of its chief. Fanatical priests made use of the bull to alarm timid consciences, and well-meaning but un-enlightened ecclesiastics considered it a sacred duty to act in conformity with the instructions of the pope. It was in the confessional that Luther had commenced his struggle against Rome; it was in the confessional that Rome contended against the reformer's adherents. Scouted in the face of the world, the bull became powerful in these solitary tribunals. "Have you read Luther's works?" asked the confessors; "do you possess any of them? do you regard them as true or heretical?" And if the penitent hesitated to pronounce the anathema, the priest refused absolution. Many consciences were troubled. Great agitation prevailed among the people. This skillful maneuver bade fair to restore to the papal yoke the people already won over to the gospel. Rome congratulated herself on having in the thirteenth century erected this tribunal, so skillfully adapted to render the free consciences of Christians the slaves of the priests.

Luther was informed of these proceedings. What could he do, unaided, to baffle this maneuver? The Word, the Word proclaimed loudly and courageously, should be his weapon. The Word would find access to those alarmed consciences, those terrified souls, and give them strength. A powerful impulse was necessary, and Luther's voice made itself heard. He addressed the penitents with fearless dignity, with a noble disdain of all secondary considerations. "When you are asked whether you approve of my books or not," said he, "reply: 'You are a confessor, and not an inquisitor or a gaoler. My duty is to confess what my conscience leads me to say: yours is not to sound and extort the secrets of my heart. Give me absolution, and then dispute with Luther, with the pope, with whomsoever you please; but do not convert the sacrament of penance into a quarrel and a combat.' And if the confessor will not give way, then [continues Luther] I would rather go without absolution. Do not be uneasy: if man does not absolve you, God will. Rejoice that you are absolved by God's will. Rejoice that you are absolved by God Himself, and appear at the altar without fear. At the last judgment the priest will have to give an account of the absolution he has refused you. They may deprive us of the sacrament, but they cannot deprive us of the strength and grace that God has connected with it. It is not in their will or in their power, but in our own faith, that God has placed salvation. Dispense with the sacrament, altar, priest, and church; the Word of God, condemned by the bull, is more than all these things. The soul can do without the sacrament, but it cannot live without the Word. Christ, the true Bishop, will undertake to give you spiritual food."

Thus did Luther's voice sink into every alarmed conscience, and make its way into every troubled family, imparting courage and faith. But he was not content simply with defending himself; he felt that he ought to become the assailant. A Romish theologian, Ambrose Catharinus, had written against him. "I will stir up the bile of this Italian beast," said Luther. He kept his word. In his reply, he proved, by the revelations of Daniel and St. John, by the epistles of St. Paul, St. Peter, and St. Jude, that the reign of Antichrist, predicted and described in the Bible, was the papacy. I know for certain," said he in conclusion, "that our Lord Jesus Christ lives and reigns. Strong in this assurance, I should not fear many thousands of popes. May God visit us at last according to His infinite power, and show forth the day of the glorious advent of His Son, in which He will destroy the wicked one. And let all the people say, Amen!"

And all the people did say, Amen! A holy terror seized upon their souls. It was Antichrist whom they beheld seated on the pontifical throne. This new idea, which derived greater strength from the prophetic descriptions launched forth by Luther into the midst of his contemporaries, inflicted the most terrible blow on Rome. Faith in the Word of God took the place of that faith which the Church alone had hitherto enjoyed; and the power of the pope, long the object of adoration among nations, had now become a source of terror and detestation.

Germany replied to the papal bull by overwhelming Luther with its acclamations. Although the plague was raging at Wittenberg, new students arrived every day, and from four to six hundred disciples habitually sat at the feet of Luther and Melancthon in the halls of the academy. The two churches belonging to the convent and the city were not large enough for the crowd that hung listening to the reformer's words. The prior of the Augustines was fearful that these temples would fall under the weight of the hearers. But this spiritual movement was not confined within the walls of Wittenberg; it spread through Germany. Princes, nobles, and learned men from every quarter, addressed Luther in letters breathing consolation and faith. The doctor showed the chaplain more than thirty such.

The Margrave of Brandenburg came one day to Wittenberg, with several other princes, to visit Luther. "They desired to see the man," said the latter. In truth, all were desirous of seeing the man whose words had moved the people.

The enthusiasm of Luther's friends increased every day. "What unheard-of foolishness in Emser," exclaimed Melancthon, "who has ventured to measure himself with our Hercules, not perceiving the finger of God in every one of Luther's actions, as Pharaoh would not see it in those of Moses." The gentle Melancthon found words of power to arouse those who seemed to be retrograding or even remaining stationary. "Luther has stood up for the truth," wrote he to John Hess, "and yet you keep silence! . . . He is alive and prospering still, although the lion (Leo) is chafing and roaring. Bear in mind that it is impossible for Roman impiety to approve of the gospel. How can this age be wanting in men like Judas, Caiaphas, Pilate, or Herod? Arm yourself, therefore, with the weapons of God's Word against such adversaries."

All Luther's writings, his *Lord's Prayer,* and particularly his new edition of the *German Theology,* were perused with avidity. Reading clubs were formed for the circulation of his works among their members. His friends reprinted them, and got them distributed by hawkers. They were recommended from the pulpit. There was a general wish for a German Church; and the people demanded that no one should henceforth be invested with any ecclesiastical dignity, unless he could preach to the people in the vulgar tongue, and that in every quarter the bishops of Germany should resist the papal power.

Nor was this all: biting satires against the principal ultramontanists were circulated throughout the provinces of the empire. The opposition rallied all its forces around this new doctrine, which gave it precisely what it stood in need of . . . a justification in the eyes of religion. Most of the lawyers, wearied by the encroachments of the ecclesiastical tribunals, attached themselves to the reform, but the Humanists, in particular, eagerly embraced this party. Ulrich Hütten was indefatigable. He addressed letters to Luther, to the legates, and to the most considerable men in Germany. "I tell you, and repeat it, Marino," said he to the legate Caraccioli, in one of his works, "the darkness with which you had covered our eyes is dispersed; the gospel is preached; the truth is proclaimed; the absurdities of Rome are overwhelmed with contempt; your decrees languish and die; liberty is beginning to dawn upon us!"

Not content with employing prose, Hütten had recourse to verse also. He published his *Outcry on the Lutheran Conflagration*, in which, appealing to Jesus Christ, he beseeches Him to consume with the brightness of His countenance all who dared deny His authority. Above all, he set about writing in German. "Hitherto," said he, "I have written in Latin, a tongue not intelligible to everyone; but now I address all my fellow countrymen!" His German rhymes unveiled to the people the long and disgraceful catalog of the sins of the Roman court. But Hütten did not wish to confine himself to mere words; he was eager to interfere in the struggle with the sword; and he thought that the vengeance of God should be accomplished by the swords and halberds of those valiant warriors of whom Germany was so proud. Luther opposed this mad project: "I desire not," said he, "to fight for the gospel with violence and bloodshed. I have written to Hütten to this effect."

The celebrated painter, Lucas Cranach, published, under the title of the Passion of Christ and Antichrist, a set of engravings which represented on one side the glory and magnificence of the pope, and on the other the humiliation and sufferings of the Redeemer. The inscriptions were written by Luther. These engravings, designed with considerable skill, produced an effect beyond all previous example. The people withdrew from a Church that appeared in every respect so opposed to the spirit of its Founder. "This is a very good work for the laity," said Luther.

The students at Wittenberg, taking advantage of the license of the carnival, dressed up one of their number in a costume similar to the pope's, and paraded him with great pomp through the streets of the city, but in a manner somewhat too ludicrous, as Luther observes. When they reached the great square, they approached the river, and some, pretending a sudden attack, appeared desirous of throwing the pope into the water. But the pontiff, having little inclination for such a bath, took to his heels; his cardinals, bishops, and familiars imitated his example, dispersing into every quarter of the city. The students pursued them through the streets; and there was hardly a corner in Wittenberg where some Roman dignitary had not taken refuge from the shouts and laughter of the excited populace. "The enemy of Christ," says Luther, "who makes a mockery of kings, and even of Christ, richly deserves to be thus mocked himself." In our opinion he is wrong; truth is too beautiful to be thus profaned. She should combat without the aid of ballads, caricatures, and the masquerades of a carnival. Perhaps, without these popular demonstrations, her success would be less apparent; but it would be purer, and consequently more lasting. However that may be, the imprudent and prejudiced conduct of the Roman court had excited universal antipathy; and this very bull, by which the papacy thought to crush the whole reformation, was precisely that which made the revolt burst out in every quarter.

Yet the reformer did not find intoxication and triumph in everything. Behind that chariot in which he was dragged by a people excited and transported with admiration, there was not wanting the slave to remind him of his miserable state. Some of his friends seemed inclined to retrace their steps. Staupitz, whom he designated his father, appeared shaken. The pope had accused him, and Staupitz had declared his willingness to submit to the decision of his holiness.

"I fear," wrote Luther to him, "that by accepting the pope for judge, you seem to reject me and the doctrines I have maintained. If Christ loves you, He will constrain you to recall your letter. Christ is condemned, stripped, and blasphemed; this is a time not to fear, but to raise the voice. For this reason, while you exhort me to be humble, I exhort you to be proud; for you have too much humility, as I have too much pride. The world may call me proud, covetous, an adulterer, a murderer, antipope, one who is guilty of every crime. . . . What matters it! provided I am not reproached with having wickedly kept silence at the moment our Lord said with sorrow: 'I looked on my right hand, and beheld, but there was no man that would know me' (Ps. 142). The Word of Jesus Christ is a Word not of peace but of the sword. If you will not follow Jesus Christ, I will walk alone, will advance alone, and alone will I carry the fortress."

Thus Luther, like a general at the head of an army, surveyed the whole field of battle; and while his voice inspirited new soldiers to the conflict, he discovered those of his troops who appeared weak, and recalled them to the line of duty. His exhortations were heard everywhere. His letters rapidly followed each other. Three presses were constantly occupied in multiplying his writings. His words ran through the people, strengthening the alarmed consciences in the confessionals, upholding in the convents timid souls that were ready to faint, and maintaining the rights of truth in the palaces of princes.

"In the midst of the storms that assail me," wrote Luther to the elector, "I hoped to find peace at last. But now I see that this was the vain thought of a man. From day to day the waters rise, and already I am entirely surrounded by the waves. The tempest is bursting upon me with frightful tumult. In one hand I grasp the sword, with the other I build up the walls of Zion." His ancient ties were broken: the hand that had hurled against him the thunders of excommunication had snapped them asunder. "Excommunicated by the bull," said he, "I am absolved from the authority of the pope and of the monastic laws. Joyfully do I welcome this deliverance. But I shall neither quit the habit of my order nor the convent." And yet, amid this agitation, he did not lose sight of the dangers to which his soul was exposed in the struggle. He perceived the necessity of keeping a strict watch over himself. "You do well to pray for me," wrote he to Pellican, who resided at Basle. "I cannot devote sufficient time to holy exercises; life is a cross to me. You do well to exhort me to modesty: I feel its necessity; but I am not master of myself; I am carried away by mysterious impulses. I wish no one ill; but my enemies press on me with such fury, that I do not sufficiently guard against the temptations of Satan. Pray, then, for me!"

Thus the reformer and the Reformation were hastening towards the goal whither God called them. The agitation was gaining ground. The men who seemed likely to be most faithful to the hierarchy began to be moved. "Those very persons," says Eck ingenuously enough, "who hold the best livings and the richest prebends from the pope, remain as mute as fishes. Many of them even extol Luther as a man filled with the divine spirit, and style the defenders of the pope mere sophists and flatterers." The Church, apparently full of vigor, supported by treasures, governments, and armies, but in reality exhausted and feeble, having no love for God, no Christian life, no enthusiasm for the truth, found itself face to face with men who were simple but courageous, and who, knowing that God is with those who contend in behalf of His Word, had no doubt of victory. In every age it has been seen how great is the strength of an idea to penetrate the masses, to stir up nations, and to hurry them, if required, by thousands to the battlefield and to death.

But if so great be the strength of a human idea, *what power must not a heaven-descended idea possess, when God opens to it the gates of the heart!* The world has not often seen so much power at work; it was seen, however, in the early days of Christianity, and in the time of the Reformation; and it will be seen in the future. Men who despised the riches and grandeur of the world, who were contented with a life of sorrow and poverty, began to be moved in favor of all that was holiest upon earth—the doctrine of faith and of grace. All the religious elements were fermenting beneath the agitated surface of society; and the fire of enthusiasm urged souls to spring forward with courage into this new life, this epoch of renovation, which had just opened before them with so much grandeur, and toward which Providence was hurrying the nations.

Chapter 46

THE DIET OF WORMS

THE REFORMATION, commenced by the struggles of a humble spirit in the cell of a cloister at Erfurt, had continually increased. An obscure individual, bearing in his hand the Word of Life, had stood firm before the mighty ones of the world, and they had shaken before him. He had wielded this arm of the Word of God, first against Tetzel and his numerous army; and those greedy merchants, after a brief struggle, had fled away; he next employed it against the Roman legate at Augsburg; and the legate in amazement had allowed the prey to escape him; somewhat later with its aid he contended against the champions of learning in the halls of Leipzig; and the astonished theologians had beheld their syllogistic weapons shivered in their hands: and, lastly, with this single arm, he had opposed the pope, when the latter, disturbed in his slumbers, had risen on his throne to condemn the unfortunate monk with his thunders; and this same Word had paralyzed all the power of this head of Christendom. A final struggle remained to be undergone. The Word was destined to triumph over the emperor of the West, over the kings and the princes of the earth; and then, victorious over all the powers of the world, to uprise in the Church, and reign as the very Word of God.

The entire nation was agitated. Princes and nobles, knights and citizens, clergy and laity, town and country—all participated in the struggle. A mighty religious revolution, of which God Himself was the prime mover, but which was also deeply rooted in the lives of the people, threatened to overthrow the long-venerated chief of the Roman hierarchy. A new generation of a serious, deep, active, and energetic spirit, filled the universities, cities, courts, castles, rural districts, and frequently even the cloisters. A presentiment that a great transformation of society was at hand inspired all minds with holy enthusiasm. What would be the position of the emperor with regard to this movement of the age? And what would be the end of this formidable impulse by which all men were carried along? . . .

A solemn diet was about to be opened: this was the first assembly of the empire over which Charles was to preside. As Nuremberg, where it should have been held, in accordance with the Golden Bull, was suffering from the plague, it was convoked to meet at Worms on the sixth of January, 1521. Never before had so many princes met together in diet; each one was desirous of participating in this first act of the young emperor's government, and was pleased at the opportunity of displaying his power. The youthful landgrave Philip of Hesse, among others, who was afterwards to play so important a part in the Reformation, arrived at Worms, about the middle of January, with six hundred horsemen, among whom were warriors celebrated for their valor.

But a much stronger motive inclined the electors, dukes, archbishops, landgraves, margraves, counts, bishops, barons, and lords of the empire, as well as the deputies of the towns, and the ambassadors of the kings of Christendom, to throng with their brilliant trains the roads that led to Worms. It had been announced that, among other important matters to be laid before the diet, would be the nomination of a council of regency to govern the empire during Charles's absence, and the jurisdiction of the imperial chamber; but public attention was more particularly directed to another question, which the emperor had also mentioned in his letters of convocation: that of the Reformation. The great interests of worldly policy grew pale before the cause of the monk of Wittenberg. It was this which formed the principal topic of conversation between the noble personages who arrived at Worms.

Everything announced that the diet would be stormy and difficult to manage. Charles, who was hardly twenty years of age, was pale, of weak health, and yet a graceful horseman, able to break a lance like others of his time; his character was as yet undeveloped; his air was grave and melancholy, although of a kindly expression, and he had not hitherto shown any remarkable talent and did not appear to have adopted any decided line of conduct. The skillful and active William de Croi, lord of Chièvres, his high chamberlain, tutor, and prime minister, who enjoyed an absolute authority at court, died at Worms: numerous ambitions here met; many passions came into collision; the Spaniards and the Belgians vied with each other in their exertions to insinuate themselves into the councils of the young prince; the nuncios multiplied their intrigues; the German princes spoke out boldly. It might easily be foreseen that the underhanded practices of parties would have a principal share in the struggle.

But over all these scenes of agitation hovered a terrible will—the Roman papacy, which, inflexible as the destiny of the ancients, had unceasingly crushed for ages past every doctor, king, or people that had opposed its tyrannous progress. A letter written at Rome in the month of January, 1521, and by a Roman citizen, reveals its intentions. "If I am not mistaken, the only business in your diet will be this affair of Luther, which gives us much more trouble than the Turk himself. We shall endeavor to gain over the young emperor by threats, by prayers, and feigned caresses. We shall strive to win the Germans by extolling the piety of their ancestors, and by making them rich presents, and by lavish promises. If these methods do not succeed, we shall depose the emperor; absolve the people from their obedience; elect another (and he will be one that suits us) in his place; stir up civil war among the Germans, as we have just done in Spain; and summon to our aid the armies of the kings of France, England, and all the nations of the earth. Probity, honor, religion, Christ—we shall make light of all, provided our tyranny be saved." A very slight familiarity with history is sufficient to show that these words are a faithful description. It is identically what Rome has always done.

Charles opened the diet on January 28, 1521, the festival of Charlemagne. His mind was filled with the high importance of the imperial dignity. He said, in his opening discourse, that no monarchy could be compared with the Roman empire, to which nearly the whole world had submitted in former times; that unfortunately this empire was a mere shadow of what it once had been; but that, by means of his kingdoms and powerful alliances, he hoped to restore it to its ancient glory.

But numerous difficulties immediately presented themselves to the young emperor. What must he do, placed between the papal nuncio and the elector to whom he was indebted for his crown? How can he avoid displeasing either Aleander or Frederick? The first entreated the emperor to execute the pope's bull, and the second besought him to take no steps against the monk until he had been heard. Desirous of pleasing both parties, the young prince, during his stay at Oppenheim, had written to the elector to bring Luther with him to the diet, assuring him that no injustice should be shown to the reformer, that no violence should be used towards him, and that learned men should confer with him.

This letter, accompanied by others from Chièvres and the count of Nassau, threw the elector into great perplexity. At every moment the alliance of the pope might become necessary to the young and ambitious emperor, and then Luther's fate would be sealed. If Frederick should take the reformer to Worms, he might be leading him to the scaffold. And yet Charles's orders were precise. The elector commanded Spalatin to communicate to Luther the letters he had received. "The adversaries," said the chaplain to him, "are making every exertion to hasten on this affair."

Luther's friends were alarmed, but he himself did not tremble. His health was at that time very weak; but that was a trifling matter for him. "If I cannot go to Worms in good health," replied he to the elector, "I will be carried there, sick as I am. For if the emperor calls me, I cannot doubt that it is the call of God Himself. If they desire to use violence against me, and that is very probable (for it is not for their instruction that they order me to appear), I place the matter in the Lord's hands. He still lives and reigns who preserved the three young men in the burning fiery furnace. If He will not save me, my life is of little consequence. Let us only prevent the gospel from being exposed to the scorn of the wicked, and let us shed our blood for it, for fear they should triumph. It is not for me to decide whether my life or my death will contribute most to the salvation of all. Let us pray God that our young emperor may not begin his reign by imbruing his hands in my blood. I would rather perish by the sword of the Romans. You know what chastisement was inflicted on the Emperor Sigismund after the murder of John Huss. You may expect everything from me . . . except flight and recantation. Fly I cannot, and still less retract!"

Before receiving Luther's reply, the elector had formed his resolution. This prince, who was advancing in the knowledge of the gospel, now became more decided in his conduct. He felt that the conference at Worms would not have a favorable result. "It appears a difficult matter," he wrote in reply to Charles, "to bring Luther with me to Worms; I beseech you to relieve me from this anxiety. Furthermore, I have never been willing to defend his doctrine, but only to prevent his being condemned without a hearing. The legates, without waiting for your orders, have permitted themselves to take a step at once dishonoring Luther and myself; and I much fear that they thus provoked him to commit a very imprudent act which might expose him to great danger, if he were to appear before the diet." The elector alluded to the burning of the papal bull.

But the rumor of Luther's coming was already current through the city. Men eager for novelty were delighted; the emperor's courtiers were alarmed; but none showed greater indignation than the papal legate. On his journey, Aleander had been able to discover how far the gospel announced by Luther had found an echo in all classes of society. Men of letters, lawyers, nobles, the inferior clergy, the regular orders, and the people, were gained over to the Reformation. These friends of the new doctrine walked boldly with heads erect; their language was fearless and daring; an invincible terror froze the hearts of the partisans of Rome. The papacy was still standing, but its buttresses were tottering; for their ears already distinguished a presage of destruction, like that indistinct murmur heard ere the mountain falls and crumbles into dust.

Aleander on the road to Worms was frequently unable to contain himself. If he desired to dine or sleep in any place, neither the learned, the nobles, nor the priests, even among the supposed partisans of Rome, dared receive him; and the haughty nuncio was obliged to seek a lodging at inns of the lowest class. Aleander was frightened, and began to think his life in danger. Thus he arrived at Worms, and to his Roman fanaticism was then superadded the feeling of the personal indignities he had suffered. He immediately used every exertion to prevent the appearance of the bold and formidable Luther. "Would it not be scandalous," said he, "to behold laymen examining anew a cause already condemned by the pope?" Would not Luther's powerful eloquence, which had already committed such ravages, drag many princes and lords into inevitable destruction? Aleander pressed Charles closely: he entreated, threatened, and spoke as the nuncio of the head of the Church. Charles submitted, and wrote to the elector that the time accorded to Luther having already elapsed, this monk lay under the papal excommunication, so that, if he would not retract what he had written, Frederick must leave him behind at Wittenberg.

But this prince had already quitted Saxony without Luther. "I pray the Lord to be favorable to our elector," said Melancthon, as he saw him depart. "It is on him all our hopes for the restoration of Christendom repose. His enemies will dare anything, and they will not leave a stone unturned; but God will confound the councils of Ahithophel. As for us, let us maintain our share of the combat by our teaching and by our prayers." Luther was deeply grieved at being forbidden to come to Worms.

It was not sufficient for Aleander that Luther did not appear at Worms; he desired his condemnation. He was continually soliciting the princes, prelates, and different members of the diet; he accused the Augustine monk not only of disobedience and heresy, but even of sedition, rebellion, impiety, and blasphemy. But the very tone of his voice betrayed the passions by which he was animated. "He is moved by hatred and vengeance, much more than by zeal and piety," was the general remark; and frequent and violent as were his speeches, he made no converts to his sentiments. Some persons observed to him that the papal bull had only condemned Luther conditionally; others could not altogether conceal the joy they felt at this humiliation of the haughtiness of Rome. The emperor's ministers on the one hand, the ecclesiastical electors on the other, showed a marked coldness; the former, that the pope might feel the necessity of leaguing with their master; the latter that the pontiff might purchase their support at a dearer price. A feeling of Luther's innocence predominated in the assembly; and Aleander could not contain his indignation.

But the coldness of the diet made the legate less impatient than the coldness of Rome. Rome, which had had so much difficulty in taking a serious view of this quarrel of a "drunken German," did not imagine that the bull of the sovereign pontiff would be ineffectual to humiliate and reduce him. She had resumed all her carelessness, and sent neither additional bulls nor money. But how could they bring this matter to an issue without money? Rome must be awakened. Aleander uttered a cry of alarm. "Germany is separating from Rome," wrote he to the Cardinal de Medicis; "the princes are separating from the pope. Yet a little more delay, yet a little more negotiation, and hope will be gone. Money! money! or Germany is lost."

Rome awoke at this cry; the vassals of the papacy, casting off their torpor, hastily forged their redoubtable thunderbolts in the Vatican. The pope issued a new bull; and the excommunication, with which the heretical doctor had as yet been only threatened, was decidedly pronounced against him and all his adherents. Rome, by breaking the last tie which still bound him to the Church, augmented Luther's liberty, and with increased liberty came an increase of strength. Cursed by the pope, he took refuge with fresh love at the feet of Christ. Ejected from the outward courts of the temple, he felt more strongly that he was himself a temple in which dwelt the living God.

"It is a great glory," said he, "that we sinners, by believing in Christ, and by eating His flesh, possess within us, in all their vigor, His power, wisdom, and righteousness, as it is written, 'Whoso believeth in me, in him do I dwell.' Wonderful abiding place! marvelous tabernacle! far superior to that of Moses, and magnificently adorned within, with beautiful hangings, curtains of purple, and ornaments of gold; while without, as on the tabernacle that God commanded to be built in the desert of Sinai, we perceive nought but a rude covering of goats' hair and rams' skins. Often do Christians stumble, and, to look at them outwardly, they seem all weakness and reproach. But this matters not, for beneath this weakness and this foolishness dwells in secret a power that the world cannot know, and which yet overcometh the world; for Christ dwelleth in us. I have sometimes beheld Christians walking lamely and with great feebleness; but when came the hour of conflict or of appearing before the bar of the world, Christ suddenly stirred within them, and they became so strong and so resolute that Satan fled away frightened from before their face."

Such an hour would soon strike for Luther; and Christ, in whose communion he dwelt, could not fail him. Meantime Rome rejected him with violence. The reformer and all his partisans were accursed, whatever their rank and power, and dispossessed, with their inheritors, of all their honors and goods. Every faithful Christian, who valued the salvation of his soul was to flee at the sight of this accursed band. Wherever the heresy had been introduced, the priests were enjoined, on Sundays and festivals, at the hour when the churches were thronged with worshipers, to publish the excommunication with due solemnity. The altars were to be stripped of their ornaments and sacred vessels; the cross to be laid on the ground; twelve priests holding tapers in their hands were first to light them, and immediately dashing them violently to the earth, to extinguish them under their feet; the bishop was then to proclaim the condemnation of these unbelievers; all the bells were to be rung; the bishops and priests were to utter their anathemas and maledictions, and preach boldly against Luther and his adherents.

The excommunication had been published in Rome twenty-two days, but probably had not yet reached Germany, when Luther, being informed that there was some talk of summoning him to Worms, wrote a letter to the elector, drawn up in such a manner that Frederick might show it to the diet. Luther was desirous of correcting the erroneous ideas of the princes, and of frankly laying before this august tribunal the true nature of a cause so misunderstood. "I rejoice with all my heart, most serene Lord," says he, "that his imperial majesty desires to summon me before him touching this affair. I call Jesus Christ to witness that it is the cause of the whole German nation, of the universal Church, of the Christian world, nay, of God Himself . . . and not of an individual, especially such a one as myself. I am ready to go to Worms, provided I have a safe-conduct, and learned, pious, and impartial judges. I am ready to answer . . . for it is not from a presumptuous spirit, or with any view to personal advantage, that I have taught the doctrine with which I am reproached: it is in obedience to my conscience and to my oath as doctor of the Holy Scriptures: it is for the glory of God, for the salvation of the Christian Church, for the good of the German nation, and for the extirpation of so much superstition, abuse, evil, scandal, tyranny, blasphemy, and impiety."

This declaration, drawn up at a moment so solemn for Luther, merits particular attention. Such were the motives of his actions and the inward springs that led to the revival of Christian society. This is very different from the jealousy of a monk or the desire of marriage!

Chapter 47

ALEANDER'S ACTIVITY
AND ACCUSATIONS

B UT ALL THIS was of little consequence to politicians. However noble might have been the idea Charles had formed of the imperial dignity, Germany was not the center of his interests and of his policy. He understood neither the spirit nor the language of Germany. He was always a Duke of Burgundy who to many other scepters had united the first crown of Christendom. It was a remarkable circumstance that, at the moment of its most intimate transformation, Germany should elect a foreign prince, to whom the necessities and tendencies of the nation were but of secondary importance. Undoubtedly the emperor was not indifferent to the religious movement, but it had no meaning in his eyes, except so far as it threatened the pope.

War between Charles and Francis I was inevitable; the principal scene of that war would be Italy. The alliance of the pope became therefore daily more necessary to Charles's projects. He would have preferred detaching Frederick from Luther, or satisfying the pope without offending Frederick. Many of his courtiers manifested in the affair of the Augustine monk that disdainful coldness which politicians generally affect when there is any question of religion. "Let us avoid all extreme measures," said they. "Let us entangle Luther by negotiations, and reduce him to silence by some trifling concessions. The proper course is to stifle and not to fan the flame. If the monk falls into the net, we are victorious! By accepting a compromise, he will silence himself and ruin his cause. For form's sake we will decree certain exterior reforms; the elector will be satisfied: the pope will be gained; and matters will resume their ordinary course."

Such was the project formed by the emperor's confidants. The Wittenberg doctors seem to have divined this new policy. "They are trying to win men over secretly," said Melancthon, "and are working in the dark." Charles's confessor, John Glapio, a man of great weight, a skillful courtier, and a wily monk, took upon himself the execution of the scheme. Glapio possessed the full confidence of Charles; and this prince, imitating the Spanish customs in this particular, intrusted him almost entirely with the care of matters pertaining to religion. As soon as Charles had been named emperor, Leo hastened to win over Glapio by favors which the confessor very gratefully acknowledged. He could make no better return to the pontiff's generosity than by crushing this heresy, and he applied himself to the task.

Among the elector's councilors was Gregory Bruck, or Pontanus, the chancellor, a man of intelligence, decision, and courage, who was a better theological scholar than many doctors, and whose wisdom was capable of resisting the wiles of the monks in Charles's court. Glapio, knowing the chancellor's influence, requested an interview with him, and introducing himself as if he had been a friend of the reformer, said with an air of kindness: "I was filled with joy, in reading Luther's first writings; I thought him a vigorous tree, which had put forth goodly branches, and gave promise to the Church of the most precious fruit. Many people, it is true, have entertained the same views before his time; yet no one but himself has had the noble courage to publish the truth without fear. But when I read his book on the *Captivity of Babylon,* I felt like one overwhelmed with blows from head to foot. I do not think," added the monk, "that brother Martin will acknowledge himself to be the author of it; I do not find in it either his usual style or learning." After some discussion, the confessor continued: "Introduce me to the elector, and in your presence I will show him Luther's errors."

The chancellor replied that the business of the diet left his highness no leisure, and besides he did not mix himself up with this matter. The monk was vexed at seeing his demand rejected. "Nevertheless," continued the chancellor, "since you say there is no evil without a remedy, explain yourself."

Assuming a confidential air, the confessor replied: "The emperor earnestly desires to see a man like Luther reconciled with the

Church; for his books (previous to the publication of the treatise on the *Captivity of Babylon*) were rather agreeable to his majesty. . . . The irritation caused by the bull no doubt excited Luther to write the latter work. Let him then declare that he had no intention of troubling the repose of the Church, and the learned of every nation will side with him. Procure me an audience with his highness."

The chancellor went to Frederick. The elector well knew that any retractation whatsoever was impossible: "Tell the confessor," answered he, "that I cannot comply with his request; but continue your conference."

Glapio received this message with every demonstration of respect; and changing his line of attack, he said: "Let the elector name some confidential persons to deliberate on this affair."

The Chancellor—"The elector does not profess to defend Luther's cause."

The Confessor—"Let Luther deny that he wrote the *Captivity of Babylon*."

The Chancellor—"But the pope's bull condemns all his other writings."

The Confessor—"That is because of his obstinacy. If he disclaims this book, the pope in his omnipotence can easily pardon him. What hopes may we not entertain now that we have so excellent an emperor!"

Perceiving that these words had produced some effect on the chancellor, the monk hastily added: "Luther always desires to argue from the Bible. The Bible . . . it is like wax, you may stretch it and bend it as you please. I would undertake to find in the Bible opinions more extravagant even than Luther's. He is mistaken when he changes every word of Christ into a commandment." And then, wishing to act upon the fears of his hearer, he added: "What would be the result if today or tomorrow the emperor should have recourse to arms? Reflect upon this." He then permitted Pontanus to retire.

The confessor laid fresh snares. "A man might live ten years with him, and not know him at last," said Erasmus.

"What an excellent book is that of Luther's on *Christian Liberty*," said he to the chancellor, whom he saw again a few days after; "what wisdom! what talent! what wit! It is thus that a real scholar ought to write. . . . Let both sides choose men of irreproachable character, and let the pope and Luther refer the whole matter to their decision. There is no doubt that Luther would come off victorious on many points. I will speak about it to the emperor. Believe me, I do not mention these things solely on my own authority. I have told the emperor that God would chastise him and all the princes if the Church, which is the Spouse of Christ, be not cleansed from all the stains that defile her. I added, that God Himself had sent Luther, and commissioned him to reprove men for their offenses, employing him as a scourge to punish the sins of the world."

The chancellor, on hearing these words (which reflected the feelings of the age, and showed the opinion entertained of Luther even by his adversaries), could not forbear expressing his astonishment that his master was not treated with more respect. "There are daily consultations with the emperor on this affair," said he, "and yet the elector is not invited to them. He thinks it strange that the emperor, who is not a little indebted to him, should exclude him from his councils."

The Confessor—"I have been present only once at these deliberations, and then heard the emperor resist the solicitations of the nuncios. Five years hence it will be seen what Charles has done for the reformation of the Church."

"The elector," answered Pontanus, "is unacquainted with Luther's intentions. Let him be summoned and have a hearing."

The confessor replied with a deep sigh: "I call God to witness how ardently I desire to see the reformation of Christendom accomplished."

To protract the affair and to keep the reformer silent was all that Glapio proposed. In any case, Luther must not come to Worms. A dead man returning from the other world and appearing in the midst of the diet would have been less alarming to the nuncios, the monks, and all the papal host, than the presence of the Wittenberg doctor.

"How many days does it take to travel from Wittenberg to Worms?" asked the confessor with an assumed air of indifference; and then, begging Pontanus to present his most humble salutations to the elector, he retired.

Such were the maneuvers resorted to by the courtiers. They were disconcerted by the firmness of Pontanus. That just man was immovable as a rock during all these negotiations. The Roman monks themselves fell into the snares they had laid for their enemies. "The Christian," said Luther in his figurative language, "is like a bird tied near a trap. The wolves and foxes prowl round it, and spring on it to devour it; but they fall into the pit and perish, while the timid bird remains unhurt. It is thus the holy angels keep watch around us, and those devouring wolves, the hypocrites and persecutors, cannot harm us." Not only were the artifices of the confessor ineffectual, but his admissions still more confirmed Frederick in his opinion that Luther was right, and that it was his duty to protect him.

Men's hearts daily inclined more and more towards the gospel. A Dominican prior suggested that the emperor, the kings of France, Spain, England, Portugal, Hungary, and Poland, with the pope and the electors, should name representatives to whom the arrangement of this affair should be confided. "Never," said he, "has implicit reliance been placed on the pope alone." The public feeling became such that it seemed impossible to condemn Luther without having heard and confuted him.

Aleander grew uneasy, and displayed unusual energy. It was no longer against the elector and Luther alone that he had to contend. He beheld with horror the secret negotiations of the confessor, the proposition of the prior, the consent of Charles's ministers, the extreme coldness of Roman piety, even among the most devoted friends of the pontiff, "so that one might have thought," says Pallavicini, "that a torrent of iced water had gushed over them." He had at length received from Rome the money he had demanded; he held in his hand the energetic briefs addressed to the most powerful men in the empire. Fearing to see his prey escape, he felt that now was the time to strike a decisive blow. He forwarded the briefs, scattered the money profusely, and made the most alluring promises; "and, armed with this threefold weapon," says the historian, Cardinal Pallavicini, "he made a fresh attempt to bias the wavering assembly of electors in the pope's favor." But around the emperor in particular he laid his snares. He took advantage of the dissensions existing between the Belgian and Spanish ministers. He besieged the monarch unceasingly. All the partisans of Rome, awakened by his voice, solicited Charles. "Daily deliberations," wrote the elector to his brother John, "are held against Luther; they demand that he shall be placed under the ban of the pope and of the emperor; they endeavor to injure him in every way. Those who parade in their red hats, the Romans, with all their followers, display indefatigable zeal in this task."

Aleander did in reality urge the condemnation of the reformer with a violence that Luther characterizes as marvelous fury. The apostate nuncio, as Luther styles him, transported by anger beyond the bounds of prudence, one day exclaimed: "If you Germans pretend to shake off the yoke of obedience to Rome, we will act in such a manner that, exterminated by mutual slaughter, you shall perish in your own blood."

But such was not Luther's language. He asked nothing for himself. "Luther is ready," said Melancthon, "to purchase at the cost of his own life the glory and advancement of the gospel." But he trembled when he thought of the calamities that might be the consequence of his death. He pictured to himself a misled people revenging perhaps his martyrdom in the blood of his adversaries, and especially of the priests. He shrank from so dreadful a responsibility. "God," said he, "checks the fury of His enemies; but if it breaks forth . . . then shall we see a storm burst upon the priests like that which has devastated Bohemia. . . . My hands are clear of this, for I have earnestly entreated the German nobility to oppose the Romans by wisdom, and not by the sword. To make war upon the priests,—a class without courage or strength,—would be to fight against women and children."

Charles V could not resist the solicitations of the nuncio. His Belgian and Spanish devotion had been developed by his preceptor Adrian, who afterwards occupied the pontifical throne. The pope had addressed him in a brief, entreating him to give the power of law to the bull by an imperial edict. "To no purpose will God have invested you with the sword of the supreme power," said he, "if you do not employ it, not only against the infidels, but against the heretics also, who are far worse than they." Accordingly, one day in the beginning of February, at the moment when every one in Worms was making preparations for a splendid tournament, and when the emperor's tent was already erected, the princes who were arming themselves to take part in the brilliant show were summoned to the imperial palace. After listening to the reading of the papal bull, a stringent edict was

laid before them, enjoining its immediate execution. "If you can recommend any better course," added the emperor, following the usual
custom, "I am ready to hear you."

An animated debate immediately took place in the assembly. "This
monk," wrote a deputy from one of the free cities of Germany, "gives
us plenty of occupation. Some would like to crucify him, and I
think that he will not escape; only it is to be feared that he will rise
again the third day." The emperor had imagined that he would be
able to publish his edict without opposition from the states; but such
was not the case. Their minds were not prepared. It was necessary to
gain over the diet. "Convince this assembly," said the youthful monarch to the nuncio. This was all that Aleander desired; and he was
promised a hearing before the diet on the thirteenth of February.

The nuncio prepared for this solemn audience. This was an important duty, but Aleander was not unworthy of it. He was not only
ambassador from the sovereign pontiff, and surrounded with all the
splendor of his high office, but also one of the most eloquent men of
his age. The friends of the Reformation looked forward to this sitting
with apprehension. The elector, pretending indisposition, was not
present; but he gave some of his councilors orders to attend, and take
notes of the nuncio's speech.

When the day arrived, Aleander proceeded toward the assembly of
the princes. The feelings of all were excited; many were reminded of
Annas and Caiaphas going to Pilate's judgment-seat and calling for
the death of this Fellow who perverted the nation. "Just as the nuncio was about to cross the threshold, the usher of the diet," says Pallavicini, "approaching him rudely, thrust him back by a blow on the
breast." "He was a Lutheran at heart," adds the Romanist historian.
If this story be true, it shows no doubt an excess of passion; but at
the same time it furnishes us with a standard by which to measure
the influence that Luther's words had excited even in those who
guarded the doors of the imperial council. The proud Aleander, recovering himself with dignity, walked forward and entered the hall.
Never had Rome been called to make its defense before so august an
assembly. The nuncio placed before him the documents that he had
judged necessary, namely, Luther's works and the papal bulls; and, as
soon as the diet was silent, he began:

"Most august emperor, most mighty princes, most excellent deputies! I appear before you in defense of a cause for which my heart glows with the most ardent affection. It is to retain on my master's head that triple crown which you all adore: to maintain that papal throne for which I should be willing to deliver my body to the flames, if the monster that has engendered this growing heresy that I am now to combat, could be consumed at the same stake and mingle his ashes with mine.

"No! the whole difference between Luther and the pope does not turn on the papal interests. I have Luther's books before me, and a man only needs have eyes in his head to see that he attacks the holy doctrines of the Church. He teaches that those alone communicate worthily whose consciences are overwhelmed with sorrow and confusion because of their sins, and that no one is justified by baptism if he has not faith in the promise of which baptism is the pledge. He denies the necessity of works to obtain heavenly glory. He denies that we have the liberty and power of obeying the natural and divine law. He asserts that we sin of necessity in every one of our actions. Has the arsenal of hell ever sent forth weapons better calculated to break the bonds of decency? . . . He preaches in favor of the abolition of monastic vows. Can we imagine any greater sacrilegious impiety? . . . What desolation should we not witness in the world, were those who are the salt of the earth to throw aside their sacred garments, desert the temples that re-echo with their holy songs, and plunge into adultery, incest, and every vice! . . .

"Shall I enumerate all the crimes of this Augustine monk? He sins against the dead, for he denies purgatory; he sins against heaven, for he says that he would not believe even an angel from heaven; he sins against the Church, for he maintains that all Christians are priests; he sins against the saints, for he despises their venerable writings; he sins against councils, for he designates that of Constance an assembly of devils; he sins against the world, for he forbids the punishment of death to be inflicted on any who have not committed a deadly sin. Some of you may say that he is a pious man. . . . I have no desire to attack his private life, but only to remind this assembly that the devil often deceives people in the garb of truth."

Aleander, having spoken of the doctrine of purgatory condemned by the Council of Florence, laid at the emperor's feet the papal bull on this council. The Archbishop of Mentz took it up, and gave it to the Archbishops of Treves and Cologne, who received it reverently, and passed it to the other princes. The nuncio, after having thus accused Luther, proceeded to the second point, which was to justify Rome:

"At Rome, says Luther, the mouth promises one thing, the hand does another. If this were true, must we not come to the very opposite conclusion? If the ministers of a religion live conformably to its precepts, it is a sign that the religion is false. Such was the religion of the ancient Romans. . . . Such is that of Mahomet and of Luther himself; but such is not the religion which the Roman pontiffs teach us. Yes, the doctrine they profess condemns them all, as having committed faults; many, as guilty; and some (I will speak frankly) as criminal. . . . This doctrine exposes their actions to the censure of men during their lives, to the brand of history after their death. Now, I would ask what pleasure or profit could the popes have found in inventing such a religion?

"The Church, it may be said, was not governed by the Roman pontiffs in the primitive ages. What conclusion shall we draw from this? With such arguments we might persuade men to feed on acorns, and princesses to wash their own linen."

But his adversary—the reformer—was the special object of the nuncio's hatred. Boiling with indignation against those who said that he ought to be heard, he exclaimed: "Luther will not allow himself to be instructed by anyone. The pope had already summoned him to Rome, and he did not comply. Next, the pope cited him before the legate at Augsburg, and he did not appear until he had procured a safe-conduct, that is to say, after the legate's hands were tied, and his tongue alone was left unfettered. . . . Ah!" said Aleander, turning towards Charles V, "I entreat your imperial Majesty to do nothing that may lead to your reproach. Do not interfere in a matter which does not concern the laity. Perform your own duties! Let Luther's doctrines be interdicted by you throughout the length and breadth of the empire: let his writings be burned everywhere. Fear not! In Luther's errors there is enough to burn a hundred thousand heretics. . . . And what have we to fear? The multitude? . . . Its insolence makes it appear terrible before the conflict, but in the battle its cowardice renders it contemptible. Foreign princes? . . . But the King of France has forbidden the introduction of Luther's doctrines into his kingdom; and the King of England is preparing an assault with his own royal hand. You know what are the sentiments of Hungary, Italy, and Spain, and there is not one of your neighbors, however much he may hate you, who wishes you so much evil as this heresy would cause you. For if our adversary's house adjoins our own, we may desire it to be visited with fever, but not with the plague. . . .

"What are all these Lutherans? A crew of insolent pedagogues, corrupt priests, dissolute monks, ignorant lawyers, and degraded nobles, with the common people, whom they have misled and perverted. How far superior to them is the Catholic party in number, ability, and power! A unanimous decree from this illustrious assembly will enlighten the simple, warn the imprudent, decide the wavering, and give strength to the weak. . . . But if the axe is not laid to the roots of this poisonous tree, if the death-blow is not struck, then . . . I see it overshadowing the heritage of Jesus Christ with its branches, changing our Lord's vineyard into a gloomy forest, transforming the kingdom of God into a den of wild beasts, and reducing Germany to that frightful state of barbarism and desolation which has been brought upon Asia by the superstition of Mahomet."

The nuncio was silent. He had spoken for three hours. The enthusiasm of his language had produced a deep impression on the assembly. The princes looked at each other, excited and alarmed, says Cochloeus, and murmurs soon arose from every side against Luther and his partisans. If the eloquent Luther had been present; if he had been able to reply to this speech; if, profiting by the avowals extorted from the Roman nuncio by the recollection of his former master, the infamous Borgia, he had shown that these very arguments, intended to defend Rome, were of themselves its condemnation; if he had shown that the doctrine which proved its iniquity was not invented by him, as the orator said, but was that religion which Christ had given to the world, and which the Reformation was re-establishing in its primitive splendor; if he had presented a faithful and animated picture of the errors and abuses of the papacy, and had shown how the religion of Christ had been made an instrument of self-interest and rapacity; the effect of the nuncio's harangue would have been instantly nullified. But no one rose to speak. The assembly remained under the impression produced by this speech; and, agitated and transported, showed itself ready to extirpate Luther's heresy by force from the soil of the empire.

Nevertheless, it was a victory only in appearance. It was among the purposes of God that Rome should have an opportunity of displaying her reasons and her power. The greatest of her orators had spoken in the assembly of the princes; he had given utterance to all that Rome had to say. But it was precisely this last effort of the papacy that became a signal of defeat in the eyes of many who had listened to it. *If a bold confession is necessary for the triumph of truth, the surest means of destroying error is to make it known without reserve.* Neither the one nor the other, to run its course, should be concealed. The light tests all things.

Chapter 48

LUTHER REFLECTS ON THE MAGNIFICAT

A FEW DAYS were sufficient to dissipate the first impression, as it is ever the case when an orator conceals the emptiness of his arguments by high-sounding words.

The majority of the princes were ready to sacrifice Luther; but no one desired to immolate the rights of the empire and the grievances of the Germanic nation. They were very ready to give up the insolent monk who had dared speak so boldly; but they were the more resolved to make the pope feel the justice of a reform demanded by the chiefs of the nation. It was accordingly Luther's most determined personal enemy, Duke George of Saxony, who spoke with the greatest energy against the encroachments of Rome. The grandson of Podiebrad, king of Bohemia, although offended by the doctrine of grace preached by the reformer, had not yet lost the hope of a moral and ecclesiastical reform. The principal cause of his irritation against the monk of Wittenberg was, that by his despised doctrines he was spoiling the whole affair. But now, seeing the nuncio affecting to involve Luther and the reform of the Church in one and the same condemnation, George suddenly rose in the assembly of the princes, to the great astonishment of those who knew his hatred of the reformer.

"The diet," said he, "must not forget its grievances against the court of Rome. How many abuses have crept into our states! The annates, which the emperor granted voluntarily for the good of Christianity, now exacted as a due; the Roman courtiers daily inventing new regulations to monopolize, sell, and lease the ecclesiastical * benefices; a multitude of transgressions connived at; rich transgressors

* ecclesiastical living, especially a rectory, vicarage.

393

undeservedly tolerated, while those who have no money to purchase impunity are punished without mercy; the popes continually bestowing on their courtiers reversions and reserves, to the detriment of those to whom the benefices belong; the *commendams* of the abbeys and convents of Rome conferred on cardinals, bishops, and prelates, who appropriate their revenues, so that not a single monk is to be found in a convent where there should be twenty or thirty; stations multiplied to infinity, and stalls for the sale of indulgences set up in every street and public place of our cities—stalls of Saint Anthony, of the Holy Ghost, of Saint Hubert, of Saint Cornelius, of Saint Vincent, and so forth; companies purchasing at Rome the right to hold such markets, then buying permission of their bishop to display their wares, and squeezing and draining the pockets of the poor to obtain money; the indulgence, that ought only to be granted for the salvation of souls, and that should be earned by prayer, fasting, and works of charity, sold according to a tariff; the bishops' officials oppressing the lowly with penances for blasphemy, adultery, debauchery, and the violation of any festival, but not even reprimanding the clergy who commit similar crimes; penalties imposed on those who repent, and devised in such a manner that they soon fall again into the same error and give more money: . . .

"These are some of the abuses that cry out against Rome. All shame has been put aside, and their only object is . . . money! money! money! . . . so that the preachers who should teach the truth utter nothing but falsehoods, and are not only tolerated, but rewarded, because the greater their lies the greater their gain. It is from this foul spring that such tainted waters flow. Debauchery stretches out the hand to avarice. The officials invite women to their dwellings under various pretexts, and endeavor to seduce them, at one time by threats, at another by presents, or if they cannot succeed, they ruin their good fame. Alas! it is the scandal caused by the clergy that hurls so many poor souls into eternal condemnation! A general reform must be effected. An ecumenical council must be called to bring about this reform. For these reasons, most excellent princes and lords, I humbly entreat you to take this matter into your immediate consideration." Duke George then handed in a list of the grievances he had enumerated. This was some days after Aleander's speech. The important catalog was placed in the archives of Weimar.

Even Luther had not spoken with greater force against the abuses of Rome; but he had done something more. The duke pointed out the evil; Luther had pointed out both the cause and the remedy. He had demonstrated that the sinner receives the true indulgence, that which cometh from God, solely by faith in the grace and merits of Jesus Christ; and this simple but powerful doctrine had overthrown all the markets established by the priests. "How can a man become pious?" asked he one day. "A gray friar will reply, By putting on a gray hood and girding yourself with a cord. A Roman will answer, By hearing mass and by fasting. But a Christian will say, Faith in Christ alone justifies and saves. Before works, we must have eternal life. But when we are born again, and made children of God by the Word of Grace, then we perform good works."

The duke's speech was that of a secular prince; Luther's that of a reformer. The great evil in the Church had been its excessive devotion to outward forms, its having made of all its works and graces mere external and material things. The indulgences were the extreme point of this course; and that which was most spiritual in Christianity, namely, pardon, might be purchased in shops like any other commodity. Luther's great work consisted in employing this extreme degeneration of religion to lead men and the Church back to the primitive sources of life, and to restore the kingdom of the Holy Ghost in the sanctuary of the heart. Here, as often happens in other cases, the remedy was found in the disease itself, and the two extremes met. From that time forward, the Church, that for so many centuries had been developed externally in human ceremonies, observances, and practices, began to be developed internally in faith, hope and charity.

The duke's speech produced a proportionally greater impression, as his hostility to Luther was notorious. Other members of the diet brought forward their respective grievances, which received the support of the ecclesiastical princes themselves. "We have a pontiff who loves only the chase and his pleasures," said they; "the benefices of the German nation are given away at Rome to gunners, falconers, footmen, ass-drivers, grooms, guardsmen, and other people of this class, ignorant, inexperienced, and strangers to Germany."

The diet appointed a committee to draw up all these grievances; they were found to amount to a hundred and one. A deputation, composed of secular and ecclesiastical princes, presented the report to the emperor, conjuring him to see them rectified, as he had engaged to do in his capitulation. "What a loss of Christian souls!" said they to Charles V; "what depredations! what extortions, on account of the scandals by which the spiritual head of Christendom is surrounded! It is our duty to prevent the ruin and dishonor of our people. For this reason we most humbly but most urgently entreat you to order a general reformation, and to undertake its accomplishment." There was at that time in Christian society an unknown power operating on princes and people alike, a wisdom from on high, influencing even the adversaries of the Reformation, and preparing for that emancipation whose hour was come at last.

Charles could not be insensible to the remonstrances of the empire. Neither he nor the nuncio had expected them. Even his confessor had threatened him with the vengeance of heaven unless he reformed the Church. The emperor immediately recalled the edict commanding Luther's writings to be burned throughout the empire, and substituted a provisional order to deliver these books into the keeping of the magistrates.

This did not satisfy the assembly, which desired the appearance of the reformer. It is unjust, said his friends, to condemn Luther without a hearing, and without learning from his own mouth whether he is the author of the books that are ordered to be burned. His doctrines, said his adversaries, have so taken hold of men's minds, that it is impossible to check their progress, unless we hear them from himself. There shall be no discussion with him; and if he avows his writings, and refuses to retract them, then we will all with one accord, electors, princes, estates of the holy empire, true to the faith of our ancestors, assist your majesty to the utmost of our power in the execution of your decrees.

Aleander in alarm, and fearing everything from Luther's intrepidity and the ignorance of the princes, instantly strained every nerve to prevent the reformer's appearance. He went from Charles's ministers to the princes most favorably inclined to the pope, and from them to the emperor himself. "It is not lawful," said he, "to question what the sovereign pontiff has decreed. There shall be no discussion with Luther, you say; but," continued he, "will not the energy of this audacious man, the fire of his eyes, the eloquence of his language, and the mysterious spirit by which he is animated, be sufficient to excite a tumult? Already many adore him as a saint, and in every place you may see his portrait surrounded with a glory like that which encircles the heads of the blessed. . . . If you are resolved to summon him before you, at least do not put him under the protection of the public faith!" These latter words were meant either to intimidate Luther, or to prepare the way for his destruction.

The nuncio found an easy access to the noblemen of Spain. In Spain, as in Germany, the opposition to the Dominican inquisitors was national. The yoke of the inquisition, that had been thrown off for a time, had just been replaced on their necks by Charles. A numerous party in that peninsula sympathized with Luther; but it was not thus with the noblemen, who had discovered on the banks of the Rhine what they had hated beyond the Pyrenees. Inflamed with the most ardent fanaticism, they were impatient to destroy the new heresy. Frederick, duke of Alva, in particular, was transported with rage whenever he heard the Reformation mentioned. He would gladly have waded in the blood of all these sectarians. Luther was not yet summoned to appear, but already his mere name had powerfully stirred the lords of Christendom assembled at Worms.

The man who thus moved all the powers of the earth seemed alone undisturbed. The news from Worms was alarming. Luther's friends were terrified. "There remains nothing for us but your good wishes and prayers," wrote Melancthon to Spalatin. "Oh! that God would deign to purchase at the price of our blood the salvation of the Christian world!" But Luther was a stranger to fear; shutting himself up in his quiet cell, he there meditated on and applied to himself those words in which Mary, the mother of Jesus, exclaimed: "My soul doth magnify the Lord, and my spirit hath rejoiced in God my Saviour. For he that is mighty hath done to me great things; and holy is his name. He hath showed strength with his arm; he hath put down the mighty from their seats, and exalted them of low degree." These are some of the reflections that filled Luther's heart: " 'He that is mighty,' said Mary. What great boldness on the part of a young girl! With a single word she brands all the strong with weakness, all the mighty with feebleness, all the wise with folly, all those whose name is glorious upon earth with disgrace, and casts all strength, all might, all wisdom, and all glory at the feet of God. 'His arm,' continued she, meaning by this the power by which He acts of Himself, without the aid of any of His creatures: myterious power! . . . which is exerted in secrecy and in silence until His designs are accomplished. Destruction is at hand, when no one has seen it coming: relief is there, and no one had suspected it. He leaves His children in oppression and weakness, so that every man says, They are lost! . . . But it is then He is strongest; for where the strength of men ends, there begins the strength of God. Only let faith wait upon Him. . . . And, on the other hand, God permits His adversaries to increase in grandeur and power. He withdraws His support, and suffers them to be puffed up with their own. He empties them of His eternal wisdom, and lets them be filled with their own, which is but for a day. And while they are rising in the brightness of their power, the arm of the Lord is taken away, and their work vanishes as a bubble bursting in the air."

It was on the tenth of March, at the very moment when the imperial city of Worms was filled with dread at his name, that Luther concluded this explanation of the Magnificat.

He was not left quiet in his retreat. Spalatin, in conformity with the elector's orders, sent him a note of the articles which he would be required to retract. A retractation, after his refusal at Augsburg! . . . "Fear not," wrote he to Spalatin, "that I shall retract a single syllable, since their only argument is that my works are opposed to the rites of what they call the Church. If the Emperor Charles summons me only that I may retract, I shall reply that I will remain here, and it will be the same as if I had gone to Worms and returned. But, on the contrary, if the emperor summons me that I may be put to death as an enemy of the empire, I am ready to comply with his call; for, with the help of Christ, I will never desert the Word on the battlefield. I am well aware that these bloodthirsty men will never rest until they have taken away my life. Would that it were the papists alone that would be guilty of my blood!"

Chapter 49

THE SAFE-CONDUCT TO WORMS

At last the emperor made up his mind. Luther's appearance before the diet seemed the only means calculated to terminate an affair which engaged the attention of all the empire. Charles V resolved to summon him, but without granting him a safe-conduct. Here Frederick was again compelled to assume the character of a protector. The dangers by which the reformer was threatened were apparent to all. Luther's friends, says Cochloeus, feared that he would be delivered into the pope's hands, or that the emperor himself would put him to death, as undeserving, on account of his heresy, that any faith should be kept with him. On this question there was a long and violent debate between the princes. Struck at last by the extensive agitation then stirring up the people in every part of Germany, and fearing that during Luther's journey some unexpected tumult or dangerous commotion might burst forth in favor of the reformer, the princes thought the wisest course would be to tranquillize the public feelings on this subject; and not only the emperor, but also the Elector of Saxony, Duke George, and the Landgrave of Hesse, through whose territories he would have to pass, gave him each a safe-conduct.

On the sixth of March, 1521, Charles V signed the following summons addressed to Luther:

"Charles, by the grace of God Emperor elect of the Romans, always August, etc., etc.

"Honorable, well-beloved, and pious! We and the States of the Holy Empire here assembled, having resolved to institute an inquiry touching the doctrine and the books that thou hast lately published, have issued, for thy coming hither and thy return to a place of security, our safe-conduct and that of the empire, which we send thee herewith. Our sincere desire is, that thou shouldst prepare immediately for this journey, in order that within the space of the twenty-one days fixed by our safe-conduct, thou mayst without fail be present before us. Fear neither injustice nor violence. We will firmly abide by our aforesaid safe-conduct, and expect that thou wilt comply with our summons. In so doing, thou wilt obey our earnest wishes.

"Given in our imperial city of Worms, this sixth day of March, in the year of our Lord 1521, and the second of our reign. Charles."

"By order of my Lord and Emperor, witness my hand, Albert, Cardinal of Mentz, High-chancellor.

"Nicholas Zwil."

The safe-conduct contained in the letter was directed: "To the honorable, our well-beloved and pious Doctor Martin Luther, of the order of Augustines."

It began thus:

"We, Charles, the fifth of that name, by the grace of God Emperor elect of the Romans, always August, King of Spain, of the Two Sicilies, of Jerusalem, of Hungary, of Dalmatia, of Croatia, &c., Archduke of Austria, Duke of Burgundy, Count of Hapsburg, of Flanders, of the Tyrol," etc., etc.

Then the king of so many states, intimating that he had cited before him an Augustine monk named Luther, enjoined all princes, lords, magistrates, and others, to respect the safe-conduct which had been given him, under pain of the displeasure of the emperor and the empire.

Thus did the emperor confer the titles of "well-beloved, honorable, and pious," on a man whom the head of the Church had excommunicated. This document had been thus drawn up, purposely to remove all distrust from the mind of Luther and his friends. Gaspard Sturm was commissioned to bear this message to the reformer, and accompany him to Worms. The elector, apprehending some outburst of public indignation, wrote on the twelfth of March to the magistrates of Wittenberg to provide for the security of the emperor's officer, and to give him a guard, if it was judged necessary. The herald departed.

Thus were God's designs fulfilled. It was His will that this light, which He had kindled in the world, should be set upon a hill; and emperor, kings, and princes, immediately began to carry out His purpose without knowing it. It costs Him little to elevate what is lowliest. A single act of His power suffices to raise the humble native of Mansfeldt from an obscure cottage to the palaces in which kings were assembled. In His sight there is neither small nor great, and, in His good time, Charles and Luther met.

But would Luther comply with this citation? His best friends were doubtful about it. "Doctor Martin has been summoned here," wrote the elector to his brother on the twenty-fifth of March; "but I do not know whether he will come. I cannot augur any good from it." Three weeks later (on the sixteenth of April), this excellent prince, seeing the danger increase, wrote again to Duke John: "Orders against Luther are placarded on the walls. The cardinals and bishops are attacking him very harshly: God grant that all may turn out well! Would to God that I could procure him a favorable hearing!"

While these events were taking place at Worms and Wittenberg, the papacy redoubled its attacks. On the twenty-eighth of March (which was the Thursday before Easter), Rome re-echoed with a solemn excommunication. It was the custom to publish at that season the terrible bull, *In Coena Domini,* which is a long series of maledictions. On that day the approaches to the temple in which the sovereign pontiff was to officiate were early occupied with the papal guards, and by a crowd of people that had flocked together from all parts of Italy to receive the benediction of the holy father. Branches of laurel and myrtle decorated the open space in front of the cathedral; tapers were lighted on the balcony of the temple, and there the remonstrance was elevated. On a sudden the air re-echoed with the loud pealing of bells; the pope, wearing his pontifical robes, and borne in an armchair, appeared on the balcony; the people knelt down, all heads were uncovered, the colors were lowered, the soldiers grounded their arms, and a solemn silence prevailed. A few moments after, the pope slowly stretched out his hands, raised them toward heaven, and then as slowly bent them toward the earth, making the sign of the cross. Thrice he repeated this movement. Again the noise of bells reverberated through the air, proclaiming far and wide the benediction of the pontiff; some priests hastily stepped forward, each holding a lighted taper in his hand: these they reversed, and after tossing them violently, dashed them away, as if they were the flames of hell; the people were moved and agitated; and the words of malediction were hurled down from the roof of the temple.

As soon as Luther was informed of this excommunication, he published its tenor, with a few remarks written in that cutting style of which he was so great a master. Although this publication did not appear till sometime afterwards, we will insert in this place a few of its most striking features. We shall hear the high-priest of Christendom on the balcony of the cathedral, and the Wittenberg monk answering him from the farthest part of Germany.

There is something characteristic in the contrast of these two voices.

The Pope—"Leo, bishop. . . ."

Luther—"Bishop! . . . yes, as the wolf is a shepherd: for the bishop should exhort according to the doctrine of salvation, and not vomit forth imprecations and maledictions. . . ."

The Pope—"Servant of all the servants of God. . . ."

Luther—"At night, when we are drunk; but in the morning, our name is Leo, lord of all lords."

The Pope—"The Roman bishops, our predecessors, have been accustomed on this festival to employ the arms of righteousness. . . ."

Luther—"Which, according to your account, are excommunication and anathema; but, according to Saint Paul, long-suffering, kindness, and love" (II Cor. 6:6,7).

The Pope—"According to the duties of the apostolic office, and to maintain the purity of the Christian faith. . . ."

Luther—"That is to say, the temporal possessions of the pope."

The Pope—"And its unity, which consists in the union of the members with Christ, their Head,—and with His vicar. . . ."

Luther—"For Christ is not sufficient: we must have another besides."

The Pope—"To preserve the holy communion of believers, we follow the ancient custom, and excommunicate and curse, in the name of Almighty God, the Father. . . ."

Luther—"Of whom it is said: God sent not his Son into the world to condemn the world" (John 3:17).

The Pope—"The Son, and the Holy Ghost, and according to the power of the apostles Peter and Paul . . . and our own. . . ."

Luther—"Our own! says the ravenous wolf, as if the power of God was too weak without him."

The Pope—"We curse all heretics—Garasi, Patarins, Poor Men of Lyons, Arnoldists, Speronists, Passageni, Wycliffites, Hussites, Fraticelli. . . ."

Luther—"For they desired to possess the Holy Scriptures, and required the pope to be sober and preach the Word of God."

The Pope—"And Martin Luther, recently condemned by us for a similar heresy, as well as all his adherents, and all those whosoever they may be, who show him any countenance. . . ."

Luther—"I thank thee, most gracious pontiff, for condemning me along with all these Christians! It is very honorable for me to have my name proclaimed at Rome on a day of festival, in so glorious a manner, that it may run through the world in conjunction with the names of these humble confessors of Jesus Christ."

The Pope—"In like manner, we excommunicate and curse all pirates and corsairs. . . ."

Luther—"Who can be a greater corsair and pirate than he that robs souls, imprisons them, and puts them to death?"

The Pope—"Particularly those who navigate our seas. . . ."

Luther—"Our seas! . . . Saint Peter, our predecessor, said: 'Silver and gold have I none' (Acts 3:6); and Jesus Christ said: 'The kings of the Gentiles exercise lordship over them; but ye shall not be so' (Luke 22:25). But if a wagon filled with hay must give place on the road to a drunken man, how much more must Saint Peter and Christ Himself give way to the pope!"

The Pope—"In like manner we excommunicate and curse all those who falsify our bulls and our apostolical letters. . . ."

Luther—"But God's letters, the Holy Scriptures, all the world may condemn and burn."

The Pope—"In like manner we excommunicate and curse all those who intercept the provisions that are coming to the court of Rome. . . ."

Luther—"He snarls and snaps, like a dog that fears his bone will be taken from him."

The Pope—"In like manner we condemn and curse all those who withhold any judiciary dues, fruits, tithes, or revenues, belonging to the clergy. . . ."

Luther—"For Christ has said: 'If any man will sue thee at the law, and take away thy coat, let him have thy cloak also' (Matt. 5:40), and this is our commentary."

The Pope—"Whatever be their station, dignity, order, power, or rank; were they even bishops or kings. . . ."

Luther—"For there shall be false teachers among you, who despise dominion and speak evil of dignities, says Scripture" (Jude 8).

The Pope—"In like manner we condemn and curse all those who, in any manner whatsoever, do prejudice to the city of Rome, the kingdom of Sicily, the islands Sardinia and Corsica, the patrimony of St. Peter in Tuscany, the duchy of Spoleto, the marquisate of Ancona, the Campagna, the cities of Ferrara and Benevento, and all other cities or countries belonging to the Church of Rome."

Luther—"O Peter! thou poor fisherman! whence didst thou get Rome and all these kingdoms? all hail, Peter! king of Sicily! and fisherman at Bethsaida!"

The Pope—"We excommunicate and curse all chancellors, councilors, parliaments, procurators, governors, officials, bishops, and others, who oppose our letters of exhortation, invitation, prohibition, mediation, execution. . . ."

Luther—"For the holy see desires only to live in idleness, in magnificence, and debauchery; to command, to intimidate, to deceive, to lie, to dishonor, to seduce, and commit every kind of wickedness in peace and security. . . .

"O Lord, arise! it is not as the papists pretend; Thou hast not forsaken us; Thou has not turned away Thine eyes from us!"

Thus spoke Leo at Rome and Luther at Wittenberg.

The pontiff having ended these maledictions, the parchment on which they were written was torn in pieces, and the fragments scattered among the people. Immediately the crowd began to be violently agitated, each one rushing forward and endeavoring to seize a scrap of this terrible bull. These were the holy relics that the Papacy offered to its faithful adherents on the eve of the great day of grace and expiation. The multitude soon dispersed, and the neighborhood of the cathedral became deserted and silent as before. Let us return to Wittenberg.

Chapter 50

LUTHER'S COURAGE

IT WAS now the twenty-fourth of March. At last the imperial herald had passed the gate of the city in which Luther resided. Gaspard Sturm waited upon the doctor, and delivered the citation from Charles V. What a serious and solemn moment for the reformer! All his friends were in consternation. No prince, without excepting Frederick the Wise, had declared for him. The knights, it is true, had given utterance to their threats; but them the powerful Charles despised. Luther, however, was not discomposed. "The papists," said he, on seeing the anguish of his friends, "do not desire my coming to Worms, but my condemnation and my death. It matters not! Pray, not for me, but for the Word of God. Before my blood has grown cold, thousands of men in the whole world will have become responsible for having shed it! The most holy adversary of Christ, the father, the master, the generalissimo of murderers, insists on its being shed. So be it! Let God's will be done! Christ will give me His Spirit to overcome these ministers of error. I despise them during my life; I shall triumph over them by my death. They are busy at Worms about compelling me to retract; and this shall be my retractation: I said formerly that the pope was Christ's vicar; now I assert that he is our Lord's adversary, and the devil's apostle."

And when he was apprized that all the pulpits of the Franciscans and Dominicans resounded with imprecations and maledictions against him: "Oh! what deep joy do I feel!" exclaimed he. He knew that he had done God's will, and that God was with him; why then should he not set out with courage? Such purity of intention, such liberty of conscience, is a hidden but incalculable support that never fails the servant of God, and renders him more invulnerable than if protected by coats of mail and armed hosts.

At this time there arrived at Wittenberg a man who, like Melancthon, was destined to be Luther's friend all his life, and to comfort him at the moment of his departure. This was a priest named Bugenhagen, thirty-six years of age, who had fled from the severities which the Bishop of Camin and Prince Bogislas of Pomerania exercised on the friends of the gospel, whether ecclesiastics, citizens. or men of letters. Sprung from a senatorial family, and born at Wollin in Pomerania (whence he is commonly called Pomeranus), Bugenhagen had been teaching at Treptow from the age of twenty. The young eagerly crowded around him; the nobles and the learned emulated each other in courting his society. He diligently studied the Holy Scriptures, praying God to enlighten him.

One day towards the end of December, 1520, Luther's book on the *Captivity of Babylon* was put into his hands as he sat at supper with several of his friends. "Since the death of Christ," said he, after running his eye over the pages, "many heretics have infested the Church; but never yet has there existed such a pest as the author of this work." Having taken the book home and perused it two or three times, all his opinions were changed; truths quite new to him presented themselves to his mind; and on returning some days after to his colleagues, he said, "The whole world is lying in the thickest darkness. This man alone sees the light." Several priests, a deacon, and the abbot himself, received the pure doctrine of salvation, and in a short time, by the power of their preaching, they led their hearers (says an historian) back from human superstitions to the sole and effectual merits of Jesus Christ. Upon this a persecution broke out. Already the prisons re-echoed with the groans of many individuals. Bugenhagen fled from his enemies and arrived at Wittenberg. "He is suffering for love to the gospel," wrote Melancthon to the elector's chaplain. "Whither could he fly but to our asylum, and to the protection of our prince?"

But no one welcomed Bugenhagen with greater joy than Luther. It was agreed between them that, immediately after the departure of the reformer, Bugenhagen should begin to lecture on the Psalms. It was thus divine Providence led this able man to supply in some measure the place of him whom Wittenberg was about to lose. A year later, Bugenhagen was placed at the head of the Church in this city, over which he presided thirty-six years. Luther styled him in an especial manner "The Pastor."

Luther was about to depart. His friends, in alarm, thought that if God did not interpose in a miraculous manner, he was going to certain death. Melancthon, far removed from his native town, was attached to Luther with all the affection of a susceptible heart. "Luther," said he, "supplies the place of all my friends; he is greater and more admirable for me than I can dare express. You know how Alcibiades admired Socrates; but I admire Luther after another and in a Christian fashion." He then added these beautiful and sublime words: "Every time I contemplate Luther, I find him constantly greater than himself." Melancthon desired to accompany Luther in his dangers; but their common friends, and no doubt the doctor himself, opposed his wishes. Ought not Philip to fill his friend's place? And if the latter never returned, who then would there be to direct the work of the Reformation? "Would to God," said Melancthon, resigned, yet disappointed, "that he had allowed me to go with him."

The impetuous Amsdorff immediately declared that he would accompany the doctor. His strong mind found pleasure in confronting danger. His boldness permitted him to appear fearlessly before an assembly of kings. The elector had invited to Wittenberg, as professor of jurisprudence, Jerome Schurff, the son of a physician at St. Gall, a celebrated man, of gentle manners, and very intimate with Luther. "He has not yet been able to make up his mind," said Luther, "to pronounce sentence of death on a single malefactor." This timid man, however, desired to assist the doctor by his advice in this perilous journey. A young Danish student, Peter Suaven, who resided with Melancthon, and who afterwards became celebrated by his evangelical labors in Pomerania and Denmark, likewise declared that he would accompany his master. The youth of the schools were also to have their representative at the side of the champion of truth.

Germany was moved at the sight of the perils that menaced the representative of her people. She found a suitable voice to give utterance to her fears. Ulrich of Hütten shuddered at the thought of the blow about to be inflicted on his country. On the first of April, he wrote to Charles V himself: "Most excellent emperor," said he, "you are on the point of destroying us, and yourself with us. What is proposed to be done in this affair of Luther's except to ruin our liberty, and to crush your power? In the whole extent of the empire there is not a single upright man that does not feel the deepest interest in this matter. The priests alone set themselves against Luther, because he has opposed their enormous power, their scandalous luxury, and their depraved lives; and because he has pleaded, in behalf of Christ's doctrine, for the liberty of our country, and for purity of morals.

"O emperor! discard from your presence these Roman ambassadors, bishops, and cardinals, who desire to prevent all reformation. Did you not observe the sorrow of the people as they saw you arrive on the banks of the Rhine, surrounded by these red-hatted gentry . . . and by a band of priests, instead of a troop of valiant warriors? . . .

"Do not surrender your sovereign majesty to those who desire to trample it under foot! Have pity on us! Do not drag yourself and the whole nation into one common destruction. Lead us into the midst of the greatest dangers, under the weapons of your soldiers, to the cannon's mouth; let all nations conspire against us; let every army assail us, so that we can show our valor in the light of day, rather than that we should be thus vanquished and enslaved obscurely and stealthily, like women, without arms and unresisting. . . . Alas! we had hoped that you would deliver us from the Roman yoke, and overthrow the tyranny of the pontiff. God grant that the future may be better than these beginnings!

"All Germany falls prostrate at your feet; with tears we entreat and implore your help, your compassion, your faithfulness; and by the holy memory of those Germans who, when all the world was subject to Rome, did not bow their heads before that haughty city, we conjure you to save us, to restore us to ourselves, to deliver us from bondage, and take revenge upon our tyrants!"

Thus, by the mouth of this knight, spoke the German nation to Charles V. The emperor paid no attention to this epistle, and probably cast it disdainfully to one of his secretaries. He was a Fleming, and not a German. His personal aggrandizement, and not the liberty and glory of the empire, was the object of all his desires.

Chapter 51

LUTHER AT ERFURT

IT WAS now the second of April, and Luther had to take leave of his friends. After apprizing Lange, by a note, that he would spend the Thursday or Friday following at Erfurt, he bade farewell to his colleagues. Turning to Melancthon, he said with an agitated voice, "My dear brother, if I do not return, and should my enemies put me to death, continue to teach, and stand fast in the truth. Labor in my stead, since I shall no longer be able to labor for myself. If you survive, my death will be of little consequence." Then, committing his soul to the hands of Him who is faithful, Luther got into the car and quitted Wittenberg. The town council had provided him with a modest conveyance, covered with awning which the travelers could set up or remove at pleasure. The imperial herald, wearing his robe of office, and carrying the imperial eagle, rode on horseback in front, attended by his servant. Next came Luther, Schurff, Amsdorff, and Suaven, in the car. The friends of the gospel and the citizens of Wittenberg were deeply agitated,—and, invoking God's aid, burst into tears. Thus Luther began his journey.

He soon discovered that gloomy presentiments filled the hearts of all he met. At Leipzig no respect was shown him, and the magistrates merely presented him with the customary cup of wine. At Naumburg he met a priest, probably J. Langer, a man of stern zeal, who carefully preserved in his study a portrait of the famous Jerome Savonarola (who was burned at Florence in 1498 by order of Pope Alexander VI), as a martyr to freedom and morality, as well as a confessor of the evangelical truth. Having taken down the portrait of the Italian martyr, the priest approached Luther, and held it out to him in silence. The latter understood what this mute representation was intended to announce, but his intrepid soul remained firm. "It is Satan," said he, "that would prevent by these terrors, the confession of the truth in the assembly of princes, for he foresees the blow it would inflict upon his kingdom." "Stand firm in the truth thou hast proclaimed," said the priest solemnly, "and God will as firmly stand by thee!"

After passing the night at Naumburg, where he had been hospitably entertained by the burgomaster, Luther arrived the next evening at Weimar. He had hardly been a minute in the town, when he heard loud cries in every direction: it was the publication of his condemnation. "Look there!" said the herald. He turned his eyes, and with astonishment saw the imperial messengers going from street to street, everywhere posting up the emperor's edict commanding his writings to be deposited with the magistrates. Luther doubted not that this unseasonable display of severity was intended to frighten him from undertaking the journey, so that he might be condemned as having refused to appear. "Well, doctor! will you proceed?" asked the imperial herald in alarm. "Yes!" replied Luther; "although interdicted in every city, I shall go on! I rely upon the emperor's safe-conduct."

At Weimar, Luther had an audience with Duke John, brother to the Elector of Saxony, who resided there. The prince invited him to preach, and the reformer consented. Words of life flowed from the doctor's agitated heart. A Franciscan monk, who heard him, by name John Voit, the friend of Frederick Myconius, was then converted to the evangelical doctrine. He left his convent two years after, and somewhat later became professor of theology at Wittenberg. The duke furnished Luther with the money necessary for his journey.

From Weimar the reformer proceeded to Erfurt. This was the city of his youth. Here he hoped to meet his friend Lange, if, as he had written to him, he might enter the city without danger. When about three or four leagues from the city, near the village of Nora, he perceived a troop of horsemen approaching in the distance. Were they friends or enemies? In a short time Crotus, rector of the university, Eobanus Hesse, the friend of Melancthon, and whom Luther styled the prince of poets, Euricius Cordus, John Draco, and others, to the number of forty, senators, members of the university, and burghers, greeted him with acclamations. A multitude of the inhabitants of Erfurt thronged the road and gave utterance to their joy. All were eager to see the man who had dared to declare war against the pope.

A man about twenty-eight years old, by name Justus Jonas, had outstripped the cavalcade. Jonas, after studying the law at Erfurt, had been appointed rector of that university in 1519. Receiving the light of the gospel, which was shining forth in every direction, he had entertained the desire of becoming a theologian. "I think," wrote Erasmus to him, "that God has elected you as an instrument to make known the glory of His Son Jesus." All his thoughts were turned towards Wittenberg and Luther. Some years before, when he was as yet a law-student, Jonas, who was a man of active and enterprising spirit, had set out on foot in company with a few friends, and had crossed forests infested with robbers, and cities devastated by the plague, in order to visit Erasmus, who was then at Brussels. Should he hesitate to confront other dangers by accompanying the reformer to Worms? He earnestly begged the favor to be granted him, and Luther consented. Thus met these two doctors, who were to labor together all their lives in the task of renovating the Church. Divine Providence gathered round Luther men who were destined to be the light of Germany: Melancthon, Amsdorff, Bugenhagen, and Jonas. On his return from Worms, Jonas was elected provost of the Church of Wittenberg, and doctor of divinity. "Jonas," said Luther, "is a man whose life is worth purchasing at a large price, in order to retain him on earth." No preacher ever surpassed him in his power of captivating his hearers. "Pomeranus is a critic," said Melanchthon; "I am a dialectician, Jonas is an orator. Words flow from his lips with admirable beauty, and his eloquence is full of energy. But Luther surpasses us all." It appears that about this time a friend of Luther's childhood, and also one of his brothers increased the number of his escort.

The deputation from Erfurt had turned their horses's heads. Luther's carriage entered within the walls of the city, surrounded by horsemen and pedestrians. At the gate, in the public places, in the streets where the poor monk had so often begged his bread, the crowd of spectators was immense. Luther alighted at the convent of the Augustines, where the gospel had first given consolation to his heart.

Lange joyfully received him; Usingen, and some of the elder fathers, showed him much coldness. There was a great desire to hear him preach; the pulpit had been forbidden him, but the herald, sharing the enthusiasm of those about him, gave his consent.

On the Sunday after Easter the church of the Augustines of Erfurt was filled to overflowing. This friar, who had been accustomed in former times to unclose the doors and sweep out the church, went up into the pulpit, and opening the Bible, read these words: "Peace be unto you. And when he had so said, he showed unto them his hands and his side" (John 20:19,20). "Philosophers, doctors, and writers," said he, "have endeavored to teach men the way to obtain everlasting life, and they have not succeeded. I will now tell it to you."

This has been the great question in every age; accordingly Luther's hearers redoubled their attention.

"There are two kinds of works," continued the reformer: "works not of ourselves, and these are good; our own works, and they are of little worth. One man builds a church; another goes on a pilgrimage to St. Jago of Compostella or St. Peter's; a third fasts, prays, takes the cowl, and goes barefoot; another does something else. All these works are nothingness, and will come to nought; for our own works have no virtue in them. But I am now going to tell you what is the true work. God has raised one man from the dead, the Lord Jesus Christ, that He might destroy death, extirpate sin, and shut the gates of hell. This is the work of salvation. The devil thought he had the Lord in his power, when he saw Him hanging between two thieves, suffering the most disgraceful martyrdom, accursed of God and of men. . . . But the Godhead displayed its power, and destroyed death, sin, and hell. . . .

"Christ has vanquished! this is the joyful news! and we are saved by His work, and not by our own. The pope says differently: but I affirm that the holy mother of God herself was saved, neither by her virginity, nor by her maternity, nor by her purity, nor by her works, but solely by the instrumentality of faith and the works of God."

While Luther was speaking, a sudden noise was heard; one of the galleries cracked, and it was feared that it would break down under the pressure of the crowd. This incident occasioned a great disturbance in the congregation. Some ran out from their places; others stood motionless through fright. The preacher stopped a moment, and then stretching out his hand, exclaimed with a loud voice: "Fear nothing! there is no danger: it is thus the devil seeks to hinder me from proclaiming the gospel, but he will not succeed." At these words, those who were flying halted in astonishment and surprise; the assembly again became calm, and Luther, undisturbed by these efforts of the devil, continued thus: "You say a great deal about faith (you may perhaps reply to me): show us how we may obtain it. Well, I will teach you. Our Lord Jesus Christ said: 'Peace be unto you! behold my hands,' that is to say, Behold, O man! it is I, I alone, who have taken away thy sin, and ransomed thee; and now thou hast peace, saith the Lord.

"I have not eaten of the fruit of the forbidden tree," resumed Luther, "nor have you; but we have all partaken of the sin that Adam has transmitted to us, and have gone astray. In like manner, I have not suffered on the cross, neither have you; but Christ has suffered for us; we are justified by God's work, and not by our own. . . . I am (saith the Lord) thy righteousness and thy redemption.

"Let us believe in the gospel and in the epistles of St. Paul, and not in the letters and decretals of the popes."

After proclaiming faith as the cause of the sinner's justification, Luther proclaims works as the consequence and manifestation of salvation.

"Since God has saved us," continued he, "let us so order our works that they may be acceptable to Him. Art thou rich? let thy goods administer to the necessities of the poor! Art thou poor? let thy services be acceptable to the rich! If thy labor is useful to thyself alone, the service that thou pretendest to render unto God is a lie."

In the whole of this sermon there is not a word about himself; not a single allusion to the circumstances in which he is placed: nothing about Worms, or Charles, or the nuncios; he preaches Christ, and Christ only. At this moment, when the eyes of all the world are upon him, he has no thought of himself: this stamps him as a true servant of God.

Luther departed from Erfurt, and passed through Gotha, where he preached another sermon. Myconius adds, that as the people were leaving the church, the devil threw down from the pediment some stones that had not moved for two hundred years. The doctor slept at the convent of the Benedictines at Reinhardsbrunn, and from thence proceeded to Eisenach, where he felt indisposed. Amsdorff, Jonas, Schurff, and all his friends were alarmed. He was bled; they tended him with the most affectionate anxiety, and John Oswald, the schultheiss of the town, brought him a cordial. Luther having drunk a portion fell asleep, and reinvigorated by this repose he was enabled to continue his journey on the following morning.

His progress resembled that of a victorious general. The people gazed with emotion on this daring man, who was going to lay his head at the feet of the emperor and the empire. An immense crowd flocked eagerly around him. "Ah!" said some, "there are so many bishops and cardinals at Worms! . . . They will burn you, and reduce your body to ashes, as they did with John Huss." But nothing frightened the monk. "Though they should kindle a fire," said he, "all the way from Worms to Wittenberg, the flames of which reached to heaven, I would walk through it in the name of the Lord—I would appear before them—I would enter the jaws of this Behemoth, and break his teeth, confessing the Lord Jesus Christ."

One day, just as he had entered an inn, and the crowd was pressing around him as usual, an officer advanced and said: "Are you the man that has undertaken to reform the papacy? How can you hope to succeed?"—"Yes," replied Luther, "I am the man; I trust in God Almighty, whose Word and commandment I have before me." The officer was touched, and looking at him with a milder air, said: "My dear friend, what you say is a great matter. I am the servant of Charles, but your Master is greater than mine. He will aid and preserve you." Such was the impression produced by Luther. Even his enemies were struck at the sight of the multitudes that thronged around him; but they depicted his journey in far different colors. The doctor arrived at Frankfurt on Sunday the fourteenth of April.

Chapter 52

LUTHER APPEARS BEFORE THE DIET OF WORMS

ALREADY the news of Luther's journey had reached Worms. The friends of the pope had thought that he would not obey the emperor's summons. Albert, cardinal archbishop of Mentz would have given anything to stop him on the road. New intrigues were put in motion to attain this result.

As soon as Luther arrived in Frankfurt, he took some repose, and afterwards gave intelligence of his approach to Spalatin, who was then at Worms with the elector. This was the only letter he wrote during his journey. "I am coming," said he, "although Satan endeavored to stop me on the road by sickness. Since I left Eisenach I have been in a feeble state, and am still as I never was before. I learn that Charles has published an edict to frighten me. But Christ lives, and I shall enter Worms in despite of all the gates of hell, and of the powers of the air. Have the goodness, therefore, to prepare a lodging for me."

The next day Luther went to visit the school of the learned William Nesse, a celebrated geographer of that period. "Apply to the study of the Bible, and to the investigation of truth," said he to the pupils. And then putting his right hand on one of the children, and his left upon another, he pronounced a benediction on the whole school.

If Luther blessed the young, he was also the hope of the aged. Catherine of Holzhausen, a widow far advanced in years, and who served God, approached him and said: "My parents told me that

God would raise up a man who should oppose the papal vanities and preserve His Word. I hope thou art that man, and I pray for the grace and Holy Spirt of God upon thy work."

These were far from being the general sentiments in Frankfurt. John Cochloeus, dean of the church of Our Lady, was one of the most devoted partisans of the papacy. He could not repress his apprehensions when he saw Luther pass through Frankfurt on his road to Worms. He thought that the Church had need of devoted champions. It is true no one had summoned him; but that mattered not. Luther had scarcely quitted the city, when Cochloeus followed him, ready (said he) to sacrifice his life in defense of the honor of the Church.

The alarm was universal in the camp of the pope's friends. The heresiarch was arriving; every day and every hour brought him nearer to Worms. If he entered, all might perhaps be lost. Archbishop Albert, the confessor Glapio, and the politicians who surrounded the emperor, were confounded. How could they hinder this monk from coming? To carry him off by force was impossible, for he had Charles's safe-conduct. Stratagem alone could stop him. These artful men immediately conceived the following plan. The emperor's confessor and his head chamberlain, Paul of Amsdorff, hastily quitted Worms. They directed their course towards the castle of Ebernburg, about ten leagues from the city, the residence of Francis of Sickingen —that knight who had offered an asylum to Luther. Bucer, a youthful Dominican, chaplain to the elector-palatine, and who had been converted to the evangelical doctrine by the disputation at Heidelberg, had taken refuge in this "resting place of the righteous." The knight, who did not understand much about religious matters, was easily deceived, and the character of the palatine chaplain facilitated the confessor's designs. In fact, Bucer was a man of pacific character. Making a distinction between fundamental and secondary points, he thought that the latter might be given up for the sake of unity and peace.

The chamberlain and Charles's confessor began their attack. They gave Sickingen and Bucer to understand that Luther was lost if he entered Worms. They declared that the emperor was ready to send a few learned men to Ebernburg to confer with the doctor. "Both parties," said they to the knight, "will place themselves under your protection." "We agree with Luther on all essential points," said they to Bucer; "it is now a question of merely secondary matters, and you shall mediate between us." The knight and the doctor were staggered. The confessor and the chamberlain continued: "Luther's invitation must proceed from you," said they to Sickingen, "and Bucer shall carry it to him." Everything was arranged according to their wishes. Only let the too credulous Luther go to Ebernburg, his safe-conduct would soon expire, and then who would defend him?

Luther had arrived at Oppenheim. His safe-conduct was available for only three days more. He saw a troop of horsemen approaching him, and at their head soon recognized Bucer, with whom he had held such intimate conversations at Heidelberg. "These cavaliers belong to Francis of Sickingen," said Bucer, after the first interchange of friendship; "he has sent me to conduct you to his castle. The emperor's confessor desires to have an interview with you. His influence over Charles is unlimited; everything may yet be arranged. But beware of Aleander!" Jonas, Schurff, and Amsdorff knew not what to think. Bucer was pressing; but Luther felt no hesitation. "I shall continue my journey," replied he to Bucer; "and if the emperor's confessor has anything to say to me, he will find me at Worms. I go whither I am summoned."

In the meanwhile, Spalatin himself began to be anxious and to fear. Surrounded at Worms by the enemies of the Reformation, he heard it said that the safe-conduct of a heretic ought not to be respected. He became alarmed for his friend. At the moment when the latter was approaching the city, a messenger appeared before him, with this advice from the chaplain: "Do not enter Worms!" And this from his best friend—the elector's confidant—from Spalatin himself! . . . But Luther, undismayed, turned his eyes on the messenger, and replied; "Go and tell your master that even should there be as many devils in Worms as tiles on the housetops, still I would enter it!" Never, perhaps, has Luther been so sublime! The messenger returned to Worms with this astounding answer. "I was then undaunted," said Luther, a few days before his death; "I feared nothing. God can indeed render a man intrepid at any time; but I know not whether I should now have so much liberty and joy." "When our cause is good," adds his disciple Mathesius, "the heart expands, and gives courage and energy to evangelists as well as to soldiers."

At length, on the morning of the sixteenth of April, Luther discovered the walls of the ancient city. All were expecting him. One
absorbing thought prevailed in Worms. Some young nobles, Bernard
of Hirschfeldt, Albert of Lindenau, with six knights and other gentlemen in the train of the princes, to the number of a hundred (if
we may believe Pallavicini), unable to restrain their impatience, rode
out on horseback to meet him, and surround him, to form an escort
at the moment of his entrance. He drew near. Before him pranced
the imperial herald, in full costume. Luther came next in his modest
car. Jonas followed him on horseback, and the cavaliers were on both
sides of him. A great crowd was waiting for him at the gates. It was
near midday when he passed those walls, from which so many persons had predicted he would never come forth alive. Everyone was at
table; but as soon as the watchman on the tower of the cathedral
sounded his trumpet, all ran into the streets to see the monk. Luther
was now in Worms.

Two thousand persons accompanied him through the streets of
the city. The citizens eagerly pressed forward to see him: every moment the crowd was increasing. It was much greater than at the public entry of the emperor. On a sudden, says an historian, a man
dressed in a singular costume, and bearing a large cross, such as is
employed in funeral processions, made way through the crowd, advanced towards Luther, and then with a loud voice, and in that
plaintive, measured tone in which mass is said for the repose of the
soul, he sang these words, as if he were uttering them from the abode
of the dead:—

Advenisti, O desiderabilis!
Quem expectabamus in tenebris! [1]

Thus a requiem was Luther's welcome to Worms. It was the court
fool of one of the dukes of Bavaria, who, if the story be true, gave
Luther one of those warnings, replete at once with sagacity and irony,
of which the history of these individuals furnishes so many examples. But the shouts of the multitude soon drowned the *de profundis*
of the cross-bearer. The procession made its way with difficulty
through the crowd. At last, the herald of the empire stopped before

[1] At last thou'rt come, long looked-for one, whom we have waited for in the
darkness of the grave.

the hotel of the knights of Rhodes. There resided the two councilors of the elector, Frederick of Thun and Philip of Feilitsch, as well as the marshal of the empire, Ulrich of Pappenheim. Luther alighted from his car, and said as he touched the ground: "God will be my defense." "I entered Worms in a covered wagon, and in my monk's gown," said he at a later period. "All the people came out into the streets to get a sight of Friar Martin."

The news of his arrival filled both the Elector of Saxony and Aleander with alarm. The young and graceful Archbishop Albert, who kept a middle position between the two parties, was confounded at such boldness. "If I had possessed no more courage than he," said Luther, "it is true they would never have seen me at Worms."

Charles V immediately summoned his council. The emperor's privy-councilors hastily repaired to the palace, for the alarm had reached them also. "Luther is come," said Charles; "what must we do?"

Modo, bishop of Palermo, and chancellor of Flanders, replied, if we may credit the testimony of Luther himself: "We have long consulted on this matter. Let your imperial majesty get rid of this man at once. Did not Sigismund cause John Huss to be burned? We are not bound either to give or to observe the safe-conduct of a heretic." "No!" said Charles, "we must keep our promise." They submitted, therefore, to the reformer's appearance before the diet.

While the councils of the great were thus agitated on account of Luther, there were many persons in Worms who were delighted at the opportunity of at length beholding this illustrious servant of God. Capito, chaplain and councilor to the Archbishop of Mentz, was the foremost among them. This remarkable man, who, shortly before, had preached the gospel in Switzerland with great freedom, thought it becoming the station he then filled to act in a manner which led to his being accused of cowardice by the Evangelicals, and of dissimulation by the Romanists. Yet at Mentz he had proclaimed the doctrine of grace with much clearness. At the moment of his departure, he had succeeded in supplying his place by a young and zealous preacher named Hedio. The Word of God was not bound in that city, the ancient seat of the primacy of the German Church. The gospel was listened to with eagerness; in vain did the monks endeavor to preach from the Holy Scriptures after their manner, and employ all the means in their power to check the impulse given to men's minds: they could not succeed.

But while proclaiming the new doctrine, Capito attempted to remain friendly with those who persecuted it. He flattered himself, as others did who shared in his opinions, that he might in this way be of great service to the Church. To judge by their talk, if Luther was not burned, if all the Lutherans were not excommunicated, it was owing to Capito's influence with the Archbishop Albert. Cochloeus, dean of Frankfurt, who reached Worms about the same time as Luther, immediately waited on Capito. The latter, who was, outwardly at least, on very friendly terms with Aleander, presented Cochloeus to him, thus serving as a link between the two greatest enemies of the reformer. Capito no doubt thought he was advancing Christ's cause by all these temporizing expedients, but we cannot find that they led to any good result. The event almost always baffles these calculations of human wisdom, and proves that a decided course, while it is the most frank, is also the wisest.

Meantime, the crowd still continued round the hotel of Rhodes, where Luther had alighted. To some he was a prodigy of wisdom, to others a monster of iniquity. All the city longed to see him. They allowed him, however, a few hours after his arrival to recruit his strength, and to converse with his most intimate friends. But as soon as the evening came, counts, barons, knights, gentlemen, ecclesiastics, and citizens, flocked about him. All, even his greatest enemies, were struck with the boldness of his manner, the joy that seemed to animate him, the power of his language, and that imposing elevation and enthusiasm which gave this simple monk an irresistible authority. But while some ascribed this grandeur to something divine, the friends of the pope loudly exclaimed that he was possessed by a devil. Visitors rapidly succeeded each other, and this crowd of curious individuals kept Luther from his bed until a late hour of the night.

On the next morning, Wednesday the seventeenth of April, the hereditary marshal of the empire, Ulrich of Pappenheim, cited him to appear at four in the afternoon before his imperial majesty and the states of the empire. Luther received this message with profound respect.

Thus everything was arranged; he was about to stand for Jesus

Christ before the most august assembly in the world. Encouragements were not wanting to him. The impetuous knight, Ulrich Hütten, was then in the castle of Ebernburg. Unable to visit Worms (for Leo X had called upon Charles V to send him bound hand and foot to Rome), he resolved at least to stretch out the hand of friendship to Luther; and on this very day (April 17) he wrote to him, adopting the language of a king of Israel: "'The Lord hear thee in the day of trouble; the name of the God of Jacob defend thee; send thee help from the sanctuary, and strengthen thee out of Zion. . . . Grant thee according to thine own heart, and fulfill all thy counsel.' Dearly beloved Luther! my venerable father! . . . fear not, and stand firm. The counsel of the wicked has beset you, and they have opened their mouths against you like roaring lions. But the Lord will arise against the unrighteous, and put them to confusion. Fight, therefore, valiantly in Christ's cause. As for me, I too will combat boldly. Would to God that I were permitted to see how they frown. But the Lord will purge His vineyard, which the wild boar of the forest has laid waste. . . . May Christ preserve you!" Bucer did what Hütten was unable to do; he came from Ebernburg to Worms, and did not leave his friend during the time of his sojourn in that city.

Four o'clock arrived. The marshal of the empire appeared; Luther prepared to set out with him. He was agitated at the thought of the solemn congress before which he was about to appear. The herald walked first; after him the marshal of the empire; and the reformer came last. The crowd that filled the streets was still greater than on the preceding day. It was impossible to advance; in vain were orders given to make way; the crowd still kept increasing. At length the herald, seeing the difficulty of reaching the town hall, ordered some private houses to be opened, and led Luther through the gardens and private passages to the place where the diet was sitting. The people who witnessed this, rushed into the houses after the monk of Wittenberg, ran to the windows that overlooked the gardens, and a great number climbed on the roofs. The tops of the houses and the pavements of the streets, above and below, all were covered with spectators.

Having reached the town hall at last, Luther and those who accompanied him were again prevented by the crowd from crossing the threshold. They cried, "Make way! make way!" but no one moved.

Upon this the imperial soldiers by main force cleared a road, through which Luther passed. As the people rushed forward to enter with him, the soldiers kept them back with their halberds. Luther entered the interior of the hall; but even there every corner was crowded. In the antechambers and deep recesses of the windows there were more than five thousand spectators,—Germans, Italians, Spaniards, and others. Luther advanced with difficulty. At last, as he drew near the door which was about to admit him into the presence of his judges, he met a valiant knight, the celebrated George of Freundsberg, who four years later, at the head of his German lansquenets, bent the knee with his soldiers on the field of Pavia, and then charging the left of the French army, drove it into the Ticino, and in a great measure decided the captivity of the King of France. The old general, seeing Luther pass, tapped him on the shoulder, and shaking his head, blanched in many battles, said kindly: "Poor monk! Poor monk! thou art now going to make a nobler stand than I or any other captains have ever made in the bloodiest of our battles! But if thy cause is just, and thou art sure of it, go forward in God's name, and fear nothing! God will not forsake thee!" A noble tribute of respect paid by the courage of the sword to the courage of the mind! "He that ruleth his spirit [is greater] than he that taketh a city," were the words of a king (Prov. 16:32).

At length the doors of the hall were opened. Luther went in, and with him entered many persons who formed no portion of the diet. Never had man appeared before so imposing an assembly. The Emperor Charles V, whose sovereignty extended over great part of the old and new world; his brother the Archduke Ferdinand; six electors of the empire, most of whose descendants now wear the kingly crown; twenty-four dukes, the majority of whom were independent sovereigns over countries more or less extensive, and among whom were some whose names afterwards became formidable to the Reformation —the Duke of Alva and his two sons; eight margraves; thirty archbishops, bishops, and abbots; seven ambassadors, including those from the kings of France and England; the deputies of ten free cities; a great number of princes, counts, and sovereign barons; the papal nuncios—in all two hundred and four persons; such was the imposing court before which Martin Luther appeared.

This appearance was of itself a signal victory over the papacy. The pope had condemned the man, and yet there he stood before a tribunal which, by this very act, set itself above the pope. The pope had laid him under an interdict, and cut him off from all human society; and yet he was summoned in respectful language, and received before the most august assembly in the world. The pope had condemned him to perpetual silence, and yet he was now about to speak before thousands of attentive hearers drawn together from the farthest parts of Christendom. An immense revolution had thus been effected by Luther's instrumentality. Rome was already descending from her throne, and it was the voice of a monk that caused this humiliation.

Some of the princes, when they saw the emotion of this son of the lowly miner of Mansfeldt in the presence of this assembly of kings, approached him kindly, and one of them said to him: " 'Fear not them which kill the body, but are not able to kill the soul.' " And another added: " 'When ye shall be brought before governors and kings for my sake, the spirit of your Father shall speak in you.' " Thus was the reformer comforted with his Master's words by the princes of this world.

Meanwhile the guards made way for Luther. He advanced and stood before the throne of Charles V. The sight of so august an assembly appeared for an instant to dazzle and intimidate him. All eyes were fixed on him. The confusion gradually subsided, and a deep silence followed. "Say nothing," said the marshal of the empire to him, "before you are questioned." Luther was left alone.

After a moment of solemn silence, the chancellor of the Archbishop of Treves, John ab Eck, who was the friend of Aleander and who must not be confounded with the theologian of the same name, rose and said with a loud and clear voice, first in Latin and then in German: "Martin Luther! his sacred and invincible imperial majesty has cited you before his throne, in accordance with the advice and counsel of the states of the holy Roman empire, to require you to answer two questions: First, Do you acknowledge these books to have been written by you?" At the same time the imperial speaker pointed with his finger to about twenty volumes placed on a table in the middle of the hall, directly in front of Luther. "I do not know how they could have procured them," said Luther, relating this circumstance. It was Aleander who had taken this trouble. "Secondly," continued the chancellor, "Are you prepared to retract these books, and their contents, or do you persist in the opinions you have advanced in them?"

Luther, having no mistrust, was about to answer the first of these questions in the affirmative, when his counsel, Jerome Schurff, hastily interrupting him, exclaimed aloud: "Let the titles of the books be read!"

The chancellor approached the table and read the titles. There were among their number many devotional works, quite foreign to the controversy.

Their enumeration being finished, Luther said first in Latin, and then in German:

"Most gracious emperor! Gracious princes and lords!

"His imperial majesty has asked me two questions.

"As to the first, I acknowledge as mine the books that have just been named: I cannot deny them.

"As to the second, seeing that it is a question which concerns faith and the salvation of souls, and in which the Word of God, the greatest and most precious treasure either in heaven or earth, is interested, I should act imprudently were I to reply without reflection. I might affirm less than the circumstance demands, or more than truth requires, and so sin against this saying of Christ: 'Whosoever shall deny me before men, him will I also deny before my Father which is in heaven.' For this reason I entreat your imperial majesty, with all humility, to allow me time, that I may answer without offending against the Word of God."

This reply, far from giving grounds to suppose that Luther felt any hesitation, was worthy of the reformer and of the assembly. It was right that he should appear calm and circumspect in so important a matter, and lay aside everything in this solemn moment that might cause a suspicion of passion or rashness. Besides, by taking reasonable time, he would give a stronger proof of the unalterable firmness of his resolution. In history we read of many men who by a hasty expression have brought misfortunes upon themselves and upon the world. Luther restrained his own naturally impetuous disposition; he controlled his tongue, ever too ready to speak, he checked himself at a time when all the feelings by which he was animated were eager for utterance. This restraint, this calmness, so surprising in such a man, multiplied his strength a hundredfold, and put him in a position to reply, at a later period, with such wisdom, power, and dignity, as to deceive the expectations of his adversaries, and confound their malice and their pride.

And yet, because he had spoken in a respectful manner, and in a low tone of voice, many thought that he hesitated, and even that he was dismayed. A ray of hope beamed on the minds of the partisans of Rome. Charles, impatient to know the man whose words had stirred the empire, had not taken his eyes off him. He turned to one of his courtiers, and said disdainfully, "Certainly this man will never make a heretic of me." Then rising from his seat, the youthful emperor withdrew with his ministers into a council room; the electors with the princes retired into another; and the deputies of the free cities, into a third. When the diet assembled again, it was agreed to comply with Luther's request. This was a great miscalculation in men actuated by passion.

"Martin Luther," said the Chancellor of Treves, "his imperial majesty, of his natural goodness, is very willing to grant you another day, but under condition that you make your reply viva voce, and not in writing."

The imperial herald now stepped forward and conducted Luther back to his hotel. Menaces and shouts of joy were heard by turns on his passage. The most sinister rumors circulated among Luther's friends. "The diet is dissatisfied," said they; "the papal envoys have triumphed; the reformer will be sacrificed." Men's passions were inflamed. Many gentlemen hastened to Luther's lodgings: "Doctor," said they, with emotion, "what is this? It is said they are determined to burn you!" "If they do so," continued these knights, "it will cost them their lives!" "And that certainly would have happened," said Luther, as, twenty years after, he quoted these words at Eisleben.

On the other hand, Luther's enemies exulted. "He has asked for time," said they; "he will retract. At a distance, his speech was arrogant; now his courage fails him. . . . He is conquered."

Perhaps Luther was the only man that felt tranquil at Worms. Shortly after his return from the diet, he wrote to Cuspianus, the imperial councilor: "I write to you from the midst of the tumult [alluding probably to the noise made by the crowd in front of the hotel]. I have just made my appearance before the emperor and his brother. . . . I confessed myself the author of my books, and declared that I would reply tomorrow touching my retractation. With Christ's help, I shall never retract one tittle of my works."

The emotion of the people and of the foreign soldiers increased every hour. While the opposing parties were proceeding calmly in the diet, they were breaking out into acts of violence in the streets. The insolence of the haughty and merciless Spanish soldiers offended the citizens. One of these myrmidons of Charles, finding in a bookseller's shop the pope's bull with a commentary written by Hütten, took the book and tore it in pieces, and then throwing the fragments on the ground, trampled them underfoot. Others having discovered several copies of Luther's writing on the *Captivity of Babylon*, took them away and destroyed them. The indignant people fell upon the soldiers and compelled them to take to flight. At another time, a Spaniard on horseback pursued, sword in hand, through one of the principal streets of Worms, a German who fled before him, and the affrighted people dared not stop the furious man.

Some politicians thought they had found means of saving Luther. "Retract your doctrinal errors," said they; "but persist in all that you have said against the pope and his court, and you are safe." Aleander shuddered with alarm at this counsel. But Luther, immovable in his resolution, declared that he had no great opinion of a political reform that was not based upon faith.

Glapio, the Chancellor ab Eck, and Aleander, by Charles's order, met early on the morning of the eighteenth to concert the measures to be taken with regard to Luther.

Chapter 53

"BUT THE CAUSE IS THINE!"

For a moment Luther had felt dismay, when he was about to appear the preceding day before so august an assembly. His heart had been troubled in the presence of so many great princes, before whom nations humbly bent the knee. The reflection that he was about to refuse to submit to these men, whom God had invested with sovereign power, disturbed his soul; and he felt the necessity of looking for strength from on high. "The man who, when he is attacked by the enemy, protects himself with the shield of faith," said he one day, "is like Perseus with the Gorgon's head. Whoever looked at it fell dead. In like manner should we present the Son of God to the snares of the devil." On the morning of April 18, he was not without his moments of trial, in which the face of God seemed hidden from him. His faith grew weak; his enemies multiplied before him; his imagination was overwhelmed at the sight. . . . His soul was as a ship tossed by a violent tempest, which reels and sinks to the bottom of the abyss, and then mounts up again to heaven. In this hour of bitter sorrow, in which he drank the cup of Christ, and which was to him a little garden of Gethsemane, he fell to the earth, and uttered these broken cries, which we cannot understand unless we can figure to ourselves the depth of the anguish whence they ascend to God:

"O Almighty and Everlasting God! How terrible is this world! Behold, it openeth its mouth to swallow me up, and I have so little trust in Thee! . . . How weak is the flesh, and how powerful is Satan! If it is in the strength of this world only that I must put my trust, all is over! . . . My last hour is come, my condemnation has been pronounced! . . . O God! O God! . . . O God! do Thou help

427

me against all the wisdom of the world! Do this; Thou shouldest do this. . . . Thou alone . . . for this is not my work, but Thine. I have nothing to do here, nothing to contend for with these great ones of the world! I should desire to see my days flow on peaceful and happy. But the cause is Thine . . . and it is a righteous and eternal cause. O Lord! help me! Faithful and unchangeable God! In no man do I place my trust. It would be vain! All that is of man is uncertain; all that cometh of man fails. . . . O God! my God, hearest Thou me not? . . . My God, art Thou dead? . . . No! Thou canst not die! Thou hidest Thyself only! Thou has chosen me for this work. I know it well! . . . Act, then, O God . . . stand at my side, for the sake of Thy well-beloved Jesus Christ, who is my defense, my shield, and my strong tower."

After a moment of silent struggle, he thus continued:

"Lord! where stayest Thou? . . . O my God! where art Thou? . . . Come! come! I am ready! . . . I am ready to lay down my life for Thy truth . . . patient as a lamb. For it is the cause of justice—it is Thine! . . . I will never separate myself from Thee, neither now nor through eternity! . . . And though the world should be filled with devils,—though my body, which is still the work of Thy hands, should be slain, be stretched upon the pavement, be cut in pieces . . . reduced to ashes . . . my soul is Thine! . . . Yes! I have the assurance of Thy Word. My soul belongs to Thee! It shall abide forever with Thee. . . . Amen! . . . O God! help me! . . . Amen!"

This prayer explains Luther and the Reformation. History here raises the veil of the sanctuary, and discloses to our view the secret place whence strength and courage were imparted to this humble and despised man, who was the instrument of God to emancipate the soul and the thoughts of men, and to open a new era. Luther and the Reformation are here brought before us. We discover their most secret springs. We see whence their power was derived. This outpouring of a soul that offers itself up in the cause of truth is to be found in a collection of documents relative to Luther's appearance at Worms, under Number XVI, in the midst of safe-conducts and other papers of a similar nature. One of his friends had no doubt overheard it, and has transmitted it to posterity. In our opinion, it is one of the most precious documents in all history.

After he had thus prayed, Luther found that peace of mind without which man can effect nothing great. He then read the Word of God, looked over his writings, and sought to draw up his reply in a suitable form. The thought that he was about to bear testimony to Jesus Christ and His Word in the presence of the emperor and of the empire, filled his heart with joy. As the hour for his appearance was not far off, he drew near the Holy Scriptures that lay open on the table, and with emotion placed his left hand on the sacred volume, and raising his right towards heaven, swore to remain faithful to the gospel, and freely to confess his faith, even should he seal his testimony with his blood. After this he felt still more at peace.

At four o'clock the herald appeared and conducted him to the place where the diet was sitting. The curiosity of the people had increased, for the answer was to be decisive. As the diet was occupied, Luther was compelled to wait in the court in the midst of an immense crowd, which heaved to and fro like the sea in a storm, and pressed the reformer with its waves. Two long hours elapsed, while the doctor stood in this multitude so eager to catch a glimpse of him. "I was not accustomed," said he, "to those manners and to all this noise." It would have been a sad preparation, indeed, for an ordinary man. But God was with Luther. His countenance was serene; his features tranquil; the Everlasting One had raised him on a rock. The night began to fall. Torches were lighted in the hall of the assembly. Their glimmering rays shone through the ancient windows into the court. Everything assumed a solemn aspect. At last the doctor was introduced. Many persons entered with him, for everyone desired to hear his answer. Men's minds were on the stretch; all impatiently awaited the decisive moment that was approaching. This time Luther was calm, free, and confident, without the least perceptible mark of embarrassment. His prayer had born fruit. The princes having taken their seats, though not without some difficulty, for many of their places had been occupied, and the monk of Wittenberg finding himself again standing before Charles V, the chancellor of the Elector of Treves began by saying:

"Martin Luther! yesterday you begged for a delay that has now expired. Assuredly it ought not to have been conceded, as every man, and especially you, who are so great and learned a doctor in the Holy Scriptures, should always be ready to answer every question touching his faith. . . . Now, therefore, reply to the question put by his majesty, who has behaved to you with so much mildness. Will you defend your books as a whole, or are you ready to disavow some of them?"

After having said these words in Latin, the chancellor repeated them in German.

"Upon this, Dr. Martin Luther," say the Acts of Worms, "replied in the most submissive and humble manner. He did not bawl, or speak with violence; but with decency, mildness, suitability, and moderation, and yet with much joy and Christian firmness."

"Most serene emperor! illustrious princes! gracious lords!" said Luther, turning his eyes on Charles and on the assembly, "I appear before you this day, in conformity with the order given me yesterday, and by God's mercies I conjure your majesty and your august highnesses to listen graciously to the defense of a cause which I am assured is just and true. If, through ignorance, I should transgress the usages and proprieties of courts, I entreat you to pardon me; for I was not brought up in the palaces of kings, but in the seclusion of a convent.

"Yesterday, two questions were put to me on behalf of his imperial majesty: the first, if I was the author of the books whose titles were enumerated; the second, if I would retract or defend the doctrine I had taught in them. To the first I then made answer, and I persevere in that reply.

"As for the second, I have written works on many different subjects. There are some in which I have treated of faith and good works, in a manner at once so pure, so simple, and so scriptural, that even my adversaries, far from finding anything to censure in them, allow that these works are useful, and worthy of being read by all pious men. The papal bull, however violent it may be, acknowledges this. If, therefore, I were to retract these, what should I do? . . . Wretched man! Among all men, I alone should abandon truths that friends and enemies approve, and I should oppose what the whole world glories in confessing. . . .

"Secondly, I have written books against the papacy, in which I have attacked those who, by their false doctrine, their evil lives, or their scandalous example, afflict the Christian world, and destroy both body and soul. The complaints of all who fear God are confirmatory of this. Is it not evident that the laws and human doctrines of the popes entangle, torment, and vex the consciences of believers, while the crying and perpetual extortions of Rome swallow up the wealth and the riches of Christendom, and especially of this illustrious nation? . . .

"Were I to retract what I have said on this subject, what should I do but lend additional strength to this tyranny, and open the floodgates to a torrent of impiety? Overflowing with still greater fury than before, we should see these insolent men increase in number, behave more tyrannically, and domineer more and more. And not only would the yoke that now weighs upon the Christian people be rendered heavier by my retractation, but it would become, so to speak, more legitimate, for by this very retractation it would receive the confirmation of your most serene majesty and of all the states of the holy empire. Gracious God! I should thus become a vile cloak to cover and conceal every kind of malice and tyranny! . . .

"Lastly, I have written books against individuals who desired to defend the Romish tyranny and to destroy the faith. I frankly confess that I may have attacked them with more acrimony than is becoming my ecclesiastical profession. I do not consider myself a saint; but I cannot disavow these writings, for by so doing I should sanction the impiety of my adversaries, and they would seize the opportunity of oppressing the people of God with still greater cruelty.

"Yet I am but a mere man, and not God; I shall therefore defend myself as Christ did. 'If I have spoken evil, bear witness of the evil,' said He (John 18:23). How much more should I, who am but dust and ashes, and who may so easily go astray, desire every man to state his objections to my doctrine!

"For this reason, most serene emperor, and you, most illustrious princes, and all men of every degree, I conjure you, by the mercy of God, to prove from the writings of the prophets and apostles that I have erred. As soon as I am convinced of this, I will retract every error, and be the first to lay hold of my books and throw them into the fire.

"What I have just said plainly shows, I hope, that I have carefully weighed and considered the dangers to which I expose myself; but, far from being dismayed, I rejoice to see that the gospel is now, as in former times, a cause of trouble and dissension. This is the character—this is the destiny of the Word of God. 'I came not to send peace [on earth], but a sword,' said Jesus Christ (Matt. 10:34). God is wonderful and terrible in His counsels; beware lest, by presuming to quench dissensions, you should persecute the holy Word of God, and draw down upon yourselves a frightful deluge of insurmountable dangers, of present disasters, and eternal desolation. . . . You should fear lest the reign of this young and noble prince, on whom (under God) we build such lofty expectations, not only should begin, but continue and close under the most gloomy auspices. I might quote many examples from the oracles of God," continued Luther, speaking with a noble courage in the presence of the greatest monarch of the world: "I might speak of the Pharaohs, the kings of Babylon, and those of Israel, whose labors never more effectually contributed to their own destruction than when they sought by counsels, to all appearance most wise, to strengthen their dominion. God removeth mountains, and they know it not; which overturneth them in his anger (Job 9:5).

"If I say these things, it is not because I think that such great princes need my poor advice, but because I desire to render unto Germany what she has a right to expect from her children. Thus, commending myself to your august majesty and to your most serene highnesses, I humbly entreat you not to suffer the hatred of my enemies to pour out upon me an indignation that I have not merited."

Luther had pronounced these words in German with modesty, but with great warmth and firmness; he was ordered to repeat them in Latin. The emperor did not like the German tongue. The imposing assembly that surrounded the reformer, the noise, and his own emotion, had fatigued him. "I was in a great perspiration," said he, "heated by the tumult, standing in the midst of the princes." Frederick of Thun, privy councilor to the Elector of Saxony, who was stationed by his master's orders at the side of the reformer, to watch over him that no violence might be employed against him, seeing the condition of the poor monk, said: "If you cannot repeat what you have said, that will do, doctor." But Luther, after a brief pause to take breath, began again, and repeated his speech in Latin with the same energy as at first.

"This gave great pleasure to the Elector Frederick," says the reformer.

When he had ceased speaking, the Chancellor of Treves, the orator of the diet, said indignantly: "You have not answered the question put to you. You were not summoned hither to call in question the decisions of councils. You are required to give a clear and precise answer. Will you, or will you not, retract?" Upon this Luther replied without hesitation: "Since your most serene majesty and your high mightinesses require from me a clear, simple, and precise answer, I will give you one, and it is this: I cannot submit my faith either to the pope or to the councils, because it is clear as the day that they have frequently erred and contradicted each other. Unless therefore I am convinced by the testimony of Scripture, or by the clearest reasoning—unless I am persuaded by means of the passages I have quoted—and unless they thus render my conscience bound by the Word of God, I cannot and I will not retract, for it is unsafe for a Christian to speak against his conscience." And then, looking round on this assembly before which he stood, and which held his life in its hands, he said: "Here I stand, I can do no other; May God help me! Amen!"

Luther, constrained to obey his faith, led by his conscience to death, impelled by the noblest necessity, the slave of his belief, and under this slavery still supremely free, like the ship tossed by a violent tempest which, to save that which is more precious than itself, runs and is dashed upon the rocks, thus uttered these sublime words which still thrill our hearts at an interval of three centuries. Thus spoke a monk before the emperor and the mighty ones of the nation; and this feeble and despised man, alone, but relying on the grace of the Most High, appeared greater and mightier than them all. His words contained a power against which all these mighty rulers could do nothing. This is the weakness of God, which is stronger than man. The empire and the Church on the one hand, and this obscure man on the other, had met. God had brought together these kings and these prelates publicly to confound their wisdom. The battle was lost, and the consequences of this defeat of the great ones of the earth would be felt among every nation and in every age to the end of time.

The assembly was thunderstruck. Many of the princes found it difficult to conceal their admiration. The emperor, recovering from his first impression, exclaimed: "This monk speaks with an intrepid heart and unshaken courage." The Spaniards and Italians alone felt confounded, and soon began to ridicule a greatness of soul which they could not comprehend.

"If you do not retract," said the chancellor, as soon as the diet had recovered from the impression produced by Luther's speech, "the emperor and the states of the empire will consult what course to adopt against an incorrigible heretic." At these words Luther's friends began to tremble; but the monk repeated: "May God be my helper; for I can retract nothing."

After this Luther withdrew, and the princes deliberated. Each one felt that this was a critical moment for Christendom. The Yes or the No of this monk would decide, perhaps for ages, the repose of the Church and of the world. His adversaries had endeavored to alarm him, and they had only exalted him before the nation; they had thought to give greater publicity to his defeat, and they had but increased the glory of his victory. The partisans of Rome could not decide to submit to this humiliation. Luther was again called in, and the orator of the diet said to him: "Martin, you have not spoken with the modesty becoming your position. The distinction you have made between your books was futile; for if you retracted those that contained your errors, the emperor would not allow the others to be burned. It is extravagant in you to demand to be refuted by Scripture, when you are reviving heresies condemned by the general council of Constance. The emperor, therefore, calls upon you to declare simply, Yes or No, whether you presume to maintain what you have advanced, or whether you will retract a portion?" "I have no other reply to make than that which I have already made," answered Luther calmly. His meaning was understood. Firm as a rock, all the waves of human power dashed ineffectually against him. The strength of his words, his bold bearing, his piercing eyes, the unshaken firmness legible on the rough outlines of his truly German features, had produced the deepest impression on this illustrious assembly. There was no longer any hope. The Spaniards, the Belgians, and even the Romans, were dumb. The monk had vanquished these great ones of the earth. He had said No to the Church and to the empire. Charles V arose, and all the assembly with him: "The diet will meet again tomorrow to hear the emperor's opinion," said the chancellor with a loud voice.

Chapter 54

CHARLES KEEPS HIS WORD

Night had closed in. Each man retired to his home in darkness. Two imperial officers formed Luther's escort. Some persons imagined that his fate was decided, that they were leading him to prison, whence he would never come forth but to mount the scaffold: an immense tumult broke out. Several gentlemen exclaimed: "Are they taking him to prison?" "No," replied Luther, "they are accompanying me to my hotel." At these words the agitation subsided. Some Spanish soldiers of the emperor's household followed this bold man through the streets by which he had to pass, with shouts and mockery, while others howled and roared like wild beasts robbed of their prey. But Luther remained calm and firm.

Such was the scene at Worms. The intrepid monk, who had hitherto boldly braved all his enemies, spoke on this occasion, when he found himself in the presence of those who thirsted for his blood, with calmness, dignity, and humility. There was no exaggeration, no mere human enthusiasm, no anger; overflowing with the liveliest emotion, he was still at peace; modest, though withstanding the powers of the earth; great in presence of all the grandeur of the world. This is an indisputable mark that Luther obeyed God, and not the suggestions of his own pride. In the hall of the diet there was One greater than Charles and greater than Luther. "When ye shall be brought before governors and kings for my sake, take no thought how or what ye shall speak," saith Jesus Christ, "for it is not ye that speak." Never perhaps had this promise been more clearly fulfilled.

A profound impression had been produced on the chiefs of the empire. This Luther had noticed, and it had increased his courage. The pope's ministers were provoked because John ab Eck had not sooner interrupted the guilty monk. Many lords and princes were won over to a cause supported with such conviction. With some, it is true, the impression was transient; but others, on the contrary, who concealed their sentiments at that time, at an after period declared themselves with great courage.

Luther had returned to his hotel, seeking to recruit his body fatigued by so severe a trial. Spalatin and other friends surrounded him, and all together gave thanks to God. As they were conversing, a servant entered, bearing a silver flagon filled with Eimbeck beer. "My master," said he, as he offered it to Luther, "invites you to refresh yourself with this draught." "Who is the prince," said the Wittenberg doctor, "who so graciously remembers me?" It was the aged Duke Eric of Brunswick. The reformer was affected by this present from so powerful a lord, belonging to the pope's party. "His highness," continued the servant, "has condescended to taste it before sending it to you." Upon this Luther, who was thirsty, poured out some of the duke's beer, and after drinking it, he said: "As this day Duke Eric has remembered me, so may our Lord Jesus Christ remember him in the hour of his last struggle." It was a present of trifling value; but Luther, desirous of showing his gratitude to a prince who remembered him at such a moment, gave him such as he had—a prayer. The servant returned with this message to his master. At the moment of his death the aged duke called these words to mind, and addressing a young page, Francis of Kramm, who was standing at his bedside: "Take the Bible," said he, "and read it to me." The child read these words of Christ, and the soul of the dying man was comforted: "Whosoever shall give you a cup of water to drink in my name, because ye belong to Christ, verily I say unto you, he shall not lose his reward."

Hardly had the Duke of Brunswick's servant gone away, when a messenger from the Elector of Saxony came with orders for Spalatin to come to him immediately. Frederick had gone to the diet filled with great uneasiness. He had imagined that in the presence of the emperor, Luther's courage would fail him; and hence he had been deeply moved by the resolute bearing of the reformer. He was proud of being the protector of such a man. When the chaplain arrived, the table was spread; the elector was just sitting down to supper with his court, and already the servants had brought in the water for their hands. As he saw Spalatin enter, he motioned him to follow, and as soon as he was alone with the chaplain in his bedchamber, he said: "Oh! how Father Luther spoke before the emperor, and before all the states of the empire! I only trembled lest he should be too bold." Frederick then formed the resolution of protecting the doctor more courageously in the future.

Aleander saw the impression Luther had produced; there was no time to lose; he must induce the emperor to act with vigor. The opportunity was favorable; war with France was imminent. Leo X, desirous of enlarging his states, and caring little for the peace of Christendom, was secretly negotiating two treaties at the same time—one with Charles against Francis, the other with Francis against Charles. In the former, he claimed of the emperor, for himself, the territories of Parma, Placentia, and Ferrara; in the second, he stipulated with the king for a portion of the kingdom of Naples, which would thus be taken from Charles. The latter felt the importance of gaining Leo to his side, in order to have his alliance in the war against his rival of France. It was a mere trifle to purchase the mighty pontiff's friendship at the cost of Luther's life.

On the day following Luther's appearance (Friday, April 19), the emperor ordered a message to be read to the diet, which he had written in French with his own hand. "Descended from the Christian emperors of Germany," said he, "from the Catholic kings of Spain, from the archdukes of Austria, and from the dukes of Burgundy, who have all been renowned as defenders of the Roman faith, I am firmly resolved to imitate the example of my ancestors. A single monk, misled by his own folly, has risen against the faith of Christendom. To stay such impiety I will sacrifice my kingdoms, my treasures, my friends, my body, my blood, my soul, and my life. I am about to dismiss the Augustine Luther, forbidding him to cause the least disorder among the people; I shall then proceed against him and his adherents, as contumacious heretics, by excommunication, by interdict, and by every means calculated to destroy them. I call on the members of the states to behave like faithful Christians."

This address did not please everyone. Charles, young and hasty, had not complied with the usual forms; he should first have consulted the diet. Two extreme opinions immediately declared themselves.

The creatures of the pope, the Elector of Brandenburg, and several ecclesiastical princes, demanded that the safe-conduct given to Luther should not be respected. "The Rhine," said they, "should receive his ashes, as it had received those of John Huss a century ago." Charles, if we may credit an historian, bitterly repented in after years that he did not adopt this infamous suggestion. "I confess," said he, towards the close of his life, "that I committed a great fault by permitting Luther to live. I was not obliged to keep my promise with him; that heretic had offended a Master greater than I—God Himself. I might and I ought to have broken my word, and to have avenged the insult he had committed against God: it is because I did not put him to death that heresy has not ceased to advance. His death would have stifled it in the cradle."

So horrible a proposition filled the elector and all Luther's friends with dismay. "The punishment of John Huss," said the elector-palatine, "has brought too many misfortunes on the German nation for us ever to raise such a scaffold a second time." "The princes of Germany," exclaimed even George of Saxony, Luther's inveterate enemy, "will not permit a safe-conduct to be violated. This diet, the first held by our new emperor, will not be guilty of so base an action. Such perfidy does not accord with the ancient German integrity." The princes of Bavaria, though attached to the Church of Rome, supported this protest. The prospect of death that Luther's friends had already before their eyes appeared to recede.

The rumor of these discussions, which lasted two days, circulated through the city. Party-spirit ran high. Some gentlemen, partisans of the reform, began to speak firmly against the treachery solicited by Aleander. "The emperor," said they, "is a young man whom the papists and bishops by their flatteries manage at their will." Pallavicini speaks of four hundred nobles ready to enforce Luther's safe-conduct with the sword. On Saturday morning placards were seen posted on the gates of houses and in the public places, some against Luther, and others in his favor. On one of them might be read merely these expressive words of the Preacher: "Woe to thee, O land! when thy king is a child . . ." (Eccles. 10:16). Sickingen, it was reported, had assembled at a few leagues from Worms, behind the impregnable ramparts of his stronghold, many knights and soldiers, and was only waiting to know the result of the affair before proceeding to action.

The enthusiasm of the people, not only in Worms, but also in the most distant cities of the empire; the intrepidity of the knights; the attachment felt by many princes to the cause of the reformer, were all of a nature to show Charles and the diet that the course suggested by the Romanists might compromise the supreme authority, excite revolts, and even shake the empire. It was only the burning of a simple monk that was in question; but the princes and the partisans of Rome had not, all together, sufficient strength or courage to do this. There can be no doubt, also, that Charles V, who was then young, feared to commit perjury. This would seem to be indicated by a saying, if it is true, which, according to some historians, he uttered on this occasion: "Though honor and faith should be banished from all the world, they ought to find a refuge in the hearts of princes." It is mournful to reflect that he may have forgotten these words when on the brink of the grave. But other motives besides may have influenced the emperor. The Florentine Vettori, the friend of Leo X and of Machiavelli, asserted that Charles spared Luther only that he might thus keep the pope in check.

In the sitting of that Saturday, the violent propositions of Aleander were rejected. Luther was beloved; there was a general desire to preserve this simple-minded man, whose confidence in God was so affecting; but there was also a desire to save the Church. Men shuddered at the thought of the consequences that might ensue, as well from the triumph as from the punishment of the reformer. Plans of conciliation were put forward; it was proposed to make a new effort with the doctor of Wittenberg. The Archbishop-elector of Mentz himself, the young and extravagant Albert, more devout than bold, says Pallavicini, had become alarmed at the interest shown by the people and nobility toward the Saxon monk. Capito, his chaplain, who during his sojourn at Basle had formed an intimacy with the evangelical priest of Zurich, named Zwingli, a bold man in the defense of truth, and of whom we have already had occasion to speak, had also, there can be no doubt, represented to Albert the justice of the reformer's cause. The worldly archbishop had one of those returns to Christian sentiments which we sometimes notice in his life, and consented to wait on the emperor, to ask permission to make a last attempt. But Charles refused everything. On Monday, the twenty-second of April, the princes went in a body to repeat Albert's request. "I will not depart from what I have determined," replied the emperor. "I will authorize no one to communicate officially with Luther. But," added he, to Aleander's great vexation, "I will grant that man three days for reflection; during which time, you may exhort him privately." This was all that they required. The reformer, thought they, elevated by the solemnity of his appearance before the diet, will give way in a more friendly conference, and perhaps will be saved from the abyss into which he is about to fall.

The Elector of Saxony knew the contrary, and hence was filled with apprehension. "If it were in my power," wrote he the next day to his brother Duke John, "I should be ready to defend Luther. You cannot imagine how far the partisans of Rome carry their attacks against me. Were I to tell you all, you would hear some most astonishing matters. They are resolved upon his destruction; and whoever manifests any interest for his safety, is immediately set down as a heretic. May God, who never abandons the cause of justice, bring all things to a happy end!" Frederick, without showing his kindly feelings toward the reformer, confined himself to observing every one of his movements.

It was not the same with men of every rank in society who were then at Worms. They fearlessly displayed their sympathy. On Friday a number of princes, counts, barons, knights, gentlemen, ecclesiastics, laymen, and of the common people, collected before the hotel where the reformer was staying; they went in and out one after another, and could hardly satisfy themselves with gazing on him. He had become the man of Germany. Even those who thought him in error were affected by the nobleness of soul that led him to sacrifice his life to the voice of his conscience. With many persons then present at Worms, the chosen men of the nation, Luther held conversations abounding in that "salt" with which all his words were seasoned. None quitted him without feeling animated by a generous enthusiasm for the truth. "How many things I shall have to tell you!" wrote George Vogler, private secretary to Casimir, margrave of Brandenburg, to one of his friends. "What conversations, how full of piety and kindness, has Luther had with me and others! What a charming person he is!"

One day a young prince, seventeen years of age, came prancing into the court of the hotel; it was Philip, who for two years had ruled in Hesse. This youthful sovereign was of prompt and enterprising character, wise beyond his years, warlike, impetuous, and unwilling to be guided by any ideas but his own. Struck by Luther's speeches, he wished to have a nearer view of him. "He, however, was not yet on my side," said Luther, as he related this circumstance. He leaped from his horse, unceremoniously ascended to the reformer's chamber, and addressing him, said: "Well! dear doctor, how goes it?" "Gracious lord," answered Luther, "I hope all will go well." "From what I hear of you, doctor," resumed the landgrave smiling, "you teach that a woman may leave her husband and take another, when the former is become too old!" It was some members of the imperial court who had told this story to the landgrave. The enemies of truth never fail to invent and propagate fables on the pretended doctrines of Christian teachers. "No, my lord," replied Luther seriously; "I entreat your highness not to talk thus!" Upon this the young prince hastily held out his hand to the doctor, shook it heartily, and said: "Dear doctor, if you are in the right, may God help you!" He then left the room, mounted his horse, and rode off. This was the first interview between these two men, who were afterwards destined to be at the head of the Reformation, and to defend it—the one with the sword of the Word, the other with the sword of princes.

Chapter 55

LUTHER'S DEPARTURE FROM WORMS

RICHARD of Greiffenklau, archbishop of Treves, had with the permission of Charles V undertaken the office of mediator. Richard, who was on very intimate terms with the Elector of Saxony, and a good Roman Catholic, desired by settling this affair to render a service to his friend as well as to his Church. On Monday evening (April 22), just as Luther was sitting down to eat, a messenger came from the archbishop, informing him that this prelate desired to see him on the next morning but one (Wednesday) at six o'clock.

The chaplain and Sturm, the imperial herald, waited on Luther before six o'clock on that day. But as early as four in the morning, Aleander had sent for Cochloeus. The nuncio had soon discovered in the man whom Capito had introduced to him a devoted instrument of the court of Rome, on whom he might count as upon himself. As he could not be present at this interview, Aleander desired to find a substitute. "Go to the residence of the Archbishop of Treves," said he to the Dean of Frankfurt; "do not enter into discussion with Luther, but listen attentively to all that is said, so as to give me a faithful report." The reformer with some of his friends arrived at the archbishop's, where he found the prelate surrounded by Joachim, margrave of Brandenburg, Duke George of Saxony, the bishops of Brandenburg and Augsburg, with several nobles, deputies of the free cities, lawyers, and theologians, among whom were Cochloeus and Jerome Wehe, chancellor of Baden. This skillful lawyer was anxious for a reformation in morals and discipline; he even went further: "The Word of God," said he, "that has been so long hidden under a bushel, must reappear in all its brightness." It was this conciliatory person who was charged with the conference. Turning kindly to Luther, he said, "We have not sent for you to dispute with you, but to exhort you in a fraternal tone. You know how carefully the Scriptures call upon us to beware of 'the arrow that flieth by day, and the destruction that wasteth at noonday.' That enemy of mankind has excited you to publish many things contrary to true religion. Reflect on your own safety and that of the empire. Beware lest those whom Christ by His blood has redeemed from eternal death should be misled by you, and perish everlastingly. . . . Do not oppose the holy councils. If we did not uphold the decrees of our fathers, there would be nothing but confusion in the Church. The eminent princes who hear me feel a special interest in your welfare; but if you persist, then the emperor will expel you from the empire, and no place in the world will offer you an asylum. . . . Reflect on the fate that awaits you!"

"Most serene princes," replied Luther, "I thank you for your solicitude on my account; for I am but a poor man, and too mean to be exhorted by such great lords." He then continued: "I have not blamed all the councils, but only that of Constance, because by condemning this doctrine of John Huss, that the Christian Church is the assembly of all those who are predestined to salvation, it has condemned this article of our faith, I believe in the Holy Catholic Church, and the Word of God itself. It is said my teaching is a cause of offense," added he; "I reply that the gospel of Christ cannot be preached without offense. Why then should the fear or apprehension of danger separate me from the Lord and from that divine Word which alone is truth? No! I would rather give up my body, my blood, and my life!"

The princes and doctors having deliberated, Luther was again called in, and Wehe mildly resumed: "We must honor the powers that be, even when they are in error, and make great sacrifices for the sake of charity." And then with greater earnestness of manner, he said: "Leave it to the emperor's decision, and fear not."

Luther—"I consent with all my heart that the emperor, the princes, and even the meanest Christian should examine and judge my works; but on one condition, that they take the Word of God for their standard. Men have nothing to do but to obey it. Do not offer violence to my conscience, which is bound and chained up with the Holy Scriptures."

The Elector of Brandenburg—"If I rightly understand you, doctor, you will acknowledge no other judge than the Holy Scriptures?"

Luther—"Precisely so, my lord, and on them I take my stand."

Upon this the princes and doctors withdrew; but the excellent Archbishop of Treves could not make up his mind to abandon his undertaking. "Follow me," said he to Luther, as he passed into his private room; and at the same time ordered John ab Eck and Cochloeus on the one side, and Schurff and Amsdorff on the other, to come after. "Why do you always appeal to Scripture?" asked Eck with warmth. "It is the source of all heresies." But Luther, says his friend Mathesius, remained firm as a rock, which is based on the true Rock—the Word of the Lord. "The pope," replied he, "is no judge in the things belonging to the Word of God. Every Christian should see and decide for himself how he ought to live and die." They separated. The partisans of the papacy felt Luther's superiority, and attributed it to there being no one present capable of answering him. "If the emperor had acted wisely," says Cochloeus, "when summoning Luther to Worms, he would also have invited theologians to refute his errors."

The Archbishop of Treves repaired to the diet, and announced the failure of his mediation. The astonishment of the young emperor was equal to his indignation. "It is time to put an end to this business," said he. The archbishop pressed for two days more; all the diet joined in the petition; Charles V gave way. Aleander, no longer able to restrain himself, burst out into violent reproaches.

While these scenes were passing in the diet, Cochloeus burned to gain a victory in which kings and prelates had been unsuccessful. Although he had from time to time dropped a few words at the archbishop's, he was restrained by Aleander's injunction to keep silence. He resolved to find compensation, and as soon as he had rendered a faithful account of his mission to the papal nuncio, he called on Luther. He went up to him in the most friendly manner, and expressed the vexation he felt at the emperor's resolution. After dinner, the conversation became animated. Cochloeus urged Luther to retract. The latter shook his head. Several nobles who were at the table with him could hardly contain themselves. They were indignant that the partisans of Rome should insist, not upon convincing Luther by Scripture, but on constraining him by force. "Well, then," said Cochloeus to Luther, impatient under these reproaches, "I offer to dispute publicly with you, if you will renounce your safe-conduct."

All that Luther demanded was a public disputation. What ought he to do? To renounce the safe-conduct would be to endanger his life; to refuse this challenge would appear to throw doubts on the justice of his cause. His guests perceived in this proposal a plot framed with Aleander, whom the Dean of Frankfurt had just quitted. One of them, Vollrat of Watzdorf by name, extricated Luther from the embarrassment occasioned by so difficult a choice. This fiery lord, indignant at a snare, the sole object of which was to deliver Luther into the hands of the executioner, rose hastily, seized the frightened priest, and pushed him out of the room; and blood no doubt would have been spilled, if the other guests had not left the table at the same moment and mediated between the furious knight and Cochloeus, who trembled with alarm. The latter retired in confusion from the hotel of the Knights of Rhodes. Most probably it was in the heat of discussion that these words had fallen from the dean, and there had been no preconcerted plan formed between him and Aleander to entice Luther into so treacherous a snare. This Cochloeus denied, and we are inclined to credit his testimony. And yet just before going to Luther's lodging he had been in conference with Aleander.

In the evening, the Archbishop of Treves assembled at supper the persons who had attended that morning's conference: he thought that this would be a means of unbending their minds, and bringing them closer together. Luther, so firm and intrepid before arbitrators and judges, in private life was so good-humored and jovial, that they might reasonably hope anything from him. The archbishop's chancellor, who had been so formal in his official capacity, lent himself to this new essay, and towards the end of the repast proposed Luther's health. The latter prepared to return the compliment; the wine was poured out, and, according to his usual custom, he had made the sign of the cross on his glass, when suddenly it burst in his hands, and the wine was spilled upon the table. The guests were astonished. "It must have contained poison!" exclaimed some of Luther's friends aloud. But the doctor, without betraying any agitation, replied with a smile: "My dear Sirs, either this wine was not intended for me, or else it would have disagreed with me." And then he added calmly: "There is no doubt the glass broke because after washing it, it was dipped too soon into cold water." These words, although so simple, under such circumstances are not devoid of grandeur, and show an unalterable peace of mind. We cannot imagine that the Roman Catholics would have desired to poison Luther, especially under the roof of the Archbishop of Treves. This repast neither estranged nor approximated the two parties. Neither the favor nor the hatred of men had any influence over the reformer's resolution: it proceeded from a higher Source.

On the morning of Thursday, the twenty-fifth of April, the Chancellor Wehe, and Doctor Peutinger of Augsburg, the emperor's councilor, who had shown great affection for Luther at the period of his interview with De Vio, repaired to the hotel of the Knights of Rhodes. The Elector of Saxony sent Frederick of Thun and another of his councilors to be present at the conference. "Place yourself in our hands," pleaded Wehe and Peutinger, who would willingly have made every sacrifice to prevent the division that was about to rend the Church. "We pledge you our word, that this affair shall be concluded in a Christian-like manner." "Here is my answer in two words," replied Luther. "I consent to renounce my safe-conduct. I place my person and my life in the emperor's hands, but the Word of God . . . never!"

Frederick of Thun rose in emotion, and said to the envoys: "Is not this enough? Is not the sacrifice large enough?" And after declaring he would not hear a single word more, he left the room. Upon this, Wehe and Peutinger, hoping to succeed more easily with the doctor, came and sat down by his side. "Place yourself in the hands of the diet," said they. "No," replied he, "for cursed be the man that trusteth in man!" (Jer. 17:5). Wehe and Peutinger became more earnest in their exhortations and attacks; they urged the reformer more pressingly. Luther, exhausted, rose and dismissed them, saying: "I will never permit any man to set himself above the Word of God." "Reflect upon our proposal," said they, as they withdrew; "we will return in the evening."

They came; but feeling convinced that Luther would not give way, they brought a new proposition. Luther had refused to acknowledge, first the pope, then the emperor, and lastly the diet; there still remained one judge whom he himself had once demanded: a general council. Doubtless such a proposal would have offended Rome: but it was their last hope of safety. The delegates offered a council to Luther. The latter might have accepted it without specifying anything. Years would have passed away before the difficulties could have been set aside which the convocation of a council would have met with on the part of the pope. To gain time was for the reformer and the Reformation to gain everything. God and the lapse of years would have brought about great changes. But Luther set plain dealing above all things; he would not save himself at the expense of truth, even were silence alone necessary to dissemble it. "I consent," replied he, "but [and to make such a request was to refuse a council] on condition that the council shall decide only according to Scripture."

Peutinger and Wehe, not imagining that a council could decide otherwise, ran quite overjoyed to the archbishop: "Doctor Martin," said they, "submits his books to a council." The archbishop was on the point of carrying these glad tidings to the emperor, when he felt some doubt, and ordered Luther to be brought to him.

Richard of Greiffenklau was alone when the doctor arrived. "Dear doctor," said the archbishop, with great kindness and feeling, "my doctors inform me that you consent to submit, unreservedly, your cause to a council."—"My lord," replied Luther, "I can endure everything, but I cannot abandon the Holy Scriptures." The bishop perceived that Wehe and Peutinger had stated the matter incorrectly. Rome could never consent to a council that decided only according to Scripture. "It was like telling a short-sighted man," says Pallavicini, "to read very small print, and at the same time refusing him a pair of spectacles." The worthy archbishop sighed: "It was a fortunate thing that I sent for you," said he. "What would have become of me, if I had immediately carried this news to the emperor?" Luther's immovable firmness and inflexibility, doubtless surprising, will be understood and respected by all those who know the law of God. Seldom has a nobler homage been paid to the unchangeable Word from heaven; and that, too, at the peril of the liberty and life of the man who bore this testimony.

"Well, then," said the venerable prelate to Luther, "point out a remedy yourself."

Luther, after a moment's silence. "My lord, I know no better than this of Gamaliel: 'If this work be of men, it will come to nought: but if it be of God, ye cannot overthrow it; lest haply ye be found even to fight against God.' Let the emperor, the electors, the princes, and states of the empire, write this answer to the pope."

The Archbishop. "Retract at least some articles."

Luther. "Provided they are none of those which the Council of Constance has already condemned."

The Archbishop. "I am afraid it is precisely those that you would be called upon to retract."

Luther. "In that case I would rather lose my life,—rather have my arms and legs cut off, than forsake the clear and true Word of God."

The archbishop understood Luther at last. "You may retire," said he, still with the same kind manner. "My lord," resumed Luther, "may I beg you to have the goodness to see that his majesty provides me with the safe-conduct necessary for my return?"—"I will see to it," replied the good archbishop, and so they parted.

Thus ended these negotiations. The whole empire had turned toward this man with the most ardent prayers and with the most terrible threats, and he had not faltered. His refusal to bend beneath the iron yoke of the pope emancipated the Church and began the new times. The interposition of Providence was manifest. This is one of those grand scenes in history over which hovers and rises the majestic presence of the Divinity. Luther withdrew in company with Spalatin, who had arrived at the Archbishop's during the interview. John Minkwitz, councilor to the Elector of Saxony, had fallen ill at Worms. The two friends went to visit him. Luther gave the sick man the most affectionate consolations. "Farewell!" said he, as he retired, "tomorrow I shall leave Worms."

Luther was not deceived. Hardly had he returned three hours to the hotel of the Knights of Rhodes, when the Chancellor ab Eck, accompanied by the imperial chancellor and a notary, appeared before him.

The chancellor said to him: "Martin Luther, his imperial majesty, the electors, princes, and states of the empire, having at sundry times and in various forms exhorted you to submission, but always in vain, the emperor, in his capacity of advocate and defender of the Catholic faith, finds himself compelled to resort to other measures. He therefore commands you to return home in the space of twenty-one days, and forbids you to disturb the public peace on your road, either by preaching or by writing."

Luther felt clearly that this message was the beginning of his condemnation: "As the Lord pleases," answered he meekly, "blessed be the name of the Lord!" He then added: "Before all things, humbly and from the bottom of my heart do I thank his majesty, the electors, princes, and other states of the empire, for having listened to me so kindly. I desire, and have ever desired, but one thing—a reformation of the Church according to Holy Scripture. I am ready to do and to suffer everything in humble obedience to the emperor's will. Life or death, evil or good report—it is all the same to me, with one reservation—the preaching of the gospel; for, says St. Paul, 'the Word of God must not be bound.'" The deputies retired.

On the morning of Friday the twenty-sixth of April, the friends of the reformer with several lords met at Luther's hotel. They were delighted at seeing the Christian firmness with which he had opposed Charles and the empire; and recognized in him the features of that celebrated portrait of antiquity:

> Justum ac tenacem propositi virum,
> Non civium ardor prava jubentium,
> Non vultus instantis tyranni
> Mente quatit solida. . . .[1]

They desired once more, perhaps for the last time, to say farewell to this intrepid monk. Luther partook of a humble repast. But now he had to take leave of his friends, and fly far from them, beneath a sky lowering with tempests. This solemn moment he desired to pass in the presence of God. He lifted up his soul in prayer, blessing those who stood around him. As it struck ten, Luther issued from the hotel with the friends who had accompanied him to Worms. Twenty gentlemen on horseback surrounded his car. A great crowd of people accompanied him beyond the walls of the city. Some time after he was overtaken by Sturm, the imperial herald, at Oppenheim, and on the next day they arrived at Frankfurt.

[1] The man that's resolute and just,
Firm to his principles and trust,
Nor hopes nor fears can bind;
Nor parties, for revenge engaged,
Nor threatenings of a court enraged,
Can shake his steady mind.—Horace

Chapter 56

THE EDICT OF WORMS

Thus had Luther escaped from these walls of Worms, that seemed destined to be his sepulcher. With all his heart he gave God the glory. "The devil himself," said he, "guarded the pope's citadel; but Christ has made a wide breach in it, and Satan was constrained to confess that the Lord is mightier than he."

"The day of the Diet of Worms," says the pious Mathesius, Luther's disciple and friend, "is one of the greatest and most glorious days given to the earth before the end of the world." The battle that had been fought at Worms resounded far and wide, and at its noise which spread through all Christendom, from the regions of the North to the mountains of Switzerland, and the towns of England, France, and Italy, many eagerly grasped the powerful weapons of the Word of God.

Luther, who reached Frankfurt on the evening of Saturday, the twenty-seventh of April, took advantage the next day of a leisure moment, the first that he had enjoyed for a long time, to write a familiar and expressive note to his friend at Wittenberg, the celebrated painter Lucas Cranach. "Your servant, dear gossip Lucas," said he. "I thought his majesty would have assembled some fifty doctors at Worms to convict the monk outright. But not at all.—Are these your books?—Yes!—Will you retract them?—No!—Well, then, be gone! —There's the whole history. O blind Germans! . . . how childishly we act, to allow ourselves to be the dupes and sport of Rome! . . . The Jews must sing their Yo! Yo! Yo! But a day of redemption is coming for us also, and then will we sing hallelujah! . . . For a season we must suffer in silence. 'A little while, and ye shall not see me: and again a little while, and ye shall see me,' said Jesus Christ (John 16:16). I hope that it will be the same with me. Farewell. I commend you all to the Lord. May He preserve in Christ your understanding and your faith against the attacks of the wolves and the dragons of Rome. Amen!"

After having written this somewhat enigmatical letter, Luther, as the time pressed, immediately set out for Friedberg, which is six leagues distant from Frankfurt. On the next day Luther again collected his thoughts. He desired to write once more to Charles, as he had no wish to be confounded with guilty rebels. In his letter to the emperor he set forth clearly what is the obedience due to kings, and that which is due to God, and what is the limit at which the former should cease and give place to the latter. As we read this epistle, we are involuntarily reminded of the words of the greatest autocrat of modern times: "My dominion ends where that of conscience begins." [1]

"God, who is the searcher of hearts, is my witness," said Luther, "that I am ready most earnestly to obey your majesty, in honor or in dishonor, in life or in death, and with no exception save the Word of God, by which man lives. In all the affairs of this present life, my fidelity shall be unshaken, for here to lose or to gain is of no consequence to salvation. But when eternal interests are concerned, God wills not that man should submit unto man. For such submission in spiritual matters is a real worship, and ought to be rendered solely to the Creator."

Luther wrote also, but in German, a letter addressed to the states of the empire. Its contents were nearly similar to that which he had just written to the emperor. In it he related all that had passed at Worms. This letter was copied several times and circulated throughout Germany. "Everywhere," says Cochloeus, "it excited the indignation of the people against the emperor and the superior clergy."

Early the next day Luther wrote a note to Spalatin, enclosing the two letters he had written the evening before; he sent back to Worms the herald Sturm, won over to the cause of the Gospel; and after embracing him, departed hastily for Grunberg.

On Tuesday, at about two leagues from Hirschfeldt, he met the chancellor of the prince-abbot of that town, who came to welcome

[1] Napoleon to the Protestant deputation after his accession to the empire.

him. Soon after there appeared a troop of horsemen with the abbot at their head. The latter dismounted, and Luther got out of his wagon. The prince and the reformer embraced, and afterwards entered Hirschfeldt together. The senate received them at the gates of the city. The princes of the Church came out to meet a monk anathematized by the pope, and the chief men of the people bent their heads before a man under the ban of the emperor.

"At five in the morning we shall be at church," said the prince at night as he rose from the table to which he had invited the reformer. The abbot insisted on his sleeping in his own bed. The next day Luther preached, and this dignitary of the church, with all his train, escorted him on his way.

In the evening Luther reached Eisenach, the scene of his childhood. All his friends in this city surrounded him, entreating him to preach, and the next day accompanied him to the church. Upon this the priest of the parish appeared, attended by a notary and witnesses; he came forward trembling, divided between the fear of losing his place, and of opposing the powerful man that stood before him. "I protest against the liberty that you are taking," said the priest at last, in an embarrassed tone. Luther went up into the pulpit, and that voice which, twenty-three years before, had sung in the streets of this town, to procure a morsel of bread, sounded beneath the arched roof of the ancient church those notes that were beginning to agitate the world. After the sermon, the priest with confusion went up to Luther. The notary had drawn up the protest, the witnesses had signed it, all was properly arranged to secure the incumbent's place. "Pardon me," said he to the doctor humbly; "I am acting thus to protect me from the resentment of the tyrants who oppress the Church."

And there were in truth strong grounds for apprehension. The aspect of affairs at Worms was changed: Aleander alone seemed to rule there. "Banishment is Luther's only prospect," wrote Frederick to his brother, Duke John: "nothing can save him. If God permits me to return to you, I shall have matters to relate that are almost beyond belief. It is not only Annas and Caiaphas, but Pilate and Herod also, that have combined against him." Frederick had little desire to remain longer at Worms; he departed, and the elector-palatine did the same. The elector-archbishop of Cologne also quitted the diet. Their example was followed by many princes of inferior rank. As they deemed it impossible to avert the blow, they preferred (and in this perhaps they were wrong) abandoning the place. The Spaniards, the Italians, and the most ultra-montane German princes alone remained.

The field was now free—Aleander triumphed. He laid before Charles the outline of an edict intended by him as a model of that which the diet ought to issue against the monk. The nuncio's project pleased the exasperated emperor. He assembled the remaining members of the diet in his chamber, and there had Aleanders' edict read over to them; it was accepted (Pallavicini informs us) by all who were present.

The next day, which was a great festival, the emperor went to the cathedral, attended by all the lords of his court. When the religious ceremonies were over, and a crowd of people still thronged the sanctuary, Aleander, robed in all the insignia of his dignity, approached Charles V. He held in his hand two copies of the edict against Luther, one in Latin, the other in German, and kneeling before his imperial majesty, entreated him to affix to them his signature and the seal of the empire. It was at the moment when the sacrifice had been offered, when the incense still filled the temple, while the sacred chants were still re-echoing through its long-drawn aisles, and as it were in the presence of the Deity, that the destruction of the enemy of Rome was to be sealed. The emperor, assuming a very gracious air, took the pen and wrote his name. Aleander withdrew in triumph, immediately sent the decree to the printers, and forwarded it to every part of Christendom. This crowning act of the toils of Rome had cost the papacy no little trouble. Pallavicini himself informs us, that this edict, although bearing date the eighth of May, was not signed till later; but it was antedated to make it appear that the signature was affixed at a period when all the members of the diet were assembled.

"We, Charles The Fifth," said the emperor (and then came his titles), "to all electors, princes, prelates, and others whom it may concern. The Almighty having confided to us, for the defense of the holy faith, more kingdoms and greater authority than He has ever given to any of our predecessors, we purpose employing every means in our power to prevent our holy empire from being polluted by any heresy.

"The Augustine monk, Martin Luther, notwithstanding our exhortation, has rushed like a madman on our holy Church, and attempted to destroy it by books overflowing with blasphemy. He has shamefully polluted the indestructible law of holy matrimony; he has endeavored to excite the laity to dye their hands in the blood of the clergy; and, setting at nought all authority, has incessantly urged the people to revolt, schism, war, murder, robbery, incendiarism, and to the utter ruin of the Christian faith. . . . In a word, not to mention his many other evil practices, this man, who is in truth not a man, but Satan himself under the form of a man and dressed in a monk's frock, has collected into one stinking slough all the vilest heresies of past times, and has added to them new ones of his own. . . .

"We have therefore dismissed from our presence this Luther, whom all pious and sensible men deem a madman, or one possessed by the devil; and we enjoin that, on the expiration of his safe-conduct, immediate recourse be had to effectual measures to check his furious rage.

"For this reason, under pain of incurring the penalties due to the crime of high-treason, we forbid you to harbor the said Luther after the appointed term shall be expired, to conceal him, to give him food or drink, or to furnish him, by word or by deed, publicly or secretly, with any kind of succor whatsoever. We enjoin you, moreover, to seize him, or cause him to be seized, wherever you may find him, to bring him before us without any delay, or to keep him in safe custody, until you have learned from us in what manner you are to act towards him, and have received the reward due to your labors in so holy a work.

"As for his adherents, you will apprehend them, confine them, and confiscate their property.

"As for his writings, if the best nutriment becomes the detestation of all men as soon as one drop of poison is mingled with it, how much more ought such books, which contain a deadly poison for the soul, be not only rejected, but destroyed! You will therefore burn them, or utterly destroy them in any other manner.

"As for the authors, poets, printers, painters, buyers or sellers of placards, papers, or pictures, against the pope or the Church, you will seize them, body and goods, and will deal with them according to your good pleasure.

"And if any person, whatever be his dignity, should dare act in contradiction to the decree of our imperial majesty, we order him to be placed under the ban of the empire.

"Let every man behave according to this decree."

Such was the edict signed in the cathedral of Worms. It was more than a bull of Rome, which, although published in Italy, could not be executed in Germany. The emperor himself had spoken, and the diet had ratified his decree. All the partisans of Rome burst into a shout of triumph. "It is the end of the tragedy!" exclaimed they. "In my opinion," said Alphonso Valdez, a Spaniard at Charles's court, "it is not the end, but only the beginning." Valdez perceived that the movement was in the Church, in the people, and in the age, and that, even should Luther perish, his cause would not perish with him. But no one was blind to the imminent and inevitable danger in which the reformer himself was placed; and the great majority of superstitious persons were filled with horror at the thought of that incarnate devil, covered with a monk's hood, whom the emperor pointed out to the nation.

The man against whom the mighty ones of the earth were thus forging their thunderbolts had quitted the church of Eisenach, and was preparing to bid farewell to some of his dearest friends. He did not take the road to Gotha and Erfurt, but proceeded to the village of Mora, his father's native place, once more to see his aged grandmother, who died four months after, and to visit his uncle, Henry Luther, and some other relations. Schurff, Jonas, and Suaven set out for Wittenberg; Luther got into the wagon with Amsdorff, who still remained with him, and entered the forests of Thuringia.

The same evening he arrived at the village of his sires. The poor old peasant clasped in her arms that grandson who had withstood Charles the emperor and Leo the pope. Luther spent the next day with his relations, happy, after the tumult at Worms, in this sweet tranquillity. On the next morning he resumed his journey, accompanied by Amsdorff and his brother James. In this lonely spot the reformer's fate was to be decided. They skirted the woods of Thuringia, following the road to Waltershausen. As the wagon was moving through a hollow way, near the deserted church of Glisback, at a short distance from the castle of Altenstein, a sudden noise was heard, and immediately five horsemen, masked and armed from head to foot, sprang upon the travelers. His brother James, as soon as he caught sight of the assailants, leaped from the wagon and ran away as fast as his legs would carry him, without uttering a single word. The driver would have resisted. "Stop!" cried one of the strangers with a terrible voice, falling upon him and throwing him to the ground. A second mask laid hold of Amsdorff and kept him at a distance. Meanwhile the three remaining horsemen seized upon Luther, maintaining a profound silence. They pulled him violently from the wagon, threw a military cloak over his shoulders, and placed him on a horse. The two other masks now quitted Amsdorff and the wagoner; all five leaped to their saddles—one dropped his hat, but they did not even stop to pick it up—and in the twinkling of an eye vanished with their prisoner into the gloomy forest.

At first they took the road to Broderode, but soon retraced their steps by another path; and without quitting the wood, made so many windings in every direction as utterly to baffle any attempt to track them. Luther, little accustomed to be on horseback, was soon overcome with fatigue. They permitted him to alight for a few minutes; he lay down near a beech tree, where he drank some water from a spring which is still called after his name. His brother James, continuing his flight, arrived at Waltershausen in the evening. The affrighted wagoner jumped into the car, which Amsdorff had again mounted, and whipping his horses, drove rapidly away from the spot, and conducted Luther's friend to Wittenberg. At Waltershausen, at Wittenberg, in the country, villages, and towns along their road, they spread the news of the violent abduction of the doctor. This intelligence, which delighted some, struck the greater number with astonishment and indignation. A cry of grief soon resounded through all Germany: "Luther has fallen into the hands of his enemies!"

After the violent combat that Luther had just sustained, God had been pleased to conduct him to a place of repose and peace. After having exhibited him on the brilliant theater of Worms, where all the powers of the reformer's soul had been strung to so high a pitch, He gave him the secluded and humiliating retreat of a prison. God draws from the deepest seclusion the weak instruments by which He purposes to accomplish great things; and then, when He has permitted them to glitter for a season with dazzling brilliancy on an illustrious stage, He dismisses them again to the deepest obscurity. The Reformation was to be accomplished by other means than violent struggles or pompous appearances before diets. It is not thus that the leaven penetrates the mass of the people: the Spirit of God seeks more tranquil paths. The man, whom the Roman champions were persecuting without mercy, was to disappear for a time from the world. It was requisite that this great individuality should fade away in order that the revolution then accomplishing might not bear the stamp of an individual. It was necessary for the man to retire, that God might remain alone to move by His Spirit upon the deep waters in which the darkness of the Middle Ages was already engulfed, and to say: "Let there be light," so that there might be light.

As soon as it grew dark, and no one could track their footsteps, Luther's guards took a new road. About one hour before midnight they reached the foot of a mountain. The horses ascended slowly. On the summit was an old castle, surrounded on all sides, save that by which it was approached, by the black forests that cover the mountains of Thuringia.

It was to this lofty and isolated fortress, named the Wartburg, where in former times the ancient landgraves had sheltered themselves, that Luther was conducted. The bolts were drawn back, the iron bars fell, the gates opened; the reformer crossed the threshold; the doors were closed behind him. He dismounted in the court. One of the horsemen, Burkhardt of Hund, lord of Altenstein, withdrew; another, John of Berlepsch, provost of the Wartburg, led the doctor into the chamber that was to be his prison, and where he found a knight's uniform and a sword. The three other cavaliers, the provost's attendants, took away his ecclesiastical robes, and dressed him in the military garments that had been prepared for him, enjoining him to let his beard and hair grow, in order that no one in the castle might discover who he was. The people in the Wartburg were to know the prisoner only by the name of Knight George. Luther scarcely recognized himself in his new dress. At last he was left alone, and his mind could reflect by turns on the astonishing events that had just taken place at Worms, on the uncertain future that awaited him, and on his new and strange residence. From the narrow loopholes of his turret, his eye roamed over the gloomy, solitary, and extensive forests that surrounded him. "It was there," says Mathesius, his friend and biographer, "that the doctor abode, like St. Paul in his prison at Rome."

Frederick of Thun, Philip Feilitsch, and Spalatin, in a private conversation they had had with Luther at Worms by the elector's orders, had not concealed from him that his liberty must be sacrificed to the anger of Charles and of the pope. And yet this abduction had been so mysteriously contrived, that even Frederick was for a long time ignorant of the place where Luther was shut up. The grief of the friends of the Reformation was prolonged. The spring passed away; summer, autumn, and winter, succeeded; the sun had accomplished its annual course, and still the walls of the Wartburg enclosed their prisoner. Truth had been interdicted by the diet; its defender, confined within the ramparts of a castle, had disappeared from the stage of the world, and no one knew what had become of him: Aleander triumphed; the reformation appeared lost. . . . But God reigns, and the blow that seemed as if it would destroy the cause of the gospel, did but contribute to save its courageous minister and to extend the light of faith to distant countries.

Chapter 57

LUTHER'S CAPTIVITY
IN THE WARTBURG

HITHERTO the Reformation had been centered in the person of Luther. His appearance before the Diet of Worms was doubtless the sublimest day of his life. His character appeared at that time almost spotless; and it is this which has given rise to the observation, that if God, who concealed the reformer for ten months within the walls of the Wartburg, had that instant removed him forever from the eyes of the world, his end would have been as an apotheosis. But God designs no apotheosis for His servants; and Luther was preserved to the Church, in order to teach, by his very faults, that the faith of Christians should be based solely on the Word of God. He was transported suddenly far from the stage on which the great revolution of the sixteenth century was taking place; the truth, that for four years he had so powerfully proclaimed, continued in his absence to act upon Christendom; and the work, of which he was but the feeble instrument, henceforward bore the seal not of man, but of God Himself.

Germany was moved at Luther's captivity. The most contradictory rumors were circulated in the provinces. The reformer's absence excited men's minds more than his presence could have done. In one place it was said that friends from France had placed him in safety on the other bank of the Rhine; in another, that he had fallen by the dagger of the assassin. Even in the smallest villages inquiries were made about Luther; travelers were stopped and questioned, and groups collected in the public places. At times some unknown orator would recount in a spirit-stirring narrative how the doctor had been carried off; he would describe the cruel horsemen tying their prisoner's hands, spurring their horses, and dragging him after them on foot, until his stength was exhausted, stopping their ears to his cries, and forcing the blood from his limbs. "Luther's body," added he, "has been seen pierced through and through." As they heard this, the listeners uttered cries of sorrow. "Alas!" said they, "we shall never see or hear that noble-minded man again, whose voice stirred our very hearts!" Luther's friends trembled with indignation, and swore to avenge his death.

Women, children, men of peace, and the aged beheld with affright the prospect of new struggles. Nothing could equal the alarm of the partisans of Rome. The priests and monks, who at first had not been able to conceal their exultation, thinking themselves secure of victory because one man was dead, and who had raised their heads with an insulting air of triumph, would now have fled far from the threatening anger of the people. These men, who, while Luther was free, had given the rein to their fury, trembled now that he was a captive. Aleander, especially, was astounded. "The only remaining way of saving ourselves," wrote a Roman Catholic to the archbishop of Mentz, "is to light torches and hunt for Luther through the whole world, to restore him to the nation that is calling for him." One might have said that the pale ghost of the reformer, dragging his chains, was spreading terror around, and calling for vengeance. "Luther's death," exclaimed some, "will cause torrents of blood to be shed."

In no place was there such commotion as in Worms itself; resolute murmurs were heard among both people and princes. Ulrich Hütten and Hermann Busch filled the country with their plaintive strains and songs of battle. Charles V and the nuncios were publicly accused. The nation took up the cause of the poor monk, who, by the strength of his faith, had become their leader.

At Wittenberg, his colleagues and friends, and especially Melancthon, were at first sunk in the deepest affliction. Luther had imparted to this young scholar the treasures of that holy theology which had thenceforward wholly occupied his mind. Luther had given substance and life to that purely intellectual cultivation which Melancthon had brought to Wittenberg. The depth of the reformer's teaching had struck the youthful Hellenist, and the doctor's courage in maintaining the rights of the everlasting gospel against all human authority had filled him with enthusiasm. He had become a partner in his labors; he had taken up the pen, and with that purity of style which he derived from the study of the ancients, had successively, and with a hand of power, humbled the authority of the fathers and councils before the sovereign Word of God.

Melancthon showed the same decision in his learning that Luther displayed in his actions. Never were there two men of greater diversity, and at the same time of greater unity. "Scripture," said Melancthon, "imparts to the soul a holy and marvelous delight: it is the heavenly ambrosia." "The Word of God," exclaimed Luther, "is a sword, a war, a destruction; it falls upon the children of Ephraim like a lioness in the forest." Thus, one saw in the Scriptures a power to console, and the other a violent opposition against the corruptions of the world. But both esteemed it the greatest thing on earth; and hence they agreed in perfect harmony. "Melancthon," said Luther, "is a wonder; all men confess it now. He is the most formidable enemy of Satan and the schoolmen, for he knows their foolishness, and Christ the Rock. The little Grecian surpasses even me in divinity; he will be as serviceable to you as many Luthers." And he added that he was ready to abandon any opinion of which Philip did not approve. On his part, too, Melancthon, filled with admiration at Luther's knowledge of Scripture, set him far above the Fathers of the Church. He would make excuses for the jests with which Luther was reproached, and compared him to an earthen vessel that contains a precious treasure beneath its coarse exterior. "I should be very unwilling to reprove him inconsiderately in this matter," said Melancthon.

But now, these two hearts, so closely united, were separated. These two valiant soldiers could no longer march side by side to the deliverance of the Church. Luther disappeared; perhaps he was lost forever. The consternation at Wittenberg was extreme: it was like that of an army, with gloomy and dejected looks, before the blood-stained body of their general who was leading them on to victory.

Suddenly more comforting news arrived. "Our beloved father lives," exclaimed Philip in the joy of his soul; "take courage and be firm." But it was not long before their dejection returned. Luther was alive, but in prison. The edict of Worms, with its terrible proscriptions, was circulated by thousands throughout the empire, and even among the mountains of the Tyrol. Would not the Reformation be crushed by the iron hand that was weighing upon it? Melancthon's gentle spirit was overwhelmed with sorrow.

But the influence of a mightier hand was felt above the hand of man; God Himself deprived the formidable edict of all its strength. The German princes, who had always sought to diminish the power of Rome in the empire, trembled at the alliance between the emperor and the pope, and feared that it would terminate in the destruction of their liberty. Accordingly, while Charles in his journey through the Low Countries greeted with an ironical smile the burning piles which flatterers and fanatics kindled on the public places with Luther's works, these very writings were read in Germany with a continually increasing eagerness, and numerous pamphlets in favor of the reform were daily inflicting some new blow on the papacy. The nuncios were distracted at seeing this edict, the fruit of so many intrigues, producing so little effect. "The ink with which Charles V signed his arrest," said they bitterly, "is scarcely dry, and yet the imperial decree is everywhere torn in pieces." The people were becoming more and more attached to the admirable man who, heedless of the thunders of Charles and of the pope, had confessed his faith with the courage of a martyr. "He offered to retract," said they, "if he were refuted, and no one dared undertake the task. Does not this prove the truth of his doctrines?" Thus the first movement of alarm was succeeded in Wittenberg and the whole empire by a movement of enthusiasm. Even the Archbishop of Mentz, witnessing this outburst of popular sympathy, dared not give the Cordeliers permission to preach against the reformer. The university, that seemed on the point of being crushed, raised its head. The new doctrines were too firmly established for them to be shaken by Luther's absence; and the halls of the academy could hardly contain the crowd of hearers.

Chapter 58

HIS LABORS WHILE A CAPTIVE

MEANTIME the Knight George, for by that name Luther was called in the Wartburg, lived solitary and unknown. "If you were to see me," wrote he to Melancthon, "you would take me for a soldier, and even you would hardly recognize me." Luther at first indulged in repose, enjoying a leisure which had not hitherto been allowed him. He wandered freely through the fortress, but could not go beyond the walls. All his wishes were attended to, and he had never been better treated. A crowd of thoughts filled his soul; but none had power to trouble. By turns he looked down upon the forests that surrounded him, and raised his eyes towards heaven. "A strange prisoner am I," exclaimed he, "a captive with and against my will!"

"Pray for me," wrote he to Spalatin; "your prayers are the only thing I need. I do not grieve for anything that may be said of me in the world. At last I am at rest." This letter, as well as many others of the same period, is dated from the island of Patmos. Luther compared the Wartburg to that celebrated island to which the wrath of Domitian in former times had banished the apostle John.

In the midst of the dark forests of Thuringia the reformer reposed from the violent struggles that had agitated his soul. There he studied Christian truth, not for the purpose of contention, but as a means of regeneration and life. The beginning of the Reformation was of necessity polemical; new times required new labors. After cutting down the thorns and the thickets, it was requisite to sow the Word of God peaceably in the heart. If Luther had been incessantly called upon to fight fresh battles, he would not have accomplished a durable work in the Church. Thus by his captivity he escaped a danger which might possibly have ruined the Reformation—that of always attacking and destroying without ever defending or building up.

This humble retreat had a still more precious result. Uplifted by his countrymen, as on a shield, he was on the verge of the abyss; the least giddiness might have plunged him into it headlong. Some of the first promoters of the Reformation both in Germany and Switzerland, ran upon the shoal of spiritual pride and fanaticism. Luther was a man very subject to the infirmities of our nature, and he was unable to escape altogether from these dangers. The hand of God, however, delivered him for a time, by suddenly removing him from the sphere of intoxicating ovations, and throwing him into an unknown retreat. There his soul was wrapt in pious meditation at God's footstool; it was again tempered in the waters of adversity; its sufferings and humiliation compelled him to walk, for a time at least, with the humble; and the principles of a Christian life were thenceforward evolved in his soul with greater energy and freedom.

Luther's calmness was not of long duration. Seated in loneliness on the ramparts of the Wartburg, he remained whole days lost in deep meditation. At one time the Church appeared before him, displaying all her wretchedness; at another, directing his eyes hopefully towards heaven, he exclaimed: "Wherefore, O Lord, hast thou made all men in vain?" (Ps. 89:47). And then, giving way to despair, he cried with dejection: "Alas! there is no one in this latter day of His anger, to stand like a wall before the Lord, and save Israel!" Then, recurring to his own destiny, he feared lest he should be accused of deserting the field of battle; and this supposition weighed down his soul. "I would rather," said he, "be stretched on coals of fire, than lie here half-dead."

Transporting himself in imagination to Worms and Wittenberg, into the midst of his adversaries, he regretted having yielded to the advice of his friends, that he had quitted the world, and that he had not presented his bosom to the fury of men. "Alas!" said he, "there is nothing I desire more than to appear before my cruelest enemies."

Gentler thoughts, however, brought a truce to such anxiety. Everything was not storm and tempest for Luther; from time to time his agitated mind found tranquillity and comfort. Next to the certainty of God's help, one thing consoled him in his sorrows: it was the recollection of Melancthon. "If I perish," wrote he, "the gospel will lose nothing: you will succeed me as Elisha did Elijah, with a double portion of my spirit." But calling to mind Philip's timidity, he exclaimed with energy: "Minister of the Word! keep the walls and towers of Jerusalem until you are struck down by the enemy. As yet we stand alone upon the field of battle; after me, they will aim their blows at you."

The thought of the final attack Rome was about to make on the infant Church, renewed his anxieties. The poor monk, solitary and a prisoner, had many a combat to fight alone. But a hope of deliverance speedily dawned upon him. It appeared to him that the assaults of the papacy would raise the whole German nation, and that the victorious soldiers of the gospel would surround the Wartburg, and restore the prisoner to liberty.

"If the pope," said he, "lays his hand on all those who are on my side, there will be a disturbance in Germany; the greater his haste to crush us, the sooner will come the end of the pope and his followers. And I . . . I shall be restored to you. God is awakening the hearts of many, and stirring up the nations. Only let our enemies clasp our affair in their arms and try to stifle it; it will gather strength under their pressure, and come forth ten times more formidable."

But sickness brought him down from those high places on which his courage and his faith had placed him. He had already suffered much at Worms; his disease increased in solitude. He could not endure the food at the Wartburg, which was less coarse than that of his convent; they were compelled to give him the meager diet to which he had been accustomed. He passed whole nights without sleep. Anxieties of mind were superadded to the pains of the body. No great work is ever accomplished without suffering and martyrdom. Luther, alone upon his rock, endured in his strong frame a passion that the emancipation of the human race rendered necessary. "Seated by night in my chamber," says he, "I uttered groans, like a woman in her travail; torn, wounded, and bleeding. . . ." Then breaking off his complaints, touched with the thought that his sufferings were a blessing from God, he exclaimed with love: "Thanks be to Thee, O Christ, that Thou wilt not leave me without the precious marks of Thy cross!" But soon, growing angry with himself, he cried out: "Madman and hard-hearted that I am! Woe is me! I pray seldom, I seldom wrestle with the Lord, I groan not for the Church of God! Instead of being fervent in spirit, my passions take fire; I live in idleness, in sleep, and indolence!" Then, not knowing to what he should attribute this state, and accustomed to expect everything from the affection of his brethren, he exclaimed in the desolation of his heart: "O my friends! do you then forget to pray for me, that God is thus far from me?"

Those who were around him, as well as his friends at Wittenberg and at the elector's court, were uneasy and alarmed at this state of suffering. They feared lest they should see the life they had rescued from the flames of the pope and the sword of Charles V decline sadly and expire. Was the Wartburg destined to be Luther's tomb? "I fear," said Melancthon, "that the grief he feels for the Church will cause his death. A fire has been kindled by him in Israel; if he dies, what hope will remain for us? Would to God, that at the cost of my own wretched life, I could retain in the world that soul which is its fairest ornament!—Oh! what a man!" exclaimed he, as if already standing beside his grave; "we never appreciated him rightly!"

What Luther denominated the shameful indolence of his prison was a task that almost exceeded the strength of one man. "I am here all the day," wrote he on May 14, "in idleness and pleasures [alluding doubtless to the better diet that was provided him at first]. I am reading the Bible in Hebrew and Greek; I am going to write a treatise in German on Auricular Confession; I shall continue the translation of the Psalms, and compose a volume of sermons, so soon as I have received what I want from Wittenberg. I am writing without intermission." And yet this was but a part of his labors.

His enemies thought that, if he were not dead, at least they should hear no more of him; but their joy was not of long duration, and there could be no doubt that he was alive. A multitude of writings, composed in the Wartburg, succeeded each other rapidly, and the beloved voice of the reformer was everywhere hailed with enthusiasm. Luther published simultaneously works calculated to edify the Church, and polemical tracts which troubled the too eager exultation of his enemies. For nearly a whole year, he by turns instructed, exhorted, reproved, and thundered from his mountain retreat; and his amazed adversaries asked one another if there was not something supernatural, some mystery, in this prodigious activity. "He could never have taken any rest," says Cochloeus.

But there was no other mystery than the imprudence of the partisans of Rome. They hastened to take advantage of the edict of Worms, and to strike a decisive blow at the Reformation; while Luther, condemned, under the ban of the empire, and a prisoner in the Wartburg, undertook to defend the sound doctrine, as if he were still victorious and at liberty. It was especially at the tribunal of penance that the priests endeavored to rivet the chains of their docile parishioners; and accordingly the confessional was the object of Luther's first attack. "They bring forward," said he, "these words of St. James: 'Confess your faults to one another.' Singular confessor! his name is One Another. Whence it would follow that the confessors should also confess themselves to their penitents; that each Christian should be, in his turn, pope, bishop, priest; and that the pope himself should confess to all!"

Luther had scarcely finished this tract when he began another. A theologian of Louvain, by name Latomus, already notorious by his opposition to Reuchlin and Erasmus, had attacked the reformer's opinions. In twelve days, Luther's refutation was ready, and it was a masterpiece. He cleared himself of the reproach that he was wanting in moderation. "The moderation of the day," said he, "is to bend the knee before sacrilegious pontiffs and impious sophists, and to say to them: 'Gracious lord! excellent master!' Then, when you have so done, you may put anyone you please to death; you may even convulse the world, and you will be none the less a man of moderation. . . . Away with such moderation! I would rather be frank and deceive no one. The shell may be hard, but the kernel is soft and tender."

As Luther's health continued feeble, he thought of leaving the place of his confinement. But how could he manage? To appear in public would be exposing his life. The back of the mountain on which the fortress stood was crossed by numerous footways, bordered by tufts of strawberries. The heavy gate of the castle opened, and the prisoner ventured, not without fear, to gather some of the fruit. By degrees he grew bolder, and in his knight's garb began to wander through the surrounding country, attended by one of the guards of the castle, a worthy but somewhat churlish man. One day, having entered an inn, Luther threw aside his sword, which encumbered him, and hastily took up some books that lay there. His nature got the better of his prudence. His guardian trembled lest a movement, so extraordinary in a soldier, should excite suspicions that the doctor was not really a knight. At another time the two comrades alighted at the convent of Reinhardsbrunn, where Luther had slept a few months before on his road to Worms. Suddenly one of the lay-brothers uttered a cry of surprise. Luther was recognized. His attendant perceived it, and dragged him hastily away; and they galloped far from the cloister before the astonished brother recovered from his amazement.

The military life of the doctor had at intervals something about it truly theological. One day the nets were made ready—the gates of the fortress opened—the long-eared dogs rushed forth. Luther desired to taste the pleasures of the chase. The huntsmen soon grew animated; the dogs sprang forward, driving the game from the covers. In the midst of all this uproar, the Knight George stands motionless: his mind is occupied with serious thoughts; the objects around him fill his heart with sorrow. "Is not this," says he, "the image of the devil setting on his dogs—that is, the bishops, those representatives of Antichrist, and urging them in pursuit of poor souls?" A young hare was caught: delighted at the prospect of liberating it, he wrapped it carefully in his cloak, and set it down in the midst of a thicket; but hardly had he taken a few steps away from the spot before the dogs scented the animal and killed it. Luther, attracted by the noise, uttered a groan of sorrow, and exclaimed: "O pope! and thou, too, Satan! thus it is ye endeavor to destroy even those souls that have been saved from death!"

Chapter 59

LUTHER ABANDONS MONACHISM

WHILE THE DOCTOR of Wittenberg, thus dead to the world, was seeking relaxation in these sports in the neighborhood of the Wartburg, the work was going on as if of itself: the Reform was beginning; it was no longer restricted to doctrine, it entered deeply into men's actions. Bernard Feldkirchen, pastor of Kemberg, the first under Luther's directions to attack the errors of Rome, was also the first to throw off the yoke of its institutions. He married.

The Germans are fond of social life and domestic joys; and hence, of all the papal ordinances, compulsory celibacy was that which produced the saddest consequences. This law, which had been first imposed on the heads of the clergy, had prevented the ecclesiastical fiefs from becoming hereditary. But when extended by Gregory VII to the inferior clergy, it was attended with the most deplorable results. Many priests had evaded the obligations imposed upon them by the most scandalous disorders, and had drawn contempt and hatred on the whole body; while those who had submitted to Hildebrand's law were inwardly exasperated against the Church, because, while conferring on its superior dignitaries so much power, wealth, and earthly enjoyment, it bound its humbler ministers, who were its most useful supporters, to a self-denial so contrary to the gospel.

"Neither popes nor councils," said Feldkirchen and another pastor named Seidler, who had followed his example, "can impose any commandment on the Church that endangers body and soul. The obligation of keeping God's law compels me to violate the traditions of men." The re-establishment of marriage in the sixteenth century was a homage paid to the moral law. The ecclesiastical authority became alarmed, and immediately fulminated its decrees against these two priests. Seidler, who was in the territories of Duke George, was given up to his superiors, and died in prison. But the Elector Frederick refused to surrender Feldkirchen to the Archbishop of Magdeburg. "His highness," said Spalatin, "declines to act the part of a constable." Feldkirchen therefore continued pastor of his flock, although a husband and a father.

The first emotion of the reformer when he heard of this was to give way to exultation: "I admire this new bridegroom of Kemberg," said he, "who fears nothing, and hastens forward in the midst of the uproar." Luther was of opinion that priests ought to marry. But this question led to another—the marriage of monks; and here Luther had to support one of those internal struggles of which his whole life was composed; for every reform must first be won by a spiritual struggle. Melancthon and Carlstadt, the one a layman, the other a priest, thought that the liberty of contracting the bonds of wedlock should be as free for the monks as for the priests. The monk Luther did not think so at first. One day the governor of the Wartburg brought him Carlstadt's theses on celibacy: "Gracious God!" exclaimed he, "our Wittenbergers then will give wives even to the monks!" . . . This thought surprised and confounded him; his heart was troubled. He rejected for himself the liberty that he claimed for others. "Ah!" said he indignantly, "they will not force me at least to take a wife." This expression is doubtless unknown to those who assert that Luther preached the Reformation that he might marry. Inquiring for truth, not with passion, but with uprightness of purpose, he maintained what seemed to him true, although contrary to the whole of his system. He walked in a mixture of error and truth until error had fallen and truth remained alone.

There was, indeed, a great difference between the two questions. The marriage of priests was not the destruction of the priesthood; on the contrary, this of itself might restore to the secular clergy the respect of the people; but the marriage of monks was the downfall of monachism. It became a question, therefore, whether it was desirable to disband and break up that powerful army which the popes had under their orders. "Priests," wrote Luther to Melancthon, "are of divine appointment, and consequently are free as regards human commandments. But of their own free will the monks adopted celibacy; they are not therefore at liberty to withdraw from the yoke they voluntarily imposed on themselves."

The reformer was destined to advance and carry by a fresh struggle this new position of the enemy. Already had he trodden under foot a host of Roman abuses, and even Rome herself; but monachism still remained standing. Monachism, that had once carried life into so many deserts, and which, passing through so many centuries, was now filling the cloisters with sloth, and often with licentiousness, seemed to have embodied itself, and gone to defend its rights in that castle of Thuringia, where the question of its life and death was discussed in the conscience of one man. Luther struggled with it: at one moment he was on the point of gaining the victory, at another he was nearly overcome. At length, unable longer to maintain the contest, he flung himself in prayer at the feet of Jesus Christ, exclaiming: "Teach us, deliver us, establish us, by Thy mercy, in the liberty that belongs to us; for of a surety we are Thy people!"

He had not long to wait for deliverance; an important revolution was effected in the reformer's mind; and again it was the doctrine of justification by faith that gave him victory. That arm which had overthrown the indulgences, the practices of Rome, and the pope himself, also wrought the downfall of the monks in Luther's mind and throughout Christendom. Luther saw that monachism was in violent opposition to the doctrine of salvation by grace, and that a monastic life was founded entirely on the pretended merits of man. Feeling convinced, from that hour, that Christ's glory was interested in this question, he heard a voice incessantly repeating in his conscience: "Monachism must fall!" "So long as the doctrine of justification by faith remains pure and undefiled in the Church, no one can become a monk," said he. This conviction daily grew stronger in his heart, and about the beginning of September he sent "to the bishops and deacons of the Church of Wittenberg," the following theses, which were his declaration of war against a monastic life:

" 'Whatsoever is not of faith is sin' (Rom. 14:23).

"Whosoever maketh a vow of virginity, of chastity, of service to God without faith, maketh an impious and idolatrous vow—a vow to the devil himself.

"To make such vows is worse than the priests of Cybele or the vestals of the pagans; for the monks make their vows in the thought of being justified and saved by these vows; and what ought to be ascribed solely to the mercy of God is thus attributed to meritorious works.

"We must utterly overthrow such convents, as being the abodes of the devil.

"There is but one order that is holy and makes man holy, and that is Christianity or faith.

"For convents to be useful they should be converted into schools, where children should be brought up to man's estate; instead of which they are houses where adult men become children, and remain so forever."

We see that Luther would still have tolerated convents as places of education; but erelong his attacks against these establishments became more violent. The immorality and shameful practices that prevailed in the cloisters recurred forcibly to his thoughts. "I am resolved," wrote he to Spalatin on the eleventh of November, "to deliver the young from the hellish fires of celibacy." He now wrote a book against monastic vows, which he dedicated to his father:

"Do you desire," said he in his dedication to the old man at Mansfeldt, "do you still desire to rescue me from a monastic life? You have the right, for you are still my father, and I am still your son. But that is no longer necessary: God has been beforehand with you, and has Himself delivered me by His power. What matters is whether I wear or lay aside the tonsure and the cowl. Is it the cowl—is it the tonsure—that makes the monk? 'All things are yours,' says St. Paul, 'and you are Christ's.' I do not belong to the cowl, but the cowl to me. I am a monk, and yet not a monk; I am a new creature, not of the pope, but of Jesus Christ. Christ, alone and without any go-between, is my Bishop, my Abbot, my Prior, my Lord, my Father, and my Master; and I know no other. What matters it to me if the pope should condemn me and put me to death? He cannot call me from the grave and kill me a second time. . . . The great day is drawing near in which the kingdom of abominations shall be overthrown. Would to God that it were worth while for the pope to put us all to death! Our blood would cry out to heaven against him, and thus his condemnation would be hastened, and his end be near."

The transformation had already been effected in Luther himself; he was no longer a monk. It was not outward circumstances, or earthly passions, or carnal precipitation that had wrought this change. There had been a struggle: at first Luther had taken the side of monachism; but truth also had gone down into the lists, and monachism had fallen before it. The victories that passion gains are ephemeral; those of truth are lasting and decisive.

Chapter 60

THE IDOL OF HALLE

WHILE LUTHER was thus preparing the way for one of the greatest revolutions that were destined to be effected in the Church, and the Reformation was beginning to enter powerfully into the lives of Christians, the Romish partisans, blind as those generally are who have been long in the possession of power, imagined that, because Luther was in the Wartburg, the Reform was dead and forever extinct; they fancied they should be able quietly to resume their ancient practices that had been for a moment disturbed by the monk of Wittenberg. Albert, elector-archbishop of Mentz, was one of those weak men who, all things being equal, decide for the truth; but who, as soon as their interest is put in the balance, are ready to take part with error. His most important aim was to have a court as brilliant as that of any prince in Germany, his equipages as rich, and his table as well furnished: the traffic in indulgences served admirably to promote this object.

Accordingly, the decree against Luther had scarcely issued from the imperial chancery, before Albert, who was then residing with his court at Halle, summoned the vendors of indulgences, who were still alarmed at the words of the reformer, and endeavored to encourage them by such language as this: "Fear nothing, we have silenced him; let us begin to shear the flock in peace; the monk is a prisoner; he is confined by bolts and bars; this time he will be very clever if he comes again to disturb us in our affairs." The market was reopened, the merchandise was displayed for sale, and again the churches of Halle re-echoed with the speeches of the mountebanks.

But Luther was still alive, and his voice was powerful enough to pass beyond the walls and gratings behind which he had been hidden. Nothing could have roused his indignation to a higher pitch. What! the most violent battles had been fought: he had confronted every danger: the truth remained victorious, and yet they dared trample it underfoot, as if it had been vanquished! . . . That voice would again be heard, which had once put an end to this criminal traffic. "I shall enjoy no rest," wrote he to Spalatin, "until I have attacked the idol of Mentz with its brothel at Halle."

Luther set to work immediately; he cared little about the mystery with which some sought to envelop his residence in the Wartburg. He was like Elijah in the desert forging fresh thunderbolts against the impious Ahab. On the first of November he finished his treatise, *Against the New Idol of Halle.*

Intelligence of Luther's plans reached the archbishop. Alarmed at the very idea, he sent (about the middle of October) two of his attendants (Capito and Auerback) to Wittenberg to avert the storm. "Luther must moderate his impetuosity," said they to Melancthon, who, although mild himself, was not one of those who imagine that wisdom consists in perpetual concession, tergiversation, and silence. "It is God who moves him," replied he, "and our age needs a bitter and pungent salt." Upon this Capito turned to Jonas, and endeavored through him to act upon the court. The news of Luther's intention was already known there, and produced great amazement. "What!" said the courtiers: "rekindle the fire that we have had so much trouble to extinguish! Luther can only be saved by being forgotten, and yet he is rising up against the first prince in the empire!" "I will not suffer Luther to write against the Archbishop of Mentz, and thus disturb the public tranquillity," said the elector.

Luther was annoyed when these words were repeated to him. Was it not enough to imprison his body, but would they enchain his mind also, and the truth with it? . . . Did they fancy that he hid himself through fear, and that his retirement was an avowal of defeat? He maintained that it was a victory. Who dared stand up against him at Worms and oppose the truth? Accordingly when the captive in the Wartburg had read the chaplain's letter informing him of the prince's sentiments, he flung it aside, determined to make no reply. But he could not long contain himself; he took up the epistle and wrote to Spalatin: "The elector will not suffer! . . . and I too will not suffer the elector not to permit me to write. . . . Rather would I destroy yourself, the elector, nay, every creature in the world! If I have resisted the pope, who is the creator of your cardinal, why should I give way before his creature? It is very fine, forsooth, to hear you say that we must not disturb the public tranquillity, while you allow the everlasting peace of God to be disturbed! . . . Spalatin, it shall not be so! Prince, it shall not be so! I send you a book I had already prepared against the cardinal when I received your letter. Forward it to Melancthon."

Spalatin trembled as he read this manuscript; again he represented to the reformer how imprudent it would be to publish a work that would force the imperial government to lay aside its apparent ignorance of Luther's fate, and punish a prisoner who dared attack the greatest prince in the empire and the Church. If Luther persevered in his designs, the tranquillity would again be disturbed, and the Reformation perhaps be lost. Luther consented to delay the publication of his treatise, and even permitted Melancthon to erase the most violent passages. But, irritated at his friend's timidity, he wrote to the chaplain: "The Lord lives and reigns, that Lord in whom you courtfolks do not believe, unless He so accommodate His works to your reason that there is no longer any necessity to believe." He then resolved to write direct to the cardinal.

It was the whole episcopal body that Luther thus brought to the bar in the person of the German primate. His words were those of a bold man, ardent in zeal for the truth, who felt that he was speaking in the name of God Himself.

"Your electoral highness," wrote he from the depth of the retreat in which he was hidden, "has set up again in Halle the idol that swallows the money and the souls of poor Christians. You think, perhaps, that I am disabled, and that the emperor will easily stifle the cries of the poor monk. . . . But know that I shall discharge the duties that Christian charity has imposed upon me, without fearing the gates of hell, and much less the pope, his bishops, and cardinals.

"For this reason my humble prayer is, that your electoral highness would remember the beginning of this affair—how from one tiny spark proceeded so terrible a conflagration. All the world was at that time in a state of security. This poor begging friar (thought they), who unaided would attack the pope, is too weak for such an undertaking. But God interposed; and He caused the pope more labor and anxiety that he had ever felt since he had taken his place in the temple of God to tyrannize over the Church. This same God still lives: let none doubt it. He will know how to withstand a cardinal of Mentz, even were he supported by four emperors; for He is pleased above all things to hew down the lofty cedars and to abase the haughty Pharaohs.

"For this reason I inform your highness by letter, that if the idol is not thrown down, I must, in obedience to God's teaching, publicly attack your highness, as I have attacked the pope himself. Let your highness conduct yourself in accordance with this advice; I shall wait a fortnight for an early and favorable reply. Given in my wilderness, the Sunday after St. Catherine's day (November 15), 1521.

"From your electoral highness's devoted and obedient servant,
"Martin Luther."

This letter was sent to Wittenberg, and from Wittenberg to Halle, where the cardinal-elector was then residing; for no one ventured to intercept it, foreseeing the storm that would be aroused by so daring an act. But Melancthon accompanied it by a letter addressed to the prudent Capito, in which he endeavored to prepare the way for a favorable termination of this difficult business.

It is impossible to describe the feelings of the youthful and weak archbishop on receiving the reformer's letter. The work announced against the idol of Halle was like a sword suspended over his head. And, at the same time, what anger must have been kindled in his heart by the insolence of this peasant's son—of this excommunicated monk—who dared make use of such language to a prince of the house of Brandenburg, the primate of the German Church? Capito besought the archbishop to satisfy the monk. Alarm, pride, and the voice of conscience which he could not stifle, struggled fearfully in Albert's bosom. At length dread of the book, and perhaps remorse also, prevailed; he humbled himself: he put together all he thought calculated to appease the man of the Wartburg, and a fortnight had barely elapsed when Luther received the following letter, still more astonishing than his own terrible epistle:

"My dear Doctor,—I have received and read your letter, and have taken it in good part. But I think the motive that has led you to write me such an epistle has long ceased to exist. I desire, with God's help, to conduct myself as a pious bishop and a Christian prince, and I confess my need of the grace of God. I do not deny that I am a sinner, liable to sin and error, sinning and erring daily. I am well assured that without God's grace I am worthless and offensive mire, even as other men, if not more so. In replying to your letter, I would not conceal this gracious disposition; for I am more than desirous of showing you all kindness and favor, for love of Christ. I know how to receive a Christian and fraternal rebuke.

"With my own hand.   ALBERT."

Such was the language addressed to the excommunicated monk of the Wartburg by the Elector-archbishop of Mentz and Magdeburg, commissioned to represent and maintain in Germany the constitution of the Church. Did Albert, in writing it, obey the generous impulses of his conscience, or his slavish fears? In the first case, it is a noble letter; in the second, it merits our contempt. We would rather suppose it originated in the better feelings of his heart. However that may be, it shows the immeasurable superiority of God's servants over all the great ones of the earth. While Luther alone, a prisoner and condemned, derived invincible courage from his faith, the archbishop, elector and cardinal, environed with all the power and favors of the world, trembled on his throne. This contrast appears continually, and is the key to the strange enigma offered by the history of the Reformation. The Christian is not called upon to count his forces and to number his means of victory. The only thing he should be anxious about is to know whether the cause he upholds is really that of God and whether he looks only to his Master's glory. Unquestionably he has an inquiry to make; but this is wholly spiritual, —the Christian looks at the heart, and not the arm; he weighs the justice of his cause and not its outward strength. And when this question is once settled, his path is clear. He must move forward boldly, were it even against the world and all its armed hosts, in the unshaken conviction that God Himself will fight for him.

The enemies of the Reformation thus passed from extreme severity to extreme weakness; they had already done the same at Worms; and these sudden transitions are of continual occurrence in the battle that error wages against truth. Every cause destined to fall is attacked with an internal uneasiness which makes it tottering and uncertain, and drives it by turns from one pope to the other. Steadiness of purpose and energy are far better; they would thus perhaps precipitate its fall, but at least if it did fall, it would fall with glory.

One of Albert's brothers, Joachim I, elector of Brandenburg, gave an example of that strength of character which is so rare, particularly in our own times. Immovable in his principles, firm in action, knowing how to resist when necessary the encroachments of the pope, he opposed an iron hand to the progress of the Reformation. At Worms he had insisted that Luther should not be heard, and that he ought to be punished as a heretic, despite his safe-conduct. Scarcely had the Edict of Worms been issued when he ordered that it should be strictly enforced throughout his states. Luther could appreciate so energetic a character, and making a distinction between Joachim and his other adversaries, he said: "We may still pray for the Elector of Brandenburg." The disposition of this prince seemed to have been communicated to his people. Berlin and Brandenburg long remained closed against the Reformation. But what is received slowly is held faithfully. While other countries, which then hailed the gospel with joy—Belgium for instance, and Westphalia—were soon to abandon it, Brandenburg, the last of the German states to enter on the narrow way of faith, was destined in afteryears to stand in the foremost ranks of the Reformation.

Luther did not read Cardinal Albert's letter without a suspicion that it was dictated by hypocrisy, and in accordance with the advice of Capito. He kept silence, however, being content with declaring to the latter, that so long as the archbishop, who was hardly capable of managing a small parish, did not lay aside his cardinal's mask and episcopal pomp, and become a simple minister of the Word, it was impossible that he could be in the way of salvation.

Chapter 61

THE TRANSLATION OF THE BIBLE

WHILE LUTHER was thus struggling against error, as if he were
still in the midst of the battle, he was also laboring in his retirement of the Wartburg, as if he had no concern in what was going
on in the world. The hour had come in which the Reformation, from
being a mere theological question, was to become the life of the people; and yet the great engine by which this progress was to be effected
was not yet in being. This powerful and mighty instrument, destined
to hurl its thunderbolts from every side against the proud edifice of
Rome, throw down its walls, cast off the enormous weight of the papacy under which the Church lay stifled, and communicate an impulse to the whole human race which would still be felt until the
end of time,—this instrument was to go forth from the old castle of
the Wartburg, and enter the world on the same day that terminated
the reformer's captivity.

The farther the Church was removed from the time when Jesus,
the true Light of the world, was on the earth, the greater was her
need of the torch of God's Word, ordained to transmit the brightness
of Jesus Christ to the men of the latter days. But this Divine Word
was at that time hidden from the people. Several unsuccessful attempts at translation from the Vulgate had been made in 1477,
1490, and in 1518; they were almost unintelligible and, because of
their high price, beyond the reach of the people. It had even been
prohibited to give the German Church the Bible in the vulgar
tongue. Besides this, the number of those who were able to read did
not become considerable until there existed in the German language
a book of lively and universal interest.

Luther was called to present his nation with the Scriptures of God. That same God who had conducted St. John to Patmos, there to write his revelation, had confined Luther in the Wartburg, there to translate His Word. This great task, which it would have been difficult for him to have undertaken in the midst of the cares and occupations of Wittenberg, was to establish the new building on the primitive rock and, after the lapse of so many ages, lead Christians back from the subtleties of the schoolmen to the pure Fountain-head of redemption and salvation.

The wants of the Church spoke loudly; they called for this great work; and Luther, by his own inward experience, was to be led to perform it. In truth, he discovered in faith that repose of the soul which his agitated conscience and his monastic ideas had long induced him to seek in his own merits and holiness. The doctrine of the Church, the scholastic theology, knew nothing of the consolations that proceed from faith; but the Scriptures proclaim them with great force, and there it was that he had found them. Faith in the Word of God had made him free. By it he felt emancipated from the dogmatical authority of the Church, from its hierarchy and traditions, from the opinions of the schoolmen, the power of prejudice, and from every human ordinance. Those strong and numerous bonds which for centuries had enchained and stifled Christendom, were snapped asunder, broken in pieces, and scattered round him; and he nobly raised his head freed from all authority except that of the Word. This independence of man, this submission to God, which he had learned in the Holy Scriptures, he desired to impart to the Church. But before he could communicate them, it was necessary to set before it the revelations of God. A powerful hand was wanted to unlock the massive gates of that arsenal of God's Word from which Luther had taken his arms, and to open to the people against the day of battle those vaults and antique halls which for many ages no foot had ever trod.

Luther had already translated several fragments of the Holy Scripture; the seven penitential Psalms had been his first task. John the Baptist, Christ Himself, and the Reformation, had begun alike by calling men to repentance. It is the principle of every regeneration in the individual man, and in the whole human race. These essays had been eagerly received; men longed to have more; and this voice of the people was considered by Luther as the voice of God Himself. He resolved to reply to the call. He was a prisoner within those lofty walls—what of that! He would devote his leisure to translating the Word of God into the language of his countrymen. Erelong this Word would be seen descending from the Wartburg with him; circulating among the people of Germany and putting them in possession of those spiritual treasures hitherto shut up within the hearts of a few pious men. "Would that this one book," exclaimed Luther, "were in every language, in every hand, before the eyes, and in the ears and hearts of all men!" Admirable words, which, after a lapse of three centuries an illustrious body, translating the Bible into the mother-tongue of every nation upon earth, has undertaken to realize. "Scripture without any comment," said he again, "is the sun whence all teachers receive their light."

Such are the principles of Christianity and of the Reformation. According to these venerable words, we should not consult the Fathers to throw light upon Scripture, but Scripture to explain the Fathers. The reformers and the apostles set up the Word of God as the only Light, as they exalt the sacrifice of Christ as the only righteousness. By mingling any authority of man with this absolute authority of God, or any human righteousness with this perfect righteousness of Christ, we vitiate both the foundations of Christianity. These are the two fundamental heresies of Rome, which, although doubtless in a smaller degree, some teachers were desirous of introducing into the bosom of the Reformation.

Luther opened the Greek originals of the evangelists and apostles and undertook the difficult task of making these divine teachers speak his mother tongue. Important crisis in the history of the Reformation! From that time the Reformation was no longer in the hands of the reformer. The Bible came forward; Luther withdrew. God appeared, and man disappeared. The reformer placed *The Book* in the hands of his contemporaries. Each one may now hear the voice of God for himself; as for Luther, henceforth he mingled with the crowd, and took his station in the ranks of those who come to draw from the common Fountain of light and life.

In translating the Holy Scriptures, Luther found that consolation and strength of which he stood so much in need. Solitary, in ill health, and saddened by the exertions of his enemies and the extravagances of some of his followers,—seeing his life wearing away in the gloom of that old castle, he had occasionally to endure terrible struggles. In those times, men were inclined to carry into the visible world the conflicts that the soul sustains with its spiritual enemies; Luther's lively imagination easily embodied the emotions of his heart, and the superstitions of the Middle Ages had still some hold upon his mind, so that we might say of him, as it has been said of Calvin with regard to the punishment inflicted on heretics: there was yet a remnant of popery in him. Satan was not in Luther's view simply an invisible though real being; he thought that this adversary of God appeared to men as he had appeared to Jesus Christ. Although the authenticity of many of the stories on this subject contained in the *Table Talk* and elsewhere is more than doubtful, history must still record this failing in the reformer.

Never was he more assailed by these gloomy ideas than in the solitude of the Wartburg. In the days of his strength he had braved the devil in Worms; but now all the reformer's power seemed broken and his glory tarnished. He was thrown aside; Satan was victorious in his turn, and in the anguish of his soul Luther imagined he saw his giant form standing before him, lifting his finger in threatening attitude, exulting with a bitter and hellish sneer, and gnashing his teeth in fearful rage. One day especially, it is said, as Luther was engaged on his translation of the New Testament, he fancied he beheld Satan, filled with horror at his work, tormenting him, and prowling round him like a lion about to spring upon his prey. Luther, alarmed and incensed, snatched up his inkstand and flung it at the head of his enemy. The figure disappeared, and the missile was dashed in pieces against the wall.

Luther's sojourn in the Wartburg began to be insupportable to him. He felt indignant at the timidity of his protectors. Sometimes he would remain a whole day plunged in deep and silent meditation, and awakened from it only to exclaim, "Oh, that I were at Wittenberg!" At length he could hold out no longer; there had been caution enough; he must see his friends again, hear them, and converse with them. True, he ran the risk of falling into the hands of his enemies, but nothing could stop him. About the end of November, he secretly quitted the Wartburg, and set out for Wittenberg.

A fresh storm had just burst upon him. At last the Sorbonne had spoken out. That celebrated school of Paris, the first authority in the Church after the pope, the ancient and venerable source whence theological learning had proceeded, had given its verdict against the Reformation.

The following are some of the propositions condemned by this learned body. Luther had said, "God ever pardons and remits sins gratuitously, and requires nothing of us in return, except that in future we should live according to righteousness." And he had added, "Of all deadly sins, this is the most deadly, namely, that anyone should think he is not guilty of a damnable and deadly sin before God." He had said in another place, "Burning heretics is contrary to the will of the Holy Ghost."

To these three propositions, and to many others besides, which they quoted, the theological faculty of Paris replied, "Heresy!—let him be accursed!"

But a young man, twenty-four years of age, of short stature, diffident, and plain in appearance, dared take up the gauntlet which the first college in the world had thrown down. They knew pretty well at Wittenberg what should be thought of these pompous censures: they knew that Rome had yielded to the suggestions of the Dominicans, and that the Sorbonne had been misled by two or three fanatical doctors who were designated at Paris by satirical nicknames. Accordingly, in his *Apology*, Melancthon did not confine himself to defending Luther; but, with the boldness which characterizes his writings, carried the war into the enemy's camp. "You say he is a Manichean!—he is a Montanist!—let fire and faggot repress his foolishness! And who is Montanist? Luther, who would have us believe in Holy Scripture alone, or you, who would have men believe in the opinions of their fellow-creatures rather than in the Word of God?"

To ascribe more importance to the word of a man than to the Word of God was in very truth the heresy of Montanus, as it still is that of the pope and of all those who set the hierarchical authority of the Church or the interior inspirations of mysticism far above the positive declarations of the Sacred Writings. Accordingly the youthful master of the arts, who had said, "I would rather lay down my life than my faith," did not stop there. He accused the Sorbonne of having obscured the gospel, extinguished faith, and substituted an empty philosophy in the place of Christianity. After this work of

Melancthon's, the position of the dispute was changed; he proved unanswerably that the heresy was at Paris and Rome, and the catholic truth at Wittenberg.

Meanwhile Luther, caring little for the condemnations of the Sorbonne, was proceeding in his military equipment to the university. He was greatly distressed by various reports which reached him on the road of a spirit of impatience and independence that was showing itself among some of his adherents. At length he arrived at Wittenberg without being recognized, and stopped at Amsdorff's house. Immediately all his friends were secretly called together; and Melancthon among the first, who had so often said, "I would rather die than lose him."

They came! What a meeting! what joy! The captive of the Wartburg tasted in their society all the sweetness of Christian friendship. He learned the spread of the Reformation, the hopes of his brethren; and, delighted at what he saw and heard, offered up a prayer, returned thanks to God, and then with brief delay returned to the Wartburg.

Chapter 62

EMANCIPATION OF THE MONKS—
THE FALL OF THE MASS

LUTHER'S JOY was well-founded. The work of the Reformation was then making great strides. Feldkirchen, always in the van, had led the assault; now the main body was in motion, and that power which carried the Reformation from the doctrine it had purified into the worship, life, and constitution of the Church, now manifested itself by a new explosion, more formidable to the papacy than even the first had been.

Rome, having got rid of the reformer, thought the heresy was at an end. But in a short time everything was changed. Death removed from the pontifical throne the man who had put Luther under the ban of the Church. Disturbances occurred in Spain and compelled Charles to visit his kingdom beyond the Pyrenees. War broke out between this prince and Francis I, and as if that were not enough to occupy the emperor, Suleiman made an incursion into Hungary. Charles, thus attacked on all sides, was forced to forget the monk of Worms and his religious innovations.

About the same time, the vessel of the Reformation, which, driven in every direction by contrary winds, was on the verge of foundering, righted itself and floated proudly above the waters.

It was in the convent of the Augustines at Wittenberg that the Reformation broke out. We ought not to be surprised at this: it is true the reformer was there no longer; but no human power could drive out the spirit that had animated him.

For some time the Church in which Luther had so often preached re-echoed with strange doctrines. Gabriel Zwilling, a zealous monk and chaplain to the convent, was there energetically proclaiming the Reformation. As if Luther, whose name was at that time everywhere celebrated, had become too strong and too illustrious, God selected feeble and obscure men to begin the Reformation which that renowned doctor had prepared. "Jesus Christ," said the preacher, "instituted the sacrament of the altar in remembrance of His death, and not to make it an object of adoration. To worship it is a real idolatry. The priest who communicates alone commits a sin. No prior has the right to compel a monk to say mass alone. Let one, two, or three officiate, and let the others receive the Lord's sacrament under both kinds."

This is what Friar Gabriel required, and this daring language was listened to approvingly by the other brethren, and particularly by those who came from the Low Countries. They were disciples of the gospel, and why should they not conform in everything to its commands? Had not Luther himself written to Melancthon in the month of August: "Henceforth and forever I will say no more private masses"? Thus the monks, the soldiers of the hierarchy, emancipated by the Word, boldly took part against Rome.

At Wittenberg they met with a violent resistance from the prior. Calling to mind that all things should be done in an orderly manner, they gave way, but with a declaration that to uphold the mass was to oppose the gospel of God.

The prior had gained the day: one man had been stronger than them all. It might seem, therefore, that this movement of the Augustines was one of those caprices of insubordination so frequently occurring in monasteries. But it was in reality the Spirit of God Himself which was then agitating all Christendom. A solitary cry, uttered in the bosom of a convent, found its echo in a thousand voices; and that which men would have desired to confine within the walls of a cloister went forth and took a bodily form in the very midst of the city.

Rumors of the dissensions among the friars soon spread through the town. The citizens and students of the university took part, some with, some against the mass. The elector's court was troubled. Frederick in surprise sent his chancellor Pontanus to Wittenberg with orders to reduce the monks to obedience, by putting them, if necessary, on bread and water; and on the twelfth of October, at seven in the morning, a deputation from the professors, of which Melancthon formed a part, visited the convent, exhorting the brethren to attempt no innovations, or at least to wait a little longer. Upon this all their zeal revived: as they were unanimous in their faith, except the prior who combated them, they appealed to Scripture, to the understanding of believers, and to the conscience of the theologians; and two days after handed in a written declaration.

The doctors now examined the question more closely and found that the monks had truth on their side. They had gone to convince, and were convinced themselves. What ought they to do? Their consciences cried aloud; their anxiety kept increasing: at last, after long hesitation, they formed a courageous resolution.

On the twentieth of October, the university made their report to the elector. "Let your electoral highness," said they, after setting forth the errors of the mass, "put an end to every abuse, lest Christ in the day of judgment should rebuke us as He did the people of Capernaum."

Thus it is no longer a few obscure monks who are speaking; it is that university which for several years has been hailed by all the wise as the school of the nation; and the very means employed to check the Reformation are those which will now contribute to its extension.

Melancthon, with that boldness which he carried into learning, published fifty-five propositions calculated to enlighten men's minds.

"Just as looking at a cross," said he, "is not performing a good work, but simply contemplating a sign that reminds us of Christ's death;

"Just as looking at the sun is not performing a good work, but simply contemplating a sign that reminds us of Christ and of His gospel;

"So, partaking of the Lord's Supper is not performing a good work, but simply making use of a sign that reminds us of the grace that has been given us through Christ.

"But here is the difference, namely, that the symbols invented by men simply remind us of what they signify; while the signs given us by God not only remind us of the things themselves, but assure our hearts of the will of God.

"As the sight of a cross does not justify, so the mass does not justify.

"As the sight of a cross is not a sacrifice either for our sins or for the sins of others, so the mass is not a sacrifice.

"There is but one sacrifice, but one satisfaction—Jesus Christ. Besides Him there is none.

"Let such bishops as do not oppose the impiety of the mass be accursed."

Thus spoke the pious and gentle Philip.

The elector was amazed. He had desired to reduce some young friars,—and now the whole university, headed by Melancthon, rose in their defense. To wait seemed to him in all things the surest means of success. He did not like sudden reforms, and desired that every opinion should make its way without obstruction. "Time alone," thought he, "clears up all things and brings them to maturity." And yet in spite of him the Reformation was advancing with hasty steps, and threatened to carry everything along with it. Frederick made every exertion to arrest its progress. His authority, the influence of his character, the reasons that appeared to him the most convincing, were all set in operation. "Do not be too hasty," said he to the theologians; "your number is too small to carry such a reform. If it is based upon the gospel, others will discover it also, and you will put an end to abuses with the aid of the whole Church. Talk, debate, preach on these matters as much as you like, but keep up the ancient usages."

Such was the battle fought on the subject of the mass. The monks had bravely led the assault; the theologians, undecided for a moment, had soon come to their support. The prince and his ministers alone defended the place. It has been asserted that the Reformation was accomplished by the power and authority of the elector; but far from that, the assailants shrank back at the sound of his voice, and the mass was saved for a few days.

The heat of the attack had already been directed against another point. Friar Gabriel still continued his heart-stirring sermons in the Church of the Augustines. Monachism was now the object of his reiterated blows; if the mass was the stronghold of the Roman doctrines, the monastic orders were the support of the hierarchy. These, then, were the two first positions that must be carried.

"No one," said Gabriel, according to the prior's report, "no dweller in the convents keeps the commandments of God; no one can be saved under a cowl; every man that enters a cloister enters it in the name of the devil. The vows of chastity, poverty, and obedience are contrary to the gospel."

This extraordinary language was reported to the prior, who avoided going to church for fear he should hear it.

"Gabriel," said they, "desires that every exertion should be made to empty the cloisters. He says if a monk is met in the streets, the people should pull him by the frock and laugh at him; and that if they cannot be driven out of the convents by ridicule, they should be expelled by force. Break open, pull down, utterly destroy the monasteries (says he), so that not a single trace of them may remain; and that not one of those stones, that have contributed to shelter so much sloth and superstition, may be found in the spot they so long occupied."

The friars were astonished; their consciences told them that Gabriel's words were but too true, that a monkish life was not in conformity with the will of God, and that no one could dispose of their persons but themselves.

Thirteen Augustines quitted the convent together, and laying aside the costume of their order, assumed a lay dress. Those who possessed any learning attended the lectures of the university in order one day to be serviceable to the Church; and those whose minds were uncultivated endeavored to gain a livelihood by the work of their own hands, according to the injunctions of the apostle and the example of the good citizens of Wittenberg. One of them who understood the business of a joiner applied for the freedom of the city, and resolved to take a wife.

If Luther's entry into the Augustine convent at Erfurt had been the germ of the Reformation, the departure of these thirteen monks from the convent of the Augustines at Wittenberg was the signal of its entering into possession of Christendom. For thirty years past Erasmus had been unveiling the uselessness, the folly, and the vices of the monks; and all Europe laughed and grew angry with him: but sarcasm was required no longer. Thirteen high-minded and bold men returned into the midst of the world, to render themselves profitable to society and fulfill the commandments of God. Feldkirchen's marriage had been the first defeat of the hierarchy; the emancipation of these thirteen Augustines was the second. Monachism, which had arisen at the time when the Church entered upon its period of enslavement and error, was destined to fall at the dawning of liberty and truth.

This daring step excited universal ferment in Wittenberg. Admiration was felt toward those men who thus came to take their part in the general labors, and they were received as brethren. At the same time a few outcries were heard against those who persisted in remaining lazily sheltered behind the walls of their monastery. The monks who remained faithful to their prior trembled in their cells; and the latter, carried away by the general movement, stopped the celebration of the low masses.

The smallest concession in so critical a moment necessarily precipitated the course of events. The prior's order created a great sensation in the town and university, and produced a sudden explosion. Among the students and citizens of Wittenberg were found some of those turbulent men whom the least excitement arouses and hurries into criminal disorders. They were exasperated at the idea of the low masses, which even the superstitious prior had suspended, still being said in the parish church; and on Tuesday, the third of December, as the mass was about to be read, they suddenly advanced to the altar, took away the books, and drove the priests out of the chapel. The council and university were annoyed, and met to punish the authors of these misdeeds. But the passions once aroused are not easily quelled. The Cordeliers had not taken part in this movement of the Augustines. On the following day, the students posted a threatening placard on the gates of their convent; after that forty students entered their church, and although they refrained from violence, they ridiculed the monks, so that the latter dared not say mass except in the choir. Toward evening the fathers were told to be upon their guard: "The students are resolved to attack the monastery!" The frightened religioners, not knowing how to shelter themselves from these real or supposed attacks, hastily besought the council to protect them; a guard of soldiers was sent, but the enemy did not appear. The university caused the students who had taken part in these disturbances to be arrested. It was discovered that some were from Erfurt, where they had become notorious for their insubordination. The penalties of the university were inflicted upon them.

And yet the necessity was felt of inquiring carefully into the lawfulness of monastic vows. A chapter of Augustine monks from Misnia and Thuringia assembled at Wittenberg in the month of December. They came to the same opinion as Luther. On the one hand they declared that monastic vows were not criminal, but on the other that they were not obligatory. "In Christ," said they, "there is neither layman nor monk; each one is at liberty to quit the monastery or to stay in it. Let him who goes forth beware lest he abuse his liberty; let him who remains obey his superiors, but through love." They next abolished mendicancy and the saying of masses for money; they also decreed that the best instructed among them should devote themselves to the teaching of the Word of God, and that the rest should support their brethren by the work of their own hands.

Thus the question of vows appeared settled; but that of the mass was undecided. The elector still resisted the torrent, and protected an institute which he saw standing in all Christendom. The orders of so indulgent a prince could not long restrain the public feeling. Carlstadt's head in particular was affected by the general fermentation. Zealous, upright, and bold, ready, like Luther, to sacrifice everything for the truth, he was inferior to the reformer in wisdom and moderation; he was not entirely exempt from vainglory, and with a disposition inclined to examine matters to the bottom, he was defective in judgment and in clearness of ideas. Luther had dragged him from the mire of scholasticism, and directed him to the study of Scripture; but Carlstadt had not acknowledged with his friend the all-sufficiency of the Word of God. Accordingly he was often seen adopting the most singular interpretations. So long as Luther was at his side, the superiority of the master kept the scholar within due bounds. But now Carlstadt was free. In the university, in the church, everywhere in Wittenberg, this little dark-featured man, who had never excelled in eloquence, might be heard proclaiming with great fervor ideas that were sometimes profound, but often enthusiastic and exaggerated. "What madness," exclaimed he, "to think that one must leave the Reformation to God's working alone! A new order of things is beginning. The hand of man should interfere. Woe be to him who lags behind, and does not mount the breach in the cause of the Almighty."

The archdeacon's language communicated to others the impatience he felt himself. "All that the popes have ordained is impious," said certain upright and sincere men who followed his example. "Let us not become partakers in those abominations by allowing them to subsist any longer. What is condemned by the Word of God ought to be put down in the whole of Christendom, whatever may be the ordinances of men. If the heads of the State and of the Church will not do their duty, let us do ours. Let us renounce all negotiations, conferences, theses, and disputations, and let us apply the effectual remedy to so many evils. We need a second Elijah to throw down the altars of Baal."

The re-establishment of the Lord's Supper, in this moment of ferment and enthusiasm, unquestionably could not present the solemnity and holiness of its first institution by the Son of God, on the eve of His death, and almost at the foot of the cross. But if God now made use of weak and perhaps passionate men, it was nevertheless His hand that revived in the Church the feast of His love.

In the previous October, Carlstadt had already celebrated the Lord's Supper in private with twelve of his friends, in accordance with Christ's institution. On the Sunday before Christmas he gave out from the pulpit that on the day of our Lord's circumcision (the first day of the year) he would distribute the eucharist in both kinds (bread and wine) to all who might present themselves at the altar; that he would omit all useless forms, and in celebrating this mass would wear neither cope nor chasuble.

The affrighted council entreated the councilor Beyer to prevent such a flagrant irregularity; and upon this Carlstadt resolved not to wait until the appointed time. On Christmas Day, 1521, he preached in the parish church on the necessity of quitting the mass and receiving the sacrament in both kinds. After the sermon he went to the altar, pronounced the words of consecration in German, and then turning towards the attentive people, said with a solemn voice: "Whosoever feels the burden of his sins, and hungers and thirsts for the grace of God, let him come and receive the body and blood of our Lord." And then, without elevating the host, he distributed the bread and wine to all, saying; "This is the cup of my blood, the blood of the new and everlasting Covenant."

Conflicting sentiments prevailed in the assembly. Some, feeling that a new grace from God had been given to the Church, approached the altar in silence and emotion. Others, attracted chiefly by the novelty, drew nigh with a certain sense of agitation and impatience. Five communicants alone had presented themselves in the confessional: the rest simply took part in the public confession of sins. Carlstadt gave a public absolution to all, imposing on them no other penance than this: "Sin no more." They concluded with singing the Agnus Dei.

No one opposed Carlstadt; these reforms had already obtained general assent. The archdeacon administered the Lord's Supper again on New Year's Day, and on the Sunday following, and from that time it was regularly celebrated. Einsidlen, one of the elector's councilors, having reproached Carlstadt with seeking his own glory rather than the salvation of his hearers: "Mighty lord," replied he, "there is no form of death that can make me withdraw from Scripture. The Word has come upon with such promptitude. . . . Woe be to me if I preach it not!" Shortly after, Carlstadt married.

In January, 1522, the council and University of Wittenberg regulated the celebration of the Lord's Supper according to the new ritual. They were, at the same time, engaged on the means of reviving the moral influence of religion; for the Reformation was destined to restore simultaneously faith, worship, and morality. It was decreed not to tolerate mendicants, whether they were begging friars or not; and that in every street there should be some pious man commissioned to take care of the poor, and summon open sinners before the university and the council.

Thus fell the mass—the principal bulwark of Rome; thus the Reformation passed from simple teaching into public worship. For three centuries the mass and transubstantiation had been peremptorily established. From that period everything in the Church had taken a new direction; all things tended to the glory of man and the worship of the priest. The Holy Sacrament had been adored; festivals had been instituted in honor of the sublimest of miracles; the adoration of Mary had acquired a high importance; the priest who, on his consecration, received the wonderful power of "making the body of Christ," had been separated from the laity, and had become, according to Thomas Aquinas, a mediator between God and man; celibacy had been proclaimed as an inviolable law; auricular confession had been enforced upon the people, and the cup denied them; for how could humble laymen be placed in the same rank as priests invested with the most august ministry? The mass was an insult to the Son of

God: it was opposed to the perfect grace of the cross, and the spotless glory of His everlasting kingdom. But if it lowered the Saviour, it exalted the priest, whom it invested with the unparalleled power of reproducing, in his hand and at his will, the Sovereign Creator. From that time the Church seemed to exist not to preach the gospel, but simply to reproduce Christ bodily. The Roman pontiff, whose humblest servants created at pleasure the body of God Himself, sat as God in the temple of God, and claimed a spiritual treasure, from which he drew at will indulgences for the pardon of souls.

Such were the gross errors which, for three centuries, had been imposed on the Church in conjunction with the mass. When the Reformation abolished this institution of man, it abolished these abuses also. The step taken by the archdeacon of Wittenberg was therefore one of a very extended range. The splendid festivals that used to amuse the people, the worship of the Virgin, the pride of the priesthood, the authority of the pope—all tottered with the mass. The glory was withdrawn from the priests, to return to Jesus Christ, and the Reformation took an immense stride in advance.

Chapter 63

THE NEW PROPHETS

PREJUDICED MEN might have seen nothing in the work that was going on but the effects of an empty enthusiasm. The very facts were to prove the contrary, and demonstrate that there is a wide gulf between a Reformation based on the Word of God and a fanatical excitement.

Whenever a great religious ferment takes place in the Church, some impure elements always appear with the manifestations of truth. We see the rise of one or more false reforms proceeding from man, and which serve as a testimony or countersign to the real reform. Thus many false messiahs in the time of Christ testified that the real Messiah had appeared. The Reformation of the sixteenth century could not be accomplished without presenting a similar phenomenon. In the small town of Zwickau it was first manifested.

In that place there lived a few men who, agitated by the great events that were then stirring all Christendom, aspired at direct revelations from the Deity, instead of meekly desiring sanctification of heart, and who asserted that they were called to complete the Reformation so feebly sketched out by Luther. "What is the use," said they, "of clinging so closely to the Bible? The Bible! always the Bible! Can the Bible preach to us? Is it sufficient for our instruction? If God had designed to instruct us by a book, would He not have sent us a Bible from heaven? It is by the Spirit alone that we can be enlightened. God Himself speaks to us. God Himself reveals to us what we should do and what we should preach." Thus did these fanatics, like the adherents of Rome, attack the fundamental principle on which the entire Reformation is founded—the all-sufficiency of the Word of God.

A simple clothier, Nicholas Storch by name, announced that the angel Gabriel had appeared to him during the night, and that after communicating matters which he could not yet reveal, said to him: "Thou shalt sit on my throne." A former student of Wittenberg, one Mark Stubner, joined Storch, and immediately forsook his studies; for he had received direct from God (said he) the gift of interpreting the Holy Scriptures. Another weaver, Mark Thomas, was added to their number; and a new adept, Thomas Munzer, a man of fanatical character, gave a regular organization to this rising sect. Storch, desirous of following Christ's example, selected from among his followers twelve apostles and seventy-two disciples. All loudly declared, as a sect in our own day has done, that apostles and prophets were at length restored to the Church of God.

The new prophets, pretending to walk in the footsteps of those of old, began to proclaim their mission: "Woe! woe!" said they; "a Church governed by men so corrupt as the bishops cannot be the Church of Christ. The impious rulers of Christendom will be overthrown. In five, six, or seven years, a universal desolation will come upon the world. The Turk will seize upon Germany; all the priests will be put to death, even those who are married. No ungodly man, no sinner will remain alive; and after the earth has been purified by blood, God will then set up a kingdom; Storch will be put in possession of the supreme authority, and commit the government of the nations to the saints. Then there will be one faith, one baptism. The day of the Lord is at hand, and the end of the world draweth nigh. Woe! woe! woe!" Then declaring that infant baptism was valueless, the new prophets called upon all men to come and receive from their hands the true baptism, as a sign of their introduction into the new Church of God.

This language made a deep impression on the people. Many pious souls were stirred by the thought that prophets were again restored to the Church, and all those who were fond of the marvelous threw themselves into the arms of the fanatics of Zwickau.

But scarcely had this old heresy, which had already appeared in the days of Montanism and in the Middle Ages, found followers, when it met with a powerful antagonist in the Reformation. Nicholas

Hausmann, of whom Luther gave this powerful testimony, "What we preach, he practices," was pastor of Zwickau. This good man did not allow himself to be misled by the pretensions of the false prophets. He checked the innovations that Storch and his followers desired to introduce, and his two deacons acted in unison with him. The fanatics, rejected by the ministers of the Church, fell into another extravagance. They formed meetings in which revolutionary doctrines were professed. The people were agitated, and disturbances broke out. A priest, carrying the host, was pelted with stones; the civil authority interfered, and cast the ringleaders into prison. Exasperated by this proceeding and eager to vindicate themselves and to obtain redress, Storch, Mark Thomas, and Stubner repaired to Wittenberg.

They arrived there December 27, 1521. Storch led the way with the gait and bearing of a trooper. Mark Thomas and Stubner followed him. The disorder then prevailing in Wittenberg was favorable to their designs. The youths of the academy and the citizens, already profoundly agitated and in a state of excitement, were a soil well fitted to receive these new prophets.

Thinking themselves sure of support, they immediately called on the professors of the university, in order to obtain their sanction. "We are sent by God to instruct the people," said they. "We have held familiar conversations with the Lord; we know what will happen; in a word, we are apostles and prophets, and appeal to Dr. Luther." This strange language astonished the professors. "Who has commissioned you to preach?" asked Melancthon of his old pupil Stubner, whom he received into his house. "The Lord our God." "Have you written any books?" "The Lord our God has forbidden me to do so." Melancthon was agitated: he grew alarmed and astonished.

"There are, indeed, extraordinary spirits in these men," said he; "but what spirits? . . . Luther alone can decide. On the one hand, let us beware of quenching the Spirit of God, and, on the other, of being led astray by the spirit of Satan."

Storch, being of a restless disposition, soon quitted Wittenberg. Stubner remained. Animated by an eager spirit of proselytism, he went through the city, speaking now to one, then to another; and many acknowledged him as a prophet from God. He addressed himself more particularly to a Swabian named Cellarius, a friend of Melancthon's who kept a school in which he used to instruct a great number of young people, and who soon fully acknowledged the mission of the new prophets.

Melancthon now became still more perplexed and uneasy. It was not so much the visions of the Zwickau prophets that disturbed him as their new doctrine on baptism. It seemed to him conformable with reason, and he thought that it was deserving examination; "for" said he, "we must neither admit nor reject anything lightly."

Such is the spirit of the Reformation. Melancthon's hesitation and anxiety are a proof of the uprightness of his heart, more honorable to him perhaps than any systematic opposition would have been.

The elector himself, whom Melancthon styled "the lamp of Israel," hesitated. Prophets and apostles in the electorate of Saxony as in Jerusalem of old! "This is a great matter," said he; "and as a layman, I cannot understand it. But rather than fight against God, I would take a staff in my hand, and descend from my throne."

At length he informed the professors, by his councilors, that they had sufficient trouble in hand at Wittenberg; that in all probability these pretensions of the Zwickau prophets were only a temptation of the devil; and that the wisest course, in his opinion, would be to let the matter drop of itself; nevertheless that, under all circumstances, whenever his highness should clearly perceive God's will, he would take counsel of neither brother nor mother, and that he was ready to suffer everything in the cause of truth.

Luther in the Wartburg was apprized of the agitation prevailing in the court and at Wittenberg. Strange men had appeared, and the source whence their mission proceeded was unknown. He saw immediately that God had permitted these afflicting events to humble his servants, and to excite them by trials to strive more earnestly after sanctification.

"Your electoral grace," wrote he to Frederick, "has for many years been collecting relics from every country. God has satisfied your desire, and has sent you, without cost or trouble, a whole cross, with nails, spears, and scourges. . . . Health and prosperity to the new relic! . . . Only let your highness fearlessly stretch out your arm, and suffer the nails to enter your flesh! . . . I always expected that Satan would send us this plague."

But at the same time nothing appeared to him more urgent than to secure for others the liberty that he claimed for himself. He had not two weights and two measures. "Beware of throwing them into prison," wrote he to Spalatin. "Let not the prince dip his hand in the blood of these new prophets." Luther went far beyond his age, and even beyond many other reformers, on the subject of religious liberty.

Circumstances were becoming every day more serious in Wittenberg.

Carlstadt rejected many of the doctrines of the new prophets, and particularly their anabaptism; but there is a contagion in religious enthusiasm that a head like his could not easily resist. From the arrival of the men of Zwickau in Wittenberg, Carlstadt accelerated his movements in the direction of violent reforms. "We must fall upon every ungodly practice, and overthrow them all in a day," said he. He brought together all the passages of Scripture against images, and inveighed with increasing energy against the idolatry of Rome. "They fall down—they crawl before these idols," exclaimed he; "they burn tapers before them, and make them offerings. . . . Let us arise and tear them from the altars!"

These words were not uttered in vain before the people. They entered the churches, carried away the images, broke them in pieces, and burned them. It would have been better to wait until their abolition had been legally proclaimed; but some thought that the caution of the chiefs would compromise the Reformation itself.

To judge by the language of these enthusiasts, there were no true Christians in Wittenberg save those who went not to confession, who attacked the priests, and who ate meat on fast days. If anyone was suspected of not rejecting all the rites of the Church as an invention of the devil, he was set down as a worshiper of Baal. "We must form a Church," cried they, "composed of saints only!"

The citizens of Wittenberg laid before the council certain articles which it was forced to accept. Many of these regulations were conformable to evangelical morals. They required more particularly that all houses of public amusement should be closed.

But Carlstadt soon went still farther: he began to despise learning; and the old professor was heard from his chair advising his pupils to return home, to take up the spade, to guide the plough, and quietly cultivate the earth, because man was ordained to eat bread in the sweat of his brow. George Mohr, the master of the boys' school at Wittenberg, led away by the same fanaticism, called to the assembled citizens from the window of his schoolroom to come and take away their children. Why should they be made study, since Storch and Stubner had never been at the university, and yet they were prophets? . . . A mechanic, therefore, was as well qualified as all the doctors in the world, and perhaps better, to preach the gospel.

Thus arose doctrines in direct opposition to the Reformation, which had been prepared by the revival of letters. It was with the weapons of theological learning that Luther had attacked Rome; and the enthusiasts of Wittenberg, like the fanatical monks with whom Erasmus and Reuchlin had contended, presumed to trample all human learning underfoot. If this vandalism succeeded in holding its ground, the hopes of the world were lost; and another irruption of barbarians would extinguish the light that God had kindled in Christendom.

The results of these strange discourses soon showed themselves. Men's minds were absorbed, agitated, diverted from the gospel; the university became disorganized; the demoralized students broke the bonds of discipline and dispersed; and the governments of Germany recalled their subjects. Thus the men who desired to reform and vivify everything, were on the point of ruining all. One struggle more (exclaimed the friends of Rome, who on all sides were regaining their confidence), one last struggle, and all will be ours!

Promptly to check the excesses of these fanatics was the only means of saving the Reformation. But who could do it? Melancthon? He was too young, too weak, too much agitated himself by these strange phenomena. The elector? He was the most pacific man of his age. To build castles at Altenburg, Weimar, Lochau, and Coburg; to adorn churches with the beautiful pictures of Lucas Cranach; to improve the singing in the chapels; to advance the prosperity of his university; to promote the happiness of his subjects; to stop in the midst of the children whom he met playing in the streets, and give them little presents—such were the gentle occupations of his life. And now in his advanced age, would he contend with fanatics—would he oppose violence to violence? How could the good and pious Frederick make up his mind to this?

The disease continued to spread, and no one stood forward to check it. Luther was far from Wittenberg. Confusion and ruin had taken hold of the city. The Reformation had seen an enemy spring from its own bosom more formidable than popes and emperors. It was on the very verge of the abyss.

Luther! Luther! was the general and unanimous cry at Wittenberg. The citizens called for him earnestly; the professors desired his advice; the prophets themselves appealed to him. All entreated him to return.

We may imagine what was passing in the reformer's mind. All the terrors of Rome were nothing in comparison with what now wrung his heart. It was from the very midst of the Reformation that its enemies went forth. It was preying upon its own vitals; and that doctrine which alone had brought peace to his troubled heart became the occasion of fatal disturbances to the Church.

"If I knew," he had once said, "that my doctrine injured one man, one single man, however lowly and obscure (which it cannot, for it is the gospel itself), I would rather die ten times than not retract it." And now a whole city, and that city Wittenberg, was falling into disorder! True, his doctrine had no share in this; but from every quarter of Germany voices were heard accusing him of it. Pains more keen than he had ever felt before assailed him now, and new temptations agitated him. "Can such then be the end of this great work of the Reformation?" said he to himself. Impossible!—he rejected these doubts. God had begun, . . . God would perfect the work. "I creep in deep humility to the grace of the Lord," exclaimed he, "and beseech Him that His name may remain attached to this work; and that if anything impure be mixed up with it, He will remember that I am a sinful man."

The news communicated to Luther of the inspiration of these new prophets and of their sublime interviews with God did not stagger him one moment. He knew the depth, the anguish, the humiliation of the spiritual life: at Erfurt and Wittenberg he had made trial of the power of God, and those experiences did not so easily permit him to believe that God appeared to His creatures and conversed with them. "Ask these prophets," wrote he to Melancthon, "whether they have felt those spiritual torments, those creations of God, those deaths and hells, which accompany a real regeneration. . . . And if they speak to you only of agreeable things, of tranquil impressions, of devotion and piety, as they say, do not believe them, although they should pretend to have been transported to the third heaven. Before

Christ could attain His glory, He was compelled to suffer death; and in like manner the believer must go through the bitterness of sin before he can obtain peace. Do you desire to know the time, place, and manner in which God talks with men? Listen: 'As a lion so will he break all my bones' (Isa. 38:13); I am cast out from before his face, and my soul is abased even to the gates of hell. . . . No! The Divine Majesty (as they call Him) does not speak face to face with men so that they may see Him; for no man (says He) can see my face and live."

But his firm conviction of the delusion under which these prophets were laboring served but to augment Luther's grief. Had the great truth of salvation by grace so quickly lost its charms that men turned aside from it to follow fables? He began to feel that the work was not so easy as he had thought at first. He stumbled at the first stone that the deceitfulness of the human heart had placed in his path; he was bowed down by grief and anxiety. He resolved, at the hazard of his life, to remove it out of the way of his people, and decided on returning to Wittenberg.

At that time he was threatened by imminent dangers. The enemies of the Reformation fancied themselves on the very eve of destroying it. George of Saxony, equally indisposed toward Rome and Wittenberg, had written, as early as the sixteenth of October, 1521, to Duke John, the elector's brother, to draw him over to the side of the enemies of the Reformation. "Some," said he, "deny that the soul is immortal. Others (and these are monks!) attach bells to swine and set them to drag the relics of St. Anthony through the streets, and then throw them into the mire. All this is the fruit of Luther's teaching! Entreat your brother the elector either to punish the ungodly authors of these innovations, or at least publicly to declare his opinion of them. Our changing beard and hair remind us that we have reached the latter portion of our course and urge us to put an end to such great evils."

After this George departed to take his seat in the imperial government at Nuremberg. He had scarcely arrived when he made every exertion to urge it to adopt measures of severity. In effect, on the twenty-first of January, this body passed an edict in which it complained bitterly that the priests said mass without being robed in their sacerdotal garments, consecrated the sacrament in German, administered it without having received the requisite confession from the communicants, placed it in the hands of laymen, and were not even careful to ascertain that those who stood forward to receive it were fasting.

Accordingly the imperial government desired the bishops to seek out and punish severely all the innovators within their respective dioceses. The latter hastened to comply with these orders.

Such was the moment selected by Luther for his reappearance on the stage. He saw the danger; he foreboded incalculable disasters. "Erelong," said he, "there will be a disturbance in the empire, carrying princes, magistrates, and bishops before it. The people have eyes: they will not, they cannot be led by force. All Germany will run blood. Let us stand up as a wall to preserve our nation in this dreadful day of God's anger."

Chapter 64

LUTHER RETURNS TO WITTENBERG

SUCH WERE Luther's thoughts; but he beheld a still more imminent danger. At Wittenberg, the conflagration, far from dying away, became fiercer every day. From the heights of the Wartburg, Luther could perceive in the horizon the frightful gleams, the signal of devastation, shooting at intervals through the air. Was not he the only one who could give aid in this extremity? Should he not throw himself into the midst of the flames to quench their fury? In vain, his enemies prepared to strike the decisive blow; in vain the elector entreated him not to leave the Wartburg, and to prepare his justification against the next diet. He had a more important task to perform—to justify the gospel itself. "More serious intelligence reaches me every day," wrote he. "I shall set out: circumstances positively require me to do so."

Accordingly, he rose on the third of March with the determination of leaving the Wartburg forever. He bade adieu to its time-worn towers and gloomy forests. He passed beyond those walls where the excommunications of Leo X and the sword of Charles V were unable to reach him. He descended the mountain. The world that lay at his feet, and in the midst of which he was about to appear again, would soon perhaps call loudly for his death. But that mattered not! he went forward rejoicing: for in the name of the Lord he was returning among his fellow men.

Time had moved on. Luther was quitting the Wartburg for a cause very different from that for which he had entered it. He had gone thither as the assailant of the old tradition and of the ancient doctors; he left it as the defender of the doctrine of the apostles against new adversaries. He had entered it as an innovator, and as an impugner of the ancient hierarchy; he left it as a conservative and champion of the faith of Christians. Hitherto Luther had seen but one thing in his work—the triumph of justification by faith; and with this weapon he had thrown down mighty superstitions. But if there was a time for destroying, there was also a time for building up. Beneath those ruins with which his strong arm had strewn the plain,—beneath those crumpled letters of indulgence, those broken tiaras and tattered cowls,—beneath so many Roman abuses and errors that lay in confusion upon the field of battle, he discerned and discovered the primitive Catholic Church, reappearing still the same, and coming forth as from a long period of trial, with its unchangeable doctrines and heavenly accents. He could distinguish it from Rome, welcoming and embracing it with joy. Luther effected nothing new in the world, as he had been falsely charged; he did not raise a building for the future that had no connection with the past; he uncovered, he opened to the light of day the ancient foundations, on which thorns and thistles had sprung up, and continuing the construction of the temple, he built simply on the foundations laid by the apostles.

Luther perceived that the ancient and primitive Church of the apostles must, on the one hand, be restored in opposition to the papacy, by which it had been so long oppressed; and on the other, be defended against enthusiasts and unbelievers who pretended to disown it, and who, regardless of all that God had done in times past, were desirous of beginning an entirely new work. Luther was no longer exclusively the man of one doctrine—that of justification—although he always assigned it the highest place; he became the man of the whole Christian theology; and while he still believed that the Church was essentially the congregation of saints, he was careful not to despise the visible Church, and acknowledge the assembly of the elect as the kingdom of God. Thus was a great change effected, at this time, in Luther's heart, in his theology, and in the work of renovation that God was carrying on in the work. The Roman hierarchy might perhaps have driven the reformer to extremes; the sects which then so boldly raised their heads brought him back to the true path of moderation. The sojourn in the Wartburg divided the history of the Reformation into two periods.

Luther was riding slowly on the road to Wittenberg: it was already the second day of his journey, and Shrove Tuesday. Toward evening a terrible storm burst forth, and the roads were flooded. Two Swiss youths, who were traveling in the same direction as himself, were hastening onwards to find a shelter in the city of Jena. They had studied at Basle, and the celebrity of Wittenberg attracted them to that university. Traveling on foot, fatigued, and wet through, John Kessler of St. Gall and his companion quickened their steps. The city was all in commotion with the amusements of the carnival; balls, masquerades, and noisy feasting engrossed the people of Jena; and when the two travelers arrived, they could find no room at any of the inns.

At last they were directed to the Black Bear, outside the city gates. Dejected and harassed, they repaired thither slowly. The landlord received them kindly. They took their seats near the open door of the public room, ashamed of the state in which the storm had placed them, and not venturing to go in. At one of the tables sat a solitary man in a knight's dress, wearing a red cap on his head and breeches over which fell the skirts of his doublet; his right hand grasped the hilt and before him lay an open book, which he appeared to be reading with great attention. At the noise made by the entrance of these two young men, he raised his head, saluted them affably, and invited them to come and sit at his table. Alluding to their accent, he said: "You are Swiss, I perceive; but from what canton?" "From St. Gall." "If you are going to Wittenberg, you will there meet with a fellow-countryman, Doctor Schurff."

Encouraged by this kind reception, they added: "Sir, could you inform us where Martin Luther is at present?"—"I know for certain," replied the knight, "that he is not at Wittenberg; but he will be there shortly. Philip Melancthon is there. Study Greek and Hebrew, that you may clearly understand the Holy Scriptures."—"If God spare our lives," observed one of the young men, "we will not return home without having seen and heard Doctor Luther; for it is on his account that we have undertaken this long journey. We know that he desires to abolish the priesthood and the mass; and as our parents destined us to the priesthood from our infancy, we should like to know clearly on what grounds he rests his proposition." The knight was silent for a moment, and then resumed: "Where have you been studying hitherto?" "At Basle." "Is Erasmus of Rotterdam still there? What is he doing?" They replied to his questions, and there was another pause. The two Swiss knew not what to think. "Is it not strange," thought they, "that this knight talks to us of Schurff, Melancthon, and Erasmus, and on the necessity of learning Greek and Hebrew." "My dear friends," said the unknown suddenly, "what do they think of Luther in Switzerland?" "Sir," replied Kessler, "opinions are very divided about him there as everywhere else. Some cannot extol him enough; and others condemn him as an abominable heretic."—"Ha! the priests, no doubt," said the stranger.

The knight's cordiality had put the students at their ease. They longed to know what book he was reading at the moment of their arrival. The knight had closed it, and placed it by his side. At last Kessler's companion ventured to take it up. To the great astonishment of the two young men, it was the Hebrew Psalter! The student laid it down immediately, and as if to divert attention from the liberty he had taken, said: "I would willingly give one of my fingers to know that language."—"You will attain your wish," said the stranger, "if you will only take the trouble to learn it."

A few minutes after, Kessler heard the landlord calling him; the poor Swiss youth feared something had gone wrong; but the host whispered to him: "I perceive that you have a great desire to see and hear Luther; well! it is he who is seated beside you." Kessler took this for a joke, and said: "Mr. Landlord, you want to make a fool of me." "It is he in very truth," replied the host; "but do not let him see that you know him." Kessler made no answer, but returned into the room and took his seat at the table, burning to repeat to his comrade what he had just heard. But how could he manage it? At last he thought of leaning forward, as if he were looking towards the door, and then whispered into his friend's ear: "The landlord assures me that this man is Luther." "Perhaps he said Hütten," replied his comrade; "you did not hear him distinctly." "It may be so," returned Kessler; "the host said, 'It is Hütten'; the two names are pretty much alike, and I mistook one for the other."

At that moment the noise of horses was heard before the inn; two merchants, who desired a lodging, entered the room; they took off their spurs, laid down their cloaks, and one of them placed beside him on the table an unbound book, which soon attracted the knight's notice. "What book is that?" asked he. "A commentary on some of the Gospels and Epistles by Doctor Luther," replied the merchant; "it is just published." "I shall procure it shortly," said the knight.

At this moment the host came to announce that supper was ready. The two students, fearing the expense of such a meal in company with the knight Ulrich of Hütten and two wealthy merchants, took the landlord aside, and begged him to serve them with something apart. "Come along, my friends," replied the landlord of the Black Bear; "take your place at table beside this gentleman; I will charge you moderately." "Come along," said the knight, "I will settle the score."

During the meal, the stranger knight uttered many simple and edifying remarks. The students and the merchants were all ears, and paid more attention to his words than to the dishes set before them. "Luther must either be an angel from heaven or a devil from hell," said one of the merchants in course of conversation; "I would readily give ten florins if I could meet Luther and confess to him."

When supper was over, the merchants left the table; the two Swiss remained alone with the knight, who, taking a large glass of beer, rose and said solemnly, after the manner of the country: "Swiss, one glass more for thanks." As Kessler was about to take the glass, the unknown set it down again, and offered him one filled with wine, saying: "You are not accustomed to beer."

He then arose, flung a military cloak over his shoulders, and extending his hand to the students, said to them: "When you reach Wittenberg, salute Dr. Schurff on my part." "Most willingly," replied they; "but what name shall we give?" "Tell him simply," added Luther, " 'He that is to come salutes you.' " With these words he quitted the room, leaving them full of admiration at his kindness and good nature.

Luther, for it was really he, continued his journey. It will be remembered that he had been laid under the ban of the empire; whoever met and recognized him might seize him. But at the time when he was engaged in an undertaking that exposed him to every risk, he was calm and serene and conversed cheerfully with those whom he met on the road.

It was not that he deceived himself: he saw the future big with storms. "Satan," said he, "is enraged, and all around are plotting death and hell. Nevertheless, I go forward, and throw myself in the way of the emperor and of the pope, having no protector save God in heaven. Power has been given to all men to kill me wherever they find me. But Christ is the Lord of all; if it be His will that I be put to death, so be it!"

On that same day, Ash Wednesday, Luther reached Borna, a small town near Leipzig. He felt it his duty to inform the prince of the bold step he was about to take; and accordingly alighted at the Guide Hotel and wrote the following letter:

"Grace and peace from God our Father, and from our Lord Jesus Christ!

"Most serene Elector, gracious Lord! The events that have taken place at Wittenberg, to the great reproach of the gospel, have caused me such pain that if I were not confident of the truth of our cause, I should have given way to despair.

"Your highness knows this, or if not, be it known to you now, that I received the gospel not from men but from heaven, through our Lord Jesus Christ. If I called for discussion, it was not because I had any doubts of the truth, but in humility and in the hope to win over others. But since my humility is turned against the gospel, my conscience compels me now to act otherwise. I have sufficiently given way to your highness by passing this year in retirement. The devil knows well that I did not do so through fear. I should have entered Worms had there been as many devils in the city as tiles on the housetops. Now Duke George, with whom your highness frightens me, is yet much less to be feared than a single devil. If that which is passing at Wittenberg were taking place at Leipzig (the duke's residence), I would immediately mount my horse to go thither, although (may your highness pardon these words) for nine whole days together it were to rain nothing but Duke Georges and each one nine times more furious than he is. What is he thinking of in attacking me? Does he take Christ my Lord for a man of straw? O Lord, be pleased to avert the terrible judgment which is impending over him!

"Be it known to your highness that I am going to Wittenberg under a protection far higher than that of princes and electors. I think not of soliciting your highness's support, and, far from desiring your protection, I would rather protect you myself. If I knew that your highness could or would protect me, I would not go to Wittenberg at all. There is no sword that can further this cause. God alone must do everything without the help or concurrence of man. He who has the greatest faith is he who is most able to protect. But I observe that your highness is still weak in faith.

"But since your highness desires to know what you have to do, I will answer with all deference: your highness has already done too much, and ought to do nothing at all. God will not and cannot endure either your cares and labors or mine. Let your highness's conduct be guided by this.

"As for what concerns me, your highness must act as an elector; you must let the orders of his imperial majesty take their course in your towns and rural districts. You must offer no resistance if men desire to seize or kill me; for no one should resist dominions except He who has established them.

"Let your highness leave the gates open, and respect safe-conducts, if my enemies in person or their envoys come in search of me into your highness's states. Everything shall be done without trouble or danger to yourself.

"I have written this letter in haste, that you may not be made uneasy at hearing of my arrival. I have to do with a very different man from Duke George. He knows me well, and I know him pretty well.

"Given at Borna, at the inn of the Guide, this Ash Wednesday, 1522.

"Your electoral highness's
"Very humble servant,
"MARTIN LUTHER."

It was thus Luther drew nigh to Wittenberg. He wrote to his prince, but not to excuse himself. An imperturbable confidence filled his heart. He saw the hand of God in this cause, and that was sufficient for him. The heroism of faith can never be carried farther. One of the editions of Luther's works has the following remark in the margin of this letter: "This is a wonderful writing of the third and last Elias!"

Chapter 65

"I PUT FORWARD GOD'S WORD"

LUTHER re-entered Wittenberg on Friday the seventh of March, having been five days on the way from Eisenach. Doctors, students, and citizens, all broke forth in rejoicings; for they had recovered the pilot who alone could extricate the vessel from the shoals among which it was entangled.

The elector, who was at Lockau with his court, felt great emotion as he read the reformer's letter. He was desirous of vindicating him before the diet: "Let him address me a letter," wrote the prince to Schurff, "explaining the motives of his return to Wittenberg, and let him say also that he returned without my permission." Luther consented.

"I am ready to incur the displeasure of your highness and the anger of the whole world," wrote he to the prince. "Are not the Wittenbergers my sheep? Has not God intrusted them to me? And ought I not, if necessary, to expose myself to death for their sakes? Besides, I fear to see a terrible outbreak in Germany by which God will punish our nation. Let your highness be well assured and doubt not that the decrees of heaven are very different from those of Nuremberg." This letter was written on the very day of Luther's arrival at Wittenberg.

On the following day, being the eve of the first Sunday in Lent, Luther visited Jerome Schurff. Melancthon, Jonas, Amsdorff, and Augustin Schurff, Jerome's brother, were there assembled. Luther eagerly questioned them, and they were informing him of all that had taken place, when two foreign students were announced, desiring to speak with Dr. Jerome. On entering this assembly of doctors, the two young men of St. Gall were at first abashed; but they soon recovered themselves on discovering the knight of the Black Bear among them. The latter immediately went up to them, greeted them as old acquaintances, and smiled as he pointed to one of the doctors: "This is Philip Melancthon, whom I mentioned to you." The two Swiss remained all day with the doctors of Wittenberg, in remembrance of the meeting at Jena.

One great thought absorbed the reformer's mind and checked the joy he felt at meeting his friends once more. Unquestionably the character in which he was now to appear was obscure: he was about to raise his voice in a small town of Saxony, and yet his undertaking had all the importance of an event which was to influence the destinies of the world. Many nations and many ages were to feel its effects. It was a question whether that doctrine which he had derived from the Word of God, and which was ordained to exert so mighty an influence on the future development of the human race, would be stronger than the destructive principles that threatened its existence. It was a question whether it were possible to reform without destroying and clear the way to new developments without annihilating the old. To silence fanatical men inspired by the energy of a first enthusiasm; to master an unbridled multitude, to calm it down, to lead it back to order, peace, and truth; to break the course of the impetuous torrent which threatened to overthrow the rising edifice of the Reformation, and to scatter its ruins far and wide—such was the task for which Luther had returned to Wittenberg. But would his influence be sufficient for this? The event alone could show.

The reformer's heart shuddered at the thought of the struggle that awaited him. He raised his head as a lion provoked to fight shakes his long mane. "We must now trample Satan underfoot, and contend against the angel of darkness," said he. "If our adversaries do not retire of their own accord, Christ will know how to compel them. We who trust in the Lord of life and of death are ourselves lords of life and of death."

But at the same time the impetuous reformer, as if restrained by a superior power, refused to employ the anathemas and thunders of the Word and became a humble pastor, a gentle shepherd of souls. "It is with the Word that we must fight," said he, "by the Word must we overthrow and destroy what has been set up by violence. I will not make use of force against the superstitious and unbelieving. Let him who believeth draw nigh! Let him who believeth not keep afar off! No one must be constrained. Liberty is the very essence of faith."

The next day was Sunday. On that day the doctor, whom for nearly a year the lofty ramparts of the Wartburg had concealed from every eye, reappeared before the people in the pulpit of the church. It was rumored in Wittenberg that Luther was come back and that he was going to preach. This news alone, passing from mouth to mouth, had already given a powerful diversion to the ideas by which the people were misled. They were going to see the hero of Worms. The people crowded together and were affected by various emotions. On Sunday morning the church was filled with an attentive and excited crowd.

Luther divined all the sentiments of his congregation; he went up into the pulpit; there he stood in the presence of the flock that he had once led as a docile sheep, but which had broken from him like an untamed bull. His language was simple, noble, yet full of strength and gentleness: one might have supposed him to be a tender father returning to his children, inquiring into their conduct and kindly telling them what report he had heard about them. He candidly acknowledged the progress they had made in faith; and by this means prepared and captivated their minds. He then continued in these words:

"But we need something more than faith; we need charity. If a man who bears a sword in his hand be alone, it is of little consequence whether it be sheathed or not; but if he is in the midst of a crowd, he should act so as to wound nobody.

"What does a mother do to her infant? At first she gives it milk, then some very light food. If she were to begin by giving it meat and wine, what would be the consequence? . . .

"So should we act towards our brethren. My friend, have you been long enough at the breast? It is well! But permit your brother to drink as long as yourself.

"Observe the sun! He dispenses two things, light and heat. There is no king powerful enough to bend aside his rays; they come straight to us: but heat is radiated and communicated in every direction. Thus faith, like light, should always be straight and inflexible; but charity, like heat, should radiate on every side, and bend to all the wants of our brethren."

Luther having thus prepared his hearers, began to press them more closely:

"The abolition of the mass, say you, is in conformity with Scripture. Agreed! But what order, what decency have you observed? It behooved you to offer up fervent prayers to the Lord and apply to the public authority; then might every man have acknowledged that the thing was of God."

Thus spake Luther. This dauntless man, who at Worms had withstood the princes of the earth, produced a deep impression on the minds of his hearers by these words of wisdom and of peace. Carlstadt and the prophets of Zwickau, so great and powerful for a few weeks, who had tyrannized over and agitated Wittenberg, had shrunk into pigmies beside the captive of the Wartburg.

"The mass," continued he, "is a bad thing; God is opposed to it; it ought to be abolished; and I would that throughout the whole world it were replaced by the Supper of the gospel. But let no one be torn from it by force. We must leave the matter in God's hands. His Word must act, and not we. And why so, you will ask? Because I do not hold men's hearts in my hand, as the potter holds the clay. We have a right to speak; we have not the right to act. Let us preach: the rest belongs unto God. Were I to employ force, what should I gain? Grimace, formality, apings, human ordinances, and hypocrisy. . . . But there would be no sincerity of heart, nor faith, nor charity. Where these three are wanting, all is wanting, and I would not give a pear-stalk for such a result.

"Our first object must be to win men's hearts; and for that purpose we must preach the gospel. Today the Word will fall into one heart, tomorrow into another, and it will operate in such a manner that each one will withdraw from the mass and abandon it. God does more by His Word alone than you and I and all the world by our united strength. God lays hold upon the heart; and when the heart is taken, all is won.

"I do not say this for the restoration of the mass. Since it is down, in God's name there let it lie! But should you have gone to work as you did? Paul, arriving one day in the powerful city of Athens, found there altars raised to false gods. He went from one to the other, and observed them without touching one. But he walked peaceably into the middle of the market place and declared to the people that all their gods were idols. His language took possession of their hearts, and the idols fell without Paul's having touched them.

"I will preach, discuss, and write; but I will constrain none, for faith is a voluntary act. See what I have done! I stood up against the pope, indulgences, and papists, but without violence or tumult. I put forward God's Word; I preached and wrote—this was all I did. The Word alone did all. If I had wished to appeal to force, the whole of Germany would perhaps have been deluged with blood. But what would have been the result? Ruin and desolation both to body and soul. I therefore kept quiet and left the Word to run through the world alone. Do you know what the devil thinks when he sees men resort to violence to propagate the gospel through the world? Seated with folded arms behind the fire of hell, Satan says, with malignant looks and frightful grin: 'Ah! how wise these madmen are to play my game!' But when he sees the Word running and contending alone on the field of battle, then he is troubled, and his knees knock together; he shudders and faints with fear."

Luther went into the pulpit again on Tuesday; and his powerful voice resounded once more through the agitated crowd. He preached again on the five succeeding days. He took a review of the destruction of images, the distinction of meats, the institution of the Lord's Supper, the restoration of the cup, the abolition of confession. He showed that these points were of far less importance than the mass, and that the originators of the disorders that had taken place in Wittenberg had grossly abused their liberty. He employed by turns the language of Christian charity and bursts of holy indignation.

He inveighed more especially against those who partook thoughtlessly of Christ's Supper. "It is not the outward manducation that maketh a Christian," said he, "but the inward and spiritual eating that worketh by faith, without which all forms are mere show and grimace. Now this faith consists in a firm belief that Jesus Christ is the Son of God; that having taken our sins and iniquities upon Himself, and having borne them on the cross, He is Himself their sole and almighty atonement; that He stands continually before God, that He reconcileth us with the Father, and that He hath given us the sacrament of His body to strengthen our faith in this unspeakable mercy. If I believe in these things, God is my defender; with Him, I brave sin, death, hell, and devils; they can do me no harm, nor disturb a single hair of my head. This spiritual bread is the consolation of the afflicted, health to the sick, life to the dying, food to the hungry, riches to the poor. He who does not groan under his sins must not approach that altar: what can he do there? Ah! let our conscience accuse us, let our hearts be rent in twain at the thought of our sins, and then we shall not so presumptuously approach the holy sacrament."

The crowd ceased not to fill the temple; people flocked from the neighboring towns to hear the new Elijah. Among others, Capito spent two days at Wittenberg and heard two of the doctor's sermons. Never had Luther and Cardinal Albert's chaplain been so well agreed. Melancthon, the magistrates, the professors, and all the inhabitants, were delighted. Schurff, charmed at the result of so gloomy an affair, hastened to communicate it to the elector. On Friday the fifteenth of March, the day on which Luther delivered his sixth sermon, he wrote: "Oh, what joy has Dr. Martin's return diffused among us! His words, through divine mercy, every day are bringing back our poor misguided people into the way of truth. It is clear as the sun that the Spirit of God is in him and that by His special providence he returned to Wittenberg."

In truth, these sermons are models of popular eloquence, but not of that which in the times of Demosthenes, or even of Savonarola, fired men's hearts. The task of the Wittenberg orator was more difficult. It is easier to rouse the fury of a wild beast than to allay it. Luther had to soothe a fanaticized multitude, to tame its unbridled passions; and in this he succeeded. In his eight discourses, the reformer did not allow one offensive word to escape him against the originators of these disorders, not one unpleasant allusion. But the greater his moderation, the greater also was his strength; the more caution he used toward these deluded men, the more powerful was his vindication of offended truth. How could the people of Wittenberg resist his powerful eloquence? Men usually ascribe to timidity, fear, and compromise, those speeches that advocate moderation. Here there was nothing of the sort. Luther appeared before the inhabitants of Wittenberg braving the excommunication of the pope and the proscription of the emperor. He had returned in despite of the prohibition of the elector, who had declared his inability to defend him. Even at Worms, Luther had not shown so much courage. He confronted the most imminent dangers; and accordingly his words were not disregarded: the man who braved the scaffold had a right to exhort to submission. That man may boldly speak of obedience to God, who, to do so, defies all the persecution of man. At Luther's voice all objections vanished, the tumult subsided, seditious cries were heard no longer, and the citizens of Wittenberg returned quietly to their dwellings.

Gabriel Didymus, who had shown himself the most enthusiastic of all the Augustine friars, did not lose one of the reformer's words. "Do you not think Luther a wonderful teacher?" asked a hearer in great emotion. "Ah!" replied he, "I seem to listen to the voice, not of a man, but of an angel." Erelong Didymus openly acknowledged that he had been deceived. "He is quite another man," said Luther.

It was not so at first with Carlstadt. Despising learning, pretending to frequent the workshops of the Wittenberg mechanics to receive understanding of the Holy Scriptures, he was mortified at seeing his work crumble away at Luther's appearance. In his eyes this was checking the reform itself. Hence his air was always dejected, gloomy, and dissatisfied. Yet he sacrificed his self-love for the sake of peace; he restrained his desires of vengeance and became reconciled, outwardly at least, with his colleague, and shortly after resumed his lectures in the university.

The chief prophets were not at Wittenberg when Luther returned. Nicholas Storch was wandering through the country; Mark Stubner had quitted Melancthon's hospitable roof. Perhaps their prophetic spirit had disappeared, and they had had neither voice nor answer, so soon as they learned that the new Elijah was directing his steps towards this new Carmel. The old schoolmaster Cellarius alone had remained. Stubner, however, being informed that the sheep of his fold were scattered, hastily returned. Those who were still faithful to "the heavenly prophecy" gathered round their master, reported Luther's speeches to him and asked him anxiously what they were to think and do. Stubner exhorted them to remain firm in their faith. "Let him appear," cried Cellarius, "let him grant us a conference—let him only permit us to set forth our doctrine, and then we shall see. . . ."

Luther cared little to meet such men as these; he knew them to be of violent, impatient, and haughty dispositions, men who could not endure even kind admonition, and who required that everyone should submit at the first word, as to a supreme authority. Such are enthusiasts in every age. And yet, as they desired an interview, the doctor could not refuse it. Besides, it might be of use to the weak ones of the flock were he to unmask the imposture of the prophets. The conference took place. Stubner opened the proceedings by explaining in what manner he desired to regenerate the Church and transform the world. Luther listened to him with great calmness. "Nothing that you have advanced," replied he at last gravely, "is based upon Holy Scripture. It is all a mere fable."

At these words Cellarius could contain himself no longer; he raised his voice, gesticulated like a madman, stamped, and struck the table with his fist, and exclaimed, in a passion, that it was an insult to speak thus to a man of God. Upon this Luther observed: "St. Paul declares that the proofs of his apostleship were made known by miracles; prove yours in like manner." "We will do so," answered the prophets. "The God whom I worship," said Luther, "will know how to bridle your gods." Stubner, who had preserved his tranquillity, then fixed his eyes on the reformer, and said to him with an air of inspiration, "Martin Luther! I will declare what is now passing in thy soul. . . . Thou art beginning to believe that my doctrine is true." Luther, after a brief pause, exclaimed: "God chastise thee, Satan!" At these words all the prophets were as if distracted. "The Spirit, the Spirit!" cried they. Luther, adopting that cool tone of contempt and that cutting and homely language so familiar to him, said, "I slap your spirit on the snout." Their clamors now increased; Cellarius, in particular, distinguished himself by his violence. He foamed and trembled with anger. They could not hear one another in the room where they met in conference. At length the three prophets abandoned the field and left Wittenberg the same day.

Thus had Luther accomplished the work for which he had left his retreat. He had made a stand against fanaticism and expelled from the bosom of the renovated Church the enthusiasm and disorder by which it had been invaded. If with one hand the Reformation threw down the dusty decretals of Rome, with the other it rejected the assumptions of the mystics and established, on the ground it had won, the living and unchangeable Word of God. The character of the Reformation was thus firmly settled. It was destined to walk forever between these two extremes, equally remote from the convulsions of the fanatics and the death-like torpor of the papacy.

A whole population excited, deluded, and unrestrained, had at once become tranquil, calm, and submissive; and the most perfect quiet again reigned in that city which a few days before had been like a troubled ocean.

Perfect liberty was immediately established at Wittenberg. Luther still continued to reside in the convent and wear his monastic dress; but everyone was free to do otherwise. In communicating at the Lord's table, a general absolution was sufficient, or a particular one might be obtained. It was laid down as a principle to reject nothing but what was opposed to the clear and formal declaration of the Holy Scriptures. This was not indifference; on the contrary, religion was thus restored to what constitutes its very essence; the sentiment of religion withdrew from the accessory forms in which it had well-nigh perished, and transferred itself to its true basis. Thus the Reformation was saved, and its teaching enabled to continue its development in the bosom of the Church in charity and truth.

Chapter 66

MELANCTHON'S THEOLOGY

TRANQUILLITY was hardly established when the reformer turned to his dear Melancthon and demanded his assistance in the final revision of the New Testament which he had brought with him from the Wartburg. As early as the year 1519, Melancthon had laid down the grand principle that the Fathers must be explained according to Scripture, and not Scripture according to the Fathers. Meditating more profoundly every day on the books of the New Testament, he felt at once charmed by their simplicity and impressed by their depth. "There alone can we find the true food of the soul," boldly asserted this man so familiar with all the philosophy of the ancients. Accordingly he readily complied with Luther's invitation; and from that time the two friends passed many long hours together studying and translating the inspired Word. Often would they pause in their laborious researches to give way to their admiration. Luther said one day, "Reason thinks, Oh! if I could once hear God speak! I would run from one end of the world to the other to hear him. . . . Listen then, my brother man! God, the Creator of the heavens and the earth, speaks to thee."

The printing of the New Testament was carried on with unexampled zeal. One would have said that the very workmen felt the importance of the task in which they were engaged. Three presses were employed in this labor, and ten thousand sheets, says Luther, were printed daily.

At length, on the twenty-first of September, 1522, appeared the complete edition of three thousand copies, in two folio volumes, with this simple title: "The New Testament—German—Wittenberg." It bore no name of man. Every German might henceforward procure the Word of God at a moderate price.

The new translation, which was written in the very tone of the Holy Writings in a language yet in its youthful vigor, and which for the first time displayed its great beauties, interested, charmed, and moved the lowest as well as the highest ranks. It was a national work, the book of the people; nay more—it was in very truth the Book of God. Even opponents could not refuse their approbation of this wonderful work, and some indiscreet friends of the reformer, impressed by the beauty of the translation, imagined they could recognize in it a second inspiration. This version served more than all Luther's writings to the spread of Christian piety. The work of the sixteenth century was thus placed on a foundation where nothing could shake it. The Bible, given to the people, recalled the mind of man, which had been wandering for ages in the tortuous labyrinth of scholasticism, to the divine fountain of salvation. Accordingly the success of this work was prodigious. In a short time every copy was sold. A second edition appeared in the month of December; and in 1533, seventeen editions had been printed at Wittenberg, thirteen at Augsburg, twelve at Basle, one at Erfurt, one at Grimma, one at Leipzig, and thirteen at Strasburg. Such were the powerful levers that uplifted and transformed the Church and the world.

While the first edition of the New Testament was going through the press, Luther undertook a translation of the Old. This labor, begun in 1522, was continued without interruption. He published his translation in parts as they were finished, the more speedily to gratify public impatience, and to enable the poor to procure the book.

From Scripture and faith, two sources which in reality are but one, the life of the gospel has flowed, and is still spreading over the world. These two principles combated two fundamental errors. Faith was opposed to the Pelagian tendency of Roman Catholicism; Scripture, to the theory of tradition and the authority of Rome. Scripture led man to faith, and faith led him back to Scripture. "Man can do no meritorious work; the free grace of God, which he receives by faith in Christ, alone saves him." Such was the doctrine proclaimed in Christendom.

But this doctrine could not fail to impel Christendom to the study of Scripture. In truth, if faith in Christ is everything in Christianity, if the practices and ordinances of the Church are nothing, it is not to the teaching of the Church that we should adhere, but to the teaching of Christ. The bond that unites to Christ will become everything to the believer. What matters to him the outward link that connects him with an outward church enslaved by the opinions of men? . . . Thus, as the doctrine of the Bible had impelled Luther's contemporaries toward Jesus Christ, so in turn the love they felt to Jesus Christ impelled them to the Bible. It was not, as has been supposed in our day, from a philosophical principle, or in consequence of doubt, or from the necessity of inquiry, that they returned to Scripture; it was because they there found the Word of Him they loved. "You have preached Christ to us," said they to the reformer, "let us now hear Him Himself." And they seized the pages that were spread before them, as a letter coming from heaven.

But if the Bible was thus gladly received by those who loved Christ, it was scornfully rejected by those who preferred the traditions and observances of men. A violent persecution was waged against this work of the reformer's. At the news of Luther's publication, Rome trembled. The pen which had transcribed the sacred oracles was really that which Frederick had seen in his dream, and which, reaching to the Seven Hills, had shaken the tiara of the papacy. The monk in his cell, the prince on his throne, uttered a cry of anger. Ignorant priests shuddered at the thought that every citizen, nay every peasant, would now be able to dispute with them on the precepts of our Lord. The King of England denounced the work to the Elector Frederick and to Duke George of Saxony. But as early as the month of November the duke had ordered his subjects to deposit every copy of Luther's New Testament in the hands of the magistrates. Bavaria, Brandenburg, Austria, and all the states devoted to Rome, published similar decrees. In some places they made sacrilegious bonfires of these sacred books in the public places. Thus did Rome in the sixteenth century renew the efforts by which paganism had attempted to destroy the religion of Jesus Christ, at the moment when the dominion was escaping from the priests and their idols. But who can check the triumphant progress of the gospel? "Even after my prohibition," wrote Duke George, "many thousand copies were sold and read in my states."

God even made use of those hands to circulate his Word that were endeavoring to destroy it. When the Romanist theologians saw that they could not prohibit the reformer's work, they themselves published a translation of the New Testament. It was Luther's version, altered here and there by the publishers. There was no hindrance to its being read. Rome as yet knew not that wherever the Word of God is established, there her power is shaken. Joachim of Brandenburg permitted all his subjects to read any translation of the Bible, in Latin or in German, provided it did not come from Wittenberg. The people of Germany, and those of Brandenburg in particular, thus made great progress in the knowledge of the truth.

The publication of the New Testament in the vulgar tongue is an important epoch in the Reformation. If Feldkirchen's marriage was the first step in the progress of the Reformation from doctrine into social life; if the abolition of monastic vows was the second; if the re-establishment of the Lord's Supper was the third,—the publication of the New Testament was perhaps the most important of all. It worked an entire change in society: not only in the presbytery of the priest, in the monk's cell, and in the sanctuary of our Lord; but also in the mansions of the great, in the houses of the citizens, and in the cottages of the peasants. When the Bible began to be read in the families of Christendom, Christendom itself was changed. Then arose other habits, other manners, other conversations, and another life. With the publication of the New Testament, the Reformation left the School and the Church to take possession of the hearts of the people.

The effect produced was immense. The Christianity of the primitive Church, drawn by the publication of the Holy Scriptures from the oblivion of centuries in which it had lain, was thus presented before the eyes of the nation; and this view was sufficient to justify the attacks that had been made against Rome. The simplest men, provided they knew how to read, women, and mechanics (our informant is a contemporary and violent opponent of the Reformation) eagerly studied the New Testament. They carried it about with them; soon they knew it by heart, and the pages of this book loudly proclaimed the perfect unison of Luther's Reformation with the divine revelation.

And yet it was only by fragments that the doctrine of the Bible and of the Reformation had been set forth hitherto. A certain truth had been put forward in one writing; a certain error attacked in an-other. On one vast plain lay scattered and confused the ruins of the old edifice and the materials of the new: but the new edifice was wanting. The publication of the New Testament undoubtedly satis-fied this want. The Reformation could say, as it gave this book: Here is my system! But as every man is at liberty to assert that his system is that of the Bible, the Reformation was called to arrange what it had found in Scripture. And this Melancthon now did in its name.

He had walked with regular but confident steps in the develop-ment of his theology, and had from time to time published the results of his inquiries. Before this, in 1520, he had declared that in several of the seven sacraments he could see nothing but an imitation of the Jewish ceremonies; and in the infallibility of the pope, a haughty presumption equally opposed to the Holy Scriptures and to good sense. "To contend against these doctrines," he had said, "we require more than one Hercules." Thus had Melancthon reached the same point as Luther, although by a calmer and more scientific process. The time had come in which he was to confess his faith in his turn.

In 1521, during Luther's captivity, Melancthon's celebrated work, *On the Commonplaces of Theology*, had presented to Christian Eu-rope a body of doctrine of solid foundations and admirable propor-tions. A simple and majestic unity appeared before the astonished eyes of the new generation. The translation of the Testament justi-fied the Reformation to the people; Melancthon's *Commonplaces* justified it in the opinion of the learned.

For fifteen centuries the Church had existed and had never seen such a work. Forsaking the ordinary developments of scholastic the-ology, Luther's friend at last gave the world a theological system de-rived solely from Scripture. In it there reigned a breath of life, a vitality of understanding, a strength of conviction, and a simplicity of statement, that form a striking contrast with the subtle and pe-dantic systems of the schools. Men of the most philosophic minds, as well as the strictest theologians, were equally filled with admiration.

Erasmus entitled this work a wondrous army drawn up in battle array against the tyrannous battalions of the false doctors; and while he avowed his dissent from the author on several points, he added, that although he had always loved him, he had never loved him so much as after reading this work. "So true it is," said Calvin when presenting it subsequently to France, "that the greatest simplicity is the greatest virtue in treating of the Christian doctrine."

But no one felt such joy as Luther. Throughout life this work was the object of his admiration. The disconnected sounds that his hand, in the deep emotion of his soul, had drawn from the harp of the prophets and apostles, were here blended together into one enchanting harmony. Those scattered stones, which he had laboriously hewn from the quarries of Scripture, were now combined into a majestic edifice. Hence he never ceased recommending the study of this work to the youths who came to Wittenberg in search of knowledge: "If you desire to become theologians," he would say, "read Melancthon."

According to Melancthon, a deep conviction of the wretched state to which man is reduced by sin is the foundation on which the edifice of Christian theology should be raised. This universal evil is the primary fact, the leading idea on which the science is based; it is the characteristic that distinguishes theology from those sciences whose only instrument is reason.

The Christian divine, diving into the heart of man, explains its laws and mysterious attractions, as another philosopher in afteryears explained the laws and attraction of bodies. "Original sin," said he, "is an inclination born with us,—a certain impulse which is agreeable to us,—a certain force leading us to sin, and which has been communicated by Adam to all his posterity. As in fire there is a native energy impelling it to mount upward, as there is in the loadstone a natural quality by which iron is attracted; so also there is in man a primitive force that inclines him to evil. I grant that in Socrates, Xenocrates, and Zeno, were found temperance, firmness, and chastity; these shadows of virtues were found in impure hearts and originated in self-love. This is why we should regard them not as real virtues, but as vices." This language may seem harsh; but not so if we apprehend Melancthon's meaning aright. No one was more willing to acknowledge virtues in the pagans that entitled them to the esteem of man; but he laid down this great truth that the sovereign law given by God to all His creatures is to love Him above all things. Now, if man, in doing that which God commands, does it not from love to God but from love of self, can God accept him for daring to substitute himself in the place of His infinite Majesty? And can there be no sinfulness in an action that is express rebellion against the supreme Deity?

The Wittenberg divine then proceeds to show how man is saved from this wretchedness. "The apostle," said he, "invites thee to contemplate the Son of God sitting at the right hand of the Father, mediating and interceding for us; and calls upon thee to feel assured that thy sins are forgiven thee, that thou art reputed righteous, and accepted by the Father for the sake of that Son who suffered for us on the cross."

The first edition of the *Commonplaces* is especially remarkable for the manner in which the theologian of Germany speaks of free will. He saw more clearly perhaps than Luther, for he was a better theologian, that this doctrine could not be separated from that which constituted the very essence of the Reformation. Man's justification before God proceeds from faith alone: this is the first point. This faith enters man's heart by the grace of God alone: here is the second. Melancthon saw clearly that if he allowed that man had any natural ability to believe, he would be throwing down in the second point that great doctrine of grace which he had stated in the first. He had too much discernment and understanding of the Holy Scriptures to be mistaken in so important a matter. But he went too far. Instead of confining himself within the limits of the religious question, he entered upon metaphysics. He established a fatalism which might tend to represent God as the author of evil,—a doctrine which has no foundation in Scripture. "As all things which happen," said he, "happen necessarily, according to the divine predestination, there is no such thing as liberty in our wills."

But the object Melancthon had particularly in view was to present theology as a system of piety. The schoolmen had so dried up the doctrine as to leave no traces of vitality in it. The task of the Reformation was therefore to reanimate this lifeless doctrine. In the subsequent editions, Melancthon felt the necessity of expounding these doctrines with greater clearness. But such was not precisely the case in 1521. "To know Christ," said he, "is to know His blessings. Paul, in his Epistle to the Romans, desiring to give a summary of the Christian doctrines, does not philosophize on the mystery of the Trinity, on the mode of incarnation, on active or passive creation; of what then does he speak?—of the law,—of sin,—of grace. On this our knowledge of Christ depends."

The publication of this body of theology was of inestimable value to the cause of truth. Calumnies were refuted; prejudices swept away. In the churches, palaces, and universities, Melancthon's genius found admirers who esteemed the graces of his character. Even those who knew not the author were attracted to his creed by his book. The roughness and occasional violence of Luther's language had often repelled many. But here was a man who explained those mighty truths whose sudden explosion had shaken the world, with great elegance of style, exquisite taste, admirable perspicuity, and perfect order. The work was sought after and read with avidity, and studied with ardor. Such gentleness and moderation won all hearts. Such nobility and force commanded their respect; and the superior classes of society, hitherto undecided, were gained over to a wisdom that made use of such beautiful language.

On the other hand, the adversaries of truth, whom Luther's terrible blows had not yet humbled, remained for a time silent and disconcerted at the appearance of Melancthon's treatise. They saw that there was another man as worthy of their hatred as Luther himself. "Alas!" exclaimed they, "unhappy Germany! to what extremity wilt thou be brought by this new birth!"

Between the years 1521 and 1595, the *Commonplaces* passed through sixty-seven editions, without including translations. Next to the Bible, this is the book that has possibly contributed most to the establishment of evangelical doctrine.

Chapter 67

HENRY VIII ATTACKS

WHILE THE "GRAMMARIAN" Melancthon was contributing by these gentle strains a powerful support to Luther, men of authority, enemies to the reformer, were turning violently against him. He had escaped from the Wartburg and reappeared on the stage of the world; and at this news the rage of his former adversaries was revived.

Luther had been three and a half months at Wittenberg when a rumor, increased by the thousand tongues of fame, brought intelligence that one of the greatest kings of Christendom had risen against him. Henry VIII, the head of the house of Tudor, a prince descended from the families of York and Lancaster, and in whose person, after so much bloodshed, the white and red roses were at length united, the mighty king of England who claimed to re-establish on the continent, and especially in France, the former influence of his crown,— had just written a book against the poor monk of Wittenberg. "There is much boasting about a little book by the King of England," wrote Luther to Lange on the twenty-sixth of June, 1522.

Henry was then thirty-one years old; "he was tall, strong-built and proportioned, and had an air of authority and empire." His countenance expressed the vivacity of his mind; vehement, presuming to make everything give way to the violence of his passions, and thirsting for glory, he at first concealed his faults under a certain impetuosity that is peculiar to youth, and flatterers were not wanting to encourage them. He would often visit, in company with his courtiers, the house of his chaplain, Thomas Wolsey, the son of an Ipswich butcher. Endowed with great skill, of overweening ambition, and of unbounded audacity, this man, protected by the Bishop of Winchester, chancellor of the kingdom, had rapidly advanced in his master's favor and allured him to his residence by the attractions of pleasures and disorders, in which the young prince would not have ventured to indulge in his own palace. This is recorded by Polydore Virgil, at that time papal sub-collector in England. In these dissolute meetings, the chaplain surpassed the licentiousness of the young courtiers who attended Henry VIII. Forgetful of the decorum befitting a minister of the Church, he would sing, dance, laugh, play the fool, fence, and indulge in obscene conversation. By these means he succeeded in obtaining the first place in the king's councils, and, as sole minister, all the princes of Christendom were forced to purchase his favor.

Henry lived in the midst of balls, banquets, and jousting, and riotously squandered the treasures his father had slowly accumulated. Magnificent tournaments succeeded each other without interval. In these sports the king, who was distinguished above all the combatants by his manly beauty, played the chief part. If the contest appeared for a moment doubtful, the strength and address of the young monarch, or the artful policy of his opponents, gave him the victory, and the lists resounded with shouts and applause in his honor. The vanity of the youthful prince was inflated by these easy triumphs, and there was no success in the world to which he thought he might not aspire.

The queen was often seen among the spectators. Her serious features and sad look, her absent and dejected air, formed a striking contrast with the noise and glitter of these festivities. Shortly after his accession to the throne, and for reasons of state, Henry VIII had espoused Catherine of Aragon, his senior by eight years: she was his brother Arthur's widow, and aunt to Charles V. While her husband followed his pleasures, the virtuous Catherine, whose piety was truly Spanish, would leave her bed in the middle of the night to take a silent part in the prayers of the monks, at which she would kneel down without cushion or carpet. At five in the morning, after taking a little rest, she would again rise, and putting on the Franciscan dress, for she had been admitted into the tertiary order of St. Francis, and hastily throwing the royal garments around her, would repair to church at six o'clock to join in the service.

Two beings, living in such different spheres, could not long continue together.

Romish piety had other representatives besides Catherine in the court of Henry VIII. John Fisher, bishop of Rochester, then nearly seventy years of age, as distinguished for learning as for the austerity of his manners, was the object of universal veneration. He had been the oldest councilor of Henry VII, and the Duchess of Richmond, grandmother to Henry VIII, calling him to her bedside, had commended to his care the youth and inexperience of her grandson. The king, in the midst of his irregularities, long continued to revere the aged bishop as a father.

A man much younger than Fisher, a layman and a lawyer, had prior to this attracted general attention by his genius and noble character. His name was Thomas More, son of one of the judges of the King's Bench. He was poor, austere, and diligent. At the age of twenty he had endeavored to quench the passions of youth by wearing a shirt of haircloth and by self-scourging. On one occasion, being summoned by Henry VIII while he was attending mass, he replied that God's service was before the king's. Wolsey introduced him to Henry, who employed him on various embassies and showed him much kindness. He would often send for him and converse with him on astronomy, about Wolsey, or on divinity.

In truth, the king himself was not unacquainted with the Romish doctrines. It would appear, that if Arthur had lived, Henry was destined for the archiepiscopal see of Canterbury. Thomas Aquinas, St. Bonaventure, tournaments, banquets, Elizabeth Blunt and others of his mistresses—all were mixed up in the mind and life of this prince, who had masses of his own composition sung in his chapel.

As soon as Henry had heard talk of Luther, he became indignant against him, and hardly was the decree of the Diet of Worms known in England, before he ordered the pontiff's bull against the reformer's works to be put into execution. On the twelfth of May, 1521, Thomas Wolsey, who, together with the office of chancellor of England, combined those of cardinal and legate of Rome, went in solemn procession to St. Paul's. This man, whose pride had attained the highest pitch, thought himself the equal of kings. He used to sit in a chair of gold, sleep in a golden bed, and a cover of cloth of gold was spread on the table during his meals.

On this occasion he displayed great magnificence. His household, consisting of eight hundred persons, among whom were barons, knights, and sons of the most distinguished families, who hoped by serving him to obtain public office, surrounded this haughty prelate. Silk and gold glittered not only on his garments (he was the first ecclesiastic who ventured to dress so sumptuously), but even on the housings and harness of the horses. Before him walked a tall priest bearing a silver column terminated by a cross; behind him, another ecclesiastic of similar height carried the archiepiscopal crosier of York; a nobleman at his side held the cardinal's hat. Lords, prelates, ambassadors from the pope and emperor, accompanied him, followed by a long line of mules bearing chests covered with the richest and most brilliant hangings. It was this magnificent procession that was carrying to the burning pile the writings of the poor monk of Wittenberg. When they reached the cathedral, the insolent priest placed his cardinal's hat on the altar. The virtuous Bishop of Rochester stationed himself at the foot of the cross, and with agitated voice preached earnestly against the heresy. After this the impious books of the heresiarch were brought together and devoutly burned in the presence of an immense crowd. Such was the first intelligence that England received of the Reformation.

Henry would not stop here. This prince, whose hand was ever upraised against his adversaries, his wives, or his favorites, wrote to the elector-palatine: "It is the devil, who, by Luther's means, has kindled this immense conflagration. If Luther will not be converted, let him and his writings be burned together!"

This was not enough. Having been convinced that the progress of heresy was owing to the extreme ignorance of the German princes, Henry thought the moment had arrived for showing his learning. The victories of his battle-axe did not permit him to doubt of those that were reserved for his pen. But another passion, vanity, ever greatest in the smallest minds, spurred the king onward. He was humiliated at having no title to oppose to that of "Catholic" and "Most Christian," borne by the kings of Spain and France, and he had been long begging a similar distinction from the court of Rome. What would be more likely to procure it than an attack upon heresy? Henry therefore threw aside the kingly purple, and descended from his throne into the arena of theological discussion. He enlisted

Thomas Aquinas, Peter Lombard, Alexander Hales, and Bonaventure into his service; and the world beheld the publication of the *Defence of the Seven Sacraments, against Martin Luther, by the* *most invincible King of England and France, Lord of Ireland, Henry* *the eighth of that name.*

"I will rush in front of the Church to save her," said the King of England in this treatise; "I will receive in my bosom the poisoned arrows of her assailants. The present state of things calls me to do so. Every servant of Christ, whatever be his age, sex, or rank, should rise up against the common enemy of Christendom.

"Let us put on a twofold breastplate; the heavenly breastplate, to conquer by the weapons of truth him who combats with those of error; but also an earthly breastplate, that if he shows himself obstinate in his malice, the hand of the executioner may constrain him to be silent, and that once at least he may be useful to the world, by the terrible example of his death."

Henry VIII was unable to hide the contempt he felt towards his feeble adversary. "This man," said the crowned theologian, "seems to be in the pangs of childbirth; after a travail without precedent, he produces nothing but wind. Remove the daring envelope of the insolent verbiage with which he clothes his absurdities, as an ape is clothed in purple, and what remains? . . . a wretched and empty sophism."

The king defended, successively, the mass, penance, confirmation, marriage, orders, and extreme unction; he was not sparing of abusive language toward his opponent; he called him by turns a wolf of hell, a poisonous viper, a limb of the devil. Even Luther's sincerity was attacked. Henry VIII crushed the mendicant monk with his royal anger "and writes as 'twere with his scepter," says a historian.

And yet it must be confessed that his work was not bad, considering the author and his age. The style is not altogether without force; but the public of the day did not confine themselves to paying it due justice. The theological treatise of the powerful King of England was received with a torrent of adulation. "It is the most learned work the sun ever saw," cried some. "We can only compare it," re-echoed others, "to the works of Augustine. He is a Constantine, a Charlemagne!" "He is more," said others, "he is a second Solomon!"

These flatteries soon extended beyond the limits of England.

Henry desired John Clarke, dean of Windsor, his ambassador at Rome, to present his book to the sovereign pontiff. Leo X received the envoy in full consistory, and Clarke laid the royal work before him, saying: "The king my master assures you that, having now refuted Luther's errors with the pen, he is ready to combat his adherents with the sword." Leo, touched with this promise, replied that the king's book could not have been written without the aid of the Holy Ghost, and conferred upon Henry the title of Defender of the Faith, which is still borne by the sovereigns of England.

The reception which this volume met with at Rome contributed greatly to increase the number of its readers. In a few months many thousand copies issued from different presses. "The whole Christian world," says Cochloeus, "was filled with admiration and joy."

Such extravagant panegyrics augmented the insufferable vanity of this chief of the Tudors. He himself seemed to have no doubt that he was inspired by the Holy Ghost. From that time he would suffer no contradiction. His papacy was no longer at Rome, but at Greenwich; infallibility reposed on his shoulders: at a subsequent period this contributed greatly to the Reformation of England.

Luther read Henry's book with a smile mingled with disdain, impatience, and indignation. The falsehood and the abuse it contained, but especially the air of contempt and compassion which the king assumed, irritated the Wittenberg doctor to the highest degree. The thought that the pope had crowned this work, and that on all sides the enemies of the gospel were triumphing over the Reformation and the reformer as already overthrown and vanquished, increased his indignation. Besides, what reason had he to temporize? Was he not fighting in the cause of a King greater than all the kings of the earth? The meekness of the gospel appeared to him unseasonable. An eye for an eye, a tooth for a tooth. He went beyond all bounds. Persecuted, insulted, hunted down, and wounded, the furious lion turned round and proudly roused himself to crush his enemy. The elector, Spalatin, Melancthon, and Bugenhagen, strove in vain to pacify him. They would have prevented his replying; but nothing could stop him.

"I will not be gentle towards the King of England," said he. "I know that it is vain for me to humble myself, to give way, to entreat, to try peaceful methods. At length I will show myself more terrible towards these furious beasts, who goad me every day with their horns.

I will turn mine upon them. I will provoke Satan until he falls down lifeless and exhausted. If this heretic does not recant, says Henry VIII the new Thomas, he must be burned alive! Such are the weapons they are now employing against me: the fury of stupid asses and swine of the brood of Thomas Aquinas; and then the stake. Well then, be it so! Let these hogs advance if they dare, and let them burn me! Here I am waiting for them. After my death, though my ashes should be thrown into a thousand seas, they will rise, pursue, and swallow up this abominable herd. Living, I shall be the enemy of the papacy; burned, I shall be its destruction. Go then, swine of St. Thomas, do what seemeth good to you. You will ever find Luther like a bear upon your road, and as a lion in your path. He will spring upon you whithersoever you go, and will never leave you at peace, until he has broken your iron heads, and ground your brazen foreheads into dust."

Luther first reproached Henry VIII with having supported his doctrines solely by the decrees and opinions of men. "As for me," said he, "I never cease crying the gospel, the gospel! Christ, Christ! And my adversaries continue to reply: Custom, custom! ordinances, ordinances! Fathers, fathers! St. Paul says: 'Let not your faith stand in the wisdom of men, but in the power of God' " (I Cor. 2:5). And the apostle by this thunderclap from heaven overthrew and dispersed all the hobgoblins of this Henry as the wind scatters the dust. Frightened and confounded, these Thomists, papists, and Henrys fell prostrate before the thunder of these words.

He then refuted the king's book in detail, and overturned his arguments one after the other, with a perspicuity, spirit, and knowledge of the Holy Scriptures and history of the Church, but also with an assurance, disdain, and sometimes violence, that ought not to surprise us.

Having reached the end of his confutation, Luther again became indignant that his opponent should derive his arguments from the Fathers only: this was the basis of the whole controversy. "To all the words of the Fathers and of men, of angels and of devils," said he, "I oppose, not old customs, not the multitude of men, but the Word of the Eternal Majesty,—the gospel, which even my adversaries are obliged to recognize. To this I hold fast, on this I repose, in this I boast, in this I exult and triumph over the papists, the Thomists, the

Henrys, the sophists, and all the swine of hell. The King of heaven is with me; for this reason I fear nothing, although a thousand Augustines, a thousand Cyprians, and a thousand of these churches which Henry defends, should rise up against me. It is a small matter that I should despise and revile a king of the earth, since he himself does not fear in his writings to blaspheme the King of heaven, and to profane His holy name by the most impudent falsehoods.

"Papists!" exclaimed he in conclusion, "will ye never cease from your idle attacks? Do what you please. Nevertheless, before that gospel which I preach down must come popes, bishops, priests, monks, princes, devils, death, sin, and all that is not Christ or in Christ."

Thus spoke the poor monk. His violence certainly cannot be excused if we judge it by the rule to which he himself appealed—by the Word of God. It cannot even be justified by alleging either the grossness of the age (for Melancthon knew how to observe decorum in his writings), or the energy of his character, for if this energy had any influence over his language, passion also exerted more. It is better, then, that we should condemn it. And yet it is but right to observe that in the sixteenth century this violence did not appear so strange as it would in our day. The learned were then an estate, as well as the princes. By becoming a writer, Henry had attacked Luther. Luther replied according to an established law in the republic of letters, that we must consider the truth of what is said, and not the quality of him that says it. Let us add also, that when this same king turned against the pope, the abuse which the Romish writers and the pope himself poured upon him far exceeded all that Luther had ever said.

Besides, if Luther called Dr. Eck an ass and Henry VIII a hog, he indignantly rejected the intervention of the secular arm; while Eck was writing a dissertation to prove that heretics ought to be burned and Henry was erecting scaffolds that he might conform with the precepts of the chancellor of Ingolstadt.

Great was the emotion at the king's court; Surrey, Wolsey, and the crowd of courtiers, put a stop to the festivities and pageantry at Greenwich to vent their indignation in abuse and sarcasm. The venerable Bishop of Rochester, who had been delighted to see the young prince, formerly confided to his care, breaking a lance in defense of the Church, was deeply wounded by the attack of the monk. He replied to it immediately. His words distinctly characterize the age and the Church. "Take us the foxes, the little foxes, that spoil the vines, says Christ in the Song of Songs. This teaches us," said Fisher, "that we must take the heretics before they grow big. Now Luther is become a big fox, so old, so cunning, and so sly, that he is very difficult to catch, What do I say? . . . a fox? He is a mad dog, a ravening wolf, a cruel bear; or rather all those animals in one; for the monster includes many beasts within him."

Sir Thomas More also descended into the arena to contend with the monk of Wittenberg. Although a layman, his zeal against the Reformation amounted to fanaticism, if it did not even urge him to shed blood. When young nobles undertake the defense of the papacy, their violence often exceeds even that of the ecclesiastics. "Reverend brother, father, tippler, Luther, runagate of the order of St. Augustine, misshapen bacchanal of either faculty, unlearned doctor of theology." Such is the language addressed to the reformer by one of the most illustrious men of his age. He then proceeded to explain in what manner Luther had composed his book against Henry VIII:

"He called his companions together, and desired them to go each his own way and pick up all sorts of abuse and scurrility. One frequented the public carriages and boats; another the baths and gambling-houses; a third the taverns and barbers' shops; a fourth the mills and brothels. They noted down in their tablets all the most insolent, filthy, and infamous things they heard; and bringing back these abominations and impurities, discharged them all into that filthy kennel which is called Luther's mind. If he retracts his falsehoods and calumnies," continues More, "if he lays aside his folly and his madness, if he swallows his own filth . . . he will find one who will seriously discuss with him. But if he proceeds as he has begun, joking, teasing, fooling, calumniating, vomiting sewers and cesspools . . . let others do what they please: as for me, I should prefer leaving the little friar to his own fury and filth." More would have done better to have restrained his own. Luther never degraded his style to so low a degree. He made no reply.

This writing still further increased Henry's attachment to More.

He would often visit him in his humble dwelling at Chelsea. After dinner, the king, leaning on his favorite's shoulder, would walk in the garden, while Mistress More and her children, concealed behind a window, could not turn away their astonished eyes. After one of these walks, More, who knew his man well, said to his wife: "If my head could win him a single castle in France, he would not hesitate to cut it off."

The king, thus defended by the Bishop of Rochester and by his future chancellor, had no need to resume his pen. Confounded at finding himself treated in the face of Europe as a common writer, Henry VIII abandoned the dangerous position he had taken, and throwing away the pen of the theologian, had recourse to the more effectual means of diplomacy.

An ambassador was despatched from the court of Greenwich with a letter for the elector and dukes of Saxony. "Luther, the real serpent fallen from heaven," wrote he, "is pouring out his floods of venom upon the earth. He is stirring up revolts in the Church of Jesus Christ, abolishing laws, insulting the powers that be, inflaming the laity against the priests, laymen and priests against the pope, and subjects against their sovereigns, and he desires nothing better than to see Christians fighting and destroying one another, and the enemies of our faith hailing this scene of carnage with a frightful grin.

"What is this doctrine which he calls evangelical, if it be not Wycliffe's? Now, most honored uncles, I know what your ancestors have done to destroy it. In Bohemia, they hunted it down like a wild beast, and driving it into a pit, they shut it up and kept it fast. You will not allow it to escape through your negligence, lest, creeping into Saxony and becoming master of the whole of Germany, its smoking nostrils should pour forth the flames of hell, spreading that conflagration far and wide which your nation hath so often wished to extinguish in its blood.

"For this reason, most worthy princes, I feel obliged to exhort you and even to entreat you in the name of all that is most sacred, promptly to extinguish the cursed sect of Luther: put no one to death if that can be avoided; but if this heretical obstinacy continues, then shed blood without hesitation, in order that the abominable heresy may disappear from under heaven."

The elector and his brother referred the king to the approaching council. Thus Henry VIII was far from attaining his end. "So great a name mixed up in the dispute," said Paul Sarpi, "served to render it more curious and to conciliate general favor towards Luther, as usually happens in combats and tournaments, where the spectators have always a leaning towards the weaker party and take delight in exaggerating the merit of his actions."

Chapter 68

PROGRESS OF THE REFORMATION

A GREAT MOVEMENT was going on. The Reformation, which, after the Diet of Worms, had been thought to be confined with its first teacher in the narrow chamber of a strong castle, was breaking forth in every part of the empire, and, so to speak, throughout Christendom. The two classes, hitherto mixed up together, were now beginning to separate; and the partisans of a monk, whose only defense was his tongue, now took their stand fearlessly in the face of the servants of Charles V and Leo X. Luther had scarcely left the walls of the Wartburg, the pope had excommunicated all his adherents, the imperial diet had just condemned his doctrine, the princes were endeavoring to crush it in most of the German states, the ministers of Rome were lowering it in the eyes of the people by their violent invectives, and the other states of Christendom were calling upon Germany to sacrifice a man whose assaults they feared even at a distance; and yet this new sect, few in numbers, and among whose members there was no organization, no bond of union, nothing in short that concentrated their common power, was already frightening the vast, ancient, and powerful sovereignty of Rome by the energy of its faith and the rapidity of its conquests.

On all sides, as in the first warm days of spring, the seed was bursting from the earth spontaneously and without effort. Every day showed some new progress. Individuals, villages, towns, whole cities, joined in this new confession of the name of Jesus Christ. There was unpitying opposition, there were terrible persecutions, but the mysterious power that urged all these people onward was irresistible; and the persecuted, quickening their steps, going forward through exile, imprisonment, and the burning pile, everywhere prevailed over their persecutors.

The monastic orders that Rome had spread over Christendom, like a net intended to catch souls and keep them prisoners, were the first to break their bonds and rapidly to propagate the new doctrine throughout the Church. The Augustines of Saxony had walked with Luther and felt that inward experience of the Holy Word which, by putting them in possession of God Himself, dethroned Rome and her lofty assumptions. But in the other convents of the order, evangelical light had dawned in like manner. Sometimes they were old men, who, like Staupitz, had preserved the sound doctrines of truth in the midst of deluded Christendom, and who now besought God to permit them to depart in peace, for their eyes had seen His salvation. At other times, they were young men, who had received Luther's teaching with the eagerness peculiar to their age. The Augustine convents at Nuremberg, Osnabrück, Dillingen, Ratisbon, Strasburg, and Antwerp, with those in Hesse and Württemberg, turned towards Jesus Christ and by their courage excited the wrath of Rome.

But this movement was not confined to the Augustines only. High-spirited men imitated them in the monasteries of other orders, and notwithstanding the clamors of the monks who would not abandon their carnal observances, notwithstanding the anger, contempt, sentences, discipline, and imprisonments of the cloister, they fearlessly raised their voices in behalf of that holy and precious truth, which they had found at last after so many painful inquiries, such despair and doubt, and such inward struggle. In the majority of the cloisters, the most spiritual, pious, and learned monks declared for the Reformation. In the Franciscan convent at Ulm, Eberlin and Kettenback attacked the slavish works of monasticism and the superstitious observances of the Church with an eloquence capable of moving the whole nation; and they called for the immediate abolition of the monasteries and houses of ill-fame. Another Franciscan, Stephen Kempe, preached the gospel at Hamburg, and, alone, presented a firm front to the hatred, envy, menaces, snares, and attacks of the priests who were irritated at seeing the crowd abandon their altars and flock with enthusiasm to hear his sermons.

Frequently the superiors of the convents were the first led away in the path of reform. At Halberstadt, Neuenwerk, Halle, and Sagan, the priors set the example to their monks, or at least declared that if a monk felt his conscience burdened by the weight of monastic vows, far from detaining him in the convent, they would take him by the shoulders and thrust him out of doors.

Indeed throughout all Germany the monks were seen laying down their frocks and cowls at the gates of the monasteries. Some were expelled by the violence of the brethren or the abbots; others, of mild and pacific character, could no longer endure the continual disputes, abuse, clamor, and hatred which pursued them even in their slumbers; the majority were convinced that the monastic life was opposed to the will of God and to a Christian life; some had arrived at this conviction by degrees; and others suddenly, by reading a passage in the Bible. The sloth, grossness, ignorance, and degradation that constituted the very nature of the mendicant orders, inspired with indescribable disgust all men of elevated mind, who could no longer support the society of their vulgar associates. One day, a Franciscan going his rounds, stopped with the box in his hand begging alms at a blacksmith's forge in Nuremberg: "Why," said the smith, "do you not gain your bread by the work of your own hands?" At these words the sturdy monk threw away his staff and seizing the hammer plied it vigorously on the anvil. The useless mendicant had become an honest workman. His box and frock were sent back to the monastery.

The monks were not the only persons who rallied round the standard of the gospel; priests in still greater numbers began to preach the new doctrines. But preachers were not required for its propagation; it frequently acted on men's minds, and aroused them from their deep slumber without anyone having spoken.

Luther's writings were read in cities, towns, and even villages; at night by the fireside the schoolmaster would often read them aloud to an attentive audience. Some of the hearers were affected by their perusal; they would take up the Scriptures to clear away their doubts, and were struck with surprise at the astonishing contrast between the Christianity of the Bible and their own. After oscillating between Rome and Scripture, they soon took refuge with that living Word which shed so new and sweet a radiance on their hearts. While they were in this state, some evangelical preacher, probably a priest or a monk, would arrive. Speaking eloquently and with conviction, he announced that Christ had made full atonement for the sins of His people, and demonstrated by Holy Scripture the vanity of works and human penances. A terrible opposition would then break out; the clergy, and sometimes the magistrates, would strain every nerve to bring back the souls they were about to lose.

But there was in the new preaching a harmony with Scripture and a hidden force that won all hearts and subdued even the most rebellious. At the peril of their goods, and of their life if need be, they ranged themselves on the side of the gospel and forsook the barren and fanatical orators of the papacy. Sometimes the people, incensed at being so long misled, compelled them to retire; more frequently the priests, deserted by their flocks, without tithes or offerings, departed voluntarily and in sadness to seek a livelihood elsewhere. And while the supporters of the ancient hierarchy retired from these places sorrowful and dejected, and sometimes bidding farewell to their old flocks in the language of anathema, the people, whom truth and liberty transported with joy, surrounded the new preachers with acclamations, and, thirsting for the Word of God, carried them as it were in triumph into the church and into the pulpit.

A word of power, proceeding from God, was at that time regenerating society. The people, or their leaders, would frequently invite some man celebrated for his faith to come and enlighten them; and he for love of the gospel would immediately abandon his interests and his family, his country and friends. Persecution often compelled the partisans of the Reformation to leave their homes: they reached some spot where it was as yet unknown; there they would find some house that offered an asylum to poor travelers; there they would speak of the gospel, read a chapter to the attentive hearers, and perhaps, by the intercession of their new friends, obtain permission to preach once publicly in the church. . . . Then indeed a fierce fire would break out in the city, and the greatest exertions were ineffectual to quench it. If they could not preach in the church, they found some other spot. Every place became a temple. At Husum in Holstein, Hermann Tast, who was returning from Wittenberg and against whom the clergy of the parish had closed the church doors, preached to an immense crowd in the cemetery, beneath the shade of two large trees, not far from the spot where, seven centuries before, Anschar had proclaimed the gospel to the heathen. At Arnstadt, Gaspard Güttel, an Augustine monk, preached in the market place.

At Danzig, the gospel was announced on a little hill outside the city. At Gosslar, a Wittenberg student taught the new doctrines in a meadow planted with lime trees; whence the evangelical Christians were denominated the Lime-tree Brethren.

While the priests were exhibiting their sordid covetousness before the eyes of the people, the new preachers said to them, "Freely we have received, freely do we give." The idea often expressed by the new preachers from the pulpit, that Rome had formerly sent the Germans a corrupted gospel, so that now for the first time Germany heard the Word of Christ in its heavenly and primal beauty, produced a deep impression on men's minds. And the noble thought of the equality of all men, of a universal brotherhood in Jesus Christ, laid strong hold upon those souls which for so long a period had groaned beneath the yoke of feudalism and of the papacy of the Middle Ages.

Often would unlearned Christians, with the New Testament in their hands, undertake to justify the doctrine of the Reformation. The Catholics who remained faithful to Rome withdrew in affright; for to priests and monks alone had been assigned the task of studying sacred literature. The latter were therefore compelled to come forward; the conference began; but erelong, overwhelmed by the declarations of Holy Scripture cited by these laymen, the priests and monks knew not how to reply. . . . "Unhappily," says Cochloeus, "Luther had persuaded his followers to put no faith in any other oracle than the Holy Scriptures." A shout was raised in the assembly, denouncing the scandalous ignorance of these old theologians who had hitherto been reputed such great scholars by their own party.

Men of the lowest station, and even the weaker sex, with the aid of God's Word, persuaded and led away men's hearts. Extraordinary works are the result of extraordinary times. At Ingolstadt, under the eyes of Dr. Eck, a young weaver read Luther's works to the assembled crowd. In this very city, the university having resolved to compel a disciple of Melancthon to retract, a woman, named Argula de Staufen, undertook his defense, and challenged the doctors to a public disputation. Women and children, artisans and soldiers, knew more of the Bible than the doctors of the schools or the priests of the altars.

Christendom was divided into two hostile bodies, and their aspects were strikingly contrasted. Opposed to the old champions of the hierarchy, who had neglected the study of languages and the cultivation of literature (as one of their own body informs us), were generous-minded youths, devoted to study, investigating Scripture, and familiarizing themselves with the masterpieces of antiquity. Possessing an active mind, an elevated soul, and intrepid heart, these young men soon acquired such knowledge that for a long period none could compete with them. It was not only the vitality of their faith which rendered them superior to their contemporaries, but an elegance of style, a perfume of antiquity, a sound philosophy, a knowledge of the world, completely foreign to the theologians "of the old leaven," as Cochloeus himself terms them. Accordingly, when these youthful defenders of the Reformation met the Romish doctors in any assembly, they attacked them with such ease and confidence that these ignorant men hesitated, became embarrassed, and fell into a contempt merited in the eyes of all.

The ancient edifice was crumbling under the load of superstition and ignorance; the new one was rising on the foundations of faith and learning. New elements entered deep into the lives of the people. Torpor and dullness were in all parts succeeded by a spirit of inquiry and a thirst for instruction. An active, enlightened, and living faith took the place of superstitious devotion and ascetic meditations. Works of piety succeeded bigoted observances and penances. The pulpit prevailed over the ceremonies of the altar; and the ancient and sovereign authority of God's Word was at length restored in the Church.

The printing press, that powerful machine invented in the fifteenth century, came to the support of all these exertions, and its terrible missiles were continually battering the walls of the enemy.

The impulse which the Reformation gave to popular literature in Germany was immense. While in the year 1513, only thirty-five publications had appeared, and thirty-seven in 1517, the number of books increased with astonishing rapidity after the appearance of Luther's theses. In 1518 we find seventy-one different works; in 1519, one hundred and eleven; in 1520, two hundred and eight; in 1521, two hundred and eleven; in 1522, three hundred and forty-seven; and in 1523, four hundred and ninety-eight. . . . And where were all these published? For the most part at Wittenberg. And who were their authors? Generally Luther and his friends. In 1522, one hundred and thirty of the reformer's writings were published; and in the year following, one hundred and eighty-three. In this same year only twenty Roman Catholic publications appeared. The literature of Germany thus saw the light in the midst of struggles, contemporaneously with her religion. Already it appeared, as later times have seen it, learned, profound, full of boldness and activity. The national spirit showed itself for the first time without alloy, and at the very moment of its birth received the baptism of fire from Christian enthusiasm.

What Luther and his friends composed, others circulated. Monks, convinced of the unlawfulness of monastic obligations, and desirous of exchanging a long life of slothfulness for one of active exertion, but too ignorant to proclaim the Word of God, traveled through the provinces, visiting hamlets and cottages where they sold the books of Luther and his friends. Germany soon swarmed with these bold colporteurs. Printers and booksellers eagerly welcomed every writing in defense of the Reformation; but they rejected the books of the opposite party, as generally full of ignorance and barbarism. If any one of them ventured to sell a book in favor of the papacy, and offered it for sale in the fairs at Frankfurt or elsewhere, merchants, purchasers, and men of letters overwhelmed him with ridicule and sarcasm. It was in vain that the emperor and princes had published severe edicts against the writings of the reformers. As soon as an inquisitorial visit was to be paid, the dealers, who had received secret intimation, concealed the books that it was intended to proscribe; and the multitude, ever eager for what is prohibited, immediately bought them up, and read them with the greater avidity. It was not only in Germany that such scenes were passing; Luther's writings were translated into French, Spanish, English, and Italian, and circulated among these nations.

Chapter 69

LUTHER'S MARRIAGE

IF THE MOST puny instruments inflicted such terrible blows on Rome, what was it when the voice of the monk of Wittenberg was heard? Shortly after the discomfiture of the new prophets, Luther, in a layman's attire, traversed the territories of Duke George in a wagon. His gown was hidden, and the reformer seemed to be a plain country gentleman. If he had been recognized, if he had fallen into the hands of the exasperated duke, perhaps his fate would have been sealed. He was going to preach at Zwickau, the birthplace of the pretended prophets. It was no sooner known at Schneeberg, Annaberg, and the surrounding places, than the people crowded around him. Fourteen thousand persons flocked into the city, and as there was no church that could contain such numbers, Luther went into the balcony of the town hall, and preached before an audience of twenty-five thousand persons who thronged the market place, some of whom had mounted on heaps of cut stones piled up near the building.

The servant of God was dilating with fervor on the election of grace, when suddenly cries were heard from the midst of the audience. An old woman of haggard mien, who had taken her station on a pile of stones, stretched out her emaciated arms, and seemed as though she would strain with her fleshless hands the crowd that was about to fall prostrate at the feet of Jesus. Her wild yells interrupted the preacher. "It was the devil," said Seckendorff, "who had taken the form of an old woman in order to excite a disturbance." But it was all in vain; the reformer's words silenced the wicked spirit, enthusiasm seized these listening thousands; glances of admiration were exchanged; hands were warmly grasped, and erelong the monks, confounded and unable to avert the storm, found it necessary to leave Zwickau.

In the castle of Freyberg dwelt Henry, brother of Duke George. His wife, a princess of Mecklenburg, had the preceding year borne him a son who had been named Maurice. With a fondness for the table and for pleasure Duke Henry combined the rudeness and coarse manners of a soldier. In other respects, he was pious after the fashion of the times, had gone to the Holy Land, and made a pilgrimage to St. Iago of Compostella. He would often say: "At Compostella I placed a hundred golden florins on the altar of the saint, and said to him: 'O St. Iago, to please thee I came hither; I make thee a present of this money; but if these knaves [the priests] take it from thee, I cannot help it; so be on your guard.'"

A Franciscan and a Dominican, both disciples of Luther, had been for some time preaching the gospel at Freyberg. The duchess, whose piety had inspired her with a horror of heresy, listened to their sermons in astonishment to find that this gentle message of a Saviour was the object she had been taught to fear. Gradually her eyes were opened and she found peace in Christ Jesus. No sooner had Duke George learned that the Gospel was preached at Freyberg than he entreated his brother to oppose these novelties. Chancellor Strehlin and the canons seconded his prayer with their fanaticism. A violent explosion took place in the court of Freyberg. Duke Henry harshly reprimanded and reproached his wife, and more than once the pious duchess watered her child's cradle with her tears. Yet by degrees her prayers and gentleness won the heart of her husband; the rough man was softened; harmony was restored between the married pair, and they were enabled to join in prayer beside their sleeping babe. Great destinies were hovering over that child; and from that cradle, where a Christian mother had so often poured forth her sorrows, God was one day to bring forth the liberator of the Reformation.

Luther's intrepidity had excited the inhabitants of Worms. The imperial decree terrified the magistrates; all the churches were closed; but in a public place, filled by an immense crowd, a preacher ascended a rudely constructed pulpit; but the storm was no sooner passed than it was immediately set up in some more secluded spot, to which the crowd again flocked to hear the Word of Christ. This temporary pulpit was every day carried from one place to another, and

served to encourage the people, who were still agitated by the emotions of the great drama lately performed in their city.

At Frankfurt-on-the-Main, one of the principal free cities of the
empire, all was in commotion. A courageous evangelist, Ibach,
preached salvation by Jesus Christ. The clergy, among whom was
Cochloeus, so notorious by his writings and his opposition, were irritated against this audacious colleague and denounced him to the
Archbishop of Mentz. The council undertook his defense, although
with timidity, but to no purpose, for the clergy discharged the evangelical minister, and compelled him to leave the town. Rome triumphed; everything seemed lost; the poor believers fancied themselves forever deprived of the Word, but at the very moment when
the citizens appeared inclined to yield to these tyrannical priests,
many nobles declared for the gospel. Max of Molnheim, Harmuth of
Cronberg, George of Stockheim, and Emeric of Reiffenstein, whose
estates lay near Frankfurt, wrote to the council: "We are constrained
to rise up against these spiritual wolves." And addressing the clergy,
they said: "Embrace the evangelical doctrine, recall Ibach, or else we
will refuse to pay our tithes!"

The people, who listened gladly to the Reformation, being encouraged by the language of the nobles, began to put themselves in motion; and one day, just as Peter Mayer, the persecutor of Ibach and
the most determined enemy of the reform, was going to preach
against the heretics, a great uproar was heard. Mayer was alarmed,
and hastily quitted the Church. This movement decided the council.
All the preachers were enjoined by proclamation to preach the pure
Word of God, or to leave the city.

The light which proceeded from Wittenberg, as from the heart of
the nation, was thus shedding its rays through the whole empire. In
the west, Berg, Cleves, Lippstadt, Munster, Wesel, Miltenberg,
Mentz, Deux Ponts, and Strasburg, listened to the gospel; on the
south, Hoff, Schlesstadt, Bamberg, Esslingen, Halle in Swabia, Heil-
brunn, Augsburg, Ulm, and many other places, received it with joy.
In the east, Pomerania, Prussia, and the duchy of Leignitz, opened
their gates to it; and in the north, Brunswick, Halberstadt, Gosslar,
Zell, Friesland, Bremen, Hamburg, Holstein, and even Denmark,
with other neighboring countries, were moved at the sounds of this
new doctrine.

The Elector Frederick had declared that he would allow the bishops to preach freely in his states, but that he would deliver no one into their hands. Accordingly, the evangelical teachers, persecuted in other countries, soon took refuge in Saxony. Ibach of Frankfurt, Eberlin of Ulm, Kauxdorf of Magdeburg, Valentine Mustoeus, whom the canons of Halberstadt had horribly mutilated, and other faithful ministers, coming from all parts of Germany, fled to Wittenberg, as the only asylum in which they could be secure. Here they conversed with the reformers; at their feet they strengthened themselves in the faith and communicated to them their own experience and the knowledge they had acquired. It is thus the waters of the rivers return by the clouds from the vast expanse of the ocean, to feed the glaciers whence they first descended to the plains.

The work which was evolving at Wittenberg, and formed in this manner of many different elements, became more and more the work of the nation, of Europe, and of Christendom. This school, founded by Frederick and quickened by Luther, was the center of an immense revolution which regenerated the Church and impressed on it a real and living unity far superior to the apparent unity of Rome. The Bible reigned at Wittenberg, and its oracles were heard on all sides. This academy, the most recent of all, had acquired that rank and influence in Christendom which had hitherto belonged to the ancient University of Paris. The crowds that flocked thither from every part of Europe made known the wants of the Church and of the nations; and as they quitted these walls, now become holy to them, they carried back with them to the Church and the people the Word of Grace appointed to heal and to save the nations.

Luther, as he witnessed this success, felt his confidence increase. He beheld this feeble undertaking, begun in the midst of so many fears and struggles, changing the aspect of the Christian world, and was astonished at the result. He had foreseen nothing of the kind when first he rose up against Tetzel. Prostrate before the God whom he adored, he confessed the work to be His, and exulted in the assurance of a victory that could not be torn from him. "Our enemies threaten us with death," said he to Harmuth of Cronberg; "if they had as much wisdom as foolishness, they would, on the contrary, threaten us with life. What an absurdity and insult to presume to threaten death to Christ and Christians, who are themselves lords and conquerors of death! . . . It is as if I would seek to frighten a man by saddling his horse and helping him to mount. Do they not know that Christ is risen from the dead? In their eyes He is still lying in the sepulcher; nay more—in hell. But we know that He lives." He was grieved at the thought that he was regarded as the author of a work in whose minutest details he beheld the hand of God. "Many believe because of me," said he. "But those alone truly believe, who would continue faithful even should they hear (which God forbid!) that I had denied Jesus Christ. True disciples believe not in Luther, but in Jesus Christ. As for myself, I do not care about Luther. Whether he is a saint or a knave, what matters it? It is not he that I preach; but Christ. If the devil can take him, let him do so! But let Christ abide with us, and we shall abide also."

And vainly, indeed, would men endeavor to explain this great movement by mere human circumstances. Men of letters, it is true, sharpened their wits and discharged their keen-pointed arrows against the pope and the monks; the shout of liberty, which Germany had so often raised against the tyranny of the Italians, again resounded in the castles and provinces; the people were delighted with the song of "the nightingale of Wittenberg," a herald of the spring that was everywhere bursting forth. But it was not a mere outward movement, similar to that effected by a longing for earthly liberty, that was then accomplishing. Those who assert that the Reformation was brought about by bribing the princes with the wealth of the convents,—the priests with permission to marry,—and the people with the prospect of freedom, are strangely mistaken in its nature. No doubt a useful employment of the funds that had hitherto supported the sloth of the monks; no doubt marriage and liberty, gifts that proceed direct from God, might have favored the development of the Reformation; but the mainspring was not there.

An interior revolution was then going on in the depths of the human heart. Christians were again learning to love, to pardon, to pray, to suffer, and even to die for a truth that offered no repose save in heaven. The Church was passing through a state of transformation. Christianity was bursting the bonds in which it had been so long confined and returning in life and vigor into a world that had forgotten its ancient power. The hand that made the world was turned toward it again; and the gospel, reappearing in the midst of the nations, accelerated its course, notwithstanding the violent and repeated efforts of priests and kings; like the ocean which, when the hand of God presses on its surface, rises calm and majestic along its shores, so that no human power is able to resist its progress.

In the monastery of Nimptsch, near Grimma in Saxony, dwelt in the year 1523 nine nuns, who were diligent in reading the Word of God and who had discovered the contrast that exists between a Christian and a cloistered life. Their names were Magdalen Staupitz, Eliza Canitz, Ava Grossen, Ava and Margaret Schonfeldt, Laneta Golis, Margaret and Catherine Zeschau, and Catherine Bora. The first impulse of these young women, after they were delivered from the superstitions of the monastery, was to write to their parents. "The salvation of our souls," said they, "will not permit us to remain any longer in a cloister." Their parents, fearing the trouble likely to arise from such a resolution, harshly rejected their prayers. The poor nuns were dismayed. How could they leave the monastery? Their timidity was alarmed at so desperate a step. At last, the horror caused by the papal services prevailed, and they promised not to leave one another, but to repair in a body to some respectable place, with order and decency. Two worthy and pious citizens of Torgau, Leonard Koppe and Wolff Tomitzsch, offered their assistance, which was accepted as coming from God Himself, and they left the convent of Nimptsch without any opposition and as if the hand of the Lord had opened the doors to them. Koppe and Tomitzsch received them in their wagon; and on the seventh of April, 1523, the nine nuns, amazed at their own boldness, stopped in great emotion before the gate of the old Augustine convent in which Luther resided.

"This is not my doing," said Luther, as he received them; "but would to God that I could thus rescue all captive consciences, and empty all the cloisters!—the breach is made!" Many persons offered to receive these nuns into their houses, and Catherine Bora found a welcome in the family of the burgomaster of Wittenberg.

If Luther at that time thought of preparing for any solemn event, it was to ascend the scaffold, and not to approach the altar. Many months after this, he still replied to those who spoke to him of marriage: "God may change my heart, if it be His pleasure; but now at least I have no thought of taking a wife; not that I do not feel any attractions in that estate; I am neither a stock nor a stone; but every day I expect the death and the punishment of a heretic."

Yet everything in the Church was advancing. The habits of a monastic life, the invention of man, were giving way in every quarter to those of domestic life, appointed by God. On Sunday, the ninth of October, 1524, Luther, having risen as usual, laid aside the frock of the Augustine monk and put on the dress of a secular priest; he then made his appearance in the church, where this change caused a lively satisfaction. Renovated Christendom hailed with transport everything that announced that the old things were passed away.

Shortly after this, the last monk quitted the convent; but Luther remained; his footsteps alone re-echoed through the long galleries; he sat silent and solitary in the refectory that had so lately resounded with the babbling of the monks. An eloquent silence, attesting the triumphs of the Word of God! The convent had ceased to exist. About the end of December, 1524, Luther sent the keys of the monastery to the elector, informing him that he should see where it might please God to feed him. The elector gave the convent to the university and invited Luther to continue his residence in it. The abode of the monks was destined erelong to be the sanctuary of a Christian family.

Luther, whose heart was formed to taste the sweets of domestic life, honored and loved the marriage state; it is even probable that he had some liking for Catherine Bora. For a long while his scruples and the thought of the calumnies which such a step would occasion had prevented his thinking of her; and he had offered the poor Catherine, first to Baumgartner of Nuremberg, and then to Dr. Glatz of Orlamund. But when he saw Baumgartner refuse to take her, and when she had declined to accept Glatz, he asked himself seriously whether he ought not to think of marrying her himself.

His aged father, who had been so grieved when he embraced a monastic life, was urging him to enter the conjugal state. But one idea above all was daily present before Luther's conscience, and with greater energy: marriage is an institution of God—celibacy an institution of man. He had a horror of everything that emanated from Rome. He would say to his friends, "I desire to retain nothing of my papistical life." Day and night he prayed and entreated the Lord to deliver him from his uncertainty. At last a single thought broke the last links that still held him captive. To all the motives of propriety and personal obedience which led him to apply to himself this declaration of God, "It is not good that man should be alone," was added a motive of a higher and more powerful nature. He saw that if he was called to the marriage-state as a man, he was also called to it as a reformer; this decided him.

"If this monk should marry," said his friend Schurff the lawyer, "he will make all the world and the devil himself burst with laughter, and will destroy the work that he has begun." This remark made a very different impression on Luther from what might have been supposed. To brave the world, the devil, and his enemies, and, by an action which they thought calculated to ruin the cause of the Reformation, prevent its success being in any measure ascribed to him— this was all he desired. Accordingly, boldly raising his head, he replied, "Well, then, I will do it; I will play the devil and the world this trick; I will content my father, and marry Catherine!"

Luther, by his marriage, broke off still more completely from the institutions of the papacy; he confirmed the doctrine he had preached, by his own example, and encouraged timid men to an entire renunciation of their errors. Rome appeared to be recovering here and there the ground she had lost; she flattered herself with the hope of victory; and now a loud explosion scattered terror and surprise through her ranks and still more fully disclosed to her the courage of the enemy she fancied she had crushed. "I will bear witness to the gospel," said Luther, "not by my words only, but also by my works. I am determined, in the face of my enemies who already exult and raise the shout of victory, to marry a nun, that they may see and know that they have not conquered me. I do not take a wife that I may live long with her; but seeing the nations and the princes letting lose their fury against me, foreseeing that my end is near, and that after my death they will again trample my doctrine underfoot, I am resolved, for the edification of the weak, to bear a striking testimony to what I teach here below."

On the eleventh of June, 1525, Luther went to the house of his friend and colleague Amsdorff. He desired Pomeranus, whom he styled "The Pastor," to bless his union. The celebrated painter Lucas Cranach and Doctor John Apella witnessed the marriage. Melancthon was not present.

No sooner was Luther married than all Europe was disturbed. He was overwhelmed with accusations and calumnies from every quarter. But while Luther was thus assailed, many wise and moderate men, whom the Roman Church still counted among her members, undertook his defense. "Luther," said Erasmus, "has taken a wife from the noble family of Bora, but she has no dowry." A more valuable testimony was now given in his favor. The master of Germany, Philip Melancthon, whom this bold step had at first alarmed, said with that grave voice to which even his enemies listened with respect: "It is false and slanderous to maintain that there is anything unbecoming in Luther's marriage. I think that in marrying he must have done violence to himself. A married life is one of humility, but it is also a holy state, if there be any such in the world, and the Scriptures everywhere represent it as honorable in the eyes of God."

Luther was troubled at first when he saw such floods of anger and contempt poured out upon him; Melancthon became more earnest in friendship and kindness towards him; and it was not long before the reformer could see a mark of God's approbation in this opposition of man. "If I did not offend the world," said he, "I should have cause to fear that what I have done is displeasing to God."

Eight years had elapsed between the time when Luther had attacked the indulgences and his marriage with Catherine Bora. It would be difficult to ascribe, as is still done, his zeal against the abuses of the Church to an "impatient desire" for wedlock. He was then forty-two years old, and Catherine Bora had already been two years in Wittenberg.

Luther was happy in this union. "The best gift of God," said he, "is a pious and amiable wife, who fears God, loves her family, with whom a man may live in peace and in whom he may safely confide." Some months after his marriage he informed one of his friends of Catherine's pregnancy, and a year after they came together she gave birth to a son. The sweets of domestic life soon dispersed the storms that the exasperation of his enemies had at first gathered over him. His Ketha, as he styled her, manifested the tenderest affection towards him, consoled him in his dejection by repeating passages from the Bible, exonerated him from all household cares, sat near him during his leisure moments, worked his portrait in embroidery, reminded him of the friends to whom he had forgotten to write, and often amused him by the simplicity of her questions. A certain dignity appears to have marked her character, for Luther would sometimes call her, "My Lord Ketha." One day he said playfully that if he were tᵣ marry again, he would carve an obedient wife for himself out of ᵣ block of stone, for, added he, "it is impossible to find such a onᵣ ·n reality." His letters overflowed with tenderness for Catherinᵣ ᵣe called her "his dear and gracious wife, his dear and amiable Kᵣᵗha." Luther's character became more cheerful in Catherine's socieᵣv, and this happy frame of mind never deserted him afterwards, everᵣ ᵣn the midst of his greatest trials.

The almost universal corruption of the clergy had brought the priesthood into general contempt, from which the isolated virtues of a few faithful servants of God had been unable to extricate it. Domestic peace and conjugal fidelity, those surest foundations of happiness here below, were continually disturbed in town and country by the gross passions of the priests and monks. No one was secure from those attempts at seduction. They took advantage of the access allowed them into every family, and sometimes even of the confidence of the confessional, to instill a deadly poison into the souls of their penitents, and to satisfy their guilty desires. The Reformation, by abolishing the celibacy of the ecclesiastics, restored the sanctity of the conjugal state. The marriage of the clergy put an end to an immense number of secret crimes. The reformers became the models of their flocks in the most intimate and important relations of life; and the people were not slow in rejoicing to see the ministers of religion once more husbands and fathers.

* * * *

Luther arrived at Eisleben on January 28, 1546, and, although very ill, he took part in the conferences which ensued, up to February 17. He preached four times and revised certain ecclesiastical regulations. At supper that day he spoke a great deal about his approaching death. Someone asked him whether we should recognize one another in the next world. He replied he thought we should. On retiring he was accompanied by the master of the house and his sons. He went to the window and remained there for a considerable time in silent prayer. Two other friends joined him, and to those present he expressed a desire to sleep if only for a half hour for the good it would do him. Resting upon his bed he did fall asleep for an hour and a half. On awaking he said to those in the room, "What! are you still there? Will you not go, dear friends, and rest yourselves?" They told him they would remain with him and then he began to pray, "Into thy hands I commend my spirit: Thou hast redeemed me, O Lord, God of truth."

After requesting of the others that prayer be made for the extension of the gospel, he fell asleep again for about an hour. Awaking he expressed a feeling of great illness. Dr. Jonas sought to give some assurance of help, but he said he was getting worse and prayed again: "O my Father, Thou, the God of our Lord Jesus Christ, Thou, the source of all consolation, I thank Thee for having revealed unto me Thy well-beloved Son, in whom I believe, whom I have preached, and acknowledged, and made known; whom I have loved and celebrated. I commend my soul to Thee, O my Lord Jesus Christ! I am about to quit this terrestrial body, I am about to be removed from this life, but I know that I shall abide eternally with Thee."

He then repeated three times: "Into Thy hands I commend my spirit: Thou hast redeemed me, O Lord, God of truth." He closed his eyes and fell back on his pillow. Efforts were made to revive him, and this question was put to him: "Reverend father, do you die firm in the faith you have taught?" Luther opened his eyes, looked at Dr. Jonas, and replied, firmly and distinctly: "Yes." He then fell asleep, his breathing was more and more faint: at length he sighed deeply, and the great reformer was gone.

His body was conveyed in a leaden coffin to Wittenberg, where it was interred on February 22, 1546, with the greatest honors. He sleeps in the castle church, at the foot of the pulpit.

* * * *

Luther's will, dated January 6, 1542, reads:

"I, the undersigned Martin Luther, doctor of divinity, do hereby give and grant unto my dear and faithful wife, Catherine, as dower to be enjoyed by her during her life, at her own will and pleasure, the farm at Zeilsdorf, with all the improvements and additions I have made thereto; the house called *Brun*, which I purchased under the name of Wolff; and all my silver goblets, and other valuables, such as rings, chains, gold and silver medals, etc., to the amount of about a thousand florins.

"I make this disposition of my means, in the first place, because my Catherine has always been a gentle, pious, and faithful wife to me, has loved me tenderly, and has, by the blessing of God, given me, and brought up for me, five children, still, I thank God, living, beside others who are now dead. Secondly, that out of the said means she may discharge my debts, amounting to about four hundred and fifty florins, in the event of my not paying them myself before my death. In the third place, and more especially, because I would not have her dependent on her children, but rather that her children should be dependent on her—honoring her, and submissive to her, according to God's command; and that they should not act as I have seen some children act, whom the devil has excited to disobey the ordinance of God in this respect, more particularly in cases when their mother has become a widow, and they themselves have married. I consider, moreover, that the mother will be the best guardian of these means in behalf of her children, and I feel that she will not abuse this confidence I place in her, to the detriment of those who are her own flesh and blood, whom she has borne in her bosom.

"Whatever may happen to her after my death, (for I cannot foresee the designs of God) I have, I say, full confidence that she will ever conduct herself as a good mother toward her children, and will conscientiously share with them whatever she possesses.

"And here I beg all my friends to testify to the truth, and to defend my dear Catherine, should it happen as is very possible, that ill tongues should charge her with retaining for her own private use, separate from the children, any money they may say I left concealed. I hereby certify that we have no ready money, no treasure of coin of any description. Nor will it appear surprising to any who shall consider that I have no income beyond my salary, and a few presents now and then, and that, yet, with this limited revenue, we have built a good deal, and maintained a large establishment. I consider it, indeed, a special favor of God, and I thank Him daily, therefore, that we have been able to manage as we have done, and that our debts are not greater than they are . . .

"I pray my gracious lord, duke John Frederick, elector, to confirm and maintain the present deed, even though it should not be exactly in the form required by law.

"Signed,   MARTIN LUTHER

"Witnesses, Melancthon, Cruciger, Bugenhagen."

Moody Press, a ministry of the Moody Bible Institute, is designed for education, evangelization and edification. If we may assist you in knowing more about Christ and the Christian life, please write us without obligation to: Moody Press, c/o MLM, Chicago, Illinois 60610.